FEMINIST PERSPECTIVES ON SOCIAL RESEARCH

Edited by

SHARLENE NAGY HESSE-BIBER
Boston College

MICHELLE L. YAISER
New England Institute of Art

New York Oxford
OXFORD UNIVERSITY PRESS
2004

Oxford University Press

Oxford New York
Auckland Bangkok Buenos Aires Cape Town Chennai
Dar es Salaam Delhi Hong Kong Istanbul Karachi Kolkata
Kuala Lumpur Madrid Melbourne Mexico City Mumbai
Nairobi São Paulo Shanghai Taipei Tokyo Toronto

Published by Oxford University Press, Inc.
198 Madison Avenue, New York, New York 10016
http://www.oup-usa.org

Oxford is a registered trademark of Oxford University Press

Library of Congress Cataloging-in-Publication Data
Feminist perspectives on social research / edited by Sharlene Nagy Hesse-Biber, Michelle L. Yaiser.
p. cm.
Includes bibliographical references.
ISBN 978-0-19-517174-7 ISBN 978-0-19-515811-3

1. Women—Social conditions—Research. 2. Women—Social conditions. 3. Women's studies—Research. 4. Feminism. I. Hesse-Biber, Sharlene Nagy. II. Yaiser, Michelle L.

HQ1180.F455 2003
304.42—dc21 2003041938

Printed in the United States of America
on acid-free paper

For the women from whose rich everyday lives we learn so much,
and for Dorothy Smith and Sandra Harding, who have personally inspired us to be feminist researchers

Contents

Acknowledgments

In the work toward this book, we appreciate the help of a number of people who supported the endeavor. Thanks to Christine Hughes, Karen Goldfeder, Lindsey Lathinghouse, Laura MacFee, and Paul Sacco for helping with the proofing of the previously published articles in the manuscript. For their thoughtful reading and comments on a preliminary draft of the introductions we are grateful to Patricia Arend, Denise Leckenby, and Abigail Brooks.

A special heartfelt thanks to Amanda Berger for her research assistance, for her attention to the fine details of the preparation of the manuscript for production, and for her invaluable assistance with the day-to-day operations of putting together an edited volume.

We are also grateful to all our students who inspired us to think and teach from an interdisciplinary perspective. Sharlene Nagy Hesse-Biber wants to especially thank the students in her graduate Feminist Methodology and Qualitative Methods courses for their inspiration and thoughtful comments on the articles for the volume.

Sharlene Nagy Hesse-Biber is especially grateful to her family for their patience, love, and understanding during all phases of the preparation of this volume.

Michelle L. Yaiser is particularly thankful to Matthew Gregory for his continued love and support during the long process of creation of this book.

We especially want to thank our editors, Peter Labella and Sean Mahoney, and project editor, Lisa Grzan, at Oxford University Press for their support and encouragement.

Contributors

Kristin L. Anderson is Assistant Professor of Sociology at Western Washington University. She received her Ph.D. in sociology from the University of Texas at Austin. She has published articles on gender differences in the experiences, interpretations, and consequences of partner violence. She is currently studying the interpretations of violence and harassment offered by friends, relatives, and acquaintances of the victims and survivors of intimate partner violence and sexual assault.

Kum-Kum Bhavnani is at the University of California Santa Barbara where she is Professor of Sociology, as well as Women's Studies and Global and International Studies. She is also chair of the Women, Culture, and Development program there. From July 2000 to July 2002 she was the founding senior editor of the journal *Meridians: Feminism, Race, Transnationalism,* based at Smith College. Her publications include *Feminism and 'Race,'* and, with John Foran and Priya Kurian, she has coedited *Feminist Futures: Reimagining Women, Culture, and Development.*

Janet Saltzman Chafetz is Professor of Sociology and Departmental Chair at the University of Houston, where she has taught since 1971. She received her Ph.D. from the University of Texas in 1967. Her major areas of teaching have long been the sociology of gender and sociological theory. She combines these interests in her research, which has focused around the topic of gender theory, specifically the development of theory explaining variation in, mechanisms for the reproduction of, and change in the level of gender stratification across time and space. She has authored eight books, edited three, and written more than forty articles and book chapters. Among her books are *Masculine/Feminine or Human?; A Primer on the Construction and Testing of Theories in Sociology; Sex and Advantage: A Comparative, Macrostructural Theory of Sex Stratification*; *Female Revolt: Women's Movements in World and Historical Perspective* (with A. G. Dworkin); *Feminist Sociology: An Overview of Contemporary Theories; Gender Equity: An Integrated Theory of Stability and Change;* and *Handbook of the Sociology of Gender* (editor).

Marjorie L. DeVault is Professor of Sociology and a member of the Women's Studies Program at Syracuse University. She is the author of *Feeding the Family: The Social Organization of Caring as Gendered Work* and *Liberating Method: Feminism and Social Research.* She has also written on qualitative research methods, the social organization of interpretation, and the "women's profession" of dietetics and nutrition counseling. She is currently exploring the work of parenting, with a focus on family activities outside the home.

Antoinette Errante is Associate Professor of Comparative and Historical Studies of Education in the School of Educational Policy and Leadership at The Ohio State University. In addition to her studies of colonial and postcolonial education in Mozambique, her scholarship in Southern Africa has examined cultural practices related to violence, trauma, and healing, especially among militarized youth. A 2000–2001 National Academy of Education/Spencer Post-Doctoral Fellowship recipient, she is currently writing a book, *Power in Learning: The Place of Schooling in Colonial/Post-Colonial Childhoods in Mozambique.*

Susan Geiger was Associate Professor in the Department of History at the University of Minnesota. Her research interests included African women's history, women and African nationalism, women's life histories, and life history methodology.

Sandra Harding is a philosopher and Professor of Education and Women's Studies at the University of California at Los Angeles. She is also the coeditor of *Signs: Journal of Women in Culture and Society.* She is the author or editor of ten books including *The Science Question in Feminism* and *Is Science Multicultural? Postcolonialisms, Feminisms, and Epistemologies,* and editor of the forthcoming *The Standpoint Reader* and (with Robert Figueroa) *Science and Other Cultures: Difference Issues in the Philosophy of Science and Technology.*

Shirley A. Hill is Associate Professor and Director of Graduate Studies for the Sociology Department at the University of Kansas. She teaches courses on social inequality, the family, and medical sociology. She is also the author of two books: *Managing Sickle Cell Disease in Low-Income Families* and *African American Children: Socialization and Development in Families.* Her research focuses on gender inequality in health care, child development, and family caregiving, and she has published numerous articles in those areas.

Jocelyn A. Hollander is a faculty member in the sociology department at the University of Oregon. Her work focuses on the construction and reconstruction of gender through interaction, especially conversation. Her most recent project investigates the consequences of self-defense training for women's conceptions of self and gender. With Judith Howard, she is the author of *Gendered Situations, Gendered Selves: A Gender Lens on Social Psychology.*

Verna M. Keith is Chair and Associate Professor of Sociology at Arizona State University. She received her Ph.D. from the University of Kentucky and did postdoctoral work in the School of Public Health and the Institute of Gerontology at the University of Michigan. She is continuing her work on the implications of colorism for African Americans. She is also currently investigating the effects of supportive and problematic social relationships on mental health.

Diane Kobrynowicz, Ph.D., is Associate Professor of Psychology at The College of New Jersey. A social psychologist, her research focuses on stereotyping and prejudice, social justice, epistemology, and health.

Patricia Leavy is Assistant Professor of Sociology at Stonehill College in Easton, MA. She received her Ph.D. in Sociology at Boston College in 2002 and her B.A. from Boston University in 1997. She is coeditor of *Approaches to Qualitative Research: A Reader on Theory and Practice*. She has also published articles in the fields of popular culture, research methods, feminism, social theory, and collective memory. She is currently completing a book-length manuscript, based on her dissertation research, tentatively titled *Representational Events: Titanic and Other Events as Case Studies in Collective Memory*.

Denise Leckenby is a Ph.D. student of sociology at Boston College. Her areas of interest include qualitative methodology, feminist methodology, feminist theory, and sexuality. She is coeditor of *Women in Catholic Higher Education: Border Work, Living Experiences, and Social Justice*.

Laura Madson received her Ph.D. in social psychology from Iowa State University in 1996. She is currently Assistant Professor of Psychology at New Mexico State University. Her research interests include gender, sexuality, and the teaching of psychology. She teaches courses in the psychology of women, sexual behavior, the psychology of sexual orientation, and psychological measurement.

Nancy A. Naples is author of *Grassroots Warriors: Activist Mothering, Community Work, and the War on Poverty,* which was a finalist for the C. Wright Mills Award of the Society for the Study of Social Problems. She is also editor of *Community Activism and Feminist Politics: Organizing Across Gender, Race, and Class* and coeditor with Manisha Desai of *Women's Activism and Globalization: Linking Local Struggles with Transnational Politics*. She currently holds a joint appointment in sociology and women's studies at the University of Connecticut. Her main research interests center on exploring the development of women's political consciousness and activism; the role of the state in reproducing or challenging inequality; and how differing community contexts influence women's resistance and political activism.

Diane Reay is Senior Lecturer in Research Methods in the School of Social Science and Public Policy, King's College London. Her current research projects examine educational inequalities both within the UK and across Europe. She has published widely in the areas of gender, social class, and ethnicity. Recent publications include *Class Work: Mothers' Involvement in Their Children's Schooling*.

Mimi Schippers is Assistant Professor of Sociology at Albion College and received a Ph.D. in sociology from the University of Wisconsin-Madison. Her work focuses on how people perform and negotiate masculinity and femininity in face-to-face interaction. Her book, *Rockin' Out of the Box: Gender Maneuvering in Alternative*

Hard Rock, is a study of how people use nontraditional ideas about gender to develop a rock music subculture. Her current research is a comparative study of gender and sexuality in counterculture subcultures in Paris, France, and Chicago, Illinois. She teaches courses on the sociology of sex and gender, history of sociological thought, feminist theory, social psychology, sociology of the body, and the sociology of sexuality. She is part of the Center for Interdisciplinary Study in Ethnicity, Gender, and Global Issues and the Center for the Interdisciplinary Study of History and Culture.

Dorothy E. Smith is Professor Emeritus in the Department of Sociology and Equity Studies of the University of Toronto and adjunct professor in the Department of Sociology, University of Victoria, British Columbia. She has been preoccupied for the past twenty-five years or so with working out the implications for sociology of taking women's standpoint and has developed a research approach called "institutional ethnography" that embodies women's standpoint in a research practice. Her books include: *The Everyday World as Problematic: A Feminist Sociology; The Conceptual Practices of Power: A Feminist Sociology of Knowledge; Texts, Facts, and Femininity: Exploring the Relations of Ruling;* and *Writing the Social: Critique, Theory, and Investigations.*

Joey Sprague is Associate Professor of Sociology at the University of Kansas. Her research and writing centers on the gendered dynamics in creating knowledge and the biases embedded in current forms of knowledge. Recent publications include "Gender and Feminist Studies in Sociology," in *International Encyclopedia of the Social and Behavioral Sciences,* "Structured Knowledges and Strategic Methodologies," in *Signs: Journal of Women in Culture and Society,* and "Self-Determination and Empowerment: A Feminist Standpoint Analysis of How We Talk About Disability," (with Jeanne Hayes) in *The American Journal of Community Psychology.* She is working on a book, tentatively titled *Seeing Through Gender: A Feminist Methodology for Critical Social Research* (AltaMira Press).

Maxine S. Thompson, Associate Professor at North Carolina State University in the Department of Sociology and Anthropology, received her Ph.D. in sociology from the University of Wisconsin. Her research interests include social support for adolescent mothers, social networks and supports of family members of persons with severe mental illness, and family structure and psychological well-being among African American women.

Debra Umberson is Professor and Chair of the Department of Sociology at the University of Texas at Austin, and received her Ph.D. from Vanderbilt University. Her research focuses on structural determinants of psychological and physical health, gender and relationships, and bereavement and the family. She is now writing a book on the impact of a parent's death on adult children and families based on research supported by a FIRST award from the National Institute on Aging. She is also conducting research on gender and domestic violence.

Lynn Weber is Director of the Women's Studies Program and Professor of Sociology at the University of South Carolina. Her research and teaching explore the intersections of race, class, gender, and sexuality particularly as they are manifest in the process of upward social mobility and work, in women's health, and in the creation of an inclusive classroom environment. In 2001 she published two books, *Understanding Race, Class, Gender, and Sexuality: A Conceptual Framework,* and *Understanding Race, Class, Gender, and Sexuality: Case Studies,* which are intended to move the field of intersectional scholarship ahead by serving as a guide to facilitate intersectional analyses and to foster more integrative thinking in the classroom. Weber is also coauthor of *The American Perception of Class.*

Sue Wilkinson is Professor of Feminist and Health Studies in the Department of Social Sciences at Loughborough University, UK. She is the founding and current editor of the international journal *Feminism & Psychology* and author/editor of six books and more than sixty journal articles and chapters on feminism, sexuality, and health. Her books include *Feminist Social Psychologies,* and, with Celia Kitzinger, *Heterosexuality; Feminism and Discourse;* and *Representing the Other.* Her most recent publications are on women's experience of breast cancer, lesbian health, and the use of focus groups in feminist research.

EDITORS

Sharlene Nagy Hesse-Biber is Professor of Sociology at Boston College. She cofounded the Women's Studies Program at Boston College. She also founded and is now director of the National Association for Women in Catholic Higher Education (NAWCHE). She is author of *Am I Thin Enough Yet? The Cult of Thinness and the Commercialization of Identity* and is coauthor of *Working Women in America: Split Dreams.* She is coeditor of: *Feminist Approaches to Theory and Methodology: An Interdisciplinary Reader; Women in Catholic Higher Education: Border Work, Lived Experiences, and Social Justice;* and *Approaches to Qualitative Research.* She has published widely on the impact of sociocultural factors on women's body image and is codeveloper of HyperRESEARCH, a qualitative data analysis software package. She is recipient of the 2002 New England Sociologist of the Year Award from the New England Sociological Association. She is coauthor of two upcoming new texts, *The Practice of Qualitative Research: A Primer* and *Feminist Research Practice: A Primer.* She earned her Ph.D. in sociology at the University of Michigan.

Michelle L. Yaiser is a member of the faculty at the New England Institute of Art and a doctoral candidate in sociology at Boston College. Having previously published in the areas of feminist and qualitative social research methodologies and feminist theory, she is currently investigating the lives and careers of female musicians for her dissertation. She earned her master's degree in sociology at Boston College. In addition to her sociological work, Michelle is a clarinetist and composer.

Credits

Anderson, Kristin, and Umberson, Debra. "Gendering violence: Masculinity and power in men's accounts of domestic violence," *Gender & Society* (Vol. 15, No. 3, pp. 358–380.) Copyright © Sage Publications, Inc. Reprinted by permission.

Bhavnani, Kum-Kum. "Tracing the contours: Feminist research and feminist objectivity," *Women's Studies International Forum* (Vol. 16, No. 2, 1993, pp. 95–104.) Copyright © Elsevier Science, Ltd. Reprinted by permission.

Chafetz, Janet Saltzman. "Some thoughts by an unrepentant positivist who considers herself a feminist nonetheless," Paper presented at the 85th Annual Meeting of the American Sociology Association. Reprinted by permission.

DeVault, Marjorie. "Talking and listening from women's standpoint: Feminist strategies for interviewing and analysis," *Social Problems* (Vol. 37, No. 1, February 1990, pp. 96–116.) Copyright © The Society for the Study of Social Problems, University of California Press. Reprinted by permission.

Errante, Antoinette. "But sometimes you're not part of the story: Oral histories and ways of remembering and telling," *Educational Researcher* (Vol. 29, pp. 16–27.) Copyright © American Educational Research Association. Reprinted by permission.

Geiger, Susan. "What's so feminist about women's oral history?" *Journal of Women's History* (Spring 1990, Vol. 2, pp.169–182.) Copyright © Indiana University Press. Reprinted by permission.

Harding, Sandra. "Rethinking standpoint epistemology: What is strong objectivity?" Copyright © 1992 *Feminist Epistemologies* (pp. 49–82) by Linda Alcoff and Elizabeth Potter, eds. Reproduced by permission of Routledge, Inc., part of The Taylor & Francis Group.

Harding, Sandra. "Can men be subjects of feminist thought?" Copyright © 1998 *Men Doing Feminism* (pp. 171–195) by Tom Digby, ed. Reproduced by permission of Routledge, Inc., part of The Taylor & Francis Group.

Hill, Shirley, and Sprague, Joey. "Parenting in black and white families: The interaction of gender with race and class," *Gender & Society* (Vol. 13, No. 4, pp. 480–502.) Copyright © Sage Publications, Inc. Reprinted by permission.

Hollander, Jocelyn. "Vulnerability and dangerousness: The construction of gender through conversation about violence," *Gender & Society* (Vol. 15, No. 1, pp. 83–109.) Copyright © Sage Publications, Inc. Reprinted by permission.

Madson, Laura. "Inferences regarding the personality traits and sexual orientation of physically androgynous people," *Psychology of Women Quarterly* (Vol. 24, 2000, pp. 148–160.) Copyright © Blackwell Publishing. Reprinted by permission.

Naples, Nancy. "The outsider phenomenon," in Carolyn Smith and William Kornblum (Eds.), *In the Field* (pp. 139–149). Westport, CT: Praeger. Copyright © Greenwood Publishing Group, Inc. Reprinted by permission.

Reay, Diane. "Rethinking social class: Qualitative perspectives on class and gender," *Sociology* (Vol. 32, 1998, pp. 259–275.) Copyright © Sage Publications, Inc. Reprinted by permission.

Schippers, Mimi. "The social organization of sexuality and gender in alternative hard rock: An analysis of intersectionality," *Gender & Society* (Vol. 14, No. 6, pp. 747–764.) Copyright © Sage Publications, Inc. Reprinted by permission.

Smith, Dorothy E. "Women's perspective as a radical critique of sociology," *Sociological Inquiry* (Vol. 4, No. 1, January 1974, pp. 1–13.) Copyright © Blackwell Publishing. Reprinted by permission.

Sprague, Joey, and Kobrynowicz, Diane. "A feminist epistemology," in Janet Saltzman Chafetz (Ed.), *Handbook of the Sociology of Gender,* pp. 25–44. Copyright © Kluwer Academic/Plenum Publishers. Reprinted by permission.

Thompson, Maxine, and Keith, Verna. "The blacker the berry: Gender, skin tone, self-esteem, and self-efficacy," *Gender & Society* (Vol. 15, No. 3, pp. 336–357.) Copyright © Sage Publications, Inc. Reprinted by permission.

Weber, Lynn. "A conceptual framework for understanding race, class, gender, and sexuality," *Psychology of Women Quarterly,* (Vol. 22, 2000, pp. 13–32.) Copyright © Blackwell Publishing. Reprinted by permission.

Weston, Kathleen. "Fieldwork in lesbian and gay communities," in Families We Choose: *Lesbians, Gays, and Kinship,* pp. 2, 7–17. Copyright © Columbia University Press. Reprinted by permission.

Wilkinson, Sue. "Focus groups in feminist research: Power, interaction, and the co-construction of meaning," *Psychology of Women Quarterly* (Vol. 23, 1999, pp. 221–244.) Copyright © Blackwell Publishing. Reprinted by permission.

PART I

EPISTEMOLOGY, METHODOLOGY, METHOD

CHAPTER 1

Feminist Approaches to Research as a *Process*

Reconceptualizing Epistemology, Methodology, and Method

SHARLENE NAGY HESSE-BIBER, PATRICIA LEAVY, AND MICHELLE L. YAISER

Feminist scholarship is an exciting terrain that is built on the premise of challenging hierarchical modes of creating and distributing knowledge. Feminists employ a variety of strategies for creating knowledge about women and their social worlds which often lies hidden from mainstream society. A feminist approach to knowledge building recognizes the essential importance of examining women's experience. It often takes a critical stance toward traditional knowledge-building claims that argue for "universal truths."[1] Research conducted within a feminist framework is attentive to issues of difference, the questioning of social power, resistance to scientific oppression, and a commitment to political activism and social justice.

Since the "second wave" of the feminist movement in the 1960s, feminists began placing women's issues, experiences, and concerns at the center of disciplinary work (Hesse-Biber 2002). This is not to dismiss the efforts of the many courageous and talented feminists who contributed to knowledge building before the 1960s, but rather to create a point of departure for this writing. The abundant feminist writings of the 1960s and '70s are unique in that "they began a widespread call for a major reassessment of concepts, theories, and methods employed within and across the academic disciplines" (Hesse-Biber 2002, 57). During this time period, feminists began critiquing the research that was being done in those disciplines. These feminists asked why women were being excluded from knowledge construction. They started thinking about research from the point of view of women's lives. At the time, this was a fairly novel idea—it had usually been assumed that whatever was found to be true for men would be true for women. Researchers pointed out how androcentrically (male) biased the sciences and social sciences in fact were, and, how this bias had caused women to be left out of both the research questions and their respective "answers." Feminists made experience (or experiential knowledge) an important category of research. Feminist researchers began to add explicitly women into the research equation. This signified an important shift (expansion) in what was considered researchable and who was considered a valuable source of knowledge. Since then we have seen feminist research develop into many different theoretical, epistemological, and methodological ideas and related practices (see Harding 1987).

There has always been disagreement among feminists concerning what makes a research project "feminist" because feminism is broad in content, methodology, and epistemological positioning. Some feminists reject the scientific model of research known as "positivism," particularly the concept of "objectivity"—the idea that a social scientist should be value-free and detached from her or his research subjects. They propose instead the importance of "attachment" of the researcher to the research process (for some the researcher and researched are "on the same plane," which means that they are similarly situated within the knowledge-building process) and the role of personal experience—more specifically, gathering data on women's experience is a central aspect of the research endeavor. (Bowles and Duelli-Klein 1983; Stanley and Wise 1983; Smith 1987, 1990). Others assert that objective social science does have something to offer feminists and are not ready to dismiss positivism (Chafetz 1990; Jayaratne and Stewart 1991; Sprague and Zimmerman 1993; Oakley 1998). Some assert that it is feminist research that promises the complete reevaluation of research methods, practices, and ethics (Reinharz 1983). Still others define it differently. Despite this lack of consensus on what exactly feminist research is, most scholars acknowledge that there is a difference between feminist and traditional mainstream social science research.

To some extent, the conflicting views about feminism and feminist research provide the strongest support for what we consider to be a most important tenet of any feminist undertaking: the acceptance of the existence of not one feminism but many feminisms. This of course then requires the acceptance of many different feminists. For too long, feminism was justly criticized for being a white, middle-class undertaking here in the United States that all too often paid little attention to or flawed attention to the range of women's lives and experiences. The early feminist researchers did much in terms of revealing errors within their disciplines based on sexism. Yet, these efforts often ignored differences *among* women in terms of race, class, ethnicity, sexuality, and nationality. These studies often "added women and stirred" to preexisting methodological and epistemological frameworks. Within contemporary feminist research, there has been a growing recognition of the problematic concept of a universalized "woman" or "women" and concern about how a researcher's personal characteristics can and do affect the research project (see especially Kum-Kum Bhavnani, this section's readings, who presents a detailed research example of issues of "difference" in the research process; see also Twine and Warren 2000). The body of research produced by feminists now contains the work of scholars who previously had been silenced, including the contributions made by women of color, postcolonial feminists, lesbian, and disabled feminists (see Moraga and Anzaldua 1981; Mohanty 1988; Trinh 1989; Collins 1990; Sedgwick 1993; Mertens, et al. 1994; Perez 1999; Wing 2000).

In this introduction, we provide a brief overview of some of the *critical* concepts in the history of feminist research (feminist empiricism, feminist standpoint, and inclusion of difference) and debates surrounding epistemology, methodology, and method. In Part Two of the book we take up the issue of "difference." We explore the position of the researcher within the research process, focusing on issues of difference in terms of race, class, and gender, as well as sexual preference. In this same vein we also examine how difference impacts women's lives. In the final section of the book, we provide inductive definitions of feminist research by analyzing how feminist researchers talk about and synergistically apply their epistemology, methodology, and methods (both qualitative and quantitative) in pursuit of their research goals.

POSITIVISM

In order to understand the large-scale implications of conducting feminist research it is important to first understand "mainstream" ways of conceptualizing knowledge construction via research. In other words, when we examine classic modes of conceptualizing and creating knowledge we can then begin to unravel the challenge posed by feminists and the ultimate contributions of feminist scholarship.

Social scientific research has historically been conducted from a positivist epistemological position. This is because the social sciences initially followed the natural science model (specifically the well-respected physics model), partly, in order to gain credibility for emergent academic disciplines such as sociology.

Before reviewing the main tenets of positivism it is important to clarify the term *epistemology* because, an epistemological position shapes the entire research process. An epistemology is "a theory of knowledge" (Harding 1987, 3). It is a philosophical theory that represents a fundamental belief system about who can be a knower and what can be known (Harding 1987; Guba and Lincoln 1998). The basic assumptions a researcher brings to bear on her or his research project will influence decisions including what to study (based on what *can* be studied) and how to conduct the research (based on who *can* be a knower and what *can* be known). By first understanding the positivist epistemology that shaped the development of the social sciences, an examination of the feminist challenge to positivism and the corresponding development of the feminist research project becomes possible.

Positivism encompasses what many refer to as "the scientific method." Under this framework, "there is only *one* logic of science, to which any intellectual activity aspiring to the title of 'science' must conform" (Keat and Urry in Neuman 2000, 66). This kind of science is primarily based on deductive modes of knowledge building where objective and value-neutral researchers typically begin with a general cause and effect relationship derived from an abstract general theory. In other words, positivists develop hypotheses about causal relationships between variables. Using methods suited to this framing, such as surveys, experiments, and statistical analyses, positivists attempt to measure the relationship between the variables they have identified as credible indicators of some larger relationship. The data is quantitative, measured, and is professed to be objective. Within positivism, there is also a basic belief that an objective reality exists independent of anyone's individual perspective and thus an objective researcher can access information of social reality. Positivist logic is combined with empirical observations (ascertained through specific research methods) in order to discover and verify causal laws that can be used to predict human behavior. Positivists look for widespread occurrences or otherwise quantifiable patterns that can be presented through statistics on tables, charts, and graphs. The following is an example of how a positivist might approach a research problem.

Sociologists have long been interested in worker satisfaction: How satisfied people are at their jobs? A positivist might approach this issue by identifying a list of "indicators" of job satisfaction. The development of these indicators would be based on specific theories of job satisfaction as well as previous empirical research studies. Such indicators might include job attendance, job performance, rate of promotion, and so forth. Using these indicators a positivist would devise a scale to measure the degree of job satisfaction based on the combined rankings of each of these indicators. The researcher would then proceed to conduct an empirical investigation, for example, collecting data using a survey. In this instance one would administer this scale along with other pertinent questions to a preselected sample of workers and the results could be presented statistically on a graph or a chart. The results from the sample would then, most likely, be generalized to a larger population.

According to positivism the social world is ordered and thus predictable. Causal relationships between variables can be identified and measured, patterns can be revealed, and social behaviors can thus be predicted. We can predict whether or not people will be satisfied with their work based on a variety of indicators that result in overall patterns. An objective knower, the researcher, can access these knowable "facts" through the application of scientific methods of measurement and statistical methods of analysis in a value-neutral context. While this is a general description of positivist epistemology, one may have noticed how certain methods of data collection and analyses are "suited" toward these assumptions. This is a critical point. While research methods are discussed more specifically later, the relationship between epistemology and methods is a direct one. While positivist science has historically denied the relationship between theories of knowledge and the use of methods, thereby de-linking theory from methods, one can see that in fact positivism, like all epistemological traditions, is intimately connected to the selection and application of research methods.

ANDROCENTRICISM IN SCIENCE AND SOCIAL SCIENCE

Most socially and culturally valid undertakings, both creative and intellectual, have historically been produced within male-dominated social spheres. Science and scientific research have certainly been prime examples of this historical phenomenon. Some argue (see Keller 1978 for example) that science is more intrinsically (socially) masculine than any other human undertaking. The identification of scientific thought with masculinity is strongly rooted in Western culture and can be directly related to the dichotomy of gender stereotypes and socialization within culture (for a psychoanalytical account of this see Chodorow 1978).[2] The objective sciences are commonly dubbed "hard" and deal solely with facts. The more subjective sciences (usually the social sciences) are considered "soft" and deal more with interpretations and feelings. These distinctions invoke both sexual and gender metaphors—the masculine is hard and logical, the feminine is soft and emotional. Fox Keller argues that this dichotomy within science is a reflection of cultural gender stereotypes that results in masculine biased, androcentric science and research.

Some classic examples of feminists identifying androcentric bias in scientific work include the work of Emily Martin, Nancy Tuana, and Zuleyma Tang Halpin. Anthropologist Emily Martin has analyzed the sexist language used in medical journals to describe the female body and reproduction. She reveals, for example, that medical discourse used to depict the egg and sperm during conception in medical journals promotes an image of women's inferiority by using language in ways that make the "sperm" appear dominant. She uncovers a range of stereotypical terms employed in medical science and suggests the importance of uncovering these stereotypical cultural images so that we can "rob them of their power to naturalize our social conventions about gender" (Martin 1999, 25).

In a study similar to Martin's analysis of the language used to describe the process of conception, Tuana's analysis of the language used to describe reproductive theories shows how "scientists work within and through the worldview of their time" (Tuana 1988, 147). Using theories on reproduction from Aristotle to the preformationists, she provides support for the argument that science has frequently provided a biological explanation and justification for women being ritualistically treated by society in an inferior way. Both Martin's and Tuana's work ultimately highlighted that androcentric bias is rampant even within the "hard" sciences that we often take for granted as "scientific" and "objective." In fact, even medical knowledge is produced in a social environment—it is conducted by imprinted[3] persons in a value-laden context.

Broadening the discussion of androcentrism in science to a bias against all minorities, Halpin links scientific objectivity with a general process of "othering." Halpin states that young scientists are taught that "science is intellect and absolute 'rationality,' and that emotions and feelings must not be allowed to play any part in the process" (Halpin 1989, 285). Yet through reading the works she cites, it becomes quite clear that emotions have played a key role in science. Science has frequently passed judgment, a process that includes referring to not only one's logic, but also one's emotions. Scientists have relegated anything that is not like them, which historically means white middle- to upper-class heterosexual Christian male, to the "other" category. Since anything "other" is different than self, it has historically been assumed to be inferior. This belief, Halpin points out, is part of the reason science has been fundamental to the maintenance of a patriarchal social order.

There are some key works that have revealed androcentric bias in other disciplines such as psychology, philosophy, and sociology. Carolyn Wood Sherif outlines the androcentric history of psychology and the existence of sexist bias that was recognized by the turn of the last century. Beginning with Weisstein's 1960s thesis that "psychology has nothing to say about what women are really like, what they need and what they want, essentially because psychology does not know" (Sherif 1987, 38), Sherif criticizes psychology for its male hierarchy of status based upon type and topic of study within the discipline, its reliance upon and embracement of the traditional methods of biological and physical sciences, and its belief of its own objectivity. These characteristics of psychology were worsened by the fact that psychology only mimicked the form of the natural sciences, not their standards. This mimicking led to false beliefs about how to pursue knowledge and limited psychology's ability to study seriously and explain women and gender.

Feminist philosopher Susan Bordo (1999) provides another classic example of androcentric bias. She underscores women's exclusion from philosophical discourse and points out that "the history of philosophy can meaningfully and nonreductively be characterized as 'male'" (Bordo 1999, 30). Her work echoes Fox Keller. The assumption is that men, who have distanced themselves from their surroundings, meaning that they practiced impersonal and apolitical research, have developed the scientific method. Millman and Kanter (1987) criticize sociology and its androcentric bias in several important ways and note for example that the field of sociology assumes "the use of certain field-defining models," which can deter exploration of new areas of knowledge building. The field also tends to focus on the "public sphere" of society to the detriment of what they see as the "less dramatic, private, and invisible spheres of social life and organization." They also stress that sociology assumes a unitary society with regard to men and women—what is true for men must be true for women. They point to the lack of taking gender as a category of analysis in its own right, and the tendency of sociology to explain the "status quo." Lastly, the field favors certain methodologies (read quantitative) that prevent the discovery of "subjugated knowledges," especially women's experiences and their interpretation of them.

Reinharz (1985, 156) notes that the context and the content of sociology itself was sexist. She supported her argument by discussing how the institutions within which sociology is often conducted (universities, hospitals, and research institutes) are male centered and by giving disconcerting examples of blatant sexism in both the contemporary classic works of the discipline and in the textbooks: "My point is that the writing of sociologists reveals their view of society, a view that sees women primarily as stupid, sexually unexciting wives *or* objects of sexual desire and violence" (1985, 165).

Having reviewed some classic examples of feminists revealing androcentric bias within the sciences and social sciences, it is important to return to the example of a positivist studying worker satisfaction. Sociologists have a long history of studying this topic, and, no surprise to feminists, these efforts have traditionally produced androcentrically biased knowledge.

Early positivists studying worker satisfaction excluded women from their samples and relied solely on men. It had been assumed that men work in the paid labor force and accordingly their satisfaction is sociologically important. If women do work, then what is true for men would also be true for women. Even if women were randomly included in a research sample, the data was not differentiated based on gender (Hesse-Biber and Carter 2000). Experiences unique to women at work were not recorded. This is an example of how women have been completely excluded from the research question and consequently data gathering. Likewise, when studying the private sphere and family life men have largely been excluded from research. This is because the private sphere is viewed as less important to men—their primary role is that of worker, not father and homemaker. Women who work in the home as wives and mothers have also been excluded from this research. They simply have not been asked about their satisfaction in the home. When feminists began asking these women about their daily life experiences and satisfaction a range of issues such as depression and boredom emerged, which is precisely what Betty Friedan labeled "the problem with no name" (Friedan 1983). These examples of exclusion exemplify the complexity of gender bias within this body of research, revealing that gender serves as a master status (see Higginbotham 1992) used to produce biased knowledge. On the occasions where women have been included in job satisfaction research, androcentrically biased knowledge has persisted because of the theoretical framework imposed. When positivists have included women in their studies they have largely been working from a "social problems" model asking questions such as: "Why do women work?" (Hesse-Biber and Carter 2000, 6). The implicit assumption is that women working is an aberration from the norm—from their proper place in the home and not a subject in need of sociological research. In other words, it has not been viewed as a question of work satisfaction in the same way as research conducted on men (Hesse-Biber and Carter 2000, 6–10). The androcentrically biased knowledge that results serves to reinforce the stereotypical ways that we think about men and women, particularly in relation to their roles, responsibilities, and needs in the public and private spheres.

As more and more feminists began identifying and criticizing the androcentricism of their disciplines, the simple acknowledgment of gender was not enough. Feminists began applying their own approaches to research and ultimately began challenging the very foundation of modern science: positivism.

FEMINIST RESPONSES TO POSITIVISM AND ANDROCENTRISM

Feminist Empiricism

Initially, many feminist scholars with a commitment to eradicating sexism in the sciences became what Sandra Harding (1991) calls "feminist empiricists." These feminist scholars believed that androcentric bias can be eliminated from knowledge construction if 1) they adhere to the tenets of positivism more strictly, and 2) add women and other minorities into their research samples.

Many scholars believe that the androcentric bias in both the physical and social sciences is the result of "bad science." The biases and prejudices found in the research are a result of the guidelines, rules, and standards of science not having been implemented properly or followed closely enough. Feminist empiricists argue that sexism and all other biases can be eliminated from science if researchers would adhere strictly to the existing methodologies of science. In other words, the scientific method and positivist conceptions of objectivity can produce responsible knowledge *if* they are rigorously followed (see Eichler 1988).

Feminist empiricism challenges the assumptions of traditional empiricism in three ways (Harding 1991). First, in order to eliminate bias, the researcher has to examine the context of discovery (What are the research questions/problems addressed in this study?) as well as the context of justification (How is this research carried out? What methods are employed?) Researchers need to recognize that the cultural filters through which the world is viewed are institutionalized and may not be visible to the individual. Feminist empiricists argue that the scientific method and objectivity can (possibly) identify and eliminate individual biases, but not the ones that are held culture-wide.

Second, the scientific method is powerless to eliminate certain biases when those biases enter the project through the identification and definition of research problems. For example, viewing women at work as a social problem in need of investigation/prevention is an example of sexism defining the research topic. The hypotheses that would challenge androcentric beliefs and encourage the production of useful and accurate knowledge about women are largely ignored in traditional empiricist research. An example of an alternative hypothesis would be asking about women's job satisfaction without applying a social problems model or asking about women's satisfaction in the home, both of which have been largely ignored in traditional empiricist research. Feminist empiricists also criticize traditional epistemologies and methodologies for not placing the research project on the same plane as the research subjects. Even if someone were to identify a research problem from a woman's perspective, if the project is placed on the plane above the subjects, the inequitable power structures of society are replicated and androcentricism comes through the project unscathed. The research merely reproduces societal relations of dominance

And third, although feminist empiricists claim that bias and androcentrism can be eliminated, or at least mitigated from research by following the rules of the scientific method more rigorously, they at times acknowledge that traditional methods of data collection were designed by traditional scientists, men. The normative methods of scientific inquiry were designed by researchers to produce answers to the kinds of questions an androcentric society has. So while we traditionally think of a research method as merely a tool that can be applied by anyone, the origin and history of those tools need investigation.

Harding also discusses how feminist empiricists may help increase feminism's respect even amongst mainstream academics by using "traditional" methods and maintaining some use of "objectivity." Harding discusses the value of relying on traditional methods in feminist research as a strength of feminist empiricism:

> [F]eminist empiricism appears to leave intact much of scientists' and philosophers' conventional understanding of the principles of adequate scientific research. It appears to challenge mainly the incomplete practice of the scientific method, not the norms of science themselves . . . it conserves, preserves, and saves understandings of scientific inquiry that have been intellectually and politically powerful. (Harding 1991, 113)

By conducting their critique of sexist research with only a minimal challenge to the fundamental logic and dominant philosophies of science, feminist empiricist critiques are more widely understood and accepted into conventional bodies of knowledge with less resistance than other forms of feminism. Feminist empiricists are able to present their research findings widely within the academy simply because their methodology is accepted and respected. By using a positivist approach these scholars, who also self-identify as feminists, are still working within the dominant system, although perhaps on the margins of that system.

Without questioning and transforming the epistemological basis on which the scientific method is employed, feminist empiricists replicate more mainstream research with women "added in." Such criticisms of the initial ways feminist empiricists attempted to eliminate sexism from knowledge construction prompted a thorough and continuous interrogation of positivism and its inextricable links to hierarchical forms of knowledge. Beyond dismantling positivism, these critical feminists have created a range of epistemological and methodological alternatives to dominant science.

Feminist Challenges to the Tenets of Positivism: The Reconceptualization of Epistemology, Methodology, and Method

Once feminists opened up a dialogue about epistemology and began adding women into research projects, an interrogation of positivism followed. Critically analyzing the major tenets of positivism, feminists began to challenge traditional notions of knowledge building and to develop new feminist epistemological approaches to the research process. Feminists were asking new research questions (with new methodologies) aimed at accessing what Michel Foucault (1980) called "subjugated knowledges." In order to understand the value added by a feminist perspective, one must review the feminist critique of positivism that spawned new epistemological and methodological approaches to knowledge building.

Feminist perspectives in social research question positivism's answers to the epistemological questions of who can possess knowledge, how knowledge is or can be obtained, and what knowledge is. Many feminists conceptualize truth differently than mainstream researchers and assert that women and other marginalized groups can possess knowledge and also recognize that people may not always gather knowledge in the same way. Because there are a variety of knowledge-gathering techniques used by researchers, many feminists do not believe one method of knowledge gathering is inherently better or worse than any other.

The overall feminist critique of positivism is multifaceted. First, feminists have contemplated deeply the notion of a "worldview" or "paradigm." A paradigm is a socially constructed "worldview that guides the researcher" (Guba and Lincoln 1998, 200). First explicated by Thomas Kuhn, paradigms are worldviews through which all knowledge is filtered (1970, 175). Epistemological questions are embedded within paradigms (Guba and Lincoln 1998, 201). If you decide to study women's satisfaction in their workplace it is because you assume it to be researchable. Accordingly, feminists have pointed out that the epistemological assumptions on which positivism is based have been shaped by the larger culture and perpetuate the hierarchies that characterize social life: patriarchy, elitism, heterosexism, and racialized modes of social power. Recognizing that positivism is both a reflection and extension of the dominant worldview and is used in the service of maintaining unequal power relations, feminists began asking a question that for years had been taken for granted: What is the nature of social reality (Nielsen 1990)? This questioning led to a critical reevaluation of the assumptions embedded within positivism, which are discussed in the Sprague and Kobrynowicz essay in this volume.

Sprague and Zimmerman (1993) outline the feminist critique of positivism by stating that positivism creates false dichotomies that bias the research process. Applying this back to the discussion of feminist empiricists one can see that if feminists employ a positivist framework on/with/through their research, even if they ask questions to and about women, the resulting knowledge may remain biased. Sprague and Zimmerman detail the major dichotomies within positivism that produce dominant knowledge and argue that researchers must integrate these dualisms in order to create a feminist methodology intended to unravel dominant relations of power rather than assist in their maintenance.

Positivist science assumes a subject-object split where the researcher is taken for granted as the knowing party. The researcher and researched, or, knower and knowable, are on different planes within the research process. By privileging the researcher as the knowing party a hierarchy paralleling that of patriarchal culture is reproduced. Unequal power relations between the researcher and the research participants serve to transform the research subject into an object. This is the same process of "othering" that Halpin (1989) explained resulted in the "scientific oppression" of all who didn't resemble the researcher. Positivists traditionally *seek* knowledge in a narrow self-contained way whereas feminists aim at *developing* knowledge *with* their research subjects who bring their own experiential knowledge, concerns, and emotions to the project. As Sprague and Kobrynowicz explain in their essay included in this volume, positivism tried (unsuccessfully) to produce a "view from nowhere" whereas feminists aim at producing the "view from somewhere." Feminists are concerned with accessing different voices.

Positivism also encompasses a rational-emotional dualism. This facet of positivism assumes the researcher to be value-neutral and objective. Sprague and Zimmerman explain that this assumption, in conjunction with the subject-object split, has sustained patriarchal modes of knowledge building. The denial of values, biases, and politics is unrealistic and undesirable. Emotions and values often serve as the impetus to a research endeavor (Jaggar 1989; Sprague and Zimmerman 1993). For example, a researcher may be interested in studying women's satisfaction at their workplace because they want to help women to be empowered in their work environment or they want to produce knowledge that validates women's unique work experiences. Likewise, a researcher may wish to study working fathers' satisfaction in the home in order to validate these long silenced experiences. Additionally, when we move beyond the standard methods available to positivists and begin to consider qualitative methods such as oral histories, in-depth interviews, and ethnography, it becomes clear that many methodological choices rely on the creation of relationships between researchers and research participants. These data-yielding relationships may be emotional by necessity. In sum, positivism is based on a dichotomous research event whereas feminist research is a process that occurs on a fluid continuum.

Haraway (1988 and 1993), Harding (this volume), and Bhavnani (this volume), believe objectivity, encompassed in the subject-object and rational-emotional dichotomies, needs to be transformed into "feminist objectivity." Both Harding's and Bhavnani's articles in this section of the volume use Donna Haraway's definition of this term: "Feminist objectivity means quite simply situated knowledges" (Bhavnani 1993, 96; Harding 1993, 49). Feminist objectivity changes the strong dualism of objectivity and subjectivity into a dialectic. The nature of knowledge and truth is that it is partial, situated, subjective, power imbued, and relational. Feminist objectivity combines the goal of conventional objectivity—to conduct research completely free of social influence or personal beliefs—with the reality that no one can achieve this goal. All research occurs within a society. The society's beliefs, ideologies, traditions, structure, etc., all impact the research in multiple ways. Feminist objectivity acknowledges the fact that the researcher is going to bring the influences of society into the project. It also recognizes that objectivity can only operate within the limitations of the scientist's personal beliefs and experiences. Positivists recognize the context of discovery and the context of justification as the two phases of scientific research. The context of discovery is the process through which researchers develop research questions such as studying women's satisfaction in their workplace. The context of justification is the process through which the research questions are tested. Both Harding (1991) and Sprague and Zimmerman (1993) critique positivism and objectivity because objectivity is only applied to the context of justification. Researchers disclose *how* they studied their topic, but not *why*. Positivism is not designed to rationally explain the context of discovery because it is a "seemingly idiosyncratic and mysterious process" (Sprague and Zimmerman 1993, 259). Acknowledging the fact that objectivity is limited by the researcher's situation and is absent from the context of discovery actually strengthens objectivity, according to Harding. Conventional objectivity does not concern itself with the context of discovery, thus "it is too weak to accomplish even the goals for which it has been designed . . ." (Harding 1993, 51). By disclosing *why* sociologists study a topic, and the decisions that went into conceptualizing research design, one gains a better understanding of the varied issues pertaining to the topic and how one can continue to create reflexive research projects (research that is attentive to the complexity of power relations) in order to create larger amounts of contextualized knowledge.

Harding's work is a significant contribution to the reevaluation of scientific objectivity and so we have included her essay in Part I. Harding's concept "strong objectivity" examines not only the context of justification but also the context of discovery. It is a process of disclosing the histories, positions, influences, beliefs, morals, etc. of the researcher at every step of the research project. In other words, the researcher is obligated to disclose her own subject position throughout the research process. The subject as well as the object of knowledge is to be critically examined. Feminist objectivity is applied to the research questions and the researcher, not just the methods.

This feminist critique has linked positivistic sociology with social dominance in two ways: (1) the conduct of research is carried out through social relationships of differential power with the attendant risks of exploitation and abuse; (2) research is inherently political in facilitating particular structures of power within the larger society, either those already in existence or those through which the currently oppressed are empowered (Sprague and Zimmerman 1993, 260). Feminists state that during the actual research process, positivism makes the subject of the study an object of dominance, thus reproducing the experience of the oppressed or marginalized in the social world. In positivistic research, the subject's only input into the research is the answers she or he gives in response to the researcher's questions. The questions asked, the variables and their conceptualization, the design of the research project, and the judgment criteria used by the researcher are all an expression of a specific viewpoint or belief held by the researcher. Research is thus inherently value-laden and reflects the power structures within which the researcher operates.

The feminist critique of positivism is the starting point for many feminists to develop alternative methodologies and methods. The basic premise of almost all of the feminist methodologies is the epistemological belief that women can possess and share valuable knowledge and thus research can start from the perspective of women's lives (see Smith 1974 and 1987; Harding 1993). There is no universal truth in a hierarchal society but rather partial and context-bound truths that can be accessed through relationships with our research participants. The knowledges produced are then less generalizable; feminists aim for partial truths rather than engaging in a process of scientific distortion. Conceptualizing women as a starting point for research not only validates their knowledge and includes them in a process from which they have long been excluded, but also attempts to upend the power relations that are reproduced in traditional, positivistic, scientific research. This is also true when starting research from any traditionally "othered" position, not just the position of women, and acknowledging the complexity of positionality that shapes people's experiences and attitudes based on the intersectionality of a variety of characteristics such as race, class, gender, nationality and sexuality (see Dill 1983; King 1988; Mohanty 1988; Sandoval, 1991; Higginbotham 1992; Collins 1999).

Feminists have specific ideas about the entire research process from the formulation of the research question to the reporting of the results. One must not confuse methodology with method. The distinction between the two terms is very important. People working within the social sciences often use the terms *method* and *methodology* interchangeably. According to Harding, this lack of distinction or preoccupation with method can lead to the mystification of the most interesting aspects of feminist research processes. While Harding is quick to point out that method and methodology are not interchangeable, she also cautions that they do interact together in a dynamic process and are thus intimately linked.

In her introduction to *Feminism and Methodology,* Harding defines method as follows:

> A research *method* is a technique for (or way of proceeding in) gathering evidence. One could reasonably argue that all evidence-gathering techniques fall into one of the following three categories: listening to (or interrogation) informants, observing behavior, or examining historical traces and records. (1987, 2)

All researchers use a method or a variety of methods while conducting their research. Feminist researchers may use a wider variety of methods in a single project or use methods that may be considered unique to feminist research, but anyone may use the methods used by feminist researchers. Feminists even employ methods that have been used by androcentric researchers as evidenced by feminist empiricism. Many feminist research projects have used survey methods and quantitative data analysis—two traditionally androcentric methods—to produce women-centered results. Methods such as intensive interviewing, the collection of oral histories, and qualitative content analysis are often labeled feminist methods by "traditional" sociologists; however, studies conducted by "traditional" sociologists have also relied on these methods. One of the things that makes feminism unique is that feminists employ so many different methods and often combine quantitative and qualitative approaches in order to create multi-method designs that gather knowledge in different forms and from different perspectives. Methods are a step-by-step process for collecting data. Methods are tools that aid research. Any researcher, female or male, may follow the steps. Thus, methods can be neither gendered nor labeled feminist/nonfeminist.

Scholars create a feminist methodology by arguing against the mainstream ways research has proceeded and how theory has been applied to research questions and to data. In other words, feminists explicitly link theory with methods. A *methodology* is a theory and analysis of how research does or should proceed (Harding 1987, 3). A primary principle of feminist methodology, according to Sprague and Zimmerman, is that it retains a commitment to the empowerment of women and other oppressed people: "Thus, feminist research is connected in principle to feminist struggle" (Sprague and Zimmerman 1993, 266).

Feminist Standpoint Epistemology and Methodology

Feminist standpoint epistemology begins with research questions (methodologies) rooted in women's lives (the researched)—women's everyday existence. Standpoint theorists explain that a hierarchical society will produce different standpoints, or vantage points, from which social life is experienced. Standpoint is based on the Hegelian idea that the oppressed have developed a dual perspective: their personal perspective developed through experience and their perspective of their oppressors, which they develop to survive. Structural difference thus creates difference in experiences and beliefs. Drawing on Hegelian and Marxist theory of the master/slave relationship, Nancy Hartstock (1983) asserts that because of women's location within the sexual division of labor and because of their experience of oppression women have greater insights as researchers into the lives of other women. Members of the dominant group on the other hand, were thought to only have a partial viewpoint based on their privileged position. Standpoint is thus an achievement—it is earned based on one's position in the social order. Dorothy Smith (1987), a pioneer of women's standpoint epistemology, asserts that a way of knowing must start from women's lives, and stresses the importance of women's own understanding and experience in creating knowledge (1987, 107). Standpoint epistemology, of course, is not without its own set of challenges regarding issues of knowledge building. If knowledge should start out from the oppressed, how can one determine who is the most oppressed? Can only women understand women? Why do those at the margins have a less distorted viewpoint and how does this happen? Moreover, is the viewpoint of those historically marginalized less distorted or differently distorted?

Critics of feminist standpoint epistemology feel uncomfortable with giving up positivism's claim of universal truth. Feminist researchers, after all, embrace multiple subjectivities. Does that lead to relativism? Chaos? No. By starting with the lives of marginalized people, standpoint theory not only critically examines the marginalized groups as done in the past, but also critically examines the lives of the dominant groups. It centers on the relationship between politics and knowledge. By using the marginalized position as the starting point, *objectivity is maximized.* Knowledge can be produced for marginalized groups, rather than about marginalized groups for the use of dominant groups to maintain hierarchical power relations.

Starting research from the standpoint of the oppressed is valid because it is often the lives and experiences of oppressed people that provide significant insight and perspective. Complex human relations can become visible when research is started at the bottom of he social hierarchy. Starting at the top of the hierarchy, as traditional science has often done, can actually hide some of the daily processes, events, and experiences that occur within society. When feminists began to employ feminist standpoint epistemology and methodology research shifted, new questions were asked, new topics emerged—social scientific inquiry changed. For example, the daily lives of women who worked in the home in both paid and unpaid labor (housewives, mothers, domestic workers) had long been ignored within our culture and the academy. Standpoint theorists began to research these neglected facets of social life by beginning with the perspective of women. This research has contributed greatly to our knowledge of the hidden aspects of "women's work," such as housework, feeding the family, and mothering (see for example Smith 1987; Devault 1991).

Standpoint theory is often employed in feminist methodology because women, having been dominated by men, have formed this dual perspective.[4] They know the workings of not only the female world, but also much of the male world. Problems that women face on a daily basis are often invisible to, or ignored by, the male eye. It is these problems that are of interest to many feminist researchers. Accordingly, many feminist researchers use standpoint epistemology as a part of feminist methodology and it has become an important approach to socially just research (see O'Leary 1997).

Issues of Difference

Standpoint Theory and many other feminist theories have not historically been sensitive to issues of difference beyond gender. Feminists have complicated the idea of a single "women's experience" and now stress the importance of difference even beyond the differences in conceptualizing standpoint detailed in the articles included for Part I. Standpoint has been challenged and expanded in other important ways in an effort to deessentialize women's experiences and account for gender as an attribute that directly intersects with other socially constructed categorizations that *together* comprise one's standpoint (be it researcher or researched).

Patricia Hill Collins (1990) has been at the forefront in challenging white feminist definitions of standpoint in order to resist the false notion that gender simply subsumes other characteristics within patriarchal culture. This notion merely reflects the position of racial privilege white feminists occupy—a status that long went unrecognized within the white feminist movement and the academy. As opposed to essentializing on the basis of gender, which is, ironically, a systemic practice in patriarchal culture, feminists must complicate their definition and application of standpoint and actively resist the tendency to assume the existence of a "universal woman" or woman's experience. Patricia Hill Collins calls for an "afrocentric" feminist standpoint epistemology which looks at the intersectionality of race, class, and gender in defining a person's standpoint, thereby shaping their experiences, viewpoints, and perceptions. As Patricia Hill Collins rightfully explains, social power is not simply dichotomous within Western culture. The social order is a complex web of power relations (Foucault 1980). She refers to this as a "matrix of domination" where race, class, and gender are overdetermined in relation to each other. She conceptualizes race, class, and gender as "interlocking systems of oppression" (Collins 1990, 234; see also Dill 1983; King 1988). Perhaps returning to the example of worker satisfaction will help elucidate this critical insight.

Early standpoint theorists began asking women questions that had not previously been asked. For example, standpoint researchers have long conducted research on women's satisfaction in the private sphere, as mothers and homemakers. This research was important as it probed into otherwise underresearched areas and validated the experiences of many women; however, this work initially did little by way of addressing the multiplicity of experiences *and* the issues of import from the perspectives of women with varied backgrounds in terms of race, social class, and sexuality. Not all women have the same issues, concerns, choices, and views on family/work. For example, it has been suggested that an overall solution to the work/family issues for working women is the expansion of day care. This, on the surface seems like a good idea. But the solution raises problematic issues regarding who is going to deliver these services and who will benefit from them. Glenn (1992) notes that historically women of color and new immigrants provided such labor, often at exploitative wages, while white middle-class women received the benefits. What seemed like a good idea for one group of women may not necessarily be of immediate benefit for another group. Recognizing the diversity of women's experiences and how these are shaped not only by their gender, but also by their racial, ethnic, cultural, sexual preference, age, and economic background is crucial in guarding against a unidimensional view of the category *woman*. Likewise, not all women experience gender as their socially defining characteristic in terms of perceived impact on daily life. Patricia J. Williams (1991) eloquently describes how within her workspace (she is a law professor at a top university) there are times when the experience of her standpoint shifts its center, from woman to African American and vice versa, based on the context in which she finds herself.

Not only is one's achieved status multidimensional, it is also fluid. Understanding how difference is generated within the research process utilizing such concepts as Patricia Hill Collins's (1990) "matrix of domination" will enable feminist researchers to compose research questions and techniques aimed at generating new knowledge. Nancy Naples (1999) uses a "multidimensional" standpoint in order to develop a method for exploring women's political activism. Standpoint, she notes, is not only located within specific individuals but also within communities as well as in "how things are put together" in the actualities of women's lives (49). These are "the social relations embedded in women's everyday activities" (45). She believes a multidimensional standpoint provides useful information on how communities are structured politically and how their members promote or inhibit political activism. By understanding these processes, we can uncover the weaknesses of systems of oppression and thereby "account for the possibility of resistance—a central goal of feminist praxis" (Naples 1999, 48). Part II of this volume takes up the issues of difference in research in more detail.

Emerging Epistemologies and Methodologies: Postmodern Feminisms

Standpoint epistemology is not the only philosophical grounding from which feminists work. Critical, post-structural, postcolonial, and postmodern theories (postmodern being the umbrella category) have converged to create a new moment in scholarship that focuses on interdisciplinary practice (Denzin and Lincoln 1998). The growth of the postmodern theoretical paradigm has served as the impetus for the emergence of new epistemological and methodological practices. Feminists have been and will continue to be an integral part of these new approaches to the research process. Feminists' widespread affinity to the practice of postmodernism is easily understood when paralleling the main tenets of postmodern epistemology to feminism itself. For some contemporary feminists, postmodern theory and practice is simply congruent with the general currents within the feminist project itself. Feminists from all traditions have always been concerned with including women in their research in order to rectify the historic reliance on men as research subjects. This is a general feminist concern. Postmodern scholars are unified in their concern for bringing the "Other" into research, which some contemporary feminists thus see as an extension of the feminist project. Postmodern scholars emphasize an oppositional politics aimed at empowering previously subjugated peoples (Denzin and Lincoln 1998). Postmodern research is thus a "transformative endeavor" practiced in order to denaturalize and transform oppressive power-knowledge relations with the intent of creating a more just world (Denzin and Lincoln 1998). In particular, postmodernism uses the voice of the "Other" in highly reflexive and politically imbued ways in order to deconstruct "metanarratives" (overreaching stories) used in the domination of some over others (Denzin and Lincoln 1998). Reflexive practice is that which accounts for the dialectical and reciprocal workings of power, including: the changing position of the researcher within the research process, the sociohistorical context, and the changing relations of power within which the research participants operate. This is a different tradition than "giving voice" to the marginalized, as feminist scholars working from other epistemologies (such as standpoint) are engaged in. The postmodern framework embodies a goal of emancipation that unifies some feminist researchers, although other feminists, as discussed earlier, aim at including women in research but not transforming the larger power structure that colonizes them. Feminist researchers have drawn on the tenets of postmodern epistemology in order to develop unique methodological approaches aimed at producing research inclusive of difference.

The interface between critical and postmodern theory has been significant in developing new forms of feminism. Postmodern feminism and other forms of critical theory including postcolonial feminism aim at creating political cultural resistance to hierarchical modes of structuring social life by being attentive to the dynamics of power and knowledge. Postmodern feminism is the umbrella term we are using to discuss these emergent forms of feminism; however, it is important to realize that this is a generalization. Postcolonial feminists are primarily concerned with de-colonizing the Other from the social and political forces that colonize, subjugate, disempower, and even enslave those deemed Other in a global context. Post-structural feminists are concerned with critical deconstruction as a method of exposing and transforming oppressive power relations. Critical feminists who often also share these post-structuralist practices are wary of privileging one truth over another and thus resist recreating hierarchies by privileging their own knowledges. All of these concerns and practices are a part of the larger term *postmodernism* and so we are using the umbrella term *postmodern feminism* as a way of encompassing these feminist methodologies. Postmodern feminists often use texts (in varied forms), the products of dominant culture and signs of postmodernity, in conjunction with the view of the oppressed, as the starting point of cultural interrogation. Some of these postmodern feminists have directly drawn on French post-structural theory (which can be viewed as a current within postmodernism), and engaged in a process of critical deconstruction. Feminist scholar Luce Irigaray was at the forefront of this endeavor and details a method of "jamming the theoretical machinery" (1985, 78) not in order to reconstruct another view of the social world (an exercise in power and colonization) but rather to unravel the social processes and relations that have constructed the social world in hierarchical ways. This process of critical interrogation, or "jamming," creates resistance within the system thereby altering power-knowledge relations in an organic way. This practice is a new form of political creation that occurs by creating resistance to dominant knowledge and then allowing that resistance to disrupt the social system thereby necessitating change.

Building on postmodernist principles and this initial feminist post-structuralist scholarship, postmodern feminists have detailed specific methodologies to fit their unique research objectives. Adrien Katherine Wing (2000) highlights another important emerging epistemology called "global critical race feminism." Feminists working from this epistemology are creating a new feminism of difference drawing on postmodern conceptualizations of power and knowledge in a global and increasingly interconnected context. Wing explains that feminists working in this new tradition must account for the context of global postmodern forms of power when considering the nature and impact of intersectionality, which is the standpoint created based on a combination of locations within the social structure (i.e., race, class, gender, sexuality, geography, etc.). Drawing on the work of feminist critical scholar Audre Lorde, Wing explains the "holistic nature of identity" (2000, 10). Wing goes on to adopt Mari Matsuda's term *multiple consciousness* in order to elucidate the complexity of positionality within a global context. Multiple consciousness implies that intersectionality creates people that possess understandings of multiple locations within the social hierarchy, not just within one's culture, but also with the potential of a global awareness of difference of interconnected systems of power. The term can then be employed by feminists in order to create, implement, and move forward new politics of liberation. Many feminist scholars share the position that the feminist agenda has changed from a simple question of equality to a "feminism of difference" (Oliveira 2000, 4; Sandoval 2000; Wing 2000). This means that feminists working in this tradition are not simply interested in giving women the same "rights" as men, but accounting for the differences amongst us in terms of gender, race, ethnicity, class, and sexuality and creating a social structure that is congruent with such differences and the corresponding perspectives yielded. The term *multiple consciousness* then goes farther than the double-consciousness contained within standpoint epistemology, making this an important emergent feminist tradition.

Postmodern feminist scholar Chela Sandoval (2000) also acknowledges the importance of multiple consciousness, and, drawing on the tenets of postmodern theory goes farther by asserting that scholars must gain access to "oppositional consciousness." The implication within her term is important as it indicates that not only does the Other develop a multi-perspective based on their complex location(s) within the social structure, but that the resulting consciousness is in opposition to the dominant culture in which they are oppressed. Resistance to colonizing hierarchical forms is thus built into the vision of those Othered by such systems. Accordingly, Sandoval develops a unique methodology aimed at accessing differential consciousness. She names her methodology "a methodology of the oppressed," which is a methodology of "emancipation" from hegemonically structured modes of power. Not only is Sandoval's framework the product of her attention to postmodern epistemology, but also a result of the postmodern world in which research is now conducted. Sandoval explains that feminists must conduct research that emancipates those who are Othered by "neocolonizing postmodern global formations" within our hyperreal context. In other words, postmodern feminists must decolonize with specific attention to new and emerging formations of domination and subjugation that are particular to postmodernity. She asserts that languages of "supremacy," which are either taken for granted or, in Denzin and Lincoln's term "misrecognized" (1998), must be "ruptured" through reflexive power-attentive methodological practice. In other words, narratives of domination may be intentionally misunderstood and accordingly must be ripped apart through the research process. The feminist agenda thus involves the "decoding" of postmodern languages of "domination and resistance" (Sandoval 2000). Through interdisciplinary research feminists must "deregulate" the postmodern global system of domination and subjugation. Sandoval's methodology of the oppressed involves the reflexive application of five techniques: 1) semiotics, 2) deconstruction, 3) meta-ideologizing, 4) democratics, and 5) differential consciousness (2000).

Kum-Kum Bhavani's article (this volume) is an important piece of feminist scholarship because it discusses the complexity of women's standpoint by drawing on standpoint epistemology, postmodernism, and third world feminism. Encompassing many of the strategies Sandoval details Bhavani explores the relationship between history and "oppositional consciousness" (Perez 1999; Narayan and Harding 2000; Sandoval 2000).

Bhavani draws on the post-structural strain in postmodern feminist thought by focusing on how feminists can use history within their research as a way of "jamming" the system, or, creating apparent tensions in hierarchically informed knowledge. In this vein history can be integrated into feminist scholarship as a method of creating resistance. Sandoval explains that this "new historicism" creates new analytical spaces that are informed by world history (2000, 8). In her article in Part I Bhavani argues that the strength of feminist research, and its potential to continue to transform the way we think about the social world, lies in the feminist pursuit of thinking about knowledge construction historically while accessing "oppositional consciousness." Feminist research must contemplate historical differences *between* women and focus on the historical relationships between "science and society." Bhavani, like the other scholars presented in Part I, emphasizes that knowledge is both partial and situated but this does not mean that the knowledge we produce must be "disembodied." On the contrary, Bhavani calls for a historicization of knowledge in order to more fully account for difference, especially differences among women. She is concerned that feminist epistemologies not erase or deny the often differing interests or standpoints some women may hold on a given issue or interest. Uma Narayan, an Indian social scientist, for example, points out that even the selection of positivism as a major "target" of feminists' critique of knowledge building may be problematic for non-Western feminists. She suggests that there are many "non-positivist frameworks" within non-Western societies that are more politically oppressive to women, and central among these is religion:

> Most traditional frameworks that nonwestern feminists regard as oppressive to women are not positivist, and it would be wrong to see feminist epistemology's critique of positivism given the same political importance for nonwestern feminists that it has for western feminists. Traditions like my own, where the influence of religion is pervasive, are suffused through and through with values. We must fight not frameworks that assert the separation of fact and value but frameworks that are pervaded by values to which we, as feminists find ourselves opposed. (Narayan 1989, 260)

It is clear that feminists working from these emergent traditions employ a variety of epistemologies and methodologies. Attention to the Other within the social system, be it local or global, and the complexity of consciousness as a product of conceptualizing identity in a holistic way are two themes within these varied emergent practices. Overall, these emergent feminist traditions provide new insights into social reality. Feminists working from these epistemological positions are providing additional strategies for getting at knowledge building and as a result they are creating new knowledge with valuable social and political components. Interestingly, it is within the political feminist agenda that many other feminists pose challenges to these emergent postmodern feminists.

Standpoint epistemologists, feminist empiricists, and many other feminist researchers have been unified in their use of the category "woman" as a political tool. In other words, feminists have traditionally used the category "woman" in order to effectively fight for women's rights by urging social policy changes and so forth. The essentializing of women for the purpose of improving women's lives through social activism has long been a part of the feminist agenda; however, this form of essentialism is neglectful of the complexity of intersectionality within a global world characterized by postmodern global forms. Accordingly, feminists working within these emergent traditions often reject even the strategic use of the category "woman." So while using the Other as a focal point of inquiry is perhaps a general feminist theme, the *way* in which this is *conceptualized* differs greatly and creates tensions between postmodern feminists and feminist scholars working from other traditions.

CONCLUSION

With the development, growth and, transformations in feminist epistemologies, feminist researchers draw on a wide range of research methods to conduct their work. From narrative analyses to in-depth interviews, ethnographies and content analyses, oral histories and discourse analyses, surveys and experiments feminists apply a particular methodology when conducting their research that reflects their unique vision. They view research holistically—as a process, and thus pay attention to the synergy between the context of discovery and the context of justification. Feminists have changed conceptions of what truth is, who can be a knower, what can be known. By creating situated and partial knowledges, by attending to the intersection of gender and other categories of difference such as race, class and sexual preference in its analysis of social reality, feminist research is open to new knowledge—asking new questions. As we will see throughout this volume, this is accomplished in many ways. There are multiple feminisms, not simply one.

Mostly, feminists conduct research for women. Whether it be by seeking knowledge from and about women in order to record their valuable life experiences, or to change women's lives through social policy, a feminist methodology aims at creating knowledge that is beneficial to women and other minorities (DeVault 1999, 31). In this vein many feminists are social activists seeking to use their research to better the social position of women. While feminist scholarship varies in epistemological position and research a feminist approach to research helps give voice to the experiences, concerns, attitudes, and needs of women. Feminists working in and developing emergent traditions seek to go farther than giving voice to Others and actually aim at disrupting social systems of oppression by utilizing the complex standpoints cultivated by such systems.

NOTES

1. As you will see later in this essay not all feminists concur on this point. For example, Chafetz wrote a paper titled "Some Thoughts by an 'Unrepentant Positivist' Who Considers herself a Feminist Nonetheless" in which she argues that positivism and feminism are not mutually exclusive.

2. Feminists rely on the psychological theories of Nancy Chodorow and Carol Gilligan to understand the problems with positivism claims to rationality, more specifically scientific claims to objectivity—the idea of the split between subject and object. Nancy Chodorow's work provides feminists with an understanding of the maleness of science and the scientific stress on objectivity. Why is it that objectivity as a tenet of positivism is so deeply embedded within the scientific model? Using "object-relations theory," Chodorow offers a psychological explanation for gender differences orientation to self. Mothers relate to their daughters in a way that allows them the ability to be more emphatic—seeing themselves in relation to others. In contrast, they raise their sons to be separate from others, in essence training them to be "more objective." Carol Gilligan's research is also interested in the relationship between self and other and supports Chodorow's research. Gilligan (1997) asserts that women's experience within society gives rise to gender differences in behavior. She stresses gender differences in "moral" development. In her view, women experience a different type of so-

cial reality from men that centers around issues of attachment and separation. Women's sense of self is focused around " an ethic of care" and women see "themselves in relations of connection." Their sense of moral development revolves around the premise of taking moral responsibility. And note that in making moral decisions women are more aware of the "limitations of any particular resolution" (149) and are concerned with the conflicts that remain unresolved from such a decision.

3. The term *imprinted* refers to how each individual is impacted by her or his cultural environment.

4. The idea of double consciousness is also in the work of W. E. B. Du Bois, which complicates the notion of men dominating women by focusing on the domination of racial minorities by whites and the double consciousness the oppressed develop. This implies that such a dual perspective is the product of a system of domination and is not only specific to social hierarchies based on gender.

REFERENCES

Bhavnani, Kum-Kum. 1993. Tracing the contours: Feminist research and feminist objectivity. *Women's Studies International Forum* 16: 95–104.

Bordo, Susan. 1999. Feminist skepticism and the "maleness" of philosophy. In *Feminist approaches to theory and methodology,* ed. Sharlene Hesse-Biber, Christine Gilmartin, and Robin Lydenberg, 29–44. New York: Oxford University Press.

Bowles, Gloria, and Renate Duelli-Klein, eds. 1983. *Theories of women's studies.* London: Routledge and Kegan Paul.

Chafetz, Janet Saltman. 1990. *Some thoughts by an unrepentant "positivist" who considers herself a feminist nonetheless.* Paper presented at the annual meeting of the American Sociological Association. Washington, DC. August.

Chodorow, Nancy. 1978. *Reproduction and mothering. Psychoanalysis and the sociology of gender.* Berkeley: University of California Press.

Collins, Patricia Hill. 1990. *Black feminist thought: Knowledge, consciousness, and the politics of empowerment.* Boston: Unwin Hyman.

———. 1999. Learning from the outsider within: The sociological significance of black feminist thought. In *feminist approaches to theory and methodology,* ed. Sharlene Hesse-Biber, Christine Gilmartin, and Robin Lydenberg, 135–78. New York: Oxford University Press.

Denzin, Norman and Yvonna S. Lincoln. 1998. *The landscape of qualitative research: Theories and issues.* Thousand Oaks, CA: Sage.

Devault, Marjorie L. 1991. *Feeding the family: The social organization of caring as gendered work.* Chicago: University of Chicago Press.

———. 1999. *Liberating method: Feminism and social research.* Philadelphia: Temple University Press.

Dill, Bonnie T. 1983. Race, class, and gender: Prospects for an all-inclusive sisterhood. *Feminist Studies* 9: 131–50.

Eichler, Margrit. 1988. *Nonsexist research methods: A practical guide.* Boston: Unwin Hyman.

Foucault, Michel. 1980. Two lectures. In *Power/Knowledge: Selected interviews and other writings, 1972–77,* ed. C. Gordon, 78–108. New York: Pantheon Books.

Friedan, Betty. 1983. *Feminine Mystique.* New York: Laurel.

Gilligan, Carol. 1997. In a different voice. In *Feminisms*, ed. Sandra Kemp and Judith Squires, 146–52. New York: Oxford University Press.

Glenn, Evelyn Nakano. 1992. From servitude to service work: Historical continuities in the racial division of paid reproductive labor. *Signs* 18: 1–43.

Guba, Egon G., and Yvonna S. Lincoln. 1998. Competing paradigms in qualitative research. In *The landscape of qualitative research,* ed. Norman K. Denzin and Yvonna S. Lincoln, 195–220. Thousand Oaks, CA: Sage.

Halpin, Zuleyma Tang. 1989. Scientific objectivity and the concept of the "Other." *Women's Studies International Forum* 12: 285–94.

Haraway, Donna. 1988. Situated knowledges: The science question in feminism and the privilege of partial perspective. *Feminist Studies* 14(13): 575–99.

———. 1993. The biopolitics of postmodern bodies: Determinations of self in immune system discourse. In *American feminist thought at century's end: A reader,* ed. L. S. Kauffman, 199–233. Cambridge, MA: Blackwell.

Harding, Sandra. 1986. *The science question in feminism.* Ithaca: Cornell University Press.

———. 1987. Introduction: Is there a feminist method? In *Feminism and methodology,* ed. Sandra Harding, 1–14. Bloomington: Indiana University Press.

———. 1991. *Whose science? Whose knowledge?* Ithaca: Cornell University Press.

———. 1993. Rethinking standpoint epistemology: What is "strong objectivity"? In *Feminist epistemologies,* ed. Linda Alcoff and Elizabeth Potter, 49–82. New York: Routledge.

Hartstock, Nancy. 1983. The feminist standpoint: Developing the ground for a specifically feminist historical materialism. In *Discovering reality: Feminist perspectives on epistemology, metaphysics, methodology, and philosophy of science,* ed. Sandra Harding and Merrill Hintikka, 283–310. Dordrecht: Reidel.

Hesse-Biber, Sharlene. 2002. Feminism and interdisciplinarity. In *Women in higher education,* ed. JoAnn DiGeorgio-Lutz, 57–66. Westport, CT: Praeger.

Hesse-Biber, Sharlene and Gregg Lee Carter. 2000. *Working women in America.* New York: Oxford University Press.

Higginbotham, Evelyn Brooks. 1992. African-American women's history and the metalanguage of race. *Signs* 17(2): 251–74.

Irigaray, Luce. 1985. *This sex which is not one.* Ithaca: Cornell: Cornell University Press

Jaggar, Alison. 1989. Love and knowledge: Emotion in feminist epistemology. In *Gender/body/knowledge,* ed. Susan Bordo and Alison Jaggar. New Brunswick: Rutgers University Press.

Jayaratne, Toby Epstein, and Abigail Stewart. 1991. Quantitative and qualitative methods in social sciences: Current feminist issues and practical strategies. In *Beyond methodology: Feminist scholarship as lived research,* ed. Mary Margaret Fonow and Judith A. Cook, 85–106. Bloomington: Indiana University Press.

Keller, Evelyn Fox. 1978. Gender and science. *Psychoanalysis and Contemporary Thought: A Quarterly of Integrative and Interdisciplinary Studies* 1: 409–33.

King, D. 1988. Multiple jeopardy, multiple consciousness: The context of black feminist ideology. *Signs* 14: 42–72.

Kuhn, Thomas S. 1970. The Structure of Scientific Revolutions. Second Edition. Chicago: University of Chicago Press.

Martin, Emily. 1999. The egg and the sperm: How science has constructed a romance based on stereotypical women's roles. In *Feminist Approaches to Theory and Methodology,* ed. Sharlene Hesse-Biber, Christine Gilmartin, and Robin Lydenberg, pp. 15–28. New York: Oxford University Press.

Mertens, D. M., J. Farley, A. M. Madison, and P. Singleton. 1994. Diverse voices in evaluation practice: Feminists, minorities, and persons with disabilities. *Evaluation Practice* 15(2): 123–129.

Millman, Marcia, and Rosabeth Moss Kanter. 1987. Introduction to another voice: Feminist perspectives on social life and social science. In *Feminism and methodology,* ed. Sandra Harding, 29–36. Bloomington: Indiana University Press.

Trinh, T. Minh-ha. 1989. *Woman, native, other: Writing postcoloniality and feminism.* Bloomington: Indiana University Press.

———. 1993. The language of nativism: Anthropology as a scientific conversation of man with man. In *American feminist thought at century's end: A reader,* ed. L. S. Kauffman, 107–39. Cambridge, MA: Blackwell.

Mohanty, Chandra. 1988. Under Western eyes: Feminist scholarship and colonial discourses. *Feminist Review* 30: 61–88.

Moraga, Cherrie, and Gloria Anzaldua, eds. 1981. *This bridge called my back: Writings by radical women of color.* Watertown, MA: Persephone Press.

Naples, Nancy A. 1999. Towards comparative analyses of women's political praxis: Explicating multiple dimensions of standpoint epistemology for feminist ethnography. *Women & Politics* 20(1): 29–54.

Narayan, Uma. 1989. The Project of feminist epistemology: Perspectives from a nonwestern feminist. In *Gender/body/knowledge: Feminist reconstructions of being and knowing,* ed. Alison M. Jaggar and Susan R. Bordo, 256–69. New Brunswick: Rutgers University Press.

Narayan, Uma, and Sandra Harding, eds. 2000. *Decentering the center: Philosophy for a multicultural, poststructural, and feminist World.* Bloomington: Indiana University Press.

Neuman, W. Lawrence. 2000. *Social research method.* 4th edition. Boston: Allyn and Bacon.

Nielsen, Joyce McCarl. 1990. Introduction. In *Feminist research methods,* ed. Joyce McCarl Nielsen, 1–37. Boulder, CO: Westview Press.

Oakley, Ann. 1998. Gender, methodology, and people's ways of knowing: Some problems with feminism and the paradigm debate in social science. *Sociology* 32(4): 707–31.

O'Leary, Catherine M. 1997. Counteridentification or counterhegemony? Transforming feminist standpoint theory. *Women and Politics* 18(3): 45–72.

de Oliveira, Rosiska Darcy. 2000. *In praise of difference: The emergence of a global feminism.* New Brunswick: Rutgers University Press.

Perez, Emma. 1999. *The decolonial imaginary: Writing Chicanos into history.* Bloomington: Indiana University Press.

Reinharz, Shulamit. 1983. Experiential analysis: A contribution to feminist research. In *Theories of women's studies,* ed. Gloria Bowles and Renate Duelli-Klein, 162–91. New York: Routledge.

———. 1985. Feminist distrust: Problems of context and content in sociological work. In *The self in sociological inquiry,* ed. David Berg and Ken Smith, 153–72. Beverly Hills: Sage Publications.

Sandoval, Chela. 1991. U.S. Third World feminism: The theory and method of oppositional consciousness in the postmodern world. *Genders* 10: 1–24.

———. 2000. *Methodology of the oppressed.* Minneapolis: University of Minnesota Press.

Sedgwick, Eve Kosofsky. 1993. *Tendencies.* Durham, NC: Duke University Press.

Sherif, Carolyn Wood. 1987. Bias in psychology. In *Feminism and methodology,* ed. Sandra Harding, 37–56. Bloomington: Indiana University Press.

Smith, Dorothy. 1974. Women's perspective as a radical critique of sociology. *Sociological Inquiry* 44: 7–13.

———. 1987. *The everyday world as problematic: A feminist sociology.* Boston: Northeastern University Press.

———. 1990. *The conceptual practices of power. A feminist sociology of knowledge*. Boston: Northeastern University Press.

Sprague, Joey, and Mark Zimmerman. 1993. Overcoming dualisms: A feminist agenda for sociological methodology. In *Theory on gender/feminism on theory,* ed. Paula England, 255–80. New York: Aldine DeGruyter.

Stanley, Liz, and Sue Wise. 1993. *Breaking out again: Feminist ontology and epistemology*. London: Routledge.

Tuana, Nancy. 1988. The weaker the seed: The sexist bias of reproductive theory. *Hypatia*. 3: 147–71.

Twine, France Winddance, and Jonathan W. Warren, eds. 2000. *Racing research, researching race: Methodological dilemmas in critical race studies*. New York: New York University Press.

Williams, Patricia J. 1991. *The alchemy of race and rights*. Cambridge: Harvard University Press

Wing, Adrien Katherine, ed. 2000. *Global critical race feminism: An international reader*. New York: New York University Press.

CHAPTER 2

Women's Perspective as a Radical Critique of Sociology

DOROTHY E. SMITH

1. The women's movement has given us a sense of our right to have women's interests represented in sociology, rather than just receiving as authoritative the interests traditionally represented in a sociology put together by men. What can we make of this access to a social reality that was previously unavailable, was indeed repressed? What happens as we begin to relate to it in the terms of our discipline? We can of course think as many do merely of the addition of courses to the existing repertoire—courses on sex roles, on the women's movement, on women at work, on the social psychology of women and, perhaps somewhat different versions of the sociology of the family. But thinking more boldly or perhaps just thinking the whole thing through a little further might bring us to ask first how a sociology might look if it began from the point of view of women's traditional place in it and what happens to a sociology which attempts to deal seriously with that. Following this line of thought, I have found, has consequences larger than they seem at first.

From the point of view of "women's place" the values assigned to different aspects of the world are changed. Some come into prominence while other standard sociological enterprises diminish. We might take as a model the world as it appears from the point of view of the afternoon soap opera. This is defined by (though not restricted to) domestic events, interests, and activities. Men appear in this world as necessary and vital presences. It is not a woman's world in the sense of excluding men. But it is a women's world in the sense that it is the relevances of the women's place that govern. Men appear only in their domestic or private aspects or at points of intersection between public and private as doctors in hospitals, lawyers in their offices discussing wills and divorces. Their occupational and political world is barely present. They are posited here as complete persons, and they are but partial—as women appear in a sociology predicated on the universe occupied by men.

But it is not enough to supplement an established sociology by addressing ourselves to what has been left out, overlooked, or by making sociological issues of the relevances of the world of women. That merely extends the authority of the existing sociological procedures and makes of a women's sociology an addendum. We cannot rest at that because it does not account for the separation between the two worlds and it does not account for or analyze for us the relation between them. (Attempts to work on that in terms of biology operate within the existing structure as a fundamental assumption and are therefore straightforwardly ideological in character.)

The first difficulty is that how sociology is thought—its methods, conceptual schemes, and theories—has been based on and built up within, the male social universe (even when women have participated in its doing). It has taken for granted not just that scheme of relevances as an itemized inventory of issues or subject matters (industrial sociology, political sociology, social stratification, etc.) but the fundamental social and political structures under which these become relevant and are ordered. There is a difficulty first then of a disjunction between how women find and experience the world beginning (though not necessarily ending up) from their place and the concepts and theoretical schemes available to think about it in. Thus, in a graduate seminar last year, we discussed on one occasion the possibility of a women's sociology and two graduate students told us that in their view and their experience of functioning in experimental group situations, theories of the emergence of leadership in small groups, etc., just did not apply to what was happening as they experienced it. They could not find the correlates of the theory in their experiences.

A second difficulty is that the two worlds and the two bases of knowledge and experience don't stand in an equal relation. The world as it is constituted by men stands in authority over that of women. It is that part of the world from which our kind of society is governed and from which what happens to us begins. The domestic world stands in a dependent relation to that other and its whole character is subordinate to it.

The two difficulties are related to one another in a special way. The effect of the second interacting with the first is to impose the concepts and terms in which the world of men is thought as the concepts and terms in which women must think their world. Hence, in these terms women are alienated from their experience.

The profession of sociology is predicated on a universe which is occupied by men and is itself still largely appropriated by men as their "territory." Sociology is part of the practice by which we are all governed and that practice establishes its relevances. Thus, the institutions which lock sociology into the structures occupied by men are the same institutions which lock women into the situations in which they find themselves oppressed. To unlock the latter leads logically to an unlocking of the former. What follows then, or rather what then becomes possible—for it is of course by no means inevitable—is less a shift in the subject matter than a different conception of how it is or might become relevant as a means to understand our experience and the conditions of our experience (both women's and men's) in corporate capitalist society.

2. When I speak here of governing or ruling I mean something more general than the notion of government as political organization. I refer rather to that total complex of activities differentiated into many spheres, by which our kind of society is ruled, managed, administered. It includes that whole section which in the business world is called "management." It includes the professions. It includes of course government more conventionally defined and also the activities of those who are selecting, training, and indoctrinating those who will be its governors. The last in-

cludes those who provide and elaborate the procedures in which it is governed and develop methods for accounting for how it is done and predicting and analyzing its characteristic consequences and sequences of events, namely, the business schools, the sociologists, the economists, etc. These are the institutions through which we are ruled and through which we, and I emphasize this we, participate in ruling.

Sociology, then, I conceive as much more than ideology, much more than a gloss on the enterprise which justifies and rationalizes it, and, at the same time as much less than "science." The governing of our kind of society is done in concepts and symbols. The contribution of sociology to this is that of working up the conceptual procedures, models, and methods by which the immediate and concrete features of experience can be read into the conceptual mode in which the governing is done. What is actually observed or what is systematically recovered by the sociologist from the actualities of what people say and do, must be transposed into the abstract mode. Sociology thus participates in and contributes to the formation and facilitation of this mode of action and plays a distinctive part in the work of transposing the actualities of people's lives and experience into the conceptual currency in which it is and can be governed.

Thus, the relevances of sociology are organized in terms of a perspective on the world which is a view from the top and which takes for granted the pragmatic procedures of governing as those which frame and identify its subject matter. Issues are formulated as issues which have become administratively relevant, not as they are significant first in the experience of those who live them. The kinds of facts and events which are facts for us have already been shaped up and given their character and substance as facts, as relations, etc., by the methods and practice of governing. Mental illness, crimes, riots, violence, work satisfaction, neighbors and neighborhoods, motivation, etc., these are the constructs of the practice of government. In many instances, such as mental illness, crimes, neighborhoods, etc., they are constituted as discrete phenomena primarily by administrative procedures and others arise as problems in relation to the actual practice of government, as for example concepts of motivation, work satisfaction, etc.

The governing processes of our society are organized as social entities constituted externally to those persons who participate in and perform them. The managers, the bureaucrats, the administrators, are employees, are people who are *used.* They do not own the enterprises or otherwise appropriate them. Sociologists study these entities under the heading of formal organization. They are put together as objective structures with goals, activities, obligations, etc., other than those which its employees can have as individuals. The academic professions are also set up in a mode which externalizes them as entities vis-à-vis their practitioners. The body of knowledge which its members accumulate is appropriated by the discipline as its body. The work of members aims at contributing to that body of knowledge.

As graduate students learning to become sociologists, we learn to think sociology as it is thought and to practice it as it is practiced. We learn that some topics are relevant and some are not. We learn to discard our experienced world as a source of reliable information or suggestions about the character of the world; to confine and focus our insights within the conceptual frameworks and relevances which are given in the discipline. Should we think other kinds of thoughts or experience the world in a different way or with edges and horizons that pass beyond the conceptual we must practice a discipline which discards them or find some procedure which makes it possible to sneak them in. We learn a way of thinking about the world which is recognizable to its practitioners as the sociological way of thinking.

We learn to practice the sociological subsumption of the actualities of ourselves and of other people. We find out how to treat the world as instances of a sociological body of knowledge. The procedure operates as a sort of conceptual imperialism. When we write a thesis or a paper, we learn that the first thing to do is to latch it on to the discipline at some point. This may be by showing how it is a problem within an existing theoretical and conceptual framework. The boundaries of inquiry are thus set within the framework of what is already established. Even when this becomes, as it happily often does, a ceremonial authorization of a project which has little to do with the theory used to authorize it, we still work within the vocabularies and within the conceptual boundaries of what we have come to know as "the sociological perspective."

An important set of procedures which serve to constitute the body of knowledge of the discipline as something which is separated from its practitioners are those known as "objectivity." The ethic of objectivity and the methods used in its practice are concerned primarily with the separation of the knower from what he knows and in particular with the separation of what is known from any interests, "biases," etc., which he may have which are not the interests and concerns authorized by the discipline. I must emphasize that being interested in knowing something doesn't invalidate what is known. In the social sciences the pursuit of objectivity makes it possible for people to be paid to pursue a knowledge to which they are otherwise indifferent. What they feel and think about society can be taken apart from and kept out of what they are professionally or academically interested in.

3. The sociologist enters the conceptually ordered society when he goes to work. He enters it as a member and he enters it also as the mode in which he investigates it. He observes, analyzes, explains, and examines as if there were no problem in how that world becomes observable to him. He moves among the doings of organizations, governmental processes, bureaucracies, etc., as a person who is at home in that medium. The nature of that world itself, how it is known to him and the conditions of its existence or his relation to it are not called into question. His methods of observation and inquiry extend into it as procedures which are essentially of the same order as those which bring about the phenomena with which he is concerned, or which he is concerned to bring under the jurisdiction of that order. His perspectives and interests may differ, but the substance is the same. He works with facts and information which have been worked up from actualities and appear in the form of documents which are themselves the product of organizational processes, whether his own or administered by him, or of some other agency. He fits that information back into a framework of entities and organizational processes which he takes for granted as known, without asking how it is that he knows them or what are the social processes by which the phenomena which correspond to or provide the empirical events, acts, decisions, etc., of that world, may be recognized. He

passes beyond the particular and immediate setting in which he is always located in the body (the office he writes in, the libraries he consults, the streets he travels, the home he returns to) without any sense of having made a transition. He works in the same medium as he studies.

But like everyone else he also exists in the body in the place in which it is. This is also then the place of his sensory organization of immediate experience, the place where his coordinates of here and now before and after are organized around himself as center; the place where he confronts people face to face in the physical mode in which he expresses himself to them and they to him as more and other than either can speak. It is in this place that things smell. The irrelevant birds fly away in front of the window. Here he has indigestion. It is a place he dies in. Into this space must come as actual material events, whether as the sounds of speech, the scratchings on the surface of paper which he constitutes as document, or directly, anything he knows of the world. It has to happen here somehow if he is to experience it at all.

Entering the governing mode of our kind of society lifts the actor out of the immediate local and particular place in which he is in the body. He uses what becomes present to him in this place as a means to pass beyond it to the conceptual order. This mode of action creates then a bifurcation of consciousness, a bifurcation, of course, which is there for all those who participate in this mode of action. It establishes two modes of knowing and experiencing and doing, one located in the body and in the space which it occupies and moves into, the other which passes beyond it. Sociology is written in and aims at this second mode. Vide Bierstedt:

> Sociology can liberate the mind from time and space themselves and remove it to a new and transcendental realm where it no longer depends upon these Aristotelian categories. (1966)

Even observational work aims at its description in the categories and hence conceptual forms of the "transcendental realm."

4. Women are outside and subservient to this structure. They have a very specific relation to it which anchors them into the local and particular phase of the bifurcated world. For both traditionally and as a matter of occupational practices in our society, the governing conceptual mode is appropriated by men and the world organized in the natural attitude, the home, is appropriated by (or assigned to) women (Smith 1973).

It is a condition of a man's being able to enter and become absorbed in the conceptual mode that he does not have to focus his activities and interests upon his bodily existence. If he is to participate fully in the abstract mode of action, then he must be liberated also from having to attend to his needs, etc. in the concrete and particular. The organization of work and expectations in managerial and professional circles both constitutes and depends upon the alienation of man from his bodily and local existence. The structure of work and the structure of career take for granted that these matters are provided for in such a way that they will not interfere with his action and participation in that world. Providing for the liberation from the Aristotelian categories of which Bierstedt speaks, is a woman who keeps house for him, bears and cares for his children, washes his clothes, looks after him when he is sick, and generally provides for the logistics of his bodily existence.

The place of women, then, in relation to this mode of action is that where the work is done to create conditions which facilitate his occupation of the conceptual mode of consciousness. The meeting of a man's physical needs, the organization of his daily life, even the consistency of expressive background, are made maximally congruent with his commitment. A similar relation exists for women who work in and around the professional and managerial scene. They do those things which give concrete form to the conceptual activities. They do the clerical work, the computer programming, the interviewing for the survey, the nursing, the secretarial work. At almost every point women mediate for men the relation between the conceptual mode of action and the actual concrete forms in which it is and must be realized, and the actual material conditions upon which it depends.

Marx's concept of alienation is applicable here in a modified form. The simplest formulation of alienation posits a relation between the work an individual does and an external order which oppresses her, such that the harder she works the more she strengthens the order which oppresses her. This is the situation of women in this relation. The more successful women are in mediating the world of concrete particulars so that men do not have to become engaged with (and therefore conscious of) that world as a condition to their abstract activities, the more complete man's absorption in it, the more effective the authority of that world and the more total women's subservience to it. And also the more complete the dichotomy between the two worlds, and the estrangement between them.

5. Women sociologists stand at the center of a contradiction in the relation of our discipline to our experience of the world. Transcending that contradiction means setting up a different kind of relation than that which we discover in the routine practice of our worlds.

The theories, concepts, and methods of our discipline claim to account for, or to be capable of accounting for and analyzing the same world as that which we experience directly. But these theories, concepts, and methods have been organized around and built up out of a way of knowing the world which takes for granted the boundaries of an experience in the same medium in which it is constituted. It therefore takes for granted and subsumes without examining the conditions of its existence. It is not capable of analyzing its own relation to its conditions because the sociologist as actual person in an actual concrete setting has been cancelled in the procedures which objectify and separate him from his knowledge. Thus, the linkage which points back to its conditions is lacking.

For women those conditions are central as a direct practical matter, to be somehow solved in the decision to take up a sociological career. The relation between ourselves as practicing sociologists and ourselves as working women is continually visible to us, a central feature of experience of the world, so that the bifurcation of consciousness becomes for us a daily chasm which is to be crossed, on the one side of which is this special conceptual activity of thought, research, teaching, administration, and on the other the world of concrete practical activities in keeping things clean, managing somehow the house and household and the children, a world in which the particularities of persons in their full organic immediacy (cleaning up the vomit, changing the diapers, as well as feeding) are inescapable. Even if we don't have that as a direct contingency in our lives, we are aware of that as something that our becoming may be inserted into as a possible predicate.

It is also present for us to discover that the discipline is not one which we enter and occupy on the same terms as men enter and occupy it. We do not fully appropriate its authority, i.e., the right to author and authorize the acts and knowing and thinking which are the acts and knowing and thinking of the discipline as it is thought. We cannot therefore command the inner principles of our action. That remains lodged outside us. The frames of reference which order the terms upon which inquiry and discussion are conducted originate with men. The subjects of sociological sentences (if they have a subject) are male. The sociologist is "he." And even before we become conscious of our sex as the basis of an exclusion (*they* are not talking about *us*), we nonetheless do not fully enter ourselves as the subjects of its statements, since we must suspend our sex, and suspend our knowledge of who we are as well as who it is that in fact is speaking and of whom. Therefore, we do not fully participate in the declarations and formulations of its mode of consciousness. The externalization of sociology as a profession which I have described above becomes for women a double estrangement.

There is then for women a basic organization of their experience which displays for them the structure of the bifurcated consciousness. At the same time it attenuates their commitment to a sociology which aims at an externalized body of knowledge based on an organization of experience which excludes theirs and excludes them except in a subordinate relation.

6. An alternative approach must somehow transcend this contradiction without reentering Bierstedt's "transcendental realm" (1966). Women's perspective, as I have analyzed it here, discredits sociology's claim to constitute an objective knowledge independent of the sociologist's situation. Its conceptual procedures, methods, and relevances are seen to organize its subject matter from a determinate position in society. This critical disclosure becomes, then, the basis for an alternative way of thinking sociology. If sociology cannot avoid being situated, then sociology should take that as its beginning and build it into its methodological and theoretical strategies. As it is now, these separate a sociologically constructed world from that which is known in direct experience and it is precisely that separation which must be undone.

I am not proposing an immediate and radical transformation of the subject matter and methods of the discipline nor the junking of everything that has gone before. What I am suggesting is more in the nature of a reorganization which changes the relation of the sociologist to the object of her knowledge and changes also her problematic. This reorganization involves first placing the sociologist where she is actually situated, namely at the beginning of those acts by which she knows or will come to know; and second, making her direct experience of the everyday world the primary ground of her knowledge.

We would reject, it seems to me, a sociology aimed primarily at itself. We would not be interested in contributing to a body of knowledge the uses of which are not ours and the knowers of whom are who knows whom, but generally male—particularly when it is not at all clear what it is that is constituted as knowledge in that relation. The professional sociologist's practice of thinking it as it is thought would have to be discarded. She would be constrained by the actualities of how it happens in her direct experience. Sociology would aim at offering to anyone a knowledge of the social organization and determinations of the properties and events of their directly experienced world. Its analyses would become part of our ordinary interpretations of the experienced world, just as our experience of the sun's sinking below the horizon is transformed by our knowledge that the world turns. (Yet from where we are it seems to sink and that must be accounted for.)

The only way of knowing a socially constructed world is knowing it from within. We can never stand outside it. A relation in which sociological phenomena are objectified and presented as external to and independent of the observer is itself a special social practice also known from within. The relation of observer and object of observation, of sociologist to "subject," is a specialized social relationship. Even to be a stranger is to enter a world constituted from within as strange. The strangeness itself is the mode in which it is experienced.

When Jean Briggs (1970) made her ethnographic study of the ways in which an Eskimo people structure and express emotion, what she learned and observed emerged for her in the context of the actual developing relations between her and the family with whom she lived and other members of the group. Her account situates her knowledge in the context of those relationships. Affections, tensions, and quarrels were the living texture in which she learnt what she describes. She makes it clear how this context structured her learning and how what she learnt and can speak of became observable to her. Briggs tells us what is normally discarded in the anthropological or sociological telling. Although sociological inquiry is necessarily a social relation, we have learned to disattend our own part in it. We recover only the object of its knowledge as if that stood all by itself and of itself. Sociology does not provide for seeing that there are always two terms to this relation. An alternative sociology must be reflexive (Gouldner 1971), i.e., one that preserves in it the presence, concerns, and experience of the sociologist as knower and discoverer.

To begin from direct experience and to return to it as a constraint or "test" of the adequacy of a systematic knowledge is to begin from where we are located bodily. The actualities of our everyday world are already socially organized. Settings, equipment, "environment," schedules, occasions, etc., as well as the enterprises and routines of actors are socially produced and concretely and symbolically organized prior to our practice. By beginning from her original and immediate knowledge of her world, sociology offers a way of making its socially organized properties first observable and then problematic.

Let me make it clear that when I speak of "experience" I do not use the term as a synonym for "perspective." Nor in proposing a sociology grounded in the sociologist's actual experience, am I recommending the self-indulgence of inner exploration or any other enterprise with self as sole focus and object. Such subjectivist interpretations of "experience" are themselves an aspect of that organization of consciousness which bifurcates it and transports us into mind country while stashing away the concrete conditions and practices upon which it depends. We can never escape the circles of our own heads if we accept that as our territory. Rather, the sociologist's investigation of our directly experienced world as a problem is a mode of discovering or rediscovering the society from within. She begins from her own original but tacit knowledge and from within the acts by which she brings it into her grasp in making it observable and in understanding how it works. She aims not at a reiteration of what she already (tacitly) knows, but at an exploration through that of what passes beyond it and is deeply implicated in how it is.

7. Our knowledge of the world is given to us in the modes we enter into relations with the object of knowledge. But in this case the object of our knowledge is or originates in a "subject." The constitution of an objective sociology as an authoritative version of how things are is done from a position and as part of the practices of ruling in our kind of society. It has depended upon class and sex bases which make it possible for sociology to evade the problem that our kind of society is known and experienced rather differently from different positions within it. Our training teaches us to ignore the uneasiness at the junctures where transitional work is done—for example, the ordinary problems respondents have of fitting their experience of the world to the questions in the interview schedule. It is this exclusion which the sociologist who is a woman cannot so easily preserve, for she discovers, if she will, precisely that uneasiness in her relation to her discipline as a whole. The persistence of the privileged sociological version (or versions) relies upon a substructure which has already discredited and deprived of authority to speak, the voices of those who know the society differently. The objectivity of a sociological version depends upon a special relation with others which makes it easy for the sociologist to remain outside the other's experience and does not require her to recognize that experience as a valid contention.

Riding a train not long ago in Ontario I saw a family of Indians, woman, man, and three children standing together on a spur above a river watching the train go by. There was (for me) that moment—the train, those five people seen on the other side of the glass. I saw first that I could tell this incident as it was, but that telling as a description built in my position and my interpretations. I have called them a family; I have said they were watching the train. My understanding has already subsumed theirs. Everything may have been quite other for them. My description is privileged to stand as what actually happened, because theirs is not heard in the contexts in which I may speak. If we begin from the world as we actually experience it, it is at least possible to see that we are located and that what we know of the other is conditional upon that location as part of a relation comprehending the other's location also. There are and must be different experiences of the world and different bases of experience. We must not do away with them by taking advantage of our privileged speaking to construct a sociological version which we then impose upon them as their reality. We may not rewrite the other's world or impose upon it a conceptual framework which extracts from it what fits with ours. Our conceptual procedures should be capable of explicating and analyzing the properties of their experienced world rather than administering it. Their reality, their varieties of experience must be an unconditional datum.

8. My experience in the train epitomizes a sociological relation. The observer is already separated from the world as it is experienced by those she observes. That sep-

aration is fundamental to the character of that experience. Once she becomes aware of how her world is put together as a practical everyday matter and of how her relations are shaped by its concrete conditions (even in so simple a matter as that she is sitting in the train and it travels, but those people standing on the spur do not) the sociologist is led into the discovery that she cannot understand the nature of her experienced world by staying within its ordinary boundaries of assumption and knowledge. To account for that moment on the train and for the relation between the two experiences (or more) and the two positions from which those experiences begin involves positing a total socio-economic order "in back" of that moment. The coming together which makes the observation possible as well as how we were separated and drawn apart as well as how I now make use of that here—these properties are determined elsewhere than in that relation itself.

Further, how our knowledge of the world is mediated to us becomes a problem. It is a problem in knowing how that world is organized for us prior to our participation as knowers in that process. As intellectuals we ordinarily receive it as a media world, of documents, images, journals, books, talk as well as in other symbolic modes. We discard as an essential focus of our practice other ways of knowing. Accounting for that mode of knowing and the social organization which sets it up for us again leads us back into an analysis of the total socio-economic order of which it is part. It is not possible to account for one's directly experienced world or how it is related to the worlds which others directly experience who are differently placed by remaining within the boundaries of the former.

If we address the problem of the conditions as well as the perceived forms and organization of immediate experience, we should include in it the events as they actually happen or the ordinary material world which we encounter as a matter of fact—the urban renewal project which uproots four hundred families; how it is to live on welfare as an ordinary, daily practice; cities as the actual physical structures in which we move; the organization of academic occasions such as that in which this paper originated. When we examine them, we find that there are many aspects of how these things come about of which we have little as sociologists to say. We have a sense that the events which enter our experience originate somewhere in a human intention, but we are unable to track back to find it and to find out how it got from there to here. Or take this room in which I work or that room in which you are reading and treat that as a problem. If we think about the conditions of our activity here, we could track back to how it is that there are chairs, table, walls, our clothing, our presence; how these places (yours and mine) are cleaned and maintained, etc. There are human activities, intentions, and relations which are not apparent as such in the actual material conditions of our work. The social organization of the setting is not wholly available to us in its appearance. We bypass in the immediacy of the specific practical activity, a complex division of labor which is an essential precondition to it. Such preconditions are fundamentally mysterious to us and present us with problems in grasping social relations in our kind of society with which sociology is ill equipped to deal. Our experience of the world is of one which is largely incomprehensible beyond the limits of what is known in a common sense. No amount of observation of face-to-face relations, no amount of analysis of commonsense knowledge of everyday life, will take us beyond our essential ignorance of how it is put together. Our direct experience of it constitutes it (if we will) as a problem, but it does not offer any answers. The matrix of direct experience as that from which sociology might begin discloses that beginning as an "appearance" the determinations of which lie beyond it.

We might think of the "appearances" of our direct experience as a multiplicity of surfaces, the properties and relations among which are generated by a social organization which is not observable in its effects. The structures which underlie and generate the characteristics of our own directly experienced world are social structures and bring us into unseen relations with others. Their experience is necessarily different from ours. Beginning from our experienced world and attempting to analyze and account for how it is, necessitates positing others whose experience is different.

Women's situation in sociology discloses to her a typical bifurcate structure with the abstracted conceptual practices on the one hand and the concrete realizations, the maintenance routines, etc., on the other. Taking each for granted depends upon being fully situated in one or the other so that the other does not appear in contradiction to it. Women's direct experience places her a step back where we can recognize the uneasiness that comes in sociology from its claim to be about the world we live in and its failure to account for or even describe its actual features as we find them in living them. The aim of an alternative sociology would be to develop precisely that capacity from that beginning so that it might be a means to anyone of understanding how the world comes about for her and how it is organized so that it happens to her as it does in her experience.

9. Though such a sociology would not be exclusively for or done by women it does begin from the analysis and critique originating in their situation. Its elaboration therefore depends upon a grasp of that which is prior to and fuller than its formulation. It is a little like the problem of making a formal description of the grammar of a language. The linguist depends and always refers back to the competent speakers' sense, etc. In her own language she depends to a large extent upon her own competence. Women are native speakers of this situation and in explicating it or its implications and realizing them conceptually, they have that relation to it of knowing it before it has been said.

The incomprehensibility of the determinations of our immediate local world is for women a particularly striking metaphor. It recovers an inner organization in common with their typical relation to the world. For women's activities and existence are determined outside them and beyond the world which is their "place." They are oriented by their training and by the daily practices which confirm it, towards the demands and initiations and authority of others. But more than that, the very organization of the world which has been assigned to them as the primary locus of their being is determined by and subordinate to the corporate organization of society (Smith 1973). Thus, as I have expressed her relation to sociology, its logic lies elsewhere. She lacks the inner principle of her own activity. She does not grasp how it is put together because it is determined elsewhere than where she is. As a sociologist, then, the grasp and exploration of her own experience as a method of discovering society restores to her a center which in this enterprise at least is wholly hers.

REFERENCES

Briggs, Jean L. 1970. *Never in anger.* Cambridge, MA: Harvard University Press.

Bierstedt, Robert. 1966. Sociology and general education. In *Sociology and contemporary education,* ed. Charles H. Page. New York: Random House.

Gouldner, Alvin. 1971. *The coming crisis in Western sociology.* London: Heinemann Educational Books.

Smith, Dorothy E. 1973. Women, the family and corporate capitalism. In *Women in Canada,* ed. M. L. Stephenson. Toronto: Newpress.

CHAPTER 3

Rethinking Standpoint Epistemology

What Is "Strong Objectivity"?

SANDRA HARDING

"Feminist objectivity means quite simply situated knowledges."

—DONNA HARAWAY[1]

BOTH WAYS

For almost two decades, feminists have engaged in a complex and charged conversation about objectivity. Its topics have included which kinds of knowledge projects have it, which don't, and why they don't; whether the many different feminisms need it, and if so why they do; and if it is possible to get it, how to do so.[2] This conversation has been informed by complex and charged prefeminist writings that tend to get stuck in debates between empiricists and intentionalists, objectivists and interpretationists, and realists and social constructionists (including poststructuralists).[3]

Most of these feminist discussions have *not* arisen from attempts to find new ways either to criticize or carry on the agendas of the disciplines. Frequently they do not take as their problematics the ones familiar within the disciplines. Instead, these conversations have emerged mainly from two different and related concerns. First, what are the causes of the immense proliferation of theoretically and empirically sound results of research in biology and the social sciences that have discovered what is not supposed to exist: rampant sexist and androcentric bias—"politics"!—in the dominant scientific (and popular) descriptions and explanations of nature and social life? To put the point another way, how should one explain the surprising fact that politically guided research projects have been able to produce less partial and distorted results of research than those supposedly guided by the goal of value-neutrality? Second, how can feminists create research that is *for* women in the sense that it provides less partial and distorted answers to questions that arise from women's lives and are not only about those lives but also about the rest of nature and social relations? The two concerns are related because recommendations for future scientific practices should be informed by the best accounts of past scientific successes. That is, how one answers the second question depends on what one thinks is the best answer to the first one.

Many feminists, like thinkers in the other new social liberation movements, now hold that it is not only desirable but also possible to have that apparent contradiction in terms—socially situated knowledge. In conventional accounts, socially situated beliefs only get to count as opinions. In order to achieve the status of knowledge, beliefs are supposed to break free of—to transcend—their original ties to local, historical interests, values, and agendas. However, as Donna Haraway has put the point, it turns out to be possible "to have *simultaneously* an account of radical historical contingency for all knowledge claims and knowing subjects, a critical practice for recognizing our own 'semiotic technologies' for making meanings, and a no-nonsense commitment to faithful accounts of a 'real' world . . ."[4]

The standpoint epistemologists—and especially the feminists who have most fully articulated this kind of theory of knowledge—have claimed to provide a fundamental map or "logic" for how to do this: "start thought from marginalized lives" and "take everyday life as problematic."[5] However, these maps are easy to misread if one doesn't understand the principles used to construct them. Critics of standpoint writings have tended to refuse the invitation to "have it both ways" by accepting the idea of real knowledge that is socially situated. Instead they have assimilated standpoint claims either to objectivism or some kind of conventional foundationalism or to ethnocentrism, relativism, or phenomenological approaches in philosophy and the social sciences.

Here I shall try to make clear how it really is a misreading to assimilate standpoint epistemologies to those older ones and that such misreadings distort or make invisible the distinctive resources that they offer. I shall do so by contrasting the grounds for knowledge and the kinds of subjects/agents of knowledge recommended by standpoint theories with those favored by the older epistemologies. Then I shall show why it is reasonable to think that the socially situated grounds and subjects of standpoint epistemologies require and generate stronger standards for objectivity than do those that turn away from providing systematic methods for locating knowledge in history. The problem with the conventional conception of objectivity is not that it is too rigorous or too "objectifying," as some have argued, but that it is *not rigorous or objectifying enough;* it is too weak to accomplish even the goals for which it has been designed, let alone the more difficult projects called for by feminisms and other new social movements.[6]

FEMINIST STANDPOINT VERSUS SPONTANEOUS FEMINIST EMPIRICIST EPISTEMOLOGIES

Not all feminists who try to explain the past and learn lessons for the future of feminist research in biology and the social sciences are standpoint theorists. The distinctiveness of feminist standpoint approaches can be emphasized by contrasting them with what I shall call "spontaneous feminist empiricist epistemology."[7]

By now, two forms of feminist empiricism have been articulated: the original "spontaneous" feminist empiricism and a recent philosophical version. Originally, feminist empiricism arose as the "spontaneous consciousness" of feminist researchers in biology and the social sciences who were trying to explain what was and what wasn't different about their research process in comparison with the standard procedures in their field.[8] They thought that they were just doing more carefully and rigorously what any good scientist should do; the problem they saw was one of "bad science." Hence, they did not give a special name to their philosophy of science; I gave it the name "feminist empiricism" in *The Science Question in Feminism* to contrast feminist standpoint theory with the insistence of empiricism's proponents that sexism and androcentrism could be eliminated from the results of research if scientists would just follow more rigorously and carefully the existing methods and norms of research—which, for practicing scientists, are fundamentally empiricist ones.

Recently, philosophers Helen Longino and Lynn Hankinson Nelson have developed sophisticated and valuable feminist empiricist philosophies of science (Longino calls hers "contextual empiricism") that differ in significant respects from what most prefeminist empiricists and probably most spontaneous feminist empiricists would think of as empiricism.[9] This is no accident, because Longino and Nelson both intend to revise empiricism, as feminists in other fields have fruitfully revised other theoretical approaches—indeed, as feminist standpoint theorists revise the theory from which they begin. Longino and Nelson incorporate into their epistemologies elements that also appear in the standpoint accounts (many would say that they have been most forcefully articulated in such accounts)—such as the inescapable but also sometimes positive influence of social values and interests in the content of science—that would be anathema to even the spontaneous feminist empiricists of the late 1970s and early 1980s as well as to their many successors today. These philosophical feminist empiricisms are constructed in opposition partly to feminist standpoint theories, partly to radical feminist arguments that exalt the feminine and essentialize "woman's experience" (which they have sometimes attributed to standpoint theorists), and partly to the prefeminist empiricists.

It would be an interesting and valuable project to contrast in greater detail these important philosophical feminist empiricisms with both spontaneous feminist empiricism and with feminist standpoint theory. But I have a different goal in this essay: to show how strongly feminist reflections on scientific knowledge challenge the dominant prefeminist epistemology and philosophy of science that are held by all of those people inside and outside science who are still wondering just what are the insights about science and knowledge that feminists have to offer. In my view, this challenge is made most strongly by feminist standpoint epistemology.

One can understand spontaneous feminist empiricism and feminist standpoint theory to be making competing arguments on two topics—scientific method and history—in order to explain in their different ways the causes of sexist and androcentric results of scientific research.[10] As already indicated, spontaneous feminist empiricists think that insufficient care and rigor in following existing methods and norms is the cause of sexist and androcentric results of research, and it is in these terms that they try to produce plausible accounts of the successes of empirically and theoretically more adequate results of research. Standpoint theorists think that this is only part of the problem. They point out that retroactively, and with the help of the insights of the women's movement, one can see these sexist or androcentric practices in the disciplines. However, the methods and norms in the disciplines are too weak to permit researchers *systematically* to identify and eliminate from the results of research those social values, interests, and agendas that are shared by the entire scientific community or virtually all of it. Objectivity has not been "operationalized" in such a way that scientific method can detect sexist and androcentric assumptions that are "the dominant beliefs of an age"—that is, that are collectively (versus only individually) held. As far as scientific method goes (and feminist empiricist defenses of it), it is entirely serendipitous when cultural beliefs that are assumed by most members of a scientific community are challenged by a piece of scientific research. Standpoint theory tries to address this problem by producing stronger standards for "good method," ones that can guide more competent efforts to maximize objectivity.[11]

With respect to history, spontaneous feminist empiricists argue that movements of social liberation such as the women's movement function much like the little boy who is the hero of the folk tale about the Emperor and his clothes. Such movements "make it possible for people to see the world in an enlarged perspective because they remove the covers and blinders that obscure knowledge and observation."[12] Feminist standpoint theorists agree with this assessment, but argue that researchers can do more than just wait around until social movements happen and then wait around some more until their effects happen to reach inside the processes of producing maximally objective, causal accounts of nature and social relations. Knowledge projects can find active ways incorporated into their principles of "good method" to use history as a resource by socially situating knowledge projects in the scientifically and epistemologically most favorable historical locations. History can become the systematic provider of scientific and epistemological resources rather than an obstacle to or the "accidental" benefactor of projects to generate knowledge.[13]

It is spontaneous feminist empiricism's great strength that it explains the production of sexist and nonsexist results of research with only a minimal challenge to the fundamental logic of research as this is understood in scientific fields and to the logic of explanation as this is understood in the dominant philosophies of science. Spontaneous feminist empiricists try to fit feminist projects into prevailing standards of "good science" and "good philosophy." This conservativism makes it possible for many people to grasp the importance of feminist research in biology and the social sciences without feeling disloyal to the methods and norms of their research traditions. Spontaneous feminist empiricism appears to call for even greater rigor in using these methods and following these norms. However, this conservatism is also this philosophy's weakness; this theory of knowledge refuses fully to address the limitations of the dominant conceptions of method and explanation and the ways the conceptions constrain and distort results of research and thought about this research even when these dominant conceptions are most rigorously respected. Nevertheless, its radical nature should not be underestimated. It argues persuasively that the sciences have been blind to their own sexist and androcentric research practices and results. And it thereby clears space for the next question: are the existing logics of research and explanation really so innocent in the commission of this "crime" as empiricism insists, or are they part of its cause?[14]

The intellectual history of feminist standpoint theory is conventionally traced to Hegel's reflections on what can be known about the master/slave relationship from the standpoint of the slave's life versus that of the master's life and to the way

Marx, Engels, and Lukacs subsequently developed this insight into the "standpoint of the proletariat" from which have been produced Marxist theories of how class society operates.[15] In the 1970s, several feminist thinkers independently began reflecting on how the Marxist analysis could be transformed to explain how the structural relationship between women and men had consequences for the production of knowledge.[16] However, it should be noted that even though standpoint arguments are most fully articulated as such in feminist writings, they appear in the scientific projects of all of the new social movements.[17] A *social* history of standpoint theory would focus on what happens when marginalized peoples begin to gain public voice. In societies where scientific rationality and objectivity are claimed to be highly valued by dominant groups, marginalized peoples and those who listen attentively to them will point out that from the perspective of marginal lives, the dominant accounts are less than maximally objective. Knowledge claims are always socially situated, and the failure by dominant groups critically and systematically to interrogate their advantaged social situation and the effect of such advantages on their beliefs leaves their social situation a scientifically and epistemologically disadvantaged one for generating knowledge. Moreover, these accounts end up legitimating exploitative "practical politics" even when those who produce them have good intentions.

The starting point of standpoint theory—and its claim that is most often misread—is that in societies stratified by race, ethnicity, class, gender, sexuality, or some other such politics shaping the very structure of a society, the *activities* of those at the top both organize and set limits on what persons who perform such activities can understand about themselves and the world around them. "There are some perspectives on society from which, however well-intentioned one may be, the real relations of humans with each other and with the natural world are not visible."[18] In contrast, the activities of those at the bottom of such social hierarchies can provide starting points for thought—for *everyone's* research and scholarship—from which humans' relations with each other and the natural world can become visible. This is because the experience and lives of marginalized peoples, as they understand them, provide particularly significant *problems to be explained* or research agendas. These experiences and lives have been devalued or ignored as a source of objectivity-maximizing questions—the answers to which are not necessarily to be found in those experiences or lives but elsewhere in the beliefs and activities of people at the center who make policies and engage in social practices that shape marginal lives.[19] So one's social situation enables and sets limits on what one can know; some social situations—critically unexamined dominant ones—are more limiting than others in this respect, and what makes these situations more limiting is their inability to generate the most critical questions about received belief.[20]

It is this sense in which Dorothy Smith argues that women's experience is the "grounds" of feminist knowledge and that such knowledge should change the discipline of sociology.[21] Women's lives (our many different lives and different experiences!) can provide the starting point for asking new, critical questions about not only those women's lives but also about men's lives and, most importantly, the causal relations between them.[22] For example, she points out that if we start thinking from women's lives, we (anyone) can see that women are assigned the work that men do not want to do for themselves, especially the care of everyone's bodies—the bodies of men, babies, children, old people, the sick, and their own bodies. And they are assigned responsibility for the local places where those bodies exist as they clean and care for their own and others' houses and work places.[23] This kind of "women's work" frees men in the ruling groups to immerse themselves in the world of abstract concepts. The more successful women are at this concrete work, the more invisible it becomes to men as distinctively social labor. Caring for bodies and the places bodies exist disappears into "nature," as, for example, in sociobiological claims about the naturalness of "altruistic" behavior for females and its unnaturalness for males or in the systematic reticence of many prefeminist Marxists actually to analyze who does what in everyday sexual, emotional, and domestic work, and to integrate such analyses into their accounts of "working class labor." Smith argues that we should not be surprised that men have trouble seeing women's activities as part of distinctively human culture and history once we notice how invisible the social character of this work is from the perspective of their activities. She points out that if we start from women's lives, we can generate questions about why it is that it is primarily women who are assigned such activities and what the consequences are for the economy, the state, the family, the educational system, and other social institutions of assigning body and emotional work to one group and "head" work to another.[24] These questions lead to less partial and distorted understandings of women's worlds, men's worlds, and the causal relations between them than do the questions originating only in that part of human activity that men in the dominant groups reserve for themselves—the abstract mental work of managing and administrating.

Standpoint epistemology sets the relationship between knowledge and politics at the center of its account in the sense that it tries to provide causal accounts of—to explain—the effects that different kinds of politics have on the production of knowledge. Of course, empiricism also is concerned with the effects politics has on the production of knowledge, but prefeminist empiricism conceptualizes politics as entirely bad. Empiricism tries to purify science of all such bad politics by adherence to what it takes to be rigorous methods for the testing of hypotheses. From the perspective of standpoint epistemology, this is *far too weak a strategy* to maximize the objectivity of the results of research that empiricists desire. Thought that begins from the lives of the oppressed has no chance to get its critical questions voiced or heard within such an empiricist conception of the way to produce knowledge. Prefeminist empiricists can only perceive such questions as the intrusion of politics into science, which therefore deteriorates the objectivity of the results of research. Spontaneous feminist empiricism, for all its considerable virtues, nevertheless contains distorting traces of these assumptions, and they block the ability of this theory of science to develop maximally strong criteria for systematic ways to maximize objectivity.

Thus, the standpoint claims that all knowledge attempts are socially situated and that some of these objective social locations are better than others as starting points for knowledge projects challenge some of the most fundamental assumptions of the scientific world view and the Western thought that takes science as its model of how to produce knowledge. It sets out a rigorous "logic of discovery" intended to maximize the objectivity of the results of research and thereby to produce knowledge that can be *for* marginalized people (and those who would know what the marginalized can know) rather than *for* the use only of dominant groups in their projects of administering and managing the lives of marginalized people.

WHAT ARE THE GROUNDS FOR KNOWLEDGE CLAIMS?

Standpoint theories argue for "starting off thought" from the lives of marginalized peoples; beginning in those determinate, objective locations in any social order will generate illuminating critical questions that do not arise in thought that begins from dominant group lives. Starting off research from women's lives will generate less partial and distorted accounts not only of women's lives but also of men's lives and of the whole social order. Women's lives and experiences provide the "grounds" for this knowledge, though these clearly do not provide foundations for knowledge in the conventional philosophical sense. These grounds are the site, the activities, from which scientific questions arise. The epistemologically advantaged starting points for research do not guarantee that the researcher can maximize objectivity in her account; these grounds provide only a necessary—not a sufficient—starting point for maximizing objectivity. It is useful to contrast standpoint grounds for knowledge with four other kinds: the "God-trick," ethnocentrism, relativism, and the unique abilities of the oppressed to produce knowledge.

Standpoint Theories versus the "God-Trick"

First, for standpoint theories, the grounds for knowledge are fully saturated with history and social life rather than abstracted from it. Standpoint knowledge projects do not claim to originate in purportedly universal human problematics; they do not claim to perform the "God-trick."[25] However, the fact that feminist knowledge claims are socially situated does not in practice distinguish them from any other knowledge claims that have ever been made inside or outside the history of Western thought and the disciplines today; all bear the fingerprints of the communities that produce them. All thought by humans starts off from socially determinate lives. As Dorothy Smith puts the point, "[W]omen's perspective, as I have analyzed it here, discredits sociology's claim to constitute an objective knowledge independent of the sociologist's situation. Its conceptual procedures, methods, and relevances are seen to organize its subject matter from a determinate position in society."[26]

It is a delusion—and a historically identifiable one—to think that human thought could completely erase the fingerprints that reveal its production process. Conventional conceptions of scientific method enable scientists to be relatively good at eliminating those social interests and values from the results of research that differ *within* the scientific community, because whenever experiments are repeated by different observers, differences in the social values of individual observers (or groups of them from different research teams) that have shaped the results of their research will stand out from the sameness of the phenomena that other researchers (or teams of them) report.[27] But scientific method provides no rules, procedures, or techniques for even identifying, let alone eliminating, social concerns and interests that are shared by all (or virtually all) of the observers, nor does it encourage seeking out observers whose social beliefs vary in order to increase the effectiveness of scientific method. Thus, culturewide assumptions *that have not been criticized within the scientific research process* are transported into the results of research, making visible the historicity of specific scientific claims to people at other times, other places, or in other groups in the very same social order. We could say that standpoint theories not only acknowledge the social situatedness that is the inescapable lot of all knowledge-seeking projects but also, more importantly, transform it into a systematically available scientific resource.

Standpoint Theories versus Ethnocentrism

Universalists have traditionally been able to imagine only ethnocentrism and relativism as possible alternatives to "the view from nowhere" that they assert grounds universal claims, so they think standpoint epistemologies must be supporting (or doomed to) one or the other of these positions. Is there any reasonable sense in which the ground for knowledge claimed by feminist standpoint theory is ethnocentric?

Ethnocentrism is the belief in the inherent superiority of one's own ethnic group or culture.[28] Do feminist standpoint theorists argue that the lives of *their own group or culture* is *superior* as a grounds for knowledge?[29] At first glance, one might think that this is the case if one notices that it is primarily women who have argued for starting thought from women's lives. However, there are several reasons why it would be a mistake to conclude from this fact that feminist standpoint theory is ethnocentric.

First, standpoint theorists themselves all explicitly argue that marginal lives that are not their own provide better grounds for certain kinds of knowledge. Thus, the claim by women that women's lives provide a better starting point for thought about gender systems is not the same as the claim that *their own* lives are the best such starting points. They are not denying that their own lives can provide important resources for such projects, but they are arguing that other, different (and sometimes oppositional) women's lives also provide such resources. For example, women who are not prostitutes and have not been raped have argued that starting thought from women's experiences and activities in such events reveals that the state is male because it looks at women's lives here just as men (but not women) do. Dorothy Smith writes of the value of starting to think about a certain social situation she describes from the perspective of Native Canadian lives.[30] Bettina Aptheker has argued that starting thought from the everyday lives of women who are Holocaust survivors, Chicana cannery workers, older lesbians, African American women in slavery, Japanese American concentration camp survivors, and others who have had lives different from hers increases our ability to understand a great deal about the distorted way the dominant groups conceptualize politics, resistance, community, and other key history and social science notions.[31] Patricia Hill Collins, an African American sociologist, has argued that starting thought from the lives of poor and in some cases illiterate African American women reveals important truths about the lives of intellectuals, both African American and European American, as well as about those women.[32] Many theorists who are not mothers (as well as many who are) have argued that starting thought in mother-work generates important questions about the social order. Of course, some women no doubt do argue that their own lives provide the one and only best starting point for all knowledge projects, but this is not what standpoint theory holds. Thus, although it is not an accident that so many women have argued for feminist standpoint approaches, neither is it evidence that standpoint claims are committed to ethnocentrism.

Second, and relatedly, thinkers with "center" identities have also argued that marginalized lives are better places from which to start asking causal and critical questions about the social order. After all, Hegel was not a slave, though he argued that the master/slave relationship could better be understood from the perspective of slaves' activities. Marx, Engels, and Lukacs were not engaged in the kind of labor that they argued provided the starting point for developing their theories about class society. There are men who have argued for the scientific and epistemic advantages of starting thought from women's lives, European Americans who understand that much can be learned about their lives as well as African American lives if they start their thought from the latter, and so on.[33]

Third, women's lives are shaped by the rules of femininity or womanliness; in this sense they "express feminine culture." Perhaps the critic of standpoint theories thinks feminists are defending femininity and thus "their own culture." But all feminist analyses, including feminist standpoint writings, are in principle ambivalent about the value of femininity and womanliness. Feminists criticize femininity on the grounds that it is fundamentally defined by and therefore part of the conceptual project of exalting masculinity; it is the "other" against which men define themselves as admirably and uniquely human. Feminist thought does not try to substitute loyalty to femininity for the loyalty to masculinity it criticizes in conventional thought. Instead, it criticizes all gender loyalties as capable of producing only partial and distorted results of research. However, it must do this while also arguing that women's lives have been inappropriately devalued. Feminist thought is forced to "speak as" and on behalf of the very notion it criticizes and tries to dismantle—women. In the contradictory nature of this project lies both its greatest challenge and a source of its great creativity. It is because the conditions of women's lives are worse than their brothers' in so many cases that women's lives provide better places from which to start asking questions about a social order that tolerates and in so many respects even values highly the bad conditions for women's lives (women's double-day of work, the epidemic of violence against women, women's cultural obligation to be "beautiful," and so on).[34] Thus, research processes that problematize how gender practices shape behavior and belief—that interrogate and criticize both masculinity and femininity—stand a better chance of avoiding such biasing gender loyalties.

Fourth, there are many feminisms, and these can be understood to be starting off their analyses from the lives of different historical groups of women. Liberal feminism initially started off its analyses from the lives of women in the eighteenth- and nineteenth-century European and U.S. educated classes; Marxist feminism, from the lives of wage-working women in the nineteenth- and early twentieth-century industrializing or "modernizing" societies; Third World feminism, from the lives of late twentieth-century women of Third World descent—and these different Third

World lives produce different feminisms. Standpoint theory argues that each of these groups of women's lives is a good place to start in order to explain certain aspects of the social order. There is no single, ideal woman's life from which standpoint theories recommend that thought start. Instead, one must turn to all of the lives that are marginalized in different ways by the operative systems of social stratification. The different feminisms inform each other; we can learn from all of them and change our patterns of belief.

Last, one can note that from the perspective of marginalized lives, it is the dominant claims that we should in fact regard as ethnocentric. It is relatively easy to see that overtly racist, sexist, classist, and heterosexist claims have the effect of insisting that the dominant culture is superior. But it is also the case that claims to have produced universally valid beliefs—principles of ethics, of human nature, epistemologies, and philosophies of science—are ethnocentric. Only members of the powerful groups in societies stratified by race, ethnicity, class, gender, and sexuality could imagine that their standards for knowledge and the claims resulting from adherence to such standards should be found preferable by all rational creatures, past, present, and future. This is what the work of Smith, Hartsock, and the others discussed earlier shows. Moreover, standpoint theory itself is a historical emergent. There are good reasons why it has not emerged at other times in history; no doubt it will be replaced by more useful epistemologies in the future—the fate of all human products.[35]

Standpoint Theory versus Relativism, Perspectivalism, and Pluralism

If there is no single, transcendental standard for deciding between competing knowledge claims, then it is said that there can be only local historical ones, each valid in its own lights but having no claims against others. The literature on cognitive relativism is by now huge, and here is not the place to review it.[36] However, standpoint theory does not advocate—nor is it doomed to—relativism. It argues against the idea that all social situations provide equally useful resources for learning about the world and against the idea that they all set equally strong limits on knowledge. Contrary to what universalists think, standpoint theory is not committed to such a claim as a consequence of rejecting universalism. Standpoint theory provides arguments for the claim that some social situations are scientifically better than others as places from which to start off knowledge projects, and those arguments must be defeated if the charge of relativism is to gain plausibility.[37]

Judgmental (or epistemological) relativism is anathema to any scientific project, and feminist ones are no exception.[38] It is not equally true as its denial that women's uteruses wander around in their bodies when they take math courses, that only Man the Hunter made important contributions to distinctively human history, that women are biologically programmed to succeed at mothering and fail at equal participation in governing society, that women's preferred modes of moral reasoning are inferior to men's, that targets of rape and battering must bear the responsibility for what happens to them, that the sexual molestation and other physical abuses children report are only their fantasies, and so on—as various sexist and androcentric scientific theories have claimed. Feminist and prefeminist claims are usually not complementary but conflicting, just as the claim that the earth is flat conflicts with the claim that it is round. *Sociological* relativism permits us to acknowledge that different people hold different beliefs, but what is at issue in rethinking objectivity is the different matter of *judgmental* or epistemological relativism. Standpoint theories neither hold nor are doomed to it.

Both moral and cognitive forms of judgmental relativism have determinate histories; they appear as intellectual problems at certain times in history in only some cultures and only for certain groups of people. Relativism is not fundamentally a problem that emerges from feminist or any other thought that starts in marginalized lives; it is one that emerges from the thought of the dominant groups. Judgmental relativism is sometimes the most that dominant groups can stand to grant to their critics—"OK, your claims are valid for you, but mine are valid for me."[39] Recognizing the importance of thinking about who such a problem belongs to—identifying its social location—is one of the advantages of standpoint theory.

Standpoint Theory versus the Unique Abilities of the Oppressed to Produce Knowledge

This is another way of formulating the charge that standpoint theories, in contrast to conventional theories of knowledge, are ethnocentric. However, in this form the position has tempted many feminists, as it has members of other liberatory knowledge projects.[40] We can think of this claim as supporting "identity science" projects—the knowledge projects that support and are supported by "identity politics." In the words of the Combahee River Collective's critique of liberal and Marxist thought (feminist as well as prefeminist) that failed to socially situate anti-oppression claims: "Focusing upon our own oppression is embodied in the concept of identity politics. We believe that the most profound and potentially the most radical politics come directly out of our own identity, as opposed to working to end somebody else's oppression."[41] (They were tired of hearing about how they should be concerned to improve others' lives and how others were going to improve theirs.)

To pursue the issue further, we will turn to examine just who is the "subject of knowledge" for standpoint theories. But we can prepare for that discussion by recollecting yet again that Hegel was not a slave, though he grasped the critical understanding of the relations between master and slave that became available only if he started off his thought from the slave's activities, and that Marx, Engels and Lukacs were not proletarians. Two questions are raised by these examples: What is the role for marginalized experience in the standpoint projects of members of dominant groups? And what are the special resources, but also limits, that the lives of people in dominant groups provide in generating the more objective knowledge claims standpoint theories call for? We shall begin to address these issues in the next section.

To conclude this one, marginalized lives provide the scientific problems and the research agendas—not the solutions—for standpoint theories. Starting off thought from these lives provides fresh and more critical questions about how the social order works than does starting off thought from the unexamined lives of members of dominant groups. Most natural and social scientists (and philosophers!) are themselves members of these dominant groups, whether by birth or through upward mobility into scientific and professional/managerial careers. Those who are paid to teach and conduct research receive a disproportionate share of the benefits of that very nature and social order that they are trying to explain. Thinking from marginal lives leads one to question the adequacy of the conceptual frameworks that the natural and social sciences have designed to explain (for themselves) themselves and the world around them. This is the sense in which marginal lives ground knowledge for standpoint approaches.

NEW SUBJECTS OF KNOWLEDGE

For empiricist epistemology, the subject or agent of knowledge—that which "knows" the "best beliefs" of the day—is supposed to have a number of distinctive characteristics. First, this subject of knowledge is culturally and historically disembodied or invisible because knowledge is by definition universal. "Science says . . ." we are told. Whose science, we can ask? The drug and cigarette companies? The Surgeon General's? The National Institute of Health's? The science of the critics of the NIH's racism and sexism? Empiricism insists that scientific knowledge has no particular historical subject. Second, in this respect, the subject of scientific knowledge is different in kind from the objects whose properties scientific knowledge describes and explains, because the latter are determinate in space and time. Third, though the subject of knowledge for empiricists is transhistorical, knowledge is initially produced ("discovered") by individuals and groups of individuals (reflected in the practice of scientific awards and honors), not by culturally specific societies or subgroups in a society such as a certain class or gender or race. Fourth, the subject is homogeneous and unitary, because knowledge must be consistent and coherent. If the subject of knowledge were permitted to be multiple and heterogeneous, then the knowledge produced by such subjects would be multiple and contradictory and thus inconsistent and incoherent.

The subjects of knowledge for standpoint theories contrast in all four respects. First, they are embodied and visible, because the lives from which thought has started are always present and visible in the results of that thought. This is true even though the way scientific method is operationalized usually succeeds in removing all personal or individual fingerprints from the results of research. But personal fingerprints are not the problem standpoint theory is intended to address. The thought of an age is *of an age,* and the delusion that one's thought can escape historical locatedness is just one of the thoughts that is typical of dominant groups in these and other ages. The "scientific world view" is, in fact, a view of (dominant groups in) modern, Western societies, as the histories of science proudly point out. Standpoint theories simply disagree with the further ahistorical and incoherent claim that the content of "modern and Western" scientific thought is also, paradoxically, not shaped by its historical location.

Second, the fact that subjects of knowledge are embodied and socially located has the consequence that they are not fundamentally different from objects of knowledge. We should assume causal symmetry in the sense that the same kinds of social forces that shape objects of knowledge also shape (but do not determine) knowers and their scientific projects.

This may appear to be true only for the objects of social science knowledge, not for the objects that the natural sciences study. After all, trees, rocks, planetary orbits, and electrons do not constitute themselves as historical actors. What they are does not depend on what they think they are; they do not think or carry on any of the other activities that distinguish human communities from other constituents of the world around us. However, this distinction turns out to be irrelevant to the point here because, in fact, scientists never can study the trees, rocks, planetary orbits, or electrons that are "out there" and untouched by human concerns. Instead, they are destined to study something different (but hopefully systematically related to what is "out there"): *nature as an object of knowledge.* Trees, rocks, planetary orbits, and electrons always appear to natural scientists only as they are already socially constituted in some of the ways that humans and their social groups are already socially constituted for the social scientist. Such objects are already effectively "removed from pure nature" into social life—they are social objects—by, first of all, the contemporary general cultural meanings that these objects have for everyone, including the entire scientific community.[42] They also become socially constituted objects of knowledge through the shapes and meanings these objects gain for scientists because of earlier generations of scientific discussion about them. Scientists never observe nature apart from such traditions; even when they criticize some aspects of them they must assume others in order to carry on the criticism. They could not do science if they did not both borrow from and also criticize these traditions. Their assumptions about what they see are always shaped by "conversations" they carry on with scientists of the past. Finally, their own interactions with such objects also culturally constitute them; to treat a piece of nature with respect, violence, degradation, curiosity, or indifference is to participate in culturally constituting such an object of knowledge. In these respects, nature as an object of knowledge simulates social life, and the processes of science themselves are a significant contributor to this phenomenon. Thus, the subject and object of knowledge for the natural sciences are also not significantly different in kind. Whatever kinds of social forces shape the subjects are also thereby shaping their objects of knowledge.

Third, consequently, communities and not primarily individuals produce knowledge. For one thing, what I believe that I thought through all by myself (in my mind), which I know, only gets transformed from my personal belief to knowledge when it is socially legitimated. Just as importantly, my society ends up assuming all the claims I make that neither I nor my society critically interrogate. It assumes the eurocentric, androcentric, heterosexist, and bourgeois beliefs that I do not critically examine as part of my scientific research and that, consequently, shape my thought and appear as part of my knowledge claims. These are some of the kinds of features that subsequent ages (and Others today) will say make my thought characteristic of my age, or society, community, race, class, gender, or sexuality. The best scientific thought of today is no different in this respect from the thought of Galileo or Darwin; in all can be found not only brilliant thoughts first expressed by individuals and then legitimated by communities but also assumptions we now regard as false that were distinctive to a particular historical era and not identified as part of the "evidence" that scientists actually used to select the results of research.[43]

Fourth, the subjects/agents of knowledge for feminist standpoint theory are multiple, heterogeneous, and contradictory or incoherent, not unitary, homogeneous, and coherent as they are for empiricist epistemology.[44] Feminist knowledge has started off from women's lives, but it has started off from many different women's lives; there is no typical or essential women's life from which feminisms start their thought. Moreover, these different women's lives are in important respects opposed to each other. Feminist knowledge has arisen from European and African women, from economically privileged and poor women, from lesbians and heterosexuals, from Protestant, Jewish, and Islamic women. Racism and imperialism, local and international structures of capitalist economies, institutionalized homophobia and compulsory heterosexuality, and the political conflicts between ethnic and religious cultures produce multiple, heterogeneous, and contradictory feminist accounts. Nevertheless, thought that starts off from each of these different kinds of lives can generate less partial and distorted accounts of nature and social life.

However, the subject/agent of feminist knowledge is multiple, heterogeneous, and frequently contradictory in a second way that mirrors the situation for women as a class. It is the thinker whose consciousness is bifurcated, the outsider within, the marginal person now located at the center,[45] the person who is committed to two agendas that are by their nature at least partially in conflict—the liberal feminist, social feminist, Sandinista feminist, Islamic feminist, or feminist scientist—who has generated feminist sciences and new knowledge. It is starting off thought from a contradictory social position that generates feminist knowledge. So the logic of the directive to "start thought from women's lives" requires that one start one's thought from multiple lives that are in many ways in conflict with each other, each of which itself has multiple and contradictory commitments. This may appear an overwhelming requirement—or even an impossible one—because Western thought has required the fiction that we have and thus think from unitary and coherent lives. But the challenge of learning to think from the perspective of more than one life when those lives are in conflict with each other is familiar to anthropologists, historians, conflict negotiators, domestic workers, wives, mothers—indeed, to most of us in many everyday contexts.

Both empiricist philosophy and Marxism could maintain the fiction that unitary and coherent subjects of knowledge were to be preferred only by defining one socially distinctive group of people as the ideal knowers and arguing that all others lacked the characteristics that made this group ideal. Thus, the liberal philosophy associated with empiricism insisted that it was the possession of reason that enabled humans to know the world the way it is and then defined as not fully rational women, Africans, the working class, the Irish, Jews, other peoples from Mediterranean cultures, and so on. It was said that no individuals in these groups were capable of the dispassionate, disinterested exercise of individual moral and cognitive reason that was the necessary condition for becoming the ideal subject of knowledge. Similarly, traditional Marxism argued that only the industrial proletariat possessed the characteristics for the ideal subject of Marxist political economy. Peasants', slaves', and women's work, as well as bourgeois activities, made these people's lives inferior starting points for generating knowledge of the political economy.[46] In contrast, the logic of standpoint theory leads to the refusal to essentialize its subjects of knowledge.

This logic of multiple subjects leads to the recognition that the subject of liberatory feminist knowledge must also be, in an important if controversial sense, the subject of every other liberatory knowledge project. This is true in the collective sense of "subject of knowledge," because lesbian, poor, and racially marginalized women are all women, and therefore all feminists will have to grasp how gender, race, class, and sexuality are used to construct each other. It will have to do so if feminism is to be liberatory for marginalized women, but also if it is to avoid deluding dominant group women about their/our own situations. If this were not so, there would be no way to distinguish between feminism and the narrow self-interest of dominant group women—just as conventional androcentric thought permits no criterion for distinguishing between "best beliefs" and those that serve the self-interest of men as men. (Bourgeois thought permits no criterion for identifying specifically bourgeois self-interest; racist thought, for identifying racist self-interest; and so on.)

But the subject of every other liberatory movement must also learn how gender, race, class, and sexuality are used to construct each other in order to accomplish their goals. That is, analyses of class relations must look at their agendas from the perspective of women's lives, too. Women, too, hold class positions, and they are not identical to their brothers'. Moreover, as many critics have pointed out, agendas of the left need to deal with the fact that bosses regularly and all too successfully attempt to divide the working class against itself by manipulating gender hostilities. If women are forced to tolerate lower wages and double-days of work, employers can fire men and hire women to make more profit. Antiracist movements must look at their issues from the perspective of the lives of women of color, and so forth. Everything that feminist thought must know must also inform the thought of every other liberatory movement, and vice versa. It is not just the women in those other movements who must know the world from the perspective of women's lives. Everyone must do so if the movements are to succeed at their own goals. Most importantly, this requires that women be active directors of the agendas of these movements. But it also requires that men in those movements be able to generate original feminist knowledge from the perspective of women's lives as, for example, John Stuart Mill, Marx and Engels, Frederick Douglass, and later male feminists have done.[47]

However, if every other liberatory movement must generate feminist knowledge, it cannot be that women are the unique generators of feminist knowledge. Women cannot claim this ability to be uniquely theirs, and men must not be permitted to claim that because they are not women, they are not obligated to produce fully feminist analyses. Men, too, must contribute distinctive forms of specifically feminist knowledge from their particular social situation. Men's thought, too, will begin first from women's lives in all the ways that feminist theory, with its rich and contradictory tendencies, has helped us all—women as well as men—to understand how to do. It will start there in order to gain the maximally objective theoretical frameworks within which men can begin to describe and explain their own and women's lives in less partial and distorted ways. This is necessary if men are to produce more than the male supremacist "folk belief" about themselves and the world they live in to which female feminists object. Women have had to learn how to substitute the generation of feminist thought for the "gender nativism" androcentric cultures encourage in them, too. Female feminists are made, not born. Men, too must learn to take historic responsibility for the social position from which they speak.

Patricia Hill Collins has stressed the importance to the development of black feminist thought of genuine dialogue across differences, and of the importance of making coalitions with other groups if that dialogue is to happen.

> While Black feminist thought may originate with Black feminist intellectuals, it cannot flourish isolated from the experiences and ideas of other groups. The dilemma is that Black women intellectuals must place our own experiences and consciousness at the center of any serious efforts to develop Black feminist thought yet not have that thought become separatist and exclusionary. . . .
>
> By advocating, refining, and disseminating Black feminist thought, other groups—such as Black men, white women, white men, and other people of color—further its development. Black women can produce an attenuated version of Black feminist thought separated from other groups. Other groups cannot produce Black feminist thought without African American women. Such groups can, however, develop self-defined knowledge reflecting their own standpoints. But the full actualization of Black feminist thought requires a collaborative enterprise with Black women at the center of a community based on coalitions among autonomous groups.[48]

It seems to me that Collins has provided a powerful analysis of the social relations necessary for the development of less partial and distorted belief by any knowledge community.

Far from licensing European Americans to appropriate African American thought or men to appropriate women's thought, this approach challenges members of dominant groups to make themselves "fit" to engage in collaborative, democratic, community enterprises with marginal peoples. Such a project requires learning to listen attentively to marginalized people; it requires educating oneself about their histories, achievements, preferred social relations, and hopes for the future; it requires putting one's body on the line for "their" causes until they feel like "our" causes; it requires critical examination of the dominant institutional beliefs and practices that systematically disadvantage them; it requires critical self-examination to discover how one unwittingly participates in generating disadvantage to them . . . and more. Fortunately, there are plenty of models available to us not only today but also through an examination of the history of members of dominant groups who learned to think from the lives of marginalized people and to act on what they learned. We can choose which historical lineage to claim as our own.

To conclude this section, we could say that since standpoint analyses explain how and why the subject of knowledge always appears in scientific accounts of nature and social life as part of the object of knowledge of those accounts, standpoint approaches have had to learn to use the social situatedness of subjects of knowledge systematically as a resource for maximizing objectivity. They have made the move from declaiming as a problem or acknowledging as an inevitable fact to theorizing as a *systematically accessible* resource for maximizing objectivity the inescapable social situatedness of knowledge claims.

STANDARDS FOR MAXIMIZING OBJECTIVITY

We are now in a position to draw out of this discussion of the innovative grounds and subject of knowledge for feminist standpoint theories the stronger standards for maximizing objectivity that such theories both require and generate. Strong objectivity requires that the subject of knowledge be placed on the same critical, causal plane as the objects of knowledge. Thus, strong objectivity requires what we can think of as "strong reflexivity." This is because culturewide (or nearly culturewide) beliefs function as evidence at every stage in scientific inquiry: in the selection of problems, the formation of hypotheses, the design of research (including the organization of research communities), the collection of data, the interpretation and sorting of data, decisions about when to stop research, the way results of research are reported, and so on. The subject of knowledge—the individual and the historically located social community whose unexamined beliefs its members are likely to hold "unknowingly," so to speak—must be considered as part of the object of knowledge from the perspective of scientific method. All of the kinds of objectivity-maximizing procedures focused on the nature and/or social relations that are the direct object of observation and reflection must also be focused on the observers and reflectors—scientists and the larger society whose assumptions they share. But a maximally critical study of scientists and their communities can be done only from the perspective of those whose lives have been marginalized by such communities. Thus, strong objectivity requires that scientists and their communities be integrated into democracy-advancing projects for scientific and epistemological reasons as well as moral and political ones.

From the perspective of such standpoint arguments, empiricism's standards appear weak; empiricism advances only the "objectivism" that has been so widely criticized from many quarters.[49] Objectivism impoverishes its attempts at maximizing objectivity when it turns away from the task of critically identifying all of those broad, historical social desires, interests, and values that have shaped the agendas, contents, and results of the sciences much as they shape the rest of human affairs.

Consider, first, how objectivism too narrowly operationalizes the notion of maximizing objectivity.[50] The conception of value-free, impartial, dispassionate research is supposed to direct the identification of all social values and their elimination from the results of research, yet it has been operationalized to identify and eliminate only those social values and interests that differ among the researchers and critics who are regarded by the scientific community as competent to make such judgments. If the community of "qualified" researchers and critics systematically excludes, for example, all African Americans and women of all races and if the larger culture is stratified by race and gender and lacks powerful critiques of this stratification, it is not plausible to imagine that racist and sexist interests and values would be identified within a community of scientists composed entirely of people who benefit—intentionally or not—from institutionalized racism and sexism. This kind of blindness is advanced by the conventional belief that the truly scientific part of knowledge seeking—the part controlled by methods of research—occurs only in the context of justification. The context of discovery, in which problems are identified as appropriate for scientific investigation, hypotheses are formulated, key concepts are defined—this part of the scientific process is thought to be unexaminable within science by rational methods. Thus, "real science" is restricted to those processes controllable by methodological rules. The methods of science—or rather, of the special sciences—are restricted to procedures for the testing of already formulated hypotheses. Untouched by these methods are those values and interests entrenched in the very statement of what problem is to be researched and in the concepts favored in the hypotheses that are to be tested. Recent histories of science are full of cases in which broad social assumptions stood little chance of identification or elimination through the very best research procedures of the day.[51] Thus, objectivism operationalizes the notion of objectivity in much too narrow a way to permit the achievement of the value-free research that is supposed to be its outcome.

But objectivism also conceptualizes the desired value-neutrality of objectivity too broadly. Objectivists claim that objectivity requires the elimination of *all* social values and interests from the research process and the results of research. It is clear, however, that not all social values and interests have the same bad effects upon the results of research. Democracy-advancing values have systematically generated less partial and distorted beliefs than others.[52]

Objectivism's rather weak standards for maximizing objectivity make objectivity a mystifying notion, and its mystificatory character is largely responsible for its usefulness and its widespread appeal to dominant groups. It offers hope that scientists and science institutions, themselves admittedly historically located, can produce claims that will be regarded as objectively valid without having to examine critically their own historical commitments from which—intentionally or not—they actively construct their scientific research. It permits scientists and science institutions to be unconcerned with the origins or consequences of their problematics and practices or with the social values and interests that these problematics and practices support. It offers the false hope of enacting what Francis Bacon erroneously promised for the method of modern science: "The course I propose for the discovery of sciences is such as leaves but little to the acuteness and strength of wits, but places all wits and understandings nearly on a level." His "way of discovering science goes far to level men's wits, and leaves but little to individual excellence, because it performs everything by surest rules and demonstrations."[53] In contrast, standpoint approaches requires the strong objectivity that can take the subject as well as the object of knowledge to be a necessary object of critical, causal—scientific!—social explanations. This program of strong reflexivity is a resource for objectivity, in contrast to the obstacle that de facto reflexivity has posed to weak objectivity.

Some feminists and thinkers from other liberatory knowledge projects have thought that the very notion of objectivity should be abandoned. They say that it is hopelessly tainted by its use in racist, imperialist, bourgeois, homophobic, and androcentric scientific projects. Moreover, it is tied to a theory of representation and concept of the self or subject that insists on a rigid barrier between subject and object of knowledge—between self and Other—which feminism and other new social movements label as distinctively androcentric or eurocentric. Finally, the conventional notion of objectivity institutionalizes a certain kind of lawlessness at the heart of science, we could say, by refusing to theorize any criteria internal to scientific goals for distinguishing between scientific method, on the one hand, and such morally repugnant acts as torture or ecological destruction, on the other. Scientists and scientific institutions disapprove of, engage in political activism against, and set up special committees to screen scientific projects for such bad consequences, but these remain ad hoc measures, extrinsic to the conventional "logic" of scientific research.

However, there is not just one legitimate way to conceptualize objectivity, any more than there is only one way to conceptualize freedom, democracy, or science. The notion of objectivity has valuable political and intellectual histories; as it is transformed into "strong objectivity" by the logic of standpoint epistemologies, it retains central features of the older conception. In particular, might should not make right in the realm of knowledge production any more than in matters of ethics. Understanding ourselves and the world around us requires understanding what others think of us and our beliefs and actions, not just what we think of ourselves and them.[54] Finally, the appeal to objectivity is an issue not only between feminist and prefeminist science and knowledge projects but also within each feminist and other emancipatory research agenda. There are many feminisms, some of which result in claims that distort the racial, class, sexuality, and gender relationships in society. Which ones generate less or more partial and distorted accounts of nature and social life? The notion of objectivity is useful in providing a way to think about the gap that should exist between how any individual or group wants the world to be and how in fact it is.[55]

AN OBJECTION CONSIDERED

"Why not just keep the old notion of objectivity as requiring value-neutrality and argue instead that the problem feminism raises is how to get it, not that the concept itself should be changed? Why not argue that it is the notion of scientific method that should be transformed, not objectivity?"

This alternative position is attractive for several reasons. For one thing, clearly feminist standpoint theorists no less than other feminists want to root out sexist and androcentric bias from the results of research. They want results of research that are not "loyal to gender"—feminine or masculine. In this sense, don't they want to maximize value-neutrality—that is, old-fashioned objectivity—in the results of research?

Moreover, in important respects an epistemology and a method for doing research in the broadest sense of the term have the same consequences or, at least, are deeply implicated in each other. What would be the point of a theory of knowledge that did not make prescriptions for how to go about getting knowledge or of a prescription for getting knowledge that did not arise from a theory about how knowledge can be and has been produced? So why not appropriate and transform what the sciences think of as scientific method, but leave the notion of objectivity intact? Why not argue that the standpoint theories have finally completed the quest for a "logic of discovery" begun and then abandoned by philosophers some decades ago? They are calling for an "operationalization" of scientific method that includes the context of discovery and the social practices of justification in the appropriate domain of its rules and recommended procedures.[56] Scientific method must be understood to begin back in the context of discovery, in which scientific "problems" are identified and bold hypotheses conjectured. Then "starting from marginalized lives" becomes part of the method of maximizing value-neutral objectivity. This possibility could gain support from the fact that some standpoint theorists consistently talk about their work interchangeably as an epistemology and a method for doing research.[57]

Attractive as this alternative is, I think it is not attractive enough to convince that only method and not also the concept of objectivity should be reconceptualized. For one thing, this strategy makes it look reasonable to think it possible to gain value-neutrality in the results of research. It implies that human ideas can somehow escape their location in human history. But this no longer appears plausible in the new social studies of science.

Second, and relatedly, this strategy leads away from the project of analyzing how our beliefs regarded as true as well as those regarded as false have social causes and thus, once again, to the assumption of a crucial difference between subjects and objects of knowledge. It would leave those results of research that are judged by the scientific community to be maximally objective to appear to have no social causes, to be the result only of nature's impressions on our finally well-polished, glassy-mirror minds. Objects of knowledge then become, once again, dissimilar for the subjects of knowledge. Subjects of real knowledge, unlike subjects of mere opinion, are disembodied and socially invisible, whereas their natural and social objects of knowledge are firmly located in social history. Thus, the "strong method" approach detached from "strong objectivity" leaves the opposition between subjects and objects firmly in place—an opposition that both distorts reality and has a long history of use in exploiting marginalized peoples. The "strong objectivity" approach locates this very assumed difference between subject and object of knowledge in social history; it calls for a scientific account of this assumption, too.

Third, this strategy leaves reflexivity merely a perpetual problem rather than also the resource into which standpoint theorists have transformed it. Observers do change the world that they observe, but refusing to strengthen the notion of objectivity leaves reflexivity always threatening objectivity rather than also as a resource for maximizing it.

Finally, it is at least paradoxical and most certainly likely to be confusing that the "strong method only" approach must activate in the process of producing knowledge those very values, interests, and politics that it regards as anathema in the results of research. It is at least odd to direct would-be knowers to go out and reorganize social life—as one must do to commit such forbidden (and difficult) acts as starting thought from marginal lives—in order to achieve value-neutrality in the results of research. Standpoint approaches want to eliminate dominant group interests and values from the results of research as well as the interests and values of *successfully colonized* minorities—loyalty to femininity as well as to masculinity is to be eliminated through feminist research. But that does not make the results of such research value-neutral. It will still be the thought of this era, making various distinctive assumptions that later generations and others today will point out to us.

On balance, these disadvantages outweigh the advantages of the "strong method only" approach.

Can the new social movements "have it both ways"? Can they have knowledge that is fully socially situated? We can conclude by putting the question another way: if they cannot, what hope is there for anyone else to maximize the objectivity of *their* beliefs?

NOTES

1. "Situated Knowledges: The Science Question in Feminism and the Privilege of Partial Perspective," *Feminist Studies* 14, 3 (1988): 581. Reprinted and revised in Donna J. Haraway, *Simians, Cyborgs, and Women* (New York: Routledge, I991). I thank Linda Alcoff and Elizabeth Potter for helpful comments on an earlier draft.

2. Important works here include Susan Bordo, *The Flight to Objectivity: Essays on Cartesianism & Culture* (Albany: SUNY Press, 1987); Anne Fausto-Sterling, *Myths of Gender* (New York: Basic Books, 1985); Elizabeth Fee, "Women's Nature and Scientific Objectivity," in *Woman's Nature: Rationalizations of Inequality,* ed. Marion Lowe and Ruth Hubbard (New York: Pergamon Press, 1981); Donna Haraway, op. cit. and *Primate Visions: Gender, Race, and Nature in the World of Modern Science* (New York: Routledge,1989); Ruth Hubbard, *The Politics of Women's Biology* (New Brunswick: Rutgers University Press, 1990); Evelyn Keller, *Reflections on Gender and Science* (New Haven: Yale University Press,1984); Helen Longino, *Science as Social Knowledge* (Princeton: Princeton University Press, 1990); and Lynn Hankinson Nelson, *Who Knows: From Quine to a Feminist Empiricism* (Philadelphia: Temple University Press, 1990). These are just *some* of the important works on the topic; many other authors have made contributions to the discussion. I have addressed these issues in *The Science Question in Feminism* (Ithaca: Cornell University Press,1986) and *Whose Science? Whose Knowledge? Thinking From Women's Lives* (Ithaca: Cornell University Press, 1991); see also the essays in Sandra Harding and Merrill Hintikka, ed., *Discovering Reality: Feminist Perspectives on Epistemology, Metaphysics, Methodology, and the Philosophy of Science* (Dordrecht: Reidel, 1983). An interesting parallel discussion occurs in the feminist jurisprudence literature in the course of critiques of conventional conceptions of what "the rational man" would do, "the objective observer" would see, and "the impartial judge" would reason; see, for example many of the essays in the special issue of *the Journal of Legal Education on Women in Legal Education—Pedagogy, Law, Theory, and Practice* 39, 1–2 (1988), ed. Carrie Menkel-Meadow, Martha Minow, and David Vernon; and Katharine T. Bartlett, "Feminist Legal Methods," *Harvard Law Review* 103, 4 (1990).

3. This literature is by now huge. For a sampling of its concerns, see Richard Bernstein, *Beyond Objectivism and Relativism* (Philadelphia: University of Pennsylvania Press, 1983); Martin Hollis and Steven Lukes, eds., *Rationality and Relativism* (Cambridge: Harvard University Press, 1982); Michael Krausz and Jack Meiland, eds., *Relativism: Cognitive and Moral* (Notre Dame: University of Notre Dame Press, 1982); and Stanley Aronowitz, *Science and Power: Discourse and Ideology in Modern Society* (Minneapolis: University of Minnesota Press, 1988).

4. Haraway, "Situated Knowledges," loc. cit., 579. In the phrase "a critical practice for recognizing our own 'semiotic technologies' for making meanings," she also raises here the troubling issue of reflexivity, to which I shall return.

5. Dorothy Smith, *The Everyday World as Problematic: A Feminist Sociology* (Boston: Northeastern University Press,1987) and *The Conceptual Practices of Power: A Feminist Sociology of Knowledge* (Boston: Northeastern University Press, 1990); Nancy Hartsock, "The Feminist Standpoint: Developing the Ground for a Specifically Feminist Historical Materialism," in Harding and Hintikka, eds., *Discovering Reality;* Hilary Rose, "Hand, Brain, and Heart: A Feminist Epistemology of the Natural Sciences," *Signs* 9, 1 (1983); and my discussion of these writings in chapter 6 of *The Science Question in Feminism.* Alison Jaggar also developed an influential account of standpoint epistemology in chapter 11 of *Feminist Politics and Human Nature* (Totowa, NJ: Rowman & Allenheld, 1983). For more recent de-

velopments of standpoint theory see Patricia Hill Collins, chapters 10 and 11 of *Black Feminist Thought: Knowledge, Consciousness, and the Politics of Empowerment* (Boston: Unwin Hyman, 1990) and chapters 5, 6, 7, and 11 of my *Whose Science? Whose Knowledge?*

6. Chapter 6 of *Whose Science?*, "'Strong Objectivity' and Socially Situated Knowledge," addresses some of the issues I raise here. However, here I develop further the differences between the "grounds" and the subject of knowledge for standpoint theory and for other epistemologies. This is partly an archeology of standpoint theory—bringing to full light the obscured aspects of its logic—and partly a reformulation of some of its claims.

7. Scientists sometimes confuse the philosophy of science called "empiricism" with the idea that it is a good thing to collect information about the empirical world. All philosophies of science recommend the latter. Empiricism is that account of such practices associated paradigmatically with Locke, Berkeley, and Hume and claiming that sensory experience is the only or fundamental source of knowledge. It contrasts with theological accounts that were characteristic of European science of the Middle Ages, with rationalism, and with Marxist philosophy of science. However, from the perspective of standpoint theory, it also shares key features with one or another of these three philosophies. For example, it borrows the monologic voice that seems proper if one assumes the necessity of a unitary and coherent subject of knowledge, as do all three.

8. Roy Bhaskar writes that although positivism mystifies the processes of science, nevertheless it has a certain degree of necessity in that it reflects the spontaneous consciousness of the lab bench—the tenets of positivism reflect how it feels like science is done when one is actually gathering observations of nature. Similarly, from the perspective of standpoint approaches, the "spontaneous" feminist empiricism I discuss here mystifies the processes of feminist research, although it has a certain necessity in that it just felt to these feminist empirical workers like what it was that they were doing as their work overturned the results of supposedly value-free prefeminist research. See Roy Bhaskar, "Philosophies as Ideologies of Science: A Contribution to the Critique of Positivism," in *Reclaiming Reality* (New York: Verso, 1989). Not all forms of empiricism are reasonably thought of as positivist, of course, but the most prevalent contemporary forms are. The philosophical feminist empiricism noted below is not positivist.

9. Longino, *Science as Social Knowledge;* Nelson, *Who Knows.*

10. There are many standpoint theorists and many spontaneous feminist empiricists. I present here ideal types of these two theories of knowledge. I have contrasted these two theories in a number of earlier writings, most recently on pp. 111–37 of *Whose Science: Whose Knowledge?* The following passage draws especially on pp. 111–20.

11. Dorothy Smith was right, I now think, to insist (in effect) that standpoint theory appropriates and transforms the notion of scientific method, not just of epistemology; see her comments on a paper of mine in *American Philosophical Association Newsletter on Feminism* 88, 3 (1989). It is interesting to note that by 1989, even the National Academy of Science—no rabble-rousing antiscience critic!—argues that the methods of science should be understood to include "the judgments scientists make about the interpretation or reliability of data . . . , the decisions scientists make about which problems to pursue or when to conclude an investigation," and even "the ways scientists work with each other and exchange information" [*On Being a Scientist* (Washington DC: National Academy Press, 1989), 5–6].

12. Marcia Millman and Rosabeth Moss Kanter, "Editor's Introduction" to *Another Voice: Feminist Perspectives on Social Life and Social Science* (New York: Anchor Books, 1975), vii. [Reprinted in S. Harding, ed., *Feminism and Methodology,* (Bloomington: Indiana University Press, 1987.)]

13. This description seems to imply that scientists are somehow outside of the history they are using—for example, capable of determining which are, in fact, the scientifically and

epistemologically most favorable historical locations. This is not so, of course, and that is why the reflexivity project Haraway refers to is so important.

14. "Of course, here and there will be found careless or poorly trained scientists, but no *real* scientist, no *good* scientist, would produce sexist or androcentric results of research." This line of argument has the consequence that there have been no real or good scientists except for feminists! See "What Is Feminist Science?," chapter 12 of *Whose Science? Whose Knowledge?*, for discussions of this and other attempts to resist the idea that feminist science is exactly good science but that refusing to acknowledge the feminist component in good science obscures what makes it good.

15. Frederic Jameson has argued that the feminist standpoint theorists are the only contemporary thinkers fully to appreciate the Marxist epistemology. See "*History and Class Consciousness* as an 'Unfinished Project,'" *Rethinking Marxism* 1 (1988): 49–72. It should be noted that empiricist explanations of Marxist accounts are common: "Marx had this puzzle. . . . He made a bold conjecture and then attempted to falsify it. . . . The facts supported his account and resolved the puzzle." These make the accounts plausible to empiricists but fail to engage both with Marx's own different epistemology and with the additional "puzzle" of the historical causes of the emergence of his account, to which Marxist epistemology draws attention.

16. See note 6.

17. Cf., for example, Edward Said, *Orientalism* (New York: Pantheon Books, 1978); Samir Amin, *Eurocentrism* (New York: Monthly Review Press, 1989); Monique Wittig, "The Straight Mind," *Feminist Issues* 1, 1 (1980); Marilyn Frye, *The Politics of Reality* (Trumansburg, NY: The Crossing Press, 1983); and Charles Mills, "Alternative Epistemologies," *Social Theory and Practice* 14, 3 (1988).

18. Hartsock, "The Feminist Standpoint," 159. Hartsock's use of the term *real relations* may suggest to some readers that she and other standpoint theorists are hopelessly mired in an epistemology and metaphysics that have been discredited by social constructionists. This judgment fails to appreciate the way standpoint theories reject *both* pure realist and pure social constructionist epistemologies and metaphysics. Donna Haraway is particularly good on this issue. (See her "Situated Knowledges," cited in note 1.)

19. We shall return later to the point that, for standpoint theorists, reports of marginalized experience or lives or phenomenologies of the "lived world" of marginalized peoples are not the *answers* to questions arising either inside or outside those lives, though they are necessary to asking the best questions.

20. For an exploration of a number of different ways in which marginal lives can generate more critical questions, see chapter 5, "What is Feminist Epistemology?" in *Whose Science? Whose Knowledge?*

21. See, for example, *The Conceptual Practices of Power: A Feminist Sociology of Knowledge*, 54.

22. The image of knowledge seeking as a journey—"starting off thought from women's lives"—is a useful corrective to misunderstandings that more easily arise from the visual metaphor—"thinking from the perspective of women's lives." The journey metaphor appears often in writings by Hartsock, Smith, and others.

23. Some women are assigned more of this work than others, but even wealthy and aristocratic women with plenty of servants are left significantly responsible for such work in ways their brothers are not.

24. Of course, body work and emotional work also require head work—contrary to the long history of sexist, racist, and class-biased views. See, for example, Sara Ruddick, *Maternal Thinking* (New York: Beacon Press, 1989). And the kind of head work required in administrative and managerial work—what Smith means by "ruling"—also involves distinctive

body and emotional work, though it is not acknowledged as such. Think of how much of early childhood education of middle-class children is really about internalizing a certain kind of (gender-specific) regulation of bodies and emotions.

25. This is Donna Haraway's phrase in "Situated Knowledges" cited in note 1.

26. Smith, "Women's Perspective as a Radical Critique of Sociology," in *Feminism and Methodology,* 91.

27. I idealize the history of science here as is indicated by recent studies of fraud, carelessness, and unconscious bias that is not detected. See, for example, Stephen Jay Gould, *The Mismeasure of Man* (New York: W. W. Norton, 1981); L. Kamin, *The Science and Politics of IQ* (Potomac, MD: Erlbaum, 1974); and William Broad and Nicholas Wade, *Betrayers of the Truth* (New York: Simon & Schuster, 1982). The issue here can appear to be one about the sins of individuals, which it is. But far more importantly, it is an issue about both the unwillingness and impotence of scientific institutions to police their own practices. They *must* do so, for any other alternative is less effective. But science institutions will not want to or be competent to do so until they are more integrated into democratic social projects.

28. Richard Rorty is unusual in arguing that because social situatedness is indeed the lot of all human knowledge projects, we might as well embrace our ethnocentrism while pursuing the conversations of mankind. His defense of ethnocentrism is a defense of a kind of fatalism about the impossibility of people ever transcending their social situation; in a significant sense this comes down to and converges with the standard definition of ethnocentrism centered in my argument here. (I thank Linda Alcoff for helping me to clarify this point.) He does not imagine that one can effectively change one's "social situation" by, for example, participating in a feminist political movement, reading and producing feminist analyses, and so on. From the perspective of his argument, it is mysterious how any woman (or man) ever becomes a feminist because our "social situation" is initially to be constrained by patriarchal institutions, ideologies, and the like. How *did* John Stuart Mill or Simone de Beauvoir ever come to think such thoughts as they did? See his *Objectivity, Relativism, and Truth* (New York: Cambridge University Press, 1991).

29. Of course a gender is not an ethnicity. Yet historians and anthropologists write of women's cultures, so perhaps it does not stretch the meaning of ethnicity too far to think of women's cultures this way. Certainly some of the critics of standpoint theory have done so.

30. "Women's Perspective," cited in note 26.

31. Bettina Aptheker, *Tapestries of Life: Women's Work, Women's Consciousness, and the Meaning of Daily Life* (Amherst: University of Massachusetts Press, 1989).

32. *Black Feminist Thought,* cited in note 6.

33. The preceding citations contain many examples of such cases.

34. "So many," but not all. African American and Latina writers have argued that in U.S. society, at least, a poor African American and Latino man cannot be regarded as better off than his sister in many important respects.

35. What are the material limits of standpoint theories? Retroactively, we can see that they require the context of scientific culture; that is, they center claims about greater objectivity, the possibility and desirability of progress, the value of causal accounts for social projects, and so on. They also appear to require that the barriers between dominant and dominated be not absolutely rigid; there must be some degree of social mobility. Some marginal people must be able to observe what those at the center do, some marginal voices must be able to catch the attention of those at the center, and some people at the center must be intimate enough with the lives of the marginalized to be able to think how social life works from the perspective of their lives. A totalitarian system would be unlikely to breed standpoint theories. So a historical move to antiscientific or to totalitarian systems would make

standpoint theories less useful. No doubt there are other historical changes that would limit the resources standpoint theories can provide.

36. See the citations in note 3.

37. All of the feminist standpoint theorists and science writers insist on distinguishing their positions from relativist ones. I have discussed the issue of relativism in several places, most recently in chapters 6 and 7 of *Whose Science? Whose Knowledge?*

38. See S. P. Mohanty, "Us and Them: On the Philosophical Bases of Political Criticism," *Yale Journal of Criticism* 2, 2 (1989); and Donna Haraway's "Situated Knowledges" for especially illuminating discussions of why relativism can look attractive to many thinkers at this moment in history, but why it should nevertheless be resisted.

39. Mary G. Belenky and her colleagues point out that the phrase "It's my opinion . . ." has different meanings for the young men and women they have studied. For men this phrase means "I've got a right to my opinion," but for women it means "It's just my opinion." Mary G. Belenky, B. M. Clinchy, N. R. Goldeberger, and J. M. Tarule, *Women's Ways of Knowing: the Development of Self, Voice, and Mind* (New York: Basic Books, 1986).

40. Critics of standpoint theories usually attribute this position to standpoint theorists. Within the array of feminist theoretical approaches, the claim that only women can produce knowledge is most often made by Radical Feminists.

41. The Combahee River Collective, "A Black Feminist Statement," in *This Bridge Called My Back: Writings by Radical Women of Color,* ed. Cherrie Moraga and Gloria Anzaldua (Latham, NY: Kitchen Table: Women of Color Press, 1983), 212.

42. For example, mechanistic models of the universe had different meanings for Galileo's critics than they have had for modern astronomers or, later, for contemporary ecologists, as Carolyn Merchant and other historians of science point out. See Carolyn Merchant, *The Death of Nature: Women, Ecology, and the Scientific Revolution* (New York: Harper & Row, 1980). To take another case, "wild animals" and, more generally, "nature" are defined differently by Japanese, Indian, and Anglo-American primatologists, as Donna Haraway points out in *Primate Visions* (cited in note 2). The cultural character of nature as an object of knowledge has been a consistent theme in Haraway's work.

43. Longino's and Nelson's arguments are particularly telling against the individualism of empiricism. See Nelson's "Who Knows," chapter 6 in *Who Knows,* and Longino's discussion of how the underdetermination of theories by their evidence ensures that "background beliefs" will function as if they were evidence in many chapters of *Science as Social Knowledge* (cited in note 2) but especially in chapters 8, 9, and 10.

44. See Elizabeth Spelman, *Inessential Woman: Problems of Exclusion in Feminist Thought* (Boston: Beacon Press, 1988) for a particularly pointed critique of essentialist tendencies in feminist writings. Most of the rest of this section appears also in "Subjectivity, Experience, and Knowledge: An Epistemology from/for Rainbow Coalition Politics," forthcoming in *Questions of Authority: The Politics of Discourse and Epistemology in Feminist Thought,* ed. Judith Roof and Robyn Weigman. I have also discussed these points in several other places.

45. These ways of describing this kind of subject of knowledge appear in the writings of, respectively, Smith ("Women's Perspective"), Collins (*Black Feminist Thought*), and bell hooks, *Feminist Theory from Margin to Center* (Boston: South End Press, 1983).

46. Consequently, a main strategy of the public agenda politics of the new social movements has been to insist that women, or peoples of African descent, or the poor, and so on do indeed possess the kinds of reason that qualify them as "rational men"; that women's, industrial, or peasant labor makes these groups also the "working men" from whose laboring lives can be generated less partial and distorted understandings of local and international economies.

47. I do not say these thinkers are perfect feminists—they are not, and no one is. But here and there one can see them generating original feminist knowledge as they think from the perspective of women's lives as women have taught them to do.

48. Collins, *Black Feminist Thought,* 35–36. Chapters 1, 2, 10, and 11 of this book offer a particular rich and stimulating development of standpoint theory.

49. See the citations in note 3. The term *objectivism* has been used to identify the objectionable notion by Bernstein, Keller, and Bordo (see earlier citations), among others.

50. The following arguments are excerpted from pp. 143–48 in my *Whose Science? Whose Knowledge?*

51. See note 27.

52. Many Americans—even (especially?) highly educated ones—hold fundamentally totalitarian notions of what democracy is, associating it with mob rule or some at least mildly irrelevant principle of representation but never with genuine community dialogue. (A physicist asked me if by democracy I really meant that national physics projects should be managed by, say, fifty-two people, one selected randomly from each state! This made me think of the wisdom of William Buckley Jr.'s desire to be governed by the first 100 people in the Boston phone book rather than the governors we have.) A good starting point for thinking about how to advance democracy is John Dewey's proposal: those who will bear the consequence of a decision should have a proportionate share in making it.

53. Quoted in Werner Van den Daele, "The Social Construction of Science," in *The Social Production of Scientific Knowledge,* ed. E. Mendelsohn, P. Weingart, and R. Whitley (Dordrecht: Reidel, 1977), 34.

54. David Mura puts the point this way in "Strangers in the Village," in *The Graywolf Annual Five: Multi-cultural Literacy*, ed. Rick Simonson and Scott Walker (St. Paul: Graywolf Press, 1988), 152.

55. These arguments for retaining the notion of objectivity draw on ones I have made several times before, most recently in *Whose Science? Whose Knowledge?,* 157–61.

56. The National Academy of Sciences recommends such an expansion, as indicated earlier.

57. For example, Smith and Hartsock, cited in note 5.

CHAPTER 4

Tracing the Contours

Feminist Research and Feminist Objectivity

KUM-KUM BHAVNANI

The projects of feminist research are frequently thought of as having epistemological concerns at their center (Le Doeuff 1987), these concerns having posed challenges to the practices and theories of the human sciences within the academy. Many writers have been working on these issues in the past two decades (Stanley and Wise 1979; Hartsock 1983; Mies 1983; Rose 1983; Smith 1987; Eichler 1988; Stacey 1988; Haraway 1989; Hill Collins 1990; Harding 1991) and it is generally agreed upon that issues of objectivity and their relationship to "science" are issues which are at the forefront of the projects of feminist research. Simultaneously, arguments which look critically at positivist approaches to knowledge have impinged upon the disciplines of sociology (Abbott and Wallace 1990), history (Alonso 1988; Passerini 1987), and social psychology (Squire 1989) to name but a few examples. These universes of discourse have been informed by feminist approaches, which means that questions are raised, for example, within psychology about the apparent objectivity of the experimental method (Wood Sherif 1987). This, in turn, has brought into focus the arguments about the limited value of quantitative analyses in providing insights into issues of human relationships (e.g., Griffin 1985) and about power inequalities within the research process (Bhavnani 1988). Such discussions frequently have focused on the *methods* deployed in the generation of insights in the human sciences. What often has flowed from these discussions are broader challenges which interrogate empiricism and positivism.

Such challenges mean that scientific activity as neutral and value free has gained academic credence (e.g., Rose and Rose 1976) although not a widespread academic acceptance. If, however, it is accepted that scientific insights are social in origin, then these origins may be analyzed by tracing the historical development of such insights. Thus, an historical approach can facilitate answers to questions such as *why* a particular issue is investigated at a particular point in time. For example, *why* was it that the end of the nineteenth and turn of the twentieth centuries saw considerable interest in relying on arguments about the brain size of black people and white women to explain apparent differences in cognitive abilities between these groups and white men (Griffiths and Saraga 1979). An historical approach may also facilitate the posing of questions as to *how* such knowledge is produced—that is, who produces it and how it becomes privileged. The logic of this argument is that a historical approach encourages questions to be raised about the political economy of knowledge production. In this way, a historical approach can eliminate the idea of total knowledges; thus, objectivity and truth come to be seen as concepts which are historically situated and situationally specific.

Knowledge production is, therefore, an historical process. My argument is that feminist epistemologies, in the process of continuing challenges against positivism, have always placed questions and issues about the historical relationships between science and society at the center of our work. Feminist theorizing has always argued that there is a necessity for scientific work to examine its practices, procedures, and theories through the use of historical insights, for it is these insights that bring into focus the ways in which knowledge production is a set of social, political, economic, and ideological processes (e.g., Acker, Barry, and Esseveld 1983).

The arguments about the historicization of knowledge, embraced by many writers (e.g., Bhaskar 1989; Fraser 1989) lead me to ask of feminist studies—is feminist work being developed with an adequate historical sense of differences amongst women?

The work in the United States of, for example, black writers such as Angela Y. Davis (1971, 1982) and Patricia Hill Collins (1990) and in Britain by writings such as those of Bryan, Dadzie, and Scafe (1985), Grewal, Kay, Landor, Lewis, and Parmar (1988), and Ware (1992) has shown that the histories of the feminist movement in both of those countries are fraught with racisms and exclusionary practices. These arguments continue by suggesting that an important consequence of these histories is that racialized, gendered, and class-based inequalities are embedded into the creation of knowledge. What often occurs in the process of presenting feminist arguments for the historicization of knowledge is that the points about racisms, exclusion, and invisibility of women of color become silenced (see Haraway 1989, for an exception). Thus, the questions that charges of exclusion and invisibility pose of feminist studies begin to disappear, the projects to create feminist knowledges become weak and fragmented, and history gets reenacted. It is sometimes implied that inclusion of racism in feminist work can lead to fragmentation of feminist projects. My argument is that far from an analysis of racism leading to fragmentation, it is the process of not engaging with the consequences of racialized inequalities which weakens the projects of feminisms.

Thus, I argue that challenges from feminist writers and analysts to positivist approaches to knowledge raise an issue central to knowledge production, namely, that such production is an historical process. I suggest, however, that many of those working on feminist epistemologies have often developed inadequate arguments about such historicity by erasing, denying, ignoring, or tokenizing the contradictory and conflicting interests which women may have—often seen most clearly in the writings of women from all over the world (see Bhavnani 1991, for a discussion of these contradictions). Conflicting interests can also mean that different standpoints develop which are in sharp opposition to each other. For example, the history of white women's suffrage in the United States demonstrates conflicting interests in that such suffrage was often argued for at the expense of black suffrage (Davis 1982). This way of writing history, that is, that conflicting interests amongst women are made *visible,* can lead to questions arising about objective knowledges. In other words, this approach can demonstrate that objective knowledges are situated and partial, not impartial or disembodied, and neither are they transcendent.

While the above arguments are not new, nor specific to feminist critiques of the social sciences, it is Donna Haraway (1988) who has recently recast and reframed them in her representation of feminist objectivity. Her sense of objectivity is in opposition to positivist discussions of this concept, and is also distant from the absolute relativism embodied in the view that all truths are equally valid. She says "Feminist objectivity means quite simply *situated knowledges*" (581). In describing feminist attempts to grapple with discussions of truth, she convincingly points to "'our' problem [which] is how to have *simultaneously* an account of radical historical contingency for all knowledge claims" (579), while still retaining a sense of the material or "real" world. She suggests that feminists could view objectivity as a "particular and specific embodiment," rather than as a "false vision promising transcendence of all limits and responsibility" (Haraway 1988, 582).

> Feminist objectivity is about limited location and situated knowledge, not about transcendence and splitting of subject and object. It allows us to become answerable for what we learn to see. (Haraway 1988, 583)

She continues later by stating that

> We seek those ruled by partial sight and limited voice—not partiality for its own sake, but, rather, for the sake of the connections and unexpected openings (which) situated knowledges make possible. Situated knowledges are about communities not about isolated individuals. (Haraway 1988, 590)

What may be derived from this is that partiality of vision need not be synonymous with partiality of theorizing, and, indeed, may be desirable, for the partiality she discusses could lead to greater insight for feminist analyses. Thus, she argues that not only are positioning and partiality two key elements of feminist objectivity, but "becom[ing] answerable for what we learn to see" requires that a third element—accountability—also be present. The strength of this argument is that she *engages* with difference, and, indeed, uses difference as the springboard from which to transform feminist arguments about objectivity.

Her emphasis on accountability, positioning, and partiality is helpful, for this accentuation can permit a clearer approach to analyzing and developing feminist insights into objectivity. Further, her argument that these elements, when emanating from feminist frameworks, can provide some dynamic and creative connections in the production of knowledges is both exciting and timely. If these elements do permit the development of creative and dynamic connections, then it is appropriate to pose the question: "by what means do these elements permit the making of such connections?" What are the implications to be drawn from the three elements—accountability, positioning, and partiality—for the ways in which knowledge production can be faithful to the notion of "feminist objectivity" outlined by Haraway? What are the principles that flow from these elements and which, in turn, indicate criteria according to which research can be evaluated as "feminist"?

This question is one which consistently haunts feminist researchers—especially those of us working within the social sciences—namely, is it possible to identify principles which could frame the development of criteria for the conduct, evaluation, and dissemination of feminist work in the social sciences? Is there, indeed, anything which is particular to feminist enquiry in the social sciences, after having specified that the main agent of the enquiry be a woman, or women? This question has been raised many times (recently by Jayaratne and Stewart 1991) and yet it has still not been thoroughly interrogated. Most readers of this article would agree that research is not necessarily feminist if it is conducted by a woman, nor that the subjects of the enquiry be only women, but surely it is valid to state that the main agent of any research which claims to be feminist must be "woman." However, while that is a necessary condition for feminist work, it is not a sufficient one. It is necessary because "feminist" is derived from "feminism," which is a political movement comprised of women, but it is not sufficient because there is a clear distinction between "woman" and "feminist." Each category is not unitary nor singular, (see Sandoval 1991), but neither are they collapsible into each other—for "feminist" is an achieved status, or, more precisely, a continuous accomplishment.

If it is not sufficient that women are the key agents in any work which is defined as feminist, then how can one identify work as feminist in the sense of furthering the aims of feminist objectivity—that is, creating situated knowledges—as laid out by Haraway? I suggest that questions be developed, and principles delineated in order to set up markers against which any social scientific enquiry could be evaluated for its claim to be feminist.

The first principle which flows from Haraway's insistence on accountability as an element within feminist objectivity is that any study whose main agent is a woman/women and which claims a feminist framework should not reproduce the researched in ways in which they are represented within dominant society—that is, the analyses can not be complicit with dominant representations which reinscribe inequality. In other words, the accountability of the research is not only to specific individuals, but also to the overall projects of feminisms. For example, feminist work often struggles to make the agency of women visible, while not presenting this agency as deviant (e.g., Essed 1990). So, when people are in positions of structural subordination, research which is defined as feminist must, at the very least, reflect upon whether the analysis presented in the work reinscribes the researched into the dominant representations of powerlessness, into being viewed as without agency, into being defined as abnormal. The questions which flow from Haraway's first element are: "Does this work/ analysis define the researched as either passive victims or as deviant?" "Does it reinscribe the researched into prevailing representations?" If that is the case, as in, for example, some studies which have been published about South Asian women living in England (see Brah 1987, for a commentary about this; and see Brah and Shaw 1992, for an example of a study which avoids such a trap), then it seems to me that regardless of whether the research focuses on women, or is conducted by women, or both, it may not be defined as being informed by *feminism.* If research is unable to achieve such a definition, then, it cannot implement the project of furthering feminist objectivity. I am not, for one second, suggesting that women researchers provide romanticized analyses of people who are frequently in positions of structural subordination. Rather, I am arguing that for feminist objectivity to be enhanced, and for knowledge production to be explicitly understood as an historical process, it is incumbent on women researchers to pose the above question of our/themselves, and to deal with it in the analysis. When this is done, then the work may be claimed as fashioning feminist objectivity.

The second question emerging from Haraway's arguments about positioning is whether the research report, however and wherever it is presented, discusses, or, at its most minimal, makes reference to the micropolitical processes which are in play during the conduct of research. In short, the question is, how and to what extent does the research conduct, write-up, and dissemination deal with the micropolitics of the research encounter—what are the relationships of domination and subordination which the researcher has negotiated and what are the means through which they are discussed in the research report?

The third question, analogous to her element of partiality, is centered upon "difference." In what ways are questions of difference dealt with in the research study—in its design, conduct, write-up, and dissemination?

It is these three questions: Are the researched reinscribed into prevailing notions of powerlessness? Are the micropolitics of the research relationships discussed? and How are questions of difference engaged with?, which I suggest flow from Haraway's discussion of feminist objectivity, and which provide reference points through which principles may be delineated and thus, research projects evaluated. The three questions generate principles and criteria which permit the creation of sufficient conditions, beyond the necessary one that the main agent is a woman. It is the combination of these necessary and sufficient conditions which then can provide the framework for evaluating research as feminist.

I shall use three questions as reference points—reinscription, micropolitics, and difference—to frame the second section of my paper. This is an examination of a research study I conducted in Britain in 1984 and 1985, whose write-up was completed in early 1988 (Bhavnani 1991). I shall use the lens of feminist objectivity combined with the questions raised above to comment on that work and to discuss in what ways it stands under the umbrella of feminist objectivity.

The research study explored the ways in which young, working class people in Britain discussed issues in the domain of the political. Much of the psychological work on young people in Britain has discussed youth as a homogeneous group, focusing on insights derived from biology and conventional psychology (e.g., Conger 1973). Such work has therefore disguised the ways in which the transition between childhood and adulthood are social transitions (Bates et al. 1984). The transition is presented as a "natural" one. From this vantage point, when the political views of young people have been discussed, most often using survey methods, young people have been presented as either politically apathetic or politically rebellious (see, e.g., Furnham 1985, for a review). The definitions which have been used to tap political views have tended to focus exclusively on the parliamentary process in Britain, as well as potential voting behavior. Whilst not *all* work with young people has done this, as, for example, the work which came out of the Centre for Contemporary Cultural Studies at the University of Birmingham in England, (see, e.g., Hall and Jefferson 1975) there is an overwhelming set of discourses about white young men in particular—much of this work had been done with men—suggesting that working class young men in Britain are not interested in politics. That is, the argument implies, young working class men are not political. In this way, the direction of such research ends up reproducing discourses which, in general, cast young working class men as social victims. The work from the Birmingham Centre, and their approach to young people, mostly men, relied on ethnographic and quasi-ethnographic methods. The use of ethnographic approaches, combined with feminist work with young women, as in, for example, the work of Angela McRobbie (1982) and Christine Griffin (1985), demonstrated to me that it was possible to take the perspective of young people seriously within an academic research project. But I did not assume that I should automatically take the young people's perspective at face value.

The study did not define "politics" only as the arena in which voting, political parties, and knowledge of the official political processes in Britain are discussed. Rather, it took as a starting point that politics is the means by which human beings regulate, attempt to regulate, and challenge, with a view to changing unequal power relationships. Such an open definition of politics required that I think hard about the topics to be discussed within the study, as well as the ways in which these topics would be discussed with young people. As a result, I conducted pilot work in Sheffield, a town in Northern England in which I used a formal questionnaire, with closed questions, as well as "hanging out"[1] in the largest shopping mall in the center of Middleton,[2] where youth often gather on weekday afternoons and on Saturdays. I also spent considerable time in youth centers in Middleton—where young people come to play pool, table tennis, listen to music, and talk. From the four months I spent immersed in this style of work, that is, a constant seven days a week engagement with young people, I quickly saw that young women, black and white, were not very present in either the malls or the youth centers, except in the latter case, when there were "girls' nights" or special sessions set up for young women of South Asian origin. As I had wanted to discuss issues within the domain of the political with both young men and young women, I decided to move the main study to schools in Central and South Middleton. I first conducted single-sex group discussions with ninety 16-year-olds in their final year of school in early 1985. The discussions covered a range of issues having "to do with society" as I explained it, and I used a frequency count of the topics which were raised by the school students to include in the individual interviews. I also wanted to discuss issues which are more frequently thought of as political, such as the parliamentary parties, and so I included this as well into the individual interviews.

The decision to move away from adopting quantitative analyses in this study was informed both by my personal history of work in developmental and social psychology and by my pilot work. The agenda for the open-ended individual interview schedule which I used was a negotiation between myself and the young people who were the potential interviewees of the study, and the use of open-ended interviews, based on prior group discussions, was a means whereby that negotiation could occur. There was no indication that the young people did not want to discuss the issues within the domain of the political which they and I had negotiated together, and so, suggestions of political apathy remain marginal for any analysis of this work. They also talked at length—as the thousands of pages of transcripts show.

I interviewed seventy-two young people in this way—half of whom were men. Approximately one-third of the interviewees were of Afro-Caribbean origin, one-third were of South Asian origin, and the remaining one-third was white. The topics covered in the individual interviews were derived from the group discussions and included employment, unemployment, training for young people, racism, democracy and voting, marriage and violence against women and children, and the miners' strike in Britain of 1984/1985. Sixty of the seventy-two interviewees were interviewed by me six months later—the issues being life since leaving school, employment, unemployment and training schemes, recent rebellions by youth in Britain, their futures, and party politics. In this way, these interviews about issues in the domain of the political were situated in the context of the movement of these young people from school to unemployment or the labor market. These 132 interviews, each of forty to forty-five minutes in length, were tape-recorded and then transcribed.

I have been reflecting on the points I made earlier about furthering the project of feminist objectivity because there have been times when I have discussed my research in public forums that I have been asked, "But what has this project got to do with your interests in 'race' (for which read difference) and gender (for which read feminist studies)?" A question which requires specification of how feminism and difference are implicated within this enquiry is certainly a helpful question, for any response to it has to lay bare some of the assumptions, and hence the criteria according to which academic work may be claimed as feminist. The criteria are clearly not obvious in this study, for apart from my self-definition as a black feminist in Britain in the past two decades, there is apparently very little in any initial outline to indicate that the work is based on and aims to develop feminist work. The research explored issues in the domain of the political—not specifically a feminist preoccupation, nor, indeed, part of that common sense of "women's issues." I also interviewed both men and women. In what ways, therefore, can it be defined as a feminist enquiry, and, hence as something which could help in the elaboration of feminist objectivity?

My previous discussion suggested three questions—focusing on reinscription, micropolitics, and difference—which generate principles and criteria from which research conducted and written by women can be evaluated for claims to feminism. Below, I shall discuss my research according to these three questions, and I shall also draw on insights from Haraway's suggestion that feminist objectivity provides unexpected openings and connections.

The first principle I discussed was that of reinscription. Let me point to the ways in which this research project may have been partly successful in avoiding reinscribing the researched as without agency, and as "politically apathetic"—that is, avoided a representation of young working class people as cultural dopes. I would not want to claim that it was totally successful, but I should like to present the reasons for my thinking that it was, partly, successful.

Many of the young people, when discussing party politics organized their arguments through the theme of intelligence ("don't think I'm a brain box," was the way in which one young woman said it). The suggestion was implied by many of the interviewees that their views about, for example, the Labor Party were not legitimate because the speaker did not see her/himself as intelligent. Thus, intelligence came to be seen as a necessary requirement for being able to comment on parliamentary parties. This link between democracy and "intelligence" provided by the interviewees led to an unexpected opening. That is, the young people in this study were not necessarily politically apathetic, but rather, that these young people understood the playing out of democracy in relation to levels of intelligence, and thus defined themselves as not intelligent enough to present *legitimate* opinions about party politics. Not that there was no interest there—just an implicit and explicit wondering whether their views were legitimate. It is this link between democracy and intelligence which provides an unexpected opening.[3] The point for the present argument is that the young people in this particular research project were not politically apathetic or politically disinterested, but rather, that there were distinct and comprehensible reasons why they appeared to not discuss many issues in the domain of the political. In taking the stated views of young people seriously, but not necessarily at face value, the research did not reinscribe the researched into dominant representations—which suggests that young working class people are social victims. In avoiding such a reinscription, the study may lay claim to furthering feminist objectivity, and therefore, suggest a more productive way of understanding the construction of politics by this group of young people.

The second question which I have suggested could be used to indicate whether the project of feminist objectivity is beginning to be implemented, is related to the micropolitics of the research process. Again, let me take my research as a case study through which I can show what I understand by this.

The power of the researcher in relation to the researched—a set of power relationships which are bounded by the imperatives of resource availability—can define the parameters of the theoretical framework, can control the design of the study, and can inform how the study is conducted, analyzed, and written up. That is, the researcher is positioned in a particular relationship of power in relation to the researched. Frequently, research which has been influenced by the arguments of feminist writers such as Helen Roberts (1981) or Liz Stanley (1989) will note this positioning of the researcher. My argument, however, is that the micropolitics of the research situation need to be analyzed and not only noted. For example, relationships within my study flowed from the socially ascribed characteristics, such as "race," gender, and class, as well as age, of the interviewer and interviewee. These socially ascribed characteristics carry hierarchical loadings of their own. Many times, the sensitive social scientist has tried to regulate this unevenness in the social characteristics by ensuring that women interview women and that black researchers interview black people. In fact, it may even have been expected that I would have designed a research study in which I set up such "matching"—that is, that I only interviewed South Asian women, or black women or black and white women. I knew however, from the start of this study that I wanted to interview white men—because I wanted to see "what would happen." Rosenthal's 1966 work on the experimenter effect is often cited to justify the matching of researcher and researched, and work such as that by Zenie-Ziegler (1988) is an example of a study which merely noted the position of the researcher in relation to the researched. I suggest that both matching and noting can take the gaze of the analyst and reader away from the micropolitics of the research encounter. This is because the processes of matching and noting cannot explicitly take account of the power relationships between the researcher and the researched, and yet both processes imply that unevenness between the two sides in a research study has been dealt with. In the research study discussed in this paper, such matching was never present—because I was always a woman who was fifteen to twenty years older than the interviewees. This age non-matching was frequently interwoven with matches or non-matches of culture, "race," and gender. For example, when interviewing young white men the frequently encountered imbalance of power between white men and black women was potentially both inverted and reproduced in the interviews. That is, when interviewing young white men, my role as student researcher, my age, and my assumed class affiliation may have been taken as sources of potential domination. However, my racialized and gendered ascriptions suggested the opposite. That is, in this instance, the interviewees and myself were inscribed within multifaceted power relations which had structural domination *and* structural subordination in play on both sides. This interplay of subordination and domination on the part of both interviewer and interviewee was a consistent feature of my study.

Let me compare this to a study for which I have considerable respect, but which, as I reflect upon it, I seem to want to add to. Paul Willis (1978) conducted an ethnographic study which deployed participant observation, discussion, and individual conversation with a group of young working class men in Britain in the mid-1970s. He wanted to analyze the ways in which, as they moved from school to the labor market, working class men obtained and stayed within "working class jobs." One part of his study showed that when the boys talked about their girlfriends, they discussed them in objectified and frequently very dismissive ways. This notion of how this group of young men discuss issues of heterosexual relationships forms part of some forms of academic conventional wisdom—white working class men are overwhelmingly and offensively sexist. None of the young men I interviewed talked about women in that way. Clearly, there is an important question to be dealt with here, which is why the young men in my study did not talk to me in the way in which they talked with Willis.

The first answer which is often presented is that "well, you're a woman and they thought they should not be rude to you, the *woman* researcher." Such a comment implies that my interviews with these young men are not authentic—and thus that work such as that of Willis is authentic about young men. This notion, that *some* kinds of work are "authentic," and, therefore, by implication, others are inauthentic has been sufficiently discredited to make that kind of explanation unsatisfactory. What such a notion does is, however, to reinscribe a Willis-type study as "natural," as *the truth.* What I am saying is that Willis, a white man, becomes a marker for a universalistic insight while I, a black woman, become particularized. (See, e.g., Barbara Christian's 1987 discussion of a similar issue when "race" and theory are under scrutiny.) In other words, I argue that the questions which may be addressed to me about my work also need to be put to Willis. When one begins to think of it in this way, then it is possible to analyze the micropolitics of the research process. That is, when the socially ascribed, hierarchically organized characteristics of the researcher and researched have structural domination and structural subordination in play on both sides in a manner which inverts the usually encountered imbalances, *this* setup can provide an opening for an analysis of the micropolitics. I am not suggesting that men interviewing women is a consequence of my argument, for that is merely a replication of the most frequently encountered power imbalances in research studies. What I am suggesting is that an inversion of this "normal" power imbalance in research studies—from the conception right through to the analysis—can permit a sharper analysis of the micropolitics of research, so that *feminist* objectivity can be implemented. So, any text which emerges in a research encounter cannot be taken for granted.

The third question which can be posed is to ask in what ways issues of difference are seen and dealt with explicitly. Ironically, this has been the one that has been the most difficult one for me to address explicitly in the context of this paper. I have again taken my lead from Donna Haraway's account of partiality, which she makes clear does not imply partiality of theorizing. Many readers will be familiar with the argument, often, but not exclusively presented by women of color that studies that have women as researchers and women as the researched group have ignored or glossed over differences amongst women (e.g., Bridenthal, Grossman, and Kaplan 1984; Hewitt 1985; Lazreg 1990). This research study did point to many continuities of experience for the young people, who had shared experiences of their schools, their housing, and the relationship of their household to the local state. However, it is clear that there were also non-shared experiences and accounts such as those of racism, culture, and gender. If difference is understood as difference of interests within this study—that is, that there are material reasons for the discontinuities of experience and identities put forward by the young people—then the ways in which the young people talked about racism provides an entry point for such a discussion. On the whole, the young white people in this study did not express explicit racism, although some of their comments were situated within discourses which can lead to a reproduction of racism. An example of this would be, "I don't care what color they are—they're just my friends." In general, however, most of the white interviewees claimed to be against racism by utilizing the theme of "we're all humans aren't we?" This appeal to a common biology and naturalness led the white interviewees to suggest that racism was also "natural." For example, many white interviewees said, "It's human nature," and, therefore, that little could be done to eliminate it by society.

In contrast, many young black people identified a number of the ways through which some of the contradictions of racism could be considered, thus indicating one type of strategy for challenging racism. Examples of the identification of contradictions were points such as, "Why do they want a tan when they criticize us because of our color?" Or reference was made to the arranged marriage between Prince Charles and Diana as being publicly lauded, while official statements in Britain about arranged marriage within South Asian cultures condemned the practice. Some of the young women of South Asian origin suggested that as marriage was a "natural" consequence in their lives, then one could defend the *concept* of arranged marriage, because the logic was that "if you're going to get married anyway," an arranged marriage was preferable to a love marriage. When asked why, one young woman said:

PN11: Cos you don't have to go out looking for someone—I couldn't.

KKB: You couldn't?

PN11: No, must be like a hunter with a spear and net, hunting for a husband.

This strategy, of pointing to contradictions within racist arguments was one that was developed by the black interviewees. This is one way of beginning to examine difference—in the sense of pointing to the contradictions within racist arguments. However, the young black people also discussed racism through suggesting explicit strategies to tackle it. Such strategies included, "I told my teacher," "I wanted to grab and choke them," and "I ignored them," this last implying that ignoring was one strategy out of a repertoire of strategies available to her. The interweaving of a concept of strategy into their discussions suggested that these speakers thought that racism could be altered by being challenged, either by pointing to the contradictions or be suggesting explicit means to tackle racism. In suggesting that patterns of racist behavior can be altered and eliminated, there is a consequent implication that, therefore, racism is not natural. That is, it is implied that racism is a result of social definitions rather than a biological inevitability of "human nature."[4] It is this discontinuity of both identity and experience which can be generated if a sense of difference is built into the research process.

In conclusion, it is clear that feminist projects which trace the contours of feminist objectivity are a central means by which it may be possible to escape from the impasse over questions of "objectivity" and "truth," which at present hound many discussions of research practices. Further, I suggest that *feminist* objectivity, with its principles of accountability, partiality, and positioning leads to a set of questions, which, in turn, frame principles and criteria for the evaluation of research studies—criteria of whether or not subjects are reinscribed into powerlessness, of how the micropolitics of the research are discussed, and of how "difference" is made integral to a research study.

The point can be made most concisely using the following extract from an interview conducted for the study:

KKB: What's your ideal job?

PN60: I'd like the job of the Queen.

KKB: Why? What does she do?

PN60: Well, put it like this, she gets paid for breaking bottles against ships and we get arrested for breaking bottles on the street!

NOTES

1. This is a common technique used in participant observation and ethnographic research where the researcher spends time with the researched on their territory, sharing their work, leisure. or home environments.

2. This is the fictional name for the large town in the north of England where I conducted the study.

3. The concept of intelligence has been widely criticized for at least the past two decades as being a means by which economic. social, and racialized inequalities are both reproduced and therefore sustained (see Richardson, Spears, and Richards 1972)—that is, that notions of intelligence can undermine the goals of a democracy. Clearly, a question which then can be raised, from the interviews with the young people, is what it is in official discourses about public-domain politics which legitimates this view.

4. One can ask why it was that the young black interviewees discussed racism with me in these ways, and why the white interviewees did so in a different way, and I have dealt with that type of argument in my discussion of Willis (1978).

REFERENCES

Abbott, Pamela, and Claire Wallace. 1990. *An introduction to sociology: Feminist perspectives.* London: Routledge.

Acker, Joan, Kate Barry, and Johanna Esseveld. 1983. Objectivity and truth problems in doing feminist research. *Women's Studies International Forum* 6(4): 423–35.

Alonso, Ana Maria. 1988. The effects of truth: Representations of the past and the imagining of community. *Journal of Historical Sociology* 1(1): 33–58.

Bates, Inge, John Clarke, Phil Cohen, Dan Finn, Robert Moore, and Paul Willis, eds. 1984. *Schooling for the dole? The new vocationalism.* London: Macmillan.

Bhaskar, Roy. 1989. *Reclaiming reality.* London: Verso.

Bhavnani, Kum-Kum. 1988. Empowerment and social research. *TEXT* 8(1): 41–51.

———. 1991. *Talking politics: A psychological framing for views from youth in Britain.* Cambridge: Cambridge University Press.

———. (in press). Talking racism and the editing of Women's Studies. In *Introducing women's studies,* ed. Diane Richardson and Vicki Robinson. London: Macmillan.

Brah, Avtar. 1987. Women of South Asian origin in Britain: Issues and concerns. *South Asia Research,* 7(1): 39–54.

Brah, Avtar, and Sobia Shaw. 1992. *Working choices: South Asian young Muslim women and the labour market.* London: Department of Employment, Research Paper No. 91.

Bridenthal, Renate, Atina Grossman, and Marion Kaplan, eds. 1984. *When biology became destiny: Women in Weimar and Nazi Germany.* New York: Monthly Review Press.

Bryan, Beverly, Sheila Dadzie, and Suzanne Scafe. 1985. *The heart of the race.* London: Virago.

Christian, Barbara. 1987. The race for theory. *Cultural Critique* 6: (Spring) 51–63.

Conger, John. 1973. *Adolescence and youth: Psychological development in a changing world.* New York: Harper International Edition.

Davis, Angela. 1971. Reflections on the role of the black woman in the community of slaves. *Black Scholar* 2: (December) 3–15.

———. 1982. *Woman race and class.* London: The Women's Press.

Eichler, Margritte. 1988. *Non-sexist research methods.* London: Allen and Unwin.

Essed, Philomena. 1990. *Everyday racism.* Claremont, CA: Hunter House.

Fraser, Nancy. 1989. *Unruly practices: Power, discourse, and gender in contemporary social theory.* Minneapolis: University of Minnesota Press.

Furnham, Adrian. 1985. Youth unemployment: A review of the literature. *Journal of Adolescence* 8: 109–24.

Grewal, Shabnam, Jackie Kay, Liliane Landor, Gail Lewis, and Pratibh Parmar, eds. 1988. *Charting the journey: Writings by Black and Third World women.* London: Sheba Feminist Publishers, 74–88.

Griffin, Christine. 1985. *Typical girls?* London: Routledge.

Griffiths, Dorothy, and Esther Saraga. 1979. Sex differences and cognitive abilities: A sterile field of enquiry? In *Sex role stereotyping,* ed. Oonagh Hartnett, Gill Boden, and Mary Fuller. 17–45. London: Tavistock.

Hall, Stuart, and Jefferson, Tony, ed. 1975. *Resistance through rituals: Youth subcultures in post-war Britain.* London: Hutchinson.

Haraway, Donna. 1988. Situated knowledges: The science question in feminism and the privilege of partial perspective. *Feminist Studies* 14(3): 575–600.
———. 1989. *Primate visions.* London: Routledge.
Harding, Sandra. 1991. *Whose science? Whose knowledge?* Ithaca: Cornell University Press.
Hartsock, Nancy. 1983. The feminist standpoint: Developing the ground for a specifically feminist historical materialism. In *Discovering reality: Feminist perspectives on epistemology, metaphysics, methodology, and philosophy of science,* ed. Sandra Harding and Merrill Hintikka, 283–310. Dodrecht: Reidel.
Hewitt, Nancy. 1985. Beyond the search for sisterhood: American Women's History in the 1980s. *Social History* 10. Reprinted in *Unequal sisters: A multicultural reader* (1–14). *U.S. women's history,* ed. Elizabeth DuBois and Vicki Ruiz. London: Routledge, 1990.
Hill Collins, Patricia. 1990. *Black feminist thought: Knowledge, consciousness, and the politics of empowerment.* Boston: Unwin Hyman.
Jayaratne, Toby Epstein, and Abigail Stewart. 1991. Quantitative and qualitative methods in social sciences: Current feminist issues and practical strategies. In *Beyond methodology: Feminist scholarship as lived research,* ed. Mary Margaret Fonow and Judith A. Cook, 85–106. Bloomington: Indiana University Press.
Lazreg, Marnia. 1990. Feminism and difference: The perils of writing as a woman on women in Algeria. In *Conflicts in feminism,* ed. Marianne Hirsch and Evelyn Fox Keller, 326–48. New York: Routledge.
LeDoeuff, Michele. 1987. Women and philosophy. In *French feminist thought: A reader,* ed. Toril Moi, 181–209. Oxford: Basil Blackwell.
McRobbie, Angela. 1982. The politics of feminist research: Between talk, text, and action. *Feminist Review* 12: 46–62.
Mies, Maria. 1983. Towards a methodology for feminist research. In *Theories of Women's Studies,* ed. Gloria Bowles and Renate Duelli-Klein, 117–39. Boston: Routledge and Kegan Paul.
Passerini, Luisa. 1987. *Fascism in popular memory.* Cambridge: Cambridge University Press.
Richardson, Ken, David Spears, and Martin Richards, ed. 1972. *Race, culture, and intelligence.* London: Penguin.
Roberts, Helen, ed. 1981. *Doing feminist research.* London: Routledge and Kegan Paul.
Rose, Hilary, and Stephen Rose, eds. 1976. *The radicalisation of science: Ideology of/in natural sciences.* New York: Macmillan.
Rosenthal, Robert. 1966. *Experimental effects in behavioural research.* New York: Appleton.
Sandoval, Chela. 1991. US Third World feminism. *Genders* 10: 1–24.
Smith, Dorothy. 1987. *The everyday world as problematic: A feminist sociology.* Milton Keynes: Open University Press.
Squire, Corinne. 1989. *Significant differences: Feminism and psychology.* London: Routledge.
Stacey, Judith. 1988. Can there be a feminist ethnography? *Women's Studies International Forum* 11(1): 21–27.
Stanley, Liz, ed. 1989. *Feminist praxis.* London: Routledge.
Stanley, Liz, and Sue Wise. 1979. Feminist research, feminist consciousness, and experience of sexism. *Women's Studies International Forum* 1(3).
Ware, Vron. 1992. *Beyond the pale.* London: Verso.
Willis, Paul. 1978. *Learning to labour.* London: Saxon House.
Wood Sherif, Carolyn. 1987. Bias in psychology. In *Feminism and methodology,* ed. Sandra Harding, 37–56. Milton Keynes: Open University.
Zenie-Ziegler, Wiedad. 1988. *In search of shadows: Conversations with Egyptian women.* London: Zed Books.

CHAPTER 5

A Feminist Epistemology

JOEY SPRAGUE AND DIANE KOBRYNOWICZ

The tradition of Western science is built on positivism, an epistemology of the fact. For both natural and social science, the world of experience is generally believed to be an objective world, governed by underlying regularities, even natural laws. Facts are empirical observations, outcroppings of these underlying regularities. If, and only if, we systematically and dispassionately observe the data of the empirical world, we can detect the patterns of which they are evidence. August Comte had such confidence in the principles of positivism that he believed it was not only possible but desirable to build a science of society, sociology, upon them.

Positivism is the hegemonic epistemology in scientific discourse, so that its specific way of connecting beliefs about knowing with research practices appears seamless: we often fail to see any distinctions among epistemology, methodology, and method. Harding's (1987) distinctions are useful in disaggregating the issues. Epistemology, Harding says, is a theory about knowledge, about who can know what and under what circumstances. A method, Harding notes, is a technique for gathering and analyzing information, for example, forms of listening, watching, or examining records. A methodology is an argument about how these two are linked, that is, about the implications of an epistemology for the practice of research.

Every epistemology, Genova (1983) says, involves assumptions about the points of a triad: the knower, the known, and the process of knowing. He describes the history of Western philosophical debates about epistemology as focused on one or another of the points on this triad. Ring (1987) identifies the same three elements, but in her representation we are drawn to their connection. Epistemologies, for Ring, are accounts of the knowing subject, the object of study, and the relationship between them. An epistemology directs us in how to approach an understanding of a phenomenon. The basic issue it resolves is the grounds for choosing one theory, or account of that phenomenon, over another (Alcoff 1989).

At the heart of positivist epistemology is the focus on objectivity. Positivism assumes that truth comes from eliminating the role of subjective judgments and interpretations, thus sharply enforcing the dichotomy between the knower and the known (Ring 1987). According to positivist epistemology, subjectivity is an obstacle to knowledge: the observer's personality and feelings introduce errors in observation. The practices of research are designed to minimize and hopefully erase any impact of the subjectivity of the researcher from the data. Observations are made through a process of objective measurement, which circumvents the subjectivity of the observer, allows for the application of statistical analyses, and makes data collection and interpretation open to replication and testing by others.

Positivism offered some clear advantages over the epistemology that prevailed prior to it, an epistemology based on faith and revelation, an authority based on tradition (Lovibond 1989). The reliance on evidence and clear, replicatable procedures for collecting and interpreting it open up the production of knowledge to many more than a chosen few. The emphasis on systematic procedures presents knowledge claims in a context that is open to critique, argument, even refutation. Positivist epistemology has generated methods with democratic potential.

However, positivism has its problems, as has been shown by scholars from Mannheim (1936) to contemporary social constructionists who have argued that official knowing as we have inherited it is not the objective, unbiased, apolitical process it represents itself to be. Rather, scholarly paradigms, like other forms of human consciousness, are the expression of specific world views.

For example, the goal of removing subjectivities has never been met. All observations are "theory-laden"; that is, making any observation requires the acceptance of background assumptions—a system of beliefs to interpret what we are seeing. Holding background assumptions thwarts the ideal of knowing pure facts outside of theory (see Bechtel 1988). Furthermore, when testing any one hypothesis, a scientist is also testing a set of auxiliary hypotheses—all the background assumptions contributing to the world view that supports the hypothesis in the first place. If a test of the hypothesis fails to achieve the predicted results, the scientist does not necessarily reject the hypothesis but can tinker with the background assumptions, arriving at a way to make sense of the data and maintaining the original thought. This process, discussed as the Quine-Duhem thesis in the philosophy of science literature, portends negatively for a pure test of scientific ideas.

Extending this line of criticism, Longino (1989) identifies another major flaw with positivist logic: the assumption that the data directly support hypotheses. She argues that the data do not say what hypothesis they are evidence for. In fact, the same data can be used to support contradictory hypotheses and which connection gets made depends on the background assumptions being made (Longino 1989; cf. Alcoff 1989). Because these background assumptions are based in values, science cannot be value neutral (Alcoff 1989). Moreover, as we will show, the values that pervade the background assumptions support the continued hegemony of privileged white men. Positivism has become the epistemology of the fathers.

The primary contender to positivist epistemology has been radical constructivism (see Jussim 1991). If positivism is the epistemology of fact, radical constructivism is an epistemology of fiction. From this perspective, reality is created through discourse about it (Weedon 1987). Thus, the object of knowledge, the truth, is the outcome of the process that "discovers" it (Alcoff 1989; Foucault 1972; Fraser 1989; Haraway 1988). Knowledge is a narrative, a text, even an act of faith based on cult membership (Haraway 1988).

Postmodernists have gone so far as to argue that in contemporary Western society knowledge and social domination are the same thing. Foucault (1972) maintains that modern knowledge amounts to intensive surveillance of individuals and groups of people, creating official standards of normality, and prompting us to monitor and discipline ourselves to try to conform to those standards (see Fraser 1989). Our subjectivity is a social construction; our values and even our sense of having a self are aspects of the way modern power works. Thus, there is no basis for rationally choosing between one theory and another. In terms of the relationship between subject and object, radical constructivism dissolves the object into the subject.

Of course, it is curious that just when women and ethnic minorities have begun to demand a voice in creating knowledge, an epistemology emerges claiming there is no truth to be known. Haraway's term for this impact is "epistemological electro-shock therapy (1988, 578)." It is easy to imagine the effects of such a stance on struggles to overcome oppression. If uniting people across diversity requires a shared world view of mutual interests, the potential for creating bonds across people evaporates when analyses of experiences are considered mere texts or subjectivities (Fraser and Nicholson 1988; Mascia-Lees, Sharpe, and Cohen 1989). Thus, we might consider radical constructivism the epistemology of the sons. But these are not our only choices.

FEMINIST STANDPOINT THEORY

Standpoint theorists begin by rejecting positivism's pretentions of creating a view from nowhere in favor of the postulate that each subject is specific, located in a particular time and place. Thus, a knower has a particular perspective on the object. At the same time, this locatedness gives access to the concrete world; knowing is not relative, as radical constructivists maintain, rather it is partial (Haraway 1988; Hartsock 1983). In most versions of standpoint theory there are certain social positions that allow for developing better understandings. Marxist epistemology generally privileges the standpoint of the working class because their role in process allows one to understand the social and relational character of production (Bar On 1993; Lukacs 1971). In feminist standpoint theory, epistemic privilege is often accorded to the standpoint of women and/or other oppressed people. We outline the arguments of Hartsock (1983; 1985), Haraway (1978; 1988; 1990; 1993), Smith (1979; 1987; 1990), and Collins (1986; 1989; 1990).

Hartsock (1983; 1985), a political scientist who pioneered the notion of standpoint, carefully distinguished a standpoint from the spontaneous subjectivity of social actors. A standpoint, she says, is "achieved rather than obvious, a mediated rather than immediate understanding" (1985, 132). Capitalists, she argues, can only know power as a commodity. However, if workers engage in class struggle and reflect on their position, they can begin to understand power as a relationship of domination.

Hartsock builds her analysis on a critique of Marxist epistemology, which, she maintains, errs in the application of its own logic. She is convinced by the logic of historical materialism that to understand people you have to start with the circumstances under which they meet their daily needs for food, clothing, and shelter. However, in privileging the standpoint of the worker, Marxist epistemology ignores the most fundamental site of production, those places where the satisfaction of people's needs is directly produced, particularly the domestic setting. Both in wage work and in the home, women's work keeps them involved in a world of directly meeting needs "in concrete, many-qualitied, changing material processes" (1985, 235). This standpoint—the one of meeting human needs, the standpoint of women—is one that Hartsock privileges. From this standpoint, she argues, we are able to understand power as potentially nonhierarchical, as a capacity.

As Hartsock faults Marxism for violating its own assumptions, Haraway (1978; 1988; 1990; 1993), an anthropologist, makes a similar critique of positivism. Haraway notes that positivism is based on the primacy of data, that is, information that is directly detectable through the senses. Positivist epistemology is, then, logically grounded in the materiality of people's bodies. Yet, positivism denies the presence of these bodies in making its claims to validity. For example, those dominating the production of knowledge in the Western tradition have, for the most part, been upper class, white, and male, and surely their observations are shaped by their specific experience. Haraway agrees with positivist arguments that it is through our sensory experience, our bodies, that we have access to the world, but that very grounding is both the basis of valid knowledge and a limit on it. She coined the term *embodied vision* to emphasize that our vision is located in some specific place, that our knowledge is "situated" and thus partial.

How can we compensate for the partiality of any perspective? Haraway says the best way to gain a critical perspective on one's situated view is to know how things look from a different position. Access to two ways of looking at a phenomenon reveals the limits and contructedness of each. Because each of us experiences life and our selves in multiple facets that are "stitched together imperfectly" (1988, 586), empathy is possible and, through it, two knowers in distinct situations can make a partial connection. By translating across distinct perspectives and connecting ever-shifting situated knowledges, we can rationally build some collective, if provisional, agreement on the whole.

Women cross boundaries between perspectives as a matter of daily life, Smith notes (1987; 1990). The sexual division of labor, both within sociology and between professional and domestic work, creates a breach between the means by which we develop our understandings of social life and the concrete work of keeping social life going. Thus, the standpoint of women in sociology offers leverage to integrate two perspectives. It gives us the opportunity to see sociology as a masculine institution that plays a role in the broader practices by which we are all organized and managed, what Smith calls "the relations of ruling."

The organization of professional work has caused men to focus on the conceptual world while ignoring their bodily existence. This has been possible only because women have been providing for their human needs and for those of their children. Similarly, at work women provide the material forms to men's conceptual work—clerical work, interviewing, taking care of patients, and so on. It is as though these men live in an ephemeral world of abstract ideas. Never does the mundane reality of physical existence impede their thoughts; their thoughts stay lofty and disconnected from reality. Women transverse the divide between this ephemeral world and the actual world of human practices, attending to these men's inevitable material needs. The better the women are at their work, the more it is invisible to men, who can thus take it for granted and have their own authority bolstered in the process.

The result is a sociology that is alienated from social life. Typical scientific practice only superficially overcomes the split between official knowledge and concrete existence. Smith's imagery is powerful: she says we reach out through our conceptual frameworks to pluck bits of the empirical world and retreat to our office to organize the data to fit our frameworks. The pictures we end up with are more likely to correspond to official organizational charts than to the daily experience of the front line actors whose practices are the stuff of social institutions. Sociological practices "convert what people experience directly in their everyday/everynight world into forms of knowledge in which people as subjects disappear and in which their perspectives on their own experience are transposed and subdued by the magisterial forms of objectifying discourse" (1990, 4). Sociology becomes an aspect of the relations of ruling.

Smith disagrees with those who say there is no difference between science and ideology, following Marx's argument that what is real is people's concerted action to address material imperatives. Creating knowledge is revealing the ways practical activity to meet human needs is shaped and constrained by social relations of domination, particularly those that go beyond the immediate context. Making ideology is letting concepts and abstractions dominate and obscure those material relations (1990, 34). We need to peer behind facts and abstractions and ask how they are the outcome of the concerted activity of specific people in concrete circumstances. For example, saying that technology is propelling us into a future outside of human control is ideology; showing how powerful elites promote specific technologies to maximize their social control is not.

Women sociologists, especially those with children, dwell in both the conceptual and the practical realms; they experience on a daily basis the concrete work of meeting human needs, coordinating with child care and schools, etc., and how these conflict with the work of sociology. The standpoint of women within sociology means we can and must work to transform its practices away from its role of supporting the relations of ruling.

Beginning from a marginalized standpoint, one that integrates the perspectives of black feminists as academic outsiders and other black women, Patricia Hill Collins (1986; 1989; 1990) develops a black feminist epistemology that exposes the systematic and particular character of hegemonic sociology at the same time it offers an alternative. Collins identifies four parameters of Black feminist epistemology (1990, 203–18). First, concrete experience and the wisdom developed out of everyday experience is valued in evaluating knowledge claims. Second, knowledge claims are not hierarchically imposed by an elite but rather worked out through dialogue with everyday social actors. Third, emotions such as empathy and attachment are incorporated into the notion of intellect. Finally, part of the assessment of an idea is via what is known about the character and biography of the person advancing it.

With this understanding of standpoint theory, we can turn a critical eye to sociology. One of our first observations is that mainstream sociology flows from the standpoint of privileged men. Before elaborating on the impact of this particular standpoint for sociology, we first describe the specifics of a privileged male standpoint.

THE STANDPOINT OF PRIVILEGED MEN

There are a variety of accounts of the ways that the experience of privileged men in the social organization of white supremacist, capitalist, patriarchal society has prompted the development of a distinct form of consciousness. The analyses of Chodorow (1978; 1991) and O'Brien (1981; 1989) operate within distinct theoretical traditions, yet display a remarkably strong degree of consensus about the parameters of hegemonic male consciousness.

Drawing on interview material from her clinical practice as a psychotherapist, Nancy Chodorow (1979; 1991) deconstructs traditional psychoanalysis to identify gendered dynamics. Chodorow argues that gender differences in structures of consciousness are the outcome of the child's development of self in gendered social arrangements: men are absent from nurturing in a culture in which gender is employed as an important organizer of social relations. Distinctions in boys' and girls' early experiences lead to development of gender differences in sense of self and relationship to others: men develop a highly individuated sense of self in opposition to others and an abstract orientation to the world; connection represents a threat of loss of identity. Women develop a connected sense of self embedded in concrete relationships.

Chodorow's analysis, like many in feminist theory, gives little attention to the dynamics of class. Her clinical data is heavily biased toward the affluent and highly educated clientele of psychoanalysis, which no doubt explains her analytic focus on the male breadwinner/female housewife nuclear family form (see Fraser and Nicholson 1988; and Lorber, Coser, Rossi, and Chodorow 1981, for critiques). Although the limits of her analysis imply caution should be used in extending it beyond the relatively privileged, those same biases make Chodorow's work particularly useful for identifying the consciousness of the privileged. Work in the literature on class and consciousness uses words such as individualistic and abstract to refer to the worldview of capitalists, in contrast with a more collective and concrete orientation in the working class (e.g., Bulmer 1975; Mann 1973; Mueller 1973; Oilman 1972). Integrating these two perspectives, we see an argument that the consciousness of economically privileged, European American men is more likely to be abstract and individuated than the worldviews of men from less privileged classes and most women.

Mary O'Brien (1981; 1989) uses a historical materialist approach to argue that differences in consciousness are the product of differences in the ways men and women have historically taken intentional action regarding the material imperative to reproduce. To assert social control over a process in which they are marginalized, men in the European traditions she is describing have historically dominated it from outside by creating and controlling the public sphere. Men's flight from involvement in the work of reproduction poses a challenge to the legitimacy of their control over the process, a challenge that is addressed by according the male role as much social significance as possible. This, O'Brien argues, is why the dominant patriarchal worldview of reproduction emphasizes intercourse and male potency and overlooks the value of reproductive labor.

Having distanced themselves from the concrete community of people who do the work of caring, O'Brien says, men have created an abstract community in the state. Alienated from the concrete history of human continuity across generations, men have constructed and sanctified a history of abstractions and ideas. The culture they have reproduced encourages a consciousness that is abstract, oppositional, and discontinuous. O'Brien's analysis resonates with the argument that the capitalistic structuring of work leads those in privileged class locations to be more individualized and have a more abstract orientation to the world (Hartsock 1985; Lukacs 1971).

In summary, whether looking through the lens of psychoanalysis or historical materialism, feminist scholars identify a privileged masculine consciousness that is highly abstract, individuated, oppositional, hierarchical, oriented to control not to nurture. These themes resonate with Hartsock's description of a masculine orientation to dominate, Haraway's critique of disembodied knowledge, Smith's account of the abstract masculine existence, and Collins's depiction of an elitist and authoritarian epistemology. They also seem to run through the kinds of criticisms feminists have raised against mainstream sociological theory and research.

FEMINIST CRITIQUES OF MAINSTREAM SOCIOLOGY

Although within sociology empirical research and social theory have long been operating on separate intellectual planes, there are interesting epistemological parallels between them. Empirical research is dominated by positivist epistemology with its assumption that science is independent of the social order in which it is conducted, that knowledge is neutral, that the observer has no particular point of view but rather merely reports empirical findings (Farganis 1986). Ring (1987) describes the epistemology guiding classic social theory as a Hegelian empiricism with similar background assumptions. Mainstream social theory constructs knowledge as a stream of ideas handed down through generations of key thinkers who, although singled out as individuals, apparently rise above their historical circumstances of gender, race, and class to identify universal rationality (Connell 1997; Smith 1990; Sprague 1997). In both theory and research, then, our attention is drawn to an objective knowledge; the contribution of the knower to the shape of the knowing is invisible (Keller 1983; Smith 1990).

Feminists have criticized sociological theory and empirical research to varying degrees, as is true of feminist critiques of science more generally (Keller 1982). Some merely say that research practice has been distorted by its gender biases. Critiques in this vein point to the relative lack of women scholars, the choice of questions that address the problems of men not women, designs that exclude women, and interpretations of data from a masculine point of view (American Sociological Association 1980). The problem from this perspective is that science has not been scientific enough. Other critiques, however, dispute the very notion of science and scholarship as a distinctive social enterprise; the claim here is that science is as socially constructed as any other element of a culture (Rosser 1988). We see these critiques expressing five kinds of concerns: 1) objectivity as process and as outcome, 2) authority in the research relationship, 3) a hierarchical ordering of the social, 4) the predominance of problematic analytic categories, and 5) the role of sociology in broader relations of social domination.

The Critique of Objectivity

Many feminists challenge the degree to which social research has succeeded in being objective and some feminists go beyond challenging whether objectivity is attainable to questioning whether it is even desirable. Likewise, Longino (1989) argues that what we hold to be rational is variable but systematically so: "[T]he only constant in Western philosophers' thinking about rationality and masculinity is their association" (263). Contemporary notions of objectivity, and the approach to rationality it represents are, it is argued, the expression of masculine psychic needs to dissociate from allegedly feminine subjectivity and the need to control the threat of connection by connecting through domination (Hartsock 1985; Haraway 1978; Keller 1982).

The first step in the practice of scientific objectivity is to carve up the continuity of lived experience to create objects, or facts, to investigate (Shiva 1995; Smith 1990). Thus, "facts" are the outcome of practices that strip phenomena of the processes that generate them, processes that are deeply social. For example, we see gender as the attribute of a person rather than as the outcome of institutionalized social practices (Lorber 1994) or of a specific form of social organization (Acker 1990; Sprague 1991, 1996).

The processes that "uncover" these facts are then hidden from view (Latour and Woolgar 1979). For example, experimental methods are held to be the best way to test a hypothesized causal relationship because of the way they control for threats to internal validity (Cook and Campbell 1979). Yet, Fine and Gordon (1989) argue that another way to describe the practices of experimentalists makes them look irrational, obsessed with the need to purge their data of the messiness of real life, contaminating details such as people's race, gender, and class. Similarly, social psychologists construct the impression of a self independent of context by posing questions such as the Twenty Statements Test's "Who am I?" and treating the answers as facts—the self is what the test has created, not a constant in people's lived experience (Markus and Kitayama 1991).

Authority in Social Research

Traditional research carves a sharp distinction between investigator and investigated and creates a hierarchical relationship between the two. Several feminists criticize scientific authority as the conceptual domination of researched by researcher: investigators turn subjects, the people they are trying to understand, into objects who are not capable of enlightening scholars about social phenomena (Collins 1989, 1990). Mies (1993) sees danger in dichotomizing subject and object: objectifying what we study can lead to justifying exploitation and abuse, for example in the development of technologies that pillage the earth of its resources and in experimentation on Jews in Nazi concentration camps.

Feminist approaches have tended to replace models of control and domination with those of connection and nurturing. An early feminist assumption was that research relationships were to be constructed as collaborations (Cook and Fonow 1986). The researcher's goal is to give voice to women who have been denied it, to express their experiences in their terms (McCall and Wittner 1989). Feminists in this camp maintain that establishing a relationship of mutuality between researcher and subject of research through self-revelation and emotional support produces better data and richer understanding (Oakley 1981).

More recently feminists have debated the limits of even a feminist investigator's empathic ability. Scholars of color have pointed out the degree to which our understandings of the dynamics of gender have been generalizations from the experience of economically privileged white women, evidence that investigators impose their own cultural frameworks on the data (Dill 1983; hooks 1981; King 1988). As a consequence of studying the oppressed through the lens of the privileged, oppressed people are objectified, represented not as people "like us" but rather as the "other." Minh-ha (1993) is describing anthropology as an ideology of imperialism but could be talking about social science more generally when she says that what presents itself as an attempt to learn the essence of human nature is in practice "mainly a conversation of 'us' with 'us' about 'them'" (1993, 125).

The reaction against "othering" has led some feminists to wonder if it is legitimate to study a category over which one has privilege, for men to study women or for whites to study people of color (see Edwards 1990; Harding 1993). Thus, although an early theme in feminist criticism of sociology was its failure to be sensitive to the pervasiveness of gender as a social force (Cook and Fonow 1986), more recent critiques have been reluctant to push any abstract category, including gender, very far.

The Hierarchy of the Social

One recurrent theme in feminist critiques of sociology is that we tend to employ a pattern of selective attention that creates a systematically masculine stratification of social life: what is important is what men do (e.g., see readings in Rosaldo and Lamphere 1974). O'Brien (1981), for example, observes that we have theories that address nearly all of the major aspects of our biological existence: providing for our physical needs (Marxism), sexuality (psychoanalysis), death (theology and secular philosophy). The stark omission, O'Brien notes, is serious consideration of the social and philosophical issues concerning human reproduction. Social theory has placed a low priority on understanding the nurturance and development of people, and on emotions and intimate relationships in general (cf. Aptheker 1989; Hillyer 1993; hooks 1990; Ruddick 1980; Smith 1987). Feminists criticize sociological accounts for essentially ignoring what Aptheker (1989) calls "the dailiness" of ordinary lives, the struggle to preserve quality of life for your family in the face of exploitation and oppression, to hold on to and nurture a positive sense of self in a culture that demeans and devalues you.

A pervasive, and much criticized, assumption in social theory is that the public and the private constitute distinct spheres of social life and that the public sphere, defined as the official economy, the polity, and related institutions, is more social than the private (cf. Fraser 1989; Mies 1986; Pateman 1983; Sprague 1997, 1988;

Ward 1993). Ironically and tellingly, the public sphere has then been constructed in such a way that it appears to be unpopulated. Interpersonal relationships at work and emotional aspects of work itself are excluded from view (Hochschild 1983). Social analyses that address large-scale social institutions from the perspective of abstract structures are labeled "macro," and are understood as most important. Those that focus on individuals and the relationships among them with an attention to process are "micro," too often with the connotation of substantive and intellectual triviality and a suspicious drift toward psychology.

The dichotomous, hierarchical opposition of public to private represents relationships as if they did not occur within and were not constrained by social structures and makes structures seem as if they had more reality than the regular relationships among people that constitute these structures (Smith 1990).

Dominant Analytic Categories

Another line of feminist critique has been to challenge the analytic categories that dominate sociological discourse. The category that has drawn the most critiques from feminists is the logical dichotomy, the tendency to make sense of phenomena by opposing them to others in a construction that is represented as mutually exclusive and exhaustive (Jay 1981). The pattern runs through the history of hegemonic Western European social thought: mind/body, city of god/city of man, capitalist/worker, nature/culture, nature/nurture, public/private, macro/micro, structure/agency (Alway 1995; Harrison 1985; hooks 1994; O'Brien 1981; Tuana 1983).

The artificiality of these dichotomies is exposed when one tries to identify the line that demarcates them empirically. Rich (1976) notes that even a dichotomy that seems as basic as me/not-me is transcended in the experience of a pregnant woman in relationship to the fetus developing within her. The demarcating line between public and private is exposed as constructed when considering state-imposed policies such as those on sexuality, reproductive freedoms, and violence within marriage (Sprague 1988). In fact, many of our most contentious political struggles can be seen as debates over where to draw the border between public and private in a particular domain of life (e.g., sexuality, parents' rights, school prayer, assisted suicide).

Another analytic approach common to social theory that has come under the criticism of feminists is what might be called abstract individuation. That is, individuals are seen in isolation from and unconnected with their interpersonal, historical, or physical context (Sprague 1997). A prime instance of this abstract individuation is the tradition of representing people as instances of just one facet of the complex intersecting social relations through which they live their lives, for example, gender, race, or class (Collins 1989; Dill 1983; hooks 1981; King 1988). In the process we tend to fall back to the hegemonic categories: when we talk about class we see men, when we talk about race we see men, and when we talk about gender we see whites (King 1988). Another example of a decontextualized individual is the model of rational man *[sic]*, an actor who establishes priorities and sets out to achieve them, evaluating options along the way in terms of an abstract value system or their utility to goal attainment (e.g., Coleman 1992). The image hides from us the degree to which most of us, especially women, find daily life an ongoing juggling of competing responsibilities emerging from the complex web of our most important relationships (England 1989; Risman and Ferree 1995; Smith 1987).

We fracture people even further into abstract attributes or personality traits. The practice has been, for example, to ask whether women are more passive or use different language than men, rather than asking whether women are more often observed in relationships in which they are relatively powerless in structural terms and are responding strategically to that structural condition (Sherif 1979). The tendency to explain problematic social behavior by resorting to syndromes (ADHD, alcoholism, chronic fatigue) and searching for biological, even genetic sources carries the fragmentation of the human being even further (Conrad 1975; Haraway 1993; Szasz 1971).

Seeing the social world through logical dichotomies and abstract individuation has generated conceptual distinctions that distort the lived experience of many people. The disciplinary division of "work" and "family" hides the work of caring for a family and the nurturing aspects of many jobs (Cancian 1985; Cancian and Oliker forthcoming; Oakley 1974). The distinction between work and leisure is not applicable to the vast majority of women who work the double shift of paid work and unpaid domestic labor (Hartmann 1981; Hochschild 1989). The distinction between paid and domestic labor is not adequate to describe the lives of many women, particularly women of color, who have historically been blocked from any waged work other than paid domestic labor and child care (Collins 1986; Glenn 1992).

The Role of Sociology in Social Domination

What is the relationship between knowledge producers and the larger society in which they work? In ironic contrast to Marx and Weber, who were deeply engaged in the politics of their time, the intellectual projects of contemporary theorists are typically understood as individual quests to maintain, develop, and extend the stream of ideas. The role of theorists is one of detachment, only abstractly connected, if at all, to any sense of responsibility to their communities. Sociological theory has, to say the least, not been engaged in contemporary policy debates; its ranks have provided us with few public intellectuals, particularly in the United States.

Mainstream sociological research has a better record in permeating public policy debates. Still, some feminists charge that sociological research is constructed in ways that facilitate social domination. Harding has observed that "there isn't such a thing as a problem without a person (or groups of them) who have this problem: a problem is always a problem for someone or other" (1987, 6). She, like Smith, argues that social scientists tend to ask the questions of those whose job is to manage people, not the questions of regular folks (cf. Fine 1994). For example, we are much more likely to ask who is likely to abuse drugs than to ask what we would need to change about social organization to make drug use less likely.

Feminists have from the beginning rejected positivism's ideal of a "value-free" science, arguing instead that the goal of research must be to help the oppressed understand and fight against their oppression (Cancian 1992; Cook and Fonow 1986; Harding 1987; Mies 1993; Smith 1987). Cancian (1992) argues that an important feminist methodology is to engage in participatory action research (PAR), working with feminist organizations on problems they have identified in a process they control. In addition to directly supporting feminist politics, Cancian submits, involvement in PAR actually generates better data by providing localized knowledge about a subject and incorporating quasi-experimental evidence.

Asking questions in hegemonic ways can have deadly consequences, as Treichler's (1993) analysis demonstrates. As the Center for Disease Control was collecting data on early AIDS cases, the organizing framework was based on the kind of person who got AIDS, not on the kind of practices that made one vulnerable to it. The result was the "4 H's" typology of risk: homosexuals, hemophiliacs, heroin addicts, and Haitians. Further, in developing their list, some codes were "master," taken as more salient than others: gay or bisexual men who injected drugs were coded by their sexuality, not their intravenous drug use. The hegemonic view that sexual practices justify categorizing people and mark sexual minorities as deviant led to analyses that no doubt created a false sense of invulnerability to this deadly disease in those who were excluded from the typology, notably women.

An important aspect of knowledge as social domination is the prevalence of "studying down," rather than "studying up." Fine reports, for example, that when her graduate students wanted to study upper-class white women they could not find much literature on them. Fine observes that these women are not surveyed by social science agencies and there is no "scholarly discourse on their dysfunctionality" (1994, 73). Some have argued that the powerless are aware that official knowledge, rather than serving their interests, often works against them. This makes them appropriately suspicious of, and therefore less than authentic with, researchers (Mies 1993; Edwards 1990).

Another way that both theoretical and empirical sociology serves the dominant interests is by communicating in a discourse that is so opaque that colleagues cannot read one another across subspecialties, much less across disciplines (Sprague 1997; Sprague and Zimmerman 1993). By using passive tense and speaking in high levels of abstraction, we hide the agency both of those we study and ourselves as researchers (hooks 1994; Hochschild 1983). "The author's activity is displaced in methods, which act on the data for the author" (Paget 1990, 158). The scientific voice also creates emotional distance. Paget (1990) notes the scholarly norm that discredits speakers who show feelings like caring, anger, or outrage in the context of scholarly communication. The text is also severed from actual human experience, distancing the reader from caring about it, much less feeling compelled to do something about it. Hochschild (1983) draws the parallel between the emotion work of creating a dispassionate text and the steps taken in an autopsy to make sure medical students will be distanced from the humanness of the corpse so as not to be disturbed by what is being done to it. The norm of disinterested discursive style, Paget (1990) notes, conflicts with the goal of communicating about knowledge, which is to persuade.

In summary, feminist critiques of sociological practices point to a detachment, both intellectual and emotional, from the daily work of keeping life going, from the people whose lives we study, and from popular political discourse. They take issue with the way we have organized the production of knowledge, noting that it serves more to control people than to nurture them. They challenge a reliance on dichotomy and high levels of abstraction. The terms of the feminist critique roughly parallel the description of privileged masculine consciousness. As Smith (1990) says, if sociology has a subject, it is a male subject.

FEMINIST ALTERNATIVES

Feminists struggling with these concerns have developed some innovative and insightful strategies. Arguing that interviewing is a hierarchical form of social relationship, feminists have worked to make that relationship more democratic. They have given interviewees control over the topics to be discussed, incorporated self-disclosure on the part of the investigator, built an interviewing relationship over time, and asked interviewees for feedback on investigators' interpretations of interviews (e.g., Acker, Barry, and Esseveld 1991; Edwards 1990; Fine 1994). Acker and her colleagues (1991) use these techniques of connection with the subjects of research in strategic alternation with more detached discussions among investigators and report this approach leads to more nuanced understanding of respondents' experience and particularly of how people change in response to social conditions.

Traditional notions of what is and is not data have also been reformed. It has been standard practice in interviewing for example, to attribute the interviewee's hesitations and questions like, "Do you know what I mean?" to inarticulateness. DeVault (1990) uses them as indicators that male-dominated language does not capture women's experience. She finds these breaks in fluid speech are fruitful gateways for exploration of the distinctive experiences of women.

The concept of valid data has been expanded in other directions as well. Aptheker (1989) and Collins (1990) respond to the elite selection bias of the usual documentary evidence by expanding the field of data to include the "documents" of those who are marginalized in official discourse. They analyze the messages, for example, in the lyrics of blues songs, poetry, quilts, and gardens, as well as oral histories and kitchen table conversations. These sources organize experience in the language of daily life, making it possible to generate analytic categories that come closer to everyday categories. For example, DeVault (1991) found that women's own word for what they do for their families, "feeding," combined the notions of work and love in a way that more formal terms like "domestic labor" or "caring" could not (cf. Yeatman 1984).

Stereotypical Feminist Ways of Knowing

By the light of accumulated stereotypes about what makes research feminist, it would be easy to conclude that feminist research involves academic feminists using qualitative methods to reveal the insights of nonacademic women. In fact, distrust of systematic measurement practices, the desire to recognize the subjectivity of those we study and the commitment to empowering women and other oppressed people have led many feminists to doubt that feminist research could be quantitative (Cook and Fonow 1986; Edwards 1990; Stacey and Thorne 1985). Reducing complex thoughts and experiences to measurable variables, these feminists argue, sacrifices any sense of the whole, objectifies those we study, and makes it likely the investigator's interpretations will support their continued domination. The assumption is that the only way to do feminist research is to begin with the lived experience of women and that requires the use of qualitative methods (e.g., Edwards 1990). This reliance on qualitative methods coincides with the reluctance to make strong, broad theoretical claims, which would necessarily be generalizing from the experience of a few.

However, other feminists point out the interpersonal and political problems inherent in this stereotype of feminist research. Interpersonally, there is an inescapable power imbalance between researchers and subjects of research: researchers have choices over their vulnerability to risk, can leave the situation when they want, can choose what to report and what to disregard, and have ultimate control over the final interpretation (Risman 1993; Sprague and Zimmerman 1989; Stacey 1988; Thorne 1983).

Qualitative researcher's reliance on personal contact in long, unstructured interviews tends to draw on small, homogeneous samples and is unlikely to represent people with inflexible jobs, heavy domestic responsibility, and less verbal confidence (Canon, Higgenbotham, and Leung 1988). Qualitative researchers have also asked the questions and reported in the categories of the hegemonic elite (Fine 1994). Quantitative methods provide some counter to both of these sources of bias through the use of representative sampling, giving respondents control over the coding of their answers, and explicit, replicable analyses (Jayaratne and Stewart 1991; Sprague and Zimmerman 1989).

Perhaps the most negative consequence of an overreliance on qualitative methods is what academic feminists have failed to contribute to a broader political movement. The point of feminist scholarship is to end the oppression of women. The purpose of knowledge is empowerment, in the sense of enabling the purposive action. Thus, we create knowledge about society in order to support people's ability to work together to make the lives they want and need. This has implications for what we call an adequate understanding. Social change requires a road map, a theory of what is and what should be (Fraser 1989; Sprague 1997). Democratic social change requires some degree of consensus on that road map, which means that scholars need to retain criteria for establishing truthfulness that do not erode "the persuasiveness of our conclusions" (Alcoff 1989, 99). Reporting the numbers can be socially empowering, indicating degrees and/or pervasiveness of inequality. Telling the stories of people's experiences can be personally empowering, supporting empathy and feelings of connection. Persuasive arguments in public discourse require both.

The explanations oppressed people want and need, then, are probably not about pure truth as much as they are about how to improve their lives (Harding 1987). To understand those lives, women and other oppressed people need to be able to see how their problems are the expression of social relations of domination (Acker et al. 1991; Mies 1993); how the irrationalities they confront are the product of the workings of "relations of ruling" that are external to their daily experience (Smith 1987). Also, since women are of many races and classes and vary in sexuality and in physical and mental abilities, ending the oppression of women requires working against all forms of oppression (Harding 1991). Precisely because the social organization of knowledge has been dominated by an elite few, the explanations people need are not the ones they are likely to employ spontaneously (Sprague and Zimmerman 1989). In other words, the goal hooks (1994) proposes for feminist pedagogy is not restricted to the classroom: to help people see the connections between their daily experience and the analytic frameworks we offer.

If we need some basis for judging among competing knowledge claims, and we know that scholars are limited by their experience and their particular interests, and we cannot blindly trust the spontaneous consciousness of any particular group, what options are open to us? We believe that a stronger, more nuanced reading of feminist standpoint epistemology suggests a way out of the trap.

IMPLICATIONS OF FEMINIST STANDPOINT EPISTEMOLOGY

Feminist standpoint epistemology transforms both the subject and the object in the epistemological relation. The subject is a collective one, strategically built on diverse experience. The object is a socially constructed one: the meaningful, coordinated activity of people in daily life is what is real. The relationship between the subject and object of knowing is historically specific and dialectic. The metaphor for feminist methodology is bridging.

The Subject is Collective

The epistemological advantage of women is that a sexist society puts them in contradictory social locations, constructing them as both subject and object. They have an "outsider within" advantage and can play on the friction created by the gap between their experience and the conceptual frameworks that are available to make sense of it (Collins 1990; Harding 1991; Smith 1987, 1990). But there is no single privileged standpoint. Because women exist in a wide diversity of social locations based on class, race, ethnicity, sexuality, disability, etc., the subject of feminist knowledge is multiple and sometimes conflicting (Bar On 1993; Bhavnani 1993; Haraway 1988; Harding 1991). Further, women cannot be the only generators of feminist knowledge; men in oppressed locations need to understand themselves and contribute to our understanding of their experience from a feminist perspective (Harding 1991).

If knowledge is grounded in experience then we need to recognize and take into account the understandings generated by people in their daily life. However, we also need to recognize the authority that comes from the experience of having studied something, having reflected on it, and paid attention to the reflections of others. That is, those who are scholars have to take responsibility for the authority of our experience.

The Object of Knowledge Is Socially Constructed

The "thing" we are trying to know from the point of view of standpoint epistemology is more than a constructivist text but less than a positivist open book. Haraway argues that we need to see the world not as an object over which we have control but as a "coding trickster" with which we try to have conversations using the methods, or "prosthetic devices," that help us see (1988, 594). The world including humanity is socially constructed, a product of history and technology (Haraway 1993, 1990).

To say something is socially constructed is not to say it is not real—merely a language game as social constructivists say—but rather to say it is the product of human activity. If the grounding of knowledge is our experience in the empirical world, then practical activity, the work of supporting continued human life, is the bedrock of that knowledge. Human activity in the world is real, O'Brien (1989) submits, and so are the structures that humans devise to meet the challenges they face. If categories are used to direct human social action, those categories are real because we are making them real: race, gender, and class are real in their consequences.

Nonetheless, if something is socially constructed it is not the durable, detached web of lawlike operations that positivism conjures up. It is—and we are—historically specific and changeable. Rational knowledge is open-ended because the world is open-ended.

The Relation between Subject and Object is Dialectical

Given these notions of subject and object, how are feminist scholars to work on producing knowledge? Feminist standpoint epistemology implies that the relation between knower and object of knowledge is, as Ring (1987) says, dialectical. Our methodology must center on "the dynamic between human experience and the material world" and assume "constant change, that is, human history" (Ring 1987, 766). Truth, Ring (1987) argues, will be attained when we have finally eliminated the conflicts between subject and object, expressed as the oppositions of ideas to material reality, of consciousness to history, of thought to action. That is, truth is the outcome of our acting in the world freely, consciously, and intentionally. If we are a diverse community, truth implies working consensus on practical activity.

To do this, we must strategically structure our discourse, both listening to and learning from the perspectives of diverse subjects and diverse scholars. This is why Haraway's notion of splitting—making a connection between two knowers in one self—is important. Mies makes a similar point in calling us to "conscious partiality," balancing empathy with distancing in a "limited identification with the subjects of research" (1993, 38).

Because each standpoint and what can be seen from it is limited, we need to construct our discourse as a critical conversations. Longino (1989) argues we construct a context for feminist rationality by removing the obstacles to criticism. These obstacles include repetitive and unproductive debates about background assumptions, overemphasis on novelty and originality at the expense of critical work, and restriction of our communities to those who share the same background assumptions. We have to find the courage to disagree with "correct" positions and/or persons and the commitment to engage one another to work toward consensus. We must be willing to disagree and use those disagreements as an access to better understanding.

Finally, feminist standpoint epistemology implies that academics are not individual producers of texts and courses. We are in a social relationship with the rest of the community. In the social division of labor, we are cultural workers; our product is understandings. Because the community in which we live and work is organized in relations of social domination, the work we do—the questions we pursue, the strategies we use to gather and interpret evidence, and the forms and venues in which we communicate our findings—connects us in valenced ways with either the powerful or with the oppressed. If we continue to do it as it has been done before, we will connect with the powerful, not with the oppressed, whether we choose to consciously or not.

REFERENCES

Acker, J. 1990. Hierarchies, jobs, bodies: A theory of gendered organizations. *Gender and Society* 4: 139–58.

Acker, J., K. Barry, and J. Esseveld. 1991. Objectivity and truth: Problems in doing feminist research. In *Beyond methodology: Feminist scholarship as lived research,* ed. M. M. Fonow and J. A. Cook, 133–53. Bloomington: University of Indiana Press.

Alcoff, L. 1989. Justifying feminist social science. In *Feminism and science,* ed. N. Tuana, 85–103. Bloomington: Indiana University Press.

Alway, J. 1995. The trouble with gender: Tales of the still-missing feminist revolution in sociological theory. *Sociological Theory* 13: 209–28.

American Sociological Association Committee on the Status of Women in Sociology. 1980. Sexist biases in sociological research: Problems and issues. Footnotes (January). Washington DC.

Aptheker, B. 1989. *Tapestries of everyday life: Women's work, women's consciousness, and the meaning of daily experience.* Amherst: University of Massachusetts Press.

Bar On, B. O. 1993. Marginality and epistemic privilege. In *Feminist epistemologies,* ed. L. Alcoff and E. Porter, 83–100. New York: Routledge.

Bechtel, W. 1988. *Philosophy of science: An overview for cognitive science.* Hillsdale, NJ: Lawrence Erlbaum.

Bhavnani, K. K. 1993. Tracing the contours: Feminist research and feminist objectivity. *Women's Studies International Forum* 16(2): 95–104.

Bulmer, M. 1975. *Working-class images of society.* London: Routledge and Kegan Paul.

Cancian, F. 1985. Gender politics: Love and power in the private and public spheres. In *Gender and the life course,* ed. A. S. Rossi. New York: Aldine.

Cancian, F. and S. Oliker. forthcoming. *For love and money: A gendered view of caring.* Thousand Oaks, CA: Pine Forge.

Cancian, F. M. 1992. Feminist science: methodologies that challenge inequality. *Gender and Society* 6: 623–42.

Canon, L. W., E. Higgenbotham, and M. L. A. Leung. 1988. Race and class bias in qualitative research on women. *Gender and Society* 2: 449–62.

Chodorow, N. 1978. *The reproduction of mothering: Psychoanalysis and the sociology of gender.* Berkeley: University of California Press.

———. 1991. *Feminism and psychoanalytic theory.* New Haven: Yale University Press.

Coleman, J. S. 1992. The rational reconstruction of society. *American Sociological Review* 58: 1–15.

Collins, P. H. 1986. Learning from the outsider within: The sociological significance of black feminist thought. *Social Problems* 33: 514–30.

———. 1989. The social construction of Black feminist thought. *Signs* 14: 745–73.
———. 1990. *Black feminist thought: Knowledge, consciousness, and the politics of empowerment.* London: HarperCollins.
Connell, R. W. 1997. Why is classical theory classical? *American Journal of Sociology* 102: 1511–57.
Conrad, P. 1975. The discovery of hyperkinesis: Notes on the medicalization of deviant behavior. *Social Problems* 23: 12–21.
Cook, T. D., and D. T. Campbell. 1979. *Quasi-experimentation: Design and analysis for field settings.* Boston: Houghton Mifflin Co.
Cook, J. A., and M. M. Fonow. 1986. Knowledge and women's interests: Issues of epistemology and methodology in feminist sociological research. *Sociological Inquiry* 56: 2–29.
DeVault, M. L. 1990. Talking and listening from women's standpoint: Feminist strategies for interviewing and analysis. *Social Problems* 37: 96–116.
———. 1991. *Feeding the family: The social organization of caring as gendered work.* Chicago: University of Chicago Press.
Dill, B. T. 1983. Race, class, and gender: Prospects for an all-inclusive sisterhood. *Feminist Studies* 9: 131–50.
Edwards, R. 1990. Connecting method and epistemology: A White woman interviewing Black women. *Women's Studies Forum* 13: 477–90.
England, P. 1989. A feminist critique of rational-choice theories: Implications for sociology. *The American Sociologist* 20: 14–28.
Farganis, S. 1986. Social theory and feminist theory: The need for dialogue. *Sociological Inquiry* 56: 50–68.
Fine, M. 1994. Working the hyphens: Reinventing self and other in qualitative research. In *Handbook of qualitative research,* ed. N. K. Denzin and Y. S. Lincoln, 70–82. Thousand Oaks, CA: Sage.
Fine, M., and S. M. Gordon. 1989. Feminist transformations of/despite psychology. In *Gender and thought: Psychological perspectives,* ed. M. Crawford and M. Gentry, 146–74. New York: Springer-Verlag.
Foucault, M. 1972. Truth and power. In *Power/Knowledge: Selected interviews and other writings, 1972–1977,* ed. C. Gordon, 109–33. New York: Pantheon.
Fraser, N. 1989. *Unruly practices: Power, discourse, and gender in contemporary social theory.* Minneapolis: University of Minnesota Press.
Fraser, N., and L. Nicholson. 1988. Social criticism without philosophy: An encounter between feminism and postmodernism. *Communication* 10: 345–66.
Genova, A. C. 1983. The metaphysical turn in contemporary philosophy. *Southwest Philosophical Studies* IX: 1–22.
Glenn, E. N. 1992. From servitude to service work: Historical continuities in the racial division of paid reproductive labor. *Signs* 18: 1–43.
Haraway, D. 1978. Animal sociology and a natural economy of the body polit, part I: A political sociology of dominance. *Signs* 4: 21–36.
———. 1988. Situated knowledges: The science question in feminism and the privilege of partial perspective. *Feminist Studies* 14: 575–99.
———. 1990. A manifesto for cyborgs: Science, technology, and Socialist Feminism in the Last Quarter. In *Feminism and postmodernism,* ed. L. Nicholson, 580–671.
———. 1993. The biopolitics of postmodern bodies: Determinations of self in immune system discourse. In *American feminist thought at century's end: A reader,* ed. L. S. Kauffman, 199–233. Cambridge, MA: Blackwell.
Harding, S. 1987. Introduction: Is there a feminist method? In *Feminism and methodology,* 1–14. Bloomington: Indiana University Press.

———. 1991. *Whose science? Whose knowledge? Thinking from women's lives.* Ithaca: Cornell University Press.

———. 1993. Reinventing ourselves as other: More new agents of history and knowledge. In *American feminist though at century's end: A reader,* ed. L. Kauffman, 140–64. Cambridge, MA and Oxford: Blackwell.

Harrison, B. W. 1985. The power of anger in the work of love: Christian ethics for women and other strangers. In *Making the connections: Essays in feminist social ethics,* ed. C. S. Robb. Boston: Beacon.

Hartmann, H. 1981. The family as the locus of gender, class, and political struggle: The example of housework. *Signs* 6: 366–94.

Hartsock, N. C. M. 1983. The feminist standpoint: Developing the ground for a specifically feminist historical materialism. In *Discovering reality: Feminist perspectives on epistemology, metaphysics, methodology, and philosophy of science,* ed. S. Harding and M. Hintikka, 283–310. Dordrecht: D. Reidel.

Hartsock, N. C. 1985. *Money, sex, and power: Toward a feminist historical materialism.* Boston: Northeastern.

Hillyer, N. 1993. *Feminism and disability.* Norman: University of Oklahoma Press.

Hochschild, A. R. 1983. *The managed heart: Commercialization of human feeling.* Berkeley: University of California Press.

———. 1989. *The second shift: Working parents and the revolution at home.* New York: Viking.

hooks, b. 1981. *Ain't I a woman? Black women and feminism.* Boston: South End Press.

———. 1990. *Yearning: Race, gender, and culture politics.* Boston: South End Press.

———. 1994. *Teaching to transgress: Education as the practice of freedom.* New York: Routledge.

Howard, J. A., and J. Hollander. 1997. *Gendered situations, gendered selves.* Thousand Oaks, CA: Pine Forge.

Jay, N. 1981. Gender and dichotomy. *Feminist studies* 7: 38–56.

Jayaratne, T. E., and A. J. Stewart. 1991. Quantitative and qualitative methods in the social sciences. In *Beyond methodology: Feminist scholarship as lived research,* ed. M. M. Fonow and J. A. Cook, 86–106. Bloomington: Indiana University Press.

Jussim, L. 1991. Social perception and social reality: A reflection-construction model. *Psychological Review* 98: 54–73.

Keller, E. F. 1982. Feminism and science. *Signs* 14: 42–72.

———. 1983. *A feeling for the organism: The life work of Barbara McClintock.* New York: Freedman.

King, D. 1988. Multiple jeopardy, multiple consciousness: The context of black feminist ideology. *Signs* 14: 42–72.

Latour, B., and S. Woolgar. 1979. *Laboratory life: The social construction of scientific facts.* New York: Sage Publications.

Longino, H. E. 1989. Feminist critiques of rationality: Critiques of science or philosophy of science? *Women's Studies International Forum* 12: 261–69.

Lorber, J. 1994. Paradoxes of gender. New Haven: Yale University Press.

Lorber, J., R. L. Coser, A. Rossi, and N. Chodorow. 1981. On the reproduction of mothering: A methodological debate. *Signs* 6: 482–514.

Lovibond, S. 1989. Feminism and postmodernism. *New Left Review* 178(Nov/Dec).

Lukacs, G. 1971. *History and class consciousness.* Cambridge: MIT Press.

Mann, M. 1973. *Consciousness and action among the Western working class.* New York: Macmillan.

Mannheim, K. 1936. *Ideology and utopia.* NY: Harcourt, Brace, and World.

Markus, H., and S. Kitayama. 1991. Culture and the self: Implications for cognition, emotion, and motivation. *Psychological Review* 98: 224–53.

Mascia-Lees, F. E., P. Sharpe, and C. B. Cohen. 1989. The postmodern turn in anthropology: Cautions from a feminist perspective. *Signs* 15: 7–33.

McCall, M. and J. Wittner. 1989. The good news about life histories. In *Cultural studies and symbolic interaction,* ed. H. Becker and M. McCall. Chicago: University of Chicago Press.

Mies, M. 1986. *Patriarchy and accumulation on a world scale: Women in the international division of labor.* Atlantic Highlands, NJ: Zed Books.

———. 1993. Feminist research: Science, violence, and responsibility. In *Ecofeminism,* ed. M. Mies and V. Shiva. London: Zed Books.

Minh-ha, T. T. 1993. The language of nativism: Anthropology as a scientific conversation of man with man. In *American feminist thought at century's end: A reader,* ed. L. S. Kauffman, 107–39. Cambridge, MA: Blackwell.

Mueller, C. 1973. *The politics of communication: A study in the political sociology of language, socialization, and legitimation.* New York: Oxford University Press.

O'Brien, M. 1981. *The politics of reproduction.* Boston: Routledge and Kegan Paul.

———. 1989. *Reproducing the world: Essays in feminist theory.* Boulder, CO: Westview.

Oakley, A. 1981. Interviewing women: A contradiction in terms. In *Doing feminist research,* ed. H. Roberts, 30–61. London: Routledge and Kegan Paul.

———. 1974. *The sociology of housework.* New York: Pantheon.

Ollman, B. 1972. Toward class consciousness next time: Marx and the working class. *Politics and Society* 3: 1–24.

Paget, M. A. 1990. Unlearning to not speak. *Human Studies* 13: 147–61.

Pateman, C. 1983. Feminist critiques of the public-private dichotomy. In *The public and private in social life,* ed. S. I. Benn and G. F. Gaus. New York: St. Martin's.

Rich, A. 1976. *Of woman born: Motherhood as experience and institution.* New York: Norton.

Ring, J. 1987. Toward a feminist epistemology. *American Journal of Political Science* 31: 753–72.

Risman, B. 1993. Methodological implications of feminist scholarship. *The American Sociologist* 24: 15–25.

Risman, B., and M. M. Ferree. 1995. Making gender visible. *American Sociological Review* 60: 775–82.

Rosaldo, M., and L. Lamphere, eds. 1974. *Woman, culture, and society.* Stanford: Stanford University Press.

Rosser, S. V. 1988. Good science: Can it ever be gender free? *Women's Studies International Forum* 11: 13–19.

Ruddick, S. 1980. Maternal thinking. *Feminist Studies* 6: 342–67.

Sherif, C. W. 1979. Bias in psychology. In *The prism of sex: Essays in the sociology of knowledge,* ed. J. A. Sherman and E. T. Beck. Madison: University of Wisconsin Press.

Shiva, V. 1995. Reductionism and regeneration: A crisis in science. In *Ecofeminism,* ed. M. Mies and V. Shiva, 22–35. London: Zed Books.

Smith, D. E. 1979. A sociology for women. In *The prism of sex: Essays in the sociology of knowledge,* ed. J. A. Sherman and E. T. Beck. Madison: University of Wisconsin Press.

———. 1987. *The everyday world as problematic: A feminist sociology.* Boston: Northeastern University Press.

———. 1990. *The conceptual practices of power: A feminist sociology of knowledge.* Boston: Northeastern University Press.

Sprague, J. 1988. The other side of the banner: Toward a feminization of politics. In *Seeing female: Social roles and personal lives,* ed. S. S. Brehm. New York: Greenwood.

———. 1991. Gender, class, and political thinking. *Research in Political Sociology* 5: 111–39.

———. 1996, August. Seeing gender as social structure. Paper presented at the annual meeting of the American Sociological Association, New York.

———. 1997. Holy men and big guns: The Can[n]on in social theory. *Gender and Society* 11: 88–107.

———. and M. K. Zimmerman. 1989. Quantity and quality: Reconstructing feminist methodology. *The American Sociologist* 20: 71–86.

———. 1993. Overcoming dualisms: A feminist agenda for sociological methodology. In *Theory on gender/Feminism on theory,* ed. P. England, 255–80. New York: Aldine De Gruyter.

Stacey, J. 1988. Can there be a feminist ethnography? *Women's Studies International Forum* 11: 21–27.

Stacey, J. and B. Thorne. 1985. The missing feminist revolution in sociology. *Social Problems* 32: 301–16.

Szasz, T. S. 1971. The sane slave: An historical note on the use of medical diagnosis as justificatory rhetoric. *American Journal of Psychotherapy* 25: 228–39.

Thomas, W. I., and D. Thomas. 1928. *The child in America.* New York: Knopf.

Thorne, B. 1983. Political activist as participant-observer: Conflicts of commitment in a study of the draft resistance movement of the 1960's. In *Contemporary field research: A collection of readings,* ed. R. Emerson, 216–34. Prospect Heights, IL: Waveland Press.

Treichler, P. A. 1993. AIDS, gender, and biomedical discourse: Current contests for meaning. In *American feminist thought at century's end,* ed. L. S. Kauffman, 281–354. Cambridge, MA: Blackwell.

Tuana, N. 1983. Re-fusing nature/nurture. *Women's studies international forum* 6: 621–32.

Ward, K. B. 1993. Reconceptualizing world system theory to include women. In *Theory on gender/Feminism on theory,* ed. P. England, 43–68. New York: Aldine De Gruyter.

Weedon, C. 1987. *Feminist practice and poststructuralist theory.* Cambridge, MA: Basil Blackwell, Inc.

Yeatman, A. 1984. Gender and the differentiation of social life into public and domestic domains. *Social Analysis* 15: 32–49.

PART II

STRATEGIES ON ISSUES OF RACE, CLASS, GENDER, AND SEXUALITY

CHAPTER 6

Difference Matters

Studying Across Race, Class, Gender, and Sexuality

SHARLENE NAGY HESSE-BIBER AND MICHELLE L. YAISER

How could a social science which isn't for all women be a feminist social science?

SANDRA HARDING,
FEMINISM AND METHODOLOGY

Feminists of color have revealed to white middle-class feminists the extent of their own racism.

HIRSCH AND KELLER,
"PRACTICING CONFLICT IN FEMINIST THEORY"

Feminism was transformed by its interactions with other disciplines including post-colonialism, post-structuralism, postmodernism, and black studies. Women both within and outside the feminist community began using the lenses of these other disciplines to examine feminist scholarship. Many feminists realized that issues of difference concerning race, class, gender, sexuality, sexual orientation, nationality, and ethnic background frequently were not included in feminist scholarship (Hesse-Biber 2002). When issues of difference were included, feminist scholarship frequently failed to analyze the important interrelationships among these categories within specific historical locations (see, for example, Anzaldua 1987; Mohanty 1988; hooks 1989; 1990; Hesse-Biber 2002). Because of the failure to incorporate difference, many scholars, both feminist and nonfeminist, criticized feminist scholarship for being racist, classist, heterosexist, and the like.

In response to this criticism, feminists working in and across many disciplines began developing new ways of thinking about, writing about, and researching women and their lives. For example in the late 1980s early 1990s, sociologist Patricia Hill Collins (1999) began uncovering black women's subjugated knowledge when she created a black women's epistemological standpoint she termed the "outsider within." With this epistemology she criticized the white middle-class feminists who overgeneralized without reference to the diversity of women's lives. To provide a framework for examining the interconnections between systems of oppression and domination, Patricia Hill Collins also developed the concept of a "matrix of domination" (Collins 1990; see also, King 1988). She argued that gender, race, and class are socially constructed and are connected and interlocked in terms of an individual's lived experience.

In addition to Patricia Hill Collins, many other feminists were revolutionizing and continue to revolutionize the way a range of widely used disciplinary concepts addressed issues of difference. Michel Foucault's (1979; 1981) concepts of "power" and "resistance" are discussed by Monique Deveaux's work (1999), which also shows how these concepts are transformed when feminists begin to "historicize" them via their everyday use in the varieties of women's daily lives (including their experiences of dominance and violence). The problems of disciplinary constructions being "universal" are examined by historian Deniz Kandiyoti (1999). She also looks at how Western feminists do not deal with the ethnocentrism hidden within important concepts such as patriarchy. She calls for a historical-comparative approach in analyzing patriarchy across Western and non-Western societies. In a similar fashion, historian Joan Scott (1999) is critical of "personal experience" as historical fact and suggests that historians view experience discursively—as a socially constructed "linguistic" event (Hesse-Biber 2002). These are only a few of the many feminist scholars who have continued to force the issue of difference upon those who would otherwise ignore it.

THE ISSUE OF DIFFERENCE: WHICH WOMEN?

Prior to this inclusion of difference, feminism and feminists often paid little or flawed attention to the diversity of women's lives and experiences. Rarely did feminists (or anyone else) ask "which women?" Most of the research focused on the differences between men and women and ignored the differences among women (and among men). Although white, middle-class, heterosexual feminists are most frequently criticized for ignoring difference, some "other" feminists also ignored issues of diversity. For example, in addition to criticizing Western feminists for their narrow view of non-Western women, Mohanty (1988) also criticized non-Western feminists for ignoring the class and geographic location of many of the women they were studying. Ladner (1987) questioned traditional social science research methods that caused a colonial political relationship to be replicated even when the research was conducted by a researcher who belonged to the same dominated social group as the research subjects. When feminists are criticized for not asking which women and thus ignoring difference in this introduction, we (the authors) are referring to *any* feminist who is guilty of this omission, regardless of race, class, orientation, religion, etc.

Although the importance of asking "which women" will become apparent throughout the course of the following discussions, Michael Kimmel and Michael Messner (2001) provide personal experience to illustrate the significance of difference. Kimmel witnessed a black woman and a white woman discussing whether their similarities as women were greater than their racial differences as black and white.

> "When you wake up in the morning and look in the mirror, what do you see?" she asked.
>
> "I see a woman," replied the white woman.

> "That's precisely the issue," replied the black woman. "I see a black woman. For me, race is visible every day, because it is how I am not privileged in this culture. Race is invisible to you, which why our alliance will always seem somewhat false to me."

After hearing this conversation, Kimmel, a white man, realized that he had seen himself as a human being. Race and gender had been invisible to him. His privileged position within society had obscured the social mechanisms that had afforded him that privilege. Being blinded by privilege is not uncommon and is one of the factors that can lead to research that ignores difference. Asking "which women" is one of the ways that researchers can shed light upon social structures, institutions, and systems that might otherwise be difficult to see.

The Strategic Use of Essentialism and Its Limitations

Although the use of a universal and essential woman is problematic, it is also important to note an empowering use of the universal category. Feminist philosopher Susan Bordo argues for the strategic use of "essentialism." She suggests that "too relentless a focus on historical heterogeneity . . . can obscure the transhistorical hierarchical patterns of white, male privilege that have informed the creation of the Western intellectual tradition" (Bordo 1990, 149). Bordo bases her argument on the notion that it is politically important at times to minimize the many differences among women in order to promote the political agenda of women as a group (see also Spivak 1990, 10).

Spalter-Roth and Hartmann's (1999) research on social welfare policy is illustrative of what Bordo is advocating. They present a "dualistic perspective" on social policy research that combines the diversity of women's "lived experience," with research methods embedded in the scientific method. In her study of Third World women, Chandra Talpade Mohanty (1999) also argues for the "strategic use" of essentialism. Despite their differences in social class, race, and nationality, she had the women in her project identify with each other as "women" around their shared material interests as "workers." Using three case studies of Third World women involved in the global division of labor, she shows how ideologies of domesticity, femininity, and race are employed by capitalists to socially construct the "domesticated woman worker"—how they are perceived as "dependent housewives" allows the capitalist to pay them low wages. She argues for a rethinking of Third World women as agents rather than victims. And she argues for political solidarity among women workers as a potential "revolutionary basis for struggles against capitalist recolonization" (Hesse-Biber 2002).

The use of homogeneity, or sameness, within a political agenda may be advantageous; however, an examination of feminist research will show that the use of the universal category of woman also allows the researcher to create an inferior "Other," making interactions between men and women the primary social relation. Such a perspective supports the assumption that one methodology will allow the researcher to collect meaningful data from all research subjects.

The universal woman erases the differences among women. "Women" are presented as a coherent, homogeneous group in which everyone has identical interests and desires. Women are bound together by a shared oppression (Mohanty 1988, 65). As such, Mohanty argues, every woman's story of her life is a story of either victimization within a patriarchal system or of resistance to that system. Women as real, material subjects of history, society, structure, etc. are either ignored or do not exist. Within this universal category, differences in race, ethnicity, gender, sexual orientation, culture, and patriarchy are ignored. "Women" are white, middle or upper class, heterosexual, and Western.

As Western feminist researchers began examining women of other countries and cultures, they did not acknowledge their privileged position as Western feminists. They created a Third World Woman as a singular monolithic subject that desired the same freedoms from oppression that Western women enjoyed. Mohanty (1988) criticizes Western feminists for not examining their personal role and the role their scholarship plays within the global economic and political frameworks, thereby ignoring the "complex interconnections between first- and third-world economies and the profound effect of this on the lives of women in *all* countries." (63). Although feminism is supposed to improve the social conditions for all women, the research and activism based upon the universal "Woman" was only benefiting the universal "Woman."

Feminist research based upon the universal "Woman" created a universal "Man" as the oppressor. Just as the differences among women were ignored, the differences among men were also ignored. This research made the relations between men and women the primary social relation. The system of patriarchy was the primary system of power and domination. The relations between men and women created a set of lived experiences that were more important than the lived experiences created by other systems of oppression.

By using this universal woman in feminist research, researchers were able to assume that "one size fits all" when choosing a method of data collection. With many feminist researchers choosing to use qualitative methods and wanting to give women a voice that they have not had before, interviewing and oral histories became popular methods for feminist projects. One of the underlying assumptions with feminist interviewing and oral history, was that women can understand women and that this shared experience of oppression helps to create or co-create meaning and understanding. The shared oppression and understanding created by it was thought to be sufficient to produce bias-free research.

Many researchers have struggled with the validity of this assumption. They found the process of conducting feminist interviewing and oral history projects frustrating and confusing even though women were interviewing women. These researchers didn't find the shared meaning and understanding that was supposed to exist. In a project exploring women's experience of marital separation, Riessman (1987) found that just being a woman was not enough to understand the narrative accounts of other women. Her position as an Anglo interviewer, although female, prevented her from fully understanding the Hispanic, working-class women that she interviewed. Beoku-Betts (1994) found similar problems while doing field research among Gullah women. As a black female researcher, she theoretically had insider status with the population she was studying; however, she found that insider status was dependent upon other factors such as class and culture and was based upon a process of negotiation. It was not until she completed the negotiation process that she had full access to some of the research subjects and could begin to co-create meaning and understanding.

Yvonne Tixier y Vigil and Nan Elsasser (1976) tested the impact of ethnicity upon interview data. Tixier y Vigil, a Chicana researcher, and Elsasser, a white researcher, both interviewed the same Chicana women asking the same questions. The intensive textual analysis of the transcripts showed that the Chicana women were more open about sex and the body with the white interviewer than with the Chicana interviewer. When it came to discussing discrimination, they talked more freely with the Chicana interviewer than with the white interviewer. Although both researchers used the same method for all of the respondents, they each received important, but very different data based upon their positionality within the community. This study demonstrates that difference must be taken into account when selecting a methodology for a research project.

Kath Weston (1998, included in this section) found that being a woman and a lesbian made the lesbian population of San Francisco more visible and accessible to her than it had to previous male researchers. Her lesbian identity further helped her establish "trust" and "rapport" with her subjects, many of whom told her they would not have talked to her had she been straight. However, she found that many participants' topics of discussion were influenced by her lesbian identity. Participants spent little time discussing anti-gay stereotypes, instead focusing much of the discussion on more controversial topics—butch/fem, gay marriage, sadomasochism (s/m), and drag queens. While her shared identity enabled access to a community and data that was previously unavailable, Weston found that a shared identity complicated her research by leaving cultural notions implicit. She had to work to get people to state, explain, and situate the obvious.

"Adding Difference and Stirring"

When difference was finally recognized in the late 1970s and early 1980s, it was brought into feminist research in a way similar to when women were first brought into androcentric research: researchers simply began "adding difference and stirring." Yet as Harding (1991) points out, if adding women and stirring was a problem, then isn't adding women of color and stirring a problem? The adding women of color and stirring created more specific, multiple "universals." Although it was recognized that the use of the universal woman could only produce a partial and distorted account of the lives of women and that difference mattered, each difference became its own universal. Women of color told one story (Harding 1991). Third World women were treated as a singular monolithic subject (Mohanty 1988). Mohanty (1988) argues that middle-class and urban researchers (especially in the Third World) assumed their own middle-class, urban culture as the norm, classifying working-class and rural women as Other. This scholarship also created a universal or essential oppressor by not looking at the difference among oppressors as they were beginning to look at the difference among the oppressed. When studying gender (sex and gender difference), there was a single masculinity that was treated as a fixed biological essence of men (Zinn, Hondagneu-Sotelo, and Messner 2000).

Commonly, only *one* difference was added into the mix—black women, working-class women, etc. As discussed in the introduction to Part I of this volume, "adding and stirring" did not change the epistemological paradigm, it simply added different subjects to the existing paradigm. Although this research did recognize difference, it was still very problematic.

> . . . "adding difference and stirring." The result may be a lovely mosaic, but like a patchwork quilt it still tends to overemphasize boundaries, rather than highlighting bridges of interdependency. In addition, this approach too often does not explore the ways that social constructions of femininities and masculinities are passed on, and reproduce relations power. In short, we think that the substantial quantity of research that has now been done on various groups and subgroups needs to be analyzed within a framework that emphasizes differences and inequalities not as discrete areas of separation, but as interrelated bands of color that together make up a spectrum. (Zinn, Hondagneu-Sotelo, and Messner 2000, 6–7)

Within this solely additive model, the "Other" that had been created by the universal "Woman" becomes exotic and exciting. bell hooks discusses the consequences of adding "Otherness" to mainstream culture and the resulting desires and fantasies about the "Other" (1992). Some of what she talks about can be applied to social research as well. By just adding difference into the analysis, the researcher reinscribes and maintains the status quo of the social hierarchy. The researcher maintains their dominant position as the one with the power to add the difference. By just adding difference (especially just adding a single difference), the researcher decontextualizes the "Others" life. Their experience is free from the history and social processes in which they live their daily lives. The primary social relations are again sex-based and the oppression suffered due to these relations is the most important. Although difference is acknowledge, there is still no recognition that differences are socially constructed and connected.

The De-Valuing of Difference within Traditional Research

> Within a positivist paradigm, research can never be deemed valid if objectivity is not maintained throughout the entire research process.
>
> It is that separation between the subject and the object that can cause the difference among women to be ignored or forgotten and the universal category used. On the simplest level, this gap compromised the amount of understanding a researcher can have for her object. It allows distortion to occur. Thus research with this gap is "likely to be an expression of patriarchal ideology." (Sprague and Zimmerman 1993, 256).

This separation between the researcher and the researched is a basic tenet of positivism and not only limits our understanding and leads to distortion, but it places the power structures and hierarchies of society at the center of the research project. Positivism makes the object of the study an object of dominance, thus reproducing the experience of the oppressed or marginalized in the social world. The questions asked, the variables and their conceptualization, the design of the research project, and the judgment criteria used by the researcher are all an expression of a specific viewpoint or belief held by the researcher.

Ladner (1987) equates the power relationship between the researcher and the researched to a colonial power relationship—the oppressor defines the problem, the nature of the research, and to some extent the quality of interaction between him and his subjects (1987, 77). Research is thus inherently value-laden and reflects the power structures within which the researcher exists. It can maintain, perpetuate, create, and recreate the power and hierarchies operating in society.

Because science is a form of power within our culture, the specific viewpoints and power relations that exist within a scientific study are oftentimes elevated to the status of being the correct or only viewpoint within society (see our discussion of Kuhn in the introduction to Part III of this book). If these viewpoints and power relations are part of the dominant paradigm, the elevation occurs quickly and is not questioned until the paradigm itself is questioned. Many of the research questions within such a paradigm frequently arise from the desire to pacify, control, exploit, or manipulate the oppressed group. Thus, consciously or unconsciously scientists may produce research that allows and facilitates the dominant group to maintain their dominance.

> Scientific research does not exist in a vacuum. Its theory and practice reflect the structure and values of society. In capitalist America, where massive inequalities in wealth and power exist between classes and racial groups, the processes of social research express both race and class oppression. The control, exploitation, and privilege that are generic components of social oppression exist in the relation of researchers to researched, even though their manifestations may be subtle and masked by professional ideologies. (Blauner and Wellman 1973, 314–15)

By using the universal, essential "Woman," the dominant paradigm, positivism, was left intact and unquestioned. By adding difference and stirring, the dominant group maintained their control of subordinate groups.

Even as feminist researchers began thinking about research in new ways and developing viable alternatives to positivism, the imbalance of power remained. In spite of attempts to equalize power in the research project, the researcher's location within society's hierarchies outside the research project has not changed (Wolf 1996, 35).

Judith Stacey further complicates the discussion of power by challenging feminists to be more honest and reflexive about themselves. Regardless of any selfless, virtuous self-portrayal, many feminist researchers desire power and privilege (in Wolf 1996, 36).

As seen in Part I of this volume, Positivism and its major assumption of objectivity have been strongly criticized by feminists. Alternative research paradigms had been developed, but many feminists continued to work within research traditions that led them to use the universal, essential category "Woman" and to "add difference and stir" although difference had been acknowledged. The reason many feminists continued to work within research traditions is connected to the issues of acceptance and respect—two things that are necessary for a successful academic career that many feminists (and feminist research) struggle to achieve. Many feminists have found that by using "traditional" methods and maintaining some use of "objectivity" their research is more quickly accepted and deemed valid by their disciplinary colleagues. By conducting their research with only a minimal challenge to the fundamental logic and dominant philosophies of science, feminist research projects are more widely understood and accepted into conventional bodies of knowledge with less resistance. (Harding 1991, 113)

In addition to relying on traditional methods, Harding discusses the total abandonment of objectivity called for by some feminists. Although she believes the reasons for this abandonment are valid, one of her arguments against such abandonment is the fact that because objectivity is a tenet of positivism, new forms of objectivity will benefit from that history. "The notion of objectivity has valuable political and intellectual histories; as it is transformed into 'strong objectivity' by the logic of standpoint epistemologies, it retains central features of the older concept" (Harding 1993, 72). Although traditional objectivity and strong objectivity have very different implications in research, feminist research that uses any type of objectivity may gain a little more acceptance and respect from the dominant research group. These two practices are not only important for the acceptance of feminist research into conventional science and knowledge, they are also important to the women scientists conducting feminist research. The structure and hierarchy of the sciences is still hostile toward women and feminist research in many ways. It has taken more than a century for women scientists (feminist or not) to receive the same access to funding, teaching appointments, and laboratory time that men have always enjoyed. In many places within the academy that struggle yet continues (see Douglas 1999; Massachusetts Institute of Technology 1999). Being able to conduct feminist research while still maintaining disciplinary respect is a necessity for these women to continue their careers. Asking "which women?" and analyzing difference as part of a dynamic social process was not yet a possibility.

THE TURN TOWARD DIFFERENCE RESEARCH

Recent scholarship has recognized the limitations of previous research dealing with difference and has set out not only to correct the problems but also to create an ongoing debate about the most productive ways of conceptualizing race, class, gender, and sexuality; how they relate to each other, and how they are revealed in everyday life (Weber 1998, 15). This new scholarship emphasizes both historical and social possibilities of these differences and their basis in power relations. In "A Conceptual Framework for Understanding Race, Class, Gender and Sexuality," Lynn Weber (this volume) outlines the six themes in this new scholarship.

First, that race, class, gender, and sexuality are contextual. They are never fixed, but are constantly undergoing change as the economy changes, politics shift, and new ideological processes, trends, and events occur. Understanding race, class, gender, and sexuality in this context requires researchers to avoid attempting to find language and meaning that would apply to these concepts across all times and all places. Researchers, scholars, activists, policy analysts, etc. need to work with dynamic, fluid definitions, theories, and labels that are a reflection of society and include political, historical, and social significance.

The second theme Weber identified is that race, class, gender, and sexuality are socially constructed. Their meanings and interpretations grow out of struggles between groups to control socially valuable, yet scarce, resources. The dominant group defines, through culture, these categories as dichotomous to create a system of social ranking. The dichotomies (white versus nonwhite, man versus woman, etc.) are then tied to biology to imply that the hierarchies are permanent and natural. Through understanding the social construction of these inequalities, we can begin to see, critique, and potentially change a system of domination that might otherwise seem impervious.

Acknowledgment of the social construction of race, class, gender, and sexuality also implies that we can not fully understand their social significance by including them as variables in quantitative projects. When treated as variables, each of these inequalities are broken down into mutually exclusive and exhaustive attributes. Individuals living in society are then assigned one location along each dimension of inequality. This quantitative research process does not and cannot recognize individuals who exist at more than one location in each dimension (multiracial individuals for example) or whose location changes (class).

Perhaps the most important theme in current race, class, gender, and sexuality scholarship, according to Weber, is that not only are these inequalities socially constructed and historically specific, they are systems of power relations. They are hierarchies in which one group controls another. At the center of these relationships is the exploitation of the oppressed group by the dominant group so that the dominant group receives a greater share of society's valued resources. By seeing these inequalities as systems of relational power, we are forced to examine privilege as well as oppression. For example, McIntosh (1995) examines the privilege (and problems) of whiteness and Messner (2000) examines the privilege (and problems) of masculinity.

Fourth, Weber continues, to fully understand the importance of race, class, gender, and sexuality in society, we must examine them in both the social structure (macro) and the social psychological (micro) contexts. There are important linkages between both the macro and micro contexts. People in different social locations live their lives very differently due to different social structures, trends, and events. People internalize social oppression differently and as such, have different survival processes. All of these and the connections between the social and the psychological must be examined.

Current scholarships also emphasize how race, class, gender, and sexuality operate simultaneously. At the structural level, these hierarchies of oppression are connected and embedded in all social institutions. We can each exist at different locations along all dimensions, leading to the possibility that we can be both dominant and subordinate at the same time. We can be both constrained and enabled by the social structure of inequalities.

Finally, Weber notes that race, class, gender and sexuality scholarship emphasizes the interdependence of knowledge and activism. Much of the research is conducted in an effort to understand oppression and effect social change. The value of the scholarship is frequently judged by a standard of empowerment. Can oppressed groups use the knowledge generated to empower themselves in seeking social justice?

Although it is impossible to separate the systems of domination from one other, to attempt to look at all of the possible combinations of domination based upon difference within one project or discussion can be daunting and overwhelming if not frustrating and impractical. Within the realm of feminist research, race, class, gender, and sexuality are the differences that receive the most attention in both theory and research. However, there are social systems of power and domination based upon other differences such as religion, age, geographic location (rural versus urban for example), physical characteristics, etc. By focusing on race, class, gender, and sexuality, this discussion is in no way underestimating the effects the other systems of domination have on people. It is instead reflecting the body of feminist research. Also, in an attempt to keep the discussion somewhat concise and coherent, each of the differences will be discussed in a somewhat separate manner.

Conceptualizing Gender and Difference

Although this belief has been criticized, sex and/or gender has long been regarded as the most important difference in feminist research. Women should have the same access to resources and power within society as men. The difference between men and women was often seen as an essential biological one. The social construction of men and women and, subsequently, masculinity and femininity was easily ignored or dismissed. As discussed above, the use of the universal "Woman" also assumed the usage of a universal "Man" as oppressor. Yet the categories of men and women have multiple meanings within and between cultures. Neither masculinity nor femininity is a fixed, biological essence. Rather, they are social constructions that shift and change over time. Each individual expresses his masculinity or her femininity in a variety of ways. And individuals may cross gender boundaries and express the opposite gender for their physical sex. What it means to be a man and what it means to be a woman are constantly changing. One only has to look at the ways in which the roles and expectations for men and women within the family and the workplace have changed over the past few decades to see how the definitions of men and women and masculinity and femininity reflect social and economic shifts.

Not only are masculinity and femininity socially constructed they are also relational. Masculinity is largely focused on expressing difference from and superiority over anything considered feminine (Zinn, Hondagneu-Sotelo, Messner 2000). This relational definition is also interconnected with other social structures such as race, class, sexuality, and nationality. For example, voting laws in the United States initially only applied to white men. When women received the right to vote, only white women were allowed to vote. Another historical example is the portrayal of black women as "beasts of burden." This portrayal stands in direct contradiction to the American stereotypical ideal of woman as "fragile and not too bright." The contradiction disappears when one realizes that the ideal woman is white (Dill 1987).

The lack of recognition of the social construction of sex and gender has, until recently, left out a large portion of the population from being subjects of feminist knowledge and research: men. Digby (1998) argues that skepticism about men being feminist and doing feminist work is derived from the fact that most men are *socialized* into identities that are hostile to feminism. As long as manhood is defined as not just different from, but as opposite and opposed to womanhood, the notion of a feminist man is difficult to accept for most people. Thus, Digby argues, even in contemporary society, the widespread popular perception is that the relation between feminism and men is necessarily antagonistic. Men are expected to resist feminism and feminists are expected to hate men. This opposition and antagonism are based upon the gender binary that is typical in patriarchal cultures. Within these cultures, there are two mutually exclusive and exhaustive categories for physical sex: male and female (Stoltenberg 2003). In the resulting social set of characteristics, behaviors, and expectations, masculinity and femininity are also mutually exclusive and exhaustive. When this social construction of both sex and gender are examined and understood, one can see that the "necessarily" antagonistic relationship between men and feminism is no longer necessary. Men cannot only be the objects of feminist thought and research, they can be the subjects.

The Harding article "Can Men Be Subjects of Feminist Thought?" included in this section, provides a strong argument for the affirmative answer to that question. In the article she shows how men can make valid contributions to the feminist cause not only as activists, but also as producers of feminist knowledge. Feminist men can inhabit valued positions within feminist empiricism, socialist feminism, liberal feminism, and even radical feminism. The hesitation to consider men feminists or allow them to be subjects of feminist thought produces gaps and inconsistencies within feminist theory and practice. By not allowing men to be feminists and subjects of feminist thought, feminists are arguing that men are incapable of using the insights of women and producing feminist thought just because they are biologically men. It is the opposing side of the essential argument used to keep women oppressed within the patriarchal system. Using such an essential argument is hypocritical and paradoxical. Most Western feminists do not question their ability to use the insights of women from other cultures to create antiracist and anti-imperialist feminist work. "So how could it be that no men can create anti-sexist, anti-androcentric, feminist thought?" (Harding 1998, included in this section). As more and more research is demonstrating how sexism and patriarchy can be as damaging to men as women, the importance of men within feminism becomes more apparent. "One will want to appreciate the importance of solidarity, not unity, among groups with different but partially overlapping interests" (Harding 1998, included in this section).

Conceptualizing Sexuality and Difference

Directly connected to issues of sex and gender are the issues of sexuality and sexual orientation. Just as our understanding of sex and gender are socially constructed, so too are our understandings of sexuality. Definitions of heterosexual and homosexual (and even the presence of such concepts) and their consequential roles and behaviors vary from culture to culture. They are directly related to the cultural definitions of masculinity and femininity. Our understandings of what is and is not a sex act are also socially constructed (see for example, Bordo 2000; Frye 2000; and Messner 2000). In spite of the unbreakable ties between sexuality, sex, and gender, there has been little written on the complex issues of studying across the difference of sexuality, specifically, the significant impact that the privileged position a heterosexual researcher has upon the research project when studying the lives of homosexuals and bisexuals and their nonprivileged location within the social structure (Rhoads 1997). Like other "outsiders" in research, heterosexual researchers frequently have to develop a cultural competency in order to have constructive and meaningful conversations with gays, lesbians, and bisexuals. If the research is focusing on the identity struggles experienced by gays, lesbians, and bisexuals, the difficulty in reaching a shared understanding between a heterosexual researcher and a non-heterosexual respondent may be greater. In her research in the San Francisco Bay area on gay families, Kath Weston (1998, included in this section) found that many issues related to gay and lesbian identities were frequently not made clear to straight individuals. Coming-out stories, which were an important part of identity formation for her participants, were frequently a meaningful way to make connections with other gay men and lesbians, often being told to new acquaintances. These stories were specifically constructed and told for the benefit of other gay men and lesbians, not for a heterosexual audience. Participants were very open in discussing controversial issues such as butch/fem, gay marriage, sadomasochism, and drag queens. When talking with heterosexuals, these topics were frequently shadowed by a discussion of antigay stereotypes. These very significant issues may not have been as visible to or as easily understood by a heterosexual researcher. Weston's common frame of reference and shared identity as a lesbian also helped her gain trust and rapport with her participants. A few even told her that they would not have talked to her if she had been straight.

In addition to issues surrounding the development of cultural competency and co-constructing meaning, Rhoads discusses the significant issue of a heterosexual researcher's identity and homophobia. Studying across differences in sexual orientation and sexual identity can present "complexities that other cultural differences do not present." (Rhoads 1997, 16). Unlike race or sex or other cultural differences, there are no physical characteristics that separate gay from straight. Sexual identity cannot be discerned from one's appearance. Especially for heterosexual male researchers, homophobia may then get in the way of understanding. "Because the border between gay and straight is constructed as the most permeable; anyone at all can become gay, especially me, so the only way to defend my identity is to turn away with irrational disgust" (Young in Rhoads 1997, 16). Rhoads argues that this homophobic thinking is one of the biggest reasons there is so little research on sexual identity conducted by heterosexual researchers. It is directly connected to the cultural assumption that anyone who does study sexual identity is homosexual. Not only are the identities of the those being studied socially constructed, the identity of the researcher himself or herself is also constructed by society.

Although there are no physical characteristics that determine sexual identity, the social construction of sexuality is tied to a person's anatomical sex. There is a correlation between the social and physical. The same is true for race. A person's skin color and/or other physical features may determine his or her race physically (at least in the eyes of others), but their experience of being that race is socially constructed. Race is a social construction that is based upon the recognition of difference. It creates a system that both distinguishes groups and then positions them in relation to one another. Race is a relational system of power rather than an inherent property of people. It both creates and maintains a social structure of domination and control.

Interconnections of Race, Gender, and Class

Within the large body of feminist literature on race, the complex interconnections between gender and race is made clear (see for example any of the works of Patricia Hill Collins 1999 and bell hooks 1989, 1990, 1992, among others). The criticism of feminism as being white and middle class was initially made by black feminists whose experience of gender and patriarchal oppression was very different from that being written about by mainstream feminists. Their experience was different, they argued, because they were not just women, they were black women. "In societies where racial demarcation is endemic to the sociocultural fabric and heritage, gender identity is inextricably linked to and even determined by racial identity" (Higginbotham 1992, 254).

Shirley Hill and Joey Sprague (1999, included in this section) focus on how race and gender interact in the gender socialization process that takes place in families. By starting with the widely accepted belief that gender expectations and roles are communicated to children through socialization, especially within families, they ask if black families socialize their children into the same gender constructions as white families. Using data from surveys completed by a nonrandom sample of parents in 202 African American and 204 white families in two large metropolitan school districts, the authors examine parents' self-reports of their immediate priorities and long-term goals for their children, their view of the parenting role, and their discipline strategies. The authors cite two different perspectives that have remained popular with researchers and theorists working with the connections between gender and race. The first, assimilationism, argues that black families have essentially the same gender norms and expectations as the dominant white society. These traditional gender values are the ones they pass down to their children through socialization. The second perspective, Afrocentricism, challenges assimilation. This perspective argues that the uniqueness of the black experience works against any rigid gender distinctions and therefore black children are not socialized into polarized gender expectations. The findings of the research were not consistent with either perspective. Although the data showed that a difference in gender socialization did exist based on race, social class also played a significant role in shaping the construction of gender. This research does not just simply demonstrate the social construction and connectedness of gender and race, but also the importance of incorporating class.

Class and Difference

Although Hill and Sprague demonstrate the importance of class within a conceptualization of both race and gender, Reay (1998, included in this section) argues that throughout the 1990s, most feminists rarely dealt with class as an important social division. The research that did examine the connections between class and gender was largely conducted by working-class feminists. Reay argues that in spite of the lack of scholarship dealing with class, class remains an important social process that shapes the lives of both women and men. It breaks down the traditional division between the public and the private and the family and the workplace. It also is a social structure of power and domination as the economic basis of class continues to become more and more polarized as the rich get richer and the poor get poorer.

Women from lower classes are frequently silenced in and excluded from social settings, the workplace, and the academic environment (Reay 1996; and 1998, included in this section). Although a middle-class education provides mobility for the working class, Reay argues, being educated also means failing to hold on to working-class values and attitudes. Once a working-class woman achieves a middle-class education, many of the people from her working-class background will treat her differently, at times even excluding her from activities in which she used to participate. Her new friends and acquaintances will expect her to "act" middle-class, yet, even when she does act appropriately, they may never fully accept her because she has working-class roots. Although these acts of oppression frequently happen to all women, women of the lower classes experience these more frequently at the hands of other women. Class, just as much as race, gender, and sexuality, influences peoples' daily lives and experiences. To limit the definition of class to economics neglects the variety of ways that class contributes to social inequality. "Class is part of the micropolitics of people's lives. It is lived in and through people's bodies and permeates their thinking as powerfully as gender, 'race,' age and sexuality" (Reay 1998, included in this section). Reay further argues that because of its importance, complexities, and connection to other social inequalities, class needs to be studied by combining both qualitative and quantitative methods that explore how class is lived in raced and gendered ways, and vice versa.

Weston and Rofel (1984) found that the interaction between sexual identity and class was indeed important. In their study of a labor conflict within a lesbian workplace (Amazon Auto Repair), neither class nor a lesbian identity was enough to fully understand the conflict. " . . . there is no justification at the level of concrete analysis for abstracting class from sexuality or for treating heterosexism and class hegemony as two distinct types of oppression operating along separate axes. The strike at Amazon cannot be analyzed as a textbook labor conflict precisely because the male and heterosexist bias of most scholarly texts renders them incapable of grasping this integration" (Weston and Rofel 1984, 644). The women who worked at Amazon Auto Repair were living and working within the complex connections between class and sexual identity.

The articles included in this section of the book and the other research examples discussed in this introduction all demonstrate the ways in which race, class, gender, and sexuality are not only socially constructed but are also socially connected. In different ways, the research projects included in this section of the book criticize the simple additive model of adding difference and stirring. Instead they offer an interactive, dynamic model that recognizes that not only are race, class, gender, and sexuality socially constructed, they interact with one another within what Patricia Hill Collins (Zinn and Dill 2000, 26) calls a "matrix of domination," in which difference is conceptualized as a range of interlocking inequalities. Several fundamental systems of domination and oppression work both with and through each other. People will experience race, class, gender, and sexuality differently depending upon their locations within the social structures of race, class, gender, and sexuality. In other words, two people of the same race living within the same society and culture will experience race differently if they are of different class, different genders, and/or different sexualities. A black man will experience race differently than a black women for example. Or a working-class woman experiences gender differently than a middle-class woman.

The "matrix of domination" (Collins 1999) also examines how the systems shape people's experiences and identities simultaneously. Within this matrix, race, class, gender, and sexuality are not reducible to individual attributes that can be measured and assessed for their separate, specific contributions to the individual's experiences and identities. They also should not be separated out and assessed for their specific contributions to social and behavioral outcomes. By using the "matrix of domination" as a guide throughout the research project, the researcher can begin to understand the multiple ways that women and men experience themselves as gendered, raced, classed, and sexualized within their culture and historical moment.

REFLEXIVITY: A TOOL TO STUDY ACROSS DIFFERENCE

Acknowledging that difference—race, class, gender, and sexuality—is socially constructed and connected is only the first step in successfully working with difference in a meaningful way in feminist research. What is perhaps most important in the process of asking "which women?" and successfully studying across difference is the recognition that there are multiple truths and that there is more than one social reality. Reality is complex and not simply one-dimensional as Positivism with its emphasis on objectivity would have us believe. A researcher must acknowledge that she is not the essential woman and that the other realities and truths she may discover are just as valid and valuable as her own personal ones.

Reflexivity can help a researcher both publicly and privately acknowledge that she is not the essential woman. In simple terms, reflexivity is the process through which a researcher recognizes, examines, and understands how her social background, positionality, and assumptions affect the practice of research. The researcher is as much a product of society and its structures and institutions as the participants she is studying. One's own beliefs, backgrounds, and feelings become part of the process of knowledge construction. The process of explaining and interpreting the data draws upon the researcher's knowledge and understanding, both of which have been influenced by society and one's location within its social structures (see also Hertz 1997).

Reflexivity also requires that the researcher makes visible to both the research audience and possibly the participants one's own social locations and identities. In her field research among Gullah women, Beoku-Betts (1994) found that fully informing her participants of her social positionality and background—that she was raised in a rural community with similar cultural practices—enabled her to make contacts and gain data that would otherwise have not been available. In the piece included in this book, Kath Weston (1998, this section) is very reflexive about her identity as a lesbian and how it influenced her research. She writes that although she still would have studied gay families, the project would have been very different if she were not a lesbian. Weston also recognizes that her position within the homosexual community as a lesbian was the reason she had little trouble finding lesbian participants while lesbians had remained virtually invisible to men conducting sexuality research. "In my case, being a woman also influenced how I spent my time in the field: I passed more hours in lesbian clubs and women's groups than gay men's bars or male gyms" (Weston 1998, this section).

In addition to recognizing the influence of the researcher's positionality and making this positionality known to both audience and participant, the reflexive researcher must also continually be aware of and examine the relationship between the researcher and the research participants. If necessary, the authority of the researcher may be deconstructed, creating a more mutual and collaborative research project. In order to achieve this goal of reflexivity, and to limit the social structures of dominance and power from being reproduced within the feminist project, many researchers blend the roles of the subject and the object. They often form a rapport with the participants and will, for example, answer as many questions as they ask during an intensive interview. Many feminist researchers will also have the participants read their interpretation and analysis. This process not only allows the subject to be part of the entire research process, but also helps limit the possibility of misunderstanding, misrepresentation, and the manipulation of data to support the researcher's agenda (see Gluck and Patai 1991).

This blending of the subject and the object requires the use of a different type of objectivity, most commonly, strong objectivity. Referring back to Sandra Harding's (1993, Part I of this volume) discussion of the positivist subject within traditional notions of objectivity, a contrasting subject can be constructed. This new subject is used within standpoint epistemology and relies on "strong objectivity." First, the subject has a definite culture and history and is fully embedded within each. The culture and history of the subject are always visible because the lives from which the knowledge was started are always present. Second, the subject and object of scientific knowledge are not different—both are determinate in space and time. The same social forces that manipulate the objects of study, causing it to be determinate in time and space in Positivist epistemology, are also at work on the subject of study. Third, communities produce knowledge. The personal beliefs an individual holds only become knowledge when they have been legitimated by society. Once an individual and his or her beliefs have been legitimated as subject and knowledge, all knowledge claims become assumptions of the society in which they are created. Finally, the subjects of knowledge are not homogeneous. They are heterogeneous and therefore do produce knowledge that can be contradictory, incoherent, and inconsistent. There is more than one truth, and therefore, more than one valid knowledge. These characteristics of the subject for standpoint theories, unlike the Positivist ones, do emphasize the social and historical nature of knowledge and those that possess it. They also call for the gap between the subject and the object to be diminished if not, at times, completely abolished.

Many of the articles included in this volume either fully incorporate this new subject that Harding explains, or incorporate some of its tenets. For example, in order to assess the class of the women she was interviewing, Reay (1998, included in this section), not only collected data on the women's own educational histories and those of their partners and their parents; their housing status; their income level; their own, their partner's, and their parents' occupations (all "objective" measurements frequently used to determine class); she also asked them to self-identify in class terms. If there was a conflict between the women's self-identification and the objective measurement of their class status, that contradiction was brought into Reay's analysis. By doing this, Reay was embedding her analysis and her research participants' experiences within their social and historical contexts.

This drastic shift in the roles of both the research subject and the research object are important. These new roles and positionalities aim for liberatory research practices for all women. Feminists understand how race, class, gender, and sexuality are used within society to construct one another. This shift also allows for the inclusion of men. Women cannot claim to be the unique generators of feminist knowledge. Relatedly, men cannot claim that because they are not women, they can not produce feminist analyses and therefore may not be held accountable for sexist work.

Reflexivity ensures that the process of producing knowledge is made visible. In reflexive research, difference is neither ignored nor simply added. It is analyzed and understood to be an important factor that significantly impacts all aspects of the research process from beginning to end. Being reflexive is the most important and simultaneously the most challenging approach to conducting research that not only asks the question "which women?" but answers it while allowing and encouraging the researcher to challenge essentialism, universals, and partial truths within the research process and him/herself.

CONCLUSION: DIFFERENCE MATTERS

Within feminist research, studying across difference and asking "which women?" have given researchers a tool to see into different realities that were previously invisible to the positivist, objective researcher. Although this process may not be unique to feminist research, many will argue that because feminist researchers frequently reject notions of positivism and objectivity, it is more common within feminist social research. Feminists continue to struggle with issues of difference. And they haven't always agreed. But by accepting the idea that there are multiple truths and multiple realities, feminists have also gained the courage to disagree with one another surrounding these issues.

The idea that reality is complex and multidimensional has also impacted the way feminists think about epistemology, methodology, and methods and the interaction between these three concepts. Within traditional, positivist epistemologies, the social position of the subject is frequently insignificant because all knowledge is "out there" waiting to be discovered regardless of the social. These epistemologies can not be used within a feminist research paradigm that emphasizes both the social location of the subject and the social construction of knowledge. Alternative epistemologies were developed. Alternative methodologies are also developed to match the change in epistemology. Methods are no longer viewed as neutral tools for collecting data. Instead, they are shaped by the interests and positionality of the researchers who use them.

Feminist research has taught us that it is not enough to merely acknowledge the importance of difference. Difference is critical to all aspects of the research process. It is important to incorporate difference into our views of reality, truth, and knowledge. We must examine the difference that difference makes. Difference matters.

REFERENCES

Anzalduá, Gloria. 1987. *Borderlands/La Frontera.* San Francisco: Spinsters/Aunt Lute.

Beoku-Betts, Josephine. 1994. When black is not enough: Doing field research among Gullah women. *NWSA Journal* 6(3): 413–33.

Blauner, R., and D. Wellman. 1973. Toward the decolonization of social research. In *The death of white sociology,* ed. Joyce Ladner, 312–18. New York: Vintage.

Bordo, Susan. 1990. Feminism, postmodernism, and gender-skepticism. In *Feminism/Postmodernism,* ed. Linda Nicholson, 133–56. London: Routledge.

———. 2000. Pills and power tools. In *Gender through the prism of difference,* ed. Maxine Baca Zinn, Pierrette Hondagneu-Sotelo, and Michael Messner, 168–70. Boston: Allyn and Bacon.

Collins, Patricia Hill. 1990. *Black feminist thought: Knowledge, consciousness, and the politics of empowerment.* Boston: Unwin Hyman.

———. 1999. Learning from the outsider within: The sociological significance of black feminist thought. In *Feminist approaches to theory and methodology,* ed. Sharlene Hesse-Biber, Christine Gilmartin, and Robin Lydenberg, 135–78. New York: Oxford University Press.

Deveaux, Monique. 1999. Feminism and empowerment: A critical reading of Foucault. In *Feminist approaches to theory and methodology,* ed. Sharlene Hesse-Biber, Christine Gilmartin, and Robin Lydenberg, 236–58. New York: Oxford University Press.

Digby, Tom. 1998. Introduction. In *Men doing feminism,* ed. Tom Digby, 171–95. New York: Routledge.

Dill, Bonnie Thornton. 1987. The *dialectics of black womanhood. In* Feminism and methodology, ed. Sandra Harding, 97–108. Bloomington: Indiana University Press.

Douglas, Ann. October 11, 1999. *Crashing the top.* www.salon.com/books/it/1999/10/11/douglas/index1.html

Foucault, Michel. 1979. *Discipline and punish: The birth of the prison.* Translated by Alan Sheridan. New York: Vintage.

———. 1981. *The history of sexuality, vol. l, an introduction,* Harmondsworth, England: Penguin.

Friedan, Betty. 1963. *The feminine mystique.* W. W. Norton.

Frye, Marilyn. 2000. Lesbian sex. In *Gender through the prism of difference,* ed. Maxine Baca Zinn, Pierrette Hondagneu-Sotelo, and Michael Messner, 200–204. Boston: Allyn and Bacon.

Gluck, Sherna Berger, and Daphne Patai. 1991. *Women's words: the feminist practice of oral history.* New York: Routledge.

Harding, Sandra. 1986. *The science question in feminism.* Ithaca: Cornell University Press.

———. 1987. Introduction. In *Feminism and methodology,* ed. Sandra Harding, 1–14. Bloomington: Indiana University Press.

———. 1991. *Whose science? Whose knowledge?* Ithaca: Cornell University Press.

———. 1993. Rethinking standpoint epistemology: What is "strong objectivity"? In *Feminist epistemologies,* ed. Linda Alcoff and Elizabeth Potter, 49–82. New York: Routledge.

———. 1998. Can men be subjects of feminist thought? In *Men doing feminism,* ed. Tom Digby, 1–16. New York: Routledge.

Hertz, Rosanna. 1997. *Reflexivity and voice.* Thousand Oaks, CA: Sage Publications.

Hesse-Biber, Sharlene. 2002. Feminism and interdisciplinarity. In *Women in higher education: Empowering change,* ed. JoAnn DiGeorgio-Lutz, 57–66. Westport, CT: Praeger Publications.

Higginbotham, Evelyn Brooks. 1992. African-American women's history and the metalanguage of race. *Signs* (Winter): 251–74.

Hill, Shirley, and Joey Sprague. 1999. Parenting in black and white families: The interaction of gender with race and class. *Gender & Society* 13(4): 480–502.

Hirsch, Marianne, and Evelyn Fox Keller. 1990. Practicing conflict in feminist theory. In *Conflicts in feminism,* ed. Marianne Hirsch and Evelyn Fox Keller, 370–85. New York: Routledge.

hooks, bell. 1989. *Talking back: Thinking feminist, thinking black.* Boston: South End Press.

———. 1990. *Yearning: Race, gender, and cultural politics.* Boston: South End Press.

———. 1992. *Black looks: Race and representation.* Boston: South End Press.

Kandiyoti, Deniz. 1999. Islam and patriarchy: A comparative perspective. In *Feminist approaches to theory and methodology,* ed. Sharlene Hesse-Biber, Christine Gilmartin, and Robin Lydenberg, 219–35. New York: Oxford University Press.

Kimmel, Michael, and Michael Messner. 2001. Introduction. In *Men's lives,* ed. Michael Kimmel and Michael Messner, ix–xvii. Boston: Allyn and Bacon.

King, Deborah. 1988. "Multiple jeopardy, multiple consciousness: The context of a black feminist ideology." *SIGNS: Journal of Women in Culture and Society* 14, no. 1: 42–72.

Ladner, Joyce. 1987. Introduction to "Tomorrow's tomorrow: The black woman." In *Feminism and methodology,* ed. Sandra Harding, 74–83. Bloomington: Indiana University Press.

McIntosh, Patricia. 1995. White privilege and male privilege: A personal account of coming to see correspondences through work in women's studies. In *Race, class, and gender: An anthology,* ed. Margaret Andersen and Patricia Hill Collins, 76–86. Belmont, CA: Wadsworth.

Massachusetts Institute of Technology Committee on Women Faculty. 1999. *A Study on the status of women faculty in science at MIT.* Cambridge: Massachusetts Institute of Technology.

Messner, Michael. 2000. Becoming 100% Straight. In *Gender through the prism of difference,* ed. Maxine Baca Zinn, Pierrette Hondagneu-Sotelo, and Michael Messner, 205–10. Boston: Allyn and Bacon.

Mohanty, Chandra. 1988. Under Western eyes: Feminist scholarship and colonial discourses. *Feminist Review* 30: 61–88.

———. 1999. "Women workers and capitalist scripts: Ideologies of domination, common interests, and the politics of solidarity. In *Feminist approaches to theory and methodology,* ed. Sharlene Hesse-Biber, Christine Gilmartin, and Robin Lydenberg, 362–88. New York: Oxford University Press.

Reay, Diane. 1996. Dealing with difficult differences: Reflexivity and social class in feminist research. *Feminism and Psychology* 6(3): 443–56.

———. 1998. Rethinking social class: Qualitative perspectives on class and gender. *Sociology* 32: 259–75.

Rhoads, Robert. 1997. Crossing sexual orientation borders: Collaborative strategies for dealing with issues of positionality and representation. *Qualitative Studies in Education* 10(1): 7–23.

Riessman, Catherine Kohler. 1987. When Gender is not enough: Women interviewing women. *Gender and Society* 1: 172–207.

Scott, Joan. 1999. The evidence of experience. In *Feminist approaches to theory and methodology,* ed. Sharlene Hesse-Biber, Christine Gilmartin, and Robin Lydenberg, 79–99. New York: Oxford University Press.

Spalter-Roth, Roberta, and Heidi Hartmann. 1999. Small happiness: The feminist struggle to integrate social research with social activism. In *Feminist approaches to theory and methodology,* ed. Sharlene Hesse-Biber, Christine Gilmartin, and Robin Lydenberg, 333–47. New York: Oxford University Press.

Spivak, Gayatri Chakravorty. 1990. *The postcolonial critic: Interviews, strategies, dialogue.* New York: Routledge.

Sprague, Joey, and Mark K. Zimmerman. 1993. Overcoming dualisms: A feminist agenda for sociological methodology. In *Theory on gender/Feminism on theory,* ed. Paula England, 255–80. New York: Aldine DeGruyter.

Stoltenberg, John. 2003. How men have (a) sex. In *Reconstructing gender: A multicultural anthology,* ed. Estelle Disch, 253–62. Boston: McGraw-Hill.

Tixier y Vigil, Yvonne, and Nan Elsasser. 1976. The effects of the ethnicity of the interviewer on conversation: A study of Chicana women. In *Sociology of the language of American women,* ed. Betty L. DuBois and Isabel Crouch, 161–69. San Antonio: Trinity University Press.

Weber, Lynn. 1998. A conceptual framework for understanding race, class, gender, and sexuality. *Psychology of Women Quarterly* 22: 13–32.

Weston, Kath. 1998. Fieldwork in lesbian and gay communities. In *Gender through the prism of difference,* ed. Maxine Baca Zinn, Pierrette Hondagneu-Sotelo, and Michael Messner, 79–85. Boston: Allyn and Bacon.

Weston, Kath, and Lisa Rofel. 1984. Sexuality, class, and conflict in a lesbian workplace. *Signs* 9(4): 623–46.

Wolf, Diane. 1996. Situating feminist dilemmas in fieldwork. In *Feminist dilemmas in fieldwork,* ed. Diane Wolf, 1–55. Boulder, CO: Westview Press.

Zinn, Maxine Baca, Pierrette Hondagneu-Sotelo, and Michael Messner. 2000. Introduction. In *Gender through the prism of difference,* ed. Maxine Baca Zinn, Pierrette Hondagneu-Sotelo, and Michael Messner, 1–12. Boston: Allyn and Bacon.

Zinn, Maxine Baca, and Bonnie Thornton Dill. 2000. Theorizing difference from multiracial feminism. In *Gender through the prism of difference,* ed. Maxine Baca Zinn, Pierrette Hondagneu-Sotelo, and Michael Messner, 23–29. Boston: Allyn and Bacon.

CHAPTER 7

A Conceptual Framework for Understanding Race, Class, Gender, and Sexuality

LYNN WEBER

People's real life experiences have never fit into the boundaries created by academic disciplines: Lives are much more complex and far reaching. Just as the social, political, economic, and psychological dimensions of everyday life are intertwined and mutually dependent, so too are the systems of inequality—race, class, gender, and sexuality—that limit and restrict some people while privileging others. Increasingly, interdisciplinary studies, including Women's Studies and multicultural studies, are extending the range of the curriculum; such programs are critical sites for the development of meaningful commentaries on human social and psychological realities that reflect such complexities. (Magner 1996)

It is in women's studies—not in racial or ethnic studies, not in social stratification (class) studies in sociology, not in psychology or in other traditional disciplines—that race, class, gender, and sexuality studies first emerged.[1] Because of its critical stance toward knowledge in the traditional disciplines, its interdisciplinary approach, and its orientation toward social change and social betterment, women's studies has been most open to self-critique for its exclusion of multiply oppressed groups, such as women of color, working-class women, and lesbians (Baca Zinn, Weber Cannon, Higginbotham, and Dill 1986; Weber Cannon, Higginbotham, and Leung 1988).

Since these initial writings, scholarship and college courses that simultaneously address these multiple dimensions of inequality under the rubric of race, class, gender, and, increasingly, sexuality studies have grown rapidly. Texts in most courses now consist of a set of readings selected by individual faculty and/or of one of a growing number of anthologies on the topic (Anderson and Collins 1995; Anzadula 1987a, 1987b; Baca Zinn and Dill 1994; Chow, Wilkinson, and Baca Zinn 1996; Cyrus 1993; Rothenberg 1995). The strength of these anthologies is that they demonstrate the significance of race, class, gender, and sexuality by presenting a wide array of diverse human experiences and analyses across these dimensions. Students are encouraged to move beyond thinking about major social and personal issues solely from their own viewpoints or from dominant group perspectives. The major limitation is that anthologies provide little direction in identifying the themes and assumptions that pull these diverse perspectives together. We are given little guidance about what constitutes a race, class, gender, and sexuality analysis of social reality. In part, this omission parallels the development of the field of race, class, gender, and sexuality studies, which began by revealing diverse experiences across these dimensions to counter the monolithic views of the social world put forth in both mainstream and women's studies scholarship.

Now, however, scholars are beginning to search for and to identify common themes and approaches that characterize the work in race, class, gender, and sexuality studies (cf. Baca Zinn and Dill 1996). This process should invite debate and critique, further the development of the scholarship, and help provide one or more frameworks for teaching about this work. This article presents six themes that currently characterize this scholarship. By reminding us of some questions that need to be asked in any analysis of human society, these themes can guide the race, class, gender, and sexuality analyses we conduct for our research, our teaching, and our social activism.

A BRIEF HISTORY OF RACE, CLASS, GENDER, AND SEXUALITY STUDIES

In the 1970s and 1980s, women of color, the majority of whom were poor or working class, were especially vehement in voicing their opposition to theories of and perspectives on social reality that focused on a single dimension—especially on gender, but also on race, class, or sexuality. They argued that the multidimensionality and interconnected nature of race, class, gender, and sexuality hierarchies are especially visible to those who face oppression along more than one dimension of inequality. Patricia Hill Collins (1990), author of *Black Feminist Thought,* identifies the "interlocking nature of oppression" as one of three recurring themes in the work of Black feminists. Collins notes that this theme dates back at least to Sojourner Truth, who in the mid-nineteenth century said: "There is a great stir about colored men getting their rights, and not colored women theirs. You see the colored men will be masters over the women, and it will be just as bad as before" (cited in Loewenberg and Bogin 1976, 238).

When black women began to critique recent gender scholarship for its exclusionary practices, they focused on conducting analyses that began from the experiences of black women, putting them at center stage. *The Black Woman* (Cade 1970), *Ain't I a Woman* (hooks 1981), *The Black Woman* (Rodgers-Rose 1980), "The Dialectics of Black Womanhood" (Dill 1979), and "Race, Class, and Gender: Prospects for an All Inclusive Sisterhood" (Dill 1983) were among the first critical perspectives on black women published as books or articles in major feminist journals.

The irony of ignoring groups whose experiences typically reflected the confluence of multiple major dimensions of inequality was captured in the often-cited title of one of the first anthologies in black women's studies: *All the Women Were White, All the Blacks Were Men, But Some of Us Are Brave: Black Women's Studies* (Hull, Scott, and Smith 1982). Since that time, the critique of the white middle-class bias in women's studies has been joined by a critique of the male bias in racial ethnic studies, harkening back to the words of Sojourner Truth. And the study of race, class, gender, and sexuality has been expanded by studies of other groups of women of color (cf. Amaro and Russo 1987; Anzaldua 1987b; Baca Zinn and Dill 1994); of other oppressed groups, such as gays and lesbians (cf. Barale and Halperin 1993; D'Emilio and Freedman 1988; Greene 1994); and, more recently, of privilege itself: for example, studies of the social construction of whiteness (cf. Frankenberg 1993; McIntosh 1995; Roediger 1991) or of masculinity (cf. Brod and Kaufman 1994; Connell 1995; Messner 1992).

As a recently developing field, race, class, gender, and sexuality studies has not yet produced a wide range of competing theories about the nature of race, class, gender, and sexual hierarchies. Rather, it has begun to generate debates about the most productive ways of conceptualizing race, class, gender, and sexuality; about the nature of their relationships to one another; and about their manifestations in everyday life (see, e.g., Collins et al. 1995, 491–513; West and Fenstermaker 1995, 8–37).

The scholarship has been characterized more by diversity of content and commonalities in perspective than by competing or conflicting interpretations. Perhaps these common themes arise because the field is young and the research and writing has come primarily from women of color and other marginalized groups who share an "outsider within" perspective (Collins 1991). Although inside the academy by virtue of their status as professors, writers, researchers, and scholars, these groups also have an outsider's view of the knowledge that the academy has produced because they are women of color, come from working-class backgrounds, and/or are gays and lesbians. Much of the new scholarship follows the tradition established by early writers who made women of color the center of attention, describing their everyday lives. Seeing the world through the eyes of oppressed groups raises new questions about our preconceived notions of many aspects of social reality—from the social relations of domestic work to what it takes to be a "good" mother to the American Dream that talent and hard work will produce material success (Dill 1988; Glenn 1992; Hochschild 1995; Rollins 1985).

At the same time that it questions traditional scholarship and interpretations of the lives of oppressed as well as dominant groups, the scholarship on race, class, gender, and sexuality also tends to avoid grand theorizing about the essential natures of these hierarchies. Scholars instead emphasize that these social constructs cannot be understood outside of their contexts in the real lives of real people. And, in part, because examining race, class, gender, and sexuality simultaneously forces one to acknowledge the multiple angles of vision that are brought to bear in any social situation, scholars in the field are reluctant to put forth a single unifying theory of the dynamics of these processes (Collins 1990).

Some of the dominant themes in the new scholarship, which are also emerging in gender, sexuality, and race scholarship, can be broadly subsumed under the label of social constructionist theories and in recent work on "multiracial feminism" (Baca Zinn and Dill 1996). They emphasize the historical and social contingencies of these dimensions and, to some extent, their macro social structural character and their basis in power relations (cf. Brod and Kaufman 1994; Connell 1985, 1995; Frankenberg 1993; Omi and Winant 1994; Thorne 1993; West and Fenstermaker 1995; West and Zimmerman 1987).

COMMON THEMES IN RACE, CLASS, GENDER, AND SEXUALITY SCHOLARSHIP

I have identified six common themes in this new scholarship. Five of them describe the way that race, class, gender, and sexuality are conceptualized as systems of oppression; the sixth is an epistemological assumption.

Contextual

Race, class, gender, and sexuality are contextual. Although they persist throughout history, race, class, gender, and sexuality hierarchies are never static and fixed, but constantly undergo change as part of new economic, political, and ideological processes, trends, and events. Their meanings vary not only across historical time periods, but also across nations and regions during the same period. Because race, class, gender, and sexuality must always be understood within a specific historical and global context, research tends to avoid the search for common meanings that would apply to all times and all places.

For example, in the post–Civil Rights era in the United States, the racial signifiers "Latino/a," "Asian American," "People of Color," and "Native American" developed when people from different cultures, tribes, and national origins were treated as a single racial group by a dominant culture that failed to recognize differences among "racial" ethnic groups. Many members of these groups subsequently organized politically to resist their joint oppressions, and out of those political movements new racial identities were forged (Omi and Winant 1994). These labels did not exist before the 1960s, and even today some people identify with them and others do not, signifying the fluid, political, historically specific, and social meaning of race.

Additionally, during the mid-nineteenth century, dominant cultural conceptions of femininity became associated with the warm, personal, "private" sphere of home, whereas masculinity became associated with the cold, "public" sphere of the labor market. As Carol Tavris (1992, 265) notes:

> People began to attribute to inherent male and female characteristics what were actually requirements of their increasingly separate domains. Thus, women were expected to provide warmth, nurturance, and care, and forgo achievement; men were expected to provide money and success, and forgo close attachments. The masculine ideal, tailored to fit the emerging economy, was to be an independent, self-made, financially successful man. Masculinity now required self-control: no gaudy displays of emotion; no weakness; no excessive self-indulgence in feelings. Femininity required, and soon came to embody, the opposite.

Despite the pervasiveness of these images, numerous race, class, and gender scholars have noted that not *all* women and men were included in these ideals of masculinity and femininity. Men of color were not extended a family wage, and women of color were already in the paid labor market, doing domestic work, other low-wage service work, or agricultural work. Further, the ideal traits held up for men and women of color contrasted sharply with those for white women and men. For example, after Reconstruction the ideal dominant culture image of the "good" African American man was the Sambo image: a happy-go-lucky, silly, and stupid person who was often afraid of the dark (Goings 1994). The image provided a justification for slavery and at the same time reduced the perceived physical and sexual threat posed by real African American men. The Mammy image was the female parallel to Sambo: a happy asexual slave who so loved the master's family—and slavery itself—that she would willingly give over her life to the care and nurturance of slave-owning white families (Collins 1990; Goings 1994). As the ideal white man was strong, independent, and emotionless, Sambo—like white women—was weak, dependent, and full of emotion. White women were to nurture their families, whereas emotionally strong Mammies could have no families of their own, just as they could have no sexuality. In sum, the meanings of masculinity and femininity are differently constructed throughout history for different social groups through social processes that produce and maintain a racialized, classbound, heterosexist patriarchy.

Socially Constructed

Race, class, gender, and sexuality are social constructs whose meaning develops out of group struggles over socially valued resources. The dominant culture defines the categories within race, gender, and sexuality as polar opposites—white and black (or nonwhite), men and women, heterosexual and homosexual—to create social rankings: good and bad, worthy and unworthy, right and wrong (Lorber 1994). It also links these concepts to biology to imply that the rankings are fixed, permanent, and embedded in nature. That is, dominant groups define race, gender, and sexuality as ranked dichotomies where whites, men, and heterosexuals are deemed superior. Dominant groups justify these hierarchies by claiming that the rankings are a part of the design of nature—not the design of those in power. Subordinate groups resist the binary categories, the rankings associated with them, and the biological rationales used to justify them. Critical examination of either process—polarizing or biologizing—reveals that race, gender, and sexuality are based neither in polar opposites nor in biology but are social constructs whose meanings evolve out of group struggles (Garnets and Kimmel 1991; King 1981; Lorber 1994; Omi and Winant 1994).

When we say that race, gender, and sexuality are social constructs, not fixed biological traits, we also mean that we cannot *fully* capture their meaning in everyday life in the way that social scientists often attempt to do by employing them as variables in traditional quantitative research. When race, gender, and sexuality are treated as discrete variables, individuals are typically assigned a single location along each dimension, which is defined by a set of presumably mutually exclusive and exhaustive categories. This practice reinforces the view of race, gender, and sexuality as permanent characteristics of individuals, as unchangeable, and as polarities—people can belong to one and only one category. The practice cannot grasp the relational character, the historical specificity, or the conflicting means that arise in everyday life (Omi and Winant 1994). "Mixed race" people, for example, often have no place in the schemas provided. And what of the people who see themselves as bisexual or as heterosexual at one time of life and gay or lesbian at another?

The case of social class provides an instructive contrast to race, gender, and sexuality ideologies. The dominant ideology of social class is that it is not binary, polarized, or biological. Instead, the United States is seen as having an open economic system where talent and hard work—not inherited physical traits—are the primary determinants of one's economic location (Hochschild 1995). Our system is not seen as polarized between rich and poor, capitalists and workers, or middle and working classes. Rather, it is viewed as a continuous ladder of income and resources, where people can slide up and down based on their own efforts and abilities—not on their biology (Vanneman and Weber Cannon 1987). In the final analysis, the real power of the middle and upper classes is reinforced through this ideology as well as through the race, gender, and sexuality ideologies because all obscure the forces that underlie the social hierarchy. In the case of social class, however, unfair hierarchy is obscured by referring to ability and effort rather than by referring to biological superiority. Social class ideology disavows biology and categorical binaries, yet justifies hierarchy and dominance nonetheless. The case of social class makes very clear that ideologies are created to justify hierarchies and need not be based in binaries or biology, nor need they be internally consistent or logical. To justify the power and control of the dominant group, ideologies of dominance develop in different ways over time and in different social contexts and can rest on fundamentally very different—even seemingly contradictory—beliefs.

For over a century, social expectations of women's work and family roles, for example, have been rationalized by the biological fact that women can bear children. Middle-class mothers who stay at home to care for their children are often viewed by the dominant culture as "good mothers," yet poor women who do the same are viewed as lazy or "welfare queens." How can women's reproductive capacities prescribe their roles as mothers when we have different expectations for mothers of different classes, races, and sexual orientations?

Furthermore, the biological relationship of women to children is far more complex than ever before and is even now being challenged as a basis for legally defining motherhood. Today, when women and men have so many different biological and social relationships to their children, the courts are increasingly being asked to mediate questions of who should rear children. Consider the following "mothers":

- *traditional mothers:* women who have a genetic, gestational, and legally sanctioned social relationship to the child
- *lesbian mothers:* women whose biological relationship may be the same as that of traditional mothers, yet whose legal status as mothers is often challenged because of their sexual orientation
- *surrogate mothers:* either genetic mothers who provide an egg, but do not bear the child; or gestational mothers (as in the case of Baby M) who have no genetic relationship to it, but bear the child
- *social mothers:* foster mothers, adoptive mothers, or "other" mothers who have no direct genetic or gestational relationship to the child, but play a significant role in raising the child (cf. Collins 1990).

Each of these ways of mothering is constructed in race, class, gender, and sexual hierarchies that prescribe the meanings attached to them and shape the legally prescribed rights of these mothers to rear children. Chesler (1986, 280) discusses why we have the phenomenon of surrogate mothers at all:

> Racism is the issue, and why thousands of babies are "unsuitable" (for adoption). Ownership is the issue, and the conceit of patriarchal genetics. "Barren women" are the issue, and why some women must come to feel an excruciating sense of failure because they cannot bear a child. . . . And guilt and money, and how women can earn both, are the issues that need honest attention.

Race, class, gender, and sexuality are social constructions that are constantly undergoing change both at the level of social institutions and at the level of personal identity. They are not fixed, static traits of individuals, as is implied when they are treated either as biological facts or as categorically fixed variables in a research model. They are, however, deeply embedded in the practices and beliefs that make up our major social institutions. The permanence and pervasiveness they exhibit illustrate their significance as major organizing principles of society and of personal identity.

Systems of Power Relationships

Perhaps the single most important theme is that race, class, gender, and sexuality are historically specific, socially constructed hierarchies of domination—they are power relationships. They do not merely represent different lifestyle preferences or cultural beliefs, values, and practices. They are power hierarchies in which one group exerts control over another, securing its position of dominance in the system, and in which substantial material and nonmaterial resources—such as wealth, income, or access to health care and education—are at stake (Baca Zinn and Dill 1996; Connell 1987, 1995; Glenn 1992; Vanneman and Weber Cannon 1987; Weber 1995; Weber, Hancock, and Higginbotham 1997; Wyche and Graves 1992). Race, class, gender, and sexuality are thus fundamental sources of social conflict among groups.

The centerpiece of these systems is the exploitation of one group by another for a greater share of society's valued resources. That they are based in social relationships between dominant and subordinate groups is key to understanding these systems. There can be no controlling males without women whose opinions are restricted; there can be no valued race without races that are defined as "other"; there can be no owners or managers without workers who produce the goods and services that the owners own and the managers control; and there can be no heterosexual privilege without gays and lesbians who are identified as "abnormal" or as "other."

Race, class, gender, and sexuality are not just rankings of socially valued resources—who has more income or prestige. They are power relationships—who exerts power and control over whom (Baca Zinn and Dill 1996; Connell 1987, 1995; Glenn 1992; Griscom 1992; Kahn and Yoder 1992; Vanneman and Weber Cannon 1987; Weber 1995; Weber et al. 1997; Yoder and Kahn 1992)? The groups that have power in a social system influence the allocation of many types of resources. In one sense, then, the procurement of socially valued resources can be seen as the end product—the spoils to the victors—of struggles for power. To maintain and extend their power and control in society, dominant groups can and do use the resources that they command. So socially valued resources, such as money and prestige, accrue to those in power and, once procured, serve as tools for maintaining and extending that power into future social relations.

Although scholars studying race, class, gender, and sexuality tend to see them as power relations, this perspective is not universally accepted. Ethnic approaches to race (cf. Glazer and Moynihan 1975), gradational perspectives on class (reviewed in Vanneman and Weber Cannon 1987), sex/gender differences, and gender roles (for a review, see West and Fenstermaker 1995), and moral or biological approaches to sexual orientation all conceive of these dimensions as differences that are not ultimately power based. Differences between women and men, gays and straights, and among racial and ethnic groups are taken as primarily centered in women's and men's social roles and in cultural variations in traditions such as food, clothing, rituals, speech patterns, leisure activities, child-rearing practices, and sexual practices.

These perspectives often downplay or ignore the very real struggles over scarce resources that accompany location in these different groups. A similar tradition in the field of stratification—the gradational approach—sees class inequality as represented by relative rankings along a scale of prestige or income (a ladder image), not by the struggle between opposing groups for scarce resources (for reviews see Lucal 1994; Vanneman and Weber Cannon 1987). In the gradational perspective, no oppositional relationships exist between positions on a scale; it is a continuum along which some people have more than others.

Perhaps because race, class, gender, and sexuality studies primarily emerged from the experiences and analyses of groups who face multiple dimensions of oppression, and perhaps because power relationships are simply much more apparent when more than one dimension of inequality is addressed, the cultural difference, gradational, or ranking perspective is almost nonexistent in race, class, gender, and sexuality studies. The view that power relations are central is almost universal.

Looking at the *relational* nature of these systems of inequality rather than the differences in rankings of resources that accompany these systems forces us to focus on privilege as well as on oppression. Because the one cannot exist without the other, any analysis of race, class, gender, and sexuality must incorporate an understanding of the ways in which the privilege of dominant groups is tied to the oppression of subordinate groups. Consequently, the scholarship in this field has begun to explore the social constructions of whiteness (cf. Frankenberg 1993; McIntosh 1995; Roediger 1991), of masculinity (cf. Brod and Kaufman 1994; Connell 1995; Messner 1992), and of heterosexual privilege (Giuffre and Williams 1994; Rich 1980).

Social Structural (Macro) and Social Psychological (Micro)

Race, class, and gender relations are embedded and have meaning at the micro level of individuals' everyday lives as well as at the macro level of community and social institutions. To grasp the significance of race, class, gender, and sexuality in society, we must examine their meaning in both contexts. In fact, a key aspect of such analyses involves explicating the linkages between broad societal level structures, trends, and events and the ways in which people in different social locations live their lives. In the last twenty-five years, for example, U.S. society has undergone major shifts in the distribution of wealth, income, jobs, and housing and in the health status of its people. Race, class, gender, and sexuality power relations structure the ways in which these societal trends develop and play out among different groups of people.

Macro social structural trends are often represented analytically as a set of lifeless statistics about different populations. When we look at statistics summarizing national trends in economic or health indicators, for example, it is difficult to know exactly what they mean for the way people live their lives. But when we closely follow the everyday lives of a group of people, we can learn how they live with financial constraints, how they feed their families, how they deal with the stresses they face, how they manage work and family life, how they stay healthy.

It is in families and individual lives where race, class, gender, and sexuality scholarship has made perhaps its most important contributions. This work has begun to identify the ongoing struggles of subordinate groups to resist negative and controlling images of their group—to resist internalizing the limits to self-esteem, self-valuation, and collective identity imposed by the dominant group (cf. Bookman and Morgen 1987, Collins 1990; Comas-Diaz and Greene 1994; Weber et al. 1997).

Because of the distorted images of subordinate groups that pervade society's institutions such as education and the media, subordinate groups are viewed by many as weak human beings who passively accept—and even deserve—a lesser share of society's valued resources. However, subordinate groups actively resist oppression and devaluation in numerous ways every day. Although, as a consequence of their location in subordinate social locations, they often lack institutional power, subordinate group members can and do use other forms of personal power and collective action to resist unfair treatment and to struggle for group power. Daily acts of resistance can range from the individual psychological process of rejecting negative group images and affirming positive group images to group activities designed to produce social change. Acts of resistance also range from passive forms such as work slowdowns or excessive and carefully planned use of sick leave (to ensure maximum disruption of the workplace) to active measures such as public protests, marches on Washington, strikes, or violence (Bookman and Morgen 1987). For example, through public protest and persistent demand for civil rights laws, which made racial discrimination in education, housing, employment, and other areas of society illegal, African Americans were able to shift greater educational and economic opportunity and earning power in their direction.

Although the barriers of oppression are material and ideological, the resources associated with one's social location in the matrix of dominance and subordination are both material and psychological (Collins 1990; Weber et al. 1997). Nonmaterial psychosocial resources have important consequences for social and psychological well-being that in turn affect one's ability to secure material resources. Psychosocial resources associated with one's social location include positive feelings of well-being and self-respect that result from a strong connection to and identity with a group of people who share a common history and life experiences (Comas-Diaz and Greene 1994). Developing a positive identity and feelings of self-respect is easier for dominant groups whose own experiences serve as the public model for how all people should live their lives. Because social institutions such as schools are structured to support the white middle class, such children are usually raised in families with greater access to resources to help them succeed in school. They enter school with greater expectations for success; teachers expect their success and, therefore, give them more attention. Teachers' positive orientations enhance the children's sense of self-worth, thus further improving their performance and their chances for school success (Oakes 1985; Ornstein and Levine 1989; Polakow 1993).

Occupying a subordinate location in the race, class, gender, and sexuality systems, however, does not necessarily equate with a lack of psychosocial resources (Comas-Diaz and Greene 1994). Working-class, Latino/a children, for example, growing up in the barrio may develop such intangible resources if they are surrounded by loving family members and neighbors who convey a sense of each child's special worth as an individual and as a Latino/a. And this psychosocial resource can serve as the foundation for a healthy defense against negative or rejecting messages from the dominant society. Resistance to the pressures of structured inequality within subordinate group communities can, in fact, be a psychosocial resource that can be used in a collective struggle against oppression and in a personal journey toward self-appreciation and good mental health.

The key aspect of dominance, then, is not whether people have access to psychosocial resources but whether the social order supports or constrains people's development. The concept of hegemonic ideologies refers to beliefs about what is right and proper, which reflect the dominant group's stance and pervade society. Controlling images refer to dominant culture beliefs about subordinate groups; these images serve to restrict their options and to constrain them. Although society has many conceptions of working women, for example, only one is hegemonic, taking precedence over other conceptions and serving as the standard against which the value or worth of all other conceptions of working women is measured.

When you hear the phrase "today's working woman" mentioned in the media or in a popular magazine, what kind of woman comes to mind? In all likelihood, no matter what your race, class, gender, or sexual orientation, you think of a white, heterosexual, professional woman working hard in a position of some power in the labor force. She is most likely married, but if she is single, she is certainly young. This image of today's working woman is not only atypical, it is antithetical to the reality of work for most women today. Only 28.7 percent of working women are in professional, managerial, or administrative positions, and many of those hold little real power in the workplace (U.S. Bureau of Labor Statistics 1995).

Why would such an atypical image come to mind? Because this image is the dominant, hegemonic conception of working women. It represents the image of the most powerful race, class, and sexual orientation group of women. It is grossly overrepresented in the media, because it is set up as the model, the ideal against which other working women are to be judged. By its repeated presentation in the media (e.g., most women seen on television are white, middle-class, professional women), the image distorts the public perception, leaving the impression that the attainment of positions of power among women is far more possible than is actually the case. By masking the true nature of race, class, gender, and sexuality oppression, the image helps to preserve the status quo. The image further sets up a standard for judgment that most women cannot attain. If they come to believe that their failure to measure up is a result of their personal limitations—a lack of talent, desire, or effort—they internalize the oppression. If, on the other hand, they are aware of the dominant belief system nature of and the structural barriers to attaining the "ideal," they resist internalizing the oppression and have the potential for self-definition and self-valuation, a process critical to the survival of oppressed groups.

To comprehend the human agency, resilience, creativity, and strength of oppressed group members, one must view the actions and motivations of subordinate group members through their own lenses, not through the lenses of the controlling images of the dominant culture. Recognition of the history of subordinate group resistance helps to counter the cultural myths and beliefs in the dominant culture that the subordinate place of these groups is a "natural" aspect of society.

Race, class, gender, and sexuality scholarship has clarified the notion of internalized oppression, as well as the processes within communities that enable them to survive and the individuals within them to define themselves, value themselves, and build community solidarity (Collins 1990; Weber et al. 1997). The Civil Rights movement, racial and ethnic pride, gay pride, and women's movements are collective manifestations of resistance to negative and controlling images of and structures constricting oppressed groups. Interestingly, the American labor movement has been too weak and invisible to provide a positive counterimage that workers can employ to resist oppression.

Simultaneously Expressed

Race, class, gender, and sexuality simultaneously operate in every social situation. At the social level, these systems of social hierarchies are connected to each other and are embedded in all social institutions. At the individual level, we each experience our lives and develop our identities based on our location along all dimensions, whether we are in dominant groups, subordinate groups, or both.

That almost all of us occupy both dominant and subordinate positions and experience both advantage and disadvantage in these hierarchies means that there are no pure oppressors or oppressed in our society. Thus, race, class, gender, and sexuality are not reducible to immutable personality traits or other seemingly permanent characteristics. Instead, they are social constructions that often give us power and options in some arenas while restricting our opportunities in another.

From this principle we cannot argue that we are all oppressed or that our oppressions can simply be added up and ranked to identify the most oppressed group or the most victimized individuals. We cannot say that disadvantage on any two dimensions is the same as on any other two. No simple mathematical relationship can capture the complexity of the interrelationships of these systems. And yet recognizing that each of us simultaneously experiences all of these dimensions—even if one is foregrounded in a particular situation—can help us see the often obscured ways in which we benefit from existing race, class, gender, and sexuality social arrangements, as well as the ways in which we are disadvantaged. Such an awareness can be key in working together across different groups to achieve a more equitable distribution of society's valued resources.

The final characteristic describes a common epistemology of race, class, gender, and sexuality scholarship.

Interdependence of Knowledge and Activism

Race, class, gender, and sexuality scholarship emphasizes the interdependence of knowledge and activism (Baca Zinn and Dill 1994, 1996; Collins 1990). These analyses developed as a means of understanding oppression and of seeking social change and social justice. The "truth value" or merit of this knowledge depends on its ability to reflect back to social groups their experiences in such a way that they can more effectively define, value, and empower themselves to seek social justice.

When we think of race, class, gender, and sexuality as historically specific, socially constructed power relations that simultaneously operate at both macro and micro levels, a more complex set of questions arises from analyses of a single dimension. The following is an example from everyday life that illustrates the simultaneous impact of these hierarchies on a fundamental social identity in the United States today.

RACE, CLASS, GENDER, SEXUALITY AND THE CONSTRUCTION OF MASCULINITY

Consider how masculinity is differently defined by and for heterosexual, white, middle-class males and for other groups of men, such as gays, working-class white men, and men of color. When you hear about such groups as the Michigan Militia or the Ku Klux Klan, you likely think of white working-class men. If you hear of the Crips or the Bloods, you likely think of black or Latino working-class, male gang members. Research by Kathleen Blee (1991) on *Women of the Ku Klux Klan* and by Karen Joe and Meda Chesney-Lind (1995) on female gang members has clearly documented that women are active participants in both worlds. Nonetheless, in the dominant culture ideology, these worlds are almost exclusively associated with working-class men.

How is masculine identity socially constructed for working-class males? The dominant culture portrays men in these groups as valuing physical strength, aggressive behavior, and dominance over women and as devaluing emotional sensitivity and intellectual development.

Consider now the dominant image of white professional/middle-class males. These men are deemed superior based on their positions of power and authority in the labor force, by their financial or material wealth, by their intellectual prowess and knowledge, and, increasingly today, by their emotional sensitivity—but *not* by their physical strength or aggressiveness.

In the popular documentary *Hoop Dreams* (Marx, Gilbert, Gilbert, and James 1994) and in Michael Messner's (1992) *Power at Play: Sport and the Problem of Masculinity,* we see the difference in how schools steer athletically talented working-class men toward careers in athletics. Sports represent a career that fits with racialized conceptions of what is suitable for working-class men. And because they represent one of the few legitimate avenues for upward social mobility, sports careers are sought by the working-class and lower-class men—despite the almost insurmountable odds against making a lifelong career in sports. Only 6 percent or 7 percent of high school football players ever play in college, and only 2 percent of eligible college football or basketball athletes ever sign a professional contract. The chances of attaining professional status in a sport are 4 in 100,000 for a white man, 2 in 100,000 for a black man, and 3 in 1,000,000 for a U.S.-born Latino (Messner 1992, 45).

Athletically talented, white, middle-class men, in contrast, are steered into college to achieve the academic credentials to work in the middle class—as professionals, owners, managers, or administrators. Athletics are seen as a way of building positive character traits, such as competitiveness, camaraderie, and determination, and of providing valuable avenues for social networking in the middle class. Sports are almost never considered as a career in themselves.

The dominant conception of masculinity in capitalist economies portrays "real men" as those who have power in the economic realm, where ownership, authority, competitiveness, and mental—not physical—labor are valued. Physical strength or physically aggressive behavior is not a valued method of maintaining power and control.

Sports do, however, serve an important role in constructing masculine identities for the many men who play them. As Messner's (1992) research shows, sport is an institution created by and for men. Misogyny and homophobia, as exhibited in extremely derogatory language toward women and gay men in the context of sports, serve as bonding agents for heterosexual men by separating them from anything "feminine." Expressing strong antigay sentiments enables men to be intimate without being sexual. And objectifying women through derogatory language enables men to be sexual without being intimate, a process that fits with maintaining a position of control over women and men of lower status in the race, class, gender, and sexuality hierarchies (Messner 1992).

In sum, many masculinities operate in the United States today. What it means to be a man—or a woman, a husband or a wife, a father or a mother—depends on one's *simultaneous* location in the race, class, gender, and sexuality hierarchies.

CONCLUSIONS

This conceptual framework for understanding race, class, gender, and sexuality can support our teaching by guiding the content we select for classes, the questions we bring to the analysis of course readings and materials, and the ways in which we promote positive interaction across race, class, gender, and sexuality hierarchies in the classroom. First, it provides a framework for conceptualizing and assessing the diverse readings that currently constitute courses on gender and diversity. To convey the complexities of these intersections we need to select course content—readings, lectures, films—that highlights the intersections of multiple dimensions of oppression. Providing students with a set of themes to help them review the diverse materials they read can be a useful pedagogical tool.

Second, rather than providing a set of answers, I hope these themes raise some questions and issues to consider in our analyses of social reality. I am increasingly convinced that the most important tools we bring to the analytical process are the questions we ask.

Race, class, gender, and sexuality are contextually rooted in history and geography. Ask how the dynamics we study might vary in different places and at different times. It is important to take account of the histories and global contexts of particular groups to understand their current situations. Taking a broad historical and global view also enables us to see the tremendous changes that have taken place in each of these systems over time and the diversity across social geography and thus to recognize the potential for change in situations we face every day.

These systems are socially constructed, not biologically determined. Ask if gender and race are taken to determine how people should act out of some notion of biological or social imperative. Is seeing gender or race as an immutable fact of people's lives either privileging them or relegating them to certain inferiority? How might we view a situation differently if someone of a different race, class, gender, or sexual orientation were in it?

The race, class, gender, and sexuality systems operate at the social structural (macro) and the social psychological (micro) levels. When we analyze a particular social event, the interpersonal and psychological manifestations of oppression are often more readily apparent. The broad macro level forces that shape events are more remote and abstract and are, therefore, more difficult to see. Ask about those structures.

In looking at the case of white male backlash against affirmative action, for example, we can easily see angry white men out to push back gains made by women and people of color and to maintain their position of power and control. We can dismiss them as "oppressors" or bad people. When we ask about the broader race, class, gender, and sexuality forces that shape this situation, however, we also see that the recent decline in our economy has rendered many white men vulnerable to loss of jobs, income, and health. White men's anger in part comes out of their different expectations—out of their sense of privilege. If we are to collaborate to achieve economic change that benefits most people, we must recognize the ways in which many white men, as well as other people, are vulnerable in the present economy.

These systems are simultaneously experienced. All operate to shape everyone's lives at all times. Ask about all of the systems in every situation. Although one dimension may appear to be in the foreground, go beyond the obvious and ask about the less visible dimensions.

Make the connection between activism for social justice and the analyses you conduct. Ask about the implications for social justice of the perspectives you employ, the questions you ask, and the answers you obtain. Does the analysis provide insights that in a political context would likely serve to reinforce existing power relations? Or does it illuminate processes of resistance or avenues for self-definition or self-valuation that could transform the race, class, gender, and sexuality hierarchies? How might people in different social locations react to and employ this analysis? To what ends?

Race, class, gender, and sexuality hierarchies are power relationships. Always ask who has the socially sanctioned power in this situation. What group gains and what group loses? Try not to confuse personal power with social power. Individuals can be powerful by virtue of their insight, knowledge, personalities, and other traits. They can persuade others to act in ways they want. But personal power can be achieved in spite of a lack of socially sanctioned power. It is the power that accrues from occupying a position of dominance in the race, class, gender, and sexuality hierarchies that enables large numbers of people in similar locations to have privileges/advantages in a situation. And it is their systematic and pervasive embeddedness in all our major institutions that makes race, class, gender, and sexuality such critical systems to understand.

Finally, when we change the content that we teach to be more inclusive and to address the complexities of race, class, gender, and sexuality, we need to change our pedagogy as well. Learning about diversity is most likely to take place when classroom interactions and activities promote positive intergroup interaction across race, class, gender, and sexuality. Themes in the scholarship suggest some strategies for shaping positive classroom dynamics across difference.

That race, class, gender, and sexuality are socially constructed, not fixed traits of individuals, means that we cannot accept group membership as a guarantee of the privileged knowledge or experience of any dominant or subordinate group member in our classes. The socially constructed nature of these dimensions means that the experiences and perspectives that students have—for example, even in the same racial group—vary by their age and the region and community they grew up in, as well as by their gender, class, and sexual orientation.

Acknowledging the diversity of experiences among our students need not, however, lead to an unfettered relativism that denies the significance of group membership or the greater impact of some dimensions than others on life chances and options. Because we recognize that power is the foundation on which these systems rest, we must acknowledge the differential power that dominant and subordinate groups wield in the classroom as well as in society at large. Members of dominant groups are less likely to know about subordinate groups and are more likely to rely on stereotypes (Fiske 1993), speak in class, receive eye contact, have their opinions correctly attributed, and have their contributions shape group responses to tasks (cf. Webster and Foschi 1988). Teaching strategies that acknowledge these tendencies and contradict them can upset the normative balance of power in the classroom and can increase understanding. They include ground rules to guide classroom discussion; introductions of students that acknowledge their race, ethnicity, and other statuses while identifying them as unique individuals; equal time for talking; and group projects (see Weber Cannon 1990 for discussion).

Having students address the simultaneity of race, class, gender, and sexuality can help them to understand that there are no pure oppressors nor oppressed people, and that each of them must reflect on their own privilege as well as their experiences of oppression. They cannot deny their privilege or claim absolute victim status. Recognizing their own multiple locations can open them to the complexities in the lived realities and experiences of others.

And finally, the interdependence of knowledge and activism that is central to race, class, gender, and sexuality scholarship suggests that certain kinds of learning activities can be especially effective. Active learning projects, particularly those that involve students in working together toward solutions to social problems, are especially likely to engage students and to facilitate positive group interaction.

NOTES

1. Although many scholars still refer to this growing field of study as race, class, and gender studies, I include sexuality because, as I argue, these structures of inequality and the meanings they engender are socially constructed in historically specific time frames and regional locations. Their meanings are not fixed, immutable, or universal but instead arise out of group struggles over socially valued resources, self-determination, and self-valuation. In recent years, the mass movement of gays, lesbians, and bisexuals for social power and self-determination has precipitated significant scholarly attention to sexuality. Our growing awareness and understanding of the pervasiveness and comprehensiveness of the system of compulsory heterosexuality has begun to place it at the center of political and intellectual attention along with race, class, and gender as essential elements in a comprehensive understanding of contemporary human social relationships and psychological processes. To date, however, the scholarship on sexuality is much less developed than work addressing the other dimensions, and race, class, and gender research is only beginning to integrate this new dimension.

REFERENCES

Amaro, H., and N. F. Russo, eds. 1987. Hispanic women and mental health: Contemporary research and practice [Special issue]. *Psychology of Women Quarterly* 11(4).

Andersen, M., and P. H. Collins. 1995. *Race, class, and gender: An anthology.* Belmont, CA: Wadsworth.

Anzaldúa, G. 1987a. *Borderlands/la frontera: The new mestiza.* San Francisco: Spinsters/Aunt Lute.

———., ed. 1987b. *Making faces, making soul/haciendo caras: Creative and critical perspectives by women of color.* San Francisco: Spinsters/AuntLute.

Baca Zinn, M., and B. T. Dill. 1994. *Women of color in U.S. society.* Philadelphia: Temple University Press.

———. 1996. Theorizing difference from multiracial feminism. *Feminist Studies,* 22: 321–331.

Baca Zinn, M., L. Weber Cannon, E. Higginbotham, & B. T. Dill. 1986. The costs of exclusionary practices in women's studies. *Signs: Journal of Women in Culture and Society* 11: 290–303.

Barale, M., and D. M. Halperin, eds. 1993. *The lesbian and gay studies reader.* New York: Routledge.

Blee, K. M. 1991. *Women of the Klan: Racism and gender in the 1920s.* Berkeley: University of California Press.

Bookman, A., and S. Morgen. 1987. *Women and the politics of empowerment: Perspectives for the workplace and the community.* Philadelphia: Temple University Press.

Brod, H., and M. Kaufman. 1994. *Theorizing masculinities.* Thousand Oaks, CA: Sage.

Cade, T., ed. 1970. *The Black women.* New York: Signet.

Chesler, P. 1986. *Mothers on trial: The battle for children and custody.* New York: McGraw-Hill.

Chow, E. N., D. Wilkinson, and M. Baca Zinn. 1996. *Race, class, and gender: Common bonds, different voices.* Thousand Oaks, CA: Sage.

Collins, P. H. 1990. *Black feminist thought: Knowledge, consciousness, and the politics of empowerment.* New York: Routledge.

———. 1991. Learning from the outsider within: The sociological significance of Black feminist thought. In *Beyond methodology: Feminist scholarship as lived research,* ed. M. M. Fonow and J. A. Cook, 35–59. Bloomington: Indiana University Press.

Collins, P. H., L. A. Maldonado, D. Y. Takagi, B. Thorne, L. Weber, and H. Winant. 1995. Symposium on West and Fenstermaker's "Doing difference." *Gender & Society* 9: 491–513.

Comas-Diaz, L., and B. Greene. 1994. *Women of color: Integrating ethnic and gender identities in psychotherapy.* New York: Guilford.

Connell, R. W. 1985. Theorising gender. *Sociology* 19: 260–72.

———. 1987. *Gender and power: Society, the person, and sexual politics.* Stanford: Stanford University Press.

———. 1995. *Masculinities.* Berkeley: University of California Press.

Cyrus, V. 1993. *Experiencing race, class, and gender in the United States.* Mountain View, CA: Mayfield.

D'Emilio, J., and E. Freedman. 1988. *Intimate matters: A history of sexuality in America.* New York: Harper & Row.

Dill, B. T. 1988. Our mother's grief: Racial ethnic women and the maintenance of families. *Journal of Family History* 13: 415–31.

———. 1983. Race, class, and gender: Prospects for an all-inclusive sisterhood. *Feminist Studies* 9: 131–50.

———. 1979. The dialectics of Black womanhood. *Signs: Journal of Women in Culture and Society* 4: 543–55.

Fiske, S. T. 1993. Controlling other people: The impact of power on stereotyping. *American Psychologist* 48: 621–28.

Frankenberg, R. 1993. *The social construction of whiteness: White women, race matters.* Minneapolis: University of Minnesota Press.

Garnets, L., and D. Kimmel. 1991. Lesbian and gay male dimensions in the psychological study of human diversity. In *Psychological perspectives on human diversity in America,* ed. J. Goodchilds, 143–89. Washington, DC: American Psychological Association.

Giuffre, P. A., and C. L. Williams. 1994. Boundary lines: Labeling sexual harassment in restaurants. *Gender & Society* 8: 378–401.

Glazer, N., and D. P. Moynihan, eds. 1975. *Ethnicity: Theory and experience.* Cambridge, MA: Harvard University Press.

Glenn, E. N. 1992. From servitude to service work: Historical continuities in the racial division of paid reproductive labor. *Signs: Journal of Women in Culture and Society* 18: 1–43.

Goings, K. 1994. *Mammy and Uncle Moses: Black collectibles and American stereotyping.* Bloomington: Indiana University Press.

Greene, B. L. 1994. Lesbian and gay sexual orientations: Implications for clinical training, practice, and research. In *Lesbian and gay psychology: Theory, research, and clinical application,* ed. B. Greene and G. M. Herek, 1–24. Thousand Oaks, CA: Sage.

Griscom, J. L. 1992. Women and power: Definition, dualism, and difference. *Psychology of Women Quarterly* 16: 389–414.

Higginbotham, E., and L. Weber. 1992. Moving up with kin and community: Upward social mobility for Black and White women. *Gender & Society* 6: 416–40.

Hochschild, J. 1995. *Facing up to the American dream: Race, class, and the soul of the nation.* Princeton: Princeton University Press.

hooks, b. 1981. *Ain't I a woman.* Boston: South End Press.

Hull, G., P. B. Scott, and B. Smith, eds. 1982. *All the women were White, all the Blacks were men, but some of us are brave: Black women's studies* Old Westbury, NY: Feminist Press.

Joe, K. A., and M. Chesney-Lind. 1995. "Just every mother's angle": An analysis of gender and ethnic variations in youth gang membership. *Gender & Society* 9: 408–31.

Kahn, A. S., and J. D. Yoder, eds. 1992. Women and power [Special issue]. *Psychology of Women Quarterly* 16: Whole No. 4.

King, J. 1981. *The biology of race.* Berkeley: University of California Press.

Loewenberg, B. J., and R. Bogin, eds. 1976. *Black women in the nineteenth-century life.* University Park: Pennsylvania State University.

Lorber, J. 1994. *Paradoxes of gender.* New Haven: Yale University Press.

Lucal, B. 1994. Class stratification in introductory textbooks: Relational or distributional models? *Teaching Sociology* 22: 139–50.

Magner, D. 1996 (September 16). Fewer professors believe western culture should be the cornerstone of the college curriculum. *Chronicle of Higher Education* A12–A15.

Marx, F., J. Gilbert, P. Gilbert, (Producers), and S. James, (Director). 1994. *Hoop dreams* (Film). (Available from Facets Video, 1518 W. Fullerton, Chicago, IL 60614)

McIntosh, P. 1995. White privilege and male privilege: A personal account of coming to see correspondences through work in women's studies. In *Race, class, and gender: An anthology,* ed. M. Andersen and P. H. Collins, 6–86. Belmont, CA: Wadsworth.

Messner, M. 1992. *Power at play: Sports and the problem of masculinity.* Boston: Beacon.

Oakes, J. 1985. *Keeping track: How schools structure inequality.* New Haven: Yale University Press.

Omi, M., and H. Winant. 1994. *Racial formation in the United States from the 1960s to the 1990s.* New York: Routledge.

Ornstein, A. C., and D. U. Levine. 1989. Social class, race, and school achievement: Problems and prospects. *Journal of Teacher Education* 40: 17–23.

Polakow, V. 1993. *Lives on the edge: Single mothers and their children in the other America.* Chicago: University of Chicago Press.

Rich, A. 1980. Compulsory heterosexuality and lesbian existence. *Signs: Journal of Women in Culture and Society* 5: 631–60.

Rollins, J. 1985. *Between women: Domestics and their employers.* Philadelphia: Temple University Press.

Rodgers-Rose, L., ed. 1980. *The black woman.* Beverly Hills, CA: Sage.

Roediger, D. 1991. *The wages of whiteness: Race and the making of the American working class.* London: Verso.

Rothenberg, P. S. 1995. *Race, class, and gender in the United States: An integrated study.* New York: St. Martin's Press.

Tavris, C. 1992. *The mismeasure of woman.* New York: Touchstone.

Thorne, B. 1993. *Gender play: Girls and boys in school.* New Brunswick, NJ: Rutgers University Press.

U.S. Bureau of Labor Statistics. 1995. *Employment and earnings* Vol. 45. Washington, DC: U.S. Government Printing Office.

Vanneman, R., and L. Weber Cannon. 1987. *The American perception of class.* Philadelphia: Temple University Press.

Weber Cannon, L. 1990. Fostering positive race, class, and gender dynamics in the classroom. *Women's Studies Quarterly* 17: 126–34.

Weber Cannon, L., E. Higginbotham, and M. Leung. 1988. Race and class bias in qualitative research on women. *Gender & Society* 2: 449–62.

Weber, L. 1995. Comment on "Doing difference." *Gender & Society* 9: 499–503.

Weber, L., T. Hancock, and E. Higginbotham. 1997. Women, power, and mental health. In *Women's health: Complexities and differences,* ed. S. Ruzek, V. Olesen, and A. Clark, 380–96. Columbus: Ohio State University Press.

Webster, M., Jr., and M. Roschi. 1988. *Status generalization: New theory and research.* Palo Alto: Stanford University Press.

West, C., and S. Fenstermaker. 1995. Doing difference. *Gender & Society* 9: 8–37.

West, C., and D. H. Zimmerman. 1987. Doing gender. *Gender & Society* 1: 125–51.

Wyche, K. F., and S. B. Graves. 1992. Minority women in academia: Access and barriers to professional participation. *Psychology of Women Quarterly* 16: 429–38.

Yoder, J. D., and A. S. Kahn. 1992. Toward a feminist understanding of women and power. *Psychology of Women Quarterly* 16: 381–88.

CHAPTER 8

Rethinking Social Class

Qualitative Perspectives on Class and Gender

DIANE REAY

In this article I argue that class continues to be an important part of social identity into the millennium despite a range of prevailing discourses which constitute it as irrelevant. At the same time, objective economic conditions constitute just one aspect of class rather than providing us with a comprehensive picture of the impact of social class in contemporary society (Prandy and Bottero 1995; Prandy and Blackburn 1997). Limiting class debates to the purely economic sphere results both in the marginalization of women and a neglect of the myriad ways in which social class differences contribute to social inequalities. Drawing on data from a qualitative study of mothers' involvement in their children's education, I illustrate how class remains an integral part of mothers' subjectivities and continues to powerfully influence their actions and attitudes. I argue through my data that, regardless of whether we see ourselves in class terms, class just as much as race, gender, age, and sexuality shapes, and goes on shaping, the individuals we are and the indinduals we become. I conclude that we need to rethink social class as a dynamic mobile aspect of identity that continues to permeate daily interactions despite its marginalization in prevailing contemporary discourses.

Academic class debates, whether conducted by men taking the "conventional" stance that women's social class is mediated through their relationships with men (Goldthorpe 1980, 1983; Lockwood 1986; Goldthòrpe and Marshall 1992), other men seeking to modify or replace that stance, or feminists contesting the status quo (Stanworth 1984), are all taking place in, and around, the "male" territory of the labor market. Even contemporary research which argues for the inclusion of women in classifications of social class works exclusively with women as employees in the labor market (Lampard 1995; Evans 1996). As Helen Roberts's review of the debates surrounding social class over the last two decades makes clear, the focus is firmly rooted in a view of social class as one of location; an issue of where you are situated, rather than the processes that got you there (Roberts 1993). This labor market focus neglects the key role of women in class formation. Holton and Turner point out that the continuing emphasis on occupational measurement neglects wider dimensions of social action and economic power, including any discussion of the contribution of gender to economic inequality (Holton and Turner 1994, 804). Similar criticisms are made by Breen and Rottman who argue that current debates over the relationship between class and gender challenge some of the fundamental premises through which mainstream class analysis is conducted (Breen and Rottman 1995a, 1995b).

On the evidence of critics of the conventional approach it appears that, over and above the technical problems endemic in conventional classificatory systems, simple categorization based on male labor market participation overlooks the complexity inherent in the relationship between gender and social class. A growing number of studies which look at women's relationship to class and gender inequalities (Abbort and Sapsford 1987; Cavendish 1982; Charles 1990; Coyle 1984; Skeggs 1997b; Walkerdine and Lucey 1989; Webb 1985; Westwood 1984) highlight the need to review an oversimplistic model which marginalizes women's relationship to class. Many of these studies have attempted to move beyond the boundaries of the labor market to begin to explore women's sense of class and how it is enacted in different contexts (see also Hey 1997; Reinfelder 1997).

In response to the narrow parameters of mainstream debates, and in keeping with a dissatisfaction with metanarratives more generally, feminism in the 1990s appears to have abandoned social class as an important social division (Skeggs 1995). In fact, current feminist work which examines the intersections of class and gender is almost exclusively written by feminist academics from working-class backgrounds and is not reflected in the concerns of mainstream feminisms. Nevertheless, I want to argue that we cannot walk away from class as a category because it continues, in spite of all the current arguments to the converse, to tell us something very important about *women's* and men's lives. Rather, there is a need to develop understandings that reflect rather than overlook the complexities of class in contemporary society. Pakulski and Waters (1996, 672) assert that "income inequalities have started widening in recent years after a century-long egalitarian trend"; evidence that there are growing inequalities in society that class continues to contribute to.

Although I want to argue in the rest of this paper for a view of class as social processes which break down traditional divisions between the public and the private, the family and labor market, there are powerful economic trends which also point to the continuing importance of social class. There has been a growing polarization in economic class structure over the past thirty years (Westergaard 1996). Inequalities in the area of paid work are intensifying (Rowntree 1995). Since 1980 the disposable income of the richest one-tenth of society has risen by 62 percent, while that of the poorest 10 percent has fallen by 17 percent. In the 1990s growing numbers of the middle classes were directly involved in employing the working classes. A Mintel survey conducted jn January 1997 showed that Britain would spend £4.3 billion over the course of the year on nannies, cleaners, cooks, and gardeners, four times as much as ten years earlier. However, remaining on the male terrain of structuralist analyses results in an oversimplification of what class constitutes. Class is much more than the simplistic metanarrative it is all too frequently held up to be. Before I discuss different ways of envisaging social class, I want to examine prevailing discourses on class and the ideological work that they do.

DIVERSIONARY RHETORICS: CONTEMPORARY DISCOURSES OF CLASSLESSNESS

For Jan Pakulski and Malcolm Waters, "there has been a radical dissolution of class in two senses: a decentering of economic relationships, especially property- and production-based relationships as determinants of membership, identity, and conflict, and a shift in patterns of group formation and lines of sociopolitical cleavage" (1996, 667–68). They argue (1996, 669) that class has increasingly less to say about social inequalities, which they admit "palpably persist and are even increasing despite class decomposition". Pakulski and Waters (1996, 671) argue their case, that social class is increasingly irrelevant, on the old structuralist terrain of Marxism (mixing in a bit of Weber in order to "broaden the base"): "If Weber can argue with Marx that: 'Property' and 'lack of property' are . . . the basic categories of all class situations, then this is where we should begin to examine the question of class divisions in contemporary society."

Pakulski and Waters refer to the disappearance of class discourses as an indication of the demise of class. I would contest their claim that class discourses no longer exist. Discourses of classlessness are in effect class discourses insofar as they operate in class interests. While discourses which recognize the existences of classes can operate in the interests of either the middle or the working class, both market discourses, which assert freedom of choice for all, and discourses of classlessness act in the interests of the privileged in society by denying their social advantage. As Bourdieu (1984, 483) reminds us: "The individual or collective classification struggles aimed at transforming the categories of perception and appreciation of the social world and, through this, the social world itself, are indeed a forgotten dimension of the class struggle." Dominant discourses which assert a norm of classlessness are part of this struggle.

Similarly, discourses which promote the need for a free market untrammelled by state intervention operate powerfully to privilege some classes at the expense of others. Contrary to the views of Pakulski and Waters, and Western (1995), the logic of markets does not displace the logic of class but rather masks it behind a rhetoric of freedom of choice for all. Despite the rhetoric, markets are profoundly shaped by class, culture, and consumption (Cookson 1992, 309). As Gewirtz et al. (1995) argue in relation to education, the market is a middle-class mode of social engagement. They assert that, by ignoring class interests in society, the education market acts to privilege middle-class groupings who will always be the groups most inclined to engage with the market and the best skilled and resourced to exploit it to their advantage.

Discourses of marketization and classlessness are not the only discourses which work to deny social advantage and disadvantage in society. There is a need to unpack the paradoxical elements contained within postmodernist discourses which deny "the possibility of authoritative opinions and of absolute standards of taste, and mixes aesthetics from diverse origins" (Gewirtz et al. 1995, 681). While denying authority they presume it in the delivery of their message and their attempt to institute a new orthodoxy (Baudrillard 1986). An argument can be made that they constitute yet another effective "new" middle-class strategy. There is an intrinsic deceit within discourses on popular culture which ignore the many ways in which popular culture is classed (and raced and gendered). In particular, the legitimacy and acceptance of popular culture depends on the status of the person espousing it. We only need to contrast the black working-class inner-city boy's consumption of hip-hop/rap music with that of the white public-school middle-class boy's. The former signifies very differently and is read in very different ways. Postmodern consumerist accounts "address various changes in media, style, the shift from production-orientated capitalism to an advertising- and seduction-based consumerism, etc., but they do not address the empirical question of whether in fact social relations, most basically relations of power, are undergoing fundamental transformations" (Calhoun 1995, 155).

Conceptualizing social differentiation and affiliation in terms of taste and lifestyle rather than production does not displace class but instead shifts it from the arena of production to that of consumption (Bourdieu 1984; Crompton 1993). Class relations are increasingly constructed through patterns of consumption and their associated technologies of desire (Kenway 1995). Consumption no less than production is a classed and classifying process. Bourdieu's most recent research highlights the pervasiveness of class and "race" exclusions operating through market consumption by focusing on the everyday miseries of excluded groups; the indigenous low-paid workers, the unemployed, and recent migrants to France (Bourdieu 1993).

To cite another example of discourses which operate in middle- and elite-class interests one of the most divisive exclusionary mechanisms of the 1990s was the labeling of some of the working classes, predominantly lone mothers, and their children, as an underclass; a device which operates simultaneously to strip them of their citizenship. While social subjects are not simply passively positioned in dominant discourses, and as I try to demonstrate below are actively engaged in "individual and collective self-making and sense-making" (Dehli 1996), the working classes rarely chose the discourses within which they position themselves. They are produced by the more powerful in society. While much is made of the "local" in contemporary academic writing, locally generated, working-class discourses of class lack the power to seriously challenge the imaginaries of the more powerful (Fraser 1992). Instead, they have to work with prevailing discourses of the market and individual reliance; primarily middle-class versions of social life.

THE TRIUMPH OF INDIVIDUALISM

According to Pakulski and Waters (1996, 675), the lack of any collective expression of class interests "either in terms of social and political reformation or, more prosaically, in terms of a collective effort to influence the market" is confirming evidence of the current unimportance of social class. I suggest that there are different ways to interpret the "spectacular decline" of collective action. Both the advent of "classlessness" and the lack of collective working-class action can be viewed as the product of a dominant class strategy which has been extremely successful. The pervasiveness of middle-class discourses on class within working-class groupings in society, while in part a result of changing occupational and housing structures, is also a consequence of the universalism of a media controlled by middle-class interests and the prevalence of individualistic discourses of consumerism across society. Similarly, just as Pakulski and Waters argue that the growth of trade unions during the twentieth century might be adduced as evidence of the robustness of the class structure, so their demise could be adduced to the robustness of dominant class activities through the legal system to control and restrict working-class interests.

The current orthodoxy of individualistic self-realization represents the almost universal acceptance of middle-class perspectives in society, which have replaced the collectivist inclinations of earlier eras among working-class groupings. It is difficult for working-class groups to share "the localised milieux of collective experience and opportunity out of which develop bounded lifestyles and political solidarities" (Thompson 1968) when the new social hegemony is based on individualistic consumerism. But rather than classes disappearing in response to new social discursive and material formations, they have evolved and changed. In particular, working-class groupings in society under siege from aggressive legal actions to augment the advantages of the middle classes are both in retreat and denial. They are no longer entitled to a sense of unfairness because everything from their financial situation, the state of their health, to their children's schooling, has been repackaged under late capitalism as the responsibility of the individual alone.

That fewer and fewer individuals wish to own the label "working class" is unsurprising in a period definitely post the era of "the nobility of the white manual male worker." A pervasive tendency to conceptualize middle-class experience as normative is simultaneously both a depiction of the working classes as deficient in some way and a failure to recognize the extent to which social processes are differentiated by class. In academic writing the hidden, highly politicized process of deciding who and what to write about and in what ways is elided. This subtext is masked by the seeming impartiality of the text (Pile and Thrift 1995, 371–72):

> Talk of relations of power can sometimes obscure the grinding, relentless nature of oppression and the way it forces accounts and choices which may not always be attractive to bourgeois academics. Instead of facing up to this task of description researchers have often reached for fantasies of otherness which, in classic post colonial terms, trap the colonised in the fantasies of the coloniser and which therefore play right into the hands of prevailing relations of power by silencing other actual or potential speaking positions. This effect is probably most clearly seen nowadays in the dumping overboard by many ambiguous academics of the "white working class," a strategy which closes down the task of description and also avoids more difticult emotions.

In 1990s Britain, to be working-class is increasingly to accept "a spoilt identity" (Reay and Ball 1997). Goffman, writing thirty years ago, describes how working-class people were:

> likely on occasion to find themselves functioning as stigmatised individuals, unsure of the reception awaiting them in face-to-face interaction and deeply involved in the various responses to this plight. This will be so if for no other reason than that almost all adults have to have some dealings with service organisations, both commercial and civil, where courteous, uniform treatment is supposed to prevail based on nothing more restrictive than citizenship, but where opportunity will arise

> concern about invidious expressive valuations based on a virtual middle class ideal. (1968, 173)

The new market economy in education has exacerbated social distinction of class. Not only in middle-class interviews but also in some working-class parents' own accounts they are presented as a stigmatized group (Reay and Ball 1997). As Calhoun argues, socially sustained discourses about who it is appropriate or valuable to be inevitably shape the way we look at and constitute ourselves (Calhoun 1995, 213). Working-class groupings in society have limited options. They can either accept their "spoilt identity" or reject the label "working class." At the same time, to claim middle-class status is not the same as inhabiting a middle-class identity (Reay 1997a).

NEW WAYS OF ENVISIONING CLASS?

Quantitative surveys premised on socioeconomic categorization need to be complemented by qualitative studies which explore what class means for individuals in the 1990s and the ways in which they act out class in their daily interactions. To view class simply as metanarrative clearly has no future, but that is not the only way in which class has been, and increasingly is, conceptualized (Bradley 1996; Morgan 1996; Ribbens 1992). Class is part of the micropolitics of people's lives. It is lived in and through people's bodies and permeates their thinking as powerfully as gender, "race," age, and sexuality (Kuhn 1995; Reay 1997a; Wolfe 1994). Beverley Skeggs (1997a, 134) writes about "the emotional politics of class, a politics of dis-identification, a result of classifying practices enacted on a daily basis by many of those who do not think class is an issue."

Yet, despite a pervasive denial of the continuing importance of class, class just as much as gender, age, sexuality, and ethnicity, infuses daily interactions; influencing to whom we talk and shaping what we say and how we say it (Reay 1997c). Pakulski and Waters (1996, 680) assert that "interpersonal exploitation and exclusion" based on class is disappearing. I would contest the view that overt discriminatory class practices are a thing of the past in contemporary "classless" society. Exclusionary devices are just as prevalent in the 1990s (Noden et al. 1997) as they were in the 1930s and their consequences infuse working-class lives. It is the ways in which they are manifested that have shifted and mutated. Current educational research has revealed an increasing middle-class policing of class boundaries (Gewirtz et al. 1995), which has resulted in the growth of educational segregation based on both class and ethnic divisions (Bagley 1996; Reay 1996).

While we need to question the extent to which collective class consciousness ever existed, class has always been both a social filter and a key mechanism individuals utilize in placing themselves and others, regardless of whether a majority of the population identify in class terms. It is this simultaneously wider and deeper conceptualization of social class that I want to argue for; a view of class as powerfially internalized and continually played out in interaction with others across social fields. There are parallels with "race." Within feminism black feminists have argued strongly that, despite whiteness remaining an unspoken taken-for-granted for white women (Frankenberg 1993; Collins 1990; Mirza 1997), it powerfully influences actions and attitudes. The fading away of class claims, in an era where claims-based politics are being replaced by discourses which center individual reliance (Bakker 1996), does not mean class, as a constantly changing aspect of identity, does not continue to influence actions and attitudes across society.

Current qualitative feminist research explores how class influences interweave with those of gender, "race," ethinicity, and sexuality (Mahony and Zmroczek 1997). Rather than such work "deemphasizing gender and racial inequality" (Pakulski and Waters 1996, 684), it attempts to examine the contribution of sexuality, "race," and social class to the construction of female and male identities (Reynolds 1997; Pyke 1996). Claims of the demise of class are grounded in static notions of what class constitutes. Recent poststructuralist feminist writing works with a conception of class as historically specific. What it means to be middle- or working-class, black or white, female or male shifts and changes, not only from one historical era to another, but for individuals over time as they negotiate the social world. Understandings of class need to be much broader than the economic; they need to integrate sociological and psychological perspectives with conventional views.

CLASS VERSIONS: RECOGNIZING CLASS IN INDIVIDUAL LIVES

As Bourdieu points out, "We must classify the classifiers" (1992, 242), and I would add "the declassifiers." Constructing groups in certain ways is a process underpinned by political as well as economic interests (Fowler 1996). Academic texts are always middle-class versions, my own account no less than those of the always middle-class (Lynch and O'Neill 1994). To assert working-class status within the academy is to inhabit a contradictory location. It also constitutes a denial of privilege. Academics, regardless of where they are positioned on the academic ladder, are a privileged social group. As I have written elsewhere, therein lies the dilemma of middle-class education for the working classes; the double-bind (Reny 1997b). It is collusion and complicity such as mine that provides the working classes with mobility. But just as academic success constitutes a failure to hold on to working-class values and attitudes, so remaining working-class is about failing to achieve the power to contribute to dominant discourses—or even marginal ones. It is about having to continually negotiate a social world suffused with others' versions of who you are. The working classes lack public forums in which to give their own accounts.

One consequence is that the working classes rarely have their own authoritative history of working-class oppression, just fragments from the past. I suggest that this lack of any historical analysis of class processes, and concomitantly elite and middle-class domination and working-class resistance, contributes to a pervasive working-class inability to construct an authentic working-class identity in the 1990s. Instead of the noble working class hero of the postwar 1950s when dominant discourses called for "homes fit for heroes," we now have the spoilt 1990s identities of white and black working-class boys and men (Goffman 1968). In the light of media coverage it is difficult not to feel that, for boys and men in particular, any toolkit of cultural resources has disappeared with the manufacturing industries (Bennett

1996; Cohen 1996; Moore 1996; Wainwright 1996). Increasingly for some groups of black and white working-class males the only thing that seems to be valued about oneself are testosterone-induced performances of macho masculinity (Pyke 1996). Similarly, one of the most divisive exclusionary mechanisms of the 1990s is equally gendered. I have already referred to the labeling of some of the working classes, predominantly lone mothers and their children, as an underclass. It is important to reiterate that the working classes do not chose the dominant discourses within which they have to position themselves.

Although the working classes have always been heterogeneous, fractured by divisions of gender, "race," and position in the labor market, new generations of the white working classes lack access to the broader collectivist cultures that many of their parents and grandparents grew up in. Any sense of heritage is denied them in the bleak 1990s discursive landscape. It is a terrain in which to be working-class is increasingly to be "not good enough," and there are no longer politicizing scripts of class oppression to counter the prevalence of views that it is all their own fault (Skeggs 1997b). Individualism has always worked much better for the middle than the working classes. I would contend that contemporary discourses of marketization, consumerism, and individualism, far from providing evidence of the demise of class, operate extremely successfully to ensure dominant class hegemony. However, despite a pervasive denial of class status, there are emotive intimacies of class which continue to shape individuals' everyday understandings, attitudes, and actions. These become very apparent when mothers talk about their involvement in their children's schooling.

CLASS TALK: MOTHERS MAKING SENSE

In this section I draw on data from a qualitative study of mothers' involvement in their children's education in order to illustrate how cultural identity has a specificity powerfully influenced by class positioning. The research was conducted in two London primary schools. Milner is a multiethnic, predominantly working-class school in inner London. Oak Park, three miles to the north of Milner, has a largely white, middle-class intake. My sample of thirty-three women reflected the maternal population in the two schools and constituted a diverse group of black, white, and mixed-race working- and middle-class women. One-third of my sample were lone mothers, while the rest were either cohabiting or married to their male partners. I carried out lengthy in-depth interviews at least once with all of the mothers, but most mothers were interviewed twice and a third three times over the eighteen-month period of the fieldwork.

My research looked at gender inequalities operating within families in relation to involvement in children's schooling (Reay 1995a). While earlier work looked at children's perspectives (Reay 1995b; 1995c), this article concentrates on the perspectives of the mothers. However, within a focus on mothers I wanted to examine the impact of differences among women on their relationship to their children's schooling, in particular how differences of "race," ethnicity, social class, and marital status influenced mothers' involvement (Reay 1998). Below I focus specifically on class influences. A qualitative focus does not preclude class categorization. I collected data on women's own educational histories and those of their partners and their parents; housing status; income level; women's, their partners', and their parents' occupations, as well as asking them to self-identify in class terms in order to build up a detailed picture of their class position. If the objective class criteria were confirmed by women's own self-definitions I have referred to them as either "working-" or "middle-class" in the text. Those women who were either ambivalent about attributing a class label to themselves or defined themselves in ways which contradicted objective criteria I refer to as occupying a contradictory class positioning and discuss in greater detail below. However, the emphasis on class is informed by a recognition of the ways in which social class, gender, and "race" "amplify, twist, negate, deepen and complicate each other" (Connell et al. 1982, 182). Class no less than gender, "race," and sexuality is constituted through difference.

> You'd never think from what you see on the telly and what you read in the newspapers that any decent people lived around here. You know, we're all rubbish. We don't care about our kids, we live in pig sties and if you're bringing up kids on your own then it's even worse. Don't they know there are a lot of good people out there in the inner city like me doing their best. (Lisa, white working-class lone mother)

> FRANCES: Melinda couldn't possibly go to Weedon. It is typically, well it's not typically for handicapped children but it does take a lot of low ability children.
>
> DIANE: You mean children with special educational needs.
>
> FRANCES: I suppose I mean inner city children, children who have got a lot of discipline problems. The discipline there is terrible. (white, middle-class, married mother)

Here we see how both mothers attempt, in very different ways, to make sense of the same pathologizing dominant class discourse. Throughout the two-hour interviews I conducted with Lisa and Frances neither referred directly to social class, utilizing instead euphemisms such as "inner city," and in Frances's account, "rough elements" and "children from families who don't care," which clearly carried class connotations. Yet, their narratives are suffused with understandings of themselves as classed, which are powerfully influenced by their very different social-class locations. Class may not be on the surface, part of contemporary simulacra, but it still lurks beneath the surface.

Mothers are also working with binaries of good/bad parent, which are primarily class constructions:

> Because you're deprived, because you haven't got the funds to give children the best education then they're deprived of it, so well if you haven't got the money yourself then I don't think you can expect much . . . and you end up letting your kids down. (Maria, white working-class lone mother)

Initially, Pamela, a white middle-class married mother, told me:

> I don't think supporting your child's education has really got anything to do with resources. I think the important thing, what matters is that you are there for your child, that you give them quality time.

But she goes on to elaborate a process of involvement which requires dominant cultural capital and is costly in terms of time and transport:

> Any mother can find the time to take her child to the library or visit a museum. I mean most museums are free to get into.

Although a majority of mothers did not mention social class until I asked them to self-identify in class terms, they continually drew on distinctions of "people like us" and "people unlike us" in order to differentiate between themselves and others (Bourdieu 1990). Most of the working-class mothers and those from working-class backgrounds who now saw themselves as either middle-class or "classless" used a rhetoric of "people like us," which set up a contrasting, more privileged other in their narratives to explain why they may be denied the academic success they desired for their children. Anita, a black lone mother from a working-class background, who had qualified as a school nurse, told me:

> What hopes have the likes of me got? It's parents like the ones at the school I work in who have got a choice. I work in the school and have to deal with them. They expect to get what they want. You should hear some of them talk to me, as if I was nothing, just a servant, or else they are friendly in a really condescending way. When the Government talks about parents it means parents like that.

Anita, who described herself as "once working-class but not any longer," repeatedly sets up in her text a contrastive rhetoric between herself and more privileged others that is powerfully influenced by class.

Christine was similarly ambivalent about her social-class positioning and told me when I asked her whether she would call herself working-class or middle-class:

> I don't like to think in terms of social class. It's all very difficult for me. I mean I don't think we have classes any more. I mean working-class was like when we had manual workers. I'm not sure you can call women working-class, except I suppose if they're cleaners or what. I suppose . . . well I'm not working-class any more and I'm not middle-class either. To be honest I think we're all classless now.

Both Christine's parents were manual workers but she is now credentialed and works as a beauty therapist. Yet, despite Christine's belief that she has transcended the influences of her working-class background, this is not borne out in her account of her relationship to her son's schooling:

> I really want him to achieve his full potential, but it's all so scary. I think things have changed a great deal from when I was at school and from talking to you with your experience in education you've got a much better idea of how it all works. For me, it's all rather confusing because I didn't get that far and neither did Brendan. I would like him to have those chances but I need help to find out about them. I just feel at the moment, I don't know what it is, but I feel incapable. There are certain aspects I feel I don't know enough about. Maybe it's because I work and am so busy but I feel I haven't got the stomach to tackle them. You know sometimes I can't even cope with asking other people, "What was it like for you, how did you tackle it?' I talk to my sister, I talk to Elaine whom I work with, but their children are only just coming up to the GCSE stage. It seems to me that if you've got knowledge of how the system works then you're looking ahead. A bit of me thinks why shouldn't he go to Oxford or Cambridge. But there are certain courses you should take and people like me just don't know.

Christine's words are imbued with a sense of powerlessness in relation to the educational system. Her sense of helplessness is embodied as well as psychological. She "hasn't got the stomach" to tackle things and for the most part feels ambivalent, anxious, and disenfranchised. The lack of fit between a habitus still powerfully influenced by her working-class past and the middle-class field of education generates a lack of confidence and a sense of incapacity. Although Christine no longer displays "the resignation of the inevitable" (Bourdieu 1984, 372) characteristic of working-class habitus, she still lacks the "self-certainty" of middle-class habitus (Bourdieu 1984, 66). Christine's material resources do not make up for her lack of psychological and social resources. She talks in terms of a "scary" educational system and feels unable to "cope" with asking for necessary information. She actually states that she "feels incapable."

Classes have always been to a greater or lesser degree fluid entities with movement at the edges (Bourdieu 1988). Both Anita and Christine occupy contradictory class positionings. Unlike most of the women who had grown up working-class they are now credentialed and identify, respectively, as "no longer working-class" and as "classless." However, class imagery permeates their understandings of home-school relationships. Implicit in Christine's, Anita's, and many of the working- and once working-class women's texts was a recognition of the uncertain, shifting territory they occupied; an educational landscape of "maybe" and "perhaps" where personal history shaped current consciousness and where there were none of the "taken-for-granted" certainties of conventional middle-class horizons. It is through such class processes to everyday sense making that we need to filter our theoretical understandings of class.

Class not only influences attitudes but also impacts on mothers' actions in support of children's schooling. Middle-class mothers' texts frequently demonstrated a clear intention to ensure advantaged circumstances for their own children; "pushing their children and pushing for their children in school" (Bratlinger et al. 1996, 589):

> There used to be two Special Needs teachers and he saw Mrs. Webster regularly and every term he was told he had graduated, his reading was good enough for him to stop and every term I went in and said "Oh, no it isn't. He needs it. You get him back in there." The Head would say to me "Well, I've got other children who are worse," and I'd have to say "I'm not worried about other kids that are worse. I'm worried about my child and he needs it." Other parents have got to fight for their children. But don't tell me my child is behind and needs help but because he's not one of the worst don't bother about him. Can you believe it? She told me they only give special support to children in years 3 and 4 because if they haven't caught up by then they are not going to and it's just tough. (Ruth, white, middle-class mother)

But it was not tough for Martin because Ruth's persistence and unswerving belief in her son's entitlement to scarce educational resources meant that he continued to receive one-to-one special needs support, even though officially he did not qualify for the provision because his reading age was above his chronological age.

Processes of ensuring class advantage often operated concurrently as practices of class exclusion. Only one of the middle-class mothers used the term "the right sort of girl" when justifying her preference for a selective secondary girls' school but encoded in other middle-class mothers' references to "wanting her to go somewhere where she will fit in" and, "It's important that there aren't children who will hold her back," are similar sentiments. Class preferences are simultaneously class exclusions in which middle-class mothers' preferences are for predominantly middle-class schools. Working-class mothers have to negotiate these middle-class preferences from their own position of being socially less powerful. As a result their desire for the "best" schooling for their children is infused with ambivalence:

> I did think it would be nice for her to go to Royden Girls'. I know it's got a very good reputation but then again I thought what if the other girls think she's not good enough to be there. (Betty, white working-class partnered mother)

Elaine, a working-class mixed-race married mother, discussing the same high status girls secondary school said:

> Well, after I had a chat with my mum I did think it might be difficult for Cerise to go thcre. It's a bit posh isn't it.

Juxtaposed with the attitudes of Frances, quoted above, the views of Betty and Elaine and the actions they led to (both mothers decided against Royden Girls, choosing instead a local mixed comprehensive) can be understood as tactics of working-class social survival in a class hierarchized society. Similarly, a wide range of middle-class women's activities in support of children's schooling, from ensuring their placement in top groups to insistence on a curriculum that prepared children for selective state and private school entrance exams, were also "class actions."

CONCLUSION

Educational restructuring in the 1990s co-opts and works through processes of gender, "race," *and* social class (Hey 1996). In this article I have juxtaposed contemporary academic discourses which marginalize the ways in which social class contributes to social identities with the everyday sense-making of mothers. As is evident in mothers' words and actions, mothers do and redo class on a daily basis. Their local discourses, without once mentioning class, draw powerfully on class imagery in order to make sense of the contemporary educational marketplace. Their consumption of education is also shaped by class (Allatt 1996), indicating some of the myriad ways in which "consumer behaviour is linked back into status, exchange, social transition, social class hierarchy etc." (Warde 1994, 896).

We need new ways of understanding class in which production and consumption are woven together to reveal the complex strands that make up class in contemporary society (Allart 1996). Class is a complicated mixture of the material, the discursive, psychological predispositions, and sociological dispositions that quantitative work on class location and class identity cannot hope to capture. Pierre Bourdieu has pointed us in the right direction utilizing both quantitative and qualitative methods in order to understand class inequalities in contemporary France (Bourdieu 1984, 1993). Now what is required are British-based ethnographic examinations of how class is "lived" in gendered and raced ways to complement the macro versions that have monopolized our ways of envisaging social class for far too long.

REFERENCES

Allatt, P. 1996. *Consumption matters.* Edited by Stephen Edgell. London: Sage.

Abbott, P. A., and R. J. Sapsford. 1987. *Women and social class.* London: Tavistock Publications.

Bagley, C. 1996. Black and unite or fight? The racialised dimension of schooling and parental choice. *British Educational Research Journal* 22:569–80.

Bakker, I., ed. 1996. *Rethinking restructuring: Gender and change in Canada.* Toronto: University of Toronto Press.

Baudrillard, J. 1986. Forgetting Baudrillard. *Social Text* 15: 140–44.

Bennett, C. 1996. The boys with the wrong stuff. *The Guardian,* 6 November 1996.

Bourdieu, P. 1984. *Distinction.* London: Routledge and Kegan Paul.

———. 1988. *Homo academicus.* Cambridge: Polity Press.

———. 1990. *The logic of practice.* Cambridge: Polity Press.

———. 1992. *Language and symbolic power.* Cambridge: Polity Press.

———. 1993. *La misere du monde.* Paris: Seuil.

Bradley, H. 1996. *Fractured identities: Changing patterns of inequality.* Cambridge: Polity Press.

Bratlinger, E., M-J Massoumeth, and S. L. Guskin. 1996. Self-interest and liberal educational discourse: How ideology works for middle-class mothers. *American Educational Research Journal* 33: 571–97.

Breen, R., and D. Rottman. 1995a. *Class stratification: A compararive perspective.* London: Harvester Wheatsheaf.

———. 1995b. Class analysis and class theory. *Sociology* 29: 453–74.

Calhoun, C. 1995. *Critical social theory.* Oxford: Blackwell.

Cavendish, R. 1982. *On the line.* London: Routledge and Kegan Paul.

Charles, N. 1990. Women and class—A problematic relationship? *Sociological Review* 38: 43–89.

Cohen, D. 1996. It's a guy thing. *The Guardian,* 4 May 1996.

Collins, P. H. 1990. *Black feminist thought.* London: HarperCollins.

Connell, R. W., D. J. Ashenden, S. Kessler, and G. W. Dowsett. 1982. *Making the difference.* Sydney: George Allen and Unwin.

Cookson, P. W. 1992. The ideology of consumership and the coming deregulation of the public school system. *Journal of Education Policy* 7: 301–11.

Coyle, A. 1984. *Redundant women.* London: Women's Press.

Crompton, R. 1993. *Class and stratification: An introduction to current debates.* Cambridge: Polity.

Dehli, K. 1996. Between "market" and "state"? Engendering education change in the 1990s. *Discourse: Studies in the Cultural Politics of Education* 17: 363–76.

Evans, G. 1996. Putting men and women into classes: An assessment of the cross-sex validity of the Goldthorpe Schema. *Sociology* 30: 209–34.

Fowler, B. 1996. *Pierre Bourdieu and cultural theory: Critical investigations.* London: Sage.

Frankenburg, R. 1993. *The social construcrion of whiteness: White women, race matters.* London: Routledge.

Fraser, N. 1992. The uses and abuses of French discourse theories for feminist politics. In *Cultural theory and cultural change,* ed. M. Featherstone. London: Sage.

Gewirtz, S., S. J. Ball, and R. Bowe. 1995. *Markets, choice, and equity in education.* Buckingham: Open University Press.

Goffman, E. 1968. *Stigma: Notes on the management of a spoilt identity.* London: Pelican Books.

Goldthorpe, J. H. 1980. *Social mobility and class structure in modern Britain.* Oxford: Clarendon Press.

———. 1983. Women and class analysis. *Sociology* 17: 465–88.

Goldthorpe, J. H., and G. Marshall. 1992. The promising future of class analysis: A response to recent critiques. *Sociology* 26: 381–400.

Hey, V. 1996. "A game of two halves"—A critique of some complicities: Between hegemonic and counter-hegemonic discourses concerning marketisation and education. *Discourse: Studies in the Cultural Politics of Education* 17: 351–62.

———. 1997. Northern accent and southern comfort: Subjectivity and social class. In *Class matters: Working class women's perspectives on social class,* ed. P. Mahony and C. Zmroczek. London: Taylor and Francis.

Holton, R., and B. Turner 1994. Debate and pseudo-debate in class analysis: Some unpromising aspects of Goldthorpe and Marshall's defence. *Sociology* 28: 799–804.

Kenway, J. 1995. Having a postmodernist turn. In *After postmodernism: Education, politics, and identity,* ed. R. Smith and P. Wexler. London: Falmer.

Kuhn, A. 1995. *Family secrets: Acts of memory and imagination.* London: Verso.

Lampard, R. 1995. Parents' occupations and their children's occupational attainment: A contribution to the debate on the class assignment of families. *Sociology* 29: 715–38.

Lockwood, G. 1986. Class, status, and gender, In *Gender and stratification,* ed. R. Crompton and M. Mann. Cambridge: Polity Press.

Lynch, C., and C. O'Neill. 1994. The colonisation of social class in education. *British Journal of Sociology of Education* 15: 307–24.

Mahony, P., and C. Zmroczek. 1997, eds. *Class matters: Working class women's perspectives on social class.* London: Taylor and Francis.

Mirza, H., ed. 1997. *Black British feminism: A reader.* London: Routledge.

Moore, S. 1996. Boorishness in a league of our very own. *The Guardian,* 30 May 1996.

Morgan, D. 1996. *Family connections: An introduction to family studies.* Cambridge: Polity Press.

Noden, P., A. West, M. David, and A. Edge. 1997. *Choices and destinations at transfer to secondary school.* Paper presented to the Market Forces Seminar, King's College, London.

Pakulski, J., and M. Waters. 1996. The reshaping and dissolution of social class in advanced society. *Theory and Society* 25: 667–91.

Pile, S., and N. Thrift. 1995. Mapping the subject. In *Mapping the subject: Geographies of cultural transformation,* ed. S. Pile and N. Thrift. London: Routledge.

Prandy, K., and W. Bottero. 1995. The social analysis of stratification and mobility. University of Cambridge: Sociological Research Group (Working Paper Series No. 18).

Prandy, K., and R. M. Blackburn. 1997. Putting men and women into classes: But is that where they belong? A comment on Evans. *Sociology* 31: 143–52.

Pyke, K. D. 1996. Class-based masculinities: The interdependence of gender, class, and interpersonal power. *Gender & Society* 10: 527–49.

Reay, D. 1995a. A silent majority: Mothers in parental involvement. *Women's Studies International Forum Special Issue* 18: 337–48.

———. 1995b. Using habitus to look at "race" and class in primary school classrooms. In *Anti-racism, culture, and social justice in education,* ed. M. Griffiths and B. Troyna. London: Trentham Books.

———. 1995c. "They employ cleaners to do that": Habitus in the primary classroom. *British Journal of Sociology of Education* 16: 353–71.

———. 1996. Contextualising choice. Social power and parental involvement. *British Educational Research Journal* 22: 581–96.

———. 1997a. Feminist theory, habitus, and social class: Disrupting notions of classlessness. *Women's Studies International Forum* 20: 225–33.

———. 1997b. The double-bind of the "working-class" feminist academic: The failure of success or the success of failure. In *Class matters: Working class women's perspectives on social class,* ed. P. Mahony and C. Zmroczek. London: Taylor and Francis.

———. 1997c. Just talking to the teacher? Habitus, cultural capital, and mothers' involvement in their children's primary schooling. Paper presented to international conference on Pierre Bourdieu. Southampton University.

———. 1998 forthcoming. *Class work: Mothers' involvement in their children's schooling.* London: University College Press.

Reay, D., and S. J. Ball. 1997. "Spoilt for choice": The working classes and education markets. *Oxford Review of Education* 23: 89–101.

Reinfelder, M. 1997. Switching cultures. In *Class matters: Working class women's perspectives on social class,* ed. P. Mahoney and C. Zmrocrek. London: Taylor and Francis.

Reynolds, T. 1997. Class matters. "Race" matters, gender matters. In *class matters: Working class women's perspectives on social class,* ed. P. Mahony and C. Zmrocrek. London: Taylor and Francis.

Ribbens, J. 1992. *Mothers and their children: A feminist sociology of childrearing.* London: Sage.

Roberts, H. 1993. Women and the class debate. In *Debates in sociology,* ed. D. Morgan and L. Stanley. Manchester: Manchester University Press.

Joseph Rowntree Foundation 1995. *Inquiry into income and wealth.* York.

Skeggs, B. 1995. Introduction. In *Feminist cultural theory: Process and production,* ed. B. Skeggs. Manchester: Manchester University Press.

———. 1997a. Classifying practices: Representations, capitals, and recognitions. In *Class matters: Working class women's perspectives on social class,* ed. P. Mahony and C. Zmrocrek. London: Taylor and Francis.

———. 1997b. *Formations of class and gender.* London: Sage.

Stanworth, M. 1984. Women and class analysis. *Sociology* 18: 159–70.

Thompson, E. P. 1968. *The making of the English working class.* Harmondsworth: Penguin.

Wainwright, M. 1996. Chalk and cheesed. *The Guardian,* 23 April 1996.

Walkerdine, V., and H. Lucey. 1989. *Democracy in the kitchen: Regulating mothers and Socializing Daughters.* London: Virago.

Warde, A. 1994. Consumption, identity-formation, and uncertainty. *Sociology* 28: 877–98.

Webb, S. 1985. *Counter arguments: An ethnographic look at women and class.* University of Manchester, Dept. of Sociology: Studies in Sexual Politics.

Westergaard, J. 1996. Class in Britain since 1979: Facts, theories, and ideologies. In *Conflicts about class: Debating inequality in late industrialisation,* ed. D. J. Lee and B. S. Turner. London: Longman.

Western, B. 1995. Union decline in eighteen advanced Western countries. *American Sociological Review* 60: 2.

Westwood, S. 1984. *All day every day: Factory and family in the making of women's lives.* London: Pluto-Press.

Wolfe, S. 1994. Getting class. In *Out of the class closet: Lesbians speak,* ed. J. Penelope. California: The Crossing Press.

CHAPTER 9

Parenting in Black and White Families

The Interaction of Gender with Race and Class

SHIRLEY A. HILL AND JOEY SPRAGUE

A central focus in the feminist analysis of gender has been understanding how gender is socially constructed, perpetuated, and passed on to children. Families are held to be the first agents of gender socialization; they not only pass gender norms on to children explicitly but also organize work, roles, and identities along gender lines (Chodorow 1978; Johnson 1988; Lytton and Romney 1991;Weitzman 1979). By age four or five, children have learned to prefer the behaviors and activities deemed appropriate for their sex (Bem 1983). In a summary of previous studies on gender differences in socialization, Block (1983) reported that parents typically emphasize achievement, competition, independence, and education more for sons, whereas daughters are expected to be kind, loving, well-mannered, and have good marriages. So, while it is understood that the construction of gender is an active, ongoing process throughout the life course (West and Zimmerman 1987), we also know that it is important to understand the specific construction of gender in childhood.

There is reason to ask whether the idea of gender socialization might be racially specific and may not apply to African American families. For example, scholars have argued that the gender roles prescribed by the dominant white society have never been fully institutionalized among black people because of the way race shapes social positions (Collins 1990; King 1988). Some have pointed out that a relative degree of gender neutrality exists in the socialization of black children (Lewis 1975; Ferguson Peters 1988; Reid and Trotter 1993), especially arguing that black girls are taught from an early age to be independent, strong, and resourceful (Collins 1990; Dill 1988; Scott 1993). Yet, the evidence with regard to these assertions is sketchy and inconsistent.

The literature on African Americans includes themes that imply conflicting claims about gender socialization in black families. Claims of assimilation to the dominant culture suggest African Americans will communicate hegemonic gendered expectations to children. Afrocentrists, on the other hand, maintain that the African heritage and American experience have curtailed the development of patriarchy and strict gender norms among blacks. Multicultural feminist theory may resolve the conflict. In arguing that the impact of race on gender varies by class, multicultural feminist theory implies that both assimilationism and Afrocentrism may be overgeneralizing from specific intersections of race and class.

We review what is claimed and what is known about racial diversity in gender arrangements and about gender socialization in African American families. Then we examine one set of indicators of gender socialization in families at diverse intersections of race and class. We look at parents' reports of immediate priorities and long-term goals for children, their view of the parenting role, and their discipline strategies, and whether these vary when talking about a son or a daughter.

RACE AND THE CONSTRUCTION OF GENDER

During the 1960s, gender was problematized in contrasting ways for white and black families. White feminists argued that the traditional Eurocentric conceptualization of gender was harmful, particularly the marginalized, secondary roles assigned to women and the notion of women as innately domestic, dependent, and submissive (see Weitzman 1979). Black women, on the other hand, pointed out that the Eurocentric ideology of patriarchal families and separate spheres for men and women had never become a tradition in their families. They argued that the history of labor force participation of African American women militated against full-time domesticity as the norm for black women, as did the fact that black families were often headed by women or organized around female-centered kinship networks (Jones 1985; Stack 1974). Racial discrimination and exclusion, on the other hand, presented significant barriers to black men in their attempt to become the sole economic provider for their families, and their inability to fulfill this role diminished their power, esteem, and participation in families (Ladner 1971; Stack 1974).

The failure of low-income black families to conform to dominant notions of gender was seen by some as pathological, a view that was popularized in a controversial study published by Moynihan in 1965. Moynihan attributed the perpetuation of racial inequality in the United States to blacks' confusion about gender roles, which, he said, undermined the stability of their families. In his opinion, the economic roles and authority of black men had been usurped by black women, who, freed from male control through work or welfare, had illegitimate children and ran families. Moynihan described black women as matriarchs and black men as weak and ineffective, and he suggested that black males would benefit by enlisting in the armed forces, "a world away from women, a world run by strong men of unquestioned authority" (1965, 42).

The burgeoning black family literature of the era challenged the Moynihan thesis by arguing that women were perfectly capable of heading families, that women's efforts inside and outside the home had been vital to the survival of black families, and that the broader roles of women had reduced the importance of gender in the organization of family work and in child socialization strategies (Hill 1972; Lewis 1975).

The widely held view of relative gender neutrality or equality among blacks, however, is based more on the experiential reflections of a few people than on systematic research. It rests heavily on the fact that black women often combine economic and family roles, with less analysis of whether these behaviors express ideological convictions or are solely the result of economic necessity. What research exists tends to focus on selected groups of women, especially those who are poor and/or single mothers, revealing little about how other factors, such as social class, affect gender ideologies. Most studies continue to view blacks as a monolithic group, despite evidence of growing social class diversity (Billingsley 1992).

One of the most glaring deficiencies in studies of gender among African Americans has been the failure to include the experiences of men. Black males have only rarely been accorded the esteem or power associated with masculinity in the broader society or patriarchal privileges that result from being the primary breadwinners for their families. Although there has been a proliferation of research on black women, usually emphasizing traditions of strength and independence among women (Collins 1990; Dill 1988; Giddings 1984; King 1988), little can be said about the contention of gender neutrality among blacks when men are absent from the equation. As Hunter and Davis (1992) have pointed out, it is tacitly assumed that whereas adversity and oppression led black women to forge strong, multidimensional roles, these same factors essentially stripped black men of the prerogatives of manhood. Carr and Mednick (1988) have suggested that although daughters may benefit from nontraditional gender roles, such roles lessen the achievement motivation of males.

STUDYING GENDER SOCIALIZATION AMONG BLACKS

Since the late 1960s, there has been a proliferation of research on gender socialization in families, although few studies have included adequate samples of African Americans. Two perspectives-assimilationism and Afrocentrism-persist in the literature with contrasting implications for gender socialization among blacks.

The earliest research on black families was assimilationist in focus. It argued that black families, especially those who achieved middle-class status, had essentially the same attitudes and child-rearing values as white families (Davis and Dollard 1940; Davis and Havighurst 1946). The idea that black parents embrace the values and priorities of the dominant white culture, even though poverty and social inequality make adherence to those ideals difficult, persists to the present (Allen 1981; Taylor et al. 1990; Thornton et al. 1990).

Studies of gender ideologies show that blacks are more likely than whites to support the breadwinner-homemaker family (Doyle 1989), have traditional views about the male role in the family (Binion 1990), believe that married women should not be employed (Smith and Seltzer 1992), and say a woman's real fulfillment in life comes from motherhood (Lyson 1986). Empirical research also has shown that black couples divide housework along traditional gender lines (Hossain and Roopnarine 1993; Wilson et al. 1990). These studies indicate that African Americans have accepted the gender norms of the dominant society, implying that, at least by example, they will pass these norms on to their children.

A contrasting perspective, expressed largely by ethnographic researchers and Afrocentric theorists, is that, as opposed to the Moynihanian view of culture as pathology, African and African American cultural norms have been a source of strength, resiliency, and survival for black families (Billingsley 1992; Hill 1972; Stack 1974). In the Afrocentric framework, the historic participation of black women in economic work, both in Africa (Burgess 1994) and in the United States (Dill 1988), produced greater gender role equality among black males and females. Proponents argue that gender is not a crucial factor in black child socialization and only minimally affects the behaviors children are taught and the work they are expected to perform (Nobles 1985).

In an early expression of this view, Lewis argued that "the black child, to be sure, distinguishes between males and females, but unlike the white child he *[sic]* is not inculcated with standards which polarize behavioral expectations according to sex" (1975, 228). According to Lewis, all black children are taught to "mother" and are instilled with similar traits of assertiveness, willfulness, and independence. A more recent study by Scott, focusing on the difficulty of socializing girls, pointed out that African American girls "are socialized to be at once independent and assertive as well as familistic and nurturant . . . to be sexually assertive . . . to be as authoritative, individualistic and confident as African American sons are, and as economically self-sufficient and personally autonomous as sons are" (1993, 73). More recently, Peters (1988) has argued that age and competency are more likely than sex to be the basis for defining children's roles in black families.

Some research has supported this Afrocentric view of gender equality among blacks. A recent study by Hunter and Sellers (1998) reported significant attitudinal support among black men and women for gender equality and feminist ideologies, and Reid and Trotter (1993) found black children exhibited less gender stereotypical behavior than white children.

There are three major weaknesses in this literature. First, little attention is paid to the specific question of the gender socialization of children, especially by those who argue for assimilationism. Second, especially in the area of black family scholarship, there has been an inordinate focus on the roles of black women rather than black men. Yet, research has shown that black males face numerous obstacles to success (Gibbs 1988; Madhubuti 1990; Majors and Billson 1992) and find it difficult to adhere to the gender norms of white males (Blake and Darling 1994; Cazenave 1981). Third, blacks are viewed as a monolithic group, in spite of growing class diversity.

The development of multicultural feminist theory,[1] largely by black feminists and other feminists of color, has broadened feminist theory by showing that race and class shape how gender gets played out in peoples' lives. For example, capitalism and patriarchy exploit women in race- and class-specific ways (Aptheker 1989; Davis 1993; Dill 1979; Espiritu 1997; Glen 1992; King 1988; Mies 1986). Whereas economically privileged white women were being relegated to unpaid, devalued reproductive roles in the family, and working-class white women had some hope of seeing their daughters rise above their class position, African American women were being heavily exploited for their labor, first as slaves and later by their long-term concentration in menial, low-paying labor market jobs (Davis 1993; Glenn 1992; hooks 1984). The way gender and race interacted to constrain the economic opportunities of black women made it impossible for them to be defined as weak and dependent. Indeed, as Collins (1990, 67) has pointed out, the dominant culture developed a race-specific set of gendered images to control black women by distorting and demeaning their strengths.

Multicultural feminism acknowledges that both race and class inequality have shaped the gendered options of African Americans. Black women traditionally have helped provide the nurturance and material necessities for their families and, presumably, have taught their own daughters to be strong, resourceful, and self reliant (Collins 1987; Ladner 1971). Black men, especially those who are poor, often find the route to masculinity as defined by Eurocentric gender norms to be quite narrow, since they lack the economic and social power to cash in on the "patriarchal dividend" (Connell 1995) and benefit from female subordination (Dill 1988). Even at an early age, these barriers lead many poor young black males to express their "masculinity" by rejecting the importance of conventional norms like getting a good education (Fordham and Ogbu 1986) and focusing on sexuality (Anderson 1989) or "cool pose" (Majors and Billson 1992) as alternative sources of esteem. Male denigration then becomes common, especially in low-income black communities, where men are often viewed as irresponsible and unreliable (Connor 1988; Ladner 1971; Stack 1974; Wilson 1996). This view of black manhood may shape the expectations parents have for their children along gender lines. Indeed, studies have shown that low-income black parents often have higher expectations for their daughters than for their sons (Blau 1981; Hill and Zimmerman 1995; Staples and Boulin Johnson 1993). Thus, race and social class are clearly central factors in the social construction of gender opportunities and ideology. Yet, we know little about how they affect gender socialization processes in families.

Multicultural feminist theory provides a framework that resolves the competing themes of assimilationism and Afrocentrism. The questions of whether black families teach their children gendered expectations similar to those prevalent among whites becomes transformed. We are directed to ask how the sex of a child influences parents' values and parenting strategies in different intersections of race and class.

DATA

The data used in this analysis are from surveys completed by a nonrandom sample of parents of elementary school students during the 1993–1994 school year. Seven schools in two large, urban, predominantly black school districts participated in the study.[2] Students[3] in these schools carried letters to their parents explaining the study and asking them to complete and return the survey. The survey return rate ranged from 10 to 40 percent.[4] In all cases, parents were asked to focus on *one child* in completing the survey—the child who brought the survey home.[5] Parents provided some demographic data on that child and responded to a broad array of questions on their goals and strategies in rearing that child.

We excluded three surveys that did not indicate the sex of the child and analyzed the remaining 406 surveys: 202 black parents and 204 white parents.[6] Demographic details about these families are reported in the appendix. Respondents range from twenty to sixty-seven years old and are overwhelmingly women and mothers. Although grandparents and others are also among our respondents, we will call them parents, assuming that the person who completed a form brought home from school is intimately involved in caretaking; that is, we are using "parent" to indicate a social role, not a biological relationship.

Although nearly half (49 percent) of the black parents are married, blacks are more likely to be single parenting than are white respondents, 58 percent of whom are married. The average number of children per family is 2.8, but the range is wide: The largest single category for blacks and whites is two children, with 72 percent having no more than three children. The very largest families are black, with 8 percent having eight or more children. The white families have comparable numbers of children, the only striking difference being among the outliers. The children parents described in this study were fairly evenly divided between daughters (50 percent of blacks, 46 percent of whites) and sons. The children range in age from five to eighteen, with an average age of about ten years, and more were in the fifth grade than in any other.

Economic differences between blacks and whites in this sample are less a reflection of population characteristics than an expression of the way race and class interact in residential patterns, on which school districts are organized. More black parents than white parents are employed, and black parents overall have a slightly higher education than do white parents. Although black and white parents are equally likely to have completed high school, blacks are slightly more likely to have attended or graduated from college. Family incomes for this sample are roughly comparable across race. Most families have less than $30,000 a year, and more than one-third are in the lowest income bracket, earning less than $15,000 per year. Whites are somewhat more likely than blacks to earn more than $30,000 a year.

The current research compares the responses of parents who indicated they were reporting about their rearing of sons to those who indicated their target child was a daughter. Of course, what people say is not necessarily what they do in particular situations. We are assuming that these parents are making a good faith effort to report the principles that they try to follow—no doubt imperfectly—as they go about parenting on a daily basis. Our confidence in the strength of the connection between these self-reports and daily practices is increased because our questions are posed in fairly concrete terms and use categories and language drawn from the way parents have actually discussed these matters in qualitative interviews. Still, as we shall see, we have reason to suspect that at least in some cases, parents are attempting to give a socially desirable response.

Measures of Socialization Practices

The survey administered to these parents includes several questions that can be used as indicators of their approach to parenting. The survey questions, constructed specifically for this study, draw their general structure and content from the classic child-rearing studies of Kohn (1963). They also incorporate some of the issues raised in black family studies and in-depth interviews with black parents (Hill 1999). In this article, we report an analysis of responses to four items that have parallel structures. In each case, a child-rearing issue is posed and the parent is asked to rank the relative importance to him or her of three positions on that issue. Although most parents did rank order three options from 1 (their top priority) to 3 (their lowest priority), a few parents gave a rank of 1 to more than one option in a question and a few others ranked only one or two options.[7] For this analysis, we converted each response option to a dichotomous variable with a value of 1 if the respondent indicated it as a top priority and 0 in all other cases.

Two of the questions address parents' reported goals for their children. To tap long-term parenting goals or future hopes parents have for their children, we asked parents to rank the following outcomes in terms of importance: 1) getting a good education and a good job (EDJOB), 2) having a strong, loving family (FAMILY), and 3) having a kind and compassionate personality (KIND). To get a sense of current priorities, parents were asked to rank three values in terms of how important they are for the child who brought the survey home: 1) being happy and feeling good about himself or herself (HAPPY), 2) being obedient and respectful (OBEY), and 3) doing well in school (SCHOOL). The other two questions deal with approaches to parenting. To identify respondents' understanding of their own role, they were asked to rank three parental roles in terms of their importance: 1) being a teacher and guide (TEACH), 2) being a disciplinarian (DISCIPLINE), or 3) being a provider (PROVIDE). Finally, we examine discipline strategies used by asking parents to rank three discipline strategies in terms of which they relied on the most: 1) the loss of privileges (PRIVIL), 2) spankings (SPANK), or 3) the use of reason or logic (REASON).

Measures of Independent Variables

We are using the gender of the child as an indicator of gender as a causal force. To the extent that gender is being constructed through parenting practices in these families, the responses given by parents of sons will differ from those given by parents of daughters. If parents are responding more generally and not thinking of a specific child, then we should find no relationship between the gender of the child and the responses of the parent.

However, we believe it is unlikely that the gender of the child interacts significantly with any reporting discrepancies. Although parents did indicate the sex of the child they were thinking of, it was in the context of a series of demographic questions about children and their parents. The parenting questions themselves do not suggest that gender comparisons are being made. Thus, although these data, and survey data in general, cannot accurately reflect actual parenting practices, any systematic differences between parents of sons and parents of daughters can reasonably be attributed to gendered belief systems that support gendered practices.

Race is measured by self-identification in a question that offered five response alternatives (black, white, Hispanic, Asian, and other). Sex of child (SEX) is also coded by the respondent (son, daughter). Cases with missing values on RACE and/or SEX ($n = 3$) were excluded from the analysis.

Our data include two indicators of parents' class, respondent's education, and total family income, which are strongly related, $X^2(9) = 117.6$, $p = .00$, $\gamma = 0.55$. We combined information on income and education to create a three-level measure of class.[8] The modal family in the lowest class level, which we are calling "working class," includes a high school graduate and has a household income less than $15,000. The modal "lower-middle-class" family includes a parent with some college education and has an annual income of $15,000 to $30,000. The modal "upper-middle-class" family includes a college graduate and has an income of $30,000 to $50,000. There is no relationship between race and class in this residence-based sample, $X^2(2) = 0.52$, $p = .77$.

Analyses

Multicultural feminist theory leads us to predict that gender, class, and race will all have an impact on parenting goals and strategies, in interacting ways. To examine this prediction, we need to look at parents' responses by gender, class, and race. The cross tabulation of the proportion of parents placing a top priority on a particular response option by our measures of these independent variables generates a complex (2 × 2 × 3 × 2) frequency table for each of the three choices offered in each question. The predicted interactions between race, gender, and class generate still more complexity in the data.

To get a clearer picture of the effects of each independent variable, we used log linear analysis, specifying a series of logit models using direct and interaction effects of class, race, and gender (sex of child) to predict each dichotomously coded response (see Norusis 1985; Tabachnick and Fidell 1989).[9] We then looked for the model that seemed to have the best fit across the three choices for each question. We will first report the findings by question. Then, we will look at the pattern of causal relationships that seems to emerge across questions.

RESULTS

Table 9.1 reports the rankings of all parents within each of the four child-rearing issue categories—long-term goals, current priorities, parental roles, and disciplinary strategies—both overall and by sex of child. Looking at long-term goals, most par-

TABLE 9.1 Measures of Dependent Variables, Labels, and Proportion of Parents Indicating Each as a Top Priority, Overall and by Sex of Child

Question	Label	All	Girls	Boys
Long-term goal for child				
Getting a good education and a good job	EDJOB	.53	.51	.54
Having a strong, loving family	FAMILY	.32	.34	.30
Having a kind and compassionate personality	KIND	.23	.21	.25
Current priority				
Being happy and feeling good about himself or herself	HAPPY	.58	.61	.55
Being obedient and respectful	OBEY	.29	.25	.33*
Doing well in school	SCHOOL	.23	.21	.25
Role as parent				
Being a teacher and guide	TEACH	.68	.65	.72
Being a disciplinarian	DISCIPLINE	.09	.10	.07
Being a provider	PROVIDE	.30	.30	.29
Discipline strategy				
The loss of privileges	PRIVILEGE	.43	.39	.47*
Spankings	SPANK	.05	.07	.04
The use of reason or logic	REASON	.53	.54	.52

*$p < .10$.

ents gave top priority to their child's getting a good education and a good job. The second most commonly cited long-term goal was having a strong and loving family. The least often cited priority, having a child grow to be a kind and compassionate person, was the first choice of only one in five parents. The sex of the child has no effect on parents' ranking of these goals. In evaluating more immediate priorities, the top choice for most parents is that their children be happy and feel good about themselves. Having their child be obedient and respectful was the second most important current priority for parents, with parents of boys more likely those of girls to emphasize this priority. Doing well in school was ranked as less important than obedience and respect.

The majority of parents see their primary role as that of a teacher. Only 30 percent see themselves primarily as providers, and very few see themselves as primarily disciplinarians. The most popular disciplinary strategy among these parents is the use of reason and logic. However, withdrawing privileges is favored by a substantial minority of parents. Primary reliance on spanking as a disciplinary strategy is a rare event, although social desirability biases are probably depressing this figure. Only twenty-two parents ranked spanking as their sole primary approach to discipline.

To the extent that a global form of gender socialization is occurring, parents' responses to these measures should be significantly associated with the sex of the child. However, there are only two places where gender makes a significant difference, even allowing for a generous margin of error ($\alpha = .10$). Those who place their top current priority on the child's being obedient and respectful and those who rely on the loss of privileges as a disciplinary strategy are more likely to be parents of boys. Of course, if the form of gender socialization varies by race and/or class, as multicultural feminists contend, those differences could be canceling one another out in global comparisons. Thus, we must examine the gender dynamics of these four measures in a race- and class-sensitive context.

Long-Term Goals

The distribution of parents' long-term goals for their children across race, class, and gender appears in Table 9.2. The logit analysis revealed that gender does not predict parents' long-term priorities and that class and race do in interaction.

The top panel of Table 9.2 shows that education and a job are more of a priority for black than for white parents overall, and the next three panels show that among both blacks and whites, this emphasis decreases as class increases. Lower-middle-class blacks are more likely to place a top priority on family than their white class peers. The strongest race contrasts are among the upper-middle-class parents, where family is the top priority for white parents and education and jobs are the top long-term goals for black parents. Whereas class does not have much impact on whether blacks place importance on their children growing up to be kind persons, the likelihood of making this a priority increases with class among whites.

Although class has some systematic effects—working-class parents are more likely to emphasize education and jobs—once parents get into easier economic sit-

Table 9.2 Parents' Rankings of Long-Term Goals for Their Children: Percentages by Race of Parent and Sex of Child, Overall and within Class Levels

	Parents Are		*Black Parents*		*White Parents*	
	Black	**White**	**Girls**	**Boys**	**Girls**	**Boys**
Overall						
Long-term goal						
EDJOB	58	49*	56	58	47	51
FAMILY	34	31	35	33	34	27
KIND	25	22	23	27	20	24
Within class levels						
Working class	$n = 56$	$n = 62$	$n = 33$	$n = 22$	$n = 31$	$n = 29$
Long-term goal						
EDJOB	82	71	79	86	65	79
FAMILY	20	18	18	18	19	14
KIND	21	13	15	27	13	14
Lower middle class	$n = 110$	$n = 104$	$n = 55$	$n = 54$	$n = 59$	$n = 45$
Long-term goal						
EDJOB	48	48	45	50	47	49
FAMILY	43	32*	45	41	34	29
KIND	27	22	27	28	22	22
Upper middle class	$n = 36$	$n = 38$	$n = 12$	$n = 22$	$n = 19$	$n = 19$
Long-term goal						
EDJOB	50	13***	42	50	16	11
FAMILY	28	50**	33	27	58	42
KIND	22	34	25	23	26	42

NOTE: Class and race have independent effects.
*$p < .10$. **$p < .05$. ***$p < .01$.

uations, racial differences become more striking. Black parents maintain the same ordering of priorities across class, whereas the priorities among whites in the upper middle class are quite different from other whites. This interaction effect could be expressing a more narrow, class-specific cultural difference than alleged by the Afrocentrists' perspective: differences based on culture emerge among the relatively privileged economically.

Gender has no statistically significant effect on long-term goals for either racial group, however, even when looking within levels of class. Although there are too few parents in this category to draw any conclusions, it is interesting to note that the biggest gender differences appear among upper-middle-class whites. Here, a clear majority of parents of daughters emphasize the goal of a strong family, whereas parents of sons are evenly split between having a good family and being a kind person.

Current Priorities

The distribution of parents' current priorities for their children across race, class, and gender appears in Table 9.3. This measure had detected one global gender dif-

Table 9.3 Parents' Rankings of Immediate Priorities for Their Children: Percentages by Race of Parent and Sex of Child, Overall and within Class Levels

	Parents Are		*Black Parents*		*White Parents*	
	Black	**White**	**Girls**	**Boys**	**Girls**	**Boys**
Overall						
Current Priority						
HAPPY	52	63**	53	53	69	57*
OBEY	37	21***	35	38	16	28**
SCHOOL	30	17***	26	33	17	16
Within class levels						
Working class	$n = 56$	$n = 62$	$n = 33$	$n = 22$	$n = 31$	$n = 29$
Current Priority						
HAPPY	46	48	42	50	52	48
OBEY	36	29	33	36	19	41*
SCHOOL	41	23**	33	50	26	14
Lower middle class	$n = 110$	$n = 104$	$n = 55$	$n = 54$	$n = 59$	$n = 45$
Current Priority						
HAPPY	56	65	60	54	75	53**
OBEY	39	18***	36	43	15	22
SCHOOL	28	18*	24	31	14	24
Upper middle class	$n = 36$	$n = 38$	$n = 12$	$n = 22$	$n = 19$	$n = 19$
Current Priority						
HAPPY	50	79***	50	55	79	79
OBEY	33	16*	33	27	11	21
SCHOOL	17	5	17	18	11	

NOTE: Class, race, and gender have independent effects.
*$p < .10$. **$p < .05$. ***$p < .01$.

ference: Parents of sons are more likely to emphasize obedience and respect. The logit analysis suggests that gender does enter into parents' current priorities and that race and class also have independent impacts.

Even though the best model to describe the structure of responses specifies direct effects of gender, gender differences on specific priorities reach statistical significance only among whites. In general, whites are more likely to emphasize happiness for daughters and obedience for sons. A look at the impact of class reveals that this gender difference in current priorities among whites exists among working-class whites, who emphasize obedience/respect for boys, and lower-middle-class whites, who emphasize happiness and self-esteem for daughters. Blacks seem to make fewer gender distinctions overall. This global pattern of non-gendering among blacks may be masking race- and class-specific gendering. Among the poorest black families, more parents of sons report top priorities on both being happy and doing well in school. Their white class peers are placing a greater emphasis on school for girls and obedience for boys. Then, in the lower middle class, where the largest gender distinctions exist among whites, the same pattern seems to occur in a more muted way among the black parents. Both black and white parents in the upper middle class seem to be making the fewest gender distinctions.

Overall, white parents are more likely than blacks to emphasize the child's happiness and self-esteem, whereas blacks outnumber whites among those placing top priorities on obedience or school performance. There are significant race differences at each class level. As class status increases, whites' emphasis on happiness increases while the importance of school performance decreases. On the other hand, the proportion of black parents putting top priority on happiness and obedience is relatively stable across class. The importance of school performance to black parents does decline as class increases, although it is always more important to blacks than to whites.

Several have argued that European American culture is more individualistic and focused on self-esteem whereas African American culture is more group oriented and places a higher value on education (Collins 1990; hooks 1994). White priorities on happiness and self-esteem and black priorities on obedience, respect, and doing well in school are consistent with that cultural contrast. However, class also makes a systematic difference here. Parents at higher class levels do not have to worry as much about whether their children will be able to get a good education and job; poorer parents seem to rely more on the potential for education to help their children move into higher class levels.

Parental Role

Parents' rankings of their own roles by race and class of parent and sex of child are reported in Table 9.4. Parents who identify first as disciplinarians are rare, constituting only thirty-six of the 406 parents. Because there are so few in this category, logit modeling is statistically inadvisable. However, the models that best predict the observed pattern of parents putting a top priority on being a teacher or a provider indicate that gender interacts with race and class in shaping parents' role conceptions.

There are strong gender differences among working-class whites: parents of sons are very likely to see themselves as teachers, whereas all the disciplinarians are parents of daughters. On the other hand, white parents in the other two classes do not seem to be making gender distinctions in their roles. In fact, the role priorities of upper-middle-class white parents of daughters and sons are identically distributed.

Although there are no statistically significant gender differences among black parents, there are some indications of gendering in both the lower middle class and upper middle class. In both cases, the nature of the disparity parallels that among whites—more emphasis on teaching boys and providing for girls. Although there are too few in this category to draw any conclusions, it is intriguing that the distribution of role preferences among upper-middle-class black parents of sons is very similar to that of whites in the same class. On the other hand, black upper-middle-class parents of daughters are more like black parents in other class levels.

There are global race differences in parents' role priorities. White parents are even more likely to see themselves as teachers, whereas more black than white par-

Table 9.4 Parents' Rankings of Their Own Roles: Percentages by Race of Parent and Sex of Child, Overall and within Class Levels

	Parents Are		*Black Parents*		*White Parents*	
	Black	**White**	**Girls**	**Boys**	**Girls**	**Boys**
Overall						
Role as parent						
TEACH	64	72*	61	68	69	75
DISCIPLINE	14	3***	14	13	6	1*
PROVIDE	35	25**	34	35	27	23
Within class levels						
Working class	$n = 56$	$n = 62$	$n = 33$	$n = 22$	$n = 31$	$n = 29$
Role as parent						
TEACH	52	60	45	59	42	76***
DISCIPLINE	16	8	12	18	16	**
PROVIDE	48	31**	39	59	42	21
Lower middle class	$n = 110$	$n = 104$	$n = 55$	$n = 54$	$n = 59$	$n = 45$
Role as parent						
TEACH	68	73	69	67	76	69
DISCIPLINE	15	***	18	13		
PROVIDE	33	28	31	35	25	31
Upper middle class	$n = 36$	$n = 38$	$n = 12$	$n = 22$	$n = 19$	$n = 19$
Role as parent						
TEACH	72	89*	67	82	89	89
DISCIPLINE	8	5		9	5	5
PROVIDE	19	5*	33	9	5	5

NOTE: Gender interacts with race and class as causes.
*$p < .10$. **$p < .05$. ***$p < .01$.

ents see their primary role as providing for their children. Most of the parents who identify primarily as disciplinarians are black: 14 percent of blacks compared with 3 percent of whites list as a top priority their role as disciplinarian.

Class also has a systematic impact on these choices. As class status increases among both black and white parents, there is increasing emphasis on the teacher role; as class status decreases, there is a greater tendency to emphasize the provider role. That is, the more a parent's ability to provide is threatened by his or her economic situation, the more likely to prioritize this role.

In general, then, parents' determination of their roles is shaped in complex ways by their race and class, as well as their notions about gender. Gendering takes the form of emphasizing teaching boys and providing for—and sometimes disciplining—girls. It is most salient among lower-middle-class whites, but there are signs it may be happening among working-class and upper-middle-class blacks.

Whether through constraints, opportunities, or culture, class also shapes what parents understand they can and must do for their children. Race has an impact as well. We see signs of cultural differences in the importance of discipline. We also

Table 9.5 Parents' Rankings of Disciplinary Strategies: Percentages by Race of Parent and Sex of Child, Overall and within Class Levels

	Parents Are		*Black Parents*		*White Parents*	
	Black	**White**	**Girls**	**Boys**	**Girls**	**Boys**
Overall						
Discipline strategy						
PRIVILEGE	42	44	34	49**	43	45
SPANK	8	3*	9	7	5	1
REASON	51	54	53	54	54	54
Within class levels						
Working class	*n* = 56	*n* = 62	*n* = 33	*n* = 22	*n* = 31	*n* = 29
Discipline strategy						
PRIVILEGE	32	45	24	41	45	48
SPANK	9	3	9	9	6	
REASON	61	50	55	68	48	52
Lower middle class	*n* = 110	*n* = 104	*n* = 55	*n* = 54	*n* = 59	*n* = 45
Discipline strategy						
PRIVILEGE	45	48	38	50	47	49
SPANK	6	4	4	9	5	2
REASON	51	50	58	44	51	49
Upper middle class	*n* = 36	*n* = 38	*n* = 12	*n* = 22	*n* = 19	*n* = 19
Discipline strategy						
PRIVILEGE	50	29*	42	55	26	32
SPANK	11	**	33	**		
REASON	39	71***	25	45	74	68

NOTE: Class interacts with race and gender as causal effects.
*$p < .10$. **$p < .05$. ***$p < .01$.

see that simply being in a more comfortable class location does not keep blacks from worrying about providing for their children. This may be because they have access to African American cultural discourses that help them understand that racism makes their class position insecure, and because they live in a social structure that has failed historically and is failing to meet the needs of black children.

Disciplinary Strategies

The disciplinary strategies that parents rely on, by race and class of parents and sex of child, are reported in Table 9.5. This is the other measure on which we observed a global gender difference: Parents of sons were more likely to rely on the withdrawal of privileges. Here, again, one of the options, spanking, was rarely selected as a top priority, so we cannot reliably fit a logit model to predict that choice. In the case of the other two choices, the model that best predicts the pattern of choices on each specifies that they are shaped by class in interaction with race and with gender.

In the case of disciplinary strategies, the only significant gender differences are among black parents. Overall, blacks are more likely to withdraw privileges from sons than from daughters, even though their use of reason and spanking is almost the same regardless of the sex of the child. This tendency for black parents to withdraw privileges more from sons than daughters is relatively consistent across class. The most marked differences are among upper-middle-class black parents, where the differential use of spanking on daughters is striking. White parents are not using gender to determine disciplinary strategies. The proportions of parents of sons and daughters relying on each strategy are nearly identical overall and within each class.

The only global race difference in disciplinary strategies is that blacks predominate among the very few parents who report relying on spanking. The largest race differences emerge within the upper middle class, where the vast majority of whites rely on the use of reason whereas more blacks use the withdrawal of privileges. The only upper-middle-class parents who rely on spanking to discipline are black parents of girls.

Class also seems to shape disciplinary strategies among these parents, but in different ways for blacks and whites. As class status increases, black parents decrease their reliance on reasoning with their children and increase their use of the withdrawal of privileges. Whites in the working class and lower middle class are roughly evenly balanced between using reason and withdrawing privileges. In the upper middle class, however, the vast majority of white parents rely on the use of reason. These findings tend to contradict claims that gendering is minimized among blacks, at least in the way that parents respond to problematic behavior in children. It could be that this differential withdrawal of privileges is a kind of ceiling effect of another cultural difference. If blacks accord fewer privileges to girls than boys, they have less to withdraw for disciplinary purposes.

DISCUSSION AND CONCLUSIONS

Do the self-reports of parents in this study reveal that parents' priorities, future hopes, views of the parenting role, and discipline strategies vary based on whether they are responding for a son or a daughter? What we have found is that gender does get constructed in the goals and values in black and white families, but in race- and class-specific ways.

First, we note that the overall ranking of the three options given for each child-rearing issue—long-term goals, current priorities, parenting role, and discipline strategies—are the same for black and white parents as a group. This is evidence of a common culture and significant overlap in values and beliefs. Still, white parents were significantly more likely than black parents to emphasize happiness as a current value for their children and being a teacher as their most important parenting role. Black parents, on the other hand, were significantly more likely than white parents to indicate doing well in school and obedience as their most important current values, having their children get a good education and job as their most important long-term goals, and being a disciplinarian and provider as their most important parenting roles. These findings are consistent with studies showing that black parents place a high value on the education of their children (Willie 1988) and stress the importance of discipline and obedience (McAdoo 1988; McLoyd 1990).

These global racial differences in priorities, taken together, suggest that white parents, perhaps more secure about their children's current status and future success, focus more on their children's psychological well-being and are less concerned about instilling strict conformity in their children. The child-rearing priorities of black parents, however, might be influenced by their perception of greater challenges to success: Controlling, providing for, and educating children become more salient aspects of their parenting work.

Central to our analysis is whether the sex of the child influenced the behaviors or goals of parents. Gender had some overall effect. Compared to the parents of girls, the parents of boys emphasized obedience and respect more frequently as a current value and were more likely to use loss of privileges as a discipline strategy. These overall gender differences, however, turn out to be largely the product of strong, race-specific effects. The emphasis on obedience for sons more than for daughters occurs among white parents but not among black parents. The tendency to discipline boys more than girls by withdrawing privileges appears among black parents but not among white parents. That is, these data show that gender socialization is not a monolithic phenomenon.

Yet, how much, and even in some cases the way in which, black and white parents differ on each of these issues varies quite a bit across class. When we observe differences between blacks and whites in gendering practices, we may sometimes be seeing an artifact of the way race corresponds to class in American society.

We see several instances of significant gender differences occurring at specific intersections of class and race. Poor whites are particularly likely to emphasize obedience in their sons. This emphasis seems to be a benevolent one; poor white parents of sons overwhelmingly see their own role as primarily a teacher, and none of them see themselves as disciplinarians. Poor white parents of daughters might be a little more likely to see themselves as providers and emphasize school performance. There are no statistically significant gender effects in the practices reported by poor black parents.

There is only one statistically significant gender effect among parents in the lower middle class: whites are much more likely to emphasize happiness and self-esteem for their daughters than for their sons. Across the two lower classes in this sample, we see gendering more markedly among whites than among blacks. The only exception is the overall black use of privileges as a disciplinary strategy for sons more than daughters. Among upper-middle-class parents, on the other hand, gendering seems to occur among blacks but not whites. If upper-middle-class blacks admit to spanking as a form of discipline, they do it to daughters and not to sons. In contrast, the reports of white parents on all four measures of goals and strategies tend to be remarkably similar across sex of child.

Overall, gender does not seem to be a salient feature in parents' long-term goals for their children. On the other hand, gender seems quite salient in the choice of disciplinary strategies for blacks and in current priorities for whites. Long-term goals are fairly abstract, distant from the daily experience of parents of elementary-school-age children, whereas current priorities and disciplinary strategies are much more concrete. So, one way of interpreting these findings is that gender may not be salient when parents think about their values, but it may be embedded in their daily practices, where it will have concrete consequences for children.

Studies of gender among African Americans often point to a tradition of gender neutrality in child socialization, but, as we have pointed out, most of these studies focus on expanded roles for women while ignoring the roles of males. Although some previous studies have suggested that black parents may have diminished expectations for their sons, our findings do not support that contention. We found that in each social class, there was no statistically significant difference in current priorities or long-term goals between black parents of sons and those of daughters.

There are important caveats to take into consideration about this analysis. First, these findings rely solely on the *reported* attitudes and behaviors of parents. The desire to appear in a "good light" as parents probably influenced at least some of their responses. Another consideration is the fact that respondents were overwhelmingly female. Johnson (1988) argues that it is men, not women, who impose gender socialization on children. Thus, gender socialization may be more pervasive than we see here, and what we are observing is that even among the parents who are less likely to gender their children, race and class shapes socialization priorities and practices.

These findings could be expressing a selection bias in drawing a residentially based sample when race still makes a big difference in freedom to choose a residence. It seems reasonable to ask whether upper-middle-class parents who choose to live and/or school their children in communities that are predominantly working-class and poor, especially whites, who do not have racial discrimination in housing as a barrier, may differ significantly from their class-race peers in values and practices (Massey and Denton 1993).We need to explore how parents who live in more privileged residential areas rear their children.

Finally, statistics on the fit of the logit models indicated that even when models fit very well, they do not explain much of the variation among parents on these questions. The best model, predicting EDJOB, still explains only about 14 percent of the variance using the more generous assessment. This is no doubt partially because of the errors in measurement of the variables. It also seems quite likely that there are other important independent variables we are not taking into account in these models. It may be that these unspecified variables are also artifacts of interactions between gender, race, and class.

Still, on the basis of these data, it seems reasonable to conclude that there is no simple answer to the question of how gender gets constructed in parents' childrearing practices. Parents operate within their own specific economic and social constraints. Within these constraints, they try to develop an approach that coincides with gendered expectations—both their own and the ones they read in others—of their children. In struggling within these constraints and expectations, they draw on the values they learned from their own families and communities, which are marked by race and class. In parenting, and probably in the rest of life, race, class, and gender dynamics interact.

APPENDIX 9.1

Characteristics of Sample

	Black Families		*White Families*	
	n	%	n	%
Respondent				
Mother	165	82	167	82
Father	22	11	22	11
Grandmother	4	4	6	3
Other	11	3	9	4
Marital status				
Never married	58	29	29	14
Married	98	49	113	58
Divorced	36	18	39	19
Separated	6	3	15	7
Widowed	3	2	7	3
Number of children				
1	32	16	23	11
2	75	37	70	34
3	39	19	58	28
4	30	15	37	18
5	15	7	9	4
6 or more	11	6	7	3
Gender of focus child				
Female	100	50	93	46
Male	98	49	106	53
Employment status of parent				
Employed	133	66	120	59
Unemployed	47	23	68	33
Retired	3	2	2	1
Other/not specified	19	10	14	7
Education of parent				
Did not complete high school	20	10	27	12
High school graduate	70	35	72	35
Some college	70	35	68	33
College graduate	40	20	33	16
Annual family income				
<$15,000	72	36	71	35
$15,001—$30,000	67	33	56	27
$30,001—$50,000	41	20	43	21
>$50,000	17	8	28	14

NOTES

1. This body of work has also been referred to as multiracial feminist theory and intersectional theory.

2. Of the twelve schools invited to participate in the study, five declined: Four had other studies already under way and one was not interested. The seven schools included were not randomly selected but do reflect some of the racial and class diversity in the two cities.

3. Initially, surveys were sent only with students between the ages of ten and twelve, since these are considered important developmental years. In three of the seven schools, surveys were sent home with all children.

4. The actual response rate is probably higher. Given the number of children in the families in this sample, many parents probably had more than one child at the school but were asked to completely only one survey.

5. The purpose of having a focus child was twofold: the recognition that parents of more than one child may have different strategies for different children and the necessity of identifying a specific sample of children.

6. Surveys completed by Asian Americans and Hispanics were omitted from this analysis because there were too few to analyze. We intend to analyze larger data sets in the future to allow for more complete cross-ethnic comparisons.

7. Our interpretation of these cases is that the scales' rank order requirement does not validly measure the beliefs of these parents, that they legitimately refuse to weigh one option over another. That is, these "ties" are substantive and should be retained in the analysis. Thus, the proportions reported do not always add up to 1.0.

8. To construct a measure of class, we used a cross tabulation of our measures of education and income to create a three-level variable. In the lowest level are families with an income of less than $30,000 and less than a high school diploma and families with high school graduates but an income of less than $15,000 a year. In the highest class level are those with a college degree and an income of at least $30,000 and all households with incomes over $50,000. Those cases missing on income were assigned class based on the modal income for their education level and vice versa.

9. To fit, a model had to predict cell frequencies that did not diverge too far from those observed in the data. We judged fit in two ways: globally by the likelihood chi-square statistic (where we set an alpha level of .20) and for each cell by the size of standardized residuals, where we would tolerate no more than two cells (10 percent) with a significantly poor fit. If two nested models fit the data adequately, we chose the model with fewer causal terms unless a statistical test showed that its fit was significantly poorer. Details on the fit of various models are available upon request.

REFERENCES

Allen, W. R. 1981. Moms, dads, and boys: Race and sex differences in the socialization of male children. In *Black men,* ed. L. E. Gary. Beverly Hills, CA: Sage.

Anderson, E. 1989. Sex codes and family life among poor inner city youths. *Annals of the American Academy of Political and Social Science* 501: 59–78.

Aptheker, B. 1989. *Tapestries of everyday life: Women's work, women's consciousness, and the meaning of daily experience.* Amherst: University of Massachusetts Press.

Bem, S. L. 1983. Gender schema theory and its implications for child development: Raising gender-aschematic children in a gender-schematic society. *Signs: Journal of Women in Culture and Society* 8:598–616.

Billingsley, A. 1992. *Climbing Jacob's ladder: The enduring legacy of African-American families.* New York: Simon & Schuster.

Binion, V. J. 1990. Psychological androgyny: A Black female perspective. *Sex Roles* 22:487–507.

Blake,W. M., and C. A. Darling. 1994. The dilemmas of the African American male. *Journal of Black Studies* 24:402–15.

Blau, Z. S. 1981. *Black children/white children: Competence, socialization, and social structure.* New York: Free Press.

Block, J. H. 1983. Differential premises arising from differential socialization of the sexes: Some conjectures. *Child Development* 54:1334–54.

Burgess, N. 1994. Gender roles revisited: The development of the "woman's place" among African American women in the United States. *Journal of Black Studies* 24:391–401.

Carr, Peggy G., and Martha T. Mednick. 1988. Sex role socialization and the development of achievement motivation in Black preschool children. *Sex Roles* 18:169–80.

Cazenave, N. A. 1981. Black men in America: The quest for "manhood." In *Black Families,* ed. H. P. McAdoo. Beverly Hills, CA: Sage.

Chodorow, N. 1978. *The reproduction of mothering.* Berkeley: University of California Press.

Collins, P. H. 1987. The meaning of motherhood in Black culture and Black mother-daughter relationships. *Sage* 4:3–10.

———. 1990. *Black feminist thought.* Cambridge, MA: Unwin Hyman.

Connell, R. W. 1995. *Masculinities.* Berkeley: University of California Press.

Connor, M. E. 1988. Teenage fatherhood: Issues confronting young Black males. In *Young, Black, and male in America: An endangered species,* ed. J. T. Gibbs. Dover, MA: Auburn House.

Davis, Angela Y. 1993. Outcast mothers and surrogates: Racism and reproductive politics in the nineties. In *American feminist thought at century's end,* ed. Linda S. Kauffman. Cambridge, MA: Blackwell.

Davis, A., and J. Dollard. 1940. *Children in bondage: The personality development of Negro youth in the urban South.* New York: Harper & Row.

Davis, A., and R. J. Havighurst. 1946. Social class and color differences in child-rearing. *American Sociological Review* 2:698–710.

Dill, B. T. 1979. The dialectic of Black womanhood. *Signs: Journal of Women in Culture and Society* 4:545–55.

———. 1988. Our mother's grief: Racial ethnic women and the maintenance of families. *Journal of Family History* 13:415–31.

Doyle, J. A. 1989. *The male experience.* Dubuque, IA: W. C. Brown.

Espiritu, Yen Le. 1997. *Asian American women and men.* Thousand Oaks, CA: Sage.

Fordham, S., and J. Ogbu. 1986. Black students' school successes: Coping with the "burden of 'acting white.'" *Urban Review* 18:176–206.

Gibbs, J. T. 1988. Young Black males in America: Endangered, embittered, and embattled. In *Young, Black, and male in America: An endangered species,* ed. J. T. Gibbs. Dover, MA: Auburn House.

Giddings, P. 1984. *When and where I enter: The impact of Black women on race and sex in America.* New York: Bantam Books.

Glen, E. N. 1992. From servitude to service work: Historical continuities in the racial division of paid reproductive labor. *Signs: Journal of Women in Culture and Society* 18:1–43.

Hill, R. 1972. *The strengths of Black families.* New York: Emerson Hall.

Hill, S. A. 1999. *African American children: Development and socialization in families.* Thousand Oaks, CA: Sage.

Hill, S. A., and M. K. Zimmerman. 1995. Valiant girls and vulnerable boys: The impact of gender and race on mothers' caregiving for chronically ill children. *Journal of Marriage and the Family* 57:43–53.

hooks, bell. 1984. *Feminist theory: From margin to center.* Boston: South End Press.
———. 1994. *Teaching to transgress: Education as the practice of freedom.* New York: Routledge.
Hossain, Ziarat, and Jaipaul L. Roopnarine. 1993. Division of household labor and child care in dual-earner African-American families with infants. *Sex Roles* 29:571–83.
Hunter, A. G., and J. E. Davis. 1992. Constructing gender: An exploration of Afro-American men's conceptualization of manhood. *Gender & Society* 6:464–79.
Hunter, A. G., and S. L. Sellers. 1998. Feminist attitudes among African American women and men. *Gender & Society* 12 (1): 81–99.
Johnson, Miriam. 1988. *Strong mothers, weak wives: The search for gender equality.* Berkeley: University of California Press.
Jones, J. 1985. *Labor of love, labor of sorrow: Black women, work, and the family from slavery to the present.* New York: Basic Books.
King, Deborah K. 1988. Multiple jeopardy, multiple consciousness: The contest of Black feminist ideology. *Signs: Journal of Women in Culture and Society* 14:42–72.
Kohn, Melvin L. 1963. Social class and parent-child relationships. *American Journal of Sociology* 63:471–80.
Ladner, J. A. 1971. *Tomorrow's tomorrow: The Black women.* Garden City, NY: Doubleday.
Lewis, Diane K. 1975. The Black family: Socialization and sex roles. *Phylon* 36:221–38.
Lyson, Thomas A. 1986. Race and sex differences in sex role attitudes of southern college students. *Psychology of Women Quarterly* 10:421–28.
Lytton, Hugh, and D. M. Romney. 1991. Parents' differential socialization of boys and girls: A meta-analysis. *Psychological Bulletin* 109:267–96.
Madhubuti, Haki R. 1990. *Black men: Obsolete, single, dangerous? The Afrikan American family in transition.* Chicago: Third World Press.
Majors, R., and J. M. Billson. 1992. *Cool pose: The dilemmas of Black manhood in America.* New York: Lexington Books.
Massey, D., and N. A. Denton. 1993. *American apartheid: Segregation and the making of the underclass.* Cambridge, MA: Harvard University Press.
McAdoo, J. L. 1988. The roles of Black fathers in the socialization of Black children. In *Black families,* ed. H. P. McAdoo. Newbury Park, CA: Sage.
McLoyd, V. C. 1990. The impact of economic hardship on Black families and children: Psychological distress, parenting, and socio-emotional development. *Child Development* 61:311–46.
Mies, Maria. 1986. *Patriarchy and accumulation on a world scale.* London: Zed Books.
Moynihan, D. P. 1965. *The Negro family: A case for national action.* Washington, DC: Department of Labor.
Nobles, Wade W. 1985. *Africanity and the Black family: The development of a theoretical model.* Oakland, CA: Institute for the Advanced Study of Black Family Life and Culture.
Norusis, M. 1985. *SPSS-X advanced statistics guide.* New York: McGraw-Hill.
Peters, Marie Ferguson. 1988. Parenting in Black families with young children: A historical perspective. *In Black families,* ed. H. P. McAdoo. Newbury Park, CA: Sage.
Reid, Pamela Trotman, and Katherine Hulse Trotter. 1993. Children's self-presentations with infants: Gender and ethnic comparisons. *Sex Roles* 29:171–81.
Scott, JosephW. 1993. African American daughter-mother relations and teenage pregnancy: Two faces of premarital teenage pregnancy. *Western Journal of Black Studies* 17:73–81.
Smith, Robert C., and Richard Seltzer. 1992. *Race, class, and culture: A study of Afro-American mass opinion.* Albany: State University of New York Press.

Stack, C. 1974. *All our kin: Strategies for survival in a Black community.* New York: Harper & Row.

Staples, Robert, and Leanor Boulin Johnson. 1993. *Black families at the crossroads: Challenges and prospects.* San Francisco: Jossey-Bass.

Tabachnick, B. G., and L. S. Fidell. 1989. *Using multivariate statistics.* 2d ed. New York: Harper & Row.

Taylor, Robert Joseph, Linda M. Chatters, M. Belinda Tucker, and Edith Lewis. 1990. Developments in research on Black families: A decade review. *Journal of Marriage and the Family* 52: 993–1014.

Thornton, Michael C., Linda M. Chatters, Robert Joseph Taylor, and Walter R. Allen. 1990. Sociodemographic and environmental correlates of racial socialization by Black parents. *Child Development* 61: 401–409.

Weitzman, Lenore J. 1979. *Sex role socialization: A focus on women.* Palo Alto, CA: Mayfield.

West, C., and Don Zimmerman. 1987. Doing gender. *Gender & Society* 1: 125–51.

Willie, C. 1988. *A new look at Black families.* Bayside, NY: General Hall.

Wilson,W. J. 1996. *When work disappears: The world of the new urban poor.* New York: Vintage Books.

Wilson, M. N., T.F.J. Tolson, I. D. Hinton, and M. Kiernan. 1990. Flexibility and sharing of childcare duties in Black families. *Sex Roles* 22: 409–25.

CHAPTER 10

Can Men Be Subjects of Feminist Thought?

SANDRA HARDING

HESITATIONS AND POSSIBILITIES

Can men be not just objects but also subjects of feminist thought? Can men create feminist insights for themselves and the rest of us, too? This question has vexed feminists, women and men (or "profeminist men," as the latter are sometimes called). Here I intend to show the diversity in possibilities for men's distinctive feminist subject positions that have been provided by the main "public agenda" feminist theories—those such as liberal, Marxist, radical, socialist, and others that guide attempts to change public policies.

Let me make clear what is not the issue here. Of course there have been men feminist activists. Obviously many men have played important roles in improving the conditions of women's lives through designing, advocating, and maintaining changes in social policies and practices. They have worked to advance women's control over their lives in local, national, and international government agencies, labor halls, educational institutions, and publishing houses. They have done so also as lawyers, women's employers, community activists, family members, and in all the other contexts where social policies and practices can limit or expand women's resources.

Moreover, it is clear that in the past men have made significant contributions not only to women's conditions, but also to feminist philosophy and theories in other fields. Many of us teach the insights of John Stuart Mill, Karl Marx, and Friedrick Engels as central parts of the legacy of earlier eras of feminist philosophy, political theory, and social theory. Some even teach Plato's Republic as a more progressive representation of women's abilities and recommendation of state policy than those one finds in much contemporary thought. Moreover, men researchers and scholars have made contributions to contemporary feminist thinking in philosophy, history, sociology, literature, and most other disciplines. If we did not already know that the authors of some such studies were men, we would not hesitate to refer to these authors as feminists.

But we do so hesitate—or, at least, most men and women do. As I have argued elsewhere (1987, 1991, 1995), this hesitation contributes to problematic gaps and inconsistencies in feminist thinking and practice. Are we really supposed to assume that our enthusiastic men students and colleagues are unable to think for themselves and come up with original feminist understandings, just as our women students and colleagues learn to do? Are men only supposed to parrot what women feminists say? Not only is such an assumption unreasonable in itself; it is also paradoxical since many of us assume that European American feminists are perfectly capable of using the insights of women from other parts of the world to generate important antiracist and anti-imperialist insights of our own. So how could it be that no men can create antisexist, anti-androcentric, feminist thought? Such assumptions seem to ask us to believe that in the case of sex/gender differences, biology and/or history determine our thought, even though there are no other cases where such an assumption should be made (cf. Collins 1991, ch. 1 and 2). Of course there are men's movements and men's studies, some parts of which have closer and others more distant or even oppositional relations to the history of women's feminist movements and thought (cf., i.e., Clatterbaugh 1990; Brod 1987; Brod and Kimmel 1995). Such reflections lead to the realization that issues about men feminists are part of the larger discussion of the strengths and limitations of "identity politics"—here, "identity thought" or "identity philosophies."

Perhaps it will appear to some readers that it is too formulaic to explore the possibilities for men's feminist subjectivities within the conventional way of dividing up the last two centuries of Western feminist philosophy into liberal, Marxist, radical, socialist, and the more recent public agenda feminist theoretical approaches. However, I think it is worth doing because, for one thing, this conceptual scheme locates differences in feminist thinking about male feminists in the context of the history of modern Western political philosophy. These theories are the main ones that have guided feminist demands on the state and other public institutions. The possibilities for men's feminist subjectivities have only been explored in fragmented ways within this framework. Furthermore, some of these philosophical frameworks increasingly are adopted in other parts of the world as Western-style economic and political relations continue to spread to other cultures. It is valuable explicitly to focus on the diverse options these theories make available to men so that men and women around the world can envision better how men can contribute to, or resist on progressive grounds, the ways such feminisms are being integrated into governmental and cultural policies at local, national, and international levels. Finally, this framework is familiar to hundreds or perhaps even thousands of faculty who teach feminist social and political theory. It is illuminating for our students to be able to see what these diverse legacies also offer to men in their capacities as feminist thinkers.

Let us set aside at the start several other issues that may be on readers' minds. First, nothing said below undermines the necessity of hiring women faculty. Women should be hired for many reasons regardless of whether men can also generate feminist thought—for example, accurate and fair assessments of women's research and scholarship, and the need for women and men students to be able to see women legitimated as college teachers, researchers, and scholars. Additionally, there are certain important topics for classroom discussions—especially those having to do with violence against women, sexuality, standards of beauty, and other issues about women's bodies—where women hesitate to engage in frank and illuminating discussions unless these are led by women.

Next, there seems to be a significant difference between a woman referring to a man's thinking as feminist and a man making such an attribution to his own or another man's thought. In both cases, one certainly can argue whether or not the piece of work or the individual is feminist. But the male-to-male attribution is suspicious for reasons that the female-to-male attribution may not be. Namely, men would be the least likely group to be able to detect whether their own or anyone else's (men's or women's) beliefs and actions do actually meet some set or other of feminist standards. Because the prevailing social institutions and discourses have been designed largely to match the understandings of men in the social groups that design and maintain such institutions and discourses, professional and administrative men would be least likely to be able to detect how those institutions and discourses do not serve women, or do not serve them as well as they do men. The deepest, most widespread, and most influential forms of sexism and androcentrism are neither overt nor intentional, but, rather, institutional, social, and "civilizational" or philosophic (see Scheurich and Young 1997). Some such influential assumptions are so camouflaged precisely by their pervasiveness in modern Western thought that it is a feat for any feminists to detect them. For such reasons, and others that will be identified in the analyses below, it can seem less contentious for women to attribute feminist standards to a man's thought or actions than it will for a man to do so.

Finally, "feminist" is not just a term that locates thoughts or actions within a set of familiar categories; it also attributes a certain political position to the thoughts or individuals it is said to describe. It "names" persons in ways they may not, or may not wish to, name themselves. Is it appropriate to call someone a feminist who does not claim such a label for himself? And what if he denies that he is a feminist, while continuing to advance claims that look to others like feminist claims? I do not intend to settle this issue, but simply to note that this kind of question has arisen about women also. Historians have puzzled about whether, for example, certain nineteenth-century women who did not claim feminism for themselves and in some cases explicitly denied that they were feminists could or should still be discussed as advancing ideas and programs that look feminist to us today, and perhaps even did so to some of their nineteenth-century peers.

Here I shall set these questions aside. Instead, I want to examine the different possibilities for men developing feminist subjectivities and thus making contributions to feminist thinking that are encouraged or permitted by major contemporary Western public agenda feminist theories. Such a project can have a number of benefits. As indicated earlier, it can show that the major public agenda feminist movements and their associated theoretical frameworks each do make available arguments about what can be men's distinctive contributions to feminist theory. Therefore, one would have to argue against these theories in order to deny that men can be subjects of feminist thought. Second, we shall see that the kinds of subject positions offered to men differ greatly in these theories. Such a project can enable us to identify the strengths and limitations of each such form of men's feminism, and to grasp how both strengths and limitations are outcomes of the feminist political philosophy on which each draws. We can better evaluate each proposal for men's feminist subjectivity by a comparison with the diverse possibilities envisioned by the other feminist theories.

Moreover, this project can enable us to appreciate that some of these theories (such as socialist feminism) at least imply that there are contributions to feminist thought that are more easily (in some cases uniquely) made by men—there can be distinctive feminist men's standpoints on nature and social relations that are different from those initially available to most women. For such theories, feminist thought is disadvantaged by a lack of contributions from men's feminist subjectivities.

Finally, in enabling us to see more clearly just what is problematic about the concept of feminist men, some of these theories enable us also to see more clearly what is problematic about the concept of feminist women. This particular project can contribute to ongoing feminist discussions of essentialist accounts of gender relations.

In examining the kinds of feminist subjectivity that these public agenda feminist theories offer men, I shall be focusing on each theory's epistemology. Political philosophies always have epistemological implications; they contain or assume specific theories of knowledge. This is so since political power is always distributed in part through policies and practices that determine which social groups get to produce, to legitimate, to maintain, and to use which kinds of knowledge about natural and social worlds. (And so, in turn, different epistemologies offer possibilities for different distributions of political power.) The question of this chapter is what kinds of knowledge men can produce as contributions to feminist knowledge, so it is each feminist political philosophy's theory of knowledge that will be of special interest to us. Of course this is much too big and complex a project to be completed in a single essay. But hopefully even this brief outline of main parts of such a project can indicate the diverse and rich options existing public agenda feminist theories already offer for men's feminist theorizing.

Let us first turn to liberal feminism and its empiricist epistemology.[1] What opportunities does this offer men?

BECOMING TRULY RATIONAL MEN: FEMINIST EMPIRICISM

Liberal feminism and its associated empiricist epistemologies retain the focus of seventeenth- and eighteenth-century social contract theory on the role of individuals' reason and will power, on how laws and institutional policies tend to codify custom and tradition, and on the importance of empirical tests of belief by "experience" in order to produce objective facts. They also stress the importance of professional communities of inquiry and their standards for the advance of knowledge.[2] Even when feminist philosophers creatively and usefully revise and stretch such concerns and principles to what one might think would be the limits of an empiricist terrain in order to accommodate contemporary feminist projects, clear traces of such empiricist themes still remain centered in their accounts (cf, i.e., Antony and Witt 1992; Code 1991; Lennon and Whitford 1994; Longino 1990; Nelson 1990).

From this perspective, both women and men can gain feminist subjectivities, and there is little or no difference in the thought that can emerge from women's and men's feminist thinking. In both cases the point is to achieve just practices and bias-free beliefs by eliminating sexist and androcentric assumptions. In knowledge seeking, there is only "bad science" and "good science" (or knowledge); feminist communities—ones that adopt the more rigorous standards for "bias-free" that feminists have produced—turn the former into the latter. In philosophy, feminist analyses eliminate the false and inadequate elements of existing philosophic arguments to create empirically and theoretically more reasonable and useful philosophies. Some feminist empiricists have pointed to how women's movements provide important resources for such processes since they enable everyone, women and men alike, to detect phenomena that were otherwise invisible, such as the social construction of gender, and gendered cultures and practices, including sexist and androcentric beliefs that have had extensive influence in the disciplines and in public life. Men, no less than women, can learn to identify and eliminate sexist and androcentric biases (cf. Millman and Kanter 1987).

Just as Thomas Kuhn pointed to the importance of scientific communities in producing the most fruitful context for the growth of scientific knowledge, so, too, some feminist empiricists have seen membership in feminist communities, such as women's studies programs and the readerships of feminist journals, with their combination of support for and also rigorous criticism of new ideas, as providing valuable climates for the growth of knowledge. Clearly, feminist empiricists hold that neither men nor women are doing the best philosophy of which they are capable if they do not engage appreciatively yet critically with feminist thought.

This position has great strengths. One of its greatest is that of all the feminist epistemologies developed recently, it can be inserted into the prevailing epistemologies with the least difficulty—even though it is far too radical for many conventional epistemologists. Moreover, feminist empiricists have importantly claimed that when the subject is women, sex, gender, or feminism, the ordinary clear thinking, resistance to superstitions, and critical attitude that people exhibit on other topics seems to weaken or disappear. Men, like women, can learn to exercise their critical thinking more rigorously in these areas. They can become more alert to the need to pursue vigorously ideals of rationality and objectivity on such topics. Moreover, the new facts that feminist research produces are not the products of female biology or of gendered histories that determine the emergence or acceptance of ideas. Though other theorists will see the situation as more complex than feminist empiricists imagine, there is something extremely valuable about the latters' assumption that whatever their origins, evidence of the empirical and theoretical adequacy of feminist claims must be available for anyone to inspect.

Limitations

Yet there are a number of weaknesses with the way feminist empiricism supports men's engagement in contributing to feminist thought. These appear to be characteristic of liberal feminism more generally. Such limitations will appear most sharply when this epistemology is contrasted to others below, but we can here at least mention some of the most obvious of them.

For one thing, feminist empiricism conceptualizes thought, reason, and the emotions as fundamentally properties of individual persons. Yet other epistemologies have identified patterns of these that appear to be characteristic of cultures rather than in any interesting way of the individuals in them. The kinds of thought, reason, and emotions that advance the growth of knowledge and the kinds that retard it differ from culture to culture, not just from individual to individual; and they vary in different historical periods within "the same culture" (See, i.e., Galison and Stump 1996). It is a limitation of liberalism and its empiricist epistemologies that cultures or societies are conceptualized as fundamentally merely collections of individuals. Thus, only the psychology of error—not the sociology, social history, or politics of knowledge—is imagined as relevant to epistemological concerns.

Second and relatedly, the liberal/empiricist self or person who knows is conceptualized as pre-socially constituted and essentially disembodied. The self is thus imagined to be free to choose its own beliefs and actions. Yet other approaches point to the ways cultures, political relations, and psychic genealogies make likely some and unlikely other beliefs and actions; our powers to choose rationally are far weaker than liberalism assumes. Third, empiricism tends to adopt a narrow conception of rationality that ignores the positive roles that emotions can play in the advance of knowledge, and which is itself symbolically at least assoclated with manliness (cf. Bordo 1987; Jaggar 1989; Lloyd 1984).

Fourth, empiricism's conception of objectivity as requiring value-neutrality ignores the positive role that historically local interests, discursive resources, values, and ways of organizing the production of knowledge can play in producing knowledge, not just in producing superstition or error. There are two issues here—one about men and women as feminists, and the other about men and women as gendered humans. Liberalism/empiricism must present the feminism of feminist discourses either as value-neutral (i.e., feminist science is simply "good science"), or else as not central to the production of knowledge. This strange choice points toward something contradictory in liberal feminism. Moreover, the conceptual resources that feminist empiricism has available to draw upon do not permit understanding how women's or men's distinctively different activities and the different meanings of masculinity and femininity in any particular culture provide men and women with specific resources that can make positive contributions to the growth of knowledge. Feminist empiricism's disregard of these empirical realities leaves it less empirically adequate than some of the other theories. Fifth and relatedly, such epistemologies stop short of the radical transformations of the conceptual frameworks and methods of the disciplines to which other epistemologies are led. Since such frameworks and methods are themselves constructed from male-supremacist subject-positions, feminist empiricisms leave disciplines' and cultures' deepest and most influential androcentric assumptions unchallenged. They protect from more critical feminist inspection fundamental features of social institutions, their cultures, and practices that most disadvantage women.

These problems conjoin to imply that, from a liberal/empiricist viewpoint, while men may contribute to the "good thought" that feminists can produce, they have nothing distinctive to contribute "as feminist men." Of course, feminist empiricism asserts the same for women philosophers: women feminists have nothing distinctive to offer to philosophy that men could not supply. The liberal feminist goal for each of us should be to become that truly "rational man" envisioned in the Enlightenment's liberal philosophies.

CRITICIZING BOURGEOIS, SEXIST IDEOLOGY: MARXIST FEMINISM

Where liberal feminism was originally conceptualized to confront the conditions of women in the educated classes in the eighteenth century, Marxist feminism was formulated to deal with the conditions of working-class women during the heyday of European and U.S. industrialization in the late nineteenth and early twentieth centuries.[3] Karl Marx, Friedrick Engels, and much later the Hungarian theorist Georg Lukacs developed the original standpoint epistemology in their thinking about the "standpoint of the proletariat," from which social position political economy could be grasped for the first time. The conceptual framework of this epistemology was borrowed and transformed for specifically feminist purposes by socialist feminists of the 1970s. So the discussion of this distinctive feminist epistemology and the opportunities it offers for men's subjectivities will be saved for the section on socialist feminism.

Here we can reflect on the obvious fact that the routine inclusion in introductory feminist theory courses and texts of Marx's and Engels's powerful critiques of women's exploitation under class systems clearly indicates that these men are recognized to be speaking from and occupying an important feminist subject position, though their gender presumably contributes nothing to such analyses. Of *course* men can produce feminist thought, such a positioning of these writings would seem to say. Men and women can join together to criticize the hegemonic bourgeois ideology, along with its institutions and practices, that distorts human social relations, including those between the sexes, as well as the social theories, disciplines, and institutions that naturalize or idealize these kinds of gender relations. Moreover, if men, too, do not focus on such ways that false beliefs and exploitative practices are produced, they will fail to produce maximally adequate accounts of nature and social relations. Marxian analyses and politics will suffer, Marxist feminism seems to say, from inattention to feminist issues. It should not be surprising to see that this traditional Marxist feminism shares with the liberal thought it criticizes fundamental Enlightenment assumptions about the irrelevance of the gender of the authors of feminist thought to either the fact of its production or to its character.

Limitations

The limitations of this position for developing men's feminist subjectivities are largely those of its historical era. On the one hand, it is Marxism that first begins to see family relations and social relations between the sexes as distinctive social phenomena not controlled by biology. And Marxism sees knowledge systems as products of historically specific economic and political activities. So it almost can see what—more than a century later—would be perceived as gendered thought patterns. Yet it does not do so. Thus, while it offers men the possibility of powerful feminist subjectivities of the sort Marx and Engels themselves possessed, it cannot yet offer them the possibility of gender-distinctive feminist subjectivities, as later feminist theories will. Nor can it offer men (or women) the kinds of insights about oneself and social relations that become available for all post-Freudian thinkers.

REFUSING TO BE MEN: RADICAL FEMINISM

Radical feminism emerges in the 1960s and early 1970s as a response to a very different world than the ones liberal and Marxist feminisms initially encountered. These earlier feminisms have lacked the conceptual resources to grasp the oppression of women by men that became fully visible only after World War II, not just the ignorance about and bad attitudes toward women entrenched in law and custom, or the exploitation of women's labor by capitalism that could be seen by the older theories.

Often radical feminist writings seem to imply that "feminist men" is a contradiction in terms. Here all men appear deeply and firmly implicated in women's oppression because they receive the benefits of male supremacist culture, its institutions and practices, whether or not they actively or consciously engage in sexist acts or the construction of androcentric conceptual frameworks. All men benefit from some men's control of women's bodies through the state's toleration of rape, wife abuse, incest, and other forms of violence against women. And many men benefit from the control of women's reproduction by the state, medical, and health care institutions, and from culturally sanctioned ideals of women's beauty. Moreover, because men cannot have women's experiences, they "can never really know" what it is that women can know that enables the latter to produce feminist thought. Finally, radical feminists (like socialist feminists) point out that the very standards of what passes for objectivity, rationality, fairness, and justice—standards that shape the law, public policy, and the sciences—are deeply linked to ideals of manliness and are, thus, far from maximally objective, rational, fair, or just. Radical feminism would seem to regard the idea of men feminist philosophers or theorists as a contradiction in terms.

Yet there is another way to read radical feminism's positions that offers men the possibility of developing important feminist subject positions. Moreover, such a reading of radical feminism opens into, or prefigures, some of the most important revaluations of sex and gender in post-structuralist and queer thinking, thereby highlighting this often undervalued potential in radical feminism more generally. In spite of its limitations, radical feminism remains far more radical than most of it critics have been able to detect.

For one thing, can't men use in innovative ways the kinds of insights that women gain in the kinds of cases on which radical feminism focuses? Does all radical feminist thought really issue directly from the individual experiences of its authors? Is radical feminist thought biologically or historically determined? After all, presumably not every radical feminist who offers illuminating insights about women's experiences of, and how the dominant institutions "think about," rape, incest, or battery has in fact experienced such acts. Catharine MacKinnon and others have taught me to think from the perspective of women's experiences of rape (and I do not mean to imply that she speaks from the experience of rape; she never says so), just as Patricia Hill Collins and others have taught me to think from black women's mothering experiences—experiences that I also have not had (MacKinnon 1982; Collins 1990). Shouldn't I, too, be expected to be able to teach and write in ways that are informed by, "in dialogue with" such writings (to borrow a phrase from Collins's somewhat differently focused analysis)? We all learn from, empathize with, the reports of friends' and loved ones' experiences, not to mention from such reports on television, in the newspapers, and in Plato's dialogues or William Shakespeare's plays. None of us except philosophy's imaginary solipsists are in fact isolated in our own experiences in the ways radical feminism is often presumed to hold. Cannot men, too, learn to listen in these ways and go on to use what they learn critically to rethink the institutions of society, their cultures, and practices? And will not such teaching and writing combine in novel ways insights emerging from experiences that they (and, perhaps, I) have never had?

Obviously, women's reports of their experiences must remain central resources for feminist accounts, but it is hard to see why men cannot also make important contributions to radical feminist thinking. In her illuminating consideration of who can be a black feminist and therefore produce black feminist thought, Patricia Hill Collins usefully situates her account as rejecting both the Enlightenment's idealist position that anyone can in principle know anything and everything anyone else can know, and also the excessively materialist position that only persons with certain kinds of biology or social histories can make contributions to the production of black feminist thought. Black feminism is for her a political/theoretical category, a discourse, one might say. Let us leave this issue here simply by noting that the most defensible account of who can author feminist thought will have to avoid both the excessive idealism and the excessive materialism of conventional epistemologies while retaining the strengths of these two positions. We need a better epistemology than those two choices offer (see Collins 1991, ch. 1 and 2; Roof and Weigand 1995).

Perhaps the most important resource for men to which radical feminism has drawn attention, however, is precisely the problems with manliness and womanliness per se—with these gender categories.[4] Where liberal and Marxist feminisms do not question the desirability or inevitability of gender categories, one stream of radical feminism locates the most fundamental causes of women's oppression precisely in these categories. It is not just that masculinity has been overvalued and femininity undervalued, or that each has been valued for the wrong reasons. Rather, the categories themselves serve primarily male supremacist interests. That is, it has been primarily in men's interests to distinguish their gender from femininity in order to link manliness to the distinctively human and to ideals of nationalism, race, "the worker," reason, militarism, the heroic, the ethical, etc. It is not just that such a practice overvalues masculinity and undervalues femininity, but also that the preoccupation with trying to fit so much of nature and social relations into gender categories obscures aspects of ourselves and our surroundings that do not easily fit into such categories no matter how they are evaluated.

Thus, radical feminism challenges men to transform themselves at the most fundamental levels of their identity—to refuse to be "men," as the title of John Stoltenberg's book proposes.[5] Men can refuse to respect the masculinity ideals that structure the cultures, policies, and practices of so many social institutions. When women refuse feminine ideals, public institutions can no longer function in their usual, male supremacist ways, as political scientist Cynthia Enloe has pointed out in her analyses of women's positions in international relations (cf. Enloe 1990).

Harry Brod (1987) has pointed out that ideals of masculine identity are highly dependent on public discourses. Consequently, disruption of public discourse regularly troubles men's senses of their masculine identity. For example, when the U.S. economy weakens, misogynist discourses about the excessive costs of social programs for children, women, and the poor (all coded feminine) reach a higher volume. Or when the end of the cold war results in decreased funding for scientific and technological research tied to military priorities, in the aerospace industry for example, feminist science critics are blamed for the incipient national "flight from reason" and its purportedly accompanying decreased science funding. However, one can ask if the causal relation might not go the other way, too. Could men's refusals of masculinity ideals have powerful effects on public discourses about international relations, economic strategies, national welfare systems, the research priorities of modern sciences, and so on? If men refused to regard as ideal such familiar masculinity figures as the warrior, the "worker," the "head of household," or the "rational man" of philosophy, economic theory, and jurisprudence, how would public discourses about militarism, the family, the economy, philosophy, and the law change?

One might be tempted to think that a man who refuses to become a man thereby becomes queer or even becomes a woman. Even this latter possibility now appears imaginable in the sense that transgendering, or gender-changing, has become more widespread. Some men have been able to become a "different kind of woman." Such alternatives to becoming a man conventionally have been the threats that have kept many men firmly focused on becoming as manly as possible every day in every way. But there certainly are other possibilities. A man could become "a different kind of man," or perhaps even better, a human, a person, in a truly gender-neutral sense. The very difficulty of imagining such possibilities indicates that radical feminism invites men to work out for themselves, in dialogue with women feminists, a creative transformation that could have widespread consequences for social relations. Thus, in contrast to liberal and Marxist feminisms, it can be argued that radical feminism assigns to men an innovative feminist theoretical and practical project that is both for themselves and for feminist thinking.

Limitations

The limitations of radical men's feminisms are the familiar ones of radical feminisms more generally. For one thing, radical feminist theories do not conceptualize the importance of differences among women or among men created by ethnicity, racism, imperialism, heterosexism, and other cultural forces. Such a conceptual silence marks these theories as thinking from the perspective of those privileged groups that can afford the luxury of such disconcern for the intersectional character of gender's mutually supportive relations with these other social structures and kinds of meanings. One has to suspect that radical feminist approaches also ensure essentialist assumptions about men, too, recuperating a Manichean dualism in which all women are in the same way victims, and all men to the same degree perpetrators of the oppression of women. In daily social relations, the issues are much more complex, and women often are complicitous in and sometimes initiators of the exploitation and domination of other women and of men. Moreover, class, race, ethnicity, sexuality, and other aspects of culture and history create important differences between the ways that different groups of men think about and participate in gender relations. For example, dominant and marginalized forms of masculinity (i.e., European American vs. African American and Latino, or Christian vs. Jewish and Muslim) play off each other in ways radical feminism does not have the resources to grasp (cf. Brod 1987). Of course many individual thinkers who use radical feminist insights vigorously try to correct for such limitations of these theories. However, it is the conceptual frameworks of radical feminist theories rather than the claims of any individual thinkers that are being discussed here.

Often radical feminisms' reification of oppositional relations between men and women appears to imply the obviously false claim that men are doomed to be unable to resist acting out their oppressive positions in social relations. "Refusing to be men" is one approach to this problem. However, it is worth noting that history reveals many men vigorously helping to organize suffrage or labor union campaigns, trying to institute institutional policies beneficial to women, and in other ways working to diminish the authority over women that the state or other institutions and cultural traditions offer men (Kimmel and Mosmiller 1992). This fact offers a starting point for men's feminist "resistance studies": men have a distinctive interest in asking what leads men to resist thinking and acting in the sexist and androcentric ways to which they are so entitled by the dominant institutions. Much of the field of men's studies, including its research and scholarly analyses in the disciplines, provides evidence of the important contributions that such resistances can provide to everyone's feminist understandings.

In spite of its limitations—after all, no theory is perfect for every explanatory purpose we might have—we can nevertheless conclude that radical feminism's central contention that men *as men* oppress women, not just as imperfectly rational, or as members of a bourgeoisie, draws attention to a possibility not envisioned by liberal or Marxist feminism. Namely, in refusing to be men, paradoxically men can create new kinds of post-patriarchal subjectivities of their own that promise powerful public effects.

BECOMING HISTORICALLY SITUATED FEMINIST MEN: SOCIALIST FEMINISM

Socialist feminism emerged alongside radical feminism, but encountered women's conditions in the late twentieth century through the lens provided by the older Marxian accounts. It has been able to build on the concerns of these two powerful analyses in innovative ways. Its "standpoint epistemology" enabled these analyses to "start off from women's lives" to examine how women fared in the historically supportive relations between men's roles in patriarchy and capitalism, and their roles in family relations and public life. It is in the continuing historical negotiations within each set of relations that women's destiny is kept out of women's own control as patriarchy and capitalism negotiate over who shall control and benefit from women's labor, and as women's subjection in private life is used to maintain their inferior options in public life, and vice versa. How do the politics of these two dimensions of contemporary social relations enable the production of some kinds of knowledge and limit the possibilities of other kinds?[6]

Thus, feminist standpoint epistemologists have argued that the prevailing conceptual frameworks in the disciplines and in public life have represented only the issues that interested—and were in the interests of—men in the dominant social groups. The kinds of knowledge that could advance women's interests were distorted by their representation within such conceptual frameworks, when they were represented at all. What people do and the cultural meanings that their activities have both enable and limit what they can know about natural and social worlds. Thus, for example, it has been the assignment of women to the maintenance of daily life both through their wage labor and in the domestic world that has permitted men professionals, administrators, and managers (these are the forms that "ruling" takes these days, as Dorothy Smith points out) to take as real only their abstract conceptual work. Such work hides and distorts its material preconditions, many of which are to be found in women's physical, intellectual, and emotional labors as mothers, wives, daughters, secretaries, nurses, domestic workers, service workers, etc. It takes both scientific and political struggle to bring such a fact to life, standpoint theorists have argued, since dominant ideologies are hegemonic; they structure the institutions, their cultures, and practices through which everyone's daily lives are organized and understood. Thus, women's interests could not simply be added to the dominant conceptual frameworks of social life or of research disciplines since such frameworks gained legitimacy only insofar as they could obscure both their material bases in women's activities, and their consequences for the gendered disribution of social benefits.

Feminist standpoint epistemologies have offered men the same resources for producing knowledge that they offer to women. Just as Marx and Engels were not proletarians, and yet could "think from proletarian lives" to produce their powerful analyses of how the class system worked, so, too, men can begin their thought in women's lives, with the assistance that feminist theories have provided, to produce equally powerful analyses of how the gender system works. How they can go about doing so in some respects is perfectly unproblematic. Marx and Engels produced a class analysis and laid the groundwork for standpoint epistemologies; whites have produced powerful analyses of racist systems that started off by thinking from the lives of those who suffer from such systems; therefore men can provide feminist gender analyses with thought that starts off from women's lives. Yet, as discussions of standpoint epistemologies have explored what it means to "start thought from women's lives," for knowledge to be "socially situated" in productive as well as limiting ways, and to use women's experiences in the production of knowledge, standpoint issues here have become both troubling and illuminating. Both such consequences are created by standpoint epistemology's problematization of the idealized positionlessness of liberal epistemologies. At least some of these issues can begin to be sorted out by looking at the strengths and limitations of standpoint epistemologies for creating men's feminist subject positions.

One such strength is to be found in the emphasis in standpoint epistemologies on the political struggle it takes to gain a feminist (or, in some formulations, women's) standpoint. A standpoint is not a perspective; it does not just flow spontaneously from the conditions of women's existence. It has to be wrestled out against the hegemonic dominant ideologies that structure the practices of daily life as well as dominant forms of belief, and that thus hide the very possibility of the kind of understanding that thinking from women's lives can generate. Similarly, men's political struggles against androcentrism and male supremacy in family life, in emotional relations, at work, in public agenda politics, and in the disciplines where dominant conceptual frameworks are organized and packaged all offer men possibilities for learning from the kinds of resistance that their struggles encounter. Some of these sites are completely or virtually woman-free. Such struggles can reveal to them sources and patterns of androcentrism and of resistances to feminisms that are not visible, or not so visible, to women. Thus, men can be both sources of kinds of information of interest to feminisms and also producers of analyses of this and other information.

Two other strengths of standpoint epistemologies point to two kinds of "locations" where men can develop feminist subjectivities and have access to distinctive forms of knowledge. Such locations are highlighted by the two kinds of "difference" that standpoint theories have exploited in order to mine their epistemological resources. One kind of difference is created by power relations between the genders: patriarchy assigns men power over women. The other is the "mere difference" in the activities to which men and women characteristically are assigned in each culture (class, ethnicity, etc.). Of course, in everyday life, power relations permeate all aspects of social relations, giving different value and meaning to women's and men's activities; the two kinds of difference are only analytically separable. Let us look at these two kinds of difference in turn.

Any power relations—of class, race, religion, ethnicity, sexuality, as well as gender—give standpoint advantages to the lives of the oppressed. From the standpoint of such lives (and, often, for those who live these lives) there can more easily appear a gap between their interests and how the social institutions, from the design of which women have been excluded, perceive their lives. For example, women's interests and the perceptions of women's lives by the law, managers of the economy, health care professionals, and educational systems can widely diverge when examined from the standpoint of women's lives. But such political relations can also give scientific and epistemic advantages to men who set out to resist male supremacy and its androcentrism. Can there not also be a gap opened up between such men's experiences—men's interests—in their struggles against androcentrism and the way the dominant conceptual schemes characterize men's lives in terms of, for example, ideals of manliness and men's entitlements? Men are socially situated in different places in male-supremacist social relations than are women. They have different relations to their fathers, mothers, sons, and daughters, to the "Great Men" of their disciplines, to the meanings of manliness expressed through ideals of patriotism, heroism, physical fitness, professionalism, spirituality, sexual desire and sexual skill, moral behavior, objective and rational thought, etc. Standpoint epistemologies offer opportunities for men to develop distinctive subject positions as socially situated men who have learned to think through feminist theories, descriptions, and practices that themselves started from women's lives. They, too, can come to think about their lives and about the rest of natural and social relations from a gap between how their lives are shaped by their concerns as feminists and how the dominant conceptual frameworks perceive and shape men's lives.

A second set of resources are offered by standpoint epistemologies' recognition of the opportunities for systematic knowledge created by "mere difference" in the activities in which individuals or groups characteristically engage (cf. Harding 1997 and forthcoming). Women feminists have focused here primarily on the distinctive kinds of knowledge for which women's activities create opportunities, but we can think in parallel ways about the distinctive kinds of knowledge for which feminist men's activities create opportunities. Women and men will tend to be developers of and repositories for distinctive kinds of knowledge insofar as they have different interactions with nature and social relations. There are at least four respects in which such distinctive opportunities can occur. First, women and men have different interactions with nature and social relations insofar as their bodies differ, and insofar as their activities bring them into interactions with distinctively different parts of the natural and social worlds—with babies, the bodies of sick relatives, or with motorcycles and locker rooms (to stick with stereotypes). Moreover, even when women and men interact with the "same environment," their socially assigned activities can give them different interests in it and, consequently, different patterns of systematic knowledge and systematic ignorance. For example, clothing can be manufactured to produce warmth, durability, and/or social status; children can be parented to maximize their health, their ongoing or potential income production, or their marriageability; land can be farmed for subsistence or for cash production. These different opportunities can represent culturally local gender-differing interests and, consequently, patterns of systematic knowledge and ignorance.

Third, women's and men's socially assigned activities and the symbolic meanings of masculinity and femininity give women and men different relations to their cultures' discursive resources. For example, in modern Western cultures, women tend to identify less with the "we" of authority, some observers report, more often perceiving authority to be "they" (Belenky et al. 1986). Masculinity discourses are highly dependent on public discourses, as noted earlier—for example, about nation formation and national destiny, the advance of science, the achievements of adventure, of "civilization," and of "humanity," the fate of colonial empire, or the lot of "the worker." A men's feminist subjectivity could make important contributions to our understanding of the models of gender linked to such public discourses.

Finally, women and men can tend to organize the production of knowledge differently in some respects. Evidently they sometimes organize differently the laboratories that they direct, and their publication strategies can tend to be distinctive (cf. Barinaga 1993). Insofar as there are "women's styles" of doing science or gaining knowledge more generally, then at least some of the alternatives to them, which were formerly conceptualized as the right styles or the only styles, now emerge into clarity as distinctively "men's styles." How does this fact create opportunities for men to develop feminist subjectivities?

Thus, socialist feminist theory offers men opportunities to produce distinctive feminist subject positions of their own that find resources in men's feminist opposition to patriarchal politics and thought, and in the gendered character (not the generically human character) of their distinctive interactions with nature, their interests, their relations to dominant patriarchal discourses, and their distinctive ways of organizing the production of knowledge. Some of these insights can provide valuable correctives to women's feminisms. For example, one commentator has pointed out that women's feminisms tend to overvalorize femininity, using feminine norms to evaluate men's beliefs and behaviors in spite of feminist theorists' otherwise critical assessment of the restrictiveness of feminine norms (Brod 1987, 6). Another observer points out that women feminists tend to equate masculinity with patriarchy, obliterating any possible space for a men's feminist subjectivity as a third term in the discourse otherwise restricted to women and patriarchy (Boone 1990, 21). Yet others point to the "phobic space" to which straight men are restricted in the absence of an articulated men's feminist subjectivity. Some feminist as well as male-supremacist cultures restrict straight men to the choice between participating in historical discourses of "normal manly" misogynistic representations of women, on the one hand, or the threat of homophobic accusations on the other. That is, in the absence of men's feminist subjectivities, straight men are offered the options only of "hating women" or becoming socially hated "lovers of men" (i.e., Forrester 1993). Thus, there is a need to create space for men's active thinking on feminist topics that can function as something other than confessions or alibis (Forrester 1993, 185).

How shall we conceptualize what happens here? Starting off thought from progressive men's lives, with lenses provided by feminist analyses? Using feminist discourses to think from the lives of men resistant to male supremacy? Such formulations seem convoluted, but perhaps also illuminating of issues about standpoint theory that need further exploration.

Limitations

Many of the problems plaguing radical feminism, on the one hand, and the older Marxian accounts, on the other hand, appear as problems for the early formulations of standpoint epistemologies. It would take us too far afield to do more here than merely recognize that history. Yet in its post-structuralist formulations, where "women's situation" is understood to be discursively established, not given "by nature" to our "glassy mirror minds," most of these problems recede (i.e., Henessey 1993; Harding, ch. 7 in 1991, 1992). Indeed, it is the need for understanding feminisms as discursive formations—material institutions, their practices, and cultures within which language plays a central role—that confronted the attempt above to formulate the possibility of men's distinctive feminist standpoints on nature and social relations.

However, other limitations to the usefulness of standpoint approaches arise from their own distinctive political social locations, and the interests, discursive resources, and ways of organizing the production of knowledge characteristic of such determinate sites in history. For one thing, standpoint epistemologies are committed to producing "scientific" accounts that more accurately and comprehensively describe and explain the worlds around (and within) us. Yet they thereby relegitimate discourses of scientificity. Moreover, they draw on distinctively European and European American discursive resources and ways of organizing the production of knowledge—Marxian accounts of the political economy and Marxian epistemology, distinctive modern Western problems in gender relations, current forms of feminism in Europe and North America. They draw on struggles over the role that the Enlightenment and "modernity" do and should play in the production of knowledge, and on many other local intellectual and political discussions. That is, standpoint epistemologies are historically located no less than are the standards for producing knowledge—past, present, and future—that are the objects of their study. Feminist thinkers from outside these cultures, women or men, might well prefer to use discursive resources available within their own cultural legacies for developing men's feminist subjectivities. Indeed, in some cases they might not even find the term *feminist* a resource for describing such a project, since the term has been associated primarily with bourgeois "women's rights" movements that cared little for the miserable conditions of poor women, peasant women, or women of dominated races, ethnicities, religions, or castes. Their "men's feminisms" might well best be developed in some other terms. No doubt there are other historical limitations of the standpoint epistemologies that others will be able to identify.

MORE RECENT FEMINIST DIRECTIONS; MORE OPPORTUNITIES FOR MEN

In recent decades a number of other distinctive public agenda feminist approaches to politics and theory in the disciplines have begun to flourish, and each of these also offers distinctive opportunities for men's feminisms. Multicultural and global feminisms and lesbian, gay, and queer theories are perhaps the most influential of these. They deserve extended analyses, but I must settle here for only indicating some of the most interesting opportunities for men's feminist subjectivities that these newer approaches make available.

Multicultural and global feminists share with socialist feminists interest in both the commonalities and the differences between women. In this respect, these "discourses," their institutions and practices, contrast with the three discussed earlier, for each of those could only illuminate commonalities or differences between women, not both. Liberal and radical feminisms could each, in different ways, focus only on the commonalities among women; they did not provide resources for analyzing differences between women. In contrast, Marxist feminism was interested primarily in the differences between women in different classes; proletarian and bourgeois women shared little, according to Marxian theories, and it was only with improving the conditions of proletarian women (and men) that feminists should be concerned.

Multiculturalism has been interested in the similarities and differences in women's (and men's) situations in different cultures—their situations as Chicanas, African Americans, or Jews. Global feminists have been interested in the similarities, differences, and relationships between different groups of women's (and men's) situations at different locations within global political economies. For example, they are interested in the similar and different ways that femininity is constructed for women who work in the textile industries of Taiwan or Costa Rica and the ways it is constructed for us who buy the products of their labor. Again, they are interested in the commonality that violence against women is "managed" by the dominant institutions in their respective cultures in order to keep both groups of women acting "feminine," yet it is used in very different ways against each group.

These related yet differently focused feminisms also offer distinctive resources for men's feminist subjectivities. They offer men opportunities to think critically about the commonalities, differences, and relations between, for example, the ways that dominant and subordinated masculinities are "managed" in each culture. What is shared and what is different about working-class African American, Chicano, and white ideals of masculinity? About the ways each group is expected to think about the sexuality of women of their own ethnicity and of other races/ethnicities? About what they are culturally expected to do with whatever economic resources they can access? About expected attitudes toward nationalism, or "race pride"? Multicultural and global feminisms expand the terrain of commonalities and differences between cultural groups that can offer distinctive resources for developing men's feminist subjectivities. In doing so they also reveal limitations in the ways earlier feminist theories posed their concerns. They open up new horizons for political action and social thought for men as well as women feminists.

Another group of recently developed political and theoretical approaches also opens up possibilities for men's feminist subjectivities. "Queer theories" develop further some of the themes of the older lesbian and gay approaches, and they introduce new ones of their own. Of course these are not always feminist approaches to issues. Some of the older lesbian and gay issues were overtly feminist or, in other cases, overlapped with feminist concerns; others did not. The same is true for the newer queer politics and theory.

We can briefly note just a couple of the implications for men developing distinctive feminist subjectivities to be found in some of the lesbian, gay, and queer theory concerns. For one thing, older writings made clear how cultural sanctions for misogynous attitudes in both men and women have been ideologically linked to homophobic ones. That is, dominant group models of masculinity have required "real men" to fear "femininity" in themselves, in women, and in men who refuse heterosexual masculinity. Each of these threatens to invoke the others. This is what Joseph A. Boone (1990) and Forrester (1993) were referring to when they wrote about the "phobic space" to which straight men are restricted in the absence of an articulated men's feminist subjectivity. Men are offered the choice of participating in the "normal manly" misogynistic representations of women or of suffering the threat of homophobic accusations. Such discussions point the way to the creation of distinctively masculine feminist subjectivities that refuse the absurdity of having to "hate women," having to fear "loving men," and to fear loving the "feminine" in themselves.

Queer theorists have produced accounts of the historical emergence of sexual identities per se—heterosexual as well as homosexual—as part of the emergence of bourgeois individualism and its "personal life" in Europe and the United States in the late eighteenth and early nineteenth centuries (cf. D'Emilio 1993; Halperin 1993; Katz 1995). It took thought originating from somewhere other than in the dominant conceptual frameworks to be able to see heterosexual no less than homosexual identity as historical emergents. The social sciences have barely begun to contemplate what a disruption of social theory traditions such a realization can create (cf., i.e., Sociological Theory 1994). Queer theory, too, thus uses a kind of standpoint epistemology, since it starts its thought from sex/gender-marginalized lives to look freshly at the different forms of gender and sexual relations created in different cultural contexts and at how "heteronormativity" (a form of ethnocentrism) has structured dominant institutions and the conceptual frameworks of public life and of research disciplines (cf. essays in Abelove et al. 1993 and Duberman et al. 1993).

There are many possibilities such queer theory opens up for men to develop distinctively feminist subjectivities. Gay men are, of course, "different kinds of men." So too are female-to-male transgendered and transsexed men, just as male-to-female women are a "different kind of woman."[7] Such subject positions might be thought of as "*nouveau* gendered" ones.[8] When gender comes unfixed for individuals in such ways, new insights are possible not only about gender relations, but also about all of the social institutions and their conceptual frameworks that assume fixed gender identities. However, the distinctive social situations on which queer theorists draw also offer men (and women) opportunities to abandon gender categories entirely or at least in new ways. This was the possibility that was prefigured in that strain of radical feminism considered above that insisted on the oppressiveness of gender categories per se, not just of any particular historical ideals of manliness and womanliness. Here men can develop subject positions not as "different kinds of men" or "different kinds of women" (as "*nouveau* gendered"), but as what we might think of as ex-gendered persons. Such positions are so new that we can only begin to glimpse the philosophic issues that can arise from them in an ironic way, such queer theories return full circle to transform for a later era's feminist (and other) projects the insistence of liberal feminist empiricism that gender should not be a relevant factor in shaping philosophy and social theory. It won't be when "ex-gender" comes into widespread social existence and designs philosophy and social theory, one might respond.

CONCLUSION

I have been exploring the many diverse kinds of subject positions envisioned in existing feminist (and queer) public agenda theories and their epistemologies from which men can make important contributions to feminist philosophy and social theory. One would have to argue against each of these theories—or the reading here of their assumptions and implications—to deny that men can be subjects of feminist thought. Of course each has its strengths and limitations. Some envision distinctive contributions that men can make specifically as feminist men; our feminisms are impoverished by the lack of such analyses. Others insist that gender is, should be, or could become irrelevant to the production of knowledge. Some are firmly socially located within dominant modern Western interests and discursive resources; others take advantage of the interests and resources that are available from other historical, social, and cultural locations.

Perhaps there should be a discussion here of the real concerns both women and many men have about co-optation, paternalism, appropriation, infiltration, and the like that provoke such skepticism toward putative feminist men. However, this important theme all too often blocks everyone's ability (and desire!) to reflect on the possibilities sketched out above. Rather, we could begin to think further about how to create environments nourishing the kind of respectful reflections and dialogues evident in the project of this volume itself. As some feminists of color have argued, one will want to appreciate the importance of solidarity, not unity, among groups with different but partially overlapping interests.[9]

NOTES

1. "Liberal," "radical," and the other labels here designate proper names of particular historical social movements and their characteristic theories, not merely (or perhaps in some cases, at all) everyday descriptions of individuals, groups, or ideas as liberal, radical, etc.

2. Of course, this position is much richer and more heterogeneous than this brief account can indicate. There are many different ways in which feminists in different disciplines and in different projects have tried to make empiricism work for feminist projects. However, the "ideal type" of this position on which I focus here contains central elements of all feminist empiricist epistemologies.

3. The movements of women factory workers and the working-class feminist movements in late nineteenth- and early twentieth-century United States, Germany, England, and other European countries were often called "socialist feminist" movements. However, today this term is often reserved for the movements and theories that emerged side-by-side with radical feminism after World War II, and "Marxist feminism" then used to designate the earlier movement and its theories. (see, i.e., Jaggar 1983; Jaggar and Rothenberg 1993). This later socialist feminism, like radical feminism, had to confront forms of women's oppression that became visible only after Sigmund Freud, after the massive entrance of women into higher education, after the increased percentages of working- and middle-class women with children under the age of six had entered wage-labor, etc.

4. Radical feminism is sometimes read only as valorizing the category of the feminine, which some radical feminists do. However, Alison Jaggar and Paula Rothenberg 1993, one of the most widely used women's studies texts for almost two decades, has consistently included problematization of gender categories as a radical feminist project.

5. John Stoltenberg 1990. It would take this essay on a tangent to go into Stoltenberg's actual analysis, so I am not aligning myself with everything it means to him to "refuse to be a man," but only with this interesting idea that he pursues in the book.

6. The initial feminist standpoint writings can be found in Sandra Harding 1983, 1986; Nancy Hartsock 1983; Alison Jaggar 1983; Dorothy Smith 1987, 1990; and, I would argue, Jane Flax 1983, though Flax herself might disagree. (Some of Smith's essays in these collections originally appeared in the mid-1970s.) See also the development and uses of this epistemology in Patricia Hill Collins 1991, Donna Haraway 1991, Sandra Harding 1993, and Rosemary Hennessey 1993. Significant parts of standpoint epistemology can be found in such otherwise clearly radical feminist writings as Catharine MacKinnon 1982. Moreover, this approach has a social history as well as an intellectual history. The former ensures that something like it will emerge when the "view from nowhere," or, in Haraway's phrase (cf. above), "God-trick" epistemologies are being challenged. The original standpoint arguments were class-based; race/ethnicity-based and postcolonial ones are widespread today.

7. My thinking here has been improved by conversations with Talia Bettcher, Holly De-Vor, and Jacob Hale.

8. The phrase is Tom Digby's (personal communication).

9. I thank Harry Brod, Tom Digby, and David Kahane for their helpful comments on an earlier draft of this chapter.

REFERENCES

Antony, Louise, and Charlotte Witt. 1993. *A mind of one's own: Feminist essays on reason and objectivity.* Boulder: Westview Press.

Barinaga, Marcia. 1993. Is there a "female style" in science? *Science* 260: 380–91.

Belenky, Mary, et al. 1986. *Women's ways of knowing.* New York: Basic Books.

Boone, Joseph A. 1990. Of me(n) and feminism: Who(se) is the sex that writes? In *Engendering men: The question of male feminist criticism,* ed. Joseph A. Boone and Michael Cadden. New York: Routledge.

Bordo, Susan. 1987. *The flight to objectivity: Reflections on Cartesianism and culture.* Albany: State University of New York Press.

Brod, Harry, ed. 1987. *The making of masculinities: The new men's studies.* New York: Allen & Unwin.

———, and Michael Kaufman, eds. 1994. *Theorizing masculinities.* Thousand Oaks: Sage Publications.

Clatterbaugh, Kenneth. 1990. *Contemporary perspectives on masculinity.* Boulder: Westview Press.

Code, Lorraine. 1991. *What can she know?* Ithaca: Cornell University Press.

Collins, Patricia Hill. 1991. *Black feminist thought: Knowledge, consciousness, and the politics of empowerment.* New York: Routledge.

D'Emilio, John. 1993. Capitalism and gay identity. In *The lesbian and gay studies reader,* ed. Henry Abelove Henry, Mechele Aina Barale, and David M. Halperin. New York: Routledge.

Duberman, Martin, Martha Vicinus, and George Chauncey Jr., eds. 1989. *Hidden from history: Reclaiming the gay and lesbian past.* New York: Penguin.

Enloe, Cynthia. 1990. *Bananas, beaches, and bases: Making feminist sense of international politics.* Berkeley: University of California Press.

Flax, Jane. 1983. Political philosophy and the patriarchal unconscious. In *Discovering Reality,* ed. Sandra Harding and Merrill Hintikka. Dordrecht: Reidel/Kluwer.

Forrester. 1993. What do men want? In *Between Men and Ferninism,* ed. David Porter. London: Routledge.

Galison, Peter, and David Stump, eds. 1996. *The disunity of science.* Stanford: Stanford University Press.

Halperin, David. 1993. Is there a history of sexuality? In *The lesbian and gay studies reader,* ed. Henry Abelove Henry, Mechele Aina Barale, and David M. Halperin. New York: Routledge.

Haraway, Donna. 1991. Situated knowledges, In *Simians, cyborgs, and women: The reinvention of nature.* New York: Routledge.

Harding, Sandra. 1986. *The science question in feminism.* Ithaca: Cornell University Press.

———. 1987. Is there a feminist method? In *Feminism and methodology: Social science issues,* ed. S. Harding. Bloomington: Indiana University Press.

———. 1991. *Whose science? Whose knowledge? Thinking from women's lives.* Ithaca: Cornell University Press.

———. 1992. Rethinking standpoint epistemology: What is strong objectivity? In *Feminist epistemologies,* ed. Linda Alcoff and Elizabeth Potter, 49–82. New York: Routledge.

———. 1995. Subjectivity, experience, and knowledge: An epistemology from/for rainbow coalition politics. In *Who can speak? Authority and critical identity,* ed. Judith Roof and Robyn Weigman. Urbana: University of Illinois Press.

———. 1997. Women's standpoints on nature: What makes them possible? *Osiris* 12

———. forthcoming. *Is science multicultural? Postcolonialism, femninism, and epistemology.* Bloomington: Indiana University Press.

———, and Merrill Hintikka, eds. 1983. *Discovering reality: Feminist perspectives on epistemology, metaphysics, methodology, and philosophy of science.* Dordrecht: Reidel/Kluwer.

Hartsock, Nancy. 1983. The feminist standpoint: Developing the ground for a specifically feminist historical materialism. In *Discovering reality,* ed. S. Harding and M. Hintikka. Dordrecht: Reidel/Kluwer.

Hennessey, Rosemary. 1993. *Feminist materialism and the politics of discourse.* New York: Routledge.

Jaggar, Alison. 1983. Chapter 11 of *Feminist politics and Human nature.* Totowa, NJ: Rowman and Allenheld.

———. 1989. Love and knowledge in feminist epistemology. In *Gender/body/knowledge,* ed. Alison Jaggar and Susan Bordo. New Brunswick: Rutgers University Press.

———. and Paula Rothenberg, eds. 1993. *Feminist frameworks.* 3rd ed. New York: McGraw-Hill.

Katz, Jonathan Ned. 1995. *The invention of heterosexuality.* New York: Dutton.

Lennon, Kathleen, and Margaret Whitford, eds. 1994. *Knowing the difference: Feminist perspectives in epistemology.* London: Routledge.

Lloyd, Genevieve. 1984. The man of reason: Male and female. In *Western philosophy.* Minneapolis: University of Minnesota Press.

Longino, Helen. 1990. *Science as social knowledge.* Princeton: Princeton University Press.

MacKinnon, Catherine. 1982. Feminism, Marxism, method, and the state: An agenda for theory. *Signs* 7:3.

Millman, Marcia, and Rosabeth Moss Kanter. 1987. Introduction to Another voice: Feminist perspectives on social life and social science. In *Feminism and methodology: Social science issues,* ed. S. Harding. Bloomington: Indiana University Press.

Nelson, Lynn Hankinson. 1990. *Who knows.* Philadelphia: Temple University Press.

Roof, Judith, and Robyn Weigand, eds. 1995. *Who can speak? Authority and critical identity.* Urbana: University of Illinois Press.

Scheurich, James Joseph, and Michelle D. Young. 1997. Coloring epistemologies: Are our research epistemologies racially biased? *Educational Researcher* 26(3): 4–16.

Smith, Dorothy. 1987. *The everyday world as problematic: A sociology for women.* Boston: Northeastern University Press.

———. 1990. *The conceptual practices of power: A feminist sociology of knowledge.* Boston: Northeastern University Press.

Sociological Theory. 1994. 12(2). Special cluster of papers on Queer theory/Sociology: A dialogue, ed. Steven Seidman, 166–248.

Stoltenberg, John. 1990. *Refusing to be a man.* New York: Meridian.

CHAPTER 11

Fieldwork in Lesbian and Gay Communities

KATH WESTON

This study addresses a deceptively simple set of questions: What is all this talk about gay families? Where did those families come from, and why should they appear now?

The fieldwork that provides the basis for my analysis was conducted in the San Francisco Bay Area during 1985–1986, with a follow-up visit in 1987. San Francisco is a port city with a large and extremely diverse population of lesbians and gay men, as well as a history of gay immigration that dates at least to World War II (D'Emilio 1989). A wave of lesbian and gay immigrants arrived in the Bay Area during the 1970s, when young people of all sexualities found themselves attracted by employment opportunities in the region's rapidly expanding service sector (FitzGerald 1986). Some came for the work, some for the climate, and some to be a part of "gay mecca." Others, of course, grew up in California.

Several San Francisco neighborhoods—Folsom, Polk Street, the Castro, Bernal Heights, parts of the Tenderloin, and increasingly the Mission—were recognized even by heterosexual residents as areas with high concentrations of gay men and/or lesbians.

The third tour bus in as many hours rolls through the Castro. I watch from behind the plate glass window of the donut shop, trying to imagine this neighborhood, so symbolic of "gay America," through tourist eyes. Every television reporter who covers AIDS seems to station herself somewhere on this block. The Castro used to be a place where gay men could come to cruise and enjoy one another, objects (if not always subjects) for themselves. Nowadays, says the man sitting next to me, when you see those buses coming around, you feel like you're in a museum or a zoo or something.

With its unique history and reputation as a gay city, San Francisco hardly presents a "typical" lesbian and gay population for study. Yet the Bay Area proved to be a valuable field site because it brought together gay men and lesbians from very different colors and classes, identities and backgrounds. One estimate for 1980 put San Francisco's combined self-identified lesbian, gay, and bisexual population at 17 percent. Of those who placed themselves in one of these categories, 30 percent were women and 70 percent were men (DeLeon and Brown 1980). Lesbians were a visible presence on both sides of the bay. In contrast to many smaller cities, the region supported an abundance of specialized organizations aimed at particular sectors of the gay population, from groups for people over or under a certain age to associations of individuals who played music or enjoyed hiking. With its multicultural population, the Bay Area also hosted a variety of social organizations, political groups, and informal gathering places for gay people of color.

Among lesbians and gay men in the country at large, San Francisco is known as a place that allows people to be relatively open about their sexual identities. Carol Warren (1977) has emphasized the need to be especially protective of respondents' identities when working with gay people, in light of the social stigmatization of homosexuality. Although I follow anthropological tradition by using pseudonyms throughout this study, I feel it is important to note that the vast majority of participants expressed a willingness to have their real names appear in print. Fear of losing employment and a desire to protect children's identities were the reasons offered by the few who requested assurances of anonymity. Unlike many studies of gay men and lesbians, this one assigns surnames to participants. In a Western context, introducing strangers by given names alone paradoxically conveys a sense of intimacy while subtly withholding individuality, respect, and full adult status from research participants. Because the same qualities are routinely denied to lesbians and gay men in society at large, the use of only first names can have the unintended consequence of perpetuating heterosexist assumptions.

While we sit at the bar watching women play pool, Sharon Vitrano is telling me about her experience walking home through the Tenderloin after one of the annual Gay Pride Parades. As she and a woman friend approached a group of men in front of a Mom-and-Pop grocery store, the two stopped walking arm in arm. On her mind, she says, were the tensions growing out of San Francisco's rapid gentrification, and escalating street violence linked to perceptions of gay people as wealthy real estate speculators. To Sharon's surprise and delight, one of the men shouted out, "Go ahead, hold hands! It's your day!"

In addition to the long hours of participant observation so central to anthropological fieldwork, my analysis draws on eighty in-depth interviews conducted while in the field. Interview participants were divided evenly between women and men, with all but two identifying themselves as lesbian or gay. Random sampling is clearly an impossibility for a population that is not only partially hidden or "closeted," but also lacks consensus as to the criteria for membership (Morin 1977; NOGLSTP 1986). In general, I let self-identification be my guide for inclusion. Determined to avoid the race, class, and organizational bias that has characterized so many studies of gay men and lesbians, I made my initial connections through personal contacts developed over the six years I had lived in San Francisco previous to the time the project got underway. The alternative—gaining entree through agencies, college classes, and advertisements—tends to weight a sample for "joiners," professional interviewees, the highly educated, persons with an overtly political analysis, and individuals who see themselves as central (rather than marginal) to the population in question.

By asking each person interviewed for names of potential participants, I utilized techniques of friendship pyramiding and snowball sampling to arrive at a sample varied in race, ethnicity, class, and class background. While the Bay Area is perhaps more generally politicized than other regions of the nation, the majority of interview participants would not have portrayed themselves as political activists. Approximately 36 percent were people of color; of the 64 percent who were white, eleven (or 14 percent of the total) were Jewish. Slightly over 50 percent came from working-class backgrounds, with an overlapping 58 percent employed in working-class occupations at the time of the interview.

At the outset I had intended to arrange second interviews with a portion of the sample, but decided instead to seek informal contexts for follow-up that would allow me to interact with participants as part of a group. Most of the direct quotations in this study are drawn from interviews, but some arose during dinner table conversations, birthday parties, a night out at a bar, or asides during a ball game. I strove not to select interview participants on the basis of the kind of experiences they claimed to have had. Individuals' characterizations of their personal histories ran the gamut from "boring" to "incredible," but I found these assessments a completely unreliable index of interest from an anthropological point of view.

Out of eighty-two people contacted, only two turned down my request for an interview. A few individuals made an effort to find me after hearing about the study, but most were far from self-selecting. The vast majority demanded great persistence and flexibility in scheduling (and rescheduling) on my part to convince them to participate. I believe this persistence is one reason this study includes voices not customarily heard when lesbians and gay men appear in the pages of books and journals: people who had constructed exceedingly private lives and could scarcely get over their disbelief at allowing themselves to be interviewed, people convinced that their experiences were uneventful or unworthy of note, people fearful that a researcher would go away and write an account lacking in respect for their identities or their perceptions.

To offset the tendency of earlier studies to focus on the white and wealthier sectors of lesbian and gay populations, I also utilized theoretic sampling. From a growing pool of contacts I deliberately selected people of color, people from working-class backgrounds, and individuals employed in working-class occupations.

What a busy day for a Friday, I think to myself, sinking into a chair after three back-to-back interviews. At the first apartment, stacks of papers had covered every counter, table, desk, and anything else approximating a flat surface. Before the interview began, Bernie Margolis, a Jewish man in his sixties, insisted on showing me his picture gallery. In one frame, a much younger Bernie stood next to Martin Luther King Jr.; others held snapshots of children from a previous marriage and distinguished service awards from a variety of community organizations. Before I left, he asked me to proofread a political leaflet. From his Mission district flat I traveled up to the Fillmore to meet Rose Ellis, an African American woman in her thirties. Laid off from her construction job, she was cooking a batch of blackeyed peas and watching soap operas when I arrived. After the interview, Rose asked me to play back part of the tape through her roommate's stereo system—so that she could hear what her voice sounded like. A little later I hurried home to interview Annie Sorenson, a young white woman who described herself as a "lesbian virgin" with few gay or lesbian friends. From the vantage point of an easy chair reflecting back upon the day, my initial reaction is to wonder what these three people are doing in the same book.

In any sample this diverse, with so many different combinations of identities, theoretic sampling cannot hope to be "representative." To treat each individual as a representative of his or her race, for instance, would be a form of tokenism that glosses over the differences of gender, class, age, national origin, language, religion, and ability which crosscut race and ethnicity. At the same time, I am not interested in these categories as demographic variables, or as reified pigeonholes for people, but rather as identities meaningful to participants themselves. I concentrate here on the interpretive links participants made (or did not make) between sexual identity and other aspects of who they considered themselves to be, always with the awareness that identical symbols can carry very different meanings in different contexts.

Despite my efforts to incorporate differences, the sample remains weak in several areas, most notably the age range (which tends to cluster around the twenties and thirties), the inclusion of relatively few gay parents, and a bias toward fairly high levels of education. Given the age-, gender-, and race-segregated structure of gay institutions and social organization, these results may partially have been a function of my own situation and identities. I was in my late twenties at the time of the study, had no children, and usually ran out of boxes to check when asked to number my years of education on forms or surveys. But the sample's deficiencies also indicate my emphasis during fieldwork, since its composition does not reflect other aspects of identity as a white woman from a working-class background. I made the greatest effort to achieve breadth in the areas of present class, class background, and race/ethnicity.

In retrospect, I wish I had added age to this list of priorities. Judging from the gay men and lesbians in older age cohorts that I did interview, people who came out before the social movements of the 1950s-1970s may possess distinctive perspectives on the issue of disclosing their sexual identities to others, including relatives (cf. Hall 1978). Although those movements affected people of all ages who lived through that time period, older interview participants often cast their experiences in a comparative framework, distinguishing between what it meant to pursue same-sex erotic relations "then" and "now." Life experiences had made many acutely aware of the negative social and economic consequences that can follow from disclosure of a lesbian or gay identity. In her study of lesbians over sixty, Monika Kehoe (1989) found that women who had married before they claimed a lesbian identity were likely to have maintained close ties with blood relatives (especially female kin) after coming out. Yet some of the same women had suffered ostracism at the hands of their heterosexual adult children.

To date there is conflicting evidence regarding the relationship between lesbian or gay identity and aging. Both the older gay men studied by Raymond Berger (1982b) and Kehoe's survey respondents reported loneliness and isolation, but their responses may have reflected the loneliness experienced by many people in the United States following retirement or the death of a partner. Further research needs to be conducted on the development of friendship networks among gay people over time, particularly given the high value historically placed on friendship by both lesbians and gay men. Do those networks expand, contract, or maintain their size as individuals grow older? Do gay people look more often to friendships, as opposed to other types of social relations, for support and assistance as they age? Are older gay men and lesbians participating in the discourse on gay families to the same extent as their younger counterparts? Since most existing studies compare lesbians to heterosexual women and gay men to heterosexual men within their respective age cohorts, there is also a need for research that contrasts the experiences of older lesbians and gay men.

"Are you a lesbian? Are you gay?" Every other day one of these questions greets my efforts to set up interviews over the telephone. Halfway through my fieldwork, I remark on this concern with the researcher's identity while addressing a course in anthropological field methods. "Do you think you could have done this study if you weren't a lesbian?" asks a student from the back of the classroom. "No doubt," I reply, "but then again, it wouldn't have been the same study."

As late as 1982, Raymond Berger experienced difficulty locating lesbians of any class, color, or creed for a study of older gay people. Concluding that lesbians had little in the way of a visible public community, he gave up and confined his book to men. While gay male institutions may be more apparent to the eye, lesbians have their own (actually quite accessible) organizations and establishments, most well-documented in local community newspapers. My point here is that lesbians remained invisible *to Berger;* for me, as a woman, finding male participants proved more of a challenge. Recent work in cultural anthropology has stressed the importance of recognizing the researcher as a positioned subject (Mintz 1979; Rosaldo 1989). In my case, being a woman also influenced how I spent my time in the field: I passed more hours in lesbian clubs and women's groups than gay men's bars or male gyms.

Once I started to gain referrals, my lesbian identity clearly helped me lay claim to those bywords that anthropologists like to apply to relationships in the field when information is forthcoming: "trust" and "rapport." Many participants mentioned that they would not have talked to me had I been straight, and one or two cited "bad experiences" of having had their words misinterpreted by heterosexual researchers. In interviews with me people devoted relatively little time to addressing antigay stereotypes, and spoke freely about subjects such as butch/fem, gay marriage, sadomasochism (s/m), and drag queens—all topics controversial among gay men and lesbians themselves. Occasionally, of course, the larger context of eventual publication would intrude, and individuals would qualify their statements.

Presumptions of a common frame of reference and shared identity can also complicate the anthropologist's task by leaving cultural notions implicit, making her work to get people to state, explain, and situate the obvious. To study one's own culture involves a process of making the familiar strange, more the province of the poet or phenomenologist than of fieldworkers traveling abroad to unravel what seems puzzling about other societies. Early in the research my daily routine was structured by decisions about what to record. Everything around me seemed fair game for notes: one day I was living a social reality, the next day I was supposed to document it. Unlike anthropologists who have returned from the field to write ethnographies that contain accounts of reaching "their" island or village, I saw no possibility of framing an arrival scene to represent the inauguration of my fieldwork, except perhaps by drawing on the novelty of the first friend who asked (with a sidelong glance), "Are you taking notes on this?" My task could not even be characterized as an exploration of "strangeness inside the familiar," a phrase used by Frances FitzGerald (1986) to describe her investigation of the gay Castro district. For me, doing fieldwork among gay and lesbian San Franciscans did not entail uncovering some "exotic" corner of my native culture but rather discovering the stuff of everyday life.

After three rings I put aside the interview I've been transcribing and reluctantly head for the phone. It's my friend Mara calling for the first time in months. With a certain embarrassment, she tells me about the affair she's been having with a man. Everything is over now, she assures me, maintaining that the affair has no wider implications for the lesbian identity. "The reason I'm calling," she says half in jest, "is that I need an anthropologist. How would you like to ghost-write a book about this whole thing? I'm going to call it My Year Among the Savages."

During interviews I used coming-out stories as a point of departure for investigating issues of identity and relationships with blood or adoptive relatives. Such narratives are customarily related to and for other lesbians and gay men rather than for the benefit of a heterosexual audience. Coming out stories had the advantage of representing a category meaningful to participants themselves, a category so indigenous that one woman asked, "Do you want the thirty-three or the forty-five rpm version?" Making new acquaintances was one type of occasion that often called for telling a coming-out story, and it seemed to me at times that my role as interviewer began to blend with the role of "lesbian friend of a friend."

In New York to do research at the Lesbian Herstory Archives, I notice that local news programs are dominated by coverage of the Statue of Liberty Restoration project. "Miss Liberty" and "Lady Liberty, " the newscasters call her. To people in the United States, "Mrs. Liberty" would sound like a joke.

A note on terminology is apropos here. I frequently refer to "lesbians and gay men" to remind readers of gendered differences and to undermine the all too common assumption that findings about gay men hold equally for lesbians. At times, however, I employ "gay" and "gay people" as generic terms that embrace both women and men. In the Bay Area, women themselves held different opinions regarding the application of these terms. Those who had come out in association with the women's movement were inclined to call themselves lesbians and reserve the word "gay" for men. Younger women, women who maintained social ties to gay men, and women with less connection to lesbian feminism, were more apt to describe themselves as gay. In certain contexts a broad range of people employed "gay" as a contrasting parallel to the categories "straight" and "heterosexual."

Readers may also notice the conspicuous absence of the term *American* throughout the text. A Latino participant playfully suggested the modifier "United Statesian" as a substitute that would demonstrate respect for residents of Central and South America—as well as Canada, Mexico, and the Caribbean—who also reside in the Americas name. I have elected to avoid such summary terms altogether, not only in deference to the linguistic claims of other peoples, but also because the label *American* is so bound up with nationalist sentiment ("the American way") that it defies limitation to a descriptive reference.

I have interchanged "African American" with "black," "Native American" with "American Indian," and "Mexican American" with "Chicano" and "Chicana." Preference for one or the other of these terms varied with regional origin, generation, political involvement, and personal likes or dislikes. In many contexts people referred to more specific racial and ethnic identities (Cuban American rather than Hispanic, Chinese American rather than Asian American). Occasionally, however, they appealed to a collective racial identity defined vis-à-vis the socially dominant categories "white" or "Anglo." "Minorities" is clearly unsatisfactory for describing this collectivity, since white people represent the numerical minority in many parts of the Bay Area, not to mention the world as a whole. I employ "people of color" for lack of a better term, although the phrase remains problematic. Racial identity and skin tone do not always correspond to the color symbolism used to depict race in the United States. The term *people of color* can also reinforce racist perceptions of white as the unmarked, and so more generically human, category. White, of course, is also a color, and white people are as implicated in race relations as anyone else in this society.

Defining class is always a vexed issue, especially in the United States, where class consciousness is often absent or superseded by other identities (Jackman and Jackman 1983). Rayna Rapp (1982) has astutely observed that class is a process, not a position or a place. Class in this sense cannot be indexed by income or plotted along a sociological continuum from "upper" to "lower." Nevertheless, to convey the range of the interview sample, I have organized a rough classification of participants based on occupation (or parents' occupations, in the case of class background), following a Marxist interpretation of class as a relation to processes of production. Where the term "middle class" appears in the text, it is always in quotation marks to indicate its status as an indigenous term used by people I encountered during fieldwork, rather than an analytic category of my own choosing.

REFERENCES

Berger, Raymond M. 1982a. The unseen minority: Older gays and lesbians. *Social Work* 27(3): 236–42.

———. 1982b. *Gay and gray: The older homosexual man.* Urbana: University of Illinois Press.

D'Emilio, John. 1989. Gay politics, gay community: San Francisco's experience. In *Hidden from history: Reclaiming the gay and lesbian past,* ed. Martin Bauml Duberman, Martha Vicinus, and George Chauncey Jr., 456–73. New York: New American Library.

DeLeon, Richard, and Courtney Brown. 1980. Preliminary estimates of size of gay/bisexual population in San Francisco based on combined data from January and June S.F.Charter Commission Surveys. Mimeograph.

FitzGerald, Frances. 1986. *Cities on a hill: A journey through contemporary american cultures.* New York: Simon & Schuster.

Hall, Marny. 1978. Lesbian families: Cultural and clinical issues. *Social Work* 23(4):380–85.
Kehoe, Monika. 1989. *Lesbians over 60 speak for themselves.* New York: Harrington Park Press.
Jackman, Mary R., and Robert W. Jackman. 1983. *Class awareness in the United States.* Berkeley: University of California Press.
Mintz, Sidney W. 1979. The anthropological interview and the life history. *Oral History Review* 17:18–26.
Morin, Stephen F. 1977. Heterosexual bias in psychological research on lesbianism and male homosexuality. *American Psychologist* 32: 629–37.
National Organization of Gay & Lesbian Scientists & Technical Professionals (NOGLSTP). 1986. Measuring the gay and lesbian population. Pamphlet.
Rapp, Rayna. 1982. Family and class in contemporary America: Notes toward an understanding of ideology. In *Rethinking the family,* ed. Barrie Thorne with Marilyn Yalom, 168–87. New York: Longman.
———. 1987. Toward a nuclear freeze? The gender politics of Euro-American kinship analysis. In *Gender and kinship: Essays toward a unified analysis,* ed. Jane Fishburne Collier and Sylvia Junko Yanagisako, 119–31. Stanford: Stanford University Press.
Rosaldo, Michelle Z. 1983. The shame of headhunters and the autonomy of self. *Ethos* 11(3): 135–51.
———. 1984. Toward an anthropology of self and feeling. In *Culture theory: Essays on mind, self, and emotion,* ed. Richard Shweder and Robert Levine, 137–57. New York: Cambridge University Press.
Warren, Carol A. B. 1974. *Identity and community in the gay world.* New York: Wiley.
———. 1977. Fieldwork in the gay world: Issues in phenomenological research. *Journal of Social Issues* 33(4): 93–107.

PART III

APPLICATIONS AND METHODS

CHAPTER 12

How Feminists Practice Social Research

SHARLENE NAGY HESSE-BIBER AND DENISE LECKENBY

What makes feminist research feminist? Are there particular applications of methods that are distinctly feminist? Is there a feminist method that is particular in its feminist grounding and singularly focused on feminist aims? Is there a tool that in its function does no harm to women? What are the threads of research that embody feminist epistemology and methodology? These are questions with complex and contested answers. These are some of the most critical questions central to the practice of feminist research

Like most researchers, feminists utilize diverse methods, drawing from a great number of well-established methods in the natural and social sciences. Shulamit Reinharz states that "feminism supplies the perspective and the disciplines supply the method. The feminist researcher exists at their intersection" (Reinharz 1992, 243). For many feminist researchers their location is marked by the borders of their discipline and their theoretical and epistemological perspectives as feminists. Reinharz acknowledges the efforts made by feminists to avoid a "narrowing" of method and methodological choices available to researchers; rather, feminist researchers continue to pursue the broadest collection of possible perspectives and tools for their research endeavors (Reinharz 1992, 244). Feminist researchers may use multiple tools to gain access and understanding into the world around them and may in fact use multiple methods within the same study (Tolman and Szalacha 1999). Illustrative of the dynamic plurality of feminist research, Part III of this volume locates and looks at various types of feminist research and the application of a number of methods feminist social scientists employ in conducting their research from a range of disciplinary perspectives. For each type of feminist research, the readings include a "discussion" piece in which the researcher talks about her research experience and how she went about doing her research, and an "example" piece that is the published research report of a feminist project. The selections chosen for this section are not exhaustive of all feminist research or all the methods feminists use. These selections do, however, provide a broad context within which to examine feminist research. We inductively analyze these studies looking for *common threads* that describe how methods, in the hands of feminists, interact with the world to produce what is known as feminist research. We are especially interested in looking at the dynamic interaction between all three aspects of the research process—epistemology, methodology, and method.

Feminist researchers often bring a unique epistemological and methodological lens to the question of how to do research. Within the research process, regardless of the method they have chosen, feminists are attuned to the way they frame their research questions. In this section we describe how feminist researchers approach their work from various angles, including empiricist, standpoint, postmodernist, and critical epistemological foci, using resources from multiple disciplines, including both quantitative and qualitative tools. Feminist researchers are not wedded to any one method. Like many researchers, they allow the questions they pose to guide the choices of their method. Feminists' approach to methodology allows for "new" types of questions about women's lives and those of "other/ed" marginalized groups to be addressed within their respective fields of research.

Research conducted from a feminist perspective often promotes new areas of knowledge building and can lead to the implementation of innovative methods. Epistemology, methodology and methods are not de-linked from each other but interact in dynamic ways to produce new knowledge and this openness itself is also characteristic of how feminist researchers approach their work. The methodological and epistemological assumptions are made manifest throughout the research process; they are not confined to the early stages of research design. The theoretical perspectives, methodological commitments, and method processes all engage cyclically with one another during feminist research. This interaction might take place in the method's connection with the epistemology and methodology of the researcher. This might take place through the reflexive sensitivity the researcher employs while engaging in data collection. This might be seen through the method's interaction with the research participant. This connection also impacts the ways that the research is presented and written about, where the method is explained and delineated.

In many of these selections, feminist researchers take hold of their epistemological and methodological groundings, and dynamically interact with the methods they employ in their research project. The process of interlocking epistemology, methodology, and method in feminist research shapes a *synergistic perspective of research.* This synergy, or interaction between the three elements of research, can be best understood through the emergent commonalities that arise from its energetic impact on feminist research. Through a synergistic connection between the elements of research—epistemology, methodology, and method—we find that feminist inquiry often shapes new research endeavors that are greater than the sum of their parts. In other words, while traditional research employs these components of research, the synergistic engagement of these components in feminist research interrogates the status quo, aiming to raise our consciousness about how we do research. Looking at the selections provided in this section, we are able to view feminist research, its implementation of synergistic use of epistemology, methodology, and method, and the resulting qualities of feminist research in action.

COMMON ELEMENTS OF FEMINIST RESEARCH

Asking New Questions

The way feminist researchers frame their questions, what is explicit and what goes unsaid can be linked to the methodological and epistemological core of their identity as a researcher. Through the synergistic connections of epistemological and methodological perspectives, feminist researchers are continually and cyclically interrogating their locations as both researcher and as feminist. They engage the boundaries of their multiple identities and multiple research aims through conscientious reflection. This engagement with their identities and roles impacts the earliest stages of research design. Much of feminist research design is marked by an openness to the shifting contexts and fluid intentions of the research question. Feminists root their research in their feminism, steeping the process of method in multiple phases of the research. Susan Geiger asks us what makes research questions feminist? She states:

> [O]ur objectives will obviously influence the kinds of questions we will address in collecting oral histories. In my view, questions that in their content or formulation presume the accuracy of existing partial, androcentric, or ethnocentric constructions of the lives or situations of women are not feminist.

Working within oral history traditions, Geiger guides her questions through a qualitative methodological lens, often used by feminist researchers. She delineates the uses of oral history as a feminist method as well as those that are not. She states, "[O]ral history only becomes a method in the hands of persons whose interests go beyond the immediate pleasure of hearing/learning the history being told." There is a feminist *use* of the oral history in the ways it draws questions to the mind of the researcher, rigorously attached to the feminist researcher's theoretical orientation. Geiger states that "it can only become a feminist *methodology* if its use is systematized in particular feminist ways and if the objectives for collecting the oral data are feminist." Here the feminist methodology impacts the use of the oral history method in all stages of the research, at the beginning when the subjects are chosen, in the manner in which the oral history is collected, and in the analysis and presentation of the information gained. In this section Susan Geiger, Marjorie DeVault, Kristin Anderson, and Debra Umberson all describe their methods and methodologies in detail, confronting troublesome issues, expressing their cautions, illuminating the benefits of feminist research within the frame of their research focus. The articulation of a particular method's interaction and impact on the world at large is another hallmark of feminist research design.

Research design is impacted, often powerfully, by feminist questions where method is determined from the researcher's epistemological and methodological perspective. Mimi Shippers employs ethnographic participant observation to analyze alternative rock music subculture, seeking to "demonstrate the utility and importance of analytically separating sexuality and gender." She looks at verbal and nonverbal data collected in her ethnography to understand the multiple and shifting meanings of sexuality and gender in context. *In context* is a pivotal point for Shippers' choice of method and her ability to collect information on the multilayered experience of sexualities. She looks at sexuality with regards to identity as self-identified through dialogue and interview. She looks for expressions of sexual practices, specifically nonverbal, including winking, kissing, and erotic dancing. She is continually guided by her focus "in the field . . . on the ways in which social interactions reinforced or challenged hegemonic masculinity and femininity and on whether there was sexual interaction among women or among men." Yet Shippers is open to the complexities of sexuality and sexual organization that went beyond the heterosexual/homosexual binary. She allows her research question to be open enough to seek out new theories of sexuality beyond the hetero-focused binary and into queer theory. Her research design and use of ethnography opens Shippers to the potentiality of multiple meanings within multiple contexts, providing "a robust understanding of how hegemony and resistance operated in this subculture." Through her openness, Shippers engages with her own forms of theory building, adding to the body of queer theory, while also indicating its relevance to real life situations.

Research questions range from the broadly general to highly specific. Antoinette Errante provides us with an example of how feminist questions remain open to the changing focus of the researcher. Errante actively engages with the successes and failures of her research methods, allowing for her reflexivity to impact the extension of her methods. She examines the ways negotiation and resistance impacted people's lives in colonial and postcolonial Mozambique through oral history. Her research goals were guided by her desire to understand the collective experiences that were not part of the historical record. To ensure that she was gathering collective experiences, she states, "I triangulated narrators' individual stories with each other and with other published and archival documentation." But in doing so, she finds that she has been treating these oral histories as mere documents, rather than memories that are shaped through processes of "remembering, forgetting, reconstructing, metamorphosis of memory, and vicarious memory." Initially, Errante did not realize that these processes of remembering and telling were an important part of understanding the research topic and engaging with the experiences of research participants. Remembering, both individual and collective, from the perspectives of the researcher and participants became Errante's research focus. She allowed herself to be open to the shifting focus of her research design and its fluid movement over time. Feminist research is marked by an openness to the fluidity and flux of the research question, allowing the question to be informed by shifting power relations within the research process, methodological choices, and situational changes. The questions are rooted in the epistemological and methodological perspectives of the researcher and impact the method chosen and implemented, providing an environment of open engagement between these elements of research.

Choice of Methods

Openness often marks the feminist research question and appropriateness often marks the choice of method. Feminist researchers often discuss the appropriateness of a method for a particular question or amongst a particular group of participants. Sue Wilkinson opens up discussion of what occasions might be inappropriate for the use of focus groups, from a feminist perspective. She argues that they should not be used simply as an effective way to gather a great deal of qualitative data in a short period of time. She states that from an essentialist perspective, researchers see focus groups as a way to gain access to the "individual in social context." However, Wilkinson notes, if a researcher is rooted in critical or post-structuralist epistemological framework, they must acknowledge that focus groups are "just as constructed—albeit differently—as, say, responses to an opinion poll or behavior in a laboratory setting."

Although qualitative methods are often used by feminists because of their attention to issues of power and subjugated meaning, feminists also engage quantitative methods from positivist, empirical perspectives. Janet Chafetz argues for the rigorous use of empirical methods that test theories about "universally applicable laws of human behavior." She challenges feminist social scientists to examine feminist concepts of patriarchy, sex/gender distinctions, and sexism through empirical means. She states, "[G]ender sociologists evince relatively little effort toward systematic theory testing, and especially toward testing different explanations of the same phenomenon." Rooted in positivistic epistemology, Janet Chafetz dares feminists to elaborate on the creativity and potential that has situated feminist research as a force in the social sciences, by countering the "lack of clarity, rigor, and data-based, sequential development and refinement," of their research. Maxine Thompson and Verna Keith take up the challenge Chafetz sets before them, examining "the relationship of skin tone to self-concept development" across gender through quantitative methods. They take a deductive approach to test their hypotheses, aiming for the clarity and rigor of which Chafetz speaks. The diversity of epistemological and methodological perspectives provides a window into the various forms of methods feminist research undertakes.

Chafetz further cautions feminists from avoiding positivistic quantitative research, arguing that there is "nothing in the view that patterned behaviors and processes exist, can be measured, and can be explained in substantial measure cross-culturally and panhistorically that automatically denigrates or controls people." Feminist researchers often try to avoid inflicting further exploitation or subordination of individuals either directly through the research process or indirectly through the impact research findings might have in the "real world." Chafetz sees positivistic science, where the world is knowable, understandable, and rigorously examined through empirical research, as an endeavor that can be utilized toward feminist ends. Methodological tools available to feminists should include quantitative and deductive processes according to Janet Chafetz. Working with experimental quantitative methods, Laura Madson tests hypotheses about inferences made of physically androgynous (PA) people about their personality and sexuality. She seeks to understand the assumptions her respondents made about PA people, utilizing traditional methods for feminist aims with social implications. The research design that Maxine Thompson and Verna Keith as well as Laura Madson seek to employ is powerful in its ability to produce Janet Chafetz's "careful construction and testing of theory."

Research for Women

Feminist researchers typically generate research that is for women, rather than about women and this is another critical element of feminist research. Many of the empirical examples shown in this section describe research that holds women as their focus and changing the situation for women as its aim. Mimi Shippers, Jacelyn Hollander, Maxine Thompson, Verna Keith, and Antoinette Errante all give us examples where gender is either a central concept in the organization of analysis or women are the central subject and beneficiary of the research. But this is not always the case. Utilizing open-ended interviews with men who are in treatment for domestic violence, Kristin Anderson and Debra Umberson seek a feminist framework to understand masculinity and its construction within partner abuse. These are feminist questions, utilized by feminists, but are asked of men about masculinity. They seek an understanding of the performance and empowerment of masculinity through the "denigration or erasure of alternative (feminine/gay/lesbian/bisexual) identities." Anderson and Umberson are looking at the situation of domestic violence, often examined from the woman's point of view, through the eyes of men. They are posing new questions that give rise to new understandings about lived experiences and adding to the potential for social change. The subject matter and area of interest for this research is feminist in its approach and use of feminist epistemological and methodological frameworks. Just as *adding women* into research does not make it feminist, feminist research may not have women as its subject.

Tending to Issues of Difference in the Research Process

If research about women provides a primary organizing frame for feminist research, then difference provides a second. Feminists who focus on difference challenge, for example, essentialist notions of a common gendered nature and experience which tends to obscure differences among women and men, and between women and men. Feminist research is often marked by an inclusion of the *interconnections* between the categories of gender, race, class, sexual preference, and so on. As we mentioned in "Difference Matters" (Part II), utilizing Patricia Hill Collins's concept of a "matrix of domination" (1990) we conceptualized difference as a range of interlocking inequalities, where individuals experience categories or positionality differently depending upon their social locations within the social structures of their given society. Those larger social structures are significantly and continually shaped by the society's beliefs about race, class, gender, and sexuality. Anderson and Umberson note the importance of social class and race/ethnicity in accounts of male violence. They found that white males of higher socioeconomic standing tend to frame conflict with their families in material terms and point to the economic rewards they provide for their partners and loved ones in terms of ensuring an education for their children and purchasing consumer items for their home. Those males from poorer economic backgrounds often framed conflict within families as involving fights with other men in their network of acquaintances in order to gain respect within their family circle and among their peers.

Intersections of difference provide feminist research with a densely complex view of the world and the shifting environments that can be seen from within the research process. Incorporating difference within research design is a difficult task. Feminist research walks a fine line between balancing the efforts to seek knowledge that is capable of making generalizations about women as a group and the recognition that all knowledge is socially situated. These dilemmas are negotiated through the particular researcher's field of vision informed by her epistemological groundings. But whether a feminist researcher with positivistic groundings outlined by Chafetz or a qualitative researcher with critical theoretical perspectives outlined by Devault, many feminists find it important to examine the interrelationships between gender and other categories of oppression in their efforts to understand the diversity of women's experiences.

Focus on Lived Experience, Especially Women's Experience and That of "Other" Marginalized Groups

As Dorothy Smith notes, feminist-based knowledge lost its legitimacy and authority within the social sciences as they (social sciences) followed more "traditional" and "scientific" guidelines for what constituted knowledge (Smith, 1990). Data and knowledge gained through scientific methods that could be replicated replaced knowledge gained through direct lived experience. In opposition to this mainstream epistemology, Smith's standpoint epistemology calls for starting research from women's lives, from that lived experience that was eschewed by traditional social science. She notes: "By taking up a standpoint in our original and immediate knowledge of the world, sociologists can make their discipline's socially organized properties first observable and then problematic (Smith, 1999: 390). By using this approach, a researcher can more effectively get "inside" the everyday lives of women and uncover their range of "subjective experiences" (Smith 1990). Thus, standpoint epistemology can help the researcher interpret the data of the Other more effectively. This result is significant because the lived experiences and points of view of the Other is another important element of feminist research.

Although quantitative research provides access into generalizable research findings, many qualitative feminist researchers seek access into data and voices that have been traditionally silenced. But the efforts *to listen and give voice* are not without their own complexities. Postcolonial feminist Gayatri Spivak cautions feminist researchers about their efforts to listen to and grant voice within their research, asking, "Can the subaltern speak?" She states:

> On the other side of the international division of labor, the subject of exploitation cannot know and speak the text of female exploitation even if the absurdity of the nonrepresenting intellectual making space for her to speak is achieved. The woman is doubly in shadow. (Spivak 1994, 84)

For Spivak, feminist researchers must avoid the trap of the nonrepresenting intellectual granting voice across boundaries of difference, reshaping the subaltern as object. Feminist researchers must heed the cautions of postcolonial critics to *unlearn privilege* to *speak to* the muted subjects. The feminist researcher must not ignore the power that is inherent in her own assumption of ability to grant voice to the "othered." This speaking to requires the feminist researcher to be a represented presence within the research endeavor, "rendering delirious that interior voice that is the voice of the other in us" (Spivak 1994, 104). Taking hold of Spivak's and other postcolonial feminists' cautionary tales about first world feminists' attempts to represent the voice of the "othered" requires specific attention and listening to the voice of the researcher.

Feminist researchers are taking heed of postcolonial feminist cautions, using their methods and their researcher positionality to complicate and interrogate their efforts. Methods are tools that in feminist hands often aim to listen to muted language. Methods are doorways that need not limit the scope of understanding or ability to listen to a research participant. Devault argues that feminist frameworks for research should pay attention to language, within the context of talking and listening, to ground their research focus, what is said and what is left unsaid. Such focus changes the way in which she looks at each stage of her research process, namely, the construction of topics, listening, editing, and writing. These four phases of her research are directly related to and impacted by her epistemological and methodological inclinations, informing her choice of interviewing as the method. Similarly, Sue Wilkinson argues that "focus groups enable feminist research to be 'naturalistic' insofar as they mirror the processes of communication in everyday social interaction." Devault and Wilkinson position their epistemology and methodology as central to their choice of methods, relying on their methods ability to allow them to listen to the voices of their participants.

Anderson and Umberson's use of intensive interviewing seeks to understand how men make sense of themselves, their partners, and their actions. They ask, "How do batterers talk about the violence in their relationships?" Anderson and Umberson's analyses bring them to the conclusion that "they excuse, rationalize, justify, and minimize their violence against female partners." But they listen even further, to the voices of these men and the things unsaid, where their accounts describe the performance of gender. Rather than mapping out the interview session with specific and closed-ended questions, Anderson and Umberson provide us with their seven guiding questions. These open-ended questions are the grounding point, but inherently the interviewer must listen *during* the interview to clues and openings that can be pursued further. The interviewer is not a passive receiver of the information, but rather an active participant in the interview process.

Shippers employs a specific sort of listening when viewing and collecting nonverbal data and bodily expressions of sexuality within her ethnography of the alternative music scene. She shows a particular willingness to listen to the contrasting statements her research participants give her concerning compulsory heterosexuality. She states, "[W]hen alternative hard rockers talked about sexuality, it was most often to confront or challenge homophobia or heterosexism . . . where it was uncool to be a bigot." She hears them challenging "derogatory talk about gay and lesbian people," but she also hears them use typically derogatory terms such as dyke and gay in reference to one another. But through her *listening* Shippers hears the participants challenging and resisting heterosexism through their use of these terms. She states, "Maddie used the label dyke as a marker of an alternative femininity to shift the meaning of her assertiveness." Listening is an active process for these researchers, not just during the analysis stages of research but also during the collection process, often allowing them to see what might be hidden and silenced through traditional means of data collection.

Listening adds new dimensions to research questions and design. Errante confronts listening and telling straight on, asking:

> What does it mean to collect and analyze personal narratives? How do persons voice their narratives or narrate their voice? Do conceptions of personhood differ and might this influence the nature of voice and what C. Wright Mills called, "the range of the intricate relations" between history and biography, the personal and the collective?

Errante reflexively interacts with the oral history she conducted in Mozambique, examining the role education took in "socializing persons to maintain, resist, and transform the colonizer-colonized relationship." Yet Errante, in this selection, also looks at the way people organize and express their "narratives of identity" as well as her own researcher narrative and procedures. Attention to voice becomes not just a matter of listening to the research participant's voice, but also paying attention to the researcher's. Errante states:

> I wanted my voice to be minimally heard during the oral history event, and my approach was to ask as few questions as would solicit the information I was looking for. I was interested in how narrators framed their experiences, and so, I allowed them to speak as long as they wished about something they wished to remember, even when this did not seem particularly relevant to my study.

She comments that in some of her interviews she experienced "'flow.' These are moments of optimal experience when our sense of self-efficacy is heightened and our social bonds are strong." The instances of potent and powerful connection between interviewer and respondent are in part consequences of careful listening and an openness to *feel* during the interview. Here we see the feminist researcher *present* in the oral history process, allowing herself the ability to listen to the flow of her emotions and the bonds created within the interview process.

Critiquing her past neglect during the research process, Errante states, "I was not listening precisely because I was *hunting* memories and not the present." This hunting of memories is reflective of Shulamit Reinharz's criticism of the "rape" model of research. Knowledge production through methodological practices is inlaid with power dimensions. Reinharz states, "[T]he right to study human beings cannot be taken-for-granted by the educated elite . . . research is frequently conducted on a rape model: the researchers take, hit and run" (Reinharz 1983, 80). Errante is reflexively criticizing her lack of listening; her interest in her research had caused her to lose her interest in the person. Through her reflexivity, her listening to her own self, and her ability to critique her methods and change them, she was able to gain much more by truly listening to her participants:

> I stopped listening for what I could extract from the narrative and started listening to the whole person. There is no way to translate this into a methodology; it is not an attitude you can feign; but it results in narrators feeling that they have an appreciative and respectful audience.

There is a strong emotional component that is drawn into research when flow is achieved and listening is part of the method. Listening empowers the participant and engages the researcher to be present.

Awareness of Power Dynamics and Practicing "Strong Reflexivity" in the Research Process

An important element within feminist research is the recognition that there are power dynamics in research (Wolf 1996). One of the central issues we examine in this section is the extent to which power relations between the researcher and researched exist and consequently impact the interpretation process. With regard to this issue, one might ask: How much authority should the researcher have in determining whose voice will be heard and counted? Power is fluid in the research process, given and received by both the researcher and research participant. In much of feminist research, researcher positionality and power are deconstructed either implicitly during the research process or explicitly in the writing of the researcher. Shifting power dimensions within the research setting are of primary concern for many feminists. Positivistic methods have been criticized as exploitative of the research subjects, upholding a false sense of objectivity, and distance between the researcher and the participant (Wolf 1996). Some methods directly impact the researcher's power and position by their design. For example, Wilkinson notes that focus groups

> inevitably reduce the researcher's power and control. Simply by virtue of the number of research participants simultaneously involved in the research interaction, the balance of power shifts away from the researcher.

Respondents, through volume and numbers are able to "usurp the moderator," imposing their own meanings, arguments, and control through the interview. The researcher's role is diminished, empowering the research participants in a context in which many participants are disempowered, while also leading to data that is co-constructed and local.

Anderson and Umberson echo this openness where they describe their personal questioning of their researcher position and its effects on the openness of participants and the outcome of the research. They used open-ended interviews with men who have battered their wives or partners to gain understanding about the way men construct their masculinity within their accounts of domestic violence. All interviewers were white females, while the research participants were of diverse racial and socioeconomic backgrounds. With regard to studying across gender differences, "respondents may have offered more deterministic accounts of gender and assumed more shared experiences with the interviewer had they been interviewed by men rather than women."

Concerning racial differences, Anderson and Umberson note that "there is some evidence that we attempted to impose a linear narrative structure on our interviews with some respondents who may have preferred an episodic style." They go so far as to transcribe a particular interview where the interviewer interjects into the story of the respondent, steering "him toward a sequential recounting of one particular incident rather than probing for elaboration of Andrew's perceptions of these multiple events." Anderson and Umberson are open to acknowledging the problems that might arise from the interview process across difference. They show a commitment to understand how difference and researcher positionality might impact the content of data collected. They also show a willingness to allow these concerns and reflections to be made public, written and published with their piece.

On a cautionary note, in order to balance frequently disparate power relations, Daphne Patai argues that many feminist scholars seek to return their research to the communities that made it possible, and they do so in a manner that reinforces traditional inequalities and hierarchies. They may do this as a "feel good measure" to reconcile power imbalances, and they may also abandon intellectual responsibilities in order to gain the trust and approval of their subjects, compromising academic interpretation for a degree of "sisterhood" among subjects (Patai 1991, 147).

Those critical of traditional approaches to qualitative analyses are concerned about uncovering the lived experiences and viewpoints of the Other especially those who have experienced oppression in terms of race, class, age, gender, and so forth. As a feminist researcher attempts to uncover subjective experiences, one might question the likelihood of producing such an understanding. For instance, can a white, middle-aged, female researcher accurately portray what the life of a black, poor teenager is like? Who has the power to represent oneself? Whose voice is represented through this problematic "voice granting" exchange within the research process? These questions are difficult to engage with and even more difficult to answer. Nonetheless, it is crucial to examine the shifting power dynamics within the research setting, often demanding a reflexive researcher be present in this environment.

Another important element of feminist research is the practice of what Sandra Harding terms "strong reflexivity," a process whereby researchers take a critical look at their conceptual schema or the frameworks that comprise their social locations. In other words, reflexive feminist researchers ask: What assumptions/values, for example, do they as researchers bring to their research endeavors and how does this impact the types of questions they address in their research? Harding finds that objectivity is simply not objective enough, that it blocks and limits the representation of less distorted and less destructive accounts of the world. These accounts destroy the possibility of shaping and creating resources that objective knowledge can bring, "such as fairness, honesty, detachment, and . . . advancing democracy" (Harding 1992, 574). She describes her vision of a "strong objectivity," which would "specify strategies to detect social assumptions that enter research in the identification and conceptualization of scientific problems and the formation of hypotheses about them (the 'context of discovery')" (Harding 1992, 574). Therefore strong objectivity is built upon the sustainable desire for critical self-reflection and an attempt at libratory social change. The position of Harding's researcher is important to her conception of reflexivity, where objects of research are seen and see the researcher, "in all their cultural particularity," and the researcher gazes back toward it/them. The subject/object distinction is maintained, but it is rooted in its standpoint of material history and cultural particularity, where the socially situated research project moves the research away from the daily work that the scientist does (Harding 1991).

Feminists employ reflexivity during various stages of the research experience, including during data collection, analysis, and writing (see also Hertz 1997). Feminist researchers are exploring the experience of reflexivity, what it means in practice, and the dilemmas it presents. Reflexivity changes the shape of insider/outsider positions, problematizing these categories of being while marking new spaces for work to be done and knowledge to be subverted and constructed. The research process is not simplified when reflexivity is added into the mix, requiring that the researcher continuously negotiate positionalities. Nancy Naples gives us a good example of the "messiness" that is entered into when reflexivity is employed. She examines her feelings about the elites who were participating in her research study in contrast to her feelings about the more middle-class and especially women participants. She states:

> I have less empathy with their expressions of outsiderness as I witness their power to define the lives of others. I do admit a certain bias in my empathy toward those on the margins of these small towns that most likely reflect my own feelings of marginalization in many social locations.

The understanding of and public admission to bias and empathy lay Naples open to critique about the validity and reliability of her research findings. But Naples is *present* in her research, perpetually linked to her epistemological and methodological stance, creating what might be marked as a more trustworthy study.

Where her reflexivity engages the reader we come to understand her awareness of herself, her methods, and her analysis. Finally, reflexivity is deeply involved in the writing of the research text and the writing of oneself. Voice, a theme threaded through many feminist research undertakings, is involved in reflexive efforts to express and interrogate the researcher's positionality. The voice of the researcher within the written text is a difficult achievement. There must be translation of both the content and context of the researcher, without succumbing to the desire to penetrate and saturate the text with an egocentric biography.

Reflecting on her past work with oral histories, Errante gives us insight into oral history processes across difference through her critique of her own work. She remarks that

> oral history work is a wondrous experience and I have never lost the sense of privilege I feel that close-to-perfect strangers are willing to share their lives with me. For a brief moment, such apparent openness led me to conclude that there was no individual or collective experience—no voice—that a good oral history could not capture.

In the years since her first exploration and use of oral histories, Errante's perspective has changed, concluding that there are some stories that are beyond "the oral history even because either the historian or the narrator is not part of the content of remembering in which a particular story is told." Errante found that, while her naïveté in the early years of her work in Mozambique endeared her to her research participants, her positionality as a Westerner and as a researcher made both the participants and Errante cynical toward one another. Participants' became "cynical toward the focus group and survey work conducted by internationals," where Errante noticed that both herself and her participants were frustrated by feeling "instrumentalized." Both parties were feeling used and exploited, breaking down the "interpersonal bridges" that allow the research to flow. But Errante reconnects to "what works," allowing herself and her methods to overcome these feelings of exploitation. She reflexively states:

> [W]ith every intimate, personally important memory that narrators offered, they revealed their humanity. This drew out my own humanity. . . . At the same time, my vulnerabilities—my inexperience, my youth, my stupid questions—all revealed my

> own humanity and this demystified notions narrators might have had about my power and position as a white foreign academic.

Further examining research positionality, Nancy Naples discusses the shifting locations of insiderness and outsiderness, both as the subject of her research in rural Iowa and in the context of her position as ethnographic researcher. She describes them as *fluid* concepts, where

> the apparently clear distinction between insiderness and outsiderness falls away as we confront how regional differences, as well as class, gender, age, parenting and marital status, sexuality, race, and ethnicity shape the multiple identities we identify (with) in our researcher.

Research methods are often concerned with the idea of gaining access to individuals and information as well as gaining trust to obtain what is desired through the research process. But Naples, like many feminist researchers, tries to deconstruct what we mean by access and insiderness. She finds that her "outsider status served as a means by which I became an insider to the outsider feelings of many interviewed for the study." In some senses, feminist research methods aim to accept and sometimes accentuate the differences in researcher and participant position, creating an environment where both individuals are *inside* this newly co-created space where new truths may be told. In and out, however, are places or locations, which often masquerade as pivotal points in the research process. Treated as locations, they seem to relieve the researcher from any responsibility to attend to their own interactions with power relations. When *in* and *out* are treated as processes or verbs, part of the methods employed, the researcher is immediately drawn into a reflexive discussion about the power dynamics and situational context of the moment. Through her open-ended interviews, oral histories, and focus groups, Naples examines insiderness and outsiderness in multiple contexts.

Feminist Research as Social Transformation

A final element we will address concerning the characteristics of feminist research relates to what Sandra Harding terms the move toward "emancipation," where knowledge building does not bend toward dominate interest groups but toward democratic ends (Harding 1991). Feminism throughout history and not limited to its existence within the academy, has always been concerned with action and social change. There has been a general focus on improving the situation for women. Action and change may be nurtured on the public policy stage as a direct result of research implications, or in the very way methods are used in the research process. In the spaces where feminist research and a commitment to activism meet there are a number of thematic commonalties. These are sites where there is a critical attention to the linkages between power and knowledge. There is a view of social change as a potential promise that can be worked on and through both the individual and structural levels. Space is provided for the researcher to change oneself through the co-construction of knowledge. There is also a restructuring of relations between the researcher and the participants, ideally where the subject/object dichotomy is inherently broken down and/or changed through the research process. These commonalties serve to shape the strategies of feminist research where action is a goal.

Jocelyn Hollander discusses the constructions of vulnerability and danger across difference using focus group methods. She contends that understanding the feelings and meanings individuals give to their sense of safety and/or ability to commit a violent act have consequences in the lives of individuals. She states, "[T]he fact that these constructions of vulnerability and dangerousness are framed in the language of physical bodies makes them appear natural, inevitable, and, as a result, virtually invisible." Hollander, through her research findings seeks to bring the invisible into light. Similarly, Anderson and Umberson seek new ways of understanding masculinity within the context of domestic violence, adding new dimensions to the body of work that has altered the way society understands and combats partner abuse. Errante gives us an example of the effort to create social change *within* the research process, remarking that she "was ignoring that the oral history events intersected with another running narrative: my own." Errante reflexively, and sensitively, examines her own role within the research process and the emotions and personal change that resulted from this reflexive view of herself are important parts of this feminist research project. Feminist researchers often engage in an attempt to communicate how things are done within their published works, explaining and consequently examining the process of co-creation of knowledge, and the experience of the research setting itself. This expression of experience and openness to the messy issues that arise when *doing* methods is an important part of many feminist accounts of their research practices.

While the knowledge that is produced through research is often oriented toward social change, the research situation and its methods are also targets for feminist goals of breaking down and building up new forms of empowerment and knowledge co-construction. Methods themselves are seen as wielding power within the interface of method, researcher, and participant. Liz Stanley and Sue Wise state:

> One consequence of acknowledging the social location and production of knowledge is that knowledge-claims are thereby positioned as part of a *political process* in which some knowledge-claims are seen and certified as superordinate in relation to others. Power is involved here, and of a very effective kind because apparently rooted in unseamed and incontrovertible kinds of knowledge about the world. (Stanley and Wise 1993, 192)

Reflective of the power-laden production of knowledge, Devault's strategy is organized around specific, "distinctive approaches to subverting the established procedures of disciplinary practice tied to the agendas of the powerful." Subverting the traditional uses of research methods that disempower individuals and the appropriation of traditional methods to extend feminist agendas shape the content and context of feminist research. Marjorie Devault argues that the "research generated by academic feminism" is succeeding in bringing "women into theorizing" and demonstrating "how traditional paradigms have been shaped by the concerns and relevance of a relatively small group of powerful men." Feminist research highlights, not just through critique, the angle of epistemological and methodological vision traditionally utilized by positivistic social science.

Certain methods may seemingly be more suitable to social change work than others, but certainly a case could be made for the power of all forms of research to impact people's lives. Particularly, some feminists root their research in focus groups, reminiscent of consciousness-raising groups. Wilkinson states, "the similarities between focus group discussions and the consciousness-raising sessions common in the early years of second wave feminism have fueled the interest of several feminist researchers." Each method holds its own inherent capabilities and inadequacies when it comes to creating a situation for social change. But feminists continue to seek new ways of extending their methods into the realm of action, where power dimensions are minimized, exploitation is avoided and in some cases, empowerment is achieved.

These grand goals of *doing good* across issues of difference have been concerns for some feminists. Being rooted in a critical epistemology, using feminist methodologies that aim to uncover hidden voices and empower do not prevent the researcher from doing harm. Daphne Patai draws the question of what action and social change can come about through a research endeavor. In her article, "Academics and Third World Women: Is Ethical Research Possible?" she states:

> [F]eminists imagine that merely engaging in the discourse of feminism protects them from the possibility of exploiting other women, while their routine research practices are and continue to be embedded in a situation of material inequality. (Patai 1991, 139)

These are cautionary words of experience that must be combated through the integration of reflexivity and attention to changing the dynamics of routine research practices. Material inequalities, while not the only inequalities that should be considered throughout the research process, can be managed, mismanaged, and worked through when action and social change are focuses of the research at hand. Some of the material inequalities are addressed by feminists through their return of research materials and transcripts to their respondents and dialogic processes of agenda identification and problem solving as a way of changing the underlying structures that help to reproduce power inequalities and material inequalities. With these aims, "This connection to social change makes much feminist research practical as well as scholarly" (Reinharz 1992, 252). This positions feminist research at the crossroads of intellectual endeavors within a community of academics and social change endeavors within a community of activists. At this crossroads epistemological perspectives and tangible goals for feminist research are shaped, producing a diverse, vibrant, and creative body of work.

CONCLUSION

The themes outlined here are not exhaustive of the commonalities feminist research shares and, on the other hand, not all feminists practice all of these characteristics even within the selections of this volume. There are enough characteristics, however, to identify some common themes. One commonality threaded through many of these themes is a synergistic approach to dealing with epistemology, methodology, and method within feminist research. This synergy provides motion to how feminists' approach research. Feminist researchers are taking up their epistemological positions and acting from a belief that epistemology, methodology, and method are interconnected. They are acting from a belief that research is best conducted within a synergistic framework. Feminist research, attempting to confront and understand difference that occurs in our daily lives, finds that synergy and momentum available to them is powerful and important. This synergy is intentional, requiring effort and engagement of the researcher with the phases of the research process, the participants, and the reader. Synergy does not happen automatically, but through careful, emotionally charged, and energetic intent. All research is engaged with epistemology, methodology, and method but synergistic research positions the researcher in the center of this intentional and powerful choreography of theory and practice. Synergistic research seeks an engagement with subjugated knowledge, challenging the basic status quo of scientific knowledge building. Synergistic involvement of epistemology, methodology, and method deeply challenges the basic power structures of our society. Feminist research is giving us new models for social change and knowledge building, impacting both our work and daily lives.

Many feminists seek, within their research processes, to acknowledge the importance of the political underpinnings of knowledge building. Knowledge is socially constructed and knowledge *in action* comprises a political process. Feminist methodology still resides on the margins of traditional textbook discussions about method and methodology. We might ask: To what extent can ideas of feminist epistemology/methodology/method be mainstreamed into research methods courses in science and social science disciplines? What is preventing this from happening? How acceptable is this methodology? How much legitimacy has feminist epistemology garnered within the disciplines? Feminist research is engaged in efforts for social change within the disciplinary frameworks of academia, moving toward a paradigm shift. In 1962, Thomas Kuhn published *The Structure of Scientific Revolutions.* One of Kuhn's central points was to question the commonly held standards about the progression of science. Specifically, he aimed to question the commonly held view that science is cumulative, where each advance in knowledge builds on that which preceded it. This perspective sees science achieving its present state through slow, steady increments of knowledge building. Kuhn regards this perspective as a great 'myth' and argues that it is not accumulation, but revolution that accounts for the important changes within science. Kuhn asserts that at any given point in time science is characterized by the dominance of a particular paradigm or way of thinking. Knowledge is derived from the particular model or paradigm within a particular field. Paradigms are theoretically derived worldviews, which frame how we construct and understand our world. Individuals conducting research within the dominant paradigm are rewarded by a host of institutional supports that recognize their scholarship, from tenure committees at their home institutions of higher learning to prestigious journals and grant agencies within their respective fields that often buy into the reigning paradigm's approach. As we have seen in Part I of this volume, positivism is an important epistemological paradigm through which scientific knowledge is filtered and continues to be the dominant paradigm for much of social and natural sciences. Feminist research challenges some of the basic tenets of this paradigm and also offers competing epistemological frameworks and methodologies. Feminist research's synergistic approach to science interrogates the status quo and challenges the dominant paradigm of positivism. According to Kuhn, challenges often create a "crisis," which opens space where social change for women and other subjugated groups can be uncovered. We hope that this synergistic perspective on knowledge building will continue to move research toward what Thomas Kuhn terms a reevaluation of dominant epistemological frameworks and create a "crisis" and a movement toward a "revolution" in the study of women and society. (Kuhn, 1962)

To position research within an intention toward a broad, revolutionary paradigm shift means that this type of research needs to be recognized and rewarded as legitimate scholarship within their respective disciplines and within the social and natural sciences as a whole. This means that feminist research needs to continue to tend to the issue of politics. To build knowledge is to be political. Thomas Kuhn was aware of the political process of knowledge building early on when he noted that the paradigm that emerges as the winner is the one that has the most converts to it, not necessarily the one with the greatest explanatory power (see Ritzer 1975, 10). Feminist research may need to be strategic about its mission and goals concerning how it will organize itself as a research movement toward social change for women. Issues of difference in the research process needs to be carefully addressed as this discussion proceeds. Issues dealing with power and control both within the research process and discussions of differences and similarities among different/competing feminist epistemologies and methodologies would be productive and energetic beginnings toward raising the consciousness of the feminist research communities.

REFERENCES

Collins, Patricia. 1990. Black feminist thought: Knowledge, consciousness, and the politics of empowerment. Boston: Unwin Hyman

Collins, Patricia Hill. 1999. Learning from the outsider within: The sociological significance of black feminist thought. In *Feminist approaches to theory and methodology,* ed. Sharlene Hesse-Biber, Christine Gilmartin, and Robin Lydenberg, 135–78. New York: Oxford University Press.

Harding, Sandra. 1992. After the neutrality ideal: Science, politics, and "strong objectivity." *Social Research* 59(3): 567–88.

———. 1991. *Whose science, whose knowledge? Thinking from women's lives.* Ithaca: Cornell University Press.

Hertz, Rosanna. 1997 *Reflexivity and voice.* Thousand Oaks, CA: Sage Publications.

Kuhn, Thomas. 1962. *The structure of scientific revolutions.* Chicago. University of Chicago Press.

Patai, Daphne. 1991. U.S. academics and third world women: Is ethical research possible? In *In women's words: The feminist practice of oral history,* ed. Sherna Berger Gluck and Daphne Patai, 137–53. New York: Routledge.

Reinharz, Shulamit. 1992. *Feminist methods in social research.* New York: Oxford University Press.

———. 1983. Experiential analysis: a contribution to feminist research. In *Theories of women's studies,* ed. G. Bowles, and R. D. Klein, 162–91. London: Routledge and Kegan Paul.

Ritzer, George. 1975. *Sociology: A multiple paradigm science.* Boston: Allyn & Bacon.

Smith, Dorothy. 1999. Knowing a society from within: A woman's standpoint. In *Social theory: The multicultural and classical headings,* ed. Charles Lemert, pp. 389–91. Boulder, Colorado: Westview Press.

Smith, Dorothy. 1990 [1974]. *The conceptual practices of power: A feminist sociology of knowledge.* Boston: Northeastern University Press.

Spivak, Gayatri Chakrovorty. 1994. Can the subaltern speak? In *Colonial discourse and postcolonial theory: A reader,* ed. Patrick Williams and Laura Chrismen, 66–111. New York: Columbia University Press.

Stanley, Liz, and Sue Wise. 1993. *Breaking out again: Feminist ontology and epistemology.* London: Routledge.

Tolman, Deborah L. and Laura A. Szalacha. 1999. Dimensions of desire: Bridging qualitative and quantitative methods in a study of female adolescent sexuality. *Psychology of Women Quarterly,* 23: 7–39.

Wolf, Diane. 1996. Situating feminist dilemmas in fieldwork. In *Feminist dilemmas in fieldwork,* ed. Diane Wolf, 1–55. Boulder: Westview.

CHAPTER 13

Talking and Listening from Women's Standpoint

Feminist Strategies for Interviewing and Analysis

MARJORIE L. DEVAULT

The research generated by academic feminism—involving a new and careful attention to women's experiences—is beginning to "bring women in" to theorizing. But this research also demonstrates how traditional paradigms have been shaped by the concerns and relevances of a relatively small group of powerful men. The dilemma for the feminist scholar, always, is to find ways of working within some disciplinary tradition while aiming at an intellectual revolution that will transform that tradition (Stacey and Thorne 1985). In order to transform sociology—to write women and their diverse experiences into the discipline—we need to move toward new methods for writing about women's lives and activities without leaving sociology altogether. But the routine procedures of the discipline pull us insistently toward conventional understandings that distort women's experiences (Smith 1987, 1989).

Feminist methodology should provide strategies for managing this central contradiction—strategies that will help us with the "balancing act" demanded of any scholar who attempts innovative research within a scholarly tradition. I use the term "*strategies*" to suggest that feminist methodology will not prescribe a single model or formula. Rather, I think of feminist methods as distinctive approaches to subverting the established procedures of disciplinary practice tied to the agendas of the powerful (Smith 1974). In the discussion that follows, I pursue some implications of feminism for the production and use of interview data. I do not treat questions about the ethics of interviewing or relations with informants, which have been discussed extensively by feminist researchers (e.g., Mies 1983; Oakley 1981; Reinharz 1983; Stacey 1988). In many ways, my approach is solidly grounded in a tradition of qualitative sociological inquiry and in relatively conventional methods for conducting interviews. But I will suggest that feminism gives us distinctive ways of extending the methods of this qualitative tradition.

I begin with an observation central to much feminist thinking: that language itself reflects male experiences, and that its categories are often incongruent with women's lives. This apparent obstacle to expression, I will argue, can be turned to advantage through attention to research as activity fundamentally grounded in talk.

Qualitative researchers of various sorts have become increasingly conscious in recent years of the obvious but mostly taken-for-granted feature of the data they collect: that interviews consist of talk (Paget 1983; Mishler 1986a). This new awareness is related to the insights of phenomenologists, who investigate the production of everyday consciousness (see, e.g., Psathas 1973; Darroch and Silvers 1983), and ethnomethodologists, who have taken as problematic the patterns of talk and interaction through which the members of any group constitute a shared reality (Garfinkel 1967; Heritage 1984). I will suggest that this new kind of attention to the language of research should be central to the feminist project. Assuming relatively standard procedures for interviewing, I will examine, as social interaction grounded in language, four aspects of work with interview data: constructing topics, listening, editing, and writing. My aim is to bring into the methodological discussion insights from feminist linguists about women's relation to language and to speech, and to examine, as aspects of social research, the processes of talking and listening "as women." My understanding of what it means to talk or listen "as a woman" is based on the concept of "women's standpoint" (Smith 1987; Hartsock 1981); the approach does not imply that all women share a single position or perspective, but rather insists on the importance of following out the implications of women's (and others') various locations in socially organized activities (see also DeVault 1990).

WOMEN AND LANGUAGE

Language was an early topic for feminist researchers and by now there is a large body of research on women and language (for summaries, see Thorne and Henley 1975; Lakoff 1975; Miller and Swift 1977; Spender [1980] 1985; Thorne, Kramarae, and Henley 1983). These studies demonstrate how linguistic forms (the generic "he," for example) exclude women, and how vocabulary and syntax make women deviant. The names of experiences often do not fit for women. For an example that is simple and immediate, consider the difficulties that arise in an attempt to apply the terms "work" and "leisure" to most women's lives. Many of the household activities so prominent in women's lives do not fit comfortably into either category (see, e.g., Smith 1987: 68), and many of women's activities, such as family, community, and volunteer work, are best described as "invisible work" (Daniels 1987). There are other examples—the terms "public" and "private," for example, construct a distinction that obscures women's "multiple crisscrossings" of fluid and constantly shifting boundaries (Saraceno 1984: 7). Such disjunctures between language and women's lives have been central to feminist scholarship: presumably, there are many more to be revealed. Presumably, as well, the lack of fit between women's lives and the words available for talking about experience present real difficulties for ordinary women's self-expression in their everyday lives. If words often do not quite fit, then women who want to talk of their experiences must "translate," either saying things that are not quite right, or working at using the language in non-standard ways.

To some extent, this kind of problem must exist for everyone: language can never fit perfectly with individual experience. My claim, however, is that the problems of what we might call linguistic incongruence must be greater for some groups than for others. Research on gender differences in speech provides some support for this claim, suggesting that, in at least some contexts, women face particular difficulties of speech. In mixed-sex dyads and groups, women are less listened to than men and less likely to be credited for the things they say in groups; they are interrupted more often than men; the topics they introduce into conversations are less often taken up by others; and they do more work than men to keep conversations going. Further, Candace West (1982) suggests that responses to speech are so thoroughly gendered that women cannot overcome these difficulties by simply adopting "male" styles: she found that when women did interrupt male speakers, they were more likely than male interrupters to be ignored, a pattern she speculatively attributes to a male presumption that women's speech can, in general, be treated as trivial. These and similar findings have been presented as effects of power relations between men and women. They can also be seen as manifestations of the special obstacles for women to speaking fully and truthfully.

Dale Spender, in *Man Made Language* ([1980] 1985), reviews and extends these ideas in ways I have found especially helpful. Beginning with the anthropologists Edwin and Shirley Ardener's (1975) idea that women in society are a "muted group," she traces the consequences of various ways that women are denied access to linguistic resources. The concept of "mutedness" does not imply that women are silent: in every culture, women speak, in a variety of forms and settings, and in almost all cultures, women are important transmitters of language, through their care and teaching of children. But just as muted sounds are audible but softened, women speak in ways that are limited and shaped by men's greater social power and control, exercised both individually and institutionally (and exercised to control less privileged men as well as women). Spender argues that distinctive features of women's speech should not be seen as deficiencies in linguistic skill, but as adaptive responses to these constraints on their speech. She also sees in language a potential source of power for women: she argues that woman-to-woman talk is quite different from talk in mixed groups—because women speakers are more likely to listen seriously to each other—and that it affords opportunities for women to speak more fully about their experiences. She argues, in fact, that consciousness-raising, which might be understood as woman-to-woman talk systematized, is at the heart of feminist theorizing (see also MacKinnon 1983).

Spender's discussion of "woman talk" is optimistic; she emphasizes the value of communication among women, and does not give much consideration to its difficulties. In drawing on her discussion, I do not mean to imply that women always (or even usually) understand each other easily. While understanding and familiar comfort are benefits of some of the ways that women have come together, they are not guaranteed by gender alone. Women who are positioned differently learn to speak and hear quite different versions of "woman talk," adapting to distinctive blends of power and oppression. Failures of understanding abound. Statements from feminists of color, for example, reveal not only their difficulties speaking among white feminists (e.g., hooks 1981), but also the costs for feminist research of the exclusion of their voices (e.g., Collins 1986, 1989). At the same time, feminist scholars have begun to experiment with texts that reflect the conflict and messiness of talking and listening together (e.g., Joseph and Lewis 1981; Lugones and Spelman 1983; Bulkin, Pratt, and Smith 1984). Such texts hold the promise that, with careful attention, we can learn from each other about our differences as well as our common experiences.

These ideas from feminist linguistic researchers provide the starting point for my discussion of interview talk, which will focus on the talk that occurs in interviews conducted by women with women. (I do not mean to imply that the label *feminist* can be applied only to research conducted by women and about women, but this category does include most feminist research to date. The reasons for such a pattern deserve attention, but lie beyond the scope of this chapter.) Below, I discuss the ways that these perspectives on women's talk have influenced my own thinking about interviewing. Though I draw examples primarily from my study of the work that women do within families (DeVault 1984, 1987, forthcoming a), I attempt to indicate as well how these ideas might be relevant to other projects.

CONSTRUCTING TOPICS

The categories available from the discipline construct "topics" for research do not necessarily correspond to categories that are meaningful in women's lives. Female researchers, like other women, have become accustomed to translating their experiences into standard vocabulary. But to fully describe women's experiences, we often need to go beyond standard vocabulary—not just in our analyses, but also in the ways that we actually talk with those we interview. By speaking in ways that open the boundaries of standard topics, we can create space for respondents to provide accounts rooted in the realities of their lives.

My research, for example, examines household routines for planning, cooking, and serving meals. I thought of it, in the beginning, as a study of housework. But I was also motivated by a sense that the feminist literature on housework didn't fit my experience. Analyses that took the content of household work for granted left things out, and the parts left out were somehow what made the work not only burdensome, but meaningful and compelling as well. I wanted to study a single kind of housework in detail, and for a variety of reasons that were only partly conscious, I was drawn to the work of providing food. The term is awkward and sounds odd, and in fact, there is no term that says precisely what I meant. I meant more than just cooking, more than "meal preparation" (the efficiency expert's term). And "providing" of course, has traditionally been used for what the traditional husband does—it is linked to the wage that a woman transforms into family meals. Though I knew—in at least a preliminary sense—what I wanted to study, I had no concise label for my topic. Eventually, I began to call it "the work of feeding a family," and later, just "feeding." But in the beginning, as I started to conduct interviews, I told my respondents that I wanted to talk with them about "all the housework that has to do with food—cooking, planning, shopping, cleaning up." I used my questions to show them that they should talk very specifically—"Who gets up first?" "What kind of cereal?" and so on—and in spite of my worries about "topic," these interviews were remarkably easy to conduct. Almost all of my respondents, both those who loved to cook and those who hated it, spoke easily and naturally. Looking back, I can see that I identified, in a rough way, a category that made sense to my respondents because it was a category that organized their day-to-day activity. For women who live in families and do this work, feeding is a central task and takes lots of time. Strategizing about how to do it leads to the development of routines, to frequent rearrangements and improvisations, and to pride in the "little tricks" that make the work easier. The topic is easy for women (and for men who actually do the work) to talk about. Our talk happened in a way that I and my respondents knew and were comfortable with, because such conversations among women are often settings for discussing this kind of work. Chatting about the details of household routines is a way of finding out what someone else does, reflecting on one's own practice, getting and sharing ideas or solutions to common problems. Sometimes, in fact, my respondents were uncomfortable because our talk didn't seem like an interview: several stopped in mid-sentence to ask, "Is this really what you want?" "Are you sure this is helping you?" They were prepared to translate into the vocabulary they expected from a researcher, and surprised that we were proceeding in a more familiar manner.

The point here—that feminist topics go beyond standard labels—applies to other kinds of research as well. Elizabeth Stanko, as follow-up to her book *Intimate Intrusions* (1985a), conceived a study of women's strategies for avoiding assault (Stanko 1985b, forthcoming). Her aim is examine a broad range of what we might call "defensive maneuvers"—not just learning self-defense, but choosing places to live, things to wear, routes for walking home, and times to go to the laundromat. There is no label that includes all of these—and the category is probably one that men would be less likely than women to understand. But when Stanko, as a female researcher, says to women that she is concerned with "the things we do to keep safe," she taps into a set of activities informed by knowledge and strategizing that make up a meaningful category for virtually all women in our society. (Though of course, the practices and conditions of the experience vary tremendously—in this instance, urban women are probably more at risk and more vigilant than others; and affluent women certainly find it easier to avoid risk than those with fewer material resources.)

Marianne Paget (1981), as part of a study of the practice of committed artists, has written about a barrier to creative work that she could see in the stories of women artists but not in those of men. She uses the term *ontological anguish* to refer to the conflict between these women's intense commitment to the creation of high art, and their learned sense that, as women, they are not supposed to participate in making culture. The artists themselves do not identify this problem. Paget sees it in their accounts of becoming artists—accounts that they provide in response to her questions about the work they finally came to do. This example suggests that researchers do not have to begin with a conception of expanded topic. Paget began with an interest in how artists do their work; she discovered that in order to explain their art, women artists have tell about getting over a barrier. Paget allows them to tell their own stories, gives a name to the barrier they describe, and through her analysis makes it a phenomenon that we can examine and discuss.

The household work process that I analyze and the defensive strategies that Stanko studies are activities that most women learn to take for granted, activities that are normally only partly conscious, learned without explicit attention. Similarly, Paget discusses a sort of "problem with no name" for women artists, a problem they experience in various ways and can talk about indirectly, but do not ordinarily label. The promise of feminist ethnography is that we can elicit accounts and produce descriptions of these kinds of practice and thought that are part of female consciousness but left out of dominant interpretive frames, shaped around male concerns. When this kind of topic construction is successful, we recognize the thinking that emerges from the analysis—we know the experience—but we are also surprised and learn something new. The analysis produces the "aha" or "click" of consciousness-raising that has been central to the development of feminist thinking, and that serves as a pointer toward a new way of seeing the world.

Conversation analytic researchers have investigated the construction of "topic" in everyday talk, and their findings help to illuminate the examples I have discussed by demonstrating how topics are produced collaboratively. Boden and Bielby (1986), for example, report that elderly conversation partners use a shared past as the basis for constructing conversational interaction in the present. And Maynard and Zimmerman (1984) report that unacquainted speakers often work at establishing areas of shared experience. In their study, conversation partners often developed topics out of the shared features of their immediate setting (the oddness of an arranged encounter in a social psychology lab). But speakers also investigated each other's categorical memberships (e.g., "sophomore" or "sociology major") and experiences (attending a recent concert) in "pre-topical" talk aimed at constructing a "sharedness" that could lead to topic development. Paget (1983), emphasizing the "conversational" character of intensive interviewing, discusses how an interviewer and respondent collaborate in a "search procedure." It is the interviewer's investment in finding answers, her own concern with the questions she asks and her ability to show that concern, that serves to recruit her respondents as partners in the search: the things said are responses to these words of this particular researcher. The researcher is actively involved with respondents, so that together they are constructing fuller answers to questions that cannot always be asked in simple, straightforward ways.

I claim here that a feminist sociology must open up standard topics from the discipline, building more from what we share with respondents as women than from disciplinary categories that we bring to research encounters. In order to do this, researchers need to interview in ways that allow the exploration of incompletely articulated aspects of women's experiences. Traditionally, qualitative researchers have conducted interviews that are "open-ended" and "intensive," seeking to avoid structuring the interaction in terms of the researcher's perspectives. But eliciting useful accounts of women's experiences is not simply a matter of encouraging women to talk. Most members of a society learn to interpret their experiences in terms of dominant language and meanings; thus, women themselves (researchers included) often have trouble seeing and talking clearly about their experiences. What researchers can do is to take responsibility for recognizing how the concepts we have learned as sociologists may distort women's accounts. We can return to activities conducted in specific settings as the sources for our studies, and ground our interviewing in accounts of everyday activity—in accounts of how particular women actually spend their time at home, for example, rather than a previously defined concept of "housework." Dorothy Smith (1987, 187–89) suggests that when we ground interviews in this way, we find that social organization is "in the talk" and that we can mine the talk for clues to social relations. This kind of interviewing, which does not begin from topics established in the discipline, will be more like everyday "woman talk" than like survey research.

LISTENING

I have argued above that since the words available often do not fit, women learn to "translate" when they talk about their experiences. As they do so, parts of their lives "disappear" because they are not included in the language of the account. In order to "recover" these parts of women's lives, researchers must develop methods for listening around and beyond words. I use the term "listening" in this section in a broad sense, to refer to what we do while interviewing, but also to the hours we spend later listening to tapes or studying transcripts, and even more broadly, to the ways we work at interpreting respondents' accounts. (I do not, however, attend to comparative aspects of analysis, which involve bringing together interpretations of multiple interviews.)

Spender's discussion of the special features of "woman talk," cited above, emphasizes the importance of listening. She notes that listening has been neglected in communication research in favor of research on speech, and she suggests that this imbalance results from the fact that those who control knowledge production are more concerned with airing their views than with hearing those of others (Spender [1980] 1985, 121–25). Spender argues that women (like members of other subordinate groups) are highly skilled at listening—to both men and women (see also Miller 1976, 1986)—and that women together can more easily cooperate in understanding each other than speakers in mixed groups. Presumably, these ideas have relevance for woman-to-woman interviewing, even though the interview setting is structured, and more artificial than everyday talk. When women interview women, both researcher and subject act on the basis of understandings about interviewing, and both follow the rules (or negotiate a shared version of the rules) associated with their respective roles. But changes in the role of researcher, based on incorporating rather than denying personal involvements, have been at the heart of many discussions of feminist methodology (Reinharz 1983; Stanley and Wise 1983). In fact, it is sometimes quite difficult for female researchers, and especially feminists, to maintain the role prescribed by traditional methodological strictures. Ann Oakley (1981), for example, explains how impossible it was for her to be an "ideal" interviewer in her discussions with pregnant women: she wasn't willing to respond, "I haven't really thought about it," when interviewees asked questions such as, "Which hole does the baby come out of?" or, "Why is it dangerous to leave a small baby alone in the house?" Many of these discussions suggest that women interviewing women bring to their interaction a tradition of "woman talk." They help each other develop ideas, and are typically better prepared than men to use the interview as a "search procedure" (Paget 1983), cooperating in the project of constructing meanings together.[1]

When this project involves the recovery of unarticulated experience, as so much feminist research does, researchers have another resource: they can listen for the everyday processes of "translation" that are part of women's speech. When I use the term here—as I have been doing rather loosely so far—I mean to refer to the various ways that women manage to deal with the incongruence of language in their everyday speech. Often, this means using words that are familiar and "close enough" to experience for most purposes, relying on listeners to understand—for example, calling "housework" whatever chores must be done at home. Sometimes, too, translation means trying to develop a more complex meaning, trying to respond more fully to questions that are not quite appropriate. In these cases, it may mean saying part of what is experienced, groping for words, doing the best one can. As an interviewer who is also a woman—who has also learned to translate—I can listen "as a woman," filling in from experience to help me understand the things that are incompletely said. As a researcher, my job is to listen for these translations, and to analyze the disjunctures that give rise to them. These linguistic phenomena provide "clues" to women's experiences (Frye 1983, xii).

In my research on the work of feeding a family, I was concerned to uncover neglected aspects of women's experience of housework. I wanted to examine those parts of the work of planning, cooking, and serving meals that women rarely think about, but have learned from their mothers and from ideologies of family life—those parts of housework that actually produce family life day to day. I asked the women in my study (and the few men who took major responsibility for cooking) to describe their daily routines in some detail: what they cooked and why, how they planned and managed family meals, when and where they bought food, and so on. As the interviews progressed, I became increasingly fascinated with some characteristic features of my respondents' talk. They spoke very concretely, about the mundane details of everyday life, but they often said things in ways that seemed oddly incomplete. They connected topics in ways that were sometimes puzzling and they assumed certain kinds of knowledge on my part ("Like, you know, the Thursday section of the newspaper," an implicit reference to the fact that many U.S. newspapers include recipes and features on food and diet in their Thursday editions). I coded my data in the traditional way, noting when respondents mentioned "topics" such as "planning," "nutrition," and so forth. But in many cases, the analysis really began with a particular phrase that seemed to demand investigation. I began to pay more and more attention to the ways things were said. I was especially interested in difficulties of expression—those fascinating moments when respondents got stuck, and worked at articulating thoughts they were not used to sharing: "It's kind of hard to explain. . . ."

One woman, talking about why she worked so hard at organizing regular meals for her family, told me:

> My husband sees food as something you need to live. But—I don't quite know how to describe it—I really have an emphasis on the social aspects. I mean, the food is an important part, but it's kind of in that setting.

As we talked, this woman was trying to formulate the principles that guide her activities. It is difficult because she doesn't have appropriate words. She knows what she means, but expressing it is new. Another woman echoed her idea, in a similar way:

> The initial drudgery is what you dislike. Actually going shopping, doing all the planning, chopping, cutting, what have you. And of course cleaning up. But you do it for the good parts, you know, you get enough of the good parts to keep doing it.

There are words for the physical tasks, but not for the interpersonal work that is more important for this woman—the activity she summarizes, somewhat puzzled herself, as "the good part." Again, it is clear that her experiences are inadequately coded in standard vocabulary, and that she must work at saying what she means.

Another example: although most women told me that they didn't really do much "planning," several of my respondents referred to an immediate, improvisational kind of thinking they do while shopping. They did not know quite what to call this process. One told me: "Most of the time, I kind of plan when I'm at the store, you know? Like OK, we have chicken Monday, pork chops Tuesday—I be kind of, you know, figuring out in my mind, as I shop, what's what." Another explained: "My husband likes to just get in and out, and then that's it. Whereas me, I like to look around, and just think, you know."

These kinds of comments do not constitute "good quotes" in the conventional sense: they are halting and rather inarticulate, and seem hardly to have any content. Typically, I think, they would be discarded as containing little information about what these women do. I used these women's words somewhat differently, however: not as straightforward accounts of "what happens," but as hints toward concerns and activities that are generally unacknowledged. Often, I believe, this halting, hesitant, tentative talk signals the realm of not-quite-articulated experience, where standard vocabulary is inadequate, and where a respondent tries to speak from experience and finds language wanting.[2] I tried to listen most carefully to this kind of talk. As I began to understand what these women were saying, I also began to see more clearly how standard vocabulary—the managerial term "planning," for instance—really doesn't describe what they do. I could also begin to see why the term doesn't fit: the concept of planning makes organizational sense where there is a separation of conception and execution, but housework has traditionally been organized so as to join not only conception and execution, but also work and the personality of the one who does it.

As I began to look for these difficulties of expression, I became aware that my transcripts were filled with notations of women saying to me, "you know," in sentences like "I'm more careful about feeding her, you know, kind of a breakfast." This seems an incidental feature of their speech, but perhaps the phrase is not so empty as it seems. In fact, I did know what she meant. I did not use these phrases systematically in my analyses, but I think now that I could have. Studying the transcripts now, I see that these words often occur in places where they are consequential for the joint production of our talk in the interviews. In many instances, "you know" seems to mean something like, "OK, this next bit is going to be a little tricky. I can't say it quite right, but help me out a little; meet me halfway and you'll understand what I mean." (It is perhaps similar to the collaborative use of "Uh huh" to sustain extended stretches of talk, noted by Schegloff [1982].) If this is so, it provides a new way to think about these data. "You know" no longer seems like stumbling inarticulateness, but appears to signal a request for understanding. The request was honored on the woman-to-woman level, as I nodded, "um hmm," making the interview comfortable, doing with my respondent what we women have done for generations—understanding each other. But I fear that the request is too often forgotten when, as researchers, we move from woman talk to sociology, leaving the unspoken behind. In some sense, this is a betrayal of the respondent—I say I understand, but if I later "forget," her reality is not fully there in what I write.

Finally, there were bits of speech that just seemed odd to me, that I wanted to understand. In one interview, for example, I asked what the evening meal was like. The reply was a long one; we had been talking about this woman's own parents and how they ate, and her answer gave information about her own childhood as well as the patterns she and her husband have developed. Eventually, I asked her to explain how their "family style" meals were different from those of her childhood. Again, her answer was long and specific and moved beyond the question. Her husband serves the meat, but not as well as her grandfather and her father did; this bothers her sometimes. Then she went on:

> And the service is important. You know, how the table is set and so forth. We probably, again when I was growing up we never had paper napkins except when my dad was out of town. We do now, have paper napkins, although we have cloth napkins and I like it. What I would like—maybe I will but probably not—but at one point where we lived we had cloth napkins and everybody had their own napkin ring and that way you didn't have to keep changing the napkins.

She went on to talk about other things, but I was haunted by a fragment of this excerpt: "What I would like—maybe I will but probably not—," which struck me immediately with its off-hand poignancy. The question, for me, was why anyone would say such a thing, what context produces this remark. Later I began to see how this woman was doing her work as we talked; she was, momentarily, musing and strategizing about the kind of meal she wished to produce for her family. What happens in her talk? Telling about her family routine, she mentions napkin rings, and thinks that she would like to use them again. Her wistful, automatic thought that she will do something different (again, not quite planning, but something akin to it) reveals her sense of how the material trappings of meals can become foundations for more emotional aspects of family life. And her brief comment also contains clues to the fate of her own preferences and desires: she plans and wishes, but she also recognizes that she alone is responsible for doing the work, and that in the end she will have limited time and make choices that reflect the priorities of others. I certainly could not see all these things when I noticed this remark, but I knew at least that there was something more to be said about this oddly contradictory phrase. As I thought about it, it brought back the time in my own life when I thought I might save my marriage by making better salads. And when I began to look, I found this kind of thinking in the comments of others as well.

As the last example suggests, researchers' own experiences as women serve as resources for this kind of listening. While other feminists have noted the value of personal involvement in interviewing, even researchers who value involvement have talked of it in a mostly unanalyzed way, as experience rather than as an element of method. If feminist researchers are to move toward a more disciplined use of the personal, we need to make the process one that we can consciously adopt and teach. We need to analyze more carefully the specific ways that interviewers use personal experience as a resource for listening. Here, I briefly discuss my own approach and a related example. What they have in common is a focus on attention to the unsaid, in order to produce it as topic and make it speakable.

My procedure, which I have illustrated above, involves noticing ambiguity and problems of expression in interview data, then drawing on my own experience in an investigation aimed at "filling in" what has been incompletely said. The point is not simply to reproduce my own perspective in my analysis; the clues I garner from this kind of introspection are only a beginning and should lead me back to hear respondents in new ways. What produces the analysis is the recognition that something is unsaid, and the attempt to articulate the missing parts of the account. The interpretive process is analogous to reading a narrative account, placing oneself in the narrator's position and referring to an implied context for the story that is told. It is a process that is being studied by analysts of reading and narrative, and the work of these theorists should provide one way of conceptualizing this kind of listening (for sociologists' discussions of narrative, see, e.g., Smith 1983; Mishler 1986a, b; DeVault 1990; Richardson forthcoming).

A related approach to "personal listening" can be seen in the work of Dorothy Smith and Alison Griffith, who have studied the ways that mothers' activities are shaped by the organization of schooling (Smith 1987; Griffith and Smith 1987). They interviewed mothers about what they do to help their children in school—how they get them dressed and there on time, how they teach them "basic skills," how they manage children's experiences with teachers and the institutions of schooling. Griffith and Smith have written about the ways that they have used their experiences as resources for analysis. They were aware from the beginning that their personal histories as single mothers provided impetus and direction for the study, and that they used a commonality of experience with their respondents to develop interview questions and to establish "rapport" and move the interviews ahead. But they also report that their analysis was furthered by noticing and using a particular sort of emotional response to some of their interviews. Griffith, for example, tells about returning from an interview with a middle-class, full-time mother who deploys an impressive range of material and educational resources to further her children's development. Her field notes ask:

> And where was I in all this? I was feeling that I hadn't done my own mothering *properly*. I had let my children watch T.V.; they'd never been taken to a Shakespearean play; when I was upset with the school, I had never managed to make things better for my children and indeed, at times made it worse; etc. In other words, my mothering, in relation to other women's mothering, appeared to be less than adequate on almost every count. As a consequence, I was finding the interview process very difficult emotionally. (Griffith and Smith 1987: 94)

The reaction is understandable, and might simply be treated, sympathetically, as one of the pitfalls of researching personally meaningful topics. But Griffith and Smith go beyond this kind of recognition to analyze the unnoticed matrix of social organization that constructs both the interview talk and their emotional reaction to it. They report that reflections on this kind of reaction led them to see a "moral dimension" to mothering, and to trace its sources in social organization. Analysis does not end, but rather begins with the recognition of their own emotion: Griffith and Smith went on to look for, and found, other illustrations of this aspect of mothering in the accounts of those they interviewed. But their own experience helped them find these clues to the social organization of mothering (see also Rothman 1986 on deep emotional response and its relation to the analysis of amniocentesis experiences).

Any competent listening depends on various kinds of background knowledge. I have argued above that woman-to-woman listening can be based on a particular type of unspoken knowledge. Of course, this kind of listening is not simple. It is certainly not guaranteed in any woman-to-woman interaction. Riessman (1987), in an analysis of a middle-class Anglo interviewer's misunderstandings of a Puerto Rican respondent, provides a sobering account of one woman's inability to hear another. Asked to explain how her divorce came about, the respondent provides an episodic narrative in which a series of exemplary vignettes answer the question. The interviewer, expecting a story with a linear temporal organization, is confused, and interrupts the account repeatedly in an attempt to elicit the sort of narrative she expects. It is not only a frustrating encounter, but a striking example of how difficult it can be to hear things said in unfamiliar forms, and how damaging when respondents are not heard. But Riessman's analysis of this mishearing also suggests that, with awareness and effort, it is possible to analyze such problems in the service of more skillful listening. The critical point is that feminist researchers can be conscious of listening as process, and can work on learning to listen in ways that are personal, disciplined, and sensitive to differences.

Preserving Women's Speech

I have suggested above that researchers can use women's speech to provide clues to analysis. This kind of analysis proceeds through attention to typically unnoticed features of talk, and is therefore made possible by methods of data collection and recording that preserve such features. In this section, I discuss several issues of "editing," a term I use to refer to the decisions researchers make about recording, transcribing, and excerpting from conversations with informants. Though these are usually thought of (if thought of at all) as mechanical or technical issues, researchers are increasingly aware of their substantive relevance. Each decision about these matters results in saving or losing aspects of interview talk, and some approaches to analysis depend on aspects of talk that are routinely discarded by other analysts. Concretely, the questions include: Should interviews be tape recorded? How should they be transcribed? What would constitute a "complete" transcription? When excerpting from transcripts, what (if anything) are we allowed to change? Should we "clean up" quotations? How? And why or why not? My aim in what follows is not to prescribe any particular version of transcription or presentation. Rather, I want to call attention to the questions, survey some possible answers, and suggest that for feminist researchers, "more complete" representations of talk can provide a resource for analysis built on distinctive features of women's speech.

Standard handbooks on qualitative methods stress the importance of exhaustive recording of conversation in interviews and field settings, but devote relatively little attention to methods of recording conversation or writing about it. Bogdan and Taylor (1975), for example, who discuss such issues in more detail than most authors, recommend that field workers avoid taping; they provide some hints for remembering dialogue, and they suggest including records of "dialogue accessories" such as gesture, tone, and accent, but they also reassure the reader that field notes need not include "flawless reproduction of what was said" (Bogdan and Taylor 1975: 60–61). They do suggest that researchers tape-record intensive interviews, because subjects' words are important and the situation is artificial anyway, but they omit discussion of transcription techniques. Presumably, students learn how to deal with these matters through experience and oral teaching, and by reading exemplary texts. The Bogdan and Taylor book, for example, teaches about these matters implicitly through the inclusion of exemplary field notes and finished research reports.

Fieldworkers in the symbolic interactionist tradition adopt a variety of solutions to problems of collecting and representing talk as data: some rely on memory rather than tape recordings (and indeed, some work in settings and adopt roles that make recording impractical), while others advocate taping interviews (often citing, in addition to the analytic utility of this technique, the benefit of easier concentration on the face-to-face interaction instead of on remembering what is said). Transcription, in this tradition, is typically viewed as a mechanical task, often assigned to subordinates in the research enterprise, though many researchers do acknowledge that the transcription process can afford rich insight. While some qualitative researchers insist that transcripts should include everything that is said (often mentioning, for instance, the importance of recording the interviewer's questions), many seem to edit out some material at this stage. Lillian Rubin (1979: Appendix), for example, defends the practice of organizing edited transcripts in terms of previously developed categories of interest rather than as verbatim records of the interview (though she does listen to entire tapes as she proceeds with the analysis). Further, the interactionist tradition in qualitative methods is virtually silent on methods for recording particular features of talk, taking for granted, for the most part, the adequacy of standard English spelling and punctuation. Excerpts in published reports tend to be brief—a few sentences from the respondent surrounded by analytic comment—and usually seem to have been "polished" by the sociologist, since they read more smoothly than most ordinary speech. Researchers routinely indicate that they have changed respondents' names and some details of their lives in order to protect their subjects' anonymity, but they rarely report in detail on which details they have changed and how.

In a rare discussion of these issues, Bob Blauner (1987) discusses the problems of editing "first-person" sociology. He notes that oral history and life history researchers have been more self-conscious about editing than most qualitative sociologists. Perhaps because the talk of informants is so much more prominent in their texts, life history researchers seem more conscious than others that they must make decisions about how to condense long hours of conversation, whether and how to represent dialectic and nonstandard grammar, and how much commentary to add to their subjects' words. Though Blauner limits his discussion to "personal document" texts—intended to present findings through extended personal narrative rather than through a sociologist-author's analytic discussion—every researcher working with interview data makes these editing decisions.

Blauner argues that the particular features of an individual's speech often have substantive significance. (Interestingly, his examples focus mainly on the ways that African American speakers mix standard and black English, and might be seen as linguistic phenomena corresponding to the ones I have claimed are important in women's speech.) Reporting to his own editing, he describes himself as having "some of the folklorist's purism" with respect to language and expressive style, but also as being "very free as an editor" (Blauner 1987: 50). He almost never changes any words when he quotes his informants (though he sometimes adds or deletes works to clarify meaning), but he condenses and eliminates material in ways intended to bring out the meaning and sociological relevance of a particular story. He also eliminates repetitive speech,[3] and, like most sociologists, changes personal names and details of identity in order to protect the anonymity of informants. Blauner also reports that many life history researchers edit their informants' words in order to encourage more respectful reading. Usually, the worry is that readers will be prejudiced, or simply distracted, by speech that reveals lack of education or a particular regional or class background. Blauner cites the example of Robert Coles, who translates slang and vernacular into standard English in order to highlight the content rather than the style of respondents' speech.

These approaches, while emphasizing the importance of respondents' own words, also give the researcher much authority as translator and mouthpiece. The researcher, relying on her understanding of respondents' meanings, represents their words in forms that fit into sociological text. Typically, this means interpreting, condensing, excerpting, and polishing respondents' talk. One rationale for such transformation emphasizes its benign intent: the researcher's purpose, often, is to secure a hearing for respondents who would not otherwise be heard. The purpose of editing is to cast talk into a form which is easier to read—and more compelling—than raw interview documents, which are often lengthy, rambling, repetitive and/or confusing. Another rationale emphasizes the redundancy of talk: the researcher should include only as much detail as needed to illustrate the analytic points to be made. (Howard Becker, for example, argues that tape recording interviews is usually unnecessary, explaining that he is confident of remembering those details that he needs to make an analysis [personal communication]. My work as Becker's student convinced me that I could remember "enough" from interviews to write sound and interesting sociology, and I repeat his advice to my own students, though with more ambivalence. However, my discussion elsewhere in this article suggests that memory is often inadequate.) Both rationales show that editing, though usually relatively unnoticed, is an essential and consequential part of the routine practice of producing a particular kind of sociological text.

Such "routine practices" must be thought of as the solutions to problems of representation accepted by a community of interpreters (Becker 1986). They are neither right or wrong for all time, but represent solutions that are relatively adequate for the purposes at hand. I have suggested above, however, that feminist researchers—whose purposes often include disrupting routine practice—might do well to adopt a reasoned suspicion of standard solutions to representation problems. I have argued that one purpose of feminist research is to recover and examine unnoticed experience, and that standard language and forms are likely to be inadequate for describing those experiences. Standard practice that smoothes out respondents' talk is one way that women's words are distorted; it is often a way of discounting and ignoring those parts of women's experience that are not easily expressed.

Conversation and discourse analysis provide models for representing talk much more completely. Conversation analytic researchers (see, e.g., Schenkein 1978; Atkinson and Heritage 1984) aim at discovering the recurring features of talk and interaction that produce the orderliness of social life; they take talk as the primordial grounding of social interaction. Analysis focuses on the significance of conversational features as minute (and as typically unnoticed) as indrawn breath, elongated vowel sounds, and hesitations as short as one-tenth of a second. Discourse analysis (e.g., Fisher and Todd 1983; Mishler 1986a) is typically based on longer stretches of talk, but involves a similarly close attention to the details of talk and storytelling. Feminists working in these traditions (e.g., Fishman 1978; West and Zimmerman 1983; Todd and Fisher 1988) have attended to the significance of gender as it both produces and is produced by the social relations of talk. Their work is especially useful for the kind of analysis I propose here, because they show, explicitly and in detail, the kinds of obstacles to expression that women confront in everyday interaction.

Researchers who rely on these approaches work with very detailed transcripts, which look more complicated than standard text and are usually rather difficult for the uninitiated to read. In the case of conversation analysis, they are based on a system of notation developed by Gail Jefferson (described in Shenkein 1978: xi–xvi); some researches use other, generally similar notation systems (see, e.g., several different levels of detail in the papers brought together by Todd and Fisher 1988). Although the form of such a transcript gives many readers the impression of a technical, "objective" approach to talk, insiders to the tradition view transcripts more provisionally. For these researchers, the talk itself is central; they work primarily from tapes, they play tapes when they present their work to others, and they view transcripts as subject to continual criticism and revision as they "hear the talk" more completely. Transcribing itself is a subtle and difficult craft, learned through apprenticeship and experience, and practiced improvisationally. Notation systems change as researchers attend to previously neglected features of talk.

Conversation and discourse analysts aim to study talk as it actually happens, and they certainly come closer than those who simply translate talk into standard written English. However, one of the important lessons to be drawn from conversation analysis is precisely how difficult it is to hold and study "the talk itself." While these technically sophisticated notation systems capture many features of talk left out of more conventional representations, they cannot be thought of as "complete." So far, most of them leave out gesture and "body language" (but see Goodwin 1979; Goodwin and Goodwin 1989), as well as subtle aspects of talk that have not yet been noticed and notated. They seem most useful (or at least are most used) for studying the form rather than the content of speech. In addition, these systems often have the effect of obscuring the individuality of speech. Because transcripts in this form require large investments of both production time and space in articles, analyses are based on relatively short fragments of speech, usually too short to give a sense of a speaker's characteristic style of speech. One might argue that the difficulty of reading a detailed transcript has the beneficial effect of forcing the reader to study respondents' talk more carefully than when it is represented in standard English. But because these transcripts require such concentrated reading, accent and dialect are often less effectively conveyed than through variations on more standard writing.

No transcription technique preserves all the details of respondents' speech, and no technique will be adequate for every analysis. My intention here is not to propose that feminist researchers must follow analytic programs emphasizing the details of talk, but rather to encourage strategic borrowing from these approaches. In my research on housework, for example, I did not begin with the intention of studying women's speech. I was not trained as an analyst of talk, and I did not use any specialized method for transcribing discourse. But I worked carefully from tape recordings. Without the tapes, I would not have been able to reproduce the hesitation and uncertainty of speech that have so interested me since I finished the interviewing. I doubt that I could have reproduced the delightfully individual accounts built around the significance of particular brands of breakfast cereal or particular cuts of meat—these stories contained too much detail about items too ordinary to remember with confidence. I think I would have remembered hesitation as a general phenomenon, or the fact that respondents often referred to particular preferences, but I needed their exact words as evidence, in order to show readers, in some detail, how they spoke about these matters.

As I worked with the interviews, I learned from conversation and discourse analysis to attend to the details of respondents' speech. I did not systematically transcribe details of dialect, pauses, or emphasis. But as I transcribed, I developed the rudiments of a system for preserving some of the "messiness" of everyday talk. I inserted ungrammatical commas to indicate hesitations mid-sentence. I included many (though not all) of my respondents' "um"s and "you know"s; I indicated outright laughter, but I had not yet learned to hear more attenuated out-breaths as signals of emotion. I transcribed the often confusing process of self-correction (e.g., "And I'm a lot more concerned about—well, I shouldn't say concerned, I should say aware, of what I eat."). In these ways, I recorded more of the inelegant features of my respondents' talk than is customary in the kind of interview study I conducted, and the transcripts retained at least some of the distinctiveness of women's talk about housework.

When I began to write about these interviews, I first selected illustrative excerpts that were clear and concise, and I felt free to do minor editing that made them clearer or more euphonious (eliminating a superfluous phrase, for example, when the meaning of a statement was clear). As the analysis developed, however, I became aware of the power of respondents' actual, often puzzling complex language. I began to search for more confusing rather than clearer speech and I stopped editing excerpts. The halting, unedited excerpts I produced required more analytic comment, of a different sort than I had previously provided. I began to attend more carefully to the small features of respondents' accounts, and to how their stories were situated in longer stretches of discourse. I returned, sometimes, to the original tapes, listening for and transcribing more details of the talk. Instead of relying on the routine practices of the interactionist tradition I had learned, I developed editing strategies that preserved and exploited distinctive features of respondents' talk.

Paget's work provides another example of strategic borrowing, and suggests that editing actual talk may be one of the ways that conventional sociology has suppressed emotion. In her study of artistic work (Paget 1981, 1983), she relies on a system of notation that preserves many features of naturally occurring speech: false starts and hesitations, rhythm and accent, periods of silence. In the analysis, she uses these features of the talk as signals of emotion. For example: the artist informant tells a story of long, hard times, and finally, some success. Paget presents a long excerpt from the interview transcript, and uses the sound of her respondent's account to pinpoint the artist's account of a turning point in her development: "THHEN . . . .sl(h)owly i started to meet other artists. . . . ," (Paget 1983: 84). As she develops the analysis, Paget summarizes the artist's story, and also explains how she herself understood its significance: "Then things in general got much better. 'THHEN' (line 1212) is said with special dramatic effect. It is like a beacon" (Paget 1983: 87). Paget attends to both the content and structure of speech. In her approach, features of speech like pauses and emphasis provide clues to emotion and meaning, and these in turn are building blocks for the analysis. Knowledge, Paget says, "accumulates with many turns at talk. It collects in stories, asides, hesitations, expressions of feeling, and spontaneous associations" (Paget 1983: 78). The researcher preserves the emotion in respondents' talk, and displays it for readers. "Had I edited these exchanges," she explains, "freed them of the odd and essential noises of talk's presence, I would have reworked meanings. The transcript would move forward in an orderly and formal manner. But the dynamic construction of what was said would be gone" (Paget 1983: 87).

There is increasing evidence of a fruitful interchange between traditional approaches to qualitative sociology and the newer insights of conversation and discourse analysis (e.g., Mishler 1986; Moerman 1988; Boden forthcoming). There is also evidence of a heightened awareness of transcription in linguistic research (see, e.g., Ochs 1979), and especially at the borders between conversation analysis and other qualitative approaches (e.g., Mishler 1984). Feminist work should be an important site for mutual influence. For conversation and discourse analysts, attention to the characteristic difficulties in women's speaking provides one route toward showing how the primordial "social doings" of talk and interaction form the "scaffolding of social structure" (West and Zimmerman 1987: 129, 147). For feminists working in more conventional qualitative modes, these approaches call attention to the importance of talk and its organized complexity, and provide techniques for capturing and using talk in analyses of interview data.

Writing about Women's Lives

Social scientists have become increasingly aware, during the 1980s, that writing is not a transparent medium with which researchers simply convey "truths" discovered in the field, but itself constructs and controls meaning and interpretation. In anthropology, a well-developed movement has grown up around the analysis of ethnographic texts, and has begun to stimulate its own feminist critique (see Clifford and Marcus 1986; Mascia-Lees, Sharpe, and Cohen 1989). A similar focus has begun to develop in sociology as well (Brown 1977; Richarson 1988; Van Maanen 1988; Hunter forthcoming; and, with respect to feminist writing specifically, Smith 1989), though it has been less focused and coherent than in anthropology, perhaps because sociologists write in a variety of genres. Here, I will discuss just one aspect of sociological writing, the issue of "labeling" women's experiences. But broader questions about writing should be on a feminist methodological agenda. As we modify traditions for data collection and analysis, we will need to experiment with forms and texts which allow us to fully express the insights arising from transformations in research practice.

Feminists have long been aware that naming is political—the labels attached to activities establish and justify their social worth—and that women's activities have often been labeled in ways that serve the project of controlling and subordinating women (Frye 1983). When researchers write about women's lives, whatever our methods of collecting and analyzing interview data, we confront the dangers of mislabeling that can result from the use of language that does not fit. A feminist strategy in sociology, then, must extend to the language of our texts: we must choose words carefully and creatively, with attention to the consequences of naming experience.

As housework and child care have become legitimate topics for sociologists, for example, researchers have faced the vexing problem of labeling the unpaid work of raising children. Standard vocabulary forces a set of unsatisfactory choices. Suzanne Peters (1985) discussed these problems when she organized a group of sociologists to meet and share research on "motherwork." By selecting a label that referred to mothers, she chose explicitly to "capture a certain element of present social reality . . . (that women mostly raise children)" (Peters 1985: 16). But she also recognized that any vocabulary used to describe these activities should be treated as provisional, and she invited participants in the working group to explore the implications of this and other labels. By using the term *motherwork,* for example, with its gender specificity, we might be denying even the possibility that men can do this work. We might be leaving out lesbian and gay couples who raise children. By using a single, coined term, we might be universalizing the experience, implying that an activity exists that is somehow the same everywhere and in all times. And what are the implications of talking about "work"? The concept does for mothers' activities what it had earlier done in research on housework—calls attention to the time and effort involved in mothering, and its social and economic significance. But it might also obscure "important emotional aspects of mothering, which include creating relationships and cherishing individuals" (Peters 1985: 19).

The problem is familiar, perhaps for all researchers, but especially for feminists exploring previously neglected experiences. But the problem is often defined rather narrowly, in terms of choosing a single word or phrase that will serve.[4] The assumption is that the researcher can, with reasonable care, make decisions that are politically or analytically correct, and then forge ahead, armed with the proper concept. I want to argue instead for a strategic imprecision—that researchers are not well served by deciding exactly what to call mothers' work, and that we would do better to use several different labels, sometimes more or less interchangeably, and sometimes to refer to subtle shadings of meaning that we are just beginning to interpret. This strategy recognizes that different labels will capture different parts of the reality we are working to construct. I developed such an approach in my study of housework, though I did not start out to do so. I began with the notion that I would eventually find a term for the neglected, invisible part of housework that I was most concerned with. As my analysis developed, I used a variety of labels— "family work," "caring," "the work of coordination," or "interpersonal work"— trying to indicate how thought and the construction of relationships are part of housework, but stubbornly resisting suggestions that I could capture what houseworkers really do with a term such as "management." Increasingly, as my understandings grew more complex, I gave up the search for a single label, and simply worked at producing a fuller understanding of women's household activity.

Now, I understand this problem as another manifestation of the uneasy fit between language and women's experiences. If the language is "man-made," it is not likely to provide, ready-made, the words that feminists researchers need to tell what they learn from other women. Instead of imposing a choice among several labels, none of which are quite right, feminist texts should describe women's lives in ways that move beyond standard vocabularies, commenting on the vocabularies themselves along the way (see, e.g., Reinharz 1988). Instead of agreeing on what to call women's activity, we should make our talk richer and more complex—we should use many words, and put them together in ways that force readers to imagine the reality we're describing in a new way—to taste it, try it out, turn it over, take it apart. In discussions of household and family activity, labels like "work" and "emotion" are words that channel thinking, leading the mind down old, familiar roads. And that should not be the effect of a feminist text.

There are unexpected barriers to putting this strategy of rich and complex description into practice. Many readers of social science, accustomed to more conventional analysis, are confused by a shifting vocabulary. Copy editors, whose job includes checking manuscripts for consistency, enforce the routine practice of obscuring complexity under concepts derived from (or developed in opposition to) disciplinary frames (for some examples of problems with editing and feminist discourse, see Paget forthcoming). These problems suggest that feminist researchers must continue to discuss these linguistic difficulties very explicitly whenever we write. When using a multi-layered vocabulary, quite different from those typically anchoring sociological analyses, we will need to alert readers to this strategy and intentions informing it. We will need to prepare the reader to read in new ways— not to expect neat re-definitions, but to settle in for a much longer process of shaping new meanings.

These last comments point toward the construction of an audience for feminist research as an aspect of feminist method. Texts work and move because they are read. But audiences must learn how to read texts, especially those that are "different" because they stretch and extend rhetorical convention (DeVault forthcoming b). This problem pulls writing toward the conventional, as authors strive to communicate effectively with audiences that exist. But a more transformative solution would involve more explicit attention to methods for reading innovative texts. Part of the task of feminist writing, then, should be to instruct a newly forming audience about how to read and hear our words.

DISCUSSION

I have argued that language is often inadequate for women. Its inadequacy surely takes multiple forms for women in different locations. Often, our relations to language are contradictory, because we are both subject to, and also working within, a loosely coordinated ruling apparatus (Smith 1987) with oppressive consequences for others besides women. Talk and interaction are thoroughly gendered, but women do not share a single experience of oppression through talk or a single culture of resistance. Instead, we share multiple versions of both oppression and resistance. There remains in this chapter an unresolved tension between an insistence on the importance of gender and a recognition of cross-cutting differences among women. I have relied on suggestive metaphors of language as "man-made" and of resistance through "woman talk," both of which are too simple if taken too literally. I acknowledge that difficulty here as a way of pointing to aspects of these methodological projects that need fuller development.

In spite of obstacles to women's expression, language is a resource to be used, and in use, there are many possibilities. While much feminist research in linguistics is designed to show how language and the organization of talk contribute to the subordination of women, it also shows, often, how skillfully and creatively women speakers circumvent and subvert the processes of social control, whether they do so by "talking back" (hooks 1989) or "telling it slant" (Spender [1980] 1985). It is quite difficult for most women to be speaking subjects—harder than for men—and that is true both for women as our research subjects and for us as researchers when we write and talk about our work. But women in different places and positions have long traditions of working at self-expression and understanding, using the language to talk about our lives, and working at listening. Professional training as sociologists and the routine practices of the discipline encourage us to abandon these traditions of "woman talk" in favor of a more abstract, controlled, and emotionless discourse. I have meant to suggest that as we construct feminist discourse in sociology, we can instead recognize those distinctively female traditions, borrow from them, and build upon them in our practice as researchers.

NOTES

1. Compare Paget (1983) and Mishler (1986b). Mishler, though without making gender the issue, comments perceptively on the difference between Paget's case and an example from his own interviewing. He notes that their different practices produced quite different results.

2. Carol Gilligan's analysis of women's moral reasoning relies in part on a similar "hearing" of hesitation in women's speech. See Gilligan (1982: 28–29, 31).

3. As an example, he cites the frequent use of "crutch words" such as "you know," though he warns that this kind of repetitiveness should not be confused with "controlled and conscious repetition for rhetorical effect" (Blauner 1987: 51). My discussion of the phrase "you know," above, suggests that such material can be analytically useful precisely because it is not used consciously by respondents toward some end, but rather points toward issues they cannot fully articulate.

4. Another solution to the problem—developing new vocabulary—has produced several experiments with the idea of a feminist dictionary (e.g., Daly and Caputi 1987; Kramarae and Treichler 1986). These books are resources that should encourage feminist sociologists to think about words in new ways. But, while feminists have successfully coined some new words ("sexism," for example), the usefulness of this kind of invention is limited by most of our audiences' impatience with such experimentation.

REFERENCES

Ardener, Edwin. 1975. Belief and the problem of women. In *Perceiving women,* ed. Shirley Ardner, 1–17. New York: John Wiley and Sons.

Ardener, Shirley, ed. 1975. *Perceiving women.* New York: John Wiley and Sons.

Atkinson, J. Maxwell, and John Heritage. 1984. *Structures of social action: Studies in conversation analysis.* Cambridge: Cambridge University Press.

Becker, Howard. 1986. *Doing things together ("Telling about society").* Evanston, Ill.: Northwestern University Press.

Blauner, Bob. 1987. "Problems of editing 'first-person' sociology." *Qualitative Sociology* 10: 46–64.

Boden, Deidre. Forthcoming. People are talking: conversation analysis and symbolic interaction. In *Symbolic interaction and cultural studies,* eds. Howard S. Becker and Michal M. McCall. Chicago: University of Chicago Press.

Boden, Deidre, and Denise D. Bielby. 1986. The way it was: topical organization in elderly conversation. *Language and Communication* 6: 73–89.

Bogdan, Robert, and Steven J. Taylor. 1975. *Introduction to qualitative research methods: A phenomenological approach to the social sciences.* New York: John Wiley and Sons.

Brown, Richard H. 1977. *A poetic for sociology.* Cambridge, MA: Harvard University Press.

Bulkin, Elly, Minnie Bruce Pratt, and Barbara Smith. 1984. *Yours in struggle: Three feminist perspectives on anti-semitism and racism.* New York: Long Haul Press.

Clifford, James, and George E. Marcus, eds. 1986. *Writing culture: The poetics and politics of ethnography.* Berkeley: University of California.

Collins, Patricia Hill. 1986. Learning from the outsider within: the sociological significance of black feminist thought. *Social Problem* 33: 14–32.

———. 1989. The social construction of black feminist thought. *Signs* 14: 745–73.

Daly, Mary, and Jane Caputi. 1987. *Webster's first new intergalactic wickedary of the English language.* Boston: Beacon Press.

Daniels, Arlene Kaplan. 1987. Invisible work. *Social Problems* 34: 403–15.

Darroch, Vivian, and Ronald J. Silvers, eds. 1983. *Interpretive human studies: An introduction to phenomenological research.* Lanham, Md.: University Press of America.

DeVault, Marjorie L. 1984. Women and food: housework and the production of family life. Ph.D. Dissertation. Northwestern University, Evanston, Ill.

———. 1987. Doing housework: feeding and family life. In *Families and work,* ed. Naomi Gerstel and Harriet Engle Gross, 178–91. Philadelphia: Temple University Press.

———. 1990. Novel readings: the social organization of interpretation. *American Journal of Sociology* 95: 887–921.

———. Forthcoming.[a] *Feeding the family: the social organization of caring as gendered work.* Chicago: University of Chicago Press.

———. Forthcoming.[b] *Women write sociology: Rhetorical strategies.* In *The rhetoric of sociology,* ed. Albert Hunter. New Brunswick, NJ: Rutgers University Press.

Fisher, Sue, and Alexandra Dundas Todd. 1983. *The social organization of doctor-patient communication.* Washington, DC: Center for Applied Linguistics.

Fishmen, Pamela M. 1978. Interaction: the work women do. *Social Problems* 25: 397–406.

Frye, Marilyn. 1983. *The politics of reality: Essays in feminist theory.* Trumansburg, NY: The Crossing Press.

Garfinkel, Harold. 1967. *Studies in ethnomethodology.* Englewood Cliffs, NJ: Prentice-Hall.

Gilligan, Carol. 1982. *In a different voice.* Boston: Harvard University Press.

Goodwin, Charles. 1979. The interactive construction of a sentence in natural conversation. In *Everyday language: Studies in ethnomethodology,* ed. George Psathas, 97–121. New York: Irvington.

Goodwin, Charles, and Marjorie H. Goodwin. 1989. Conflicting participation frameworks. Paper presented at the annual meetings of the American Sociological Association, San Francisco.

Griffith, Alison I., and Dorothy E. Smith. 1987. Constructing cultural knowledge: Mothering as discourse. In *Women and education: A Canadian perspective,* ed. Jane Gaskell and Arlene McLaren, 87–103. Calgary, Alberta: Detselig.

Hartsock, Nancy M. 1981. The feminist standpoint: Developing the ground for a specifically feminist historical materialism." In *Discovering reality: Feminist perspectives on epistemology, metaphysics, methodology, and philosophy of science,* ed. Sandra Harding and Merrill Hintikka, 283–310. Boston: Reidel.

Heritage, John. 1984. *Garfinkel and ethnomethodology.* Cambridge: Polity Press.

hooks, bell. 1981. *Ain't I a woman: Black women and feminism.* Boston: South End Press.

———. 1989. Talking back: Thinking feminist, thinking black. Boston: South End Press.

Hunter, Albert, ed. Forthcoming. *The rhetoric of sociology.* New Brunswick, NJ: Rutgers University Press.

Joseph, Gloria I., and Jill Lewis. 1981. *Common differences: Conflicts in black and white feminist perspectives.* Boston: South End Press.

Kramarae, Cheris, and Paula A. Treichler. 1986. *A feminist dictionary.* New York: Routledge, Chapman and Hall.

Lakoff, Robin. 1975. *Language and women's place.* New York: Harper and Row.

Lugones, Maria C., and Elizabeth V. Spelman. 1983. Have we got a theory for you! Feminist theory, cultural imperialism, and the demand for "the woman's voice." *Women's Studies International Forum* 6: 573–81.

MacKinnon, Catharine. 1983. Feminism, marxism, method, and the state: An agenda for theory. In *The signs readers,* ed. Elizabeth Abel and Emily K. Abel, 227–56. Chicago: University of Chicago Press.

Mascia-Lees, Frances E., Patricia Sharpe, and Colleen Ballerino Cohen. 1989. The postmodernist turn in anthropology: Cautions from a feminist perspective. *Signs* 15: 7–33.

Maynard, Douglas W., and Don H. Zimmerman. 1984. Topical talk, ritual, and the social organization of relationships. *Social Psychology Quarterly* 47: 301–16.

Mies, Maria. 1983. Towards a methodology for feminist research. In *Theories of women's studies,* ed. Gloria Bowles and Renate Duelli Klein, 117–39. London: Routledge and Kegan Paul.

Miller, Casey, and Kate Swift. 1977. *Words and women.* Garden City, NY: Anchor Doubleday.

Miller, Jean Baker. 1976. *Toward a new psychology of women.* Boston: Beacon.
———. 1986. What do we mean by relationships? Working Paper No. 22. Stone Center for Developmental Services and Studies. Wellesley College, Wellesley, MA.
Mishler, Elliot G. 1984. *The discourse of medicine: Dialectics of medical interviews.* Norwood, NJ: Ablex.
———. 1986a. *Research interviewing: Context and narrative.* Cambridge, MA: Harvard University Press.
———. 1986b. The analysis of interview-narratives. In *Narrative psychology: The storied nature of human conduct,* ed. Theodore R. Sarbin, 233–55. New York: Praeger.
Moerman, Michael. 1988. *Talking culture: Ethnography and conversation analysis.* Philadelphia: University of Pennsylvania Press.
Oakly, Ann. 1981. Interviewing women: A contradiction in terms. In *Doing feminist research,* ed. Helen Roberts, 30–61. London: Routledge and Kegan Paul.
Ochs, Elinor. 1979. Transcription as theory. In *Developmental pragmatics,* ed. Elinor Ochs and Bambi B. Schieffelin, 43–72. New York: Academic Press.
Paget, Marianne A. 1981. The ontological anguish of women artists. *The New England Sociologist* 3: 65–79.
———. 1983. "Experience and knowledge." *Human Studies* 6: 67–90.
———. Forthcoming. Unlearning to not speak. *Human Studies.*
Peters, Suzanne. 1985. "Reflections on studying mothering, motherwork, and mother's work." Paper presented at *The Motherwork Workshop.* Institut Simone de Beauvoir, Concordia University, Montreal.
Psathas, George. 1973. *Phenomenological sociology: Issues and applications.* New York: Wiley and Sons.
Reinharz, Shulamit. 1983. Experiential analysis: a contribution to feminist research. In *Theories of women's studies,* ed. Gloria Bowles and Renate Duelli Klein, 162–91. London: Routledge and Kegan Paul.
———. 1988. What's missing in miscarriage? *Journal of Community Psychology* 16: 84–103.
Richardson, Laurel. 1988. The collective story: Postmodernism and the writing of sociology. *Sociological Focus* 21: 199–208.
———. Forthcoming. Narrative and sociology. *Journal of Contemporary Ethnography.*
Riessman, Catherine Kohler. 1987. When gender is not enough: Women interviewing women. *Gender and Society* 1: 172–207.
Rothman, Barbara Katz. 1986. Reflections: On hard work. *Qualitative Sociology* 9: 48–53.
Rubin, Lillian B. 1979. *Women of a certain age: The mid-life search for self.* New York: Harper and Row.
Saraceno, Chiaro. 1984. Shifts in public and private boundaries: Women as mothers and service workers in Italian daycare. *Feminist Studies* 10: 7–29.
Schegloff, Emanuel A. 1982. Discourse as an interactional achievement: some uses of "uh huh" and other things that come between sentences. In *Analyzing discourse: Text and talk,* ed. Deborah Tannen, 71–93. Washington, DC: Georgetown University Press.
Schenkein, Jim, ed. 1978. *Studies in the organization of conversational interaction.* New York: Academic Press.
Smith, Dorothy E. 1974. The ideological practice of sociology. *Catalyst No.* 8: 39–54.
———. 1983. No one commits suicide: Textual analysis of ideological practices. *Human Studies* 6: 309–59.
———. 1987. *The everyday world as problematic: A feminist sociology.* Boston: Northeastern University Press.
———. 1989. Sociological theory: Methods of writing patriarchy. In *Feminism and sociological theory,* ed. Ruth A. Wallace, 34–64. Newbury Park, CA: Sage.

Spender, Dale. [1980] 1985. *Man made language*. 2d ed. with revised introduction. London: Routledge and Kegan Paul.

Stacey, Judith. 1988. Can there be a feminist ethnography? *Women's Studies International Forum* 11: 21–27.

Stacey, Judith, and Barrie Thorne. 1985. The missing feminist revolution in sociology. *Social Problems* 32: 301–16.

Stanko, Elizabeth. 1985a. *Intimate intrusions: Women's experience of male violence*. Boston: Routledge and Kegan Paul.

———. 1985b. Presentation at a meeting of the Boston area chapter of Sociologists for Women in Society, November.

———. Forthcoming. *Everyday violence*. London: Pandora Press.

Stanley, Liz, and Sue Wise. 1983. "Back into the personal" or: our attempt to construct "feminist research." In *Theories of women's studies,* ed. Gloria Bowles and Renate Duelli Klein, 192–309. London: Routledge and Kegan Paul.

Thorne, Barrie, and Nancy Henley. 1975. *Language and sex: Difference and dominance*. Rowley, MA: Newbury House.

Thorne, Barrie, Cheris Kramarae, and Nancy Henley, eds. 1983. *Language, gender, and society*. Rowley, MA: Newbury House.

Todd, Alexandra Dundas, and Sue Fisher, eds. 1988. *Gender and discourse: The power of talk*. Norwood, NJ: Ablex.

Van Maanan, John. 1988. *Tales of the field: On writing ethnography*. Chicago: University of Chicago Press.

West, Candace. 1982. Why can't a woman be more like a man? An interactional note on organizational game playing for managerial women. *Work and Occupations* 9: 5–29.

West, Candace, and Don H. Zimmerman. 1983. Small insults: A study of interruptions in cross-sex conversations between unacquainted persons. In *Language, gender, and society,* ed. Barrie Thorne, Cheris Kramarae, and Nancy Henley, 86–111. Rowley, MA: Newbury House.

———. 1987. Doing gender. *Gender and Society* 1: 125–51.

CHAPTER 14

Gendering Violence

Masculinity and Power in Men's Accounts of Domestic Violence

KRISTIN L. ANDERSON AND DEBRA UMBERSON

In the 1970s, feminist activists and scholars brought wife abuse to the forefront of public consciousness. Published in the academic and popular press, the words and images of survivors made one aspect of patriarchy visible: Male dominance was displayed on women's bruised and battered bodies (Dobash and Dobash 1979; Martin 1976). Early research contributed to feminist analyses of battery as part of a larger pattern of male domination and control of women (Pence and Paymar 1993; Yllo 1993). Research in the 1980s and 1990s has expanded theoretical understandings of men's violence against women through emphases on women's agency and resistance to male control (Bowker 1983; Kirkwood 1993); the intersection of physical, structural, and emotional forces that sustain men's control over female partners (Kirkwood 1993; Pence and Paymar 1993); and the different constraints faced by women and men of diverse nations, racial ethnic identities, and sexualities who experience violence at the hands of intimate partners (Eaton 1994; Island and Letellier 1991; Jang, Lee, and Morello-Frosch 1998; Renzetti 1992). This work demonstrates ways in which the gender order facilitates victimization of disenfranchised groups.

Comparatively less work has examined the ways in which gender influences male perpetrators' experiences of domestic violence (Yllo 1993). However, a growing body of qualitative research critically examines batterers' descriptions of violence within their relationships. Dobash and Dobash (1998), Hearn (1998), and Ptacek (1990) focus on the excuses, justifications, and rationalizations that batterers use to account for their violence. These authors suggest that batterers' accounts of violence are texts through which they attempt to deny responsibility for violence and to present nonviolent self-identities.

Dobash and Dobash (1998) identify ways in which gender, as a system that structures the authority and responsibilities assigned to women and men within intimate relationships, supports battery. They find that men use violence to punish female partners who fail to meet their unspoken physical, sexual, or emotional needs. Lundgren (1998) examines batterers' use of gendered religious ideologies to justify their violence against female partners. Hearn (1998, 37) proposes that violence is a "resource for demonstrating and showing a person is a man." These studies find that masculine identities are constructed through acts of violence and through batterers' ability to control partners as a result of their violence.

This chapter examines the construction of gender within men's accounts of domestic violence. Guided by theoretical work that characterizes gender as performance (Butler 1990, 1993; West and Fenstermaker 1995), we contend that batterers attempt to construct masculine identities through the practice of violence and the discourse about violence that they provide. We examine these performances of gender as "routine, methodical, and ongoing accomplishment[s]" that create and sustain notions of natural differences between women and men (West and Fenstermaker 1995, 9). Butler's concept of performativity extends this idea by suggesting that it is through performance that gendered subjectivities are constructed: "Gender proves to be performative—that is, constituting the identity it is purported to be. In this sense, gender is always a doing, though not a doing by a subject who may be said to preexist the deed" (1990, 25). For Butler, gender performances demonstrate the instability of masculine subjectivity; a "masculine identity" exists only as the actions of individuals who stylize their bodies and their actions in accordance with a normative binary framework of gender.

In addition, the performance of gender makes male power and privilege appear natural and normal rather than socially produced and structured. Butler (1990) argues that gender is part of a system of relations that sustains heterosexual male privilege through the denigration or erasure of alternative (feminine/gay/lesbian/bisexual) identities. West and Fenstermaker (1995) contend that cultural beliefs about underlying and essential differences between women and men, and social structures that constitute and are constituted by these beliefs, are reproduced by the accomplishment of gender. In examining the accounts offered by domestically violent men, we focus on identifying ways in which the practice of domestic violence helps men to accomplish gender. We also focus on the contradictions within these accounts to explore the instability of masculine subjectivities and challenges to the performance of gender.

DATA AND METHOD

In-depth interviews conducted in 1995–96 with thirty-three men recruited through the Family Violence Diversion Network (FVDN), a nonprofit agency located in a midsize southwestern city, serve as data for analysis. FVDN provides educational domestic violence programs and serves approximately five hundred to seven hundred men per year in this capacity. Eighty-five percent to 90 percent of the program participants are court mandated to participate in a battering program. The remaining participants are self-referred or referred by other sources such as their attorneys or therapists. FVDN's program for batterers entails twenty-one weekly meetings run by male group leaders. The first three weeks of the program consist of orientation sessions. We recruited respondents primarily through these orientation sessions to reduce the possibility that responses would be influenced by the information provided during group sessions. Potential participants were informed that the study was not connected to FVDN and that their participation was voluntary. The number of

Table 14.1 Comparison of Sample to FVDN[a] Population

	FVDN Population 7–94 to 12–94		*Sample of FVDN Participants*	
Variable	**M**	**SD**	**M**	**SD**
Sociodemographic				
Household Income	14,123	15,936	30,463	16,642
Education (years)	11	3.10	13	1.8
Age	31.51	9.00	32.07	7.88
Race/Ethnicity (%)				
African American	16.0	18.2		
European American	32.4	57.5		
Hispanic/Latino	39.7	21.2		
Other	12.1	3.0		
Marital Status (%)				
Married	40.2	42.4		
Cohabitating	23.8	27.3		
Divorced/separated	3.7	30.3		
Never married	11.4	0		
FVDN participation (%)				
Court mandated	90.3	81.5		
Voluntary	9.7	18.5		
n	219	33		

a. FVDN = Family Violence Diversion Network.

participants recruited from ten FVDN orientation meetings ranged from 5 percent to 40 percent of the men present. Participants were paid thirty to forty dollars for their participation.

We collected information about the characteristics of the FVDN participant population that allows us to compare our sample to the population. Table 14.1 presents descriptive data for the study sample and the population of all men who participated in the FVDN program from July through December 1994. A middle-class group of the population served by FVDN volunteered to participate in the present study. On average, the men who volunteered to participate were of higher socioeconomic status and were more likely to be at FVDN at their own initiative than men in the FVDN population. Our sample contained more European American men and fewer Latino men compared with the FVDN population. Six of the respondents reported an African American ethnic identity, seven men identified as Latino, nineteen men reported a European American ancestry, and one respondent reported a Native American ancestry. Five men had earned college degrees, eighteen had attended college or vocational/technical schools, six had completed high school, and four had not completed high school. Their annual household incomes ranged from $5,000 to $80,000, with a mean of $30,463.

Interviews were conducted by three white female graduate students in FVDN agency offices and lasted between one and two hours (the average length was ninety-five minutes). We asked open-ended questions about positive and negative aspects of their relationships with female partners and their children (see Appendix 14.1 for a list of the guiding questions). Following the methods used by Dobash and Dobash (1984) in their study of women's accounts of domestic violence, we asked participants to recount the worst and most recent incidents of violence in their relationships. Interviews were semistructured; interviewers were instructed to cover the topics suggested by the guiding questions and to pursue topics raised by the participants. Interviews were transcribed and thematically coded for analysis. After identifying the prevalent themes in the interviews, we reread the transcripts separately for each theme to identify the presence or absence of the theme within the individual transcripts.

The diversity in our sample enables us to examine some ways in which social class and racial ethnic locations influence accounts of violence. Moreover, we are attentive to ways in which gender and racial ethnic differences may have influenced our rapport with respondents and the content of the interviews. Appendix 14.2 presents specific demographic information about the individual participants and pseudonyms through which they are referenced.

FINDINGS

How do batterers talk about the violence in their relationships? They excuse, rationalize, justify, and minimize their violence against female partners. Like the batterers studied by previous researchers, the men in this study constructed their violence as a rational response to extreme provocation, a loss of control, or a minor incident that was blown out of proportion. Through such accounts, batterers deny responsibility for their violence and save face when recounting behavior that has elicited social sanctions (Dobash and Dobash 1998; Ptacek 1990).

However, these accounts are also about the performance of gender. That is, through their speech acts, respondents presented themselves as rational, competent, masculine actors. We examine several ways in which domestic violence is gendered in these accounts. First, according to respondents' reports, violence is gendered in its practice. Although it was in their interests to minimize and deny their violence, participants reported engaging in more serious, frequent, and injurious violence than that committed by their female partners. Second, respondents gendered violence through their depictions and interpretations of violence. They talked about women's violence in a qualitatively different fashion than they talked about their own violence, and their language reflected hegemonic notions of femininity and masculinity. Third, the research participants constructed gender by interpreting the violent conflicts in ways that suggested that their female partners were responsible for the participants' behavior. Finally, respondents gendered violence by claiming that they are victimized by a criminal justice system that constructs all men as villains and all women as victims.

Gendered Practice

Men perpetrate the majority of violence against women and against other men in the United States (Bachman and Saltzman 1995). Although some scholars argue that women perpetrate domestic violence at rates similar to men (Straus 1993), feminist scholars have pointed out that research findings of "sexual symmetry" in domestic violence are based on survey questions that fail to account for sex differences in physical strength and size and in motivations for violence (Dobash et al. 1992; Straton 1994). Moreover, recent evidence from a large national survey suggests that women experience higher rates of victimization at the hands of partners than men and that African American and Latina women experience higher rates of victimization than European American women (Bachman and Saltzman 1995).

Although the majority of respondents described scenarios in which both they and their partners perpetrated violent acts, they reported that their violence was more frequent and severe than the violence perpetrated by their female partners. Eleven respondents (33 percent) described attacking a partner who did not physically resist, and only two respondents (6 percent) reported that they were victimized by their partners but did not themselves perpetrate violence. The twenty cases (61 percent) in which the participants reported "mutual" violence support feminist critiques of "sexual symmetry":

> We started pushing each other. And the thing is that I threw her on the floor. I told her that I'm going to leave. She took my car keys, and I wanted my car keys so I went and grabbed her arm, pulled it, and took the car keys away from her. She—she comes back and tries to kick me in the back. So I just pushed her back and threw her on the floor again. (Juan)

Moreover, the respondents did not describe scenarios in which they perceived themselves to be at risk from their partners' violence. The worst injury reportedly sustained was a split lip, and only five men (15 percent) reported sustaining any injury. Female partners reportedly sustained injuries in fourteen cases (42 percent). Although the majority of the injuries reportedly inflicted on female partners consisted of bruises and scratches, a few women were hospitalized, and two women sustained broken ribs. These findings corroborate previous studies showing that women suffer more injuries from domestic violence than men (Langhinrichsen-Rohling, Neidig, and Thorn 1995). Moreover, because past studies suggest that male batterers underreport their perpetration of violence (Dobash and Dobash 1998), it is likely that respondents engaged in more violence than they described in these in-depth interviews.

Domestic violence is gendered through social and cultural practices that advantage men in violent conflicts with women. Young men often learn to view themselves as capable perpetrators of violence through rough play and contact sports, to exhibit fearlessness in the face of physical confrontations, and to accept the harm and injury associated with violence as "natural" (Dobash and Dobash 1998; Messner 1992). Men are further advantaged by cultural norms suggesting that women should pair with men who are larger and stronger than themselves (Goffman 1977). Women's less pervasive and less effective use of violence reflects fewer social opportunities to learn violent techniques, a lack of encouragement for female violence within society, and women's size disadvantage in relation to male partners (Fagot et al. 1985; McCaughey 1998). In a culture that defines aggression as unfeminine, few women learn to use violence effectively.

Gendered Depictions and Interpretations

Participants reported that they engaged in more frequent and serious violence than their partners, but they also reported that their violence was different from that of their partners. They depicted their violence as rational, effective, and explosive, whereas women's violence was represented as hysterical, trivial, and ineffectual. Of the twenty-two participants who described violence perpetrated by their partners, twelve (55 percent) suggested that their partner's violence was ridiculous or ineffectual. These respondents minimized their partners' violence by explaining that it was of little concern to them:

> I came out of the kitchen, and then I got in her face, and I shoved her. She shoved, she tried to push me a little bit, but it didn't matter much. (Adam)

> I was seeing this girl, and then a friend of mine saw me with this girl and he went back and told my wife, and when I got home that night, that's when she tried to hit me, to fight me. I just pushed her out of the way and left. (Shad)

This minimizing discourse also characterizes descriptions of cases in which female partners successfully made contact and injured the respondent, as in the following account:

> I was on my way to go to the restroom. And she was just cussing and swearing and she wouldn't let me pass. So, I nudged her. I didn't push her or shove her, I just kind of, you know, just made my way to the restroom. And, when I done that she hit me, and she drew blood. She hit me in the lip, and she drew blood. . . . I go in the bathroom and I started laughing, you know. And I was still half lit that morning, you know. And I was laughing because I think it maybe shocked me more than anything that she had done this, you know. (Ed)

Although his partner "drew blood," Ed minimized her violence by describing it as amusing, uncharacteristic, and shocking.

Even in the case of extreme danger, such as when threatened with a weapon, respondents denied the possibility that their partners' violence was a threat. During a fight described by Steve, his partner locked herself in the bathroom with his gun:

> We were battering each other at that point, and that's when she was in the bathroom. This is—it's like forty-five minutes into this whole argument now. She's in the bathroom, messing with my [gun]. And I had no idea. So I kicked the door in—in the bathroom, and she's sitting there trying to load this thing, trying to get this clip in, and luckily she couldn't figure it out. Why, I don't—you know, well, because she was drunk. So, luckily she didn't. The situation could have been a whole lot worse, you know, it could have been a whole lot worse than it was. I thank God that she didn't figure it out. When I think about it, you know, she was lucky to come out of it with just a cut in her head. You know, she could have blown her brains out or done something really stupid.

This account contains interesting contradictions. Steve stated that he had "no idea" that his partner had a gun, but he responded by kicking down the door to reach her. He then suggested that he was concerned about his partner's safety and that he kicked in the door to save her from doing "something really stupid" to herself. Similarly, Alejandro minimized the threat in his account of an incident in which his partner picked up a weapon:

> So, she got angry and got a knife, came up at me, and I kick her. *And then what happened?* Well, I kick her about four times because she—I kick her, and I say "Just stop, stay there!" and she stand up and come again and I had to kick her again. Somebody called the police, somebody called the police. I guess we were making a lot of noise. And I couldn't go out, I couldn't leave home, because I was not dressed properly to go out. And so I couldn't go, so the only alternative I had at this moment was to defend myself from the knife. So I had to kick her.

Alejandro suggested that his partner's attack with a knife was not enough of a threat to warrant his leaving the house when he was "not dressed properly to go out."

In addition to emphasizing their partners' incompetence in the practice of violence, some respondents depicted the violence perpetrated by their partners as irrational:

> She has got no control. She sees something and she don't like it, she'll go and pull my hair, scratch me, and [act] paranoid, crazy, screaming loud, make everybody look at her, and call the police, you know. Just nuts. (Andrew)

> She came back and started hitting me with her purse again so I knocked the purse out of her hand, and then, she started screaming at me to get out. I went back to the room, and she came running down the hall saying she was going to throw all my stuff out and I'd just had enough so I went and grabbed her, pulled her back. And grabbed her back to the bed and threw her on the bed and sat on her—told her I wasn't going to let her up until she came to her senses . . . she came back up again and I just grabbed her and threw her down. After that, she promised—she finally said that she had come to her senses and everything. I went into the other room, and she went out to clean up the mess she had made in the living room, and then she just started just crying all night long, or for a while. (Phil)

Phil and Andrew described their partners' acts as irrational and hysterical. Such depictions helped respondents to justify their own violence and to present themselves as calm, cool, rational men. Phil described his own behavior of throwing his partner down as a nonviolent, controlled response to his partner's outrageous behavior. Moreover, he suggests that he used this incident to demonstrate his sense of superior rationality to his partner. Phil later reported that a doctor became "very upset" about the marks on his wife's neck two days after this incident, suggesting that he was not the rational actor represented in his account.

In eight other cases (36 percent), respondents did not depict their partner's violence as trivial or ineffectual. Rather, they described their partners' behavior in matter-of-fact terms:

> Then she starts jumping at me or hitting me, or tell me "leave the house, I don't want you, I don't love you" and stuff like that. And I say, "don't touch me, don't touch me." And I just push her back. She keeps coming and hit me, hit me. I keep pushing back, she starts scratch me, so I push hard to stop her from hurting me. (Mario)

Other respondents depicted their partner's violence in factual terms but emphasized that they perceived their own violence as the greater danger. Ray took his partner seriously when he stated that "she was willing to fight, to defend herself," yet he also mentioned his fears that his own violence would be lethal: 'The worst time is when she threw an iron at me. And I'm gonna tell you, I think that was the worst time because, in defense, in retaliation, I pulled her hair, and I thought maybe I broke her neck." Only two respondents—Alan and Jim—consistently identified as victims:

> One of the worst times was realizing that she was drunk and belligerent. I realized that I needed to take her home in her car and she was not capable of driving. And she was physically abusive the whole way home. And before I could get out of the door or get out of the way, she came at me with a knife. And stupidly, I defended myself—kicked her hand to get the knife out. And I bruised her hand enough to where she felt justified enough to call the police with stories that I was horribly abusing. (Jim)

Jim reported that his partner has hit him, stabbed him, and thrown things at him. However, he also noted that he was arrested following several of these incidents, suggesting that his accounts tell us only part of the story. Moreover, like Steve and Alejandro, he did not describe feelings of fear or apprehension about his partner's use of a knife.

Although female partners were represented as dangerous only to themselves, the participants depicted their own violence as primal, explosive, and damaging to others:

> I explode for everything. This time it was trying to help my daughter with her homework, it was a Sunday, and she was not paying any attention, and I get angry with my daughter, and so I kick the TV . . . I guess broke the TV, and then I kick a bookshelf. My daughter tried to get into the middle so I pushed her away from me and I kicked another thing. So, she [his partner] called the police. I am glad she called the police because something really awful could have happened. (Alejandro)

> She said something, and then I just lost control. I choked her, picked her up off her feet, and lifted her up like this, and she was kind of kicking back and forth, and I really felt like I really wanted to kill her this time. (Adam)

> I feel that if there had been a gun in the house, I would have used it. That's one reason also why I refuse to have a gun. Because I know I have a terrible temper and I'm afraid that I will do something stupid like that. (Fred)

In contrast to their reported fearlessness when confronted by women wielding weapons, respondents constructed their own capacity for violence as something that should engender fear. These interpretations are consistent with cultural constructions of male violence as volcanic—natural, lethal, and impossible to stop until it has run its course.

Respondents' interpretations of ineffectual female violence and lethal male violence reflect actual violent practices in a culture that grants men more access to violence, but they also gender violence. By denying a threat from women's violence, participants performed masculinity and reinforced notions of gender difference. Women were constructed as incompetent in the practice of violence, and their successes were trivialized. For example, it is unlikely that Ed would have responded with laughter had his lip been split by the punch of another man (Dobash and Dobash 1998). Moreover, respondents ignored their partners' motivations for violence and their active efforts to exert change within their relationships.

In her examination of Irigaray's writings on the representation of women within the masculine economy, Butler (1993, 36) writes that "the economy that claims to include the feminine as the subordinate term in a binary opposition of masculine/feminine excludes the feminine—produces the feminine as that which must be excluded for that economy to operate." The binary representation of ineffectual, hysterical female behavior and rational, lethal male violence within these accounts erases the feminine; violence perpetrated by women and female subjectivity are effaced in order that the respondents can construct masculinities.[1] These representations mask the power relations that determine what acts will qualify as "violence" and thus naturalize the notion that violence is the exclusive province of men.

Gendering Blame

The research participants also gendered violence by suggesting that their female partners were responsible for the violence within their relationships. Some respondents did this by claiming that they did not hit women with whom they were involved in the past:

> I've never hit another woman in my life besides the one that I'm with. She just has a knack for bringing out the worst in me. (Tom)
>
> You know, I never hit my first wife. I'm married for five years—I never hit her. I never struck her, not once. (Mitchell)

Respondents also shifted blame onto female partners by detailing faults in their partners' behaviors and personalities. They criticized their partners' parenting styles, interaction styles, and choices. However, the most typically reported criticism was that female partners were controlling. Ten of the thirty-three respondents (30 percent) characterized their partners as controlling, demanding, or dominating:

> She's real organized and critiquing about things. She wanna—she has to get it like—she like to have her way all the time, you know. In control of things, even when she's at work in the evenings, she has to have control of everything that's going on in the house. And—but—you know, try to get, to control everything there. You know, what's going on, and me and myself. (Adam)
>
> You know, you're here with this person, you're here for five years, and yet they turn out to be aggressive, what is aggressive, too educated, you know. It's the reason they feel like they want to control you. (Mitchell)

In a few cases, respondents claimed that they felt emasculated by what they interpreted as their partners' efforts to control them:

> She's kind of—I don't want to say dominating. She's a good mother, she's a great housekeeper, she's an excellent cook. But as far as our relationship goes, the old traditional "man wears the pants in the family," it's a shared responsibility. There's no way that you could say that I wear the pants in the family. She's dominating in that sense. (Ted)
>
> You ask the guy sitting next door to me, the guy that's down the hall. For years they all say, "Bill, man, reach down and grab your eggs. She wears the pants." Or maybe like, "Hey man, we're going to go—Oh, Bill can't go. He's got to ask his boss first." And they were right. (Bill)

These representations of female partners as dominating enabled men to position themselves as victims of masculinized female partners. The relational construction of masculinity is visible in these accounts; women who "wear the pants" disrupt the binary opposition of masculinity/femininity. Bill's account reveals that "one is one's gender to the extent that one is not the other gender" (Butler 1990, 22); he is unable to perform masculinity to the satisfaction of his friends when mirrored by a partner who is perceived as dominating.

Moreover, respondents appeared to feel emasculated by unspecified forces. Unlike female survivors who describe concrete practices that male partners utilize to exert control (Kirkwood 1993; Walker 1984), participants were vague about what they meant by control and the ways in which their partners exerted control:

> I don't think she's satisfied unless she has absolute control, and she's not in a position to control anyway, um, mentally. . . . *When you said that, um, that she wasn't really in a position to control, what did you mean by that?* Well, she's not in a position to control, in the fact that she's not, the control that she wants, is pretty much control over me. I'm pretty much the only person that she sees every day. She wants to control every aspect of what I do, and while in the same turn, she really can't. (George)

Respondents who claimed that their partners are controlling offered nebulous explanations for these feelings, suggesting that these claims may be indicative of these men's fears about being controlled by a woman rather than the actual practices of their partners.

Finally, respondents gendered violence through their efforts to convince female partners to shoulder at least part of the blame for their violence. The following comments reflect respondents' interpretations of their partners' feelings after the argument was over:

> Finally, for once in her life, I got her to accept 50/50 blame for the reason why she actually got hit. You know, used to be a time where she could say there was never a time. But, she accepts 50/50 blame for this. (Tom)

> She has a sense that she is probably 80–90 percent guilty of my anger. (Alejandro)

Contemporary constructions of gender hold women responsible for men's aggression (Gray, Palileo, and Johnson 1993). Sexual violence is often blamed on women, who are perceived as tempting men who are powerless in the face of their primal sexual desires (Scully 1990). Although interviewees expressed remorse for their violent behavior, they also implied that it was justified in light of their partners' controlling behavior. Moreover, their violence was rewarded by their partners' feelings of guilt, suggesting that violence is simultaneously a performance of masculinity and a means by which respondents encouraged the performance of femininity by female partners.

"The Law Is for Women": Claiming Gender Bias

Participants sometimes rationalized their violence by claiming that the legal system overreacted to a minor incident. Eight of the thirty-three interviewees (24 percent) depicted themselves as victims of gender politics or the media attention surrounding the trial of O. J. Simpson:

> I think my punishment was wrong. And it was like my attorney told me—I'm suffering because of O. J. Simpson. Mine was the crime of the year. That is, you know, it's the hot issue of the year because of O. J. Two years ago they would have gone "Don't do that again." (Bill)
>
> I'm going to jail for something I haven't even done because the woman is always the victim and the guy is always the bad guy. And O.J., I think, has made it even worse—that mentality. I know that there's a lot of bad, ignorant, violent guys out there that probably think that it's wonderful to batter their wife on a regular basis, but I think there's a lot of reverse mentality going on right now. (Jim)
>
> I don't necessarily agree with the jail system, which I know has nothing to do with you guys, but you have to sign a form saying that you'll come to counseling before you've ever been convicted of a crime. And, like I said, here I am now with this [inaudible] that I have to come to for twenty-one weeks in a row—for what could amount to some girl calling—hurting herself and saying her boyfriend or husband did it. (Tom)

These claims of gender bias were sometimes directly contradicted by respondents' descriptions of events following the arrival of the police. Four participants (12 percent) reported that the police wanted to arrest their female partner along with or instead of themselves—stories that challenged their claims of bias in the system. A few of these respondents reported that they lied to the police about the source of their injuries to prevent the arrest of their partners. Ed, the respondent who sustained a split lip from his partner's punch, claimed that he "took the fall" for his partner:

> They wanted to arrest her, because I was the one who had the little split lip. And I told them that—I said, "No, man, she's seven months pregnant." I told the officer, you know, "How can you take her to jail? She's seven months pregnant!" And I said, "Look, I came in here—I started it, I pushed her. And she hit me." You know, I told them that I had shoved her. And after that they said, "Okay, well, we have to remove, move you out of this—out of this situation here." Something about the law. So, I said, "Well, you know, I started it." I told them I had started it, you know. And, they said, "Okay, well, we'll take you then." So I went to jail. (Ed)

When the police arrived, these respondents were in a double bind. They wanted to deny their own violence to avoid arrest, but they also wanted to deny victimization at the hands of a woman. "Protecting" their female partners from arrest allowed them a way out of this bind. By volunteering to be arrested despite their alleged innocence, they became chivalrous defenders of their partners. They were also, paradoxically, able to claim that "gender bias" led to their arrest and participation in the FVDN program. When Ed argued that the criminal justice system is biased toward women, we confronted him about this contradiction:

> ED: I am totally against, you know,—ever since I stepped foot in this program and I've only been to the orientation—[that] it speaks of gender, okay, and everything that—it seems like every statement that is made is directed toward

men, toward the male party . . . as I stated earlier, the law is for women. In my opinion, it—

INTERVIEWER: Although, they would have arrested her if you hadn't intervened.

ED: They would, that's right. That's another thing. That's right, that's right. They would have arrested her. But, you know even, even with her statement saying, look this is what, this is what happened, I'm not pressing charges. The state picked up those charges, and, they just took it upon themselves, you know, to inconvenience my life, is what they did.

INTERVIEWER: Okay. And the other alternative would have been that she would have been going through this process instead of you.

ED: Well, no, the other alternative, that was, that was, that would come out of this, is [that] I would have spent thirty days in jail.

Ed repeatedly dismissed the notion that the legal system would hold his partner accountable for her actions despite his own words to the contrary. His construction of men as victimized by an interfering justice system allowed him to avoid the seemingly unacceptable conclusion that either he or his partner was a victim of violence.

Another respondent, Jim, reportedly prevented his partner's arrest because he felt it to be in his best interests:

> She was drunk and behind the wheel and driving erratically while backhanding me. And a cop pulled us over because he saw her hit me. And I realized that she was gonna get a DWI [Driving While Intoxicated], which would have been her second and a major expense to me, besides, you know, I think that there's a thin line between protecting somebody and possessing somebody. But I protect her, I do. I find myself sacrificing myself for her and lying for her constantly. And I told the cops that I hit her just because they saw her hit me and I figured that if I told them that I hit her, rather than her get a DWI, that we would both go to jail over an assault thing. Which is what happened. (Jim)

When batterers "protect" their partners from arrest, their oppressor becomes a powerful criminal justice system rather than a woman. Although even the loser gains status through participation in a fight with another man, a man does not gain prestige from being beaten by a woman (Dobash and Dobash 1998). In addition, respondents who stepped in to prevent their partners from being arrested ensured that their partners remained under their control, as Jim suggested when he described "the thin line between being protected by somebody and possessing somebody." By volunteering to be arrested along with his partner, Jim ensured that she was not "taken into possession" (e.g., taken into custody) by the police.[2]

By focusing the interviews on "gender bias" in the system, respondents deflected attention from their own perpetration and victimization. Constructions of a bias gave them an explanation for their arrest that was consistent with their self-presentation as rational, strong, and nonviolent actors. Claims of "reverse mentality" also enabled participants to position themselves as victims of gender politics.

Several interviewees made use of men's rights rhetoric or alluded to changes wrought by feminism to suggest that they are increasingly oppressed by a society in which women have achieved greater rights:

> I really get upset when I watch TV shows as far as, like they got shows or TV station called Lifetime and there are many phrases "TV for women." And that kind of made me upset. Why is it TV for women? You know, it should be TV for everyone, not just women. You don't hear someone else at a different TV station saying, "TV for men." . . . As far as the law goes, changing some of the laws goes too, some of the laws that guys are pulled away from their children. I kind of felt sorry for the guys. (Kenny)

A number of recent studies have examined the increasingly angry and antifeminist discourse offered by some men who are struggling to construct masculine identities within patriarchies disrupted by feminism and movements for gay/lesbian and civil rights (Fine et al. 1997; Messner 1998; Savran 1998). Some branches of the contemporary "men's movement" have articulated a defensive and antifeminist rhetoric of "men's rights" that suggests that men have become the victims of feminism (Messner 1998; Savran 1998). Although none of our interviewees reported participation in any of the organized men's movements, their allusions to the discourse of victimized manhood suggest that the rhetoric of these movements has become an influential resource for the performance of gender among some men. Like the angry men's rights activists studied by Messner (1998), some respondents positioned themselves as the victims of feminism, which they believe has co-opted the criminal justice system and the media by creating "myths" of male domination. The interviews suggest that respondents feel disempowered and that they identify women—both the women whom they batter and women who lead movements to criminalize domestic violence—as the "Other" who has "stolen their presumed privilege" (Fine et al. 1997, 54): "Now girls are starting to act like men, or try and be like men. Like if you hit me, I'll call the cops, or if you don't do it, I'll do this, or stuff like that" (Juan). Juan contends that by challenging men's "privilege" to hit their female partners without fear of repercussions, women have become "like men." This suggests that the construction of masculine subjectivities is tied to a position of dominance and that women have threatened the binary and hierarchical gender framework through their resistance to male violence.

DISCUSSION: SOCIAL LOCATIONS AND DISCOURSES OF VIOLENCE

Respondents' descriptions of conflicts with female partners were similar across racial ethnic and class locations. Participants of diverse socioeconomic standings and racial ethnic backgrounds minimized the violence perpetrated by their partners, claimed that the criminal justice system is biased against men, and attempted to place responsibility for their violence on female partners. However, we identified some ways in which social class influenced respondents' self-presentations.[3]

Respondents of higher socioeconomic status emphasized their careers and the material items that they provided for their families throughout the interviews:

> We built two houses together and they are nice. You know, we like to see a nice environment for our family to live in. We want to see our children receive a good education. (Ted)
>
> That woman now sits in a twenty-seven hundred square foot house. She drives a Volvo. She has everything. A brand-new refrigerator, a brand-new washer and dryer. (Bill)

Conversely, economically disenfranchised men volunteered stories about their prowess in fights with other men. These interviewees reported that they engaged in violent conflicts with other men as a means of gaining respect:

> Everybody in my neighborhood respected me a lot, you know. I used to be kind of violent. I used to like to fight and stuff like that, but I'm not like that anymore. She—I don't think she liked me because I liked to fight a lot but she liked me because people respected me because they knew that they would have to fight if they disrespected me. You know I think that's one thing that turned her on about me; I don't let people mess around. (Tony)
>
> My stepson's friend was there, and he start to push me too. So I started to say, "Hey you know, this is my house, and you don't tell me nothing in my house." So I start fighting, you know, I was gonna fight him. (Mario)

The use of violence to achieve respect is a central theme in research on the construction of masculinities among disenfranchised men (Messerschmidt 1993; Messner 1992). Although men of diverse socioeconomic standings valorize fistfights between men (Campbell 1993; Dobash and Dobash 1998), the extent to which they participate in these confrontations varies by social context. Privileged young men are more often able to avoid participation in social situations that require physical violence against other men than are men who reside in poor neighborhoods (Messner 1992).

We find some evidence that cultural differences influence accounts of domestic violence. Two respondents who identified themselves as immigrants from Latin America (Alejandro and Juan) reported that they experienced conflicts with female partners about the shifting meanings of gender in the United States:

> She has a different attitude than mine. She has an attitude that comes from Mexico—be a man like, you have to do it. And it's like me here, it's fifty-fifty, it's another thing, you know, it's like "I don't have to do it." . . . I told her the wrong things she was doing and I told her, "It's not going to be that way because we're not in Mexico, we're in the United States." (Juan)

Juan's story suggests that unstable meanings about what it means to be a woman or a man are a source of conflict within his relationship and that he and his partner draw on divergent gender ideologies to buttress their positions. Although many of the respondents expressed uncertainty about appropriate gender performances in the 1990s, those who migrated to the United States may find these "crisis tendencies of the gender order" (Connell 1992, 736) to be particularly unsettling. Interestingly, Juan depicts his partner as clinging to traditional gender norms, while he embraces the notion of gender egalitarianism. However, we are hesitant to draw conclusions about this finding due to the small number of interviews that we conducted with immigrants.

Race or ethnicity, class, and gender matter in the context of the interview setting. As white, middle-class, female researchers, we were often questioning men who resided in different social worlds. Like other female researchers who have interviewed men with histories of sexual violence, we found that the interviewees were usually friendly, polite, and appeared relatively comfortable in the interview setting (Scully 1990). Unlike Ptacek, a male researcher who interviewed batterers, we did not experience a "subtext of resistance and jockeying for power beneath the otherwise friendly manner these individuals displayed in our initial phone conversations" (1990, 140). However, respondents may have offered more deterministic accounts of gender and assumed more shared experiences with the interviewer had they been interviewed by men rather than women (Williams and Heikes 1993). For example, whereas Ptacek (1990) found that 78 percent of the batterers that he interviewed justified their violence by complaining that their wives did not fulfill the obligations of a good wife, participants in this study rarely used language that explicitly emphasized "wifely duties."

Previous studies also suggest that when white, middle-class researchers interview working-class people or people of color, they may encounter problems with establishing rapport and interpreting the accounts of respondents (Edwards 1990). Riessman (1987) found that white researchers feel more comfortable with the narrative styles of white and middle-class respondents and may misinterpret the central themes raised by respondents of color. These findings suggest that shared meanings may have been less easily achieved in our interviews conducted with Latino, Native American, and African American men. For example, there is some evidence that we attempted to impose a linear narrative structure on our interviews with some respondents who may have preferred an episodic style (see Riessman 1987):

> We just started arguing more in the house. And she scratched me, and I push her away. Because I got bleeding on my neck and everything, and I push her away. And she called the police and I run away so they don't catch me there. There's a lot of worse times we argued. She tried to get me with the knife one time, trying to blame me that I did it. And the next time I told her I was going to leave her, and she tried to commit suicide by drinking like a whole bunch of bottles of Tylenol pill. And I had to rush her to the hospital, you know. That's about it. *So, in this worst fight, she scratched you and you pushed her. She called the police?* A few times she kicked me and scratched me on my neck and everything, and my arms. (Andrew)

Andrew, who identifies as Latino, recounts several episodes that are salient to his understanding of the problems within his relationship. The interviewer, however, steers him toward a sequential recounting of one particular incident rather than probing for elaboration of Andrew's perceptions of these multiple events.

In contrast, racial ethnic locations can shape what interviewers and interviewees reveal. One way in which this dynamic may have influenced the interviews was suggested by Tom, who identified as African American:

> I've never dated a Black woman before. Not me. That was my choice—that's a choice I made a long time ago. . . . I tend to find that Black women, in general, don't have any get-up-and-go, don't work. I can't say—it's just down players. But I just don't see the desire to succeed in life.

Tom introduced the issue of interracial dating without prompting and went on to invoke a variety of controlling images to represent Black women (Collins 1991). It is difficult to imagine that Tom would have shared these details if he had been interviewed by an African American woman or perhaps even a white man. Given the middle-class bias of our sample and our own social locations, future research ought to compare accounts received by differently located interviewers and a wider class and racial ethnic range of respondents.

CONCLUSIONS

Many scholars have suggested that domestic violence is a means by which men construct masculinities (Dobash and Dobash 1998; Gondolf and Hannekin 1987; Hearn 1998). However, few studies have explored the specific practices that domestically violent men use to present themselves as masculine actors. The respondents in this study used diverse and contradictory strategies to gender violence and they shifted their positions as they talked about violence. Respondents sometimes positioned themselves as masculine actors by highlighting their strength, power, and rationality compared with the "irrationality" and vulnerability of female partners. At other times, when describing the criminal justice system or "controlling" female partners, they positioned themselves as vulnerable and powerless. These shifting representations evidence the relational construction of gender and the instability of masculine subjectivities (Buder 1990).

Recently, performativity theories have been criticized for privileging agency, undertheorizing structural and cultural constraints, and facilitating essentialist readings of gender behavior: "Lacking an analysis of structural and cultural context, performances of gender can all too easily be interpreted as free agents' acting out the inevitable surface manifestations of a natural inner sex difference" (Messner 2000, 770). Findings from our study show that each of these criticisms is not necessarily valid.

First, although the batterers described here demonstrate agency by shifting positions, they do so by calling on cultural discourses (of unstoppable masculine aggression, of feminine weakness, and of men's rights). Their performance is shaped by cultural options.

Second, batterers' performances are also shaped by structural changes in the gender order. Some of the batterers interviewed for this study expressed anger and confusion about a world with "TV for women" and female partners who are "too educated." Their arrest signaled a world askew—a place where "the law is for women" and where men have become the victims of discrimination. Although these accounts are ironic in light of the research documenting the continuing reluctance of the legal system to treat domestic violence as a criminal act (Dobash and Dobash 1979), they demonstrate the ways in which legal and structural reforms in the area of domestic violence influence gender performances. By focusing attention on the "bias" in the system, respondents deflected attention from their own perpetration and victimization and sustained their constructions of rational masculinity. Therefore, theories of gender performativity push us toward analyses of the cultural and structural contexts that form the settings for the acts.

Finally, when viewed through the lens of performativity, our findings challenge the notion that violence is an essential or natural expression of masculinity. Rather, they suggest that violence represents an effort to reconstruct a contested and unstable masculinity. Respondents' references to men's rights movement discourse, their claims of "reverse discrimination," and their complaints that female partners are controlling indicate a disruption in masculine subjectivities. Viewing domestic violence as a gender performance counters the essentialist readings of men's violence against women that dominate U.S. popular culture. What one performs is not necessarily what one "is."

Disturbingly, however, this study suggests that violence is (at least temporarily) an effective means by which batterers reconstruct men as masculine and women as feminine. Participants reported that they were able to control their partners through exertions of physical dominance and through their interpretive efforts to hold partners responsible for the violence in their relationships. By gendering violence, these batterers not only performed masculinity but reproduced gender as dominance. Thus, they naturalized a binary and hierarchical gender system.

APPENDIX 14.1

Guiding Questions for In-Depth Interviews

1. First, how did you meet your wife/partner? What attracted you to her in the first place? What do you think attracted her to you?
2. What would you change about her if you could? Anything else? What do you think she would change about you? Anything else?
3. Please tell me about the *worst* time an argument with your partner became physical.
4. Please tell me about the *last* time an argument with your partner became physical.
5. What does it mean to you to be a good father? A good mother? A good child?
6. (Does/do) your own (partner/wife) (and children) fit your view of a good mother (and children)? Why or why not?
7. How do you think children should be disciplined?

APPENDIX 14.2

Pseudonyms and Sociodemographic Characteristics of the Sample

Pseudonym	Age	Education	Race/Ethnicity	Household Income	Marital Status
Jeff	25	Some college	African American	$40,000–59,999	Married
Alejandro	37	College	Latino	$25,000–29,999	Married
Steve	35	Some college	European American	$15,000–19,999	Married
Mitchell	32	Vocational	African American	$40,000–59,999	Cohabiting
Jake	37	General equivalency diploma (GED)	Native American	$5,000–9,999	Married
Adam	31	High school	European American	$40,000–59,999	Married
Alan	37	High school	European American	$25,000–29,999	Separated
Tom	26	High school	African American	$25,000–29,999	Separated
Ray	42	Some college	African American	$5,000–9,999	Married
Tony	22	Some college	Latino	$20,000–24,999	Cohabiting
Max	29	College	European American	$30,000–39,999	Cohabiting
Robert	40	Vocational	European American	$40,000–59,999	Cohabiting
Jim	38	Some college	European American	$40,000–59,999	Married
Juan	26	High school	Latino	$15,000–19,999	Married
Fred	44	Some college	European American	$40,000–59,999	Separated
Chad	40	Some college	European American/ Asian	$40,000–59,999	Cohabiting
Tim	31	Vocational	European American	$25,000–29,999	Separated
Andrew	27	<High school	Latino	$10,000–14,999	Cohabiting
Mario	33	Vocational	Latino	$20,000–24,999	Cohabiting
Kenny	23	GED	European American	$25,000–29,999	Married
Phil	45	College	European American	$60,000–79,999	Separated
Ed	30	Some college	Latino	$10,000–14,999	Cohabiting
George	21	Some college	African American	$10,000–14,999	Cohabiting
Frank	23	Vocational	European American	$30,000–39,999	Married
Eric	24	<High school	Latino	$25,000–29,999	Married
Shad	21	<High school	African American	$20,000–24,999	Divorced
Rich	47	Some college	European American	$10,000–14,999	Married
Leonard	38	Some college	European American	$25,000–29,999	Separated
Matt	31	College	European American	$10,000–14,999	Separated
Ted	41	College	European American	$40,000–59,999	Married
Ryan	22	Some college	European American	$15,000–19,999	Separated
Brandon	28	<High school	European American	$20,000–24,999	Married
Bill	34	Some college	European American	$30,000–39,999	Divorced

NOTES

1. We thank an anonymous *Gender & Society* reviewer for suggesting the relevance of Butler's theory to this analysis.

2. We are grateful to an anonymous *Gender & Society* reviewer for the suggestion that respondents "protect" female partners from arrest to maintain control of their partners.

3. We define high socioeconomic status respondents as those who earn at least $25,000 per year in personal income and who have completed an associate's degree. Seven respondents fit these criteria. We define disenfranchised respondents as those who report personal earnings of less than $15,000 per year and who have not completed a two-year college program. Nine respondents fit these criteria.

REFERENCES

Bachman, R., and L. E. Saltzman. 1995. *Violence against women: Estimates from the redesigned survey. August 1995.* NCJ-154348 special report. Washington, DC: Bureau of Justice Statistics.

Bowker, L. H. 1983. *Beating wife-beating.* Lexington, MA: Lexington Books.

Butler, J. 1990. *Gender trouble: Feminism and the subversion of identity.* New York: Routledge.

———. 1993. *Bodies that matter: On the discursive limits of sex.* New York: Routledge.

Campbell, A. 1993. *Men, women and aggression.* New York: Basic Books.

Collins, P. H. 1991. *Black feminist thought: Knowledge, consciousness, and the politics of empowerment.* New York: Routledge.

Connell, R. W. 1992. A very straight gay: Masculinity, homosexual experience, and the dynamics of gender. *American Sociological Review* 57: 735–51.

Dobash, R. E., and R. P. Dobash.1979. *Violence against wives: A case against the patriarchy.* New York: Free Press.

———. 1984. The nature and antecedents of violent events. *British Journal of Criminology* 24: 269–88.

———. 1998. Violent men and violent contexts. In *Rethinking violence against women,* edited by R. E. Dobash and R. P. Dobash. Thousand Oaks, CA: Sage.

Dobash, R. P., R. E. Dobash, M. Wilson, and M. Daly. 1992. The myth of sexual symmetry in marital violence. *Social Problems* 39: 71–91.

Eaton, M. 1994. Abuse by any other name: Feminism, difference, and intralesbian violence. In *The public nature of private violence: The discovery of domestic abuse,* edited by M. A. Fineman and R. Mykitiuk. New York: Routledge.

Edwards, R. 1990. Connecting method and epistemology: A white woman interviewing Black women. *Women's Studies International Forum* 13 (5): 477–90.

Fagot, B., R. Hagan, M. B. Leinbach, and S. Kronsberg. 1985. Differential reactions to assertive and communicative acts of toddler boys and girls. *Child Development* 56: 1499–1505.

Fine, M., L. Weis, J. Addelston, and J. Marusza. 1997. (In)secure times: Constructing white working-class masculinities in the late 20th century. *Gender & Society* 11: 52–68.

Goffman, E. 1977. The arrangement between the sexes. *Theory and Society* 4 (3): 301–31.

Gondolf, Edward W., and James Hannekin. 1987. The gender warrior: Reformed batterers on abuse, treatment, and change. *Journal of Family Violence* 2: 177–91.

Gray, N. B., G. J. Palileo, and G. D. Johnson. 1993. Explaining rape victim blame: A test of attribution theory. *Sociological Spectrum* 13: 377–92.

Hearn, J. 1998. *The violences of men: How men talk about and how agencies respond to men's violence against women.* Thousand Oaks, CA: Sage.

Island, D., and P. Letellier. 1991. *Men who beat the men who love them: Battered gay men and domestic violence.* New York: Harrington Park.

Jang, D., D. Lee, and R. Morello-Frosch. 1998. Domestic violence in the immigrant and refugee community: Responding to the needs of immigrant women. *In Shifting the center: Understanding contemporary families,* edited by S. J. Ferguson. Mountain View, CA: Mayfield.

Kirkwood, C. 1993. *Leaving abusive partners: From the scars of survival to the wisdom for change.* Newbury Park, CA: Sage.

Langhinrichsen-Rohling, J., P. Neidig, and G. Thorn. 1995. Violent marriages: Gender differences in levels of current violence and past abuse. *Journal of Family Violence* 10: 159–76.

Lundgren, E. 1998. The hand that strikes and comforts: Gender construction and the tension between body and symbol. In *Rethinking violence against women,* edited by R. E. Dobash and R. P. Dobash. Thousand Oaks, CA: Sage.

Martin, Del. 1976. *Battered wives.* New York: Pocket Books.

McCaughey, M. 1998. The fighting spirit: Women's self-defense training and the discourse of sexed embodiment. *Gender & Society* 12: 277–300.

Messerschmidt, J. 1993. *Masculinities and crime: A critique and reconceptualization of theory.* Lanham, MD: Rowman & Littlefield.

Messner, M. A. 1992. *Power at play: Sports and the problem of masculinity.* Boston: Beacon.

———. 1998. The limits of the "male sex role": An analysis of the men's liberation and men's rights movements' discourse. *Gender & Society* 12 (3): 255–76.

———. 2000. Barbie girls versus sea monsters: Children constructing gender. *Gender & Society* 14 (6): 765–84.

Pence, E., and M. Paymar. 1993. *Education groups for men who batter: The Duluth model.* New York: Springer.

Ptacek, J. 1990. Why do men batter their wives? In *Feminist perspectives on wife abuse,* edited by K. Yllo and M. Bograd. Newbury Park, CA: Sage.

Renzetti, C. M. 1992. *Violent betrayal: Partner abuse in lesbian relationships.* Newbury Park, CA: Sage.

Riessman, C. K. 1987. When gender is not enough: Women interviewing women. *Gender & Society* 1 (2): 172–207.

Savran, D. 1998. *Taking it like a man: White masculinity, masochism, and contemporary American culture.* Princeton, NJ: Princeton University Press.

Scully, D. 1990. *Understanding sexual violence: A study of convicted rapists.* Boston: Unwin Hyman.

Straton, J. C. 1994. The myth of the "battered husband syndrome." *masculinities* 2: 79–82.

Straus, M. A. 1993. Physical assaults by wives: A major social problem. In *Current controversies on family violence,* edited by R. J. Gelles and D. R. Loseke. Newbury Park, CA: Sage.

Walker, L. 1984. *The battered woman syndrome.* New York: Springer.

West, C., and S. Fenstermaker. 1995. Doing difference. *Gender & Society* 9: 8–37.

Williams, C. L., and E. J. Heikes. 1993. The importance of researcher's gender in the in-depth interview: Evidence from two case studies of male nurses. *Gender & Society* 7: 280–91.

Yllo, K. 1993. Through a feminist lens: Gender, power, and violence. In *Current controversies on family violence,* edited by R. J. Gelles and D. R. Loseke. Newbury Park, CA: Sage.

CHAPTER 15

Focus Groups

A Feminist Method

SUE WILKINSON

A family group, gathered around the TV in their living room, argues over a favorite soap opera; teenage girls sprawled over tables in a classroom swap stories about sexual harassment in high school; women waiting for appointments in a family planning clinic discuss methods of contraception—these are all potential focus group scenarios. A focus group is—at its simplest—"an informal discussion among selected individuals about specific topics" (Beck, Trombetta, and Share 1986, 73). Researchers using focus groups typically organize and run a series of small, focused, group discussions and analyze the resulting data using a range of conventional qualitative techniques. As a research method, focus groups are similar to one-to-one interviews, except that they involve more than one participant per data collection session; indeed, they are sometimes described as focus group interviews, group interviews, or group depth interviews.

Although focus groups are widely used in some fields, particularly in applied areas—such as communication/media studies (e.g., Lunt and Livingstone 1996), education (e.g., Vaughn, Schumm, and Sinagub 1996), and health care (e.g., Brems and Griffiths 1993)—few feminists (and even fewer feminist psychologists) use the method. This chapter makes the case for the value of focus groups in feminist psychology and in feminist research more generally. As such, it is a contribution to the continuing feminist debate on methodology, both within psychology (e.g., Marecek 1989; Morawski 1994; Peplau and Conrad 1989; Wilkinson 1986) and beyond it (e.g., Bowles and Klein 1983; Fonow and Cook 1991; Harding 1987; Stanley and Wise 1993; Westkott 1979). This debate considers not only the pros and cons of different methods of data collection, but also the ways in which methodological issues are intrinsically conceptual ones (cf. Unger 1983). The design and conduct of a research project, the questions that are asked, the methods of data collection, the type of analysis that takes place, the perceived implications or utility of that analysis—all of these necessarily incorporate particular assumptions, models, and values. As Jeanne Marecek (1989, 370) noted, "a method is an interpretation." The choice of one method over another is not simply a technical decision, but an epistemological and theoretical one. This means that, as feminists considering the use of innovative or unusual methods, we need (as much as with conventional methods) to be aware of the epistemological commitments and value assumptions they make (Riger, 1992). In this chapter, I introduce focus group method; I then highlight the particular advantages of focus group method for feminist researchers; finally, I evaluate the potential of focus group method for feminist research.

INTRODUCING FOCUS GROUPS

As the authors of a key text on focus groups pointed out, "what is known as a focus group today takes many different forms" (Stewart and Shamdasani 1990, 9), but centrally it involves one or more group discussions in which participants focus collectively on a topic selected by the researcher and presented to them in the form of a film, a collection of advertisements, a vignette to discuss, a "game" to play, or simply a particular set of questions. The groups (rarely more than twelve people at a time and more commonly six to eight) can consist of either preexisting clusters of people (e.g., family members, Khan and Manderson, 1992; work colleagues, J. Kitzinger 1994a, 1994b) or people drawn together specifically for the research. Many aspects of focus groups (e.g., the selections of participants, the setting in which they meet, the role of the moderator, the specific focus of the group, the structure of the discussion) are discussed in detail in the various "how to" books that address this method (e.g., Krueger 1988; Morgan 1988, 1993; Stewart and Shamdasani 1990; Vaughn et al. 1996), and I will not rehearse such discussions here. Discussions between group participants, usually audiotaped (sometimes videotaped) and transcribed, constitute the data, and methods of qualitative analysis (ranging from conventional content analysis to rhetorical or discursive techniques) are generally employed. The method is distinctive not for its analysis but for its data collection procedures. Crucially—and many commentators on the method make this point—focus groups involve the interaction of group participants with each other as well as with the researcher/moderator, and it is the collection of this kind of interactive data that distinguishes the focus group from the one-to-one interview (cf. J. Kitzinger 1994a; Morgan 1988).

In general, focus group method is well suited to exploratory, interpretive, multimethod, and phenomenological research questions (Frey and Fontana 1993). In considering whether to use focus groups, two leading experts (Morgan and Krueger 1993) suggested that the researcher should take into account not only the purpose of the study, but also the appropriateness of group discussion as a format, the match between researchers' and participants' interests, and the type of results required. In conducting a focus group study, the researcher must make critical decisions about the following key parameters, all of which fundamentally affect the design and analysis of the study: the type of participants and the number of groups to be conducted, the topic or activity on which the groups are to focus; the conduct of the sessions; recording and transcription issues; and the analytic frame to be employed (see Knodel 1993, for a useful summary discussion of design issues).

Although social psychologist Emory Bogardus (1926) used group interviews in developing his social distance scale, the invention of the focus group is usually attributed to sociologist Robert Merton, who, along with his colleagues Patricia Kendall and Majorie Fiske, developed a group approach ("the focussed group-interview") to elicit information from audiences about their responses to radio programs (Merton and Kendall 1946; Merton, Fiske, and Kendall 1956). The method is most widely used within the fields of business and marketing (Goldman and McDonald 1987), and it is only in the past five years or so that it has been described as "gaining some popularity among social scientists" (Fontana and Frey 1994, 364), so the current "resurgence of interest" (Lunt and Livingstone 1996, 79) in focus groups is a recent phenomenon. Focus groups have not been widely used in psychology, in part because "they did not fit the positivist criteria extant in the dominant research paradigm" (Harrison and Barlow 1995, 11). The method rarely appears in texts of psychological research methods (although for recent exceptions see Millward 1995; Vaughn et al. 1996), nor is it often cited in feminist research methods texts. (For an exception see Reinharz 1992. But even here there are only two paragraphs on focus groups, and the author cites just one focus group study by a feminist psychologist—and that in an unpublished dissertation.)

Despite half a century (or more) of focus group research, feminist psychologists' use of the method seems to have begun only during the 1990s. Such focus group research includes work on men talking about sex (Crawford, Kippax, and Waldby 1994), and about unemployment (Willott and Griffin 1997); immigrant/refugee women exploring sexuality and gender-related issues (Espin 1995); and sorority women talking about the threat of sexual aggression (Norris, Nurius, and Dimeff 1996). In particular, feminist psychologists at the beginning of their careers seem to be drawn to focus groups as a research method: under the heading of student "work in progress," see Barringer's (1992) work with incest survivors, Lampon's (1995) study of lesbians' perceptions of safer sex practices, and Raabe's (1993) research on young people's identities. There are, of course, other feminist psychologists who rely on conversation between groups of participants as a means of data collection but do not use the term *focus groups* or rely on the literature associated with this method. Michelle Fine's research with groups of girls (e.g., Fine 1992; Fine and Anderson 1996; Macpherson and Fine 1995) is an example of such group work; others include Billinghurst (1996), Erkut, Fields, Sing, and Marx (1996), Kissling (1996), Lovering (1995), Walkerdine (1996), and Widdicombe (1995).

ADVANTAGES OF FOCUS GROUPS FOR FEMINIST RESEARCHERS

Feminist researchers have identified a range of problems inherent in traditional psychological methods (see, e.g., critiques by Jayaratne and Stewart 1991; Reinharz 1983). Central to such critiques are the artificiality of traditional psychological methods, their decontextualized nature, and the exploitative power relations between researcher and researched. These three problems are key to feminist critiques of traditional methods, and it is precisely these problems, I argue, that can be addressed through the use of focus groups.

Artificiality

Many feminist psychologists have been critical of data generated via experimental methods (e.g., Parlee 1979; Sherif 1979/1992) and by tests and scales (e.g., Lewin and Wild 1991; Tavris 1992), urging "the abandonment of the experiment as contextually sterile and trivial in favor of more qualitative methods that are closer to actual experience" (Lott 1985, 151). Feminist researchers have argued that feminist methods should be naturalistic in the sense that they should tap into the usual "modes of communication" (Maynard 1990, 275) and the "everyday social processes" (Graham 1984, 113) that constitute people's social lives.

Decontextualization

From the beginning of second wave feminist psychology, researchers emphasized the importance of social context and insisted that feminist methods should be contextual: that is, they should avoid focusing on the individual devoid of social context or separate from interactions with others (e.g., Weisstein 1968/1993). The "context-stripping" nature of experiments and surveys was criticized because, as Janis Bohan (1992, 13) stated, "the reality of human experience—namely that it always occurs in context— . . . is lost." Feminists (along with other critical social psychologists, e.g., Gergen 1987; Pilleltensky 1989; Sampson 1988) have criticized psychology's individualism, proposing that the individual self may be characterized as "in connection" or "relational" (e.g., Jordan, Kaplan, Miller, Stiver, and Surrey 1991; Taylor, Gilligan, and Sullivan 1996) or seen primarily as a social construction, a cultural product of Western thought (e.g., C. Kitzinger 1992; Lykes 1985). "If you really want to know either of us," wrote Michelle Fine and Susan Gordon, then "do not put us in a laboratory, or hand us a survey, or even interview us separately alone in our homes. Watch me (MF) with women friends, my son, my father, my niece, or my mother and you will see what feels most authentic to me" (Fine and Gordon 1989, 159). Other (social construction and postmodernist) critics have gone further in suggesting that human experience is constructed within specific social contexts. Collective sense is made, meanings negotiated, and identities elaborated through the process of social interaction between people (e.g., Hare-Mustin and Marecek 1990; Morawski and Agronick 1991; West and Zimmerman 1987).

Exploitation

Feminist psychologists have criticized the extent to which the interests and concerns of research participants are subordinated to those of the researcher and the way in which people are transformed into "object-like subjects" (Unger 1983, 149) and have castigated the traditional hierarchy of power relations between researcher and researched (e.g., Campbell and Schram 1995, 88; Peplau and Conrad 1989, 386). In feminist research, "respecting the experience and perspective of the other" (Worell and Etaugh 1994, 444) is key. Many feminist researchers express commitment to "realizing as fully as possible women's voices in data gathering and preparing an account that transmits those voices" (Olesen 1994, 167), suggesting that feminist research is characterized by "non-hierarchical relations" (Seibold, Richard, and Simon 1994, 395), and evaluating research methods (at least partly) in terms of their adequacy in enabling feminist researchers to engage in "a more equal and reciprocal relationship with their informants" (Graham 1984, 113).

These three problems—artificiality, decontextualization, and exploitation—in conjunction have led feminist researcher frequently to advocate qualitative approaches, even to suggest that these are "quintessentially feminist" (Maynard and Purvis 1994, 3). I will not rehearse here the arguments for the use—or particular merits—of qualitative methods in feminist research, as these have been well documented elsewhere (see, e.g., Griffin 1985; Henwood and Pidgeon 1995; Marshall 1986; Reinharz 1983). Rather, I will demonstrate the particular value of focus groups as a qualitative feminist method.

AVOIDING ARTIFICIALITY: FOCUS GROUPS ARE A RELATIVELY "NATURALISTIC" METHOD

The claim that focus groups are "naturalistic" (or "ecologically valid") is commonplace in the focus group literature (e.g., Albrecht, Johnson, and Walther 1993, 54; Liebes 1984, 47). Focus groups avoid the artificiality of many psychological methods because they draw on people's normal, everyday experiences of talking and arguing with families, friends, and colleagues about events and issues in their everyday lives. It is exactly this ordinary social process that is tapped by focus group method. Everyday topics about which focus groups are invited to talk might include drinking behaviors (Beck et al. 1987), sexual decision making (Zeller 1993), labor and birth experiences (DiMatteo, Kahn, and Berry 1993), buying a new car (Stewart and Shamdasani 1990), coping with marriage breakdown (Hamon and Thiessen 1990), and experiences of friends' and acquaintances' heart attacks (Morgan and Spanish 1984). As focus group textbook author Richard Krueger (1988, 44) note, people are "social creatures who interact with others," who are "influenced by the comments of others," and who "make decisions after listening to the advice and counsel of people around them." Focus groups tap into the "natural" processes of communication, such as arguing, joking, boasting, teasing, persuasion, challenge, and disagreement. Robin Jarrett (1993, 194) described her focus groups with young women as having "the feel of rap sessions with friends. The atmosphere was exuberantly boisterous and sometimes frank in language."

Feminist researchers who have used focus groups have typically commented favorably on the extent to which they mirror everyday social interchange in a relatively naturalistic way. A study of female friends' talk about abortion involved groups of friends meeting to watch an episode of the TV program *Cagney and Lacey* in the home of one of their members, which "provided a fairly naturalistic environment for television viewing" (Press 1991, 423). Feminist psychologist Kathryn Lovering (1995), in talking about menstruation with young people at school, found that group discussions provided a context for a "relatively naturalistic conversational exchange" (16)—in this case characterized by a great deal of "embarrassment" and "giggling" (22–23). In discussing these topics, participants draw on the modes of interaction, communication, and expression common in their everyday lives.

Many focus groups use preexisting or naturally occurring social groups such as friendship groups (e.g., Liebes 1984), work colleagues (e.g., J. Kitzinger 1994a, 1994b), family members (e.g., Khan and Manderson 1992), members of clubs (J. Kitzinger 1994a, 1994b), or simply "people who have experienced the same problem, such as residents of a deteriorating neighborhood or women in a sexist organization" (Rubin and Rubin 1995, 139). According to focus group researcher Jenny Kitzinger (1994a), in a study of the effects of media messages about AIDS:

> By using pre-existing groups we were sometimes able to tap into fragments of interactions which approximated to 'naturally-occurring' data. . . . The fact that research participants already knew each other had the additional advantage that friends and colleagues could relate each others' comments to actual incidents in their shared daily lives. (105)

Feminist researchers have also drawn on people who already know each other in setting up their groups. Heterosexual college women from sorority houses at a large west coast university in the United States were invited (together with a friend) to attend group meetings to discuss the perceived threat of sexual aggression from fraternity acquaintances (Norris et al., 1996). In another project, the participants themselves decided to bring along their best friends, which worked well for the group: "The best friend pairings ensured that each girl had a familiar audience and, as it turned out, a critical one; challenges came only from the friend at first, uncritical questions came from the other girls" (Macpherson and Fine 1995, 182). Participants who know each other may recall common experiences, share half-forgotten memories, or challenge each other on contradictions between what they are professing to believe in the group and what they might have said or done outside the group ("What about the other day when you . . . ?"; "But last night you said . . . !").

The value of having people who know each other as participants in a focus group is illustrated in the following exchange between Marlene and Rebecca, two members of a focus group asked to discuss a television drama dealing with abortion as a moral issue. In the following extract, the interviewer apparently misunderstands Marlene's initial response to a question (hearing "eloquent" as "awkward") and subsequently seeks clarification of her referent. Rebecca intervenes with a shared memory, which both she and Marlene understand as contradicting Marlene's earlier statement:

> INTERVIEWER: So what did you think? In general.
>
> MARLENE: Parts of it were kind of unrealistic. . . . I think the pro-life people. . . . They're not that eloquent and I don't think they're that knowledgeable.
>
> INTERVIEWER: Not that awkward . . .
>
> MARLENE: Eloquent . . . and not that knowledgeable and also every . . .
>
> INTERVIEWER: The pro-life people?
>
> MARLENE: Yeah . . . and everyone I've talked to basically told me a lie, so . . .
>
> REBECCA: But remember the um, the false clinic that we went to . . .
>
> MARLENE: . . . that one woman . . .
>
> REBECCA: That one woman was so eloquent. (Press 1991, 432)

In this extract, Rebecca contrasts the material in the TV drama with an actual experience, which Marlene shared, and their joint memories of this particular experience provoke a detailed discussion typical of what can occur when participants already know each other.

In sum, focus groups enable feminist research to be "naturalistic" insofar as they mirror the processes of communication in everyday social interaction. This is particularly the case when group members are friends or already acquainted and/ or when they are discussing topics or issues within the range of their everyday experiences. Focus groups themselves are not, of course, "natural" (in the sense of spontaneously arising). They are facilitated by a researcher for research purposes. There are debates within the literature about to extent to which they may be considered "naturalistic" (see, e.g., Morgan 1993). However, the interactions that take place within focus groups are closer to everyday social processes than those afforded by most other research methods. The use of focus groups allows feminist researchers to better meet the feminist research objective of avoiding artificiality.

AVOIDING DECONTEXTUALIZATION: FOCUS GROUPS ARE SOCIAL CONTEXTS FOR MEANING-MAKING

A focus group participant is not an individual acting in isolation. Rather, participants are members of a social group, all of whom interact with each other. In other words, the focus group is itself a social context. As David Morgan, a leading focus group researcher, emphasized: "The hallmark of focus groups is *the explicit use of group interaction to produce data and insights that would be less accessible without the interaction found in a group*" (Morgan 1988, 12; his emphasis). These social interactions among participants constitute the primary data.

The interactive data generated by focus groups are based on the premise that "all talk through which people generate meaning is contextual" (Dahlgren 1988, 292). The social context of focus group provides an opportunity to examine how people engage in generating meaning, how opinions are formed, expressed, and (sometimes) modified within the context of discussion and debate with others. As Jenny Kitzinger (1994b, 170–71) pointed out, in focus group discussions, meanings are constantly negotiated and renegotiated:

> Participants do not just agree with each other, they also misunderstand one another, question one another, try to persuade each other of the justice of their own point of view and sometimes they vehemently disagree. . . . Such unexpected dissent [can lead] them to clarify why they thought as they did, often identifying aspects of their personal experience which had altered their opinions or specific occasions which had made them rethink their point of view. . . . People's different assumptions are thrown into relief by the way in which they challenge one another, the questions they ask, the sources they cite, and which explanations seem to sway the opinion of other members of the group.

In the focus group, people take differing individual experiences and attempt to make "collective sense" of them (Morgan and Spanish 1984, 259). It is this process of collective sense-making that occurs through the interactions among focus group participants.

In individual interviews, the interaction is between the interviewer and a single interviewee; in focus groups, "a multitude of interpersonal dynamics occur," through interactions people change their views, and " the unit of analysis becomes the group" (Crabtree, Yanoshik, Miller, and O'Connor 1993, 144). Focus groups not only provide a context for the collection of interactive data, but also offer "*the opportunity to observe directly the group process.* In the individual interview respondents *tell* how they would or did behave in a particular social situation. In the group interview, respondents react to each other, and their behavior is directly *observed*" (Goldman 1962, 62; his emphasis). An example of the way in which group processes can become a key part of the analysis is found in Michael Billig's (1992) work on talk about the British Royal family. One of Billig's concerns is the way people construct others as gullible and uncritical consumers of the media; they are used as "contrastive others" to illustrate the speaker's own critical powers and thereby enhance his or her own identity. Billig described a group discussion among four people, aged between fifty-nine and sixty-six and all related, plus the mother of one of them, aged eighty-seven, whose "contributions to the conversation were often interruptions, as she told jokes or reminisced about poverty before the war. She even broke into song once: "I'm 'Enery the Eighth I am," she sang. For periods, she remained mute, while the not-so-elderly got on with their nimble conversational business" (Billig 1992, 159). It is this woman who is constructed as the gullible other by her relatives. Billig analyzed the interactive mechanisms through which this othering (cf. Wilkinson and Kitzinger 1996) is achieved. In his presentation of the data, one can see the process of othering at work and how the elaboration of the speaker's own identity depends on the interactive production of this contrastive other. (For a more extended discussion of the way in which Billig's analysis has made full use of the group interaction, see Wilkinson 1998a.) Focus groups, then, offer the researcher the opportunity to observe directly the coconstruction of meaning in a social context via the interactions of group participants.

The few feminist researchers who have used focus groups (and other kinds of group work) have similarly taken advantage of the method to illustrate how arguments are developed and identities elaborated in a group context, typically through challenge and provocation from other members of the group. For example, after viewing a televised reconstruction of the rape and murder of a young female hitchhiker, one participant in Schlesinger, Dobash, Dobash, and Weaver's (1992, 146) research responds to another member of the focus group (who had expressed the opinion that the hitchhiker "was leading them on . . . the way she was dancing and her clothes as well . . . her top, her shirt") with the unequivocal statement: "Her clothes have got nothing to do with it." She adds, "I didn't want to say anything because my views are totally clear on this . . . ," and she then expounds them at some length. The provocation of the earlier speaker ensured that this woman's views were elicited and elaborated. Other examples of this include a (self-identified) "upper-class" teenage girl, whose remarks imply that the behavior of the working class is responsible for the problems of the class system and who is challenged by other discussion group members to defend this view (Frazer 1988, 349), and female students in an elite law school, who elaborate their experiences of profound alienation (and support each other in so doing) in the context of provocation from a male student who refers to "making a mountain out of a molehill" (Fine and Addelston 1996, 131–32).

The elaboration of meaning and identity through group interaction is also evident in an over-dinner group, in which "the text of conversation co-created by we six" (Macpherson and Fine 1995, 181) is used to elaborate racial/ethnic differences among the participants. Janet (described by the authors as "Korean American") is challenged by Shermika, when she refers to African Americans at her school:

SHERMIKA: I don't consider myself no African American.

JANET: That's the acceptable politically correct . . .

SHERMIKA: I'm full American, I've never been to Africa.

JANET: Are you black or wh[ite] . . . African American? (Sorry.)

[Janet inadvertently repeated the "black or white" dichotomy that Shermika had announced was excluding Janet.]

SHERMIKA: I'm neither one.

MICHELLE: What racial group do you consider yourself?

SHERMIKA: Negro. Not black, not African American. That's just like saying all white people come from Europe. Why don't you call 'em European American? (Macpherson and Fine 1995, 188–89)

Here, Shermika is defending and elaborating her identity (as "full American" and as "Negro") in the context of a challenge from a group member. Janet's challenge also leads Shermika to explain her reasons for these identity label choices ("I've never been to Africa"). This exchange then prompts Janet to elaborate her own identity, creating her own differences from Shermika.

In sum, then, feminist focus group researchers have shown how the social context of the focus group offers the opportunity to observe the coconstruction of meaning and the elaboration of identities through interaction. The interactive nature of focus group data produces insights that would not be available outside the group context (although there is disappointingly little evidence of sophisticated analyses by feminists of such interactive data). This emphasis on the person in context makes the focus group an ideal method for feminist psychologists who see the self as relational or socially constructed and who argue, therefore, that feminist methods should be contextual.

AVOIDING EXPLOITATION: FOCUS GROUPS SHIFT THE BALANCE OF POWER

Focus groups inevitably reduce the researcher's power and control. Simply by virtue of the number of research participants simultaneously involved in the research interaction, the balance of power shifts away from the researcher. The researcher's influence is "diffused by the very fact of being in a group rather than a one-to-one situation" (Frey and Fontana 1993, 26). As the aim of a focus group is to provide opportunities for a relatively free-flowing and interactive exchange of views, it is less amenable to the researcher's influence, compared with a one-to-one interview. Focus groups place "control over [the] interaction in the hands of the participants rather than the researcher" (Morgan 1988, 18).

In direct contrast to the goals of most feminist researchers, the reduced power and control of the researcher is typically identified as a disadvantage of the method in the mainstream focus group literature. As Richard Krueger, a leading handbook author, lamented:

> the researcher has less control in the group interview as compared to the individual interview. The focus group interview allows the participants to influence and interact with each other, and, as a result, group members are able to influence the course of the discussion. This sharing of group control results in some inefficiencies such as detours in the discussion, and the raising of irrelevant issues. (Krueger 1988, 46)

Similarly, other researchers have warned that the potential of groups to "usurp the moderator" (Watts and Ebbutt 1987, 32) may lead to "relatively chaotic data collection" (Kvale 1996, 101). The reassertion of control over focus group participants is seen as a management issue and is addressed by many of the "how to" books on focus groups, which offer advice for dealing with individual "problem" participants who do not behave in line with the researcher's requirements (e.g., Krueger 1988; Stewart and Shamdasani 1990; Vaughn et al. 1996). One focus group expert offered detailed instructions for maintaining power over participants in a section headed "Pest Control" (Wells 1974). Moderator training is seen as essential and typically focuses around "leadership" issues. According to the handbooks, such training should enable the moderator to take "the role of nominal leader" (Stewart and Shamdasani 1990, 70) and to exercise "a mild, unobtrusive control over the group" (Krueger 1988, 73).

With this emphasis on the moderator's role, the issue of power and control in interactions among group members is rarely addressed, either as a feature of focus group method or even as a management issue for the moderator/researcher. A rare exception is a footnoted comment on the researcher's ethical obligation to deal with offensive comments, bullying, or intimidation directed at other group members (J. Kitzinger 1994a, 118), also suggesting how this may be done (e.g., by considering group composition in advance, by using dissent within the group to challenge offensive remarks, or by direct intervention to silence or move on the discussion). In general, the more subtle exercise of power relations among group members (e.g., apparent collusion in constructing a particular argument or silencing a particular member) is rarely made explicit and is addressed in the focus group literature only insofar as it can be reduced to a "problem" generated by an individual group member and "solved" by direct intervention of the researcher. Billig's (1992, 159) demonstration of the process by which a family constructs its oldest member as the gullible other is therefore an unusual exception (although note that the researcher appears here only as recorder/analyst, not as a participant in the group interaction).

Some researchers do recognize that the reduction in the researcher's influence in focus groups can be seen as an advantage. David Morgan (1988, 18) pointed out that "participants' interaction among themselves replaces their interaction with the interviewer, leading to a greater emphasis on participants' points of view." Focus groups are sometimes presented as an opportunity for "listening to local voices" (Murray, Tapson, Turnbull, McCallum, and Little 1994), for learning participants' own language instead of imposing the researcher's language on them (Bers 1987; Freimuth and Greenberg 1986; Mays et al. 1992), and for gaining an insight into participants' conceptual worlds (Broom and Dozier 1990). Focus groups can allow participants much greater opportunity to set the research agenda and to "develop the themes most important to them" (Cooper, Diamond, and High 1993), which may diverge from those identified by the researcher. Compared with a one-to-one interview, it is much harder for the researcher to impose his or her own agenda in the group context.

The relative lack of power and control held by the researcher in the focus group allows the participants to challenge each other (Jarrett 1993) and to challenge—or even to undermine—the researcher, insisting on their own interpretations and agendas being heard in place of the formal requirements of the research project. The following exchange is taken from the first few minutes of a focus group session in which the moderator (a forty-five-year-old man) attempts to set the agenda for the discussion. The participants are eighteen- and nineteen-year-old women:

> MODERATOR: The discussion is on sexual decision making and interpersonal relationships between those of the female and those of male arrangements. Tomorrow night, we are talking to the guys to see what their view of this thing is.
>
> PARTICIPANT: I'd like to listen to that. [laughter]
>
> MODERATOR: There is every reason to believe that . . .
>
> PARTICIPANT: [Like] Oprah Winfrey! [laughter]
>
> MODERATOR: There is every reason to believe that girls and guys see sex differently.
>
> PARTICIPANT: I can tell you that right now. [laughter] (Zeller, 1993, 174–75)

The interruptions, laughter, jokes, badinage, and cryptic comments of the participants cut across and over the formal introduction attempted by this moderator. The apparent attempt to set particular discussion topics is undermined by the young women, who frivolously compare his agenda to that of a popular TV program or who imply that his (rather pompously presented) hypotheses are simply self-evident ("I can tell you that right now"). In this extract the participants are—collaboratively—taking control over the process of context setting and hence contributing to the determination of the subsequent course and nature of this discussion. (To be fair, this author does acknowledge the advantages of this process.)

Focus group researchers, then, are virtually unanimous that, compared with many other methods of data collection (especially the one-to-one interview), focus groups reduce the researcher's influence. For some (e.g., Krueger 1988), this is a disadvantage that, although offset by the numerous advantages of the method, needs careful management. For others (e.g., Morgan 1988), it is an advantage that enables participants to contribute to setting the research agenda, resulting in better access to their opinions and conceptual worlds. But, whether identified as a problem or a benefit, researchers concur on the relative lack of power held by the focus group researcher.

The few feminists who have used focus groups (and other kinds of group work) have similarly emphasized the shift in the balance of power—and particularly the extent to which the method enables research participants to speak in their own voice—to express their own thoughts and feelings and to determine their own agendas. In a recent article in the *Psychology of Women Quarterly,* Jeanette Norris et al. (1996, 129) claimed that: "Within feminist research, focus groups have been used to provide a 'voice' to the research participant by giving her an opportunity to define what is relevant and important to understand her experience." Feminist psychologist Oliva Espin (1995, 228), using focus groups in her exploration of immigrant/refugee women's understandings of sexuality and their internalization of cultural norms, commented that the method's "open-ended narratives allow for the expression of thoughts and feelings while inviting participants to introduce their own themes and concepts." Similarly, in a study of women's reactions to violent episodes on television, Schlesinger et al. (1992, 29) saw the group discussions as an opportunity for women to "determine their own agendas as much as possible." (See also Griffin 1986 and Frazer 1988) for examples of how group discussions led the researcher to change the research questions to address participants' concerns better.)

The following exchange arises in response to a (young, female) researcher's request to her focus group participants for examples of the excuses they use to avoid sex. Three young, heterosexual women (Lara, Cath, and Helen), challenge the researcher's implication that young women have to find excuses to avoid having sex with their male partners:

> CATH: Do you mean like really naff excuses?
>
> RESEARCHER: Well, anything that you would use.
>
> LARA: But I mean . . .
>
> CATH: But it depends how far you've got because that can go completely.
>
> HELEN: No, but . . . no, but that just gives you a few days respite doesn't it?—and then I think that after a few days you'd just feel so shitty that you had to rely on that.
>
> LARA: That's horrible, why should you have to lie on an issue that is just perfectly right and you feel strongly about, why do you have to come up with excuses?
>
> CATH: That's right.
>
> LARA: I mean, I would much rather, it would be so nice just to be able to say no, for no particular reason. I don't really know, I haven't felt the need to think about it, I just don't particularly fancy it.
>
> HELEN: I just don't feel like it at the moment.
>
> LARA: Wouldn't that be nice! (Frith, 1997)

Although these young women are evidently able to generate excuses to avoid sex, they reject the idea that this is an appropriate question for the researcher to be asking or a desirable action in which to be engaged.

In sum, feminist focus group researchers recognize that focus groups shift the balance of power and control toward the research participants, enabling them to assert their own interpretations and agendas. Despite the disadvantages of this in some contexts (particularly when researching powerful—e.g., male—groups; cf. Green, Barbour, Bernard, and Kitzinger 1993), this reduction in the relative power of the researcher also allows the researcher to access better, understand, and take account of the opinions and conceptual worlds of research participants, in line with the suggested principles of feminist research.

THE POTENTIAL OF FOCUS GROUPS FOR FEMINIST RESEARCH

As I have shown, the particular advantages of focus groups for feminist research are that they are relatively "naturalistic," that they offer a social context for meaning-making; and that they shift the balance of power away from the researcher toward the research participants. In this manner, focus groups meet the concerns of feminist researchers to avoid the problems of artificiality, decontextualization, and exploitative power relations. There are also other ways in which focus group method may benefit feminist research: for example, in the appropriateness of focus groups for use with underrepresented and severely disadvantaged social groups, their value for action research, and the role of focus groups in consciousness raising.

Work with Underrepresented Social Groups

Some focus group researchers have suggested that focus groups may be particularly useful for accessing the views of those who have been poorly served by traditional research:

> Social research has not done well in reaching people who are isolated by the daily exhausting struggles for survival, services and dignity—people who will not respond to surveys or whose experiences, insights and feelings lie outside the range of data survey methods. These people are also uncomfortable with individual interviews. We found that almost all elements in the community could be accessed in the safe and familiar context of their own turf, relations and organizations through focus groups. (Plaut, Landis, and Trevor 1993, 216)

Focus group participants have included, for example, difficult-to-reach, high-risk families in an inner city (Lengua et al. 1992); Black gay men (Mays et al. 1992), the elderly (Chapman and Johnson 1995), and village women in rural counties of China (Wong, Li, Burris, and Xiang 1995). Such use of focus groups is in line with the proposal that feminist research should pay particular attention to the needs of "those who [have] little or no societal voice" (Rubin and Rubin 1995, 36), and feminist focus group researchers have similarly used the method in researching the lives of immigrant/refugee women (Espin 1995) and urban African American preadolescents and young adolescents living in poverty (Vera, Reese, Paikoff, and Jarrett 1996).

Action Research

Some focus group researchers have suggested that the method "has promise in action research" (Vaughn et al. 1996, 32), that it can be used radically "to empower and to foster social change" (Johnson 1996, 536). For example, Raymond Padilla (1993) described a project to overcome barriers to the success of Hispanic students in a U.S. community college, based on the work of Brazilian educator Paulo Friere. He used focus groups as a "dialogical method" to empower research subjects to change their own lives as part of "a larger project of political freedom, cultural autonomy, and liberation from oppressive economic and social conditions" (154). It is the project's intent that

> By critically examining through dialogue the problematic aspects of their own lives, the subjects are able to gain the critical understanding that is necessary to identify viable alternatives to existing social arrangements and to take appropriate actions to change and improve their own lives. (Padilla 1993, 154)

Some feminists have also wanted their research to have direct practical effects in women's lives and have used focus groups (and other kinds of group work) in action research projects. For example, Maria Mies (1983), in a project aiming to make practical provisions for battered women, insisted that, in order to implement a non-hierarchical egalitarian research process, to ensure that research serves the interests of the oppressed, to develop political awareness, and to use her own relative power in the interests of the oppressed, to develop political awareness, and to use her own relative power in the interests of other women, "interviews of individuals . . . must be shifted towards group discussions, if possible at repeated intervals" (128). Mies' view is that "this collectivization of women's experience . . . helps women to overcome their structural isolation in their families and to understand that their individual sufferings have social causes" (128). Similarly, Jean Orr's (1992) project on Well Women Clinics "encourages members to see that problems are often not caused by personal inadequacy but are based in current social structure" (32), offering "support to members in changing aspects of their lives" and enabling them to "feel confident in asserting their needs to others" (32) within the Community Health Movement and beyond. (Further examples of the use of focus groups in feminist action research on health issues may be found in de Koning and Martin's [1996] edited collection.)

Consciousness Raising

The similarities between focus group discussions and the consciousness-raising sessions common in the early years of second wave feminism have fueled the interest of several feminist researchers. Noting that it was through consciousness raising that Lynn Farley (1978) came to identify and name the experience of "sexual harassment," feminist sociologist Carrie Herbert (1989) included group discussions in her work with young women on their experience of sexual harassment. Similarly, Michelle Fine (1992, 173), chronicling a set of group discussions with adolescent girls, claimed that "through a feminist methodology we call 'collective consciousness work,' we sculpted . . . a way to theorize consciousness moving from stridently individualist feminism to a collective sense of women's solidarity among difference." Feminist researchers using focus group work in this way (cf. Mies 1983; Orr 1992) hope that, through meeting together with others and sharing experience and through realizing group commonalties in what had previously been considered individual and personal problems, women will develop a clearer sense of the social and political processes through which their experiences are constructed and perhaps also a desire to organize against them. It has to be said, however, that other researchers using focus groups are less sanguine about their consciousness-raising potential. Jenny Kitzinger's (1994a) focus groups' discussions of HIV risk offer salutary counterexamples of the alleged consciousness-raising benefit of group discussion. In several groups, she said, "any attempt to address the risks HIV poses to gay men were drowned out by a ritual period of outcry against homosexuality" (J. Kitzinger 1994a, 108).

Given the advantages of focus groups, it is perhaps surprising that they are not more widely used by feminist researchers. Among the qualitative methods available to feminists, the one-to-one interview is the most commonly used technique; according to some researchers (Kelly, Burton, and Regan 1994, 34), it has become "the paradigmatic 'feminist method'." Many of the classic qualitative studies in feminist psychology use the one-to-one interview as their only or primary research tool (e.g., Belenky, Clinchy, Goldberger, and Tarule 1986; Chesler, 1972; Gilligan 1982; Walker 1979). Of the seventy-seven empirical articles published in the first six volumes (1991–1996) of the international journal *Feminism and Psychology,* forty-three (56 percent) used interviews, and no other qualitative method was used in more than 10 percent of the studies. Over a similar period, *Psychology of Women Quarterly* published twenty-five studies using interviews, although these constituted a much smaller proportion of the total number of empirical articles (only 17 percent),with no other qualitative method used in more than 2 percent of studies. Focus groups were rarely used: in the same period, there were eight focus group studies published in *F&P* and only one in *PWQ* (plus two studies that used group discussions).

I would suggest that there are many reported instances of the use of interviews in feminist research where focus groups could have met the researcher's aims better, provided fuller or more sophisticated answers to the research question, or addressed particular methodological concerns. For example, Niobe Way (1995) interviewed twelve girls individually to answer the question: "What are the various ways urban, poor, and working-class adolescent girls speak about themselves, their schools and their relationships to parents and peers over a three-year period?" (109). Given the stated assumptions of this study, including that research is "inherently relational" (109) and that "the words of adolescents cannot be separated from the cultural and societal context of which they are a part" (109), it seems that focus groups might have been a better methodological choice. It is particularly surprising that the work of the Harvard Project on Women's Psychology and Girl's Development (e.g., Brown and Gilligan 1983; Gilligan 1982; Taylor et al. 1996), which theorizes the self as fundamentally "relational," relies almost exclusively on individual interviews with young women.

Finally, although it is a pity that there is not greater use of focus groups in feminist research, it is also a pity that there is not better use of focus groups, capitalizing on their particular advantages as a method. I will close by highlighting some of the main problems in the current use of focus groups (by feminists and others) and indicate the ways in which these could be overcome, in order to maximize the value of the method as a tool for feminist research. These problems are inappropriate use of focus groups, neglect of group interactions, and insufficient epistemological warranting. I will look briefly at each.

Inappropriate Use of Focus Groups

Although the "how to" books include advice on "how not to" (and also "when not to") use focus groups (e.g., Morgan and Krueger 1993; Vaughn et al. 1996), this advice is often disregarded, not least by feminist focus group researchers. For example, although the textbooks caution against using focus groups as a quick and easy way of increasing sample size, indicating that the method is unsuitable for conducting large-scale studies, it is not uncommon for researchers to present as their rationale for using focus groups that they are "effective and economical in terms of both time and money" (Espin 1995, 228), or that they are "a means of gathering qualitative data from a relatively large sample" (Lampon 1995, 171). Similarly, although the handbooks warn against inappropriate quantification of focus group data (cf. Morgan and Krueger 1993, 14), this, too, is often apparent: for example, Geraghty (1980) offered a statistical profile of donors to a particular charity based on four focus groups, and Flexner, McLaughlin, and Littlefield (1977) presented a graph comparing three focus groups ("consumers," "potential consumers," and "providers" of abortion services) in terms of the average ranks given by members of each group to features of an abortion service. More recently, an article included in a special issue of *Qualitative Health Research,* on "Issues and Applications of Focus Groups" (Carey 1995) categorized the social service concerns of HIV-positive women and tabulated the number of responses coded under each category (Seals et al. 1995). This is despite at least two injunctions elsewhere in the special issue not to quantify focus group data.

Neglect of Group Interactions

Although interaction among group participants is supposed to be a defining characteristic of focus group methods, one review of over forty published reports of focus group studies "could not find a single one concentrating on the conversation between participants and very few that even included any quotations from more than one participant at a time" (J. Kitzinger 1994a, 104). For this chapter, I reviewed almost two hundred focus group studies ranging in date of publication from 1946 to 1996, with the same result. Focus group data are most commonly presented as if they were one-to-one interview data, with interactions among group participants rarely reported, let alone analyzed. This is despite clear statements in the focus group literature that "researchers who use focus groups and do not attend to the impact of the group setting will incompletely or inappropriately analyze their data" (Carey and Smith 1994, 125). The extracts quoted in this chapter are not, in fact, typical of the way in which focus group data are normally reported. I have deliberately sought out those rare published examples of interactive data in order to make the best possible case for the use of focus groups. In presenting these data extracts, I have often drawn attention to interactional features that are not commented on by the authors themselves. More commonly, the focus is on the content rather than the process of interaction. One wishes feminist focus group researchers were producing analyses of interactions approaching the sophistication of that offered by Billig (1992).

Insufficient Epistemological Warranting

In common with other types of qualitative data, data from focus groups are open to either essentialist or social constructionist interpretations (Guba and Lincoln 1994; cf. also C. Kitzinger and Powell 1995). For feminist researchers working within an essentialist frame, it may be the voices of individual women (speaking with, or in contradiction to, other women) that they wish to hear, and for them focus groups offer a valuable route to "the individual in social context" (Goldman 1962; Rubin and Rubin 1995, 95). The researchers may well argue that focus group data are more "authentic" or "closer to the essential meanings of women's lives" than data elicited by other methods. Within a social constructionist (or postmodernist or discursive) frame, however, focus group data are just as constructed—albeit differently—as, say, responses to an opinion poll or behavior in a laboratory setting. Viewed within this frame, the method offers access to "the patterns of talk and interaction through which the members of any group constitute a shared reality" (Devault 1990, 97). The analytic emphasis is on the construction and negotiation of persons and events, the functions served by different discourses, and—for feminists—the ways in which social inequalities are produced and perpetuated through talk (cf. Wilkinson and Kitzinger 1995, for further examples of this approach). However, focus group researchers rarely offer a clear epistemological warrant for the interpretation of their data, and there is a great deal of slippage between essentialist and social constructionist frames.

In conclusion, this chapter has argued that focus groups offer considerable potential for the future development of feminist research in and beyond psychology in ways congruent with feminist goals. I do not embrace the orthodoxy that qualitative methods are "quintessentially feminist" (Maynard and Purvis 1994, 3), nor do I believe that any particular method can be designated feminist per se (cf. Wilkinson 1986, 14). Indeed, as Peplau and Conrad (1989, 379) observed, "no method comes with a feminist guarantee." Following Peplau and Conrad (1989), I do not seek to define feminist research in psychology primarily at the methodological level but rather to evaluate a particular method—the focus group—in terms of its usefulness in the pursuit of feminist goals. Within this context, I have shown that focus groups are a valuable method for feminist research because they meet three key feminist goals: they enable relatively "naturalistic" research, give due account to social context, and shift the balance of power in research. They are also useful in work with underrepresented groups, in action research, and in consciousness raising.

In order to realize the potential of focus groups as a research method, however, feminist researchers could develop a better awareness of the appropriate uses of focus groups and the functions they can—and cannot—serve. In general, focus group method is well suited to research questions involving the elicitation and clarification of perspectives, the construction and negotiation of meanings, the generation and elaboration of hypotheses, and a whole range of exploratory analyses. It is poorly suited to research questions involving the estimation of frequencies, the testing of causal relationships, generalizations to larger populations, comparisons between population groups, and most types of inferential analysis. It would also be useful for feminist researchers to pay more attention to the interactive nature of focus groups, reporting and analyzing interactions among group participants in ways that do justice to their role in meaning-making. Finally, feminist researchers could more clearly identify the epistemological frameworks that inform their interpretations of focus group data in order to warrant the particular analyses they present.

It is true that, at present, focus groups are not widely used by feminist psychologists, perhaps because, as Jill Morawski (1994, 21–22) stated, "Attempts to study women's experiences that take seriously the transindividual, contextually embedded, or socially constructed nature of those experiences risk using methodologies that are appropriate to their mandate but that fail to meet orthodox standards of the science." We have, as psychologists, undergone training within a discipline that has "placed a high value on quantification and imbued us with suspicion of alternative methods and non-positivistic science" (Mednick 1991, 618). If, however, as feminist psychologists we agree on "the need for more interactive, contextualized methods in the service of emancipatory goals" (Riger 1992, 736), then feminist psychology needs to be bolder in its challenge to the orthodoxies of the discipline. It needs to harness "varied epistemological forces from empiricism and materialism to utopianism and postmodernism, in order to construct *feminist* science" (Morawski and Agronick 1991, 575; my emphasis), and it needs to demonstrate a commitment to "developing and testing innovative concepts, methods and applications for understanding and empowering women" (Russo 1995, 1). The continued use and further development of focus group method offer feminist psychology an excellent opportunity for the future.

ENDNOTE

I am delighted to report that the field of focus group research has developed considerably since this article was accepted for publication. Second editions of several of the classic handbooks have appeared, as well as a number of new texts. There is now a growing body of feminist focus group research, and some of the researchers referenced in this article (e.g. Niobe Way, members of the Harvard Project) have moved from exclusive reliance on one-to-one interviews to include group discussions in their work. More up-to-date reviews of the field have also been published, including two of my own, on the use of focus groups in health research (Wilkinson 1998b) and across the social sciences (Wilkinson 1998c).

REFERENCES

Albrecht, T. L., G. M. Johnson, and J. B. Walther. 1993. Understanding communication processes in focus groups. In *Successful focus groups: Advancing the state of art,* ed. D. L. Morgan, 51–64. Newbury Park, CA: Sage.

Barringer, C. E. 1992. Speaking of incest: It's not enough to say the word. *Feminism and Psychology* 2: 183–88.

Beck, L., W. Trombetta, and S. Share. 1986. Using focus group sessions before decisions are made. *North Carolina Medical Journal,* 47: 73–74.

Belenky, M., B. Clinchy, N. Goldberger, & J. Tarule. 1986. *Women's ways of knowing: The development of self, voice and mind.* New York: Basic Books.

Bers, T. H. 1987. Exploring institutional images through focus group interviews. In *Designing and using market research,* ed. R. S. Lay and J. J. Endo, 19–29. San Francisco: Jossey-Bass.

Billig, M. 1992. *Talking of the royal family.* London: Routledge.

Billinghurst, B. 1996. Theorizing women's self-blame. *Feminism and Psychology,* 6: 569–73.

Bogardus, E. 1926. The group interview. *Journal of Applied Sociology* 10: 372–82.

Bohan, J. S., ed. 1992. Prologue: Re-viewing psychology, re-placing women—An end searching for a means. In *Seldom seen, rarely heard: Women's place in psychology,* ed. J. S. Bohan, 9–53. Boulder, CO: Westview Press.

Bowles, G., and R. D. Klein. 1983. *Theories of women's studies.* London: Routledge and Kegan Paul.

Brems, S., and M. Griffiths. 1993. Health women's way: Learning to listen. In *The health of women: A global perspective,* ed. M. Koblinsky, J. Timyan, and J. Gay, 255–73. Boulder, CO: Westview Press.

Broom, G. M., and D. M. Dozier. 1990. *Using research in public relations: Application to program management.* Englewood Cliffs, NJ: Prentice-Hall.

Brown, L. M., and C. Gilligan. 1993. Meeting at the crossroads: Women's psychology and girls' development. *Feminism and Psychology* 3: 11–35.

Campbell, R., and P. J. Schram. 1995. Feminist research methods: A content analysis of psychology and social science textbooks. *Psychology of Women Quarterly* 19: 85–106.

Carey, M. A. 1995. Issues and applications of focus groups [Special issue]. *Qualitative Health Research* 5 (4).

Carey, M. A., and M. W. Smith. 1994. Capturing the group effect in focus groups: A special concern in analysis. *Qualitative Health Research* 4: 123–27.

Chapman, T., and A. Johnson. 1995. *Growing old and needing care: A health and social care needs audit.* London: Avebury.

Chesler, P. 1972. *Women and madness.* New York: Avon.

Cooper, P., I. Diamond, and S. High. 1993. Choosing and using contraceptives: Integrating qualitative and quantitative methods in family planning. *Journal of the Market Research Society* 35: 325–39.

Crabtree, B. F., M. K. Yanoshik, W. L. Miller, and P. J. O'Connor. 1993. Selecting individual or group interviews. In *Successful focus groups: Advancing the state of the art,* ed. D. L. Morgan. 137–49. Newbury, CA: Sage.

Crawford, J., S. Kippax, and C. Waldby. 1994. Women's sex talk and men's sex talk: Different worlds. *Feminism and Psychology* 4: 571–88.

Dahlgren, P. 1988. What's the meaning of this? Viewers' plural sense-making of TV news. *Media, Culture and Society* 10: 285–301.

de Koning, K., and M. Martin. 1996. *Participatory research in health: Issues and experiences.* London: Zed Books.

DeVault, M. L. 1990. Talking and listening from women's standpoint: Feminist strategies for interviewing and analysis. *Social problems* 37: 96–116.

DiMatteo, M. R., K. L. Kahn, and S. H. Berry. 1993. Narratives of birth and the postpartum: Analysis of the focus group responses of new mothers. *Birth* 20: 204–11.

Erkut, S., J. P. Fields, R. Sing, and F. Marx. 1996. Diversity in girls' experiences: Feeling good about who you are. In *Urban girls: Resisting stereotypes, creating identities,* ed. B. J. R. Leadbetter and N. Way, 53–64. New York: New York University Press.

Espin, O. M. 1995. "Race," racism, and sexuality in the life narratives of immigrant women. *Feminism and Psychology* 5: 223–38.

Farley, L. 1978. *Sexual shakedown: The sexual harassment of women on the job.* New York: Warner Books.

Fine, M. 1992. *Disruptive voices: The possibilities of feminist research.* Ann Arbor: University of Michigan Press.

Fine, M., and J. Addelston. 1996. Containing questions of gender and power: The discursive limits of "sameness" and "difference." In *Feminist social psychologies: International perspectives,* ed. S. Wilkinson, 66–86. Buckingham: Open University Press.

Fine, M., and S. M. Gordon. 1989. Feminist transformations of/despite psychology. In *Gender and thought: Psychological perspectives,* ed. M. Crawford and M. Gentry, 146–74. New York: Springer-Verlag.

Flexner, W. A., C. P. McLaughlin, and J. E. Littlefield. 1977. Discovering what the consumer really wants. *Health Care Management Review* 1: 43–49.

Fonow, M. M., and J. A. Cook, eds. 1991. *Beyond methodology: Feminist scholarship as lived research.* Bloomington: Indiana University Press.

Frazer, E. 1988. Teenage girls talking about class. *Sociology* 22: 343–58.

Freimuth, V. S., and R. Greenberg. 1986. Pretesting television advertisements for family planning products in developing countries: A case study. *Health Education Research* 1: 37–45.

Frey, J. H., and A. Fontana. 1993. The group interview in social research. In *Successful focus groups: Advancing the state of the art,* ed. D. L. Morgan, 20–34. Newbury Park, CA: Sage.

Frith, H. 1997. *Young women refusing sex.* Unpublished doctoral dissertation, Department of Social Sciences, Loughborough University, England.

Geraghty, G. 1980. Social research in Asia using focus group discussions: A case study. *Media Asia* 7: 205–11.

Gergen, K. 1987. Toward self as relationship. In *Self and identity: Psychosocial perspectives,* ed. K. Yardley and T. Honess, 52–67. Chickester: Wiley.

Goldman, A. E. 1962. The group depth interview. *Journal of Marketing* 26: 61–68.

Goldman, A. E., and S. S. McDonald. 1987. *The group depth interview: Principles and practice.* Englewood Cliffs, NJ: Prentice-Hall.

Graham, H. 1984. Surveying through stories. In *Social researching, politics, problems, practice,* ed. C. Bell and H. Roberts, 104–24. London: Routledge and Kegan Paul.

Green, G., R. S. Barbour, M. Bernard, and J. Kitzinger. 1993. "Who wears the trousers?" Sexual harassment in research settings. *Women's Studies International Forum* 16: 627–37.

Gilligan, C. 1982. In a different voice: Psychological theory and women's development. Cambridge, MA: Harvard University Press.

Griffin, C. 1985. Qualitative methods and cultural analysis: Young women and the transition from school to un/employment. In *Field methods in the study of education,* ed. R. Burgess, London: Falmer Press.

———. 1986. Qualitative methods and female experience: Young women from school to the job market. In *Feminist social psychology: Developing theory and practice,* ed. S. Wilkinson, 173–91. Milton Keynes: Open University Press.

Guba, E. G., and Y. S. Lincoln. 1994. Competing paradigms in qualitative research. In *Handbook of qualitative research,* ed. N. K. Denzin and Y. S. Lincoln, 105–17. Thousand Oaks, CA: Sage.

Hamon, R. R., and J. D. Thiessen. 1990. *Coping with the dissolution of an adult child's marriage* Report No. CG-023–311. Seattle, WA: National Council on Family Relations. (ERIC Document Reproduction Service No. ED 330 968).

Harding, S. 1987. *Feminism and methodology.* Bloomington: Indiana University Press.

Hare-Mustin, R. T., and J. Marecek, eds. 1990. *Making a difference: Psychology and the construction of gender.* New Haven: Yale University Press.

Harrison, K., and J. Barlow. 1995. Focused group discussion: A "quality" method for health research? *Health Psychology Update* 20: 11–13.

Henwood, K., and N. Pidgeon. 1995. Remaking the link: Qualitative research and feminist standpoint theory. *Feminism and Psychology* 5: 7–30.

Herbert, C. M. H. 1989. *Talking of silence: The sexual harassment of schoolgirls.* London: Falmer Press.

Jarrett, R. L. 1993. Focus group interviewing with low-income minority populations: A research experience. In *Successful focus groups: Advancing the state of art,* ed. D. L. Morgan, 184–201. Newbury Park, CA: Sage.

Jayaratne, T. E., and A. J. Stewart. 1991. Quantitative and qualitative methods in the social sciences: Current feminist issues and practical strategies. In *Beyond methodology: Feminist scholarship as lived research,* ed. M. M. Fonow and J. A. Cook, 85–106. Bloomington: Indiana University Press.

Johnson, A. 1996. "It's good to talk": The focus group and the sociological imagination. *Sociological Review* 44: 517–38.

Jordan, J. V., A. G. Kaplan, J. B. Miller, I. P. Stiver, and J. L. Surrey. 1991. *Women's growth in connection: Writings from the Stone Center.* New York: Guilford Press.

Kelly, L., S. Burton, and L. Regan. 1994. Researching women's lives or studying women's oppression? Reflections on what constitutes feminist research. In *Researching women's lives from a feminist perspective,* ed. M. Maynard and J. Purvis, 27–48. London: Taylor and Francis.

Khan, M. E., and L. Manderson. 1992. Focus groups in tropic diseases research. *Health Policy and Planning* 7: 56–66.

Kissling, E. A. 1996. Bleeding out loud: Communication about menstruation. *Feminism and Psychology* 6: 481–504.

Kitzinger, C. 1992. The individual self concept: A critical analysis of social-constructionist writing on individualism. In *Social psychology of identity and the self concept,* ed. G. M. Breakwell, 221–50. London: Surrey University Press, in association with Academic Press.

Kitzinger, C., and Powell, D. 1995. Engendering infidelity: Essentialist and social constructionist readings of a story completion task. *Feminism and Psychology* 5: 345–72.

Kitzinger, J. 1994a. The methodology of focus groups: The importance of interaction between research participants. *Sociology of Health and Illness* 16: 103–21.

———. 1994b. Focus groups: Method or madness? In *Challenge and innovation: Methodological advances in social research on HIV/AIDS,* ed. M. Boulton, 159–75. London: Taylor and Francis.

Knodel, J. 1993. The design and analysis of focus group studies. In *Successful focus groups: Advancing the state of the art,* ed. D. L. Morgan, 35–50. Newbury Park, CA: Sage.

Krueger, R. A. 1988. *Focus groups: A practical guide for applied research.* Newbury Park, CA: Sage.

Kvale, S. 1996. *InterViews: An introduction to qualitative research interviewing.* Thousand Oaks, CA: Sage.

Lampon, D. 1995. Lesbians and safer sex practices. *Feminism and Psychology* 5: 170–76.

Lengua, L. J., M. W. Roosa, E. Schupak-Neuberg, M. L. Michaels, C. N. Berg, and L. F.

Weschler. 1992. Using focus groups to guide the development of a parenting program for difficult-to-reach, high-risk families. *Family Relations* 41: 163–68.

Lewin, M., and C. L. Wild. 1991. The impacts of the feminist critique on tests, assessment, and methodology. *Psychology of Women Quarterly* 15: 581–96.

Liebes, T. 1984. Ethnocriticism: Israelis of Moroccan ethnicity negotiate the meaning of "Dallas." *Studies in Visual Communication* 10: 46–72.

Lott, B. 1985. The potential enrichment of social/personality psychology through feminist research and vice versa. *American Psychologist* 40: 155–64.

Lovering, K. M. 1995. The bleeding body: Adolescents talk about menstruation. In *Feminism and discourse: Psychological perspectives,* ed. S. Wilkinson and C. Kitzinger, 10–31. London: Sage.

Lunt, P., and Livingstone, S. 1996. Focus groups in communication and media research. *Journal of Communication,* 42: 78–87.

Lykes, M. B. 1985. Gender and individualistic versus collectivist biases for notions about the self. *Journal of Personality* 53: 356–83.

Macpherson, P., and M. Fine. 1995. Hungry for an us: Adolescent girls and adult women negotiating territories of race, gender, class, and difference. *Feminism and Psychology* 5: 181–200.

Marecek, J. 1989. Introduction. [Special Issue on Theory and Method in Feminist Psychology.] *Psychology of Women Quarterly* 13: 367–77.

Marshall, J. 1986. Exploring the experiences of women managers: Towards rigour in qualitative research. In *Feminist social psychology: Developing theory and practice,* ed. S. Wilkinson, 193–209. Milton Keynes: Open University Press.

Maynard, M. 1990. Trend report: The re-shaping of sociology? Trends in the study of gender. *Sociology* 24: 269–90.

Maynard, M., and J. Purvis. 1994. Introduction: Doing feminist research. In *Researching women's lives from a feminist perspective,* ed. M. Maynard and J. Purvis, 1–9. London: Taylor and Francis.

Mays, V. M., S. D. Cochran, G. Bellinger, R. G. Smith, N. Henley, M. Daniels, T. Tibbits, G. D. Victorianne, O. K. Osei, and D. K. Birt. 1992. The language of black gay men's sexual behavior: Implications for AIDS risk reduction. *Journal of Sex Research* 29: 425–34.

Mednick, M. T. 1991. Currents and futures in American feminist psychology: State of the art revisited. *Psychology of Women Quarterly* 15: 611–21.

Merton, R. K., and P. L. Kendall. 1946. The focused interview. *American Journal of Sociology* 51: 541–57.

Merton, R. K., M. Fiske, and P. L. Kendall. 1956. *The focused interview.* New York: Free Press.

Mies, M. 1983. Towards a methodology for feminist research. In *Theories of women's studies,* ed. G. Bowles and R. D. Klein, 117–39. London: Routledge and Kegan Paul.

Milward, L. J. 1995. Focus groups. In *Research methods in psychology,* ed. G. M. Breakwell, S. Hammond, and C. Fife-Shaw, 274–91. London: Sage.

Morawski, J. G. 1994. *Practicing feminisms, reconstructing psychology.* Ann Arbor: University of Michigan Press.

Morawski, J. G., and G. Agronick. 1991. A restive legacy: The history of feminist work in experimental and cognitive psychology. *Psychology of Women Quarterly* 15: 567–79.

Morgan, D. 1988. Focus groups as qualitative research. (Sage University Papers, Qualitative Research Methods Series, No. 16.) London: Sage.

Morgan, D. L., ed. 1993. *Successful focus groups: Advancing the state of the art.* Newbury Park, CA: Sage.

Morgan, D. L., and R. A. Krueger. 1993. When to use focus groups and why. In *Successful focus groups: Advancing the state of art,* ed. D. L. Morgan, 3–19. Newbury Park, CA: Sage.

Morgan, D. L., and M. Spanish. 1984. Focus groups: A new tool for qualitative research. *Qualitative Sociology,* 7: 253–70.

Murray, S. A., J. Tapson, L. Turnbull, J. McCallum, and A. Little. 1994. Listening to local voices: Adapting rapid appraisal to assess health and social needs in general practice. *British Medical Journal* 308: 698–700.

Norris, J., P. S. Nurius, and L. A. Dimeff. 1996. Through her eyes: Factors affecting women's perception of and resistance to acquaintances sexual aggression threat. *Psychology of Women Quarterly* 20: 123–45.

Olesen, V. 1994. Feminisms and models of qualitative research. In *Handbook of qualitative research,* ed. N. K. Denzin and Y. S. Lincoln, 158–74. Thousand Oaks, CA: Sage.

Orr, J. 1992. Working with women's health groups. In *Research into practice: A reader for nurses and the caring professions,* ed. P. Abbott and R. Sapsford, 23–38. Buckingham: Open University Press.

Padilla, R. V. 1993. Using dialogical research methods in group interviews. In *Successful focus groups: Advancing the state of the art,* ed. D. L. Morgan, 153–66. Newbury Park, CA: Sage.

Parlee, M. B. 1979. Review essay: Psychology and women. *Signs* 5: 121–29.

Peplau, L. A., and E. Conrad. 1989. Beyond nonsexist research: The perils of feminist methods in psychology. *Psychology of Women Quarterly* 13: 379–400.

Plaut, T., S. Landis, and J. Trevor. 1993. Focus groups and community mobilization: A case study from rural North Carolina. In *Successful focus groups: Advancing the state of the art,* ed. D. L. Morgan, 202–21. Newbury Park, CA: Sage.

Press, A. L. 1991. Working-class women in a middle-class world: The impact of television on modes of reasoning about abortion. *Critical Studies in Mass Communication* 8: 421–41.

Prilleltensky, I. 1989. Psychology and the status quo. *American Psychologist* 44: 795–802.

Raabe, B. 1993. Constructing identities: Young people's understandings of power and social relations. *Feminism and Psychology* 3: 369–73.

Reinharz, S. 1983. Experiential analysis: A contribution to feminist research. In *Theories of women's studies,* ed. G. Bowles and R. D. Klein, 162–91. London: Routledge and Kegan Paul.

———. 1992. *Feminist methods in social research.* New York: Oxford University Press.

Riger, S. 1992. Epistemological debates, feminist voices: Science, social values, and the study of women. *American Psychologist* 47: 730–40.

Rubin, H. J., and I. S. Rubin. 1995. *Qualitative interviewing: The art of hearing data.* Thousand Oaks, CA: Sage.

Russo, N. F. 1995. Editorial: PWQ: A scientific voice in feminist psychology. *Psychology of Women Quarterly* 19: 1–3.

Sampson, E. E. 1988. The debate on individualism: Indigenous psychologies of the individual and their role in personal and societal functioning. *American Psychologist* 43: 15–22.

Schlesinger, P., R. E. Dobash, R. P. Dobash, and C. K. Weaver. 1992. *Women viewing violence.* London: British Film Institute.

Seals, B. F., R. L. Sowell, A. S. Demi, L. Moneyham, L. Cohen, and J. Guillory. 1995. Falling through the cracks: social service concerns of women infected with HIV. *Qualitative Health Research* 5: 496–515.

Siebold, C., L. Richards, and D. Simon. 1994. Feminist method and qualitative research about midlife. *Journal of Advanced Nursing* 19: 394–402.

Sherif, C. A. 1979/1992. Bias in psychology. Reprinted in *Seldom seen, rarely heard: Women's place in psychology,* ed. J. S. Bohan 107–46. Boulder, CO: Westview Press.

Stanley, L., and Wise, S. 1993. *Breaking out again: Feminist ontology and epistemology.* London: Routledge.

Stewart, D. W., and P. N. Shamdasani. 1990. *Focus groups: Theory and practice.* London: Sage.

Tavris, C. 1992. *The mismeasure of women.* New York: Simon and Schuster.

Taylor, J. M., C. Gilligan, and A. M. Sullivan. 1996. Missing voices, changing meanings: Developing a voice-centered relational method and creating an interpretive community. In *Feminist social psychologies: International perspectives,* ed. S. Wilkinson, 233–57. Buckingham: Open University Press.

Unger, R. K. 1983. Through the looking glass: No wonderland Yet! (The reciprocal relationship between methodology and models of reality.) *Psychology of Women Quarterly* 8: 9–32.

Vaughn, S., J. S. Schumm, and J. Sinagub. 1996. *Focus group interviews in education and psychology.* Thousand Oaks, CA: Sage.

Vera, E. M., L. E. Reese, R. L. Paikoff, and R. L. Jarrett. 1996. Contextual factors of sexual risk-taking in urban African American preadolescent children. In *Urban girls: Resisting stereotypes, creating identities,* ed. B. J. R. Leadbetter and N. Way, 291–304. New York: New York University Press.

Walker, L. 1979. *The battered woman.* New York: Haper and Row.

Walkerdine, V. 1996.. Working class women: Psychological and social aspects of survival. In *Feminist social psychologies: International perspectives,* ed. S. Wilkinson, 145–62. Buckingham: Open University Press.

Watts, M., and D. Ebbutt. 1987. More than the sum of the parts: Research methods in group interviewing. *British Education Research Journal* 13: 25–34.

Way, N. 1995. "Can't you see the courage, the strength that I have?": Listening to urban adolescent girls speak about their relationships. *Psychology of Women Quarterly* 19: 107–28.

Weisstein, N. 1968/1993. Psychology constructs the female; or, The fantasy life of the male psychologist (with some attention to the fantasies of his friends, the male biologist and the male anthropologist). Reprinted in *Feminism and Psychology* 3: 195–210.

Wells, W. D. 1974. Group interviewing. In *Handbook of marketing research,* ed. R. Ferber, 2–133–2–146. New York: McGraw-Hill.

West, C., and D. H. Zimmerman. 1991. Doing gender. In *The social construction of gender,* ed. J. Lorber, S. A. Farrell et al. 13–37. Newbury Park, CA: Sage.

Westkott, M. 1979. Feminist criticism of the social sciences. *Harvard Educational Review* 49: 422–30.

Widdicombe, S. 1995. Identity, politics, and talk: A case for the mundane and the everyday. In *Feminism and discourse: Psychological perspectives,* ed. S. Wilkinson and C. Kitzinger, 106–27. London: Sage.

Wilkinson, S. 1986. Sighting possibilities: Diversity and commonality in feminist research. In *Feminist social psychology: Developing theory and practice,* ed. S. Wilkinson, 7–24. Milton Keynes: Open University Press.

———. 1988a. Focus group in feminist research: Power, interaction, and the co-construction of meaning. *Women's Studies International Forum* 21: 111–25.

———. 1998b. Focus groups in health research: Exploring the meanings of health and illness. *Journal of Health Psychology* 3: 329–48.

———. 1998c. Focus group methodology: A review. *International Journal of Social Research Methodology* 1: 181–203.

Wilkinson, S., and C. Kitzinger, eds. 1995. *Feminism and discourse: Psychological perspectives.* London: Sage.

———, eds. 1996. *Representing the other: A "Feminism and Psychology" reader.* London: Sage.

Willott, S., and C. Griffin. 1997. Wham bam, am I a man? Unemployed men talk about masculinities. *Feminism and Psychology* 7: 107–28.

Wong, G. C., V. C. Li, M. A. Burris, and Y. Xiang. 1995. Seeking women's voices: Setting the context for women's health interventions in two rural counties in Yunnan, China. *Social Science and Medicine* 41: 1147–57.

Worell, J., and C. Etaugh. 1994. Transforming theory and research with women: Themes and variations. *Psychology of Women Quarterly* 18: 433–50.

Zeller, R. A. 1993. Focus group research on sensitive topics: Setting the agenda without setting the agenda. In *Successful focus groups: Advancing the state of the art,* ed. D. L. Morgan, 167–83. Newbury Park, CA: Sage.

CHAPTER 16

Vulnerability and Dangerousness

The Construction of Gender through Conversation about Violence

JOCELYN A. HOLLANDER

> *Stacy:* I think I'm definitely impacted by violence, or the implied threat of violence, just in the atmosphere. I mean, as a woman, I'm conscious of the possibility of being assaulted whenever I go out. I always am thinking about my safety and whether or not this is a safe area or not, and I'm very conscious about who and what is around me . . . it's kind of that threat hanging over me. . . . I've never been physically assaulted, but its kind of that possibility. I'm always conscious of that. *(Group 5)*

> *Bob:* The whole thing kind of hits me as kinda weird in a way. It's like [I] listen to women talk about how they're afraid and . . . I've never had to feel that way. And I guess that's what is hitting me. I've never had to consider, walking down the street, if I'm going to get whooped or not. And I guess that'd be a damn hard feeling to have to take. *(Group 13)*

These two quotes summarize one of the most pervasive differences between the lives of women and men in the contemporary United States. As many researchers have found, women tend to report far more fear of violence than do men, in a far wider range of circumstances (Gordon and Riger 1989; Madriz 1997; Warr 1985).

Paradoxically, reported patterns of victimization do not correspond to these patterns of fear (Pain 1997). According to official statistics, men's risk of experiencing violence is much higher than women's, both overall and for every type of violence except sexual assault. Moreover, there is a disjuncture between the situations women report fearing most (assault by a stranger, away from home, at night, and outside) and the situations in which they are most likely to be at risk (in or near the home, with intimates) (Koss 1988; Tjaden and Thoennes 1998).[1] As Valentine (1992, 22) writes, there seems to be "a mismatch between the geography of violence and the geography of fear."[2]

Why are women so much more afraid than men, even though their reported risk of violence is lower?[3] A number of explanations for this seeming paradox have been suggested, including the underreporting of violence against women, especially when committed by intimates (Stanko 1992); the unique nature of sexual assault (Ferraro 1996; Warr 1985); women's experiences of everyday harassment (Brooks Gardner

1995; Sheffield 1987); and mass media depictions of violence against women (Altheide 1997; Heath and Gilbert 1996; Heath, Gordon, and LeBailly 1981).

In this article, I suggest that another, more subtle source of difference in fear has been overlooked. I argue that widely shared conceptions of gender[4] associate femininity with vulnerability and masculinity with dangerousness. Stanko (1995, 50) writes that "the reality of sexual violence . . . is a core component of being female and is experienced through a wide range of everyday, mundane situations." I make a similar argument, but with respect to potential danger, not actual engagement with violence: Vulnerability to violence is a core component of femininity, but not masculinity. Relatedly, potential dangerousness is associated with masculinity, but not femininity. As I will show below, these ideas are pervasive, widely shared, and constructed through interaction: through routine patterns of behavior and communication that replicate and reinforce existing ideas about gender.

These ideas are based, in part, on shared beliefs about gendered bodies. Female bodies are believed to be inherently vulnerable and not dangerous to others because of their smaller average size, perceived lack of strength, and physical vulnerability to rape. Male bodies, in contrast, are seen as potentially dangerous to other because of their larger size, greater strength, and potential use as a tool of sexual violence. As McCaughey (1997, 37) writes,

> Imagistic discourse suggests that men have bodies that will prevail, that are strong and impenetrable. Female bodies are not represented as active agents in this way, but instead as breakable, takeable bodies. Just as such images portray women as prey to men's violence, they allow men to imagine themselves as invulnerable, especially compared to women.

These ideas are so integral to notions of gender that they seem "natural" and thus are largely invisible in daily life. Men's perceived greater strength and women's perceived sexual vulnerability are, as I show below, taken for granted in everyday conversation. I suggest here that these beliefs about male and female bodies are as much socially constructed as they are true representations of reality (Lorber 1993). While it is obviously true that men are on average taller than women, other aspects of perceived vulnerability and dangerousness are less clear-cut. For example, women's lack of strength relative to men is the result not simply of different physiology but of gender expectations that valorize feminine delicacy and thinness and discourage athletic ability, while men's greater strength and agility are due, in part, to more extensive physical training (Burton Nelson 1994; McCaughey 1997). Similarly, the prevalence of rape among incarcerated men demonstrates that men as well as women are vulnerable to sexual assault (Mezey and King 1992), and the experiences of gay men and men of color with homophobic and racist violence, respectively, show that subordinated groups of men are targeted for violence (Stanko and Hobdell 1993). Despite the reality of violence against men, however, vulnerability is not part of shared cultural conceptions of masculinity. According to McCaughey (1997, 8), "Gender ideology is not a matter of psychology as opposed to biology. Gender ideology affects the way we interpret and experience our bodies." However, the constructed nature of these beliefs is normally invisible because of the association of physical bodies with essentialism. Since bodies are perceived to be "natural" and therefore inevitable, so too are the gendered differences that are constructed through them.

In this article, I focus on everyday talk about violence—mundane conversations that take place in a wide variety of circumstances and relationships. Through conversations, people construct and transmit particular ways of understanding social phenomena by using a variety of sources of information, including popular wisdom, experience, and media discourse (Gamson 1992; Sasson 1995). Using data from thirteen focus groups, I show how everyday discourse paints women as vulnerable and men as potentially dangerous. This may lead women to see themselves as vulnerable to violence and may lead men to see themselves as relatively invulnerable, fostering gender differences in fear (Gordon and Riger 1989; McDaniel 1993). It may also lead women to exaggerate their fear of violence in both everyday interaction and in survey responses, while it may lead men to minimize fear: To appear appropriately feminine or masculine, individuals must meet gender expectations regarding vulnerability. These perceptions and expectations have far-reaching consequences for the daily practices of women and men, in terms of the strategies they use to keep themselves safe, their interactions with others, and their freedom to move through public and private space.

RELATIONSHIP TO PAST THEORY AND RESEARCH

In the sections that follow, I argue that beliefs about dangerousness and vulnerability are central to notions of gender. This argument extends current research in three ways.

The Centrality of Violence

First, it refocuses the attention of gender scholars on violence and, as importantly, on the perceived threat of violence as central features of a gendered world. Feminist scholars have been leaders in bringing attention to men's violence against women (and against other men) and the relationship of this violence to power, inequality, and social structure (Bart and O'Brien 1985; Brownmiller 1975; Russell 1975).[5] Yet both actual violence and perceived vulnerability are curiously absent from most sociological theory about gender. For example, Lorber's (1994) widely acclaimed volume on the "paradoxes of gender" briefly mentions wife beating, sexual harassment, and rape, but it does not identify violence or the fear of it as a central component of the institution of gender. Similarly, England's (1993) edited volume on gender includes ten essays explaining gender differentiation and inequality from a broad range of theoretical frameworks. None of these essays mention male violence against women as a cause—or even a symptom—of gender inequality. The new volume *Revisioning Gender* (Marx Ferree, Lorber, and Hess 1999), which takes as its goal "explain[ing] the meaning of gender itself" (xiii), contains only one chapter that discusses violence, and this only in the context of sexuality. These and other important theoretical works on gender published in recent years neglect the centrality of violence—either actual violence or the potential of perpetration or victimization—in the lives of women and men. While there are a few writers who have put violence at the center of their theorizing about gender (e.g., Connell 1987; MacKinnon 1989; Sheffield 1987), their insights have been largely ignored: sometimes dismissed, other times acknowledged but not integrated into mainstream thinking. In this article, I suggest that violence and the fear of violence are pervasive (although often invisible) aspects of gendered social life and as such deserve a more central place in theorizing about gender.

Perceptions of Vulnerability and Dangerousness

Second, I propose two new concepts—*perceived vulnerability* and *perceived dangerousness*—to represent shared understandings of the relationship between gender and violence, understandings that may foster gender differences in fear. These concepts too build on, but extend, the work of other scholars. For example, there has been considerable attention to the relationship between aggression, passivity, and gender (e.g., Eagly and Steffen 1986). However, aggression and passivity have typically been understood either as personality traits or as patterns of behavior. In contrast, the terms *perceived vulnerability* and *perceived dangerousness,* as I use them here, refer to shared beliefs about the perceived openness of particular social groups to violent victimization on one hand and their perceived potential for perpetrating violence on the other. Both of these are commonly attributed to the seemingly innate qualities of physical bodies—their size, strength, vulnerability to rape, and ability to defend themselves against attack.

These concepts capture a different dimension of the experience of danger in everyday life than do aggression and passivity. Although aggression (actual violence) does occur, it is relatively infrequent. What is more frequently experienced in daily life is men's presumed potential for aggression, which I term *perceived dangerousness.* Even if men do not actually behave aggressively—and, in fact, many men do not regularly act out aggression—they are seen by others as having the capacity to do so. In everyday life, it is often impossible to tell from outside appearances whether an unknown (or even a known) man may be aggressive. What is important to others around him—for example, to the woman walking past him on the street—is the cultural equation of masculinity with dangerousness. Similarly, the concept of passivity (lack of resistance in the face of aggression) does not entirely capture the daily experiences many women have with violence. Rather, they perceive themselves—and are perceived by others—as vulnerable to violence, regardless of whether they might respond passively or actively to it. Indeed, in the research I report below, I found no evidence that women perceived themselves to be passive, and many participants indicated that they would respond vigorously if attacked. What was salient, however, was women's widespread lack of faith in their ability to defend themselves against men and their pervasive association of masculinity with danger. These beliefs, I suggest, contribute to the gendered distribution of fear in American society.

Intersecting Systems of Social Hierarchy

Third, I discuss the relationship of vulnerability and dangerousness not simply to gender but also to other social hierarchies, including age, race, social class, and sexual identity. These intersections have been a notable gap not only in research on gender, as many scholars have pointed out (Connell 1987; Spelman 1988), but also in research on fear of violence. While there have been studies on gender and fear (Gordon and Riger 1989; Stanko 1995;Warr 1985), race and fear (Skogan 1995; St. John and Heald-Moore 1996), and age and fear (Warr 1984; Yin 1982), few studies have examined the intersections. Notable exceptions include Madriz (1997), whose work on women and fear focuses on the differences and similarities between women of different racial groups, and Pain (1995), who has looked at the intersections of gender and age. In this article, I explore connections of vulnerability and dangerousness not only with gender but also with race, social class, age, and sexual identity. As the discussion below makes clear, these social positions are not separable in shared beliefs about vulnerability and dangerousness. While gender remains the focus of this article (because it was discussed by the participants at far greater length than any other social position), the results below demonstrate that gender's relationship to vulnerability and dangerousness cannot be analyzed in isolation from other systems of social hierarchy.

In sum, although scholars have attended to the reality of violence and have explored aggression and passivity, they have largely overlooked the centrality of beliefs about vulnerability and dangerousness. As I demonstrate below, these ideas are closely intertwined with contemporary notions of gender. In overlooking these associations, scholars have neglected one of the most important insights of early feminist work: the body and its perceived relationship to violence are fundamental to the meaning and practice of gender.

METHOD

The analysis below is based on data from thirteen focus groups conducted between April 1994 and March 1997 in Seattle, Washington. Sample selection is a complex problem for focus group research. Morgan (1988, 44–45) argues that because the small number of participants used in a typical focus group study "are never going to be representative of a large population," researchers should concentrate instead on selecting "theoretically chosen subgroups from the total population," focusing on those subgroups expected to provide the richest information. For this study, I selected subgroups that past research suggested would differ in their exposure to, or fear of, violence. Because the most consistent difference found in fear is based on gender, and because women and men report different experiences of violence, in terms of both quantity and type, I recruited approximately equal numbers of women and men. Other factors that have been found to affect exposure to violence, or the fear of it, include race, social class, sexual identity, and age. I thus made an effort to maximize the diversity on these dimensions among the sample population by recruiting participants from a variety of different locations, as described below. However, I retained as much homogeneity as possible within each focus group to facilitate disclosure and discussion (Morgan 1988).

Participants were recruited through churches, community centers, workplaces, clubs, apartment buildings, university classes, community service organizations, and other preexisting groups in the Seattle area, chosen from the Seattle phone book and

Table 16.1 Demographic Characteristics of Focus Groups

Group	Gender	Race[a]	Age Range	Sexual Identity	Household Income Range (in thousands)	Source
1	Female and male	W, L, A	21–53	Heterosexual	$10–$25	University evening class
2	Male	W	31–63	Gay	$10–$100+	Athletic club
3	Female and male	W	33–59	Heterosexual	<$10–$75	Outdoors club
4	Female and male	W	30–38	Heterosexual and lesbian	$25–$100	Workplace
5	Female	W, L, N	30–41	Lesbian	$25–$100	Athletic club
6	Male	W, N	35–60	Heterosexual	<10	Low-income hotel
7	Male	W	18–19	Heterosexual	Unknown (students)	Fraternity
8	Female	W, N, B	44–71	Heterosexual	<$10–$25	Low-income apartment
9	Male	B, W	31–70	Heterosexual	<$10–$25	Low-income apartment
10	Female and male	W	65–88	Heterosexual	<$10–$25	Apartment for elderly
11	Female	B	30–44	Heterosexual	$10–$50	Church group
12	Female	W, A	18–22	Heterosexual	<$10–$50	University day class
13	Female and male	W, L, N	21–40	[b]	<$10–$50	University day class

a. The order in which the racial categories are listed in the table indicated the relative number of participants from each category: W = white, B = black, N = Native American, A = Asian or Pacific Islander, L = Latina/o.
b. Members of this group were not asked about their sexual identity

my own and my colleagues' connections in the community. The final sample included seventy-six adult participants. Groups ranged in size from four to eight participants. Table 16.1 describes the gender, race, sexual identity, age, income range, and source of recruitment of each group.

Each group met once, for approximately two hours. Facilitators[6] followed Morgan's (1988) strategy of "self-managed groups" in which, after an initial introduction to the general themes and ground rules of the discussion, the participants themselves help to facilitate the group discussion while the facilitator says very little. This strategy was crucial because the goal of the focus groups was to explore the participants' understandings of violence rather than their reactions to the facilitator's ideas. All discussions began with the following question:

1. Do you feel that the issue of violence affects you personally or affects your friends and relatives?

The groups varied widely in terms of the quantity of discussion of this question: Some groups discussed the question for the full two hours, while in others conversation lagged after half an hour. Follow-up questions were used as needed and included the following:

2. When do other people give you warnings about dangerous situations or people? What kinds of warnings do you give others? (Groups 2, 3, 4, 5, 7, 9)
3. In what situations do you feel most vulnerable? (Groups 2, 3, 5, 6, 10, 11)
4. In what situations do you feel most safe? (Groups 1, 2, 3, 4, 6, 7, 8, 10, 11)

The discussions were audiotaped with the participants' consent, transcribed, and coded for analysis.

I used a number of strategies to increase the external validity of the findings. I compared the demographic composition of my sample with that of the city of Seattle to assess the degree to which the participants in this study were representative of other populations. In general, the demographic characteristics of the focus group participants approximated those of Seattle residents. However, there were more women, more young adults, more people with a very low yearly income, and fewer Asian Americans than in the general Seattle population. I also compared participants' responses on a number of survey questions[7] with the responses of nationally representative samples in other surveys; here too, study participants were not greatly different from the larger populations. Finally, to ensure uniformity among groups, facilitators were provided with a detailed script for the focus group, which they read essentially verbatim to the participants.

Despite these efforts, I do not claim that the participants in this study are representative of any larger population, and therefore caution is warranted in generalizing from these results. I see no reason to assume, however, that these participants differ from the larger populations from which they are drawn in ways that detract from the conclusions of this study. Moreover, the focus of this analysis is not the participants' individual experiences or behaviors but their shared ideas about vulnerability and dangerousness—ideas that, because they are shared among such a diverse group of participants, are also likely to be shared in the wider social context. Thus, while it would be inappropriate to generalize from this sample, I do suggest that the findings that are described here provide clues about more generally held social ideas.

I now turn to an analysis of these focus group conversations. First, I discuss patterns in the participants' characterizations of vulnerability and then explore their ideas about dangerousness.

VULNERABILITY

Gender and Vulnerability

Vulnerability was deeply associated with gender in the focus group discussions. Participants made many more comments about women's vulnerability than about men's. In the thirteen discussions, sixty-nine comments identified individuals (other than the speaker's self) or groups as vulnerable to violence. Of these, only 19 percent (thirteen statements) referred to men, while 81 percent (fifty-six statements) referred to women.

These statements differed in quality as well as quantity. Virtually all the comments that identified men as vulnerable focused on particular individuals and located the source of their vulnerability in specific characteristics or behaviors. For example, one speaker perceived her teenage sons to be vulnerable because "they're out late a lot"; another speaker noted that he felt vulnerable because of his below-average height. In contrast, most of the comments about women's vulnerability were quite different. They identified not simply specific women but women as a group as inherently vulnerable to violence. Of the fifty-six references to women's vulnerability, twenty-four (43 percent) were of this type; an additional eight (14 percent) identified large subgroups of women (e.g., lesbians or older women) as particularly at risk. Thus, more than half of the references to women's vulnerability identified women, or some subgroup thereof, as being by their nature vulnerable to violence.

Many of these references stated in a taken-for-granted way that women are vulnerable (all participants are identified by pseudonyms in this article):

> ERIC: I think that men are, on average, men are physically stronger, in most cases, and you know, if I was a woman, damn, I—
>
> BILL: Would you feel vulnerable?
>
> ERIC: I'm sure I'd feel vulnerable. Very vulnerable. Yes. . . . (Group 2)

> RICHARD: But as far as like a sexual type assault or a violent crime, I don't hear too much about men being assaulted sexually in the street or in a parking garage or something, where you think of a woman, that happening more often.
>
> NORA: Yeah, I think women are much more vulnerable to that type of crime than men are. I go jogging at night too, but [I go with] my two roommates. . . . I was really hesitant to jog at night when they started this. . . . I was like, "Yeah, I'm with the two of them, but still, we're only girls . . ." (Group 1)

Only once was a general statement like this made about men, in a brief discussion among seven young women about how women might respond to an assault by a man:

> MARCIA: But you never know, because if you get in that situation [being attacked by a man] your adrenaline is going. . . . You're not fully aware of what you probably could do. I always had this plan in my head, if anything were to happen like that, because men do have a weak spot, and if you know where it's at . . . (Group 12)

This comment, however, occurred in the context of an extended discussion of women's vulnerability and weakness relative to men. Usually, these kinds of generalizations were made exclusively about women. More frequent were comments that explicitly associated men with invulnerability, as in this quote from a young man:

> RICHARD: One point . . . is like my mom would tell me, "Oh Richard, you shouldn't go jogging at night," and I said, "Oh mom, don't worry. I'm a guy, no one's going to bother me." (Group 1)

Table 16.2 Relationship between Protectors and Those in Need of Protection in Comments by Focus Group Participants

	Types of People Described as Protectors						
Types of People Described as Receiving or Needing Protection	**Men**	**Women**	**General**	**Unspecified**	**Police**	**Parents**	**Total**
Men	6	0	9	1	1	0	17
Women	30	10	15	5	1	2	63
Children	0	2	0	0	0	0	2
General	5	3	4	1	0	0	13
Unspecified	1	2	0	0	0	0	3
Total	42	17	28	7	2	2	98

Whereas for men the unmarked case is invulnerability (i.e., men are generally perceived to be invulnerable, and only exceptions are vulnerable), for women the default is vulnerability. Valentine (1997) reports similar findings from interviews with children: Children of both sexes viewed girls, but not boys, as vulnerable to danger.

Another way to assess cultural ideas about vulnerability is to examine which groups are perceived to be capable of protecting others and which groups are perceived to need protection. Presumably, only those believed to be relatively invulnerable would be seen as protectors, while those who are believed to be vulnerable would be seen as especially in need of protection.

There were ninety-eight statements made during the focus groups that identified specific types of people as protectors or as in need of protection. Table 16.2 categorizes these statements according to the relationship between protectors and those they protect.

Forty-one of these ninety-eight statements identified men as protectors of others; women were identified as protectors less than half as often. Gender differences were even more notable in statements about people perceived to need protection: sixty-three statements identified women as needing protection, but only seventeen identified men. Equally telling is the relationship between the protector and the protected. The single most frequent type of comment, representing more than 30 percent of all comments, involved men's protecting women. In contrast, women were never discussed as protectors of men. Men in the focus groups tended to make statements like the following:

> BOB [in response to a woman's description of harassment by an ex-boyfriend]: I keep thinking in my mind listening to you, what anybody I know would say. They'd say, well get your brothers, your old man, go over there, haul him up like that, go over pay him a visit and bust him up a bit. You'll be surprised, he'll shut up real good. (Group 13)

> TONY: Just the other night, Jane here, she has a parking spot up here, and at eight o'clock at night she says, "Tony, would you watch me when I go to park

my truck?" And I said, "Jane, I'm not going to watch you. I'm going to go with you." (Group 10)

The first quote demonstrates that men, not women, are perceived as capable of protecting others. The speaker suggests that the woman should depend on her male relatives for protection, not take action herself. The second quote shows succinctly that both women and men see men as protectors. Jane requests protection from Tony; Tony's response confirms Jane's perceptions of herself as vulnerable and of him as a source of protection.

In contrast, only a few comments referred to women's protecting others. All of these comments referred to women's protection of other women, children, or unspecified "other people"; no comments referred to women's protecting men. These findings are consistent with Warr's (1992) study of "altruistic fear" (i.e., fear for others), which found that women are more likely than men to fear for their children, whereas men are more likely than women to fear for their spouses.

Moreover, with the exception of protecting children, women are not perceived to have the same responsibility for protecting others as men:

LINDA: I've seen guys on the bus, it's always on the bus, some guy's hassling a woman. And I traded seats with her cause she was really shy and couldn't get away from him, and I'm like, "You wanna trade seats?" and she's like "No," and I'm like, "You wanna trade seats!" [laughter] And she's like "Oh! Oh!" [laughter] and so I'm standing there glaring at this guy the whole bus ride to keep him from bothering her, and the minute he gets off, three guys go, "Are you okay?" to her, and it's like, "Where were you when he was bothering her?" (Group 13)

This speaker clearly feels that the role of protector she has stepped into should have been occupied by one of the men on the bus.

Although women's perceived inability to protect others was usually implicit, at times, women were also explicitly identified as being ineffective protectors, as in this conversation about the dangers of international travel among three young women:

SARAH: Even with another girlfriend somewhere in a foreign land or something, it's still not [safe] though.

KATRINA: And even if you're like ten girls, you're still [not safe].

JILL: No, you're not. (Group 12)

Even ten women together are not perceived to be capable of defending themselves or each other from men's violence. Thus, comments about protection, like the more general comments about vulnerability discussed in the previous section, tended to identify women as vulnerable and men as the sources of both danger and protection.

Age

Age was also associated with perceived vulnerability in the focus group discussions. However, this relationship varied depending on gender. Although discussion participants identified young children of both sexes as vulnerable, gender was not particularly salient in these comments. Rather, both young girls and young boys were believed to be vulnerable principally because of their physical and/or mental immaturity.

As they grow older, however, the perceived vulnerability of boys and girls diverges. Boys become larger and stronger and are consequently seen as less vulnerable:

> BARBARA: I know that one thing that's really changed. My son's fourteen now, and I . . . was concerned about [him going] outside until my son got old enough. . . . He's not [a] real huge towering person but just the fact that he's male and is taller. (Group 13)

As boys grow older, they become identified with stereotypes of masculinity, which center on strength and invulnerability (Goodey 1995; Valentine 1997).

While girls also become larger and stronger as they age, these changes are interpreted quite differently. Girls and women are seen as weak, regardless of their actual strength and abilities. Moreover, young women are seen as being at a peak of sexual desirability. Given the widespread misconception that sexual assaults are motivated by the victim's attractiveness, girls and young women are perceived to be at risk because of this intersection of gender, age, and sexuality. In this example, a forty-four-year-old woman describes the difference she sees between her own and her college-age daughter's vulnerability:

> ANGELA: [When] I'm walking, I'm not worried about people attacking me. . . . [But] young people, I have a feeling for young girls, when they're running, and they wear this little provocative stuff. And I make [my daughter] cover up, but you know what I'm saying? . . . I am always wanting to make sure that they are equipped when they leave because they're a lot younger than I am and people are looking at them, and I'm aware of that, too, because I was young. (Group 11)

Thus, at the same moment that young men are seen as least vulnerable, young women are seen as most vulnerable.

As women grow older, however, they move past this peak of perceived vulnerability. As the quotes above and below illustrate, middle-aged women are perceived to be less vulnerable than young women:

> BARBARA: Being older, I have the advantage of not having to put up with the crap from a twenty-two-year-old that an eighteen- or nineteen-year-old would have to. It doesn't bother me to play kinda mother to people [and] say, "Don't worry," "Back off!" . . . By being older and assuming a matronly attitude that I'm just not going to mess with any of this macho stuff. . . . It's like, they'll just kind of fold their tents and they'll go away. And it is an advantage being older, I think that's given me a lot of security. (Group 13)

Finally, as individuals grow into old age, women's and men's perceived vulnerability converges again. For example, this speaker identifies her elderly father as vulnerable:

> BARBARA: . . . My dad's seventy. I could beat my dad up. [laughter] (Group 13)

The group's laughter confirms the perceived absurdity of a woman's being seen as capable of victimizing a man. Note, however, that this quote refers to a particular old man. Although specific old men like her father are perceived to be vulnerable, older women as a group are seen as especially vulnerable, as in this statement by a seventy-one-year-old woman:

> MEG: I've noticed since I got older, particularly, that I'm much more of a target. You think as a woman you're a target, but as an older woman, you really become much more of a target. (Group 8)

Even though men's vulnerability increases in old age, women are still believed to be more vulnerable than men (Pain 1995). Aging makes women seem more vulnerable, while men move from being perceived as invulnerable to being seen as vulnerable.

Thus, while women are seen as more vulnerable than men at every age, the size and shape of this difference vary. These shifting differences provide excellent examples of how gender and age intersect in both experience and perception.

Race and Ethnicity

A number of participants made comments that associated race or ethnicity with vulnerability. Most of these comments were made by white participants who associated whiteness with vulnerability and people of color with potential danger:

> JANET: My children were raised in [a racially diverse neighborhood] where I lived for twenty years, so their friends are multiethnic. And my oldest son is actually a rap DJ. And so they get into a lot of situations that are fairly unusual for white kids. And I try to warn my older son, particularly, about being in situations where late at night or someone has too much to drink, they might be angry just because of his appearance. (Group 1)

> DAVID: I have to say that I think that race is a relevant factor . . . in that I think that one of the things that allows somebody to perpetrate violence against another person is if they believe that they're not like them, that they're different. If I'm traveling in a neighborhood that I clearly don't live in, because it's an Asian neighborhood, or a black neighborhood, and I see somebody walking down the street and they belong, they live there, and I don't, and I know that right away because they're black and I'm not, I'm going to feel more threatened. (Group 4)

These participants clearly see their vulnerability as stemming from their whiteness.

Interestingly, only one participant of color noted that she believed her race made her more vulnerable. This thirty-year-old African American woman commented that her race became a liability after moving from a large city to an all-white suburb:

> ALISSA: I know my dad moved to [the suburbs] because of the violence here [in the city] . . . he didn't want us to grow up that way. But then this opened up a whole another set of issues, you know, when you don't realize that you're different and you suddenly move somewhere else and they let you know you're different. . . . There was only one other black family. . . . And so I would go to school and I'd get beat up—I mean, I'd never even had to fight before. (Group ll)

The effects of race are contextual: Both white and black participants felt vulnerable only in a context that highlighted their racial identity (Covington and Taylor 1991).

Social Class

Only a few participants explicitly commented that social class affected perceived vulnerability, perhaps because of the relative invisibility of issues of class in the United States. Most of these comments were made by middle- and upper-middle-class participants who felt that their apparent wealth made them attractive targets for violence. For example, this exchange took place in a conversation between two white, middle-class men about how they might react when encountering dangerous-looking people on the street:

> ERIC: Now some of my Asian friends . . . would respond totally different to that. "Nobody bothers me. I look like hell, and they [potential assailants] don't give me two looks," you know? But this guy, this Caucasian white guy, he dresses in a Gap shirt or whatever casual stuff, "Oh, he's got money, let's get him."
>
> RICK: Yeah, [I could be] going for a job interview, [and] just because I have a suit on, [panhandlers] assume I have money. (Group 2)

As these quotes illustrate, it is not so much actual wealth as the appearance of wealth that makes one vulnerable. And in many cases, simply being white is perceived to be associated with wealth; race and class are not separable in these comments.

Only one participant, a wealthy white man, noted that poverty might increase one's vulnerability. It is notable that no poor or working-class participants made such comments, especially in light of the fact that other research has found that income is inversely correlated with risk (Newhart Smith and Hill 1991). However, a number of oblique comments, generally about the perceived danger level of the communities in which the participants resided, provide evidence that social class does affect perceptions of vulnerability in this way. For example, in these comments, two poor white men living in a high-crime area discussed their neighborhood:

> ERNIE: It's still bad out there, and they've still got a lot of dealers out there. . . . I tell everybody, they shouldn't go out there alone. They should always have a friend with them.
>
> HENRY: Yeah, it's a high-risk area. (Group 6)

In contrast, this middle-class white man discussed his mother's neighborhood:

> TOM: But I think that [when] you get into my mom's neighborhood, which is a middle-class neighborhood, all of a sudden you have block watch programs, single dwelling homes. You've got police who know the people who live there. And you also have a place where . . . everyone knows each other, and knows . . . who belongs and who doesn't. (Group 2)

Thus, social class does make a difference in perceived vulnerability, although these comments were more implicit than those about race or gender.

Sexual Identity

Although sexual identity was not a major topic of conversation in the focus groups, several comments associated homosexuality with vulnerability. For example, one lesbian woman said,

> JOYCE: If I'm in a group of gay people, I feel safe because I know they're not going to beat me up. But anywhere else, that's where I've experienced the most violence, where I've been assaulted. . . . And I expect most people to be violent towards me. That's sort of my feeling. And I feel like I have a double whammy because my partner, not only is she a woman but she's Jewish, and we make these little jokes like, "Okay, we're going to this town, act as married, and as Christian as you can, and maybe they won't notice." [laughter]. . . . Yeah, you know, get out the big crucifix. Because, you know, we are targets. We are targeted people, and we know that. And we're not stupid. We read the reports, and we see things. (Group 4)

In this case, gender interacts with sexual identity, ethnicity, and religion to multiply the women's perceived vulnerability. Although Joyce's proposed strategies to avoid violence ("act as married and as Christian as you can") are offered in jest, they illustrate the self-regulation that is perceived to be necessary for avoiding victimization: She and her partner attempt to appear heterosexual to prevent being targeted. However, "this self-regulation normalizes not only homophobia but gendered violence as well. Attention is displaced from the root of the problem, the workings of (hetero)normativity" (Stanko and Curry 1997, 525).

Being gay is also perceived to increase men's vulnerability. For example, this gay man notes that he perceives one of his friends to be vulnerable because he frequents a park known for anonymous sexual encounters:

> ERIC: This guy, good friend of mine, he likes to go to Volunteer Park at night. And I try to impress upon the fellow [that] it's not the safest thing to do, there's a lot of crazies out there. . . . And [the warning is] not particularly well accepted. I mean, "I am a man. Who are you telling me what I can and can't do?" . . . I mean yes, I've gone to Volunteer Park, but usually it's with a team, you know, [laughs] we've got our defenses. (Group 2)

The friend's perceived vulnerability is in part due to his sexual identity and the consequent risk of gay bashing (Connell 1987; Stanko and Hobdell 1993). However, note again that this speaker is identifying a specific man as vulnerable for a specific reason: It is by going to Volunteer Park alone that his vulnerability is magnified. In contrast, going with a "team" of other men, as the speaker himself does, offers protection.

This speaker's comment highlights the way in which vulnerability based on sexual identity is conditioned by gender. Eric suggests that men can protect themselves and each other from the danger of homophobic violence. Indeed, his friend's reaction highlights the perceived self-sufficiency of masculinity. Joyce's quote, above, offers no such sense of confidence; her vulnerability as a woman and as a lesbian magnify each other. Thus, homophobic violence cannot be conceptualized as a single phenomenon but must incorporate "a gendered understanding of violence against gay *men* and lesbian *women*" (Jenness and Broad 1994, 419).

One need not identify oneself as gay, lesbian, or bisexual to be perceived as vulnerable. Simply not meeting expectations for heterosexual appearance can be enough to increase perceived risk. This was made clear in comments by a straight man who felt that he had been threatened because other men had believed him to be gay:

> JACK: It really was a hazard, I felt shit scared, I should not walk close to those people at all. Because someone will have something to show to someone else. Some macho thing, where they'll want to show that they can, you know, say "fuck you" to the faggot and what's he going to do, because I'm such a stud. (Group 4)

In sum, gender interacts with a variety of social positions in the construction of vulnerability. Masculinity is perceived to protect men from danger, whereas femininity is perceived to be a sign of inherent vulnerability. However, race, class, sexuality, and age interact with gender in particular social contexts to increase or decrease vulnerability. Despite these interactions, gender was mentioned far more frequently than other systems of social hierarchy with respect to vulnerability. Unless there are specific extenuating circumstances, such as old age, youth, racial salience, or a proclivity to engage in behaviors perceived as risky, men are not understood to be as vulnerable to violence as women.

DANGEROUSNESS

Vulnerability does not occur in a vacuum; one is vulnerable to other people and to particular kinds of harm. In this section, I turn to the concept of perceived dangerousness: What types of people are considered dangerous?

There were 159 mentions of dangerous people during the focus group discussions, of which 121 specified the gender of the people identified as dangerous. Of these, 115 (or 95 percent) identified men as potentially dangerous, either individually or as a group:

> JANET: The most threatened I've felt in the last year is on campus when I'm going to my car after a night class, and there's nobody in sight except one guy. (Group 1)

> JOYCE: I see a bunch of guys, any age, any group, more than two and I'm scared. I don't care what color they are, what age they are, even if they're like twelve. It's like, uh oh, trouble. It's either going to be verbal assault, or it might be physical assault, or whatever. (Group 4)

In some cases, male family members and other male intimates were described as potential dangers:

> ANITA: A lot of times violent crimes happen as a result from your boyfriend, your husband . . . rather than just some stranger. (Group 1)

However, the vast majority of the comments about dangerous people referred not to intimates but to strangers—despite the fact that violence is at least as likely to occur between people who know each other (Tjaden and Thoennes 1998).

Only six comments identified women as dangerous. Moreover, of these six comments, two were meant (and received) as jokes, highlighting the perceived absurdity of a woman being seen as dangerous. Two comments involved the danger not of physical violence but of a woman's falsely accusing a man of rape. For example, a thirty-year-old man described his reactions after he picked up a female hitchhiker who subsequently threatened him:

> HAROLD: I felt that there was a risk of harm to myself, but not so much that she was going to physically injure me, more than scratching me or something like that. It was more the fact that I could end up in the newspaper. I could have harm to my reputation, people could become aware . . . that I was accused of rape by this woman. (Group 4)

This is a very different kind of danger than that believed to be posed by men.

Of the two remaining cases of women perceived as dangerous, one involved a woman wielding a gun, and the other referred to groups of young black women encountered in an area the speaker believed to be the most dangerous in Seattle. Thus, women are seen as dangerous only in extraordinary circumstances: when they are armed or when they are both members of groups perceived to be dangerous and in a context perceived as especially risky.

Race was also seen as a potent marker of dangerousness, although to a much lesser extent than gender. Of the 159 comments about dangerousness, twenty-seven associated race or particular racial groups with danger in some way. Sixteen of these identified African Americans, two identified whites, two referred to Asians or Latinos, and seven referred to "race," a "mixed group," "other cultures," or "immigration" as potentially dangerous. For example, this conversation took place between three young white men:

> SEAN: Like if I drove through one of the really, darker-skinned areas of Seattle, then I get a lot of looks. I've been through there and everyone's looking at you, and they don' look like they're happy to see you.
>
> ROB: "Whitey, get out of here." That's what I heard.
>
> ANDREW: They either think you're a chump, or they think you're such a badass that you can afford to go through there. (Group 7)

These men's projections of what people of color think about them say a great deal about their ideas about race and dangerousness, and are consistent with Madriz's (1997) findings that images of criminals are deeply racialized.

Poverty is another marker of danger. In fifteen of the 159 comments, poor people were perceived to be particularly dangerous; in contrast, danger was never associated with wealth:

> TOM: I think if you look at who you're getting the locks to lock out . . . you're not putting locks on your doors to keep out your neighbor down the street or the neighbor two blocks away. It's the person from the lesser income bracket who lives two miles away. (Group 2)

> MEG: I have a car, so basically I have to be in my parking lot by eight o'clock because if I am not, I have to go in the back door, and that is just a parking lot that is filled with a lot of homeless, sleeping in the trash barrels and the dumpsters and things like that, and I am not crazy about that . . . (Group 8)

Thus, gender, race, and class were frequently invoked when describing people perceived as dangerous. Moreover, in 22 percent of these descriptions (thirty-five of the 159), the participants identified dangerous people by reference to some combination of these social statuses. Gender was mentioned in all of these combinations, and all but one case mentioned men. In addition, one-half of these comments (seventeen) referred to men of color, especially black men, and fifteen comments referred to young men. Social class, however, was rarely mentioned in combination with other social positions, suggesting that being poor, like being male, is sufficient to be seen as dangerous. In contrast, race and age require a combination with other social positions to produce perceptions of danger.

The combination of race, gender, and age was particularly potent in the focus group discussions. In particular, young black men were most frequently identified as dangerous. For example, this conversation between two white women took place in response to a facilitator's question about when they feel most vulnerable:

> BECKY: That one's easy. [laughter] I think when I'm alone, and I walk by a group of . . . probably young black men, I would say, that would—and I know it's a stereotypical prejudiced scenario, but it still happens. It's still the first instinct, is, heart starts to go a little faster. And the second would be young punky males of any race, but those are the two. . . .
>
> LIZ: I'd like to think that they were equal, but in the questionnaire, I had the same reaction and I thought, oh God, I really feel prejudiced, and I didn't like it, but it's young Black males. (Group 3)

The white participants' self-consciousness about talking about race was clear in the discussions—as was the tenacity of their associations between people of color, especially black men, and dangerousness. This identification of poor men and men of color as more dangerous than white and wealthy men parallels findings from Brooks Gardner's (1995) study of public harassment of women. She found that women reacted much more positively to harassment when it came from high-status, attractive men than when it came from low-status men and explains this pattern in terms of the heterosexual romanticization of harassment. Women were likely to interpret harassment from high-status men as suggesting romantic interest; this interpretation served to rationalize the harassment.

DISCUSSION

Thus, in dramatic contrast to representations of vulnerability, representations of danger in the focus group conversations identified men as the main source of potential violence. In some cases, maleness is identified along with other social positions, especially race, class, and age; in the majority of cases, however, simply being a man is enough to render a person potentially dangerous in others' eyes. Women, in comparison, were only identified as dangerous in very few, particular cases and situations; the default category for women is vulnerability.

The salience of gender and other systems of social hierarchy in the talk described above is particularly remarkable in light of the fact that the focus group participants were never asked about specific social positions. This suggests that the par-

Table 16.3 Comparison of Victimization Data and Focus Group References to Victimization and Vulnerability (in percentages)

	Gender of Victims or People Perceived as Vulnerable	
Data Source	**Men**	**Women**
Violent crime victimizations[a]	58	42
Focus group references to victims	41	59
Focus group references to vulnerable people	19	81

a. Source: Bureau of Justice Statistics (1995, 231, Table 3.2).

ticipants' marked and consistent association of vulnerability with femininity and other social positions represents their actual beliefs, rather than their assumptions about what the facilitator hoped to hear.

Disjunctions between Perceived and Actual Vulnerability

The strong association between gender and vulnerability in everyday discourse is particularly fascinating in light of the wealth of contradictory empirical evidence. Table 16.3 compares victimization data from the National Crime Survey with focus group references to victims and to people perceived as vulnerable.

According to the National Crime Survey, men are more likely than women to be victimized: in 1995, men were the targets in 58 percent of all reported violent victimizations. Qualitative research on victimization has also found that men experience a great deal of violence (e.g., Stanko and Hobdell 1993). Even the focus group participants themselves discussed incidents where men were victimized nearly as often as incidents in which women were victims: 41 percent of victims mentioned by the participants were male. Nonetheless, participants still perceived men to be relatively invulnerable: Only 19 percent of the focus group comments about people perceived to be vulnerable referred to men. Thus, ideas about vulnerability do not derive directly from actual experiences of violence.

A similar observation can be made for the relationship between race and vulnerability. In the focus group discussions, whiteness was perceived as a source of vulnerability (especially when in mixed-race environments) far more often than other racial positions, but crime and victimization reports show that people of color—and especially men of color—are at greater risk of victimization than whites (Bureau of Justice Statistics 1995) and, indeed, tend to report more fear of crime in large surveys (see Skogan 1995).

The greater emphasis on gender than on race in the focus group discussions—especially the lack of comments about the vulnerability of men of color—may stem from several factors. First, the fact that the participants were drawn from the Seattle area may have resulted in less talk about race than might occur in other areas. Seattle has a relatively small number of African Americans and Latinos (10.0 percent and 3.3 percent of the city's population, respectively [U.S. Bureau of the Census 1992]) and less visible interracial conflict than many other large cities. It does have a larger Asian and Pacific Islander population (11.9 percent) than most cities, but men from these groups are not perceived to be as dangerous as other men of color. Moreover, like many other big cities, Seattle has a relatively high degree of racial segregation: African Americans, Latinos, and to a lesser extent Asians and Asian Americans, tend to live in distinct neighborhoods. This means that individuals (especially whites) may have very limited contact with members of other racial categories and spend most of their time in racially homogeneous contexts. In contrast, because gender is not a basis for spatial segregation, individuals are much more frequently in mixed-gender contexts. Thus, racial difference may have been less salient than gender difference as a marker of danger for these participants. Finally, Americans tend to talk about gender, more than race, in terms of broadly shared personality characteristics. While sensitivity to issues of racism has made it less acceptable to make generalizations about racial groups (at least in public discourse), the same is not true for gender. Thus, participants' lack of discussion about race may have stemmed from their reluctance to make comments that could be perceived as racist.

Together, this evidence shows that vulnerability is socially constructed quite independently from actual experiences (or knowledge of others' experiences) with violence. Ideas about women's vulnerability and men's invulnerability persist even when men's victimization is discussed. The focus group discussions provide a useful window on this process of construction. The talk of the participants shows how women become and remain identified with vulnerability and men with invulnerability and dangerousness. These kinds of associations, I argue, help to explain the gendered patterns of fear and vulnerability discussed above.

Vulnerability, Dangerousness, and the Body

One theme that ran throughout the focus group conversations was the relationship of vulnerability and dangerousness to human bodies. Women's vulnerability is perceived to stem from physical factors: their generally smaller size, lesser strength, and physical vulnerability to rape. These differences are believed to be natural even though, as many scholars have argued, these seemingly physiological differences are themselves socially constructed (Kessler and McKenna 1978; Lorber 1994).

The other social positions discussed above are also located at least partly in bodies. The process of aging is manifested in bodily changes: Young children and the elderly are perceived as physically less able to defend themselves against attack. In a different way, race and ethnicity are translated into vulnerability through the body, because they are a source of danger only insofar as they are visible to others. As discussed above, racial salience was perceived to increase vulnerability. Both people of color and whites reported feeling at risk in contexts where they were in the racial minority. But physical appearance mediates this effect: If a person of color can pass as white in an all-white context, he or she is perceived as less vulnerable than those who are obviously people of color. The same can be said for sexual identity: Those whose appearance signals that they are lesbian or gay are perceived to be more vulnerable than those who can pass as straight. Social class is in some cases signaled through appearance, such as dress, regardless of actual class position. Moreover, even those who are not members of targeted groups may be at risk because their appearance suggests mistakenly that they are members.

Other physical aspects of bodies are also associated with vulnerability and dangerousness. Bodily size and strength are believed to increase dangerousness and decrease vulnerability, as was evident in the focus group discussions:

> TINA: If you're five foot one and one hundred ten pounds, you can be sized up and you're a decent target. (Group 5)

> LINDA: I have a friend who's a really big guy. I don't think he's ever been in a fight, I think I've been in more fights than he has, and he's really gentle, but because of how he looks people never mess with him. (Group 13)

Note that smallness and weakness (and therefore vulnerability) are considered normative for women but the exception for men; women are believed to be inherently weak and vulnerable. Interestingly, a number of comments emphasized a man's small size, as in this quote:

> STACY: I had a male friend that was, it's not a politically correct term, but he was a midget, he was about 4'8", 4'6". And we were wrestling around, and I was about the same height and weight as I am now, and he pinned me. . . . It definitely gave me a start, and something to think about. . . . He was much smaller, weighed a lot less, but he still had some strength that, even at his size, he was able to pin me. (Group 5)

These kinds of comments served to emphasize the association of masculinity with danger: Even small men are perceived to be dangerous to women.

Although perceptions of vulnerability stem from socially constructed ideas—about gender, race, age, and so on—the markers that convey vulnerability are located in physical bodies. This fact reinforces the perceived essentialism of these differences. Because bodies are perceived to be "natural," any patterns associated with them are perceived to be inherent and therefore not changeable. This perception significantly lowers the possibility of resistance.[8]

Vulnerability, Fear, and Daily Life

These patterns of perceived vulnerability and dangerousness are not simply cognitive constructs; they have concrete consequences for the everyday lives of women and men. Many of the quotes used above illustrate these effects. Women report constantly monitoring their environment for signs of danger, hesitating to venture outside at night alone or even in the company of other women, asking men for protection, modifying their clothes and other aspects of their appearance, and restricting their activities to reduce their perceived risk of violence, thus limiting their use of public space. These strategies are simply part of daily life as a woman:

> CHRISTINE: I think most women have . . . a checklist of ten things they always do that's just in their heads. They always lock their door, they always check behind the seat when you get in the car, you always have the lights on, you always have the automatic timers set for the lights, you always have the doors locked, you always have the windows locked. (Group 4)

Men in the focus groups, however, rarely mentioned using such elaborate strategies. Stanko (1997, 489) discusses women's ongoing "safekeeping" as the "process of assessing risk as an ongoing accomplishment." This process, she argues, "is 'performative' . . . of respectable femininities." Similarly, men's lack of fear, and accompanying failure to use many safety strategies, can be seen as performative of normative masculinities. This too may have negative consequences for men. It allows them to live without the restrictions imposed by safety strategies, but it may also increase their risk of violence and may make it more difficult for them to cope with any victimization that does occur (Stanko and Hobdell 1993).

CONCLUSIONS

Ideas about gender, vulnerability, and dangerousness have consequences for both individuals and social life. These ideas affect not only those who experience violence but nonvictims (and nonperpetrators) as well. Shared ideas about bodies, in other words, affect material realities, in pervasive and far-reaching ways.

I began by posing the paradox of fear and violence: Why is there a disjunction between women's and men's reported fear of violence and their apparent risk of victimization? Others have argued that fear is imposed from the outside—from experiences of victimization, media representations, and everyday harassment. I have suggested that in addition to these external forces, people themselves construct women's vulnerability and men's dangerousness through everyday talk about violence and danger. These mundane conversations identify women as inherently open to attack and men as inherently able to both protect themselves from danger and menace others. I have also argued that these are often conversations about physical bodies—most often about what it means to have a male body or a female body, but also other types of bodies (small bodies, old bodies, bodies marked by race or sexual identity or disability). The fact that these constructions of vulnerability and dangerousness are framed in the language of physical bodies makes them appear natural, inevitable, and, as a result, virtually invisible. Although pervasive and consequential, they are rarely salient, instead forming the taken-for-granted backdrop for everyday life.

An incident from one of the focus groups illustrates this point. The group was a mixed-sex, all-white group that took place on the campus of a large company near Seattle. When the discussion ended at about 9:00 P.M., it was quite dark outside. The participants were chatting as they prepared to leave when one of the men in the group turned to me and said, "Need a walk out to your car?" (Group 4). This well-meaning offer encapsulates the ideas discussed in this article. In just a few, indirect words, this speaker suggested that women are vulnerable and unable to take care of themselves, and that therefore they need protection by men (and that men, in turn, are capable of protecting women and have a responsibility to do so). His simple question reproduces shared ideas about vulnerability and danger, and reaffirms the perceived reality of a world in which women's fear is rational and expected; only in such a reality does the statement make sense. Through everyday talk such as this, ideas about gender, vulnerability, and dangerousness are transmitted and reaffirmed. The fact that these beliefs are maintained in the face of empirical evidence to the contrary speaks to the powerful role of discourse in constructing and reproducing gender.

NOTES

1. It should be noted that women's fear does parallel their victimization in one important respect: overwhelmingly, women are both victimized by and report fearing men.

2. I do not mean to suggest that women's fears are baseless. Violence against women, especially sexual violence, is widespread. Noting the discrepancy between risk and fear does not imply that women are unnecessarily afraid; rather, it suggests that fear is created by factors other than a purely "rational" calculation of risk.

3. It is important to note that although on average women report substantially more fear than men do, this does not mean that all women are afraid (Burton 1998). The question of why some women have substantially greater fear than others is a separate question deserving of further research.

4. Gender operates at multiple, mutually reinforcing levels, including as a characteristic of individuals, an interactional activity and expectation, asocial institution and ideology, and a system of hierarchy (Lorber 1994). In this article, I use the term *gender* to refer to all of these levels. I focus, however, on the conceptual and ideological level of gender, what Lorber calls "gender imagery."

5. It should be noted, however, that in calling attention to this violence, some early feminist writers themselves inscribed vulnerability as an inherent condition of the female body and dangerousness as an inherent condition of the male body (Burton 1998).

6. The sex of the facilitator matched that of the group participants: Female facilitators conducted the all-female groups, and male facilitators conducted the all-male groups. Mixed-sex groups were also conducted by female facilitators. When possible, the facilitator also matched the participants on other salient social characteristics such as race and sexual identity.

7. All participants completed a detailed written survey before attending the focus group discussion. The survey included questions on the participants' experiences with violence, fear of violence, media exposure, and demographic characteristics. Because responses to survey questions are not analyzed in this article, I have not described the survey in great detail. See Hollander (1997) for a much fuller discussion of the survey and its administration.

8. The fact that vulnerability and dangerousness are perceived to be located in physical bodies does suggest, however, that changing beliefs about bodies may provide a way to change ideas about gender and vulnerability. For example, participation in sports and learning self-defense techniques may change women's perceptions of their physical abilities and, as a result, decrease their perceived vulnerability. This possibility is supported by other research (McCaughey 1997; McDaniel 1993) but deserves further investigation.

REFERENCES

Altheide, David L. 1997. The news media, the problem frame, and the production of fear. *Sociological Quarterly* 38: 647–68.

Bart, Pauline B., and Patricia H. O'Brien. 1985. *Stopping rape: Successful survival strategies.* Elmsford, NY: Pergamon.

Brooks Gardner, Carol. 1995. *Passing by: Gender and public harassment.* Berkeley: University of California Press.

Brownmiller, Susan. 1975. *Against our will: Men, women, and rape.* New York: Simon & Schuster.

Bureau of Justice Statistics. 1995. *Source book of criminal justice statistics 1994.* Washington, DC: U.S. Department of Justice.

Burton, Nadya. 1998. Resistance to prevention: Reconsidering feminist antiviolence rhetoric. In *Violence against women: Philosophical perspectives,* ed. S. G. French, W. Teays, and L. M. Purdy. Ithaca: Cornell University Press.

Burton Nelson, Mariah. 1994. *The stronger women get, the more men love football.* New York: Harcourt Brace.

Connell, R. W. 1987. *Gender and power: Society, the person, and sexual politics.* Stanford: Stanford University Press.

Covington, Jeanette, and Ralph B. Taylor. 1991. Fear of crime in urban residential neighborhoods: Implications of between- and within-neighborhood sources for current models. *Sociological Quarterly* 32: 23–149.

Eagly, Alice H., and Valeriel J. Steffen. 1986. Gender and aggressive behavior: A meta-analytic review of the social psychological literature. *Psychological Bulletin* 100: 309–30.

England, Paula. 1993. *Theory on gender/feminism on theory.* New York: Aldine.

Ferraro, Kenneth F. 1996. Women's fear of victimization: Shadow of sexual assault? *Social Forces* 75: 667–90.

Gamson, William A. 1992. *Talking politics.* Cambridge: Cambridge University Press.

Goodey, Jo. 1995. Fear of crime: Children and gendered socialization. In *Gender and crime,* ed. R. E. Dobash, R. P. Dobash, and L. Noaks. Cardiff, UK: University of Wales.

Gordon, Margaret T., and Stephanie Riger. 1989. *The female fear: The social cost of rape.* Urbana: University of Illinois Press.

Heath, Linda, and Kevin Gilbert. 1996. Mass media and fear of crime. *American Behavioral Scientist* 39: 379–86.

Heath, Linda, Margaret T. Gordon, and R. LeBailly. 1981. What newspapers tell us (and don't tell us) about rape. *Newspaper Research Journal* 2: 48–55.

Hollander, Jocelyn A. 1997. Discourses of danger: The construction and performance of gender through talk about violence. Ph.D. diss., University of Washington, Seattle.

Jenness, Valerie, and Kendal Broad. 1994. Antiviolence activism and the (in)visibility of gender in the gay/lesbian and women's movements. *Gender & Society* 8: 402–23.

Kessler, Susan J., and Wendy McKenna. 1978. *Gender: An ethnomethodological approach.* New York: John Wiley.

Koss, Mary P. 1988. Hidden rape: Sexual aggression and victimization in a national sample of students in higher education. In *Rape and sexual assault,* Vol. 2, ed. A. Burgess. New York: Garland.

Lorber, Judith. 1993. Believing is seeing: Biology as ideology. *Gender & Society* 7: 568–81.

———. 1994. *Paradoxes of gender.* New Haven: Yale University Press.

MacKinnon, Catherine. 1989. *Toward a feminist theory of the state.* Cambridge, MA: Harvard University Press.

Madriz, Esther I. 1997. *Nothing bad happens to good girls: Fear of crime in women's lives.* Berkeley: University of California Press.

Marx Ferree, Myra, Judith Lorber, and Beth B. Hess. 1999. *Revisioning gender.* Thousand Oaks, CA: Sage.

McCaughey, Martha. 1997. *Real knock outs: The physical feminism of women's self-defense.* New York: New York University Press.

McDaniel, Patricia. 1993. Self defense training and women's fear of crime. *Women's Studies International Forum* 16: 37–45.

Mezey, Gillian C., and Michael B. King. 1992. *Male victims of sexual assault.* Oxford: Oxford University Press.

Morgan, David L. 1988. *Focus groups as qualitative research.* Newbury Park, CA: Sage.

Newhart Smith, Lynn, and Gary D. Hill. 1991. Victimization and fear of crime. *Criminal Justice and Behavior* 18: 217–39.

Pain, Rachel H. 1995. Elderly women and fear of violent crime: The least likely victims? A reconsideration of the extent and nature of risk. *British Journal of Criminology* 35: 584–97.

Pain, R. 1997. Whither women's fear? Perceptions of sexual violence in public and private space. *International Review of Victimology* 4: 297–312.

Russell, Diana E. H. 1975. *The politics of rape: The victim's perspective.* New York: Stein and Day.

Sasson, Theodore. 1995. *Crime talk: How citizens construct a social problem.* New York: Aldine.

Sheffield, Carol J. 1987. Sexual terrorism: The social control of women. In *Analyzing gender,* ed. B. B. Hess and M. M. Ferree. Newbury Park, CA: Sage.

Skogan, Wesley G. 1995. Crime and the racial fears of white Americans. *Annals of the American Academy of Political and Social Science* 539: 59–71.

Spelman, Elizabeth V. 1988. *Inessential woman: Problems of exclusion in feminist thought.* Boston: Beacon.

St. John, Craig, and Tamara Heald-Moore. 1996. Racial prejudice and fear of criminal victimization by strangers in public settings. *Sociological Inquiry* 66: 267–84.

Stanko, Elizabeth A. 1992. The case of fearful women: Gender, personal safety, and fear of crime. *Women and Criminal Justice* 4: 117–35.

———. 1995. Women, crime, and fear. *Annals of the American Academy of Political and Social Science* 539: 46–58.

———. 1997. Safety talk: Conceptualizing women's risk assessment as a "technology of the soul." *Theoretical Criminology* 1: 479–99.

Stanko, Elizabeth A., and Paul Curry. 1997. Homophobic violence and the self "at risk": Interrogating the boundaries. *Social and Legal Studies* 6: 513–32.

Stanko, Elizabeth A., and Kathy Hobdell. 1993. Assault on men: Masculinity and male victimization. *British Journal of Criminology* 33: 400–15.

Tjaden, Patricia. and Nancy Thoennes. 1998. *Prevalence, incidence, and consequences of violence against women: Findings from the National Violence against Women Survey.* Washington, DC: National Institute of Justice.

U.S. Bureau of the Census. 1992. *1990 census of population and housing.* Washington, DC: U.S. Department of Commerce, Economies and Statistics Administration.

Valentine, Gill. 1992. Images of danger: Women's sources of information about the spatial distribution of male violence. *Area* 24: 22–29.

———. 1997. "Oh yes I can." "Oh no you can't": Children's and parents' understanding of kids' competence to negotiate public space safely. *Antipode* 29: 65–89.

Warr, Mark. 1984. Fear of victimization: Why are women and the elderly more afraid? *Social Science Quarterly* 65: 681–702.

———. 1985. Fear of rape among urban women. *Social Problems* 32: 238–50.

———. 1992. Altruistic fear of victimization in households. *Social Science Quarterly* 73: 723–36.

Yin, Peter P. 1982. Fear of crime as a problem for the elderly. *Social Problems* 30: 240–45.

CHAPTER 17

Some Thoughts by an Unrepentant "Positivist" Who Considers Herself a Feminist Nonetheless

JANET SALTZMAN CHAFETZ

I begin with my catechism, so that those of you who have strong intellectual commitments antithetical to my own strong ones can turn off your hearing aids and meditate on other issues for the next fifteen–twenty minutes if you wish.

1. I believe that a fundamental purpose of sociology is the development and testing of theory.
2. I believe that the purpose of sociological theory is to enhance our ability to explain empirical regularities—including similarities and variability among social categories/collectivities, as well as the origins, processes that maintain, and those that change patterned behavior, across time and space.
3. I believe that theoretical constructs should be defined clearly so that methods of operationalization are relatively apparent, and that constants and variables should be demarcated and conceptualized clearly as one or the other.
4. I believe that theories ought to be stated in formal terms so that they may be tested and potentially falsified or revised.
5. I believe that the application of theory to explain a set of findings is not the same as the testing of theory (or theories) and that the latter is more important than the former for theoretical development and hence the development of our discipline and substantive specialty.
6. I believe that before theoretical development can occur, empirically relevant theoretical questions must be clearly formulated.
7. I believe that the variety of extant social (including gender/feminist) theories may all offer important insights, but that whether they do is an empirical question, and one to be answered by systematically testing alternative explanations of the same phenomenon.
8. I also believe that we should abandon our almost religious commitments to particular theoretical perspectives and become more catholic in our use

and integration of the variety of available approaches to address specific questions.

9. Finally, I believe that it is very difficult to live up to these eight canons, that we all "sin" regularly, but that they provide the standards toward which we should aspire.
10. Finally, finally, I believe that our special training as sociologists means that our greatest possible contribution to feminist activism comes from developing the most intellectually cogent and empirically supported theories of gender possible; *that our major contribution is first and foremost intellectual.*

From this catechism, one may surmise a few things in which I do not believe:

1. Along with Epstein (1988) and Coser (1989), I do not believe that there is a particular method of theorizing about the social world that is inherently masculine, feminine or feminist (although there are topics, questions, interests, insights and interpretations that may sometimes reflect those labels, most especially the label "feminist").
2. I do not believe that the following kinds of discussions constitute theory (although, up to a point, they are important precursors to the development of theory and methodology): explications or critiques of extant theories; epistemological discussions; and those that concern the issues, types of variables, techniques, etc. of theorizing that ought to be used or addressed.
3. I do not believe we gender/feminist sociologists have yet made much progress in developing and testing the kind of theory I propose, although most of the theoretical and empirical tools necessary to do so have become well developed during the last twenty years.

THE UNREPENTANT "POSITIVIST"

Among sociologists, the term "positivism" seems to be used and maligned more often than it is clearly defined. In its original sociological application by Saint-Simon and Comte, it meant the search for universally applicable laws to explain empirically verifiable knowledge. It meant the abandonment of the search for absolute causes—especially theological—and a concentration on "observation of the social and physical world in the search for the laws governing them" (Ritzer 1988, 13). Underlying this is the assumption that there exist timeless and invariant properties of the social universe—human action, interaction and organization—that sociologists can come to understand (Turner 1985, 24 and 30). "Positivism" has taken on additional meanings since the nineteenth century, specifically by "antipositivist" Sociologists, including a stance of ostensible value neutrality that tends, in fact, toward social conservatism (Ritzer 1983, 261, an accusation that historically has not even been accurate according to Randall Collins, personal communication). It has become an ideologically and politically charged term in our discipline, such that few dare to apply the label to themselves for fear of being presumed to hold "suspect" sociopolitical views. But if we take it in its original meaning, the search for universally applicable laws of human behavior, I think that it remains a highly useful—albeit not the only—way to proceed with developing a sociological understanding of gender (among other topics). I am not proclaiming that humans are the same as rocks, trees, or chemicals. Nor am I asserting that unique histories and cultures are important contexts within which human action—individual and collective—must be understood.

I am, however, asserting that many regularities or uniformities do exist pan historically and cross-culturally, and that sociologists can both document and explain these with law-like statements that enter into theories (a somewhat more modest vision than that of Comte). Moreover, they exist regardless of peoples' perceptions or evaluations of them (for instance, practically all feminists agree, in their everyday, commonsense view of the world, that women are "oppressed" in "patriarchal" systems even when they exhibit "false gender consciousness" by not recognizing their "oppression"). I further assert that, while many phenomena of interest to gender sociologists do not share these properties, many important ones do and should be examined "positivistically."

For instance, there are apparently a relatively small number of constructs that explain most of the observed variance in the level of gender stratification across time and space (defined as unequal access by women, relative to male social peers, to the scarce and valued resources of their collectivity). The chief constructs of which law-like statements regarding the level of gender stratification can be/perhaps have already been developed concern features of the gender division of labor, ideology, technology, the economy, and family structure (see, for instance, Blumberg 1984; Huber 1988; Chafetz 1984). Some level—ranging from near equality to extensive stratification disadvantaging women—exists everywhere, and that level is strongly influenced by the same types of processes, regardless of whether women and/or men perceive it or how they evaluate it in particular times and places. Blumberg provides another example in her theorizing about women's relative power, and especially autonomy within marital relationships (1988). She uses as her primary explanatory construct the relative "economic power" of women, in a substantially formalized theory that she has tested cross-culturally. My own work with Dworkin (1986) suggests that there are a small number of structural variables (level of industrialization, urbanization, and size of the middle class) that serve as independent constructs in the explanation of the emergence of women's movements, the size to which they grow, and the radicalness of the dominant movement ideology, again across both time and space. We also delineated two political phenomena (repression and co-optation) that, when present, counteract the effects of the independent constructs. As a final example, in my most recent work (1990) I attempt to account for change (over time) in the level of gender inequality in any one society. I argue that change in one or more primarily economic and demographic factors affects the demand for women's resource-generating labor, which in turn (through a complex set of intervening constructs) increases or reduces gender stratification, depending on the direction of change in demand.

These examples refer to patterned regularities which take different values in different times, places, and among subpopulations in a given time and place, and to the processes that connect them. In other words, both the independent and dependent constructs are what we normally think of as structural properties. A full theory explaining structural dependent constructs (e.g., the emergence and growth of women's movements, cross-societal variation and intra-societal change in the level of gender stratification) requires social psychological and micro-interactional intervening constructs as transmission mechanisms. After all, most structural variables are abstractions from the ways in which real people usually behave in the vast multitude of concrete, everyday interactions in which they find themselves. For regular behavioral patterns to change into some other regular pattern, large numbers of people must probably change their ways of thinking, defining situations, assessing self and others, etc. But I am in no way uncomfortable in assuming that, regardless of time and place, similar structural features often produce substantially (never totally) similar individual-level definitions, reactions, cognitions, evaluations, and so on, that is, micro-level processes, which in turn induce predictably similar structural results. From my examination of the historical and cross-cultural research in the gender literature, there appears to be substantial evidence to back up this assumption.

Of course, each case, whether individuals or collectivities, will vary in some ways from other cases. Unique histories, cultures, contexts, and individual experiences *are* relevant to understanding any human phenomenon. To say that is to raise the issue of focus. If the focus is on a *deep* understanding of one or a few cases, then one must attend to all of its (their) unique elements. However, I believe that the primary purpose of theory is to understand how much can be explained while ignoring that which is unique to each case; how much variance can general, panhistorical and cross-cultural structures and processes explain? This is parallel to the distinction in the study of biological evolution between the delineation of theoretical processes, such as random mutation and natural selection, and understanding the unique and highly contingent evolution of any one specific type of organism. While unlike Comte we can assume that we will never be able to understand all the variance in any social phenomenon on the basis of general principles, I think that in many instances the amount that can be explained with reference to such generalizations is substantial. It is in this sense that I call myself an "unrepentant positivist."

THE CURRENT STATE OF GENDER THEORY

In *Feminist Sociology* (1988) I was able to show a remarkably wide range of theoretical approaches feminist sociologists have developed or used during the last twenty years. Variants of Marxist, Weberian, Freudian, Exchange, Symbolic Interactionist, Labeling, Dramaturgical, Ethnomethodological, Social Role, Social Learning, and Cognitive Developmental theories have all been revised, expanded, or just plain applied to issues of gender. Clearly, we are not lacking in theoretical tools.

Like our discipline in general, however, theory in gender sociology today is marked by several problems that impede its further development. In the remainder of my chapter I will discuss five of these: 1) the lack of a coherent and clearly defined set of conceptual terms; 2) the lack of a coherent set of clearly defined theoretical questions toward the answers to which we devote our energies; 3) the attachment of individual scholars to particular theoretical camps and therefore 4) the paucity of integrated theories that systematically incorporate the variety of perspectives at diverse levels of analysis; and finally 5) the paucity of systematic tests of alternative theoretical approaches to, or explanations of given phenomena.

Conceptual Terms

Without well-conceptualized and defined theoretical terms (constructs/concepts), theory is vague and untestable. Sociological theory abounds with poorly conceptualized terms and truth-asserting definitions, as well as the almost constant problem of reification (see Blumer 1956; Gibbs 1989). Gender sociology is heir to these same problems. Consider three of our more commonly used terms: patriarchy, sex/gender role, and sexism (everything said about these could readily be applied to another commonly used term: the oppression of women or female oppression).

Depending on the writer, "patriarchy" may refer to an ideology—secular or religious—or to one or more properties of the economy, polity and family structure, or to some combination thereof. To the extent that it subsumes more than one of these, it is truth-asserting; that is, an empirical hypothesis about the relationship between these varied phenomena is smuggled into a definition, and thereby assumed to be "true." Since the term refers to an abstract property that is distilled from human behaviors, including utterances, it is reification to use any active verb after "patriarchy" (e.g., patriarchy creates, causes, encourages, requires, needs), a frequent practice in the literature. Nor do we usually find scholars using the term quantitatively (higher or lower amounts of patriarchy). If it is a constant, how do we understand either the variability in gender inequality so clearly demonstrated by anthropologists, or change in the level of such inequality short of absolute equality? Do only two kinds of systems exist? patriarchal and non-patriarchal?

The term "sex/gender role" repeats these problems. It is never—and as far as I can see cannot ever be—used with a quantitative logic: the greater/higher the level of gender roles? In the absence of a quantitative logic, it is difficult to see how the construct can be used theoretically to understand variability among or change in gender systems. Men and women do indeed perform different *social* roles in most times and places, the specifics of which vary over space and change over time. However, the concept gender roles is not used to denote this phenomenon per se. To the extent that the term purports to refer to expected behaviors attached to the ascribed status of gender/sex, it reifies to the point of stereotyping. Not only do such expectations vary widely from one time and place to another, there is substantial variability across subpopulations (racial, class, ethnic, religious, regional) in one complex society, and probably from one context or situation to another (is gender role behavior appropriate between a woman and her male boss the same as appropriate behavior between the same woman and a male family friend? a male child? her brother? her father?). The term makes it too easy to confuse stereotypes and real behaviors, assuming the latter to reflect the former. Gender roles are sometimes defined, and especially measured in terms of a set of traits thought to characterize masculinity and femininity for a given time and place. This assumes the co-variance of such traits and is therefore truth-asserting, a conceptual problem not solved by use of scaling techniques such as factor analysis. More importantly, this practice tends to conceptually exaggerate real (observable) differences, short-shrifting or ignoring overlap in particular traits that is often so substantial that more variation exists within each gender than between most males and most females. Indeed, even when they don't employ the term "gender role," many contemporary gender theories are guilty of conceptually exaggerating male-female differences on the basis of flimsy or no empirical evidence, and ignoring the enormous variability within each gender (e.g., Chodorow 1978; Gilligan 1982; Johnson 1988; see Epstein 1988 for a discussion of this). Indeed, I think that this form of exaggeration is today one of the major impediments to the further development of gender theory.

"Sexism" is so vague as to be theoretically useless. Individuals, organizational practices, theories, books, advertisements, religions, educational practices, indeed, practically everything has been referred to somewhere along the line as "sexist." Does the term refer to prejudiced attitudes, discriminatory behaviors, institutional practices? Like "patriarchy," "sexism" is often inappropriately linked with an active verb. Such reification makes it sound like an explanation is being offered when in fact nothing concrete is being uttered. To reiterate: we cannot go very far in theorizing with terms so fraught with problems and carelessly used. Without clear analytical distinctions we are unable to pose (not to mention attempt to answer) questions concerning the processes that connect the various components of gender systems.

Theoretical Questions

Sociology in general, including our specialty, is inclined to spinning off myriad answers which go in search of an interesting and important central question or set of questions. Some theorists ask how children become engendered, while another group tries to explain the level of wives' power or autonomy in the household; still others want to understand how capitalism and patriarchy affect and support one another; some want to understand why women earn less than men or are segregated in the labor force; still others try to explain how interpersonal interactions between women and men reinforce gender arrangements; why has the women's movement emerged? what explains female antifeminism? What explains male violence against women? The list of questions is apparently endless, and they vary on a continuum from relatively abstract and general to little more than empirical-level issues specific to one or a few times/places. While these questions are interesting and of practical importance, they collectively do not add up to a coherent understanding of anything. We need to develop broader theoretical questions that subsume these particulars and place them in a context. To do so, we need constructs that are not only more precise, but sufficiently abstract to encompass a variety of the particulars involved in more narrowly focused theories.

We currently do have one broad question that appears to have achieved substantial consensus about its importance: how do race, class and gender intersect? In the last few years conferences, journal issues, and meeting sessions have devoted substantial time and space to this issue. Without for a moment denying the importance of the topic, or its theoretical promise, I suggest that it has yet to be formulated as a question about which systematic *theorizing* (as distinct from empirical, mostly descriptive research) is possible; it is simply too vaguely stated. Coming to grips with this topic at the theoretical level is probably the major agenda item for this decade.

Theoretical Camps and Lack of Theoretical Synthesis

The majority of sociological, including gender theorists pin a label on themselves: Marxist- or Socialist-Feminist, Neo-Freudian, Critical Theorist, Symbolic Interactionist, etc. While they do not totally ignore one another (Chodorow's ideas, for instance, seem to find their way into an astounding array of other types of theories), there is a paucity of attempts to genuinely integrate the rich array of theoretical insights available from these different schools. By its nature, theory always produces "blinders" by focusing attention on some phenomena and ignoring or short-shrifting others. But it seems to me that in our discipline we often go too far in this by defining our perspective as "truth" and the others as misguided, irrelevant—or worse. My impression is that gender sociologists are less bound by theoretical camps than those in many other specialties in our discipline. Nonetheless, we waste considerable time and effort criticizing other approaches rather than getting on with the business of building actual theories that attempt to explain something. Each perspective is characterized by a set of questions that differs—or at least appears to differ—from those posed by other theoretical approaches. When we ask broad enough and clear enough theoretical questions, I am confident that we will find that most of our theoretical perspectives offer important pieces in constructing the answers.

In *Feminist Sociology* (1988) I organized my review of gender theories around four broad issues: 1) the origins of gender inequality (which is probably better conceptualized as explanations of variability in the level of gender inequality); 2) mechanisms which maintain systems of gender differentiation and inequality; 3) the consequences of the gender system for other features of social life; and 4) change in systems of gender inequality. Every gender theory addresses one or more of these issues, at least implicitly. I think that if we could agree that these *are* the fundamental theoretical questions we seek to answer, we could advance our theoretical development substantially. First, we would be better able to place within one or more broad contexts the multitude of more narrow theoretical issues with which we have been dealing. For instance, theory that addresses the rise and growth of women's movements would be subsumed within a broader theory of how systems of gender stratification change. Those dealing with childhood engenderment would be incorporated into a broader theory of how systems of gender inequality maintain themselves. Second, mechanisms to integrate and synthesize existing theories would also become more readily apparent as the issues around which such integration should occur would be clear. For instance, endless discussion of the need to integrate "macro" and "micro" theories, and strategies for doing so have occurred in sociology recently—almost always in the abstract. When I confronted concrete, substantive issues while writing *Gender Equity*, techniques for such integration became apparent. Finally, remaining issues requiring theoretical development in order to enhance our understanding of the broad ones would become more obvious.

In *Gender Equity* (1990) I attempted to accomplish these goals by focusing on issues 2 and especially 4: maintenance mechanisms and change processes. I found theories from virtually every tradition, and concerning every level of analysis useful in the process. It was more or less like putting together a jigsaw puzzle, with the addition of the need to create some pieces that were not already available. For instance, I found no theory that directly dealt with the issue of how, specifically, women's movements contribute to change at the macro-level. It is normally just assumed that they do—as if by magic. I might add that in order to begin to accomplish my goals (and only you can ultimately judge how successful I may have been) I had to employ a set of constructs and definitions, many of which are not entirely conventional among gender sociologists.

Theory Testing

Finally, gender sociologists evince relatively little effort toward systematic theory testing, and especially toward testing different explanations of the same phenomenon (with the notable exception of explanations of the male-female wage gap, which, as *theoretical* issues go, is not very abstract). We routinely apply theory to a set of findings—often ex post facto. By doing this, theory is almost always "supported"; only an explicit test is likely to falsify a theory or allow us to refine it. We in fact have a number of competing explanations for various phenomena, for instance, the question of how systems of gender inequality maintain and reproduce themselves. Some theories look primarily to childhood engenderment (with substantial differences among them), others to economic/labor force phenomena, some to family structure, still others to ideological or cultural phenomena as the major independent constructs. To my knowledge, no one has begun the difficult but fundamentally important job of empirically examining which of these clusters of variables is more important in maintaining (or changing) systems of gender inequity; which constitute independent and which intervening constructs? What kinds of feedback mechanisms exist? Merely asserting that all are related to each other and all contribute to maintaining gender inequality is, while undoubtedly accurate, too vague to constitute good theory. It is intellectual laziness to proclaim that everything is related to everything, and leave it at that.

CONCLUSION

The current state of gender theory is one full of variety and rich potential, yet marred by a lack of clarity, rigor, and data-based, sequential development and refinement. I believe that these shortcomings, in turn, are in substantial measure a result of the fact that so many gender theorists reject out of hand the "positivistic" view of theory I am propounding. "Positivism" has become a dirty word in our discipline and our specialty. In part this has happened because of the erroneous confusion of this term with the kind of mindless empiricism that has marked so much sociological research. I believe that theory development and well-crafted, theoretically oriented research go hand-in-hand, and that this is in fact what "positivism" is all about.

I think that a more fundamental reason that "positivism" is a dirty word for many gender sociologists is a conviction that the kind of sociology I support, having been developed and practiced primarily by men, is therefore "masculine" and inherently antithetical to a feminist commitment or consciousness (e.g., Stacey and

Thorne 1985). "Positivism" is defined as treating research subjects as "objects" external to, and manipulated by researchers. It is said to be an instrument of control rather than of liberation (e.g., see Smith 1987, 1989; Farganis 1986). Ironically, this criticism was well-developed by the mid 1970s by many male sociologists who could scarcely be defined—nor would they have defined themselves—as feminist.

First of all, I see nothing in the view that patterned behaviors and processes exist, can be measured, and can be explained in substantial measure cross-culturally and pan-historically that *automatically* denigrates or controls people. Unless one wishes to assert that we are all potentially such totally free agents that our social environment need have no effect on us, it is incumbent upon us to examine those effects as they usually occur, and try to understand why they do. Indeed, the possibility that people can be freed from social constraints is heightened by understanding better how such constraints usually work. Despite epistemological discussions of a peculiarly feminist method of doing sociology, much feminist research in fact examines precisely the external social constraints confronted by women. In general, I think that this criticism blames the messenger for the message. There is no question that issues pertinent to women have often been ignored or addressed in a biased manner in the history of our discipline, and that as a result an inequitable gender system has been supported by much traditional sociology. However, this is not a criticism of "positivism" as much as it is of two other phenomena: 1) the people who have misapplied it (done their work poorly); and 2) the biases that result from the historical exclusion of whole categories of people, including women, whose experiences, perceptions and interests arise from different locations within the social structure from that of the white males who long dominated the field. However, we need not throw out a method or approach in order to correct the biases that historically have been associated with it (a principle widely accepted by those feminist theorists who have revised the heavily misogynistic theory developed by Freud, and Marxian theory that ignored issues of gender and reproduction).

Second, "feminism" means many different things, and about the only component that I have seen which unites all who apply that label to themselves is a general commitment to battle any practice which they perceive as disadvantaging or devaluing females. There is not even consensus over what those practices might be in some concrete instances (e.g., pornography). I see a lot of discussion of, but no consensus about or good data supporting the idea that there is a peculiarly female or feminist *method* (as distinct from topics) of thinking, doing research, or doing theory in sociology; that there are masculine and feminine ways of knowing that are distinctly different; that qualitative and case study research and interpretive theory constitute feminist sociology, while quantitative methods and structural theories are masculine. Unless we are in the business of proclaiming that, despite people's self-definitions, they aren't "really feminists" if they to not accept a particular epistemology, I doubt whether we will ever witness such consensus.

I for one remain unconvinced that our understanding of gender will be advanced by abandoning the attempt at careful construction and testing of theory along the lines that I have defined as "positivistic." The alternatives appear to me to be speculation and vague, unfalsifiable "metatheory," on the one hand, and endless description of phenomena assumed to be unique, on the other. I'm afraid we have plenty of both in our discipline and specialty. The latter is not fundamentally different from the mindless empiricism we all bemoan, even if numbers aren't crunched and the data are qualitative, historical, cultural and/or "contextual." The former sends us scurrying back to the eighteenth century and our armchairs. I believe that it is through the combined use of "positivistic" and other approaches to the study of gender that we are most likely to develop to our full potential empirically credible theory that can best inform our activist efforts toward change. Let us end the epistemological navel-gazing and use all the techniques available to us—including those of "positivism"—to advance our theoretical understanding of gender.

REFERENCES

Blumberg, Rae Lesser. 1984. A general theory of gender stratification. In *Sociological Theory,* ed. R. Collins, 23–101. San Francisco: Jossey-Bass.

———. 1988. Income under female versus male control hypotheses from a theory of gender stratification and data from the third world. *Journal of Family Issues* 9: 51–84.

Blumer, Herbert. 1956. Sociological analysis and its variables. *American Sociological Review* 21: 683–90.

Chafetz, Janet Saltzman. 1984. *Sex and advantage: A comparative macro-structural theory of sex stratification.* Totowa, NJ: Rowman and Allanheld.

———. 1988. *Feminist sociology: An overview of contemporary theories.* Itasca, IL: F.E. Peacock.

———. 1990. *Gender equity: A theory of stability and change.* Newbury Park, CA: Sage.

Chafetz, Janet Saltzman, and A. Gary Dworkin. 1986. *Female revolt: Women's movements in world and historical perspective.* Totowa, NJ: Rowman and Allanheld.

Chodorow, Nancy. 1978. *The reproduction of mothering: Psychoanalysis and the sociology of gender.* Berkeley: University of California Press.

Coser, Rose Laub. 1989. Reflections on feminist theory. In *Feminism and sociological theory,* ed. Ruth Wallace, 200–207. Newbury Park, CA: Sage.

Epstein, Cynthia Fuchs. 1988. *Deceptive distinctions: Sex, gender, and the social order.* New Haven: Yale University Press.

Farganis, Sandra. 1986. Social theory and feminist theory: The need for dialogue. *Sociological Inquiry* 56 (1): 50–68.

Gibbs, Jack P. 1989. *Control: Sociology's central notion.* Urbana, IL: University of Illinois Press.

Gilligan, Carol. 1982. *In a different voice.* Cambridge, MA: Harvard University Press.

Huber, Joan. 1988. A theory of family, economy, and gender. *Journal of Family Issues* 9 (1): 9–26.

Johnson, Miriam M. 1988. *Strong mother weak wives: The search for gender equality.* Berkeley: University of California Press.

Ritzer, George. 1983. *Sociological theory.* New York: Alfred A. Knopf.

———. 1988. *Contemporary sociological theory.* 2nd ed. New York: Alfred A. Knopf.

Smith, Dorothy. 1987. *The everyday world as problematic: A feminist sociology.* Boston: Northeastern University Press.

———. 1989. Sociological theory: Methods of writing patriarchy. In *Feminism and sociological theory,* ed. Ruth Wallace, 34–64. Newbury Park, CA: Sage.

Stacey, Judith, and Barrie Thorne. 1985. The missing feminist revolution in sociology. *Social Problems* 32: 301–16.

Turner, Jonathan. 1985. In defense of positivism. *Sociological theory* 3: 24–30.

CHAPTER 18

The Blacker the Berry

Gender, Skin Tone, Self-Esteem, and Self-Efficacy

MAXINE S. THOMPSON AND VERNA M. KEITH

> She should have been a boy, then color of skin wouldn't have mattered so much, for wasn't her mother always saying that a Black boy could get along, but that a Black girl would never know anything but sorrow and disappointment? But she wasn't a boy; she was a girl, and color did matter, mattered so much that she would rather have missed receiving her high school diploma than have to sit as she now sat, the only odd and conspicuous figure on the auditorium platform of the Boise high school . . .
>
> Get a diploma?—What did it mean to her? College?—Perhaps. A job?—Perhaps again. She was going to have a high school diploma, but it would mean nothing to her whatsoever. (Thurman 1929, 4–5)

Wallace Thurman (1929) speaking through the voice of the main character, Emma Lou Morgan, in his novel, "The Blacker the Berry," about skin color bias within the African American community, asserts that the disadvantages and emotional pain of being "dark skinned" are greater for women than men and that skin color, not achievement, determines identity and attitudes about the self. Thurman's work describes social relationships among African Americans that were shaped by their experiences in the white community during slavery and its aftermath. In the African American community, skin color, an ascribed status attribute, played an integral role in determining class distinctions. Mulattoes, African Americans with white progenitors, led a more privileged existence when compared with their Black counterparts, and in areas of the Deep South (most notably Louisiana and South Carolina), mulattoes served as a buffer class between whites and Blacks (Russell, Wilson, and Hall 1992). In *Black Bourgeoisie,* Frazier (1957) describes affluent organized clubs within the Black community called "blue vein" societies. To be accepted into these clubs, skin tone was required to be lighter than a "paper bag" or light enough for visibility of "blue veins" (Okazawa Rey, Robinson, and Ward 1987). Preferential treatment given by both Black and white cultures to African Americans with light skin have conveyed to many Blacks that if they conformed to the white, majority standard of beauty, their lives would be more rewarding (Bond and Cash 1992; Gatewood 1988).

Although Thurman's novel was written in 1929, the issue of *colorism* (Okazawa Rey, Robinson, and Ward 1987), intraracial discrimination based on skin color, continues to divide and shape life experiences within the African American community. The status advantages afforded to persons of light complexion continue despite the political preference for dark skin tones in the Black awareness movement during the 1960s. No longer an unspoken taboo, color prejudice within the African American community has been a "hot" topic of talk shows, novels, and movies and an issue in a court case on discrimination in the workplace (Russell, Wilson, and Hall 1992).[1] In addition to discussions within lay communities, research scholars have had considerable interest in the importance of skin color. At the structural level, studies have noted that skin color is an important determinant of educational and occupational attainment: Lighter-skinned Blacks complete more years of schooling, have more prestigious jobs, and earn more than darker-skinned Blacks (Hughes and Hertel 1990; Keith and Herring 1991). In fact, one study notes that the effect of skin color on earnings of "lighter" and "darker" Blacks is as great as the effect of race on the earnings of whites and all Blacks (Hughes and Hertel 1990). The most impressive research on skin tone effects is studies on skin tone and blood pressure. Using a reflectometer to measure skin color, research has shown that dark skin tone is associated with high blood pressure in African Americans with low socioeconomic status (Klag et al. 1991; Tryoler and James 1978). And at the social-psychological level, studies find that skin color is related to feelings of self-worth and attractiveness, self-control, satisfaction, and quality of life (Bond and Cash 1992; Boyd Franklin 1991; Cash and Duncan 1984; Chambers et al.1994; Neal and Wilson 1989; Okazawa Rey, Robinson, and Ward 1987).

It is important to note that skin color is highly correlated with other phenotypic features—eye color, hair texture, broadness of nose, and fullness of lips. Along with light skin, blue and green eyes, European-shaped noses, and straight as opposed to "kinky" hair are all accorded higher status both within and beyond the African American community. Colorism embodies preference and desire for both light skin as well as these other attendant features. Hair, eye color, and facial features function along with color in complex ways to shape opportunities, norms regarding attractiveness, self-concept, and overall body image. Yet, it is color that has received the most attention in research on African Americans.[2] The reasons for this emphasis are not clear, although one can speculate that it is due to the fact that color is the most visible physical feature and is also the feature that is most enduring and difficult to change. As Russell, Wilson, and Hall (1992) pointed out, hair can be straightened with chemicals, eye color can be changed with contact lenses, and a broad nose can be altered with cosmetic surgery. Bleaching skin to a lighter tone, however, seldom meets with success (Okazawa Rey, Robinson, and Ward 1987). Ethnographic research also suggests that the research focus on skin color is somewhat justified. For example, it played the central role in determining membership in the affluent African American clubs.

Although colorism affects attitudes about the self for both men and women, it appears that these effects are stronger for women than men. In early studies, dark-skinned women were seen as occupying the bottom rungs of the social ladder, least marriageable, having the fewest options for higher education and career advancement, and as more color conscious than their male counterparts (Parrish 1944; Warner, Junker, and Adams 1941). There is very little empirical research on the relationship between gender, skin color, and self-concept development. In this chapter, we evaluate the relative importance of skin color to feelings about the self for men and women within the African American community.

The literature that relates skin tone to self-image has several methodological limitations. First, with the exception of doll preference studies, there is an absence of a systematic body of research on self-concept development. This is particularly true for studies on adults. Inferences about the relationship between skin tone and attitudes about the self are drawn from findings of studies on attitudes about body image, mate or dating preferences, physical attractiveness, and skin tone satisfaction. Second, much of this literature is based on data from descriptive anecdotes of personal accounts, clinical studies, and laboratory studies that use small purposive samples of respondents. Studies using generalizable survey research methodology with nationally representative samples of respondents to examine the relationship between skin tone and self-concept development are rare. Third, the use of limited databases is often joined with a lack of adequate controls for socioeconomic status variables such as education and income. Despite the strong empirical literature that shows that skin tone is an important determinant of socioeconomic status as well as studies that argue that socioeconomic status is an important determinant of self-concept development, researchers have failed to take socioeconomic status into account. Fourth, not all studies employ an objective measure of skin tone. The use of self-reported skin tone may possibly contaminate the observed relationship between skin tone and self-concept outcomes.

Our study addresses several of these limitations. Using an adult sample of respondents who are representative of the national population, we examine the relationship of skin tone to self-concept development. Our analyses employ objective and reliable measures of skin tone, self-concept, and adequate control variables for socioeconomic status. More important, we examine the way in which gender socially constructs the impact of skin tone on self-concept development. The following sections consider the gendered relationships between skin tone and self-concept development and outline the conceptual argument and prior empirical evidence.

Skin Tone and Gender

Issues of skin color and physical attractiveness are closely linked and because expectations of physical attractiveness are applied more heavily to women across all cultures, stereotypes of attractiveness and color preference are more profound for Black women (Warner, Junker, and Adams 1941). In the clinical literature (Boyd Franklin 1991; Grier and Cobbs 1968; Neal and Wilson 1989; Okazawa Rey, Robinson, and Ward 1987), issues of racial identity, skin color, and attractiveness were central concerns of women. The "what is beautiful is good" stereotype creates a "halo" effect for light-skinned persons. The positive glow generated by physical attractiveness includes a host of desirable personality traits. Included in these positive judgments are beliefs that attractive people would be significantly more intelligent, kind, confident, interesting, sexy, assertive, poised, modest, and successful, and they appear to have higher self-esteem and self-worth (Dion, Berscheid, and Walster 1972). When complexion is the indicator of attractiveness, similar stereotypic attributes are found. There is evidence that gender difference in response to the importance of skin color to attractiveness appears during childhood. Girls as young as six are twice as likely as boys to be sensitive to the social importance of skin color (Porter 1971; Russell, Wilson, and Hall 1992, 68). In a study of facial features, skin color, and attractiveness, Neal (cited in Neal and Wilson 1989, 328) found that

> unattractive women were perceived as having darker skin tones than attractive women and that women with more Caucasoid features were perceived as more attractive to the opposite sex, more successful in their love lives and their careers than women with Negroid features.

Frequent exposure to negative evaluations can undermine a woman's sense of self. "A dark skinned Black woman who feels herself unattractive, however, may think that she has nothing to offer society no matter how intelligent or inventive she is" (Russell, Wilson, and Hall 1992, 42).

Several explanations are proffered for gender differences in self-esteem among Blacks. One is that women are socialized to attend to evaluations of others and are vulnerable to negative appraisals. Women seek to validate their selves through appraisal from others more than men do. And the media has encouraged greater negative self-appraisals for dark-skinned women. A second explanation is that colorism and its associated stressors are not the same for dark-skinned men and women. For men, stereotypes associated with perceived dangerousness, criminality, and competence are associated with dark skin tone, while for women the issue is attractiveness (Russell, Wilson, and Hall 1992, 38). Educational attainment is a vehicle by which men might overcome skin color bias, but changes in physical features are difficult to accomplish. Third, women may react more strongly to skin color bias because they feel less control of their lives. Research studies show that women and persons of low status tend to feel fatalistic (Pearlin and Schooler 1978; Turner and Noh 1983) and to react more intensely than comparable others to stressors (Kessler and McLeod 1984; Pearlin and Johnson 1977; Thoits 1982, 1984; Turner and Noh 1983). This suggests a triple jeopardy situation: Black women face problems of racism and sexism, and when these two negative status positions—being Black and being female—combine with colorism, a triple threat lowers self-esteem and feelings of competence among dark Black women.

CONCEPTUAL ARGUMENT

Skin Tone and Self-Evaluation

William James (1890) conceived of the self as an integrating social product consisting of various constituent parts (i.e., the physical, social, and spiritual selves). Body image, the aspect of the self that we recognize first, is one of the major components of the self and remains important throughout life. One can assume that if one's bodily attributes are judged positively, the impact on one's self is positive. Likewise, if society devalues certain physical attributes, negative feelings about the self are likely to ensue. Body image is influenced by a number of factors including skin color, size, and shape. In our society, dark-skinned men and women are raised to believe that "light" skin is preferred. They see very light-skinned Blacks having successful experiences in advertisements, in magazines, in professional positions, and so forth. They are led to believe that "light" skin is the key to popularity, professional status, and a desirable marriage. Russell, Wilson, and Hall (1992) argue that the African American gay and lesbian community is also affected by colorism because a light-skinned or even white mate confers status. Whether heterosexual, gay, or lesbian, colorism may lead to negative self-evaluations among African Americans with dark skin.

Self-evaluations are seen as having two dimensions, one reflecting the person's moral worth and the other reflecting the individual's competency or agency (Gecas 1989). The former refers to self-esteem and indicates how we feel about ourselves. The latter refers to self-efficacy and indicates our belief in the ability to control our own fate. These are two different dimensions in that people can feel that they are good and useful but also feel that what happens to them is due to luck or forces outside themselves.

Self-esteem and Skin Tone

Self-esteem consists of feeling good, liking yourself, and being liked and treated well.[3] Self-esteem is influenced both by the social comparisons we make of ourselves with others and by the reactions that other people have toward us (i.e., reflected appraisals). The self-concept depends also on the attributes of others who are available for comparison. Self-evaluation theory emphasizes the importance of consonant environmental context for personal comparisons; that is, Blacks will compare themselves with other Blacks in their community. Consonant environmental context assumes that significant others will provide affirmation of one's identity and that similarity between oneself and others shapes the self. Thus, a sense of personal connectedness to other African Americans is most important for fostering and reinforcing positive self-evaluations. This explains why the personal self-esteem of Blacks, despite their lower status position, was as high as that of whites (Porter and Washington 1989, 345; Rosenberg and Simmons 1971).[4] It does not explain the possible influence of colorism on self-esteem within the African American community. Evidence suggest that conflictual and dissonant racial environments have negative effects on self-esteem, especially within the working class (Porter and Washington 1989, 346; Verna and Runion 1985). The heterogeneity of skin tone hues and colorism create a dissonant racial environment and become a source of negative self-evaluation.

Self-efficacy and Skin Tone

Self-efficacy, as defined by Bandura (1977, 1982), is the belief that one can master situations and control events. Performance influences self-efficacy such that when faced with a failure, individuals with high self-efficacy generally believe that extra effort or persistence will lead to success (Bandura 1982). However, if failure is related to some stable personal characteristic such as "dark skin color" or social constraints such as blocked opportunities resulting from mainstreaming practices in the workplace, then one is likely to be discouraged by failure and to feel less efficacious than his or her lighter counterparts. In fact, Pearlin and colleagues (1981) argue that stressors that seem to be associated with inadequacy of one's efforts or lack of success are implicated in a diminished sense of self. Problems or hardships "to which people can see no end, those that seem to become fixtures of their existence" pose the most sustained affront to a sense of mastery and self-worth (Pearlin et al.1981, 345). For Bandura, however, individual agency plays a role in sustaining the self. Individuals actively engage in activities that are congenial with a positive sense of self. Self-efficacy results not primarily from beliefs or attitudes about performance but from undertaking challenges and succeeding. Thus, darker-skinned Blacks who experience success in their everyday world (e.g., work, education, etc.) will feel more confident and empowered.

Following the literature, we predict a strong relationship between skin tone and self-esteem and self-efficacy, but the mechanisms are different for the two dimensions. The effect of skin tone on self-efficacy will be partially mediated by occupation and income. The effect will be direct for self-esteem. That is, the direct effect will be stronger for self-esteem than for self-efficacy. Furthermore, we expect a stronger relationship between skin tone and self-esteem for women than men because women's self-esteem is conditioned by the appraisals of others, and the media has encouraged negative appraisals for dark-skinned women.

DATA AND METHOD

The Sample

Data for this study come from the National Survey of Black Americans (NSBA) (Jackson and Gurin 1987). The sample for the survey was drawn according to a multistage-area probability procedure that was designed to ensure that every Black household in the United States had an equal probability of being selected for the study. Within each household in the sample, one person age eighteen or older was randomly selected to be interviewed from among those eligible for the study. Only self-identified Black American citizens were eligible for the study. Face-to-face interviews were carried out by trained Black interviewers, yielding a sample of 2,107 respondents. The response rate was approximately 69 percent. For the most part, the NSBA is representative of the national Black population enumerated in the 1980 census, with the exception of a slight overrepresentation of women and older Blacks and a small underrepresentation of southerners (Jackson, Tucker, and Gurin 1987).

Measures

Dependent Variables

There are two indicators of self-evaluation: *self-esteem* and *self-efficacy*. The NSBA included six items that measure self-esteem. Two items are from Rosenberg's (1979) Self-Esteem Scale: "I feel that I am a person of worth" and "I feel I do not have much to be proud of." Two items are from the Monitoring the Future Project (Bachman and Johnson 1978): "I feel that I can't do anything right" and "I feel that my life is not very useful." Two items measure the worth dimension of self-esteem: "I am a useful person to have around" and "As a person, I do a good job these days." Respondents were asked to indicate whether the statements are *almost always true* (4), *often true* (3), *not often true* (2), and *never true* (1). Negatively worded items were reverse coded so that high values represent positive self-esteem. Items were summed to form a self-esteem scale (α = .66).

Self-efficacy measures the respondents' feelings of control and confidence in managing their own lives. The four questions asked in the NSBA are the most highly correlated (Wright 1976, 107) in a commonly used scale of personal efficacy (for validity of the scale, see J. P. Robinson and Shaver 1969, 102). Each of the four items was followed by two responses:

1. "Do you think it's better to *plan your life a good ways ahead,* or would you say life is *too much a matter of luck to plan ahead very far?*"
2. "When you do make plans ahead, do you usually *get to carry out things the way you expected or do things come up to make you change your plans?*"
3. "Have you usually *felt pretty sure* your life would work out the way you want it to, or have there been times when you *haven't been sure about it?*"
4. "Some people feel they *can run their lives* pretty much the way they want to, others feel the *problems of life are sometimes too big* for them. Which one are you most like?"

The items were summed to form a scale where high values represent a high sense of personal efficacy (α = .57). The positive responses were coded 2, and negative responses were coded 1. Hughes and Demo's (1989, 140) analysis of these data shows that the measure of self-efficacy is empirically distinct from the measure of self-esteem.

Independent Variables

Skin tone is the independent variable of primary interest in this study. Values of skin tone were based on interviewers' observations of respondents' complexions and recorded after the interview. The interviewer was asked to respond to the following: "The [respondent's] skin color is (1) *very dark brown,* (2) *dark brown,* (3) *medium brown,* (4) *light brown* (light skinned), and (5) *very light brown* (very light skinned)." Ninety-eight percent of the respondents were classified according to this scheme. Of those assigned a color rating, 8.5 percent (175) were classified as being very dark brown, 29.9 percent (617) as dark brown, 44.6 percent (922) as medium brown, 14.4 percent (298) as light brown, and 2.6 percent (54) as very light brown. This measurement scheme is similar to other studies that used objective ratings of skin color (Freeman et al. 1966; Udry, Bauman, and Chase 1969).

Three sets of independent variables are used in these analyses: sociodemographic, socioeconomic status, and body image. The sociodemographic variables include age, marital status, region of current residence, and urban area. Age of the respondent is self-reported and measured in years. Marital status is a dummy variable coded 1 for currently married, with those who are not married as the comparison category (0). Region of current residence is collapsed into two categories: South is coded 1, and non-South is coded 0. For the urbanicity variable, respondents were coded 1 if they lived in an urban area and 0 elsewhere.

The second set of variables consists of socioeconomic status variables and includes education, employment, and income. Education of respondents is measured as years of completed schooling, with eighteen categories ranging from 0 to 18 years or more of educational attainment. A dummy variable for employment status is coded 1 for working with pay and 0 for laid off or not working for pay.[5] Personal income was initially coded using seventeen categories ranging from 1 for *no income* to 17 for *income of $30,000 or more.* Each respondent was assigned scores that correspond to the midpoint of his or her income category for personal income. A Pareto curve estimate was used to derive a midpoint for the open-ended categories (see Miller 1964).

Three measures of body image are physical attractiveness, weight, and disabled health status. Interviewers were asked to indicate where the respondent fell on a semantic scale from 1 = *unattractive* to 7 = *attractive.* We recognize that interviewer perceptions of skin tone are likely to affect interviewer perceptions of attractiveness. That is, interviewers probably evaluated lighter skinned African Americans, especially women, as being more attractive. However, this was the only measure in the NSBA. The correlations between skin tone and attractiveness, however, are modest ($r = .13$, $\rho < .01$ for men and $r = .20$, $\rho < .01$ for women), suggesting that they operate somewhat independently. On this basis, we concluded that omitting this information would introduce more bias than the bias produced by their correlation. Respondents' weight is also assessed by interviewers' observations. Interviewers were asked where the respondent fell on a scale from 1 = *underweight* to 7 = *overweight.* Disabled is measured as follows: For each of thirteen medical conditions, respondents were asked, "How much does this health problem keep you from working or carrying out your daily tasks?" The responses were *a great deal* (2), *only a little* (1), or *not at all* (0). High scores indicate greater disability. Table 18.1 shows the means, standard deviations, and correlations of the independent and dependent variables for male and female respondents separately.

Data Analysis

To assess the impact of gender on the relationship between skin tone and self evaluations, we analyze the data separately for men and women.[6] Data analysis consists of a series of ordinary least squares (OLS) regression equations that assess the effects of skin tone on indicators of self-esteem and self-efficacy. A hierarchical multiple regression strategy is used to analyze the data. Successive reduced-form equations are presented for each dependent variable. The first equation looks at the bivariate relationship between skin tone and each dependent variable. Our strategy is to determine how this relationship is altered as successive groups of independent variables are controlled. Therefore, the second equation includes skin tone and the sociodemographic variables. Equation 3 includes skin tone, sociodemographic variables, and socioeconomic status variables. The fourth equation includes all the above plus the body image variables.

RESULTS

Table 18.2 shows the regression of self-efficacy on measures of skin tone, sociodemographic, socioeconomic, and body image variables for men and women sep-

Table 18.1 Correlations, Means, and Standard Deviations by Gender

	1	2	3	4	5	6	7	8	9	10	11	x	SD
Men (n = 647)													
1. Skin tone												2.62	.90
2. Age	.017											41.79	17.70
3. Urban	.089*	−.131**										.77	.42
4. South	.000	.064	−.410**									.55	.50
5. Married	.035	.186**	−.106**	.041								.52	.50
6. Income	.137**	−.023	.229**	−.229**	.257**							10.89	8.74
7. Education	.106**	−.516**	.266**	−.200**	−.001	.402**						11.00	3.76
8. Employed	.021	−.279**	.063	−.009	.148	.357**	.304**					.69	.46
9. Attractiveness	.133**	−.125**	−.017	.037	.084*	.060	.127**	.130**				4.41	1.37
10. Weight	.005	.110**	.038	−.070	.052	.034	−.039	−.012	−.151**			4.02	.91
11. Disabled	−.002	.443**	−.081*	.020	.033	−.138**	−.320**	−.350**	−.072	.107**		1.95	2.96
12. Self-efficacy	.116**	.061	.123**	−.094	.076	.160**	.159**	.017	.055	.013	−.114**	8.26	2.50
13. Self-esteem	.054	.016	−.060	.065	.089*	.123**	.071	.151**	.098*	−.004	−.161**	21.29	2.59
Women (n = 1,036)													
1. Skin tone												2.78	.90
2. Age	−.069*											42.03	17.39
3. Urban	.085**	−.101**										.78	.42
4. South	−.051	.064*	−.407**									.56	.50
5. Married	.034	.006	−.094	.034								.36	.48
6. Income	.139**	−.082**	.226**	−.219**	.044							5.95	5.45
7. Education	.154**	−.490**	.225**	−.142**	.074*	.434**						11.03	3.27
8. Employed	.085**	−.193**	.058	−.021	.087**	.437**	.340**					.52	.50
9. Attractiveness	.196**	−.076*	.017	.042	.037	.094**	.127**	.092′**				4.38	1.47
10. Weight	−.025	.061	−.019	−.008	.006	−.021	−.060	.009	−.205**			4.31	1.13
11. Disabled	−.098**	.404**	−.083**	.049	−.044	−.222**	−.399**	−.332**	−.128	.077*		2.97	3.69
12. Self-efficacy	.061*	.081**	.134**	−.103	.015	.210**	.164**	.087**	.076*	−.024	−.111**	7.75	2.60
13. Self-esteem	.100**	.107**	.012	.021	.005	.135**	.078*	.131 **	.095**	.046	−.159**	21.06	2.55

*$p \leq .05$ (two-tailed test). **$p \leq .01$ (two-tailed test).

Table 18.2 Regression Results for Predicting Self-Efficacy, by Gender

	Men (n = 647)				*Women (n = 1,036)*			
	1	**2**	**3**	**4**	**1**	**2**	**3**	**4**
Skin tone	.325**	.288**	.220*	.208t	.177*	.157t	0.063	0.029
	(.116)	(.103)	(.079)	(.074)	(.061)	(.054)	(.022)	(.010)
Age		0.009	.022***	.030***		.015***	.029***	.033***
		(.063)	(.157)	(.215)		(.100)	(.191)	(0.221)
Urban		.629*	0.406	0.406		.735***	.437*	.437*
		(.106)	(0.068)	(.068)		(.117)	(.070)	(.070)
South		−0.292	−0.137	−0.165		−.313t	−0.179	−0.201
		(−.058)	(−.027)	(−.033)		(−.060)	(−.034)	(−.038)
Married		.372t	0.218	0.206		0.139	0.010	−0.001
		(.074)	(.044)	(.041)		(.026)	(.002)	(−.000)
Income			0.015	0.014			.056***	.054***
			(.052)	(.048)			(.119)	(.114)
Education			.135***	.126***			.144***	.127***
			(.196)	(.183)			(.181)	(.160)
Employed			−0.163	−0.378			0.021	−0.093
			(−.030)	(−.070)			(.004)	(−.018)
Attractiveness				0.080				0.084
				(.043)				(.048)
Weight				0.029				−0.015
				(.010)				(−.007)
Disabled				−.136***				−.072**
				(−.161)				(−.102)
Constant	8.260	7.096	6.767	6.771	7.753	6.727	6.313	6.140
R_2	0.014	0.040	0.072	0.093	0.004	0.034	0.085	0.096
Adjusted R^2	0.012	0.033	0.061	0.077	0.003	0.029	0.078	0.086

NOTE: Standardized coefficients are in parentheses.
t$\rho < .10$. *$\rho < .05$. **$\rho < .01$. ***$\rho < .001$.

arately. Looking at column 1, we see that skin tone has a significant positive effect on self-efficacy for both men and women. A lighter complexion is associated with higher feelings of perceived mastery. Among men, each incremental change in skin color from dark to light is associated with a .33 increment in self-efficacy; for women, changes in skin color are associated with a .18 increment in self-efficacy. Thus, the skin tone effect on self-efficacy is much stronger for men. In fact, the coefficient for the skin tone effect in the equation predicting self-efficacy for men is almost twice that of the coefficient for women.

The pattern of skin tone effects for men and women begins to diverge when the sociodemographic variables are added in the second equation. Among African American men, the effect of skin tone on self-efficacy remains statistically significant, and the coefficient is reduced by 11 percent. In contrast, among women, the skin tone effect is reduced also by a similar amount, but the significance level is reduced to borderline. Adding the socioeconomic variables to the equation (column 3), we see that the effect of skin tone on self-efficacy remains statistically significant for men. Note that men's standardized coefficient for education is almost twice as large as that of skin tone, suggesting that education has a stronger effect in determining self-efficacy for them. Body image, represented by attractiveness and weight (equation 4), does not statistically alter the effect of skin tone on self-efficacy for men. Disabled health conditions, which have a significant negative effect on self-efficacy for men, do not alter the skin tone effect. When all the independent variables are accounted for (equation 4), skin tone continues to have a moderate significant effect on self-efficacy among men. By contrast, the determinants of self-efficacy for women in this study are age, education, income, disability, and urban residence. The effect of skin tone is reduced by 80 percent and is no longer statistically significant after all variables are controlled. Note that among men, skin tone, has a significant moderate effect on self-efficacy when other more robust factors such as education and age are controlled. Among women, skin tone effect on self-efficacy is largely indirect, via its consequence for income and education.

A similar analysis for the self-esteem measure is displayed in Table 18.3 and shows that the effect for skin tone on self-esteem is not statistically significant in the equation for Black men in this study. Conversely, among Black women, skin tone has a significant positive association with self-esteem, even after all other variables are controlled. These findings show that among women, a change in skin color from dark to light is associated with a .28 increment in self-esteem. The effect of skin tone on self-esteem for women is slightly enhanced when the sociodemographic controls are added to the equation (column 2) and remains constant in the face of a strong pattern of socioeconomic effects (equation 3). Education and employment have positive effects on self-esteem for African American women. Two indicators for body image have significant positive effects on self-esteem—attractiveness and weight. Disabled conditions (equation 4) have a significant negative association with self-esteem. Of these socioeconomic effects, only education remains when body image variables are controlled, but the skin tone effect remains statistically significant. The body image variables have a moderate impact on the relationship between skin tone and self-esteem, reducing it by 20 percent. Women who are rated physically attractive have higher self-esteem scores, but attractiveness is at least in part related to skin tone.

Table 18.3 Regression Results for Predicting Self-Esteem, by Gender

	Men (n = 647)				*Women (n = 1,036)*			
	1	**2**	**3**	**4**	**1**	**2**	**3**	**4**
Skin color	0.157	0.159	0.112	0.088	.283***	.303***	.235**	.187*
	(0.054)	(.055)	(.039)	(.031)	(.100)	(.017)	(.083)	(.066)
Age		−0.001	0.010	.019**		.017***	.027***	.034***
		(−.008)	(0.068)	(.132)		(.115)	(.185)	(.235)
Urban		−0.235	−0.405	−0.400		0.167	−0.020	−0.015
		(−.038)	(−.066)	(−.065)		(.027)	(−.003)	(−.002)
South		0.244	0.328	0.295		0.153	0.218	0.196
		(.047)	(.063)	(.057)		(.030)	(.042)	(.038)
Married		.429*	0.153	0.126		0.013	−0.104	−0.125
		(.083)	(.030)	(.024)		(.003)	(−.019)	(−.023)
Income			0.020	0.019			0.028	0.025
			(.069)	(.065)			(.060)	(.053)
Education			0.048	0.036			.081**	.053t
			(.067)	(.051)			(.104)	(.068)
Employed			.696**	.449t			.512**	0.292
			(.124)	(.080)			(.100)	(.057)
Attractiveness				.142t				.121*
				(.075)				(.070)
Weight				0.047				.151*
				(.017)				(.067)
Disabled				−0.148***				−.130***
				(−.169)				(−.189)
Constant	21.292	21.388	21.005	20.632	21.055	20.131	19.812	19.508
R^2	0.003	0.016	0.046	0.072	0.010	0.024	0.058	0.092
Adjusted R^2	0.001	0.008	0.034	0.056	0.009	0.019	0.051	0.082

NOTE: Standardized coefficients are in parentheses.
$t\rho \leq .10$. $^*\rho \leq .05$. $^{**}\rho \leq .01$. $^{***}\rho \leq .001$.

Although the overall models in the analysis for self-efficacy and self-esteem are modest, they compare favorably to sociological models predicting self-esteem and self-efficacy. It is most informative to look at the size of the coefficient for skin tone compared to other variables in the model. Skin tone effects are sizable in the models predicting self-efficacy for men and self-esteem for women.

Do Achievement and Body Image Condition the Effects of Skin Tone on Self-Concept?

The literature suggests that it is reasonable to expect that skin tone may interact with socioeconomic status and body image to affect self-concept (Ransford 1970; St. John and Feagin 1998). We expect that among women, the relationship between skin tone and self-esteem and skin tone and self-efficacy will be moderated by socioeconomic status and body image. That is, the relationships will be stronger for Black women from lower social classes and for Black women who are judged as unattractive. To test for these possibilities, we created interaction terms for skin color and each of the socioeconomic status variables and for skin color and each of the body image variables. As suggested by Aiken and West (1991), all variables used to compute interaction terms were centered. Each interaction term was entered into the regression equation separately. Simple slope regression analyses were then used to probe significant interactions. The results are presented in Table 18.4.

In the analyses of women's self-esteem, two significant interaction effects emerge—skin tone and personal income ($b = -.035$, $p = .025$) and skin tone and interviewer-rated attractiveness ($b = -.113$, $p = .029$). The results from the simple-slopes analyses indicate that the relationship between skin tone and personal income is positive and significant among women with the lowest incomes. In other words, among women with the lowest levels of income, self-esteem increases as color lightens. The relationship is also positive and significant for women with average levels of income, although the relationship is not as strong. There is no relationship between skin tone and self-esteem among women with the highest incomes. Thus, women who are dark and successful evaluate themselves just as positively as women who are lighter and successful. Similar to the findings for income, skin color has a significant positive effect on self-esteem among women evaluated as having low and average levels of attractiveness, although the effect is stronger for the former. Self-esteem increases as skin color becomes lighter among women judged unattractive or average. There is no relationship between skin tone and self-esteem for women who are judged highly attractive. In other words, skin tone does not have much relevance for self-esteem among women who have higher levels of income and who are attractive. Education, unlike income, has no significant effect on women's self-esteem. We are at a loss to explain this finding. Perhaps income is more important because it permits women to obtain more visible symbols of success such as clothing, cars, and living quarters. We discuss this further in the concluding section.

Skin tone and interviewer-evaluated weight combine to affect men's self-esteem ($b = .274$, $p = .012$). Results from the simple slopes regression analyses show that skin tone has a significant impact on self-esteem for men who are either

Table 18.4 Significant Interaction Effects and Summary of Simple Regression Analysis for Self-Esteem and Self-Efficacy by Gender

Gender	Interaction Effect	b^1	Value of Moderator Variable	b^2	b_0
Dependent Variable = Self-Esteem					
Women	Skin Tone* Income	−.035*	Low income	.376*	19.373
			Average income	.185*	19.552
			High income	−.005	19.732
Women	Skin Tone* Attractiveness	−.113*	Low attractiveness	.350**	19.323
			Average attractiveness	.184*	19.524
			High attractiveness	.018	19.726
Men	Skin Tone* Weight	.274*	Low weight	−1.009*	20.372
			Average weight	.092	20.621
			High weight	1.192**	20.870

Gender	Interaction Effect	b	Value of Moderator Variable	b^1	b_0
Dependent Variable = Self-Efficacy					
Men	Skin Tone* Weight	.188†	Low weight	−.545	6.603
			Average weight	.210†	6.759
			High weight	.965*	6.916

NOTE: b^1 = coefficient for the interaction effect; b^2 = coefficient represents the effects of skin tone on self-esteem/self-efficacy at low (1 SD below mean), average (at mean equals 0), and high (1 *SD* above mean) values of the moderator variable $\dagger p \leq .10$. $^{*}p \leq .05$. $^{***}p \leq .01$.

underweight or overweight, although the direction of the effects is opposite. Among underweight men, self-esteem decreases as skin tone becomes lighter. However, among overweight men, self-esteem increases as skin tone becomes lighter. We suggest that cultural definitions of weight probably interact with those of skin color and health as explanations of the observed effects. In our culture, a robust athletic body is associated with masculinity, and a thin body frame combined with light complexion might be viewed as ill health. And a negative stigma of both weight and complexion affects self-esteem for men who are overweight and dark skinned. It seems that light skin compensates for the negative stigma of weight for large body frames but enhances the negative stigma for thin frames.

In the analyses of self-efficacy, there are no significant interaction effects among women. Among men, one interaction term emerged as marginally significant—skin tone and weight ($b = .188$, $p = .072$). The simple slopes indicate that skin tone and efficacy are negatively associated for underweight men, although the relationship is not significant. The relationship is marginally significant for men judged as average and is significant and positive for men judged overweight. Among those judged overweight, lighter men are more likely to have high self-efficacy. Note additional evidence that skin tone might compensate the effect of a negative stigma of weight on self among larger men.

DISCUSSION

The data in this study indicate that gender—mediated by socioeconomic status variables such as education, occupation, and income—socially constructs the importance of skin color evaluations of self-esteem and self-efficacy. Self-efficacy results not primarily from beliefs or attitudes about performance but rather reflects an individual's competency or agency from undertaking challenges and succeeding at overcoming them. Self-esteem consists of feeling good about oneself and being liked and treated favorably by others. However, the effect of skin color on these two domains of self is different for women and men. Skin color is an important predictor of perceived efficacy for Black men but not Black women. And skin color predicts self-esteem for Black women but not Black men. This pattern conforms to traditional gendered expectations (Hill Collins 1990, 79–80). The traditional definitions of masculinity demand men specialize in achievement outside the home, dominate in interpersonal relationships, and remain rational and self-contained. Women, in contrast, are expected to seek affirmation from others, to be warm and nurturing. Thus, consistent with gendered characteristics of men and women, skin color is important in self-domains that are central to masculinity (i.e., competence) and femininity (i.e., affirmation of the self).[7]

Turning our attention to the association between skin color and self-concept for Black men, the association between skin, color and self-efficacy increases significantly as skin color lightens. And this is independent of the strong positive contribution of education—and ultimately socioeconomic status—to feelings of competence for men. We think that the effect of skin tone on self-efficacy is the result of widespread negative stereotyping and fear associated with dark-skinned men that pervade the larger society and operates independent of social class. Correspondingly, employers view darker African American men as violent, uncooperative, dishonest, and unstable (Kirschenman and Neckerman, 1998). As a consequence, employers exclude "darker" African American men from employment and thus block their access to rewards and resources.

Evidence from research on the relationship between skin tone and achievement supports our interpretation. The literature on achievement and skin tone shows that lighter-skinned Blacks are economically better off than darker skinned persons (Hughes and Hertel 1990; Keith and Herring 1991). Hughes and Hertel (1990), using the NSBA data, present findings that show that for every dollar a light-skinned African American earns, the darker skinned person earns 72 cents. Thus, it seems colorism is operative within the workplace. Lighter skinned persons are probably better able to predict what will happen to them and what doors will open and remain open, thus leading to a higher sense of control over their environment. Our data support this finding and add additional information on how that process might work, at least in the lives of Black men. Perhaps employers are looking to hire African American men who will assimilate into the work environment, who do not alienate their clients (Kirschenman and Neckerman 1998), and who are nonthreatening. One consequence of mainstreaming the workplace is that darker skinned Black men have fewer opportunities to demonstrate competence in the breadwinner role. It is no accident that our inner cities, where unemployment is highest, are filled with darker skinned persons, especially men (Russell, Wilson, and Hall 1992, 38). During adolescence, lighter skinned boys discover that they have better job prospects, appear less threatening to whites, and have a clearer sense of who they are and their competency (Russell, Wilson, and Hall 1992, 67). In contrast, darker skinned African American men may feel powerless and less able to affect change through the "normal" channels available to lighter skinned African American men (who are able to achieve a more prestigious socioeconomic status).

While skin color is an important predictor of self-efficacy for African American men, it is more important as a predictor of self-esteem for African American women. These data confirm much of the anecdotal information from clinical studies of clients in psychotherapy that have found that dark-skinned Black women have problems with self-worth and confidence. Our findings suggest that this pattern is not limited to experiences of women who are in therapy but that colorism is part of the everyday reality of Black women. Black women expect to be judged by their skin tone. No doubt messages from peers, the media, and family show a preference for lighter skin tones. Several studies cited in the literature review point out that Black women of all ages tend to prefer lighter skin tones and believe that lighter hues are perceived as most attractive by their Black male counterparts (Bond and Cash 1992; Chambers et al. 1994; Porter 1971; T. L. Robinson and Ward 1995).

Evidence from personal accounts reported by St. John and Feagin (1998, 75) in research on the impact of racism in the everyday lives of Black women supports this interpretation. One young woman describes her father's efforts to shape her expectations about the meaning of beauty in our society and where Black women entered this equation.

> Beauty, beauty standards in this country, a big thing with me. It's a big gripe, because I went through a lot of personal anguish over that, being Black and being female, it's a real big thing with me, because it took a lot for me to find a sense of self . . . in this white-male-dominated society. And just how beauty standards are so warped because like my daddy always tell me, "white is right." The whiter you are, somehow the better you are, and if you look white, well hell, you've got your ticket, and anything you want, too.

Nevertheless, the relationship between skin color and self-esteem among African American women is moderated by socioeconomic status. For example, there is no correlation between skin color and self-esteem among women who have a more privileged socioeconomic status. Consequently, women who are darker and "successful" evaluate themselves just as positively as women of a lighter color. On the other hand, the relationship between skin color and self-esteem is stronger for African American women from the less privileged socioeconomic sectors. In other words, darker skinned women with the lowest incomes display the lowest levels of self-esteem, but self-esteem increases as their skin color lightens. Why does skin color have such importance for self-regard in the context of low income or poverty?

Low income shapes self-esteem because it provides fewer opportunities for rewarding experiences or affirming relationships. In addition, there are more negative attributes associated with behaviors of individuals from less privileged socioeconomic status than with those of a more prestigious one. For example, the derisive comment "ghetto chick" is often used to describe the behaviors, dress, communication, and interaction styles of women from low-income groups. Combine stereotypes of classism and colorism, and you have a mixture that fosters an undesirable if not malignant context for self-esteem development. An important finding of this research is that skin color and income determine self-worth for Black women and especially that these factors can work together. Dark skin and low income produce Black women with very low self-esteem. Accordingly, these data help refine our understanding of gendered racism and of "triple oppression" involving race, gender, and class that places women of color in a subordinate social and economic position relative to men of color and the larger white population as well (Segura 1986). More important, the data suggest that darker skinned African American women actually experience a "quadruple" oppression originating in the convergence of social inequalities based on gender, class, race, and color. Earlier, we noted the absence of an interaction effect between skin tone and education, and we can only speculate on the explanation for this non-finding. Perhaps education does not have the same implications for self-esteem as income because it is a less visible symbol of success. Financial success affords one the ability to purchase consumer items that tell others, even at a distance, that an individual is successful. These visible symbols include the place where we live, the kind of car we drive, and the kind of clothing that we wear. Educational attainment is not as easily grasped, especially in distant social interactions—passing on the street, walking in the park, or attending a concert event. In other words, for a dark-skinned African American woman, her M.A. or Ph.D. may be largely unknown outside her immediate friends, family, and coworkers. Her Lexus or Mercedes, however, is visible to the world and is generally accorded a great deal of prestige.

Finally, the data indicate that self-esteem increases as skin color becomes lighter among African American women who are judged as having "low and average levels of attractiveness." There is no relationship between skin color and self-esteem for women who are judged "highly attractive," just as there is no correlation between skin color and self-esteem for women of higher socioeconomic status. That physical attractiveness influenced feelings of self-worth for Black women is not surprising. Women have traditionally been concerned with appearance, regardless of ethnicity. Indeed, the pursuit and preoccupation with beauty are central features of female sex-role socialization. Our findings suggest that women who are judged "unattractive" are more vulnerable to color bias than those judged attractive.

NOTES

1. In 1990, a workplace discrimination suit was filed in Atlanta, Georgia, on the behalf of a light-skinned Black female against her dark-skinned supervisor on the charge of color discrimination (for a discussion, see Russell, Wilson, and Hall 1992).

2. Skin color bias has also been investigated among Latino groups, although more emphasis has been placed on the combination of both color and European phenotype facial characteristics. Studies of Mexican Americans have documented that those with lighter skin and European features attain more schooling (Telles and Murguia 1990) and generally have higher socioeconomic status (Acre, Murguia, and Frisbie 1987) than those of darker complexion with more Indian features. Similar findings have been reported for Puerto Ricans (Rodriguez 1989), a population with African admixture.

3. Self-esteem is divided into two components: racial self-esteem and personal self-esteem. Racial self-esteem refers to group identity, and personal self-esteem refers to a general evaluative view of the self (Porter and Washington 1989). In our discussion, self-esteem is conceptualized as personal self-esteem, which is defined as "feelings of intrinsic worth, competence, and self approval rather than self rejection and self-contempt" (Porter and Washington 1989, 344).

4. Self-concept theory argued that the experience of social inequality would foster lower self-concept of persons in lower status positions compared with their higher status counterparts. However, when comparing the self-concept of African American schoolboys and schoolgirls, Rosenberg and Simmons (1971) found that their self-feelings were as high and in some instances higher than those of white schoolchildren. This "unexpected" finding was explained by strong ties and bonds within the African American community as opposed to identifying with the larger community.

5. At the suggestion of one reviewer, we estimated all equations with respondents classified as employed part-time, employed full-time, and not employed. The results remained unchanged. The not-employed group could be separated into "laid off" and "retired," but the former category had too few cases to include as a separate group. Using occupation, as one reviewer suggested, also resulted in a substantial loss of cases as many respondents (about 40 percent) were retired.

6. The decision to conduct separate analyses for men and women is based on findings of significant higher order interaction effects, which suggested, as did the literature, that the effects of skin tone on self-esteem and self-efficacy differ for men and women in complex ways. For example, in the analysis of self-esteem, we found a significant three-way interaction effect for gender, skin tone, and income ($\beta = -.288$, $p = .024$). In the analysis of self-efficacy, we found a significant three-way interaction effect for gender, skin tone, and weight ($\beta = -.832$, $p = .015$). The two-way interactions (e.g., skin tone by gender, skin tone by income, gender by income) were not significant.

7. These findings also reflect the dual nature of colorism as it pertains to Black women. Colorism is an aspect of racism that results in anti-Black discrimination in the wider society and, owing to historical patterns, also occurs within the Black community. The finding that the effects of skin tone on self-efficacy become nonsignificant when socioeconomic status variables are added suggests that the interracial discrimination aspect of colorism is more operational for Black women's self-efficacy via access to jobs and income. The finding that the effect of skin tone is more central to Black women's self-esteem indicates that colorism within the Black community is the more central mechanism. Self-esteem is derived from family, friends, and close associates.

REFERENCES

Acre, Carlos, Edward Murguia, and W. P. Frisbie. 1987. Phenotype and life chances among Chicanos. *Hispanic Journal of Behavioral Sciences* 9 (1): 19–32.

Aiken, Leona S., and Stephen G. West. 1991. *Multiple regression: Testing and interpreting interactions*. Newbury Park, CA: Sage.

Bachman, J. G., and Johnson. 1978. *The monitoring the future project: Design and procedures*. Ann Arbor: University of Michigan, Institute for Social Research.

Bandura, A.1977. Self efficacy: Towards a unifying theory of behavioral change. *Psychological Review* 84: 191–215.

———. 1982. Self efficacy mechanism in human agency. *American Psychologist* 37: 122–47.

Bond, S., and T. F. Cash.1992. Black beauty: Skin color and body images among African-American college women. *Journal of Applied Social Psychology* 22 (11): 874–88.

Boyd Franklin, N. 1991. Recurrent themes in the treatment of African-American women in group psychotherapy. *Women and Therapy* 11 (2): 25–40.

Cash, T. S., and N. C. Duncan. 1984. Physical attractiveness stereotyping among Black American college students. *Journal of Social Psychology* 1: 71–77.

Chambers, J. W., T. Clark, L. Dantzler, and J. A. Baldwin.1994. Perceived attractiveness, facial features, and African self-consciousness. *Journal of Black Psychology* 20 (3): 305–24.

Dion, K., E. Berscheid, and E. Walster. 1972. What is beautiful is good. *Journal of Personality and Social Psychology* 24: 285–90.

Frazier, E. Franklin.1957. *Black bourgeoise: The rise of the new middle class*. New York: Free Press.

Freeman, H. E., J. M. Ross, S. Armor, and R. F. Pettigrew. 1966. Color gradation and attitudes among middle class income Negroes. *American Sociological Review* 31: 365–74.

Gatewood, W. B. 1988. Aristocrat of color: South and North and the Black elite, 1880–1920. *Journal of Southern History* 54: 3–19.

Gecas, Viktor. 1989. The social psychology of self-efficacy. *Annual Review of Sociology* 15: 291–316.

Grier, W., and P. Cobbs. 1968. *Black rage*. New York: Basic Books.

Hill Collins, Patricia. 1990. *Black feminist thought: Knowledge, consciousness, and the politics of empowerment*. Boston: Unwin Hyman.

Hughes, M., and B. R. Hertel. 1990. The significance of color remains: A study of life chances, mate selection, and ethnic consciousness among Black Americans. *Social Forces* 68 (4): 1105–20.

Hughes, Michael, and David H. Demo.1989. Self perceptions of Black Americans: Self-esteem and personal efficacy. *American Journal of Sociology* 95: 132–59.

Jackson, J., and G. Gurin. 1987. *National survey of Black Americans, 1979–1980* (machine-readable codebook). Ann Arbor: University of Michigan, Inter-University Consortium for Political and Social Research.

Jackson, J. S., B. Tucker, and G. Gurin. 1987. *National survey of Black Americans 1979–1980* (MRDF). Ann Arbor: Institute for Social Research.

James, W. 1890. *The principles of psychology*. New York: Smith.

Keith, V. M., and C. Herring. 1991. Skin tone and stratification in the Black community. *American Journal of Sociology* 97 (3): 760–78.

Kessler, R. C., and J. D. McLeod. 1984. Sex differences in vulnerability to undesirable life events. *American Sociological Review* 49: 620–31.

Kirschenman, J., and K. M. Neckerman. 1998. We'd love to hire them, but. . . . In *The meaning of race for employers in working American: Continuity, conflict, and change*, ed. Amy S. Wharton. Mountain View, CA: Mayfield.

Klag, Michael, Paul Whelton, Josef Coresh, Clarence Grim, and Lewis Kuller. 1991. The association of skin color with blood pressure in US Blacks with low socioeconomic status. *Journal of the American Medical Association* 65 (5): 599–602.

Miller, Herman P. 1964. *Rich man, poor man.* New York: Crowell.

Neal, A., and M. Wilson.1989. The role of skin color and features in the Black community: Implications for Black women in therapy. *Clinical Psychology Review* 9 (3): 323–33.

Okazawa Rey, Margo, Tracy Robinson, and Janie V. Ward. 1987. *Black women and the politics of skin color and hair.* New York: Haworth.

Parrish, Charles. 1944. The significance of skin color in the Negro community. Ph.D. diss., University of Chicago.

Pearlin, L. I., and J. S. Johnson.1977. Marital status, life strains, and depression. *American Sociological Review* 42: 704–15.

Pearlin, L. I., M. A. Liberman, E. G. Menaghan, and J. T. Mullan. 1981. The stress process. *Journal of Health and Social Behavior* 22 (December): 337–56.

Pearlin, L. I., and C. Schooler. 1978. The structure of coping. *Journal of Health and Social Behavior* 19: 2–21.

Porter, J. 1971. *Black child, white child: The development of racial attitudes.* Cambridge, CA: Harvard University Press.

Porter, J. R., and R. E. Washington. 1989. Developments in research on Black identity and self esteem: 1979–88. *Review of International Psychology and Sociology* 2: 341–53.

Ransford, E. H. 1970. Skin color, life chances, and anti-white attitudes. *Social Problems* 18: 164–78.

Robinson, J. P., and P. R. Shaver.1969. *Measures of social psychological attitudes.* Ann Arbor: University of Michigan, Institute of Social Research.

Robinson, T. L., and J. V. Ward. 1995. African American adolescents and skin color. *Journal of Black Psychology* 21 (3): 256–74.

Rodriguez, Clara. 1989. *Puerto Ricans: Born in the USA.* Boston: Unwin Hyman.

Rosenberg, M. 1979. *Conceiving the self.* New York: Basic Books.

Rosenberg, M., and R. Simmons. 1971. *Black and white self-esteem: The urban school child.* Washington, DC: American Sociological Association.

Russell, Kathy, Midge Wilson, and Ronald Hall. 1992. *The color complex: The politics of skin color among African Americans.* New York: Harcourt Brace Jovanovich.

Segura, Denise. 1986. Chicanas and triple oppression in the labor force. In *Chicana voices: Intersections of class, race and gender,* ed. Teresa Cordova and the National Association of Chicana Studies Editorial Committee. Austin, TX: Center for Mexican American Studies.

St. John, Y., and J. R. Feagin. 1998. *Double burden: Black women and everyday racism.* New York: M. E. Sharpe.

Telles, Edward E., and Edward Murguia. 1990. Phenotypic discrimination and income differences among Mexican Americans. *Social Science Quarterly* 71 (4): 682–95.

Thoits, Peggy A. 1982. Life stress, social support, and psychological vulnerability: Epidemiological considerations. *Journal of Community Psychology* 10: 341–62.

———. 1984. Explaining distributions of psychological vulnerability: Lack of social support in the face of life stress. *Social Forces* 63: 452–81.

Thurman, Wallace. 1929. *The blacker the berry: A novel of Negro life.* New York: Macmillan.

Turner, R. J., and S. Noh. 1983. Class and psychological vulnerability among women: The significance of social support and personal control. *Journal of Health and Social Behavior* 24: 2–15.

Tryoler, H. A., and S. A. James. 1978. Blood pressure and skin color. *American Journal of Public Health* 58: 1170–72.

Udry, J. R., K. E. Bauman, and C. Chase. 1969. Skin color, status, and mate selection. *American Journal of Sociology* 76: 722–33.

Verna, G., and K. Runion.1985. The effects of contextual dissonance on the self concept of youth from high vs. low socially valued group. *Journal of Social Psychology* 125: 449–58.

Warner, W. L., B. H. Junker, and W. A. Adams.1941. *Color and human nature.* Washington, DC: American Council on Education.

Wright, B. 1976. *The dissent of the governed: Alienation and democracy in America.* New York: Academic Press.

CHAPTER 19

Inferences Regarding the Personality Traits and Sexual Orientation of Physically Androgynous People

LAURA MADSON

How do we draw conclusions about a person's personality? One way is to draw inferences from his or her behavior. Generally speaking, observers assume that a person's personality traits match his or her behavior (Jones, 1990; Jones and Davis 1965; Jones, Davis, and Gergen 1961). This type of inference is particularly likely when the behavior is freely chosen (Jones and Harris 1967) or unexpected (Jones and McGillis 1976).

Sometimes, however, we need information about a person's personality when we do not have an opportunity to observe the person's behavior. How do we make inferences about a person's personality in the absence of behavior? Considerable research suggests that observers use a person's physical appearance as a basis for drawing conclusions about his or her personality (e.g., Secord, Dukes, and Bevan 1954; Secord and Muthard 1955). Specifically, observers assume a person possesses personality characteristics that are consistent with his or her physical appearance. McArthur and her colleagues found that individuals with facial features generally associated with young children (i.e., baby faces) were perceived to have more childlike psychological attributes than those with more mature faces (Berry and McArthur 1985; McArthur and Apatow 1983–1984; McArthur and Berry 1987). Children who were portrayed as relatively baby-faced also elicited more baby talk from adults than those who were portrayed as relatively mature-faced (Zebrowitz, Brownlow, and Olson 1992). Similarly, perceivers assume that physically attractive individuals possess a number of other desirable traits (Dion, Berscheid, and Walster 1972). Compared to unattractive people, attractive people tend to be perceived as more successful, more intelligent, more competent, more socially skilled, and more interesting (see reviews by Calvert 1988; Eagly, Ashmore, Makhijani, and Longo 1991; Jackson 1992). In a sense, perceivers infer that physically attractive people are also psychologically or inwardly attractive. Information regarding an individual's physical appearance also affects perceivers' inferences in that they assume an individual's traits, occupation, and role behaviors match the relative masculinity or femininity of his or her physical characteristics (Deaux and Lewis 1984). For example, a person described as having stereotypically masculine physical features (e.g., tall, strong, sturdy, and broad-shouldered) was perceived as likely to possess stereotypically masculine personality traits as well (e.g., independent, can make decisions easily, competitive, self-confident).

In short, observers assume a person's personality and behavior are consistent with the type of physical characteristics he or she possesses. People with childlike facial features are assumed to have childlike psychological attributes, and people with attractive physical features are assumed to have attractive psychological attributes. Similarly, people with gender-typed physical characteristics are inferred to possess gender-typed traits and engage in gender-typed behaviors.

If observers assume that a target with masculine physical characteristics also possesses masculine personality traits and that a target with feminine physical characteristics also possesses feminine personality traits, what inferences would be made if a person's physical characteristics were neither clearly masculine nor clearly feminine? What inferences would be made about a physically androgynous (PA) person? PA people have a combination of physical characteristics that make it difficult to categorize their gender. In the three studies reported here, inferences made about PA targets were contrasted with those made about gendered targets (i.e., targets whose gender is not ambiguous).

Given that observers often assume that a person's personality matches his or her physical characteristics, I expected that observers would assume that PA people also have androgynous personality traits and behaviors (i.e., traits and behaviors that are between those of a man and a woman). In other words, PA individuals would be perceived as less masculine than a typical man but more masculine than a typical women. Similarly, I expected that PA individuals would be perceived as less feminine than a typical woman but more feminine than a typical man. Drawing on Deaux and Lewis (1984), this pattern of results was expected with respect to male and female gender-role behavior as well as male- and female-dominated occupations. Thus, PA individuals would be perceived as less likely to engage in male gender-role behaviors and male-dominated occupations than a man but more likely to engage in these behaviors and occupations than a woman. Similarly, PA individuals would be perceived as less likely to engage in female gender-role behaviors and female-dominated occupations than a woman but more likely to engage in these behaviors and occupations than a man.

If observers draw conclusions about a person's personality and behavior based on physical characteristics, might they also use appearance as a basis for inferences regarding a person's sexual orientation? Deaux and Lewis (1984) found that targets whose physical characteristics or role behaviors were not consistent with their gender label were perceived as more likely to be homosexual and less likely to be heterosexual than targets whose attributes and gender label were consistent. This pattern was particularly strong for mismatched physical characteristics. For example, a man described as having feminine physical characteristics was perceived as more likely to be homosexual and less likely to be heterosexual than a man described as having masculine physical characteristics. This kind of mismatch between gender label and physical attributes may be comparable to the stimulus conditions elicited by PA targets. Consequently, I hypothesized that PA individuals would be perceived as more likely to be homosexual and less likely to be heterosexual than gendered targets.

A series of three experiments was conducted to test the following two hypotheses. First, perceivers would infer that PA people have gender-related traits and behaviors that are between those of men and women (e.g., less masculine than a man but more masculine than a woman; less feminine than a woman but more feminine than a man). Second, PA individuals would be perceived as more likely to be homosexual and less likely to be heterosexual than gendered individuals. In each study, participants rated the personality, gender-role behavior, occupation, and sexual orientation of male, female, and PA targets. In Experiment 1, target persons were presented in color photos, and participants rated each of the four targets (i.e., one male, one female, and two PA targets) in a within-subjects design. In Experiment 2, target information was presented in verbal descriptions rather than through photos. Experiment 3 used the same verbal descriptions in a between-subjects design where each participant rated only one target person.

EXPERIMENT 1

Method

Participants

A sample of 110 undergraduate psychology students (forty-seven men, sixty-three women) at a large university in the Midwest volunteered to participate in the study in exchange for extra credit in their psychology classes. Although ethnicity was not explicitly measured, the student population at the university was largely Caucasian.

Materials

TARGET PHOTOS A separate sample of 645 undergraduate psychology students (238 men, 397 women) viewed thirty-five color photos of adults. Participants identified each person as male or female and rated their confidence in this judgment using a 7–point Likert-type scale ranging from *not at all confident* (1) *to very confident* (7). They also rated the attractiveness of each person on a 7–point Likert-type scale ranging from *not at all attractive* (1) to *very attractive* (7).

Targets were considered physically androgynous if fewer than 60 percent of participants agreed on the gender of the target (e.g., 50 percent of participants thought the target was male and 50 percent thought the target was female) and the mean confidence rating was less than 4.50. Two photos met these criteria. Targets were considered gendered (i.e., their gender was readily apparent from their appearance) if more than 95 percent of participants agreed on the gender of the target and the mean confidence rating was greater than or equal to 6.00. Fourteen photos (six men and eight women) met these criteria. Two gendered photos (one man and one woman) were selected from this set based on attractiveness ratings such that the gendered targets were as comparable as possible to the PA targets on level of attractiveness. Because the PA targets were perceived as relatively unattractive, this informal matching procedure resulted in the selection of relatively unattractive gendered targets as well. Unfortunately, the female target who was the closest match was still rated as somewhat more attractive than the androgynous targets and the male target (*M* attractiveness ratings were 2.79 and 2.78 for the PA targets and 2.62 and 3.09, respectively, for the male and female targets). In particular, women rated the female target as significantly more attractive than did men, $F(1, 630) = 3.79$, $\rho = .05$, $\eta^2 = .01$. The female target was also the only target of the four whose ethnicity was unambiguous. The female target was clearly Caucasian (i.e., she had fair skin and blond hair). The other three targets were somewhat ambiguous with respect to their ethnicity (i.e., they had darker skin and dark hair but could not be unambiguously categorized according to a particular ethnic group).

PERSONALITY SCALE Twenty adjectives were selected from Deaux and Lewis (1984), the Personal Attributes Questionnaire (Spence, Helmreich, and Stapp 1974), and the Bem Sex Role Inventory (Bem 1974). Ten adjectives represented stereotypically feminine traits (e.g., gentle, understanding of others, tactful, affectionate), and ten adjectives represented stereotypically masculine traits (e.g., competitive, aggressive, individualistic, strong). Students rated the degree to which each adjective described the target's personality using a 10-point Likert-type scale ranging from *not at all descriptive* (1) to *very descriptive* (10). The masculine and feminine personality scales were constructed by summing the ratings on the ten masculine items and the ten feminine items, respectively. Both scales had satisfactory reliability (masculine scale $\alpha = .82$; feminine scale $\alpha = .86$).

GENDER-ROLE BEHAVIORS Ten gender-role behaviors were selected from Orlofsky and O'Heron's (1987) Sex Role Behavior Scale and Deaux and Lewis (1984). Five items represented stereotypically feminine behaviors (i.e., enjoys taking care of children, is a source of emotional support for others, is responsible for cooking meals, enjoys decorating his or her home, enjoys making crafts), and five items represented stereotypically masculine behaviors (i.e., is responsible for household repairs, takes the initiative in romantic relationships, enjoys hunting, is responsible for yard work, enjoys working on cars). Students rated the likelihood that each person engaged in these gender-related role behaviors using a 10-point Likert-type scale ranging from *extremely unlikely* (1) to *extremely likely* (10). The masculine and feminine role behavior scales were constructed by summing the ratings on the five masculine items and the five feminine items, respectively. The feminine behavior scale had satisfactory reliability ($\alpha = .88$), although the reliability of the masculine behavior scale was somewhat lower ($\alpha = .59$).

SEXUAL ORIENTATION Two items assessing perceived sexual orientation were embedded in the role behavior items. One item assessed the perceived likelihood that each person was heterosexual, and the other item assessed the perceived likelihood that each person was homosexual. Ratings were made on the same 10-point Likert-type scale as the role behaviors. These ratings were treated as separate dependent variables in the analyses (i.e., they were not combined into a composite scale), and so reliability analyses were not conducted.

OCCUPATIONS Five male-dominated and five female-dominated occupations were selected from 1994 employment statistics (U.S. Department of Commerce

1994). Occupations were considered male-dominated if at least 90 percent of individuals in that occupation were men (i.e., airline pilot, auto mechanic, firefighter, engineer, carpenter). Occupations were considered female-dominated if at least 90 percent of individuals in that occupation were women (i.e., kindergarten teacher, registered nurse, dental hygienist, secretary, dietitian). Students rated the likelihood each person held these occupations using a 10-point Likert-type scale ranging from *extremely unlikely* (1) to *extremely likely* (10). The male-dominated and female-dominated occupation scales were constructed by summing the ratings on the five male-dominated and five female-dominated occupations, respectively. Each scale possessed satisfactory reliability (male-dominated $\alpha = .79$, female-dominated $\alpha = .87$).

Procedure

Participants made judgments about the gender, personality, role behaviors, sexual orientation, and occupation of each of the four targets (i.e., one male, one female, and two PA targets). They were told they would be forming impressions of other university students in order to examine individual differences in the impression formation process. Targets were presented in three-inch color photos that depicted the head and shoulders of each target. Participants completed all judgments for a single person before proceeding to the next person. Order of target presentation was counterbalanced (four different orders were used). Dependent measures were completed in the order specified previously (i.e., gender categorization, followed by judgments about the target's personality, gender-role behaviors, sexual orientation, and occupation).

Results

All hypotheses were tested using a mixed-factorial analysis of variance (ANOVA), with target (i.e., male, female, and the two PA targets) as the within-subjects factor and participant gender and order of target presentation as between-subjects factors. A priori comparisons were conducted on type of target comparing perceptions of the PA targets to the male target and perceptions of the PA targets to the female target. There were no significant main effects of, nor were there interactions with, order of presentation. Thus, the results were collapsed across this factor. Perceptions of the two PA targets also did not differ significantly, nor were there any significant interactions with this factor. Thus, the ratings of the two PA targets were collapsed. Two significant main effects and one significant two-way interaction with participant gender are discussed.

PERSONALITY TRAITS, ROLE BEHAVIORS, AND OCCUPATIONS Ratings of the PA targets were hypothesized to fall between the ratings of the male and female targets on these gender-related dimensions. Results of the six ANOVAs largely supported the hypothesis. The PA targets were perceived as significantly less masculine than the male target, $F\ (1, 83) = 39.81$, $p < .001$, $\eta^2 = .32$, although the PA targets were not perceived as significantly more masculine than the female target, $F\ (1, 83) = 2.65$, $p = .11$, $\eta^2 = .03$ (see Table 19.1). The PA targets were also perceived as less feminine than the female target, $F\ (1, 87) = 27.72$, $p < .001$,

Table 19.1 Mean Ratings for the Four Targets in Experiment 1

	Target		
Dimension	**Male**	**PA**	**Female**
Masculine personality traits	64.60_a (13.02)	55.81_b (12.56)	53.22_b (12.27)
Feminine personality traits	47.50_a (12.44)	60.41_b (13.44)	68.36_c (11.47)
Masculine role behaviors	27.34_a (6.91)	22.97_b (6.66)	20.66_c (5.82)
Feminine role behaviors	18.37_a (6.98)	26.98_b (8.41)	33.86_c (7.87)
Male-dominated occupations	24.55_a (7.43)	20.10_b (7.66)	16.70_c (7.93)
Female-dominated occupations	15.61_a (7.61)	23.43_b (9.81)	25.65_c (7.61)

Notes: Standard deviations shown in parentheses. Means in the same row that do not share subscripts differ at $p < .001$.

$\eta^2 = .24$, and more feminine than the male target, $F\,(1, 87) = 62.66$, $p < .001$, $\eta^2 = .42$. In addition, there was a gender difference among participants, with women rating all four targets as more masculine than did men, $F\,(1, 83) = 11.78$, $p = .001$, $\eta^2 = .12$. With respect to gender-role behaviors, the PA targets were perceived as less likely to engage in male gender-role behaviors than the male target, $F\,(1, 89) = 30.15$, $p < .001$, $\eta^2 = .25$, but more likely to engage in these behaviors than the female target, $F\,(1, 89) = 13.48$, $p < .001$, $\eta^2 = .13$. The PA targets were also perceived as less likely to engage in female gender-role behaviors than the female target, $F\,(1, 88) = 48.02$, $p < .001$, $\eta^2 = .35$, but more likely to engage in these behaviors than the male target, $F\,(1, 88) = 93.39$, $p < .001$, $\eta^2 = .51$. Finally, the PA targets were rated as less likely to hold male-dominated occupations than the male target, $F\,(1, 90) = 32.63$, $p < .001$, $\eta^2 = .27$, but more likely to hold these occupations than the female target, $F\,(1, 90) = 27.76$, $p < .001$, $\eta^2 = .24$. The PA targets were also rated as less likely to hold female-dominated occupations than the female target, $F\,(1, 88) = 84.76$, $p < .001$, $\eta^2 = .49$, but more likely to hold these positions than the male target, $F\,(1, 88) = 58.30$, $p < .001$, $\eta^2 = .40$.

In sum, PA targets were perceived as having psychological characteristics between that of men and women on a number of different gender-related dimensions. However, there was an alternative interpretation to these results. In these analyses, the ratings from participants who perceived the PA targets to be male were combined with the ratings from participants who perceived the targets to be female. If the participants' inferences regarding the targets' personality and behaviors were based on perceived target gender, the results could be an artifact of the perceived gender of the PA targets. For example, assume participants first categorize a PA target according to gender and then infer that the target has the corresponding personality traits (see Brewer 1988). Thus, a participant who perceived a PA target to be male would subsequently infer that the target's personality is also relatively masculine. However, keep in mind that approximately 50 percent of participants perceived the PA targets to be male and 50 percent perceived them to be female. Thus, another participant may have perceived the same target to be female and subsequently inferred that the target's personality is not particularly masculine. Combining the personality ratings from participants who perceived the PA targets to be male with those who perceived the PA target to be female could have created an artificial impression that the PA targets' characteristics were between those of the male and female targets.

To test this possibility, the analyses were repeated controlling for the perceived gender of the PA targets. This second round of analyses indicated that the perceived gender of the PA targets did not influence the pattern of results. Regardless of whether the PA targets were perceived to be male or female, their personality and behaviors were still rated between those of the two gendered targets.

SEXUAL ORIENTATION Participants were expected to assume that the PA targets were more likely to be homosexual and less likely to be heterosexual than the gendered targets. Results supported this hypothesis. PA targets were perceived as more likely to be homosexual than the male and female targets ($M = 4.56$, 3.24, and 3.26, respectively), $F\ (1, 92) = 55.86$, $p < .001$, $\eta^2 = .38$. The PA targets were also perceived as less likely to be heterosexual than the male and female targets ($M = 6.14$, 6.73, and 6.65, respectively), $F\ (1, 93) = 22.50$, $p < .001$, $\eta^2 = .19$.[2] In addition, women rated all four targets as less likely to be homosexual than did men, $F\ (1, 92) = 9.19$, $p = .003$, $\eta^2 = .09$. There was also a significant two-way interaction between participant gender and target such that there was a larger difference between men's and women's ratings with respect to the male target and the two PA targets than with respect to the female target, $F\ (1, 92) = 4.59$, $p = .04$, $\eta^2 = .05$.

Discussion

The results of Experiment 1 support the two hypotheses. PA targets were assumed to have personality traits, gender-role behaviors, and occupations that were between those of men and women. They were also perceived as more likely to be homosexual and less likely to be heterosexual than the gendered targets. These results replicate and extend Deaux and Lewis's (1984) findings by demonstrating that the effects generalize to target persons presented in photos rather than in verbal descriptions.

However, the target photos used in this study were also the source of two alternative explanations for the data. First, all four targets were perceived as relatively unattractive. Given the effects of physical attractiveness on the person perception process, perceivers' ratings may have been influenced by the relative unattractiveness of the targets. The gender of target photos was also confounded with ethnicity. Only one target (the female) was clearly Caucasian. The remaining three photos (the male and both PA targets) were somewhat ambiguous with respect to ethnicity. (This may have also accounted for the greater perceived attractiveness of the female target.) Because gender, age, and ethnicity are the basic social categories that perceivers use in the initial stages of person perception (Brewer 1988; Bruner

1957; Fiske and Neuberg 1990), the participants' ratings of the PA targets may have been influenced by the ambiguity of the targets' ethnicity in addition to the ambiguity of their gender. Experiment 1 also used only one male and one female target, and so it is unclear whether the effects would generalize beyond these targets. Experiment 2 was conducted to eliminate these alternative explanations and to replicate the basic effects using different targets.

EXPERIMENT 2

The hypotheses and dependent measures used in Experiment 2 were identical to those used in Experiment 1 with three exceptions. First, in order to overcome the confounds with attractiveness and ethnicity in Experiment 1, participants received verbal descriptions of target persons rather than were shown photos. Second, a single item assessing the likelihood that each target was bisexual was added to the sexual orientation measure to test whether the tendency to assume PA people are homosexual generalized to bisexuality. Third, because perceptions of the two PA targets used in Experiment 1 did not differ significantly, Experiment 2 used only one PA target. Thus, each participant in Experiment 2 rated three target persons (i.e., one male, one female, and one PA target). As in Experiment 1, participants completed all the judgments for a single target before proceeding to the next target, and order of target presentation was counterbalanced (six different orders were used).

Method

Participants

Participants were 101 introductory psychology students (forty-six men, fifty-five women) at a large university in the Southwest who participated in the experiment in partial fulfillment of a course requirement. Ethnicity was not explicitly measured, but the majority of the students at the university were of Caucasian or Hispanic origin.

Materials

Verbal descriptions were written for three different target persons (one male, one female, and one PA target). Descriptions focused on each target person's physical characteristics but did not explicitly specify the target person's gender or ethnicity. Target characteristics were similar but not identical to those used by Deaux and Lewis (1984). One target had stereotypically masculine physical features (i.e., "K. T. is 6'3" tall and weighs 210 lbs. K. T. has brown eyes, brown wavy hair, strong facial features, dark thick eyebrows, and a deep voice. K. T. has an athletic build with broad shoulders and muscular arms."). Another target had stereotypically feminine physical features (i.e., "D. S. is 5'4" tall and weighs 110 lbs. D. S. has green eyes, long straight blond hair, large expressive eyes, and high cheekbones. D. S. is petite with a small frame and delicate features."). The third target had physical features that were not diagnostic of the person's gender (i.e., "L. R. is 5'8" tall and weighs 155 lbs. L. R. has blue eyes, short sandy hair, tan skin, and average features. Many people have commented on L. R.'s striking appearance and pleasing voice. Most people consider L. R. to be attractive, although L. R. is sometimes mistaken for a person of the other gender."). The PA target was explicitly described as attractive and possessing desirable features (e.g., a pleasing voice) to avoid a potential confound between physical androgyny and perceived unattractiveness. (Recall that the PA targets in Experiment 1 were considered less physically attractive than the female target.) Target ethnicity was deliberately unspecified, although cues in the physical descriptions could be interpreted as indicating all three targets were Caucasian (i.e., L. R. has blue eyes, D. S. has blond hair and green eyes, K. T. has wavy hair).

The dependent measures and their order of administration were the same as those used in Experiment 1 with the exception of the added item to assess the perceived likelihood that each person was bisexual. First, to confirm the perceived gender of the target descriptions, participants identified each target as male or female. Consistent with the intended categorization, 93 percent of participants rated K. T. as male, 95 percent of participants rated D. S. as female, and 50.5 percent of participants rated L. R. as male (49.5 percent rated L. R. as female). As in Experiment 1, participants then rated the degree to which the 20 personality traits described each target's personality and rated the likelihood that each target engaged in the ten gender-role behaviors. Three items assessing each target person's perceived sexual orientation were embedded in the gender role behaviors. Again, these measures of sexual orientation were analyzed as separate variables (i.e., they were not combined into a composite scale). Finally, participants rated the likelihood that each target person held each of the male-dominated and female-dominated occupations. All six scales had satisfactory reliability (masculinity $\alpha = .83$; femininity $\alpha = .86$; masculine role behaviors $\alpha = .86$;[3] feminine role behaviors $\alpha = .83$; male-dominated occupations $\alpha = .86$; female-dominated occupations $\alpha = .85$).

Results

All hypotheses were tested using mixed-factorial ANOVAs, with target as the within-subjects factor and order of target presentation and participant gender as between-subjects factors. A priori comparisons were again conducted on type of target comparing perceptions of the PA target to the male target and perceptions of the PA target to the female target. These target effects were significant, as were two main effects of participant gender with respect to the male gender-role behaviors and male-dominated occupations. Three target by participant gender interactions were obtained when the sample was restricted to control for perceived gender of the PA target. A main effect of order of presentation with respect to the homosexuality ratings was also obtained. There were no other main effects of, nor were there interactions with, participant gender or order of presentation. With these exceptions, results were collapsed across participant gender and order of presentation.

PERSONALITY TRAITS, GENDER-ROLE BEHAVIORS, AND OCCUPATIONS Again, ratings of the PA target were expected to fall between the ratings of the male and female targets. Results of six ANOVAs supported the hypothesis (see Table 19.2). Across all six dimensions, the pattern of results found in Experi-

Table 19.2 Mean Ratings for the Three Targets in Experiment 2

	Target		
Dimension	**Male**	**PA**	**Female**
Masculine personality traits	75.13_a (11.78)	57.17_b (11.43)	50.30_c (11.90)
Feminine personality traits	46.14_a (12.11)	65.16_b (11.07)	72.62_c (12.12)
Masculine role behaviors	29.18_a (6.06)	19.61_b (5.95)	12.86_c (5.62)
Feminine role behaviors	19.19_a (7.94)	29.73_b (6.76)	34.04_c (7.91)
Male-dominated occupations	32.46_a (8.08)	21.94_b (7.87)′	16.42_c (7.73)
Female-dominated occupations	19.11_a (7.77)	25.84_b (8.18)	32.91_c (8.15)
Heterosexuality likelihood	8.25_a (2.12)	5.62_b (2.77)	7.85_a (2.31)
Homosexuality likelihood	3.01_a (2.26)	5.13_b (2.70)	3.05_a (2.27)
Bisexuality likelihood	3.13_a (2.14)	5.41_b (2.55)	4.03_a (2.50)

Notes: Standard deviations shown in parentheses. Means in the same row that do not share subscripts differ at $p < .001$.

ment 1 were replicated. Regardless of whether target information was presented in photographs or through verbal descriptions, participants inferred that the psychological characteristics of the PA target were as "in the middle" as his/her physical characteristics. Specifically, the PA target was perceived as less masculine than the male target, $F\ (1, 70) = 140.99$, $p < .001$, $\eta^2 = .67$, and more masculine than the female target, $F\ (1, 70) = 14.11$, $p < .001$, $\eta^2 = .17$. The PA target was perceived as less feminine than the female target, $F\ (1, 73) = 22.72$, $p < .001$, $\eta^2 = .24$, and more feminine than the male target, $F\ (1, 73) = 97.81$, $p < .001$, $\eta^2 = .57$. The PA target was perceived as less likely to engage in stereotypically masculine behavior than the male target, $F\ (1, 79) = 136.73$, $p < .001$, $\eta^2 = .63$, but more likely to perform these behaviors than the female target, $F\ (1, 79) = 73.11$, $p < .001$, $\eta^2 = .48$. The analogous pattern was found with respect to female gender-role behaviors, with the PA target rated as less likely to engage in behaviors such as cooking and decorating than the female target, $F\ (1, 80) = 20.10$, $p < .001$, $\eta^2 = .20$, but more likely to perform these activities than the male target, $F\ (1, 80) = 114.95$, $p < .001$, $\eta^2 = .59$. The PA target was perceived as less likely to work in male-dominated occupations than the male target, $F\ (1, 75) = 79.92$, $p < .001$, $\eta^2 = .52$, but more likely to hold these positions than the female target, $F\ (1, 75) = 34.14$, $p < .001$, $\eta^2 = .31$. Finally, the PA target was rated as less likely to work in female-dominated occupations than the female target, $F\ (1, 76) = 39.98$, $p < .001$, $\eta^2 = .38$, and more likely to hold these occupations than the male target, $F\ (1, 76) = 33.71$, $p < .001$, $\eta^2 = .31$. A significant target by participant gender interaction was also obtained with respect to female-dominated occupations, F (1, 76) = 4.51, $p = .04$, $\eta^2 = .06$. Men rated the male and the PA target as more likely to hold these occupations than did women, and women rated the female target as more likely to hold these occupations than did men. There were also two main effects of participant gender such that, compared to men, women perceived all three targets as more likely to engage in masculine gender-role behaviors, F (1, 79) = 6.74, $p = .01$, $\eta^2 = .08$, and to hold male-dominated occupations, F (1, 75) = 3.88, $p = .05$, $\eta^2 = .05$.

Because these results may have been an artifact of combining data from participants who perceived the PA target to be male with data from those who perceived the PA target to be female, the analyses were repeated to control for perceived target gender. Again, the results were replicated regardless of whether the PA target was perceived to be male or female.[4] There was a tendency for perceivers to view a PA target of their own gender as particularly unlikely to engage in gender-consistent behaviors. For example, when the sample was restricted to participants who perceived the PA target to be male, a significant target by participant gender interaction was obtained on masculine gender-role behaviors, F (1, 42) = 5.52, $p = .02$, $\eta^2 = .12$. Although both women and men rated the "male" PA target as less likely to engage in masculine gender-role behaviors than the male-gendered target, this pattern was particularly evident in the men's responses (M = 17.14 and 30.21 for men; M = 21.44 and 30.32 for women). The analogous target by participant gender interaction was obtained with regard to feminine gender-role behaviors when the sample was restricted to those participants who perceived the PA target to be female, F (1, 41) = 5.44, $p = .03$, $\eta^2 = .12$ (M = 28.00 and 32.30 for women; M = 30.92 and 33.24 for men).

Aside from these higher order interactions, participants tended to make the same pattern of inferences about PA targets perceived to be male as they did about PA targets perceived to be female, at least when the inferences about the PA target were compared to inferences about the gendered targets (e.g., when inferences about the "male" PA target were compared with inferences about the male target). Do these inferences remain the same if we change the comparison such that inferences about the "male" PA target are compared directly with inferences about the "female" PA target? Interestingly, perceptions of the "male" and "female" PA target did not differ on any of the six dimensions: masculinity, t (90) = .03, *ns;* femininity, t (88) = .83, *ns;* male gender-role behaviors, t (90) = .83, *ns;* female gender-role behaviors, t (90) = .11, *ns;* male-dominated occupations, t (85) = .01, *ns;* and female dominated-occupations, t (87) = .67, *ns.*

This is somewhat puzzling when compared with the results of the analogous analyses for the male- and female-gendered target. Compared to the female-gendered target, the male-gendered target was perceived as more masculine, F (1, 84) = 202.35, $p < .001$, $\eta^2 = .71$, more likely to perform male gender-role behaviors, F (1, 79) = 307.61, $p < .001$, $\eta^2 = .80$, and more likely to hold male-dominated occupations, F (1, 75) = 207.06, $p < .001$, $\eta^2 = .73$. Compared to the male-gendered target, the female-gendered target was perceived as more feminine, F (1, 87) = 207.59, $p < .001$, $\eta^2 = .71$, more likely to perform female gender-role behaviors, F (1, 80) = 149.91, $p < .001$, $\eta^2 = .65$, and more likely to hold female-dominated occupations, F (1, 76) = 105.02, $p < .001$, $\eta^2 = .58$. Thus, the effect of perceived target gender was very different for PA and gendered targets. For PA targets, participants made the same inferences for "male" and "female" PA targets. For gendered targets, participants made very different inferences for the male and female targets.

SEXUAL ORIENTATION As in Experiment 1, the PA target was perceived as more likely to be homosexual, $F\ (1, 83) = 42.95, \rho < .001, \eta^2 = .34$, and less likely to be heterosexual than the gendered targets, $F\ (1, 84) = 56.58, \rho < .001, \eta^2 = .40$ (see Table 19.2). The PA target was also rated as more likely to be bisexual than the gendered targets, $F\ (1,80) = 38.78, \rho < .001, \eta^2 = .33$. Interestingly, the female-gendered target was also rated as more likely to be bisexual than the male-gendered target, $F\ (1, 80) = 11.77, \rho = .001, \eta^2 = .13$, although the male- and female-gendered targets did not differ on the homosexuality and heterosexuality ratings, $F\ (1, 83) = .00$, *ns;* $F\ (1, 84) = 2.70$, *ns,* respectively. There was also a main effect of order such that participants who received the male target first tended to rate all three targets as more likely to be homosexual than participants who received the PA or the female target first, $F\ (5, 83) = 4.39, \rho = .001, \eta^2 = .21$.

DISCUSSION

As the results of Experiment 2 demonstrate, PA targets were inferred to have gender-related characteristics between that of a man and a woman regardless of whether target information was presented in verbal descriptions or through photos. Inferences regarding the sexual orientation of the PA target also replicated. The PA target was perceived as more likely to be homosexual and less likely to be heterosexual than the gendered targets. In addition, Experiment 2 demonstrated that perceived target gender had a greater effect on inferences about gendered targets than it did on PA targets. Perceivers made different inferences about the male- and female-gendered targets, but their inferences about the "male" and "female" PA target did not differ.

There are two alternative explanations for the data. First, the tendency to assume that PA targets are likely to be homosexual may be due to an illusory correlation between physical androgyny and homosexuality rather than the ambiguity of PA people's gender per se. An illusory correlation is the tendency for people to overestimate the correlation between infrequent events (Chapman, 1967; Hamilton, 1981; Hamilton and Sherman, 1994; McArthur, 1982; see also Stroessner, Hamilton, and Mackie, 1992). Because both homosexuality and physical androgyny occur relatively infrequently in the general population, perceivers may assume that these characteristics go together. If this is the case, this illusory correlation may lead individuals to infer that, if a person has a PA appearance, there is a higher probability he or she is homosexual. Given that bisexuality also occurs relatively infrequently in the general population, any effect of an illusory correlation should also occur for bisexuality judgments.

Second, both Experiment 1 and Experiment 2 used within-subjects designs such that each participant rated a male target, a female target, and at least one PA target. This created the possibility that participants compared the PA target against the gendered targets in making their inferences. Would the findings replicate in a between-subjects design where participants rate only one target? Experiment 3 repeated a segment of the original design to explore these questions.

EXPERIMENT 3

Methods

Participants

Participants were 221 introductory psychology students (121 women, 100 men) at a large university in the Southwest who participated in the experiment in partial fulfillment of a course requirement. Ethnicity was not explicitly measured, but the majority of the students at the university were of Caucasian or Hispanic origin.

Materials and Procedure

Participants received one of the verbal descriptions used in Experiment 2. Participants first indicated whether the target was male or female. Consistent with the intended categorization, 95 percent of participants rated K. T. as male, 95 percent of participants rated D. S. as female, and 69 percent of participants rated L. R. as male (31 percent rated L. R. as female). Second, participants indicated how unusual they thought the person was using a 10-point Likert-type scale ranging from *not at all unusual* (1) to *somewhat unusual* (5) to *very unusual* (10). This measure was included in order to explore the possibility of an illusory correlation between physical androgyny and perceived homosexuality. Finally, participants rated the target on the three sexual orientation items and the twenty personality traits used in Experiment 2. Measures of gender-role behaviors and occupations were not included in Experiment 3 because the hypothesized pattern of effects in Experiments 1 and 2 were consistent across the personality, gender-role behavior, and occupation items, and it seemed unlikely that inclusion of these measures in Experiment 3 would add significant new information to the results.

Results and Discussion

Ratings on the masculine traits and the feminine traits were summed as in Experiments 1 and 2. No main effects of, nor interactions with, participant gender were obtained. Results of a one-way ANOVA indicated that the findings in Experiments 1 and 2 could not be attributed to comparisons between targets. Although participants received only one target description, the personality traits of the PA target were again perceived in the middle between those of the male and female target: that is, less masculine than the male but more masculine than the female, F (2, 203) = 36.26, $p < .001$, a priori comparison, t (148) = 5.71, $p < .001$ and t (150) = 3.19, $p = .002$, respectively; less feminine than the female but more feminine than the male, F (2, 203) = 27.17, $p < .001$, a priori comparison, t (152) = 2.22, $p = .03$ and t (154) = 6.03, $p < .001$, respectively (see Table 19.3).

The findings regarding the sexual orientation ratings were also replicated for the most part. The PA target was again perceived as less likely to be heterosexual and more likely to be homosexual than the gendered targets, t (217) = 2.93, $p =$

Table 19.3 Means for the Male, Female, and PA Target in Experiment 3

	Target		
Dimension	**Male**	**PA**	**Female**
Masculine personality traits	72.56_a (12.71)	57.02_b (17.58)	48.55_c (12.06)
Feminine personality traits	50.43_a (9.65)	63.37_b (14.53)	69.00_c (16.15)
Heterosexuality likelihood	6.78_a (2.39)	5.63_b (2.33)	6.40_a (2.64)
Homosexuality likelihood	3.68_a (1.72)	4.63_b (1.97)	3.76_a (2.14)
Bisexuality likelihood	4.05_a (2.20)	4.56_a (2.30)	4.29_a (1.98)

Notes: Standard deviations shown in parentheses. Means in the same row that do not share subscripts differ at $p < .01$.

.004 and t (219) = 3.44, p = .001, respectively. However, the PA target was not perceived as significantly more likely to be bisexual, although the means were in the predicted direction, t (218) = 1.31, *ns* (see Table 19.3). Because this effect did not replicate, it seemed unlikely that there was an illusory correlation between bisexuality and physical androgyny. It remained possible, however, that an illusory correlation explained the homosexuality judgments.

If participants' tendency to assume the PA target was homosexual was due to an illusory correlation, two conditions should have occurred: (1) the PA target should have been perceived as more unusual than the gendered targets, and (2) this uniqueness rating should have mediated homosexuality judgments. The first condition was met in that the PA target was rated as more unusual than the gendered targets (M = 3.41, 3.47, and 4.34 for the male, female, and PA targets, respectively), t (212) = 2.96, p = .003.

A series of three regressions were conducted to test whether the uniqueness rating mediated homosexuality judgments. For these analyses, type of target was dummy coded with the two gendered targets as ϕ and the PA target as 1. Uniqueness rating was regressed on type of target, homosexuality judgment was regressed on type of target, and homosexuality judgment was regressed on type of target and uniqueness rating (Baron and Kenny 1986). Type of target did predict uniqueness rating, F (1, 212) = 8.76, p = .003, but the uniqueness rating did not significantly mediate homosexuality judgments (see Table 19.4). Furthermore, the correlation between uniqueness rating and homosexuality judgments was not significant for the PA target (r = −.08, *ns*) nor for the gendered targets (r = −.11, *ns*). The correlation between uniqueness rating and bisexuality judgments was also not significant for the PA target (r = −.02, *ns*) nor for the gendered targets (r = .06, *ns*). Thus, although participants assumed that the PA target was more likely to be homosexual than the gendered targets, this assumption did not appear to be the result of an illusory correlation between homosexuality and physical androgyny.

Table 19.4 Homosexuality Likelihood Regressed on Type of Target, Before and After Controlling for Uniqueness Rating

Predictor	B	SE B	*Beta*	t	p
Type of target	.90	.26	.23	3.44	.00
$R^2 = .05$					
$F (1, 219) = 11.81, p < .001$					
Uniqueness rating	−.09	.06	−.10	−1.43	*ns*
Type of target	.99	.27	.25	3.64	.00
$R^2 = .06$					
$F (2, 211) = 6.88, p = .001$					

Note: Regression analyses entered uniqueness rating and type of target simultaneously.

In sum, the results of Experiment 3 eliminated two potential alternative explanations for the findings of Experiments 1 and 2. First, perceivers inferred that PA people have gender-related traits and behaviors that are between those of a man and a woman even when they could not directly compare gendered and PA targets. Second, assumptions regarding the sexual orientation of the PA target were not due to an illusory correlation between homosexuality and physical androgyny.

GENERAL DISCUSSION

Perceivers make consistent inferences about PA targets over a wide range of characteristics and behaviors. Specifically, PA targets are assumed to be less masculine than a man but more masculine than a woman. PA targets are also assumed to be less feminine than a woman but more feminine than a man. The same pattern is evident with respect to masculine and feminine gender-role behaviors and male- and female-dominated occupations. In each case, the likelihood of PA targets performing these behaviors is perceived to be between that of a man and a woman. Perceivers also make consistent inferences regarding the sexual orientation of PA targets. Compared to gendered targets, PA targets are perceived as more likely to be homosexual and less likely to be heterosexual.

These findings hold up against the challenge of a number of alternative explanations. The pattern of results is not limited to one mode of target presentation or one set of targets, as the findings replicated using both photos and verbal descriptions. The findings with respect to personality traits and sexual orientation are also not attributable to comparisons between gendered and PA targets because the results replicated when participants were presented with only one target.[5] The tendency to assume PA targets are homosexual is not a function of an illusory correlation between physical androgyny and homosexuality because uniqueness ratings did not mediate homosexuality judgments. There is also no evidence to support the existence of an illusory correlation between bisexuality and physical androgyny. Thus, it appears unlikely that the observers' inferences regarding the sexual orientation of PA targets are attributable to the underlying frequency (or infrequency) of physical androgyny in the population.

Just as perceivers make different inferences about PA targets than gendered targets, the effect of perceived gender on these inferences is different for PA targets than gendered targets. For targets whose gender is not ambiguous, inferences correspond to the targets' gender (e.g., a male target is rated as more masculine and more likely to engage in male gender-role behaviors and occupations than a female target). For PA targets, inferences do not correspond to the targets' gender in that "male" and "female" targets are assumed to have the same characteristics (e.g., a "male" PA target is not rated as more masculine and more likely to engage in male gender-role behaviors and occupations than a "female" PA target).

This poses an interesting question for current models of impression formulation, particularly Brewer's (1988) dual process model and Fiske and Neuberg's (1990) continuum model. These models assume that gender categorization is preconscious and precedes all further information processing about an individual. Thus, under usual conditions, subsequent inferences regarding the person's characteristics can be influenced by the gender categorization. This is particularly true of Brewer's model in that it assumes that, once an individual has been categorized according to gender, all further processing remains divided according to gender. In other words, the moment we encounter another person, we have already categorized that person as being male or female. Consequently, any subsequent judgments we make about that person may be influenced by our awareness of the person's gender. We may decide the person is friendly or athletic or attractive, but all of these judgments are made in light of our categorization of the person's gender.

Given that inferences about the "male" and "female" PA targets did not differ, information processing regarding PA targets may not be completely divided in this way. Or, if perceivers are dividing PA targets according to gender, they are not making different inferences about "male" and "female" PA targets. This seems unlikely, given that the participants made very different inferences about the male- and female-gendered targets. Perhaps physical androgyny is so salient that it takes precedence over gender as a basis for making inferences such that perceivers assume anyone who is physically androgynous has more or less the same characteristics, regardless of his or her gender.

Or perhaps the assumptions we make about other people (gendered or PA) are not solely a function of gender categorization. Perhaps judgments about a target's personality and behavior are a function of the target's physical characteristics rather than the gender label.[6] If an individual's outward characteristics appear masculine, perceivers make the correspondent inference that his or her inward characteristics are also masculine (and vice versa for femininity). If an individual's outward characteristics are androgynous, perceivers make the correspondent inference that his or her inward characteristics are also androgynous. Interestingly, Deaux and Lewis (1984) found that a target's physical characteristics predicted perceiver's inferences better than direct information about the target's gender. This may be because physical characteristics (especially characteristics as gender-linked as those used by Deaux and Lewis) are usually redundant with gender. Thus, if one knows a person has a soft voice and is dainty, graceful, and soft, one may simply infer that individual is female, making explicit information about the target's gender superfluous.

Although perceivers undoubtedly do make gender categorizations, these judgments may or may not be directly involved in the inference process. This is difficult to test because most people's physical characteristics are directly indicative of their gender. Research with PA targets may afford a unique opportunity to test the role of gender categorization in the impression formation process. However, researchers need to be mindful that PA targets may be processed differently than gendered targets, precisely because of their unusual appearance. For example, perceived gender may not affect inferences about PA targets because, although perceivers categorize target gender, they are not confident in their judgments. Consequently, their inferences are driven by characteristics other than gender (e.g., physical appearance).[7] Perceived gender may have a greater influence on impressions formed about gendered targets because perceivers are more confident that their gender categorizations are accurate.

The results of these three studies may have practical implications. First, these results add empirical evidence to the abundant anecdotal evidence suggesting that people draw conclusions about someone's sexual orientation based on his or her physical characteristics, particularly if those characteristics are somewhat inconsistent with the person's gender. Second, the association between physical androgyny and homosexuality may reinforce (or be a result of) our culture's butch/fem stereotypes about lesbians and gay men. If a person with certain physical characteristics is assumed to be homosexual and to have psychological characteristics atypical of their gender (e.g., less masculine than a man but more masculine than a woman), observers may conclude that other people assumed to be homosexual also have psychological characteristics atypical of their gender. This may be related to the tendency in Western culture to confound sexual orientation with masculinity/femininity. Specifically, one defining characteristic of masculinity is to be attracted to women, and one defining characteristic of femininity is to be attracted to men (see Bem 1993; Bohan 1996). To the degree that lesbians are attracted to women, others assume they must somehow be masculine, perhaps in their physical characteristics as well as their psychological characteristics. Because gay men are attracted to men, they must somehow be feminine in their physical characteristics and/or in their psychological characteristics.

Third, because they are assumed to be gay, PA individuals may be more likely to experience homophobic responses than people with less ambiguous physical characteristics. It is possible that the perceived correlation between physical androgyny and sexual orientation is accurate, but the assumption that PA people are gay has disturbing implications regardless of whether this is the case. Because homosexuality is associated with a range of other negative characteristics in American culture, perceivers who assume that PA people are gay may also assume PA people are immoral, mentally ill, and unfit for military service or parenthood. PA people may also be subjected to a variety of negative behavior, including violence, discrimination, and negative affect.

Although Experiments 2 and 3 eliminated a number of alternative explanations, at least three limitations remain. First, the grouping of the dependent measures was the same in Experiments 1 and 2 (i.e., all participants completed the personality items, the gender-role behavior items, and the occupation items). It is possible that the coupling of the dependent measures may have influenced participants' inferences. For example, perhaps participants made consistent inferences regarding a target's personality, gender-role behaviors, and occupations because they always responded to these items as a group. If the dependent measures were separated such that each participant rated either the target's personality traits, gender-role behaviors, or occupation, participants' inferences may not have been as consistent across these dimensions. This was done in Experiment 3, where perceivers responded to only the personality items. Still, the results replicated in that they perceived the PA target's personality as falling between the male and female target in terms of masculinity and femininity. Although these data cannot address what might have happened if participants had rated only the gender-role behaviors or only the occupation items, it seems likely that inferences about these dimensions would change radically when presented in isolation, given that the personality inferences did not change. More to the point, the key results of these studies indicate differences between targets such that participants made systematically different inferences about the PA target compared to the male and female target. Given that the dependent measures were the same for the PA and the gendered targets, it is unclear how the grouping of the dependent measures in Experiments 1 and 2 could explain the between-target differences in perceivers' impressions.

The second limitation involves target attractiveness. In Experiment 1, both the PA and the gendered-target photos were rated as relatively unattractive compared to other test photos. The female target was also rated as somewhat more attractive than the male and PA targets, although this may be attributable to the ambiguous ethnicity of the male target and the PA targets. Although verbal stimuli were used in Experiments 2 and 3 in an attempt to eliminate the potential influence of perceived attractiveness on participants' inferences, perceived attractiveness was not measured in these studies. To the degree that participants in Experiments 2 and 3 concluded that some of the targets (in particular the PA target) were less attractive, their inferences could be driven by perceived unattractiveness rather than physical androgyny.

Two factors throw suspicion on this explanation. First, it is unclear how perceivers would make assumptions about the attractiveness of the targets based solely on the information in the verbal descriptions used in Experiments 2 and 3. It is also unclear why participants would assume that the PA target is less attractive than the other targets when the PA target description explicitly describes the target as attractive. Second, even if the participants did assume the PA target was less attractive than the gendered targets, why would inferences about the relative unattractiveness of a PA target lead perceivers to assume he or she is psychologically androgynous? It may be reasonable to predict that perceivers would conclude that unattractive people are more likely to be gay in that both of these characteristics are viewed somewhat negatively by portions of the population. However, it seems unlikely that a perceiver would conclude that a person is less masculine than a man but more masculine than a woman simply because that person is unattractive.

The third limitation is that the perceptions of the PA target were somewhat male-biased in Experiment 3 in that a majority of participants (69 percent) perceived the PA target to be male. This may be related to the more general tendency to assume that any person or animal with an unspecified gender is male (see Hamilton 1991). On the surface, this may seem to be a serious concern. Recall, however, the finding in Experiment 2 that participants made identical inferences about PA targets perceived to be male and those perceived to be female. In other words, the perceived gender of the PA target did not change participants' perceptions in Experiment 2. The perceived gender of the PA target also appeared to have little influence on participants' inference in Experiment 3 because the hypothesized pattern of results replicated, despite the fact that more participants perceived the PA target to be male. The tendency to perceive that PA target to be male does suggest that the participants' gender categorization in Experiments 1 and 2 (which used within-subjects designs) may have been influenced by direct comparisons across the PA and gendered targets.

These data suggest a number of possibilities for future research. Given the assumptions that are made about the personality, behavior, and sexual orientation of PA individuals, how does physical androgyny affect perceivers' behavior? It is possible that perceivers will try to avoid or minimize interaction with a PA person. It is also possible they might prolong an interaction with a PA person in an effort to gather more information about his or her gender. How might their inferences and behavior change if, as a result of this interaction, they learn the person they though was female is actually male (or vice versa)? Perceivers may experience a range of negative affect, including embarrassment and anger, and may be even more likely to assume the PA person is gay.

It would also be interesting to explore the characteristics and reactions of PA persons themselves (see Devor 1989). To what degree do PA people actually possess a psychologically androgynous mix of personality characteristics and behaviors? Perhaps perceivers' inferences are correct in that PA individuals are more psychologically androgynous and more likely to be homosexual than other people. This might be the result of personal choice or the influence of a self-fulfilling prophecy, where PA people exhibit traits and behaviors that are consistent with others' expectations.

Naturally occurring events can be useful heuristics for generating psychological hypotheses (McGuire, 1983). Physical androgyny provides a unique means to enrich our understanding of the importance of physical appearance in the impression formation process. Contrary to the old adage, it appears that perceivers are quite willing to judge a book by its cover.

NOTES

1. When the sample was restricted to those participants who perceived the PA targets to be male, these "male" PA targets were perceived as less masculine, F (1, 72) = 28.76, $p < .001$, $\eta^2 = .29$ (M = 54.85 and 63.88), less likely to perform male gender-role behaviors, F (1, 77) = 8.94, $p = .004$, $\eta^2 = .10$ (M = 23.89 and 25.91), and less likely to hold male-dominated occupations than the male target, F (1, 79) = 9.44, $p = .003$, $\eta^2 = .11$ (M = 20.75 and 23.36). When compared with the female target, the "female" PA targets were perceived as less feminine, F (1, 47) = 9.77, $p = .003$, $\eta^2 = .17$ (M = 62.19 and 68.36), less likely to engage in female gender-role behaviors, F (1, 47) = 13.05, $p = .001$, $\eta^2 = .28$ (M = 29.54 and 33.86), and less likely to engage in female-dominated occupations, F(1, 48) = 6.75, $p = .012$, $\eta^2 = .12$ (M = 27.75 and 30.96). To avoid problems with redundant effects, participant gender and order of presentation were excluded from these analyses.

2. Because sexual orientation is only indirectly tied to gender (unlike perceived personality, gender-role behavior, and gender-dominated occupations), these analyses were not repeated to control for perceived gender of the PA targets.

3. One masculine role behavior (i.e., takes the initiative in romantic relationships) was dropped from the scale due to poor reliability. Dropping this item increased the reliability from $\alpha = .76$ to $\alpha = .86$. Although the reliability of the masculine role behavior scale was also somewhat low in Experiment 1, dropping this item did not improve the reliability in Experiment 1. It is unclear why the reliability of this scale was so low in Experiment 1.

4. Compared to the male target, PA targets perceived to be male were rated as less masculine, F (1, 38) = 95.97, $\rho < .001$, $\eta^2 = .72$ (M = 56.98 and 77.75), more feminine, F (1, 41) = 52.95, $\rho < .001$, $\eta^2 = .56$ (M = 65.59 and 46.09), less likely to perform masculine gender-role behaviors, F (1, 42) = 92.80, $\rho < .001$, $\eta^2 = .69$ (M = 18.00 and 28.18), more likely to perform female gender-role behaviors, F (1, 41) = 36.96, $\rho < .001$, $\eta^2 = .47$ (M = 29.80 and 19.17), less likely to hold male-dominated occupations, F (1, 42) = 39.61, $\rho < .001$, $\eta^2 = .49$ (M = 22.02 and 32.87), and more likely to perform female-dominated occupations, F (1, 40) = 10.87, $\rho = .002$, $\eta 2 = .21$ (M = 24.80 and 19.50). Compared to the female target, PA targets perceived to be female were rated as more masculine, F (1, 36) = 10.30, $\rho = .003$, $\eta^2 = .22$ (M = 56.91 and 50.83), less feminine, F (1, 37) = 14.54, $\rho = .001$, $\eta^2 = .28$ (M = 63.68 and 71.67), more likely to perform masculine gender-role behaviors, F (1, 39) = 55.44, $\rho < .001$, $\eta^2 = .59$ (M = 20.98 and 13.23), less likely to perform female gender-role behaviors, F (1, 41) = 8.88, $\rho = .005$, $\eta^2 = .18$ (M = 29.65 and 32.82), more likely to hold male-dominated occupations, F (1, 37) = 24.61, $\rho < .001$, $\eta^2 = .40$ (M = 22.00 and 16.23), and less likely to hold female-dominated occupations, F (1, 39) = 39.92, $\rho < .001$, $\eta^2 = .51$ (M = 25.95 and 33.55). To avoid problems with redundant effects, participant gender and order of target presentation were excluded from these analyses.

5. Because Experiment 3 did not explicitly test inferences regarding gender-role behaviors and occupations, it is possible these effects are influenced by comparisons between gendered and PA targets. However, given that the same pattern of results was found with respect to traits, gender-role behaviors, and occupations in Experiments 1 and 2, it seems unlikely the results regarding behaviors and occupations are attributable to cross-target comparisons when the results regarding traits are not.

5. I thank Gary L. Wells for this suggestion.

7. I thank Linda J. Beckman for this suggestion.

REFERENCES

Baron, R. M., and D. A. Kenny. 1986. The moderator-mediator variable distinction in social psychology research: Conceptual, strategic, and statistical considerations. *Journal of Personality and Social Psychology* 51: 1173–82.

Bem, S. A. 1974. The measurement of psychological androgyny. *Journal of Consulting and Clinical Psychology* 42: 155–62.

———. 1993. *The lenses of gender: Transforming the debate on sexual inequality.* New Haven: Yale University Press.

Berry, D. S., and L. Z. McArthur. 1985. Some components and consequences of a babyface. *Journal of Personality and Social Psychology* 48: 312–23.

Bohan, J. S. 1996. *Psychology and sexual orientation: Coming to terms.* New York: Routledge.

Brewer, M. B. 1988. A dual process model of impression formation. In *Advances in social cognition: A dual process model of impression formation,* ed. T. K. Srull and R. S. Wyer Jr., Vol. 1, 1–37. Hillsdale, NJ: Erlbaum.

Bruner, J. S. 1957. On perceptual readiness. *Psychological Review 64:* 123–52.

Calvert, J. D. 1988. Physical attractiveness: A review and re-evaluation of its role in social skill research. *Behavioral Assessment* 10: 29–42.

Chapman, L. J. 1967. Illusory correlation in observational report. *Journal of Verbal Learning and Verbal Behavior* 6: 151–55.

Deaux, K., and L. L. Lewis. 1984. Structure of gender stereotypes: Interrelationships among components and gender label. *Journal of Personality and Social Psychology 46:* 991–1004.

Devor, H. 1989. *Gender blending: Confronting the limits of duality.* Bloomington: Indiana University Press.

Dion, K., E. Berscheid, and E. Walster. 1972. What is beautiful is good. *Journal of Personality and Social Psychology* 24: 285–90.

Eagly, A. H., R. D. Ashmore, M. G. Makhijani, and L. C. Longo. 1991. What is beautiful is good, but . . . : A meta-analytic review of research on the physical attractiveness stereotype. *Psychology Bulletin* 110: 109–28.

Fiske, S. T., and S. L. Neuberg. 1990. A continuum of impression formation, from category-based to individuating processes: Influences of information and motivation on attention and interpretation. *Advances in Experimental Social Psychology* 23: 1–74.

Hamilton, D. L. 1981. Illusory correlation as a basis for stereotyping. In *Cognitive processes in stereotyping and intergroup behavior,* ed. D. L. Hamilton, 115–44. Hillsdale, NJ: Erlbaum.

Hamilton, D. L., and J. W. Sherman. 1994. Stereotypes. In *Handbook of social cognition,* ed. R. S. Wyer Jr. and T. K. Srull, 2nd ed., Vol. 2, 1–68. Hillsdale, NJ: Erlbaum.

Hamilton, M. C. 1991. Masculine bias in the attribution of personhood: People = male, male = people. *Psychology of Women Quarterly* 15: 393–402.

Jackson, L. A. 1992. *Physical appearance and gender: Sociobiological and sociocultural perspectives.* Albany: State University of New York Press.

Jones, E. E. 1990. *Interpersonal perception.* New York: Freeman.

Jones, E. E., and K. E. Davis. 1965. From acts to dispositions: The attribution process in social psychology. In *Advances in experimental social psychology,* ed. L. Berkowitz, Vol. 2, 219–66. New York: Academic.

Jones, E. E., K. E. Davis, and K. J. Gergen. 1961. Role playing variations and their informational value for person perception. *Journal of Abnormal and Social Psychology* 63: 302–10.

Jones, E. E., and V. A. Harris. 1967. The attribution of attitudes. *Journal of Experimental Social Psychology* 3: 1–24.

Jones, E. E., and D. McGillis. 1976. Correspondent inferences and the attribution cube: A comparative reappraisal. In *New directions in attribution research,* ed. J. H. Harvey, W. J. Ickles, and R. F. Kidd, Vol. 1, 389–420. Hillsdale, NJ: Erlbaum.

McArthur, L. Z. 1982. Judging a book by its cover: A cognitive analysis of the relationship between physical appearance and stereotyping. In *Cognitive social psychology,* ed. A. H. Hastorf and A. M. Isen, 149–211. New York: Elsevier/North Holland.

McArthur, L. Z., and K. Apatow. 1983–1984. Impressions of baby-faced adults. *Social cognition* 2: 315–42.

McGuire, W. J. 1983. A contextualist theory of knowledge. *Advances in Experimental Social Psychology* 16: 1–33.

Orlofsky, J. L., and C. A. O'Heron. 1987. Development of a short-form Sex Role Behavior Scale. *Journal of Personality Assessment* 51: 267–77.

Secord, P. F., W. F. Dukes, and W. Bevan. 1954. Personalities in faces: I. An experiment in social perceiving. *Genetic Psychology Monographs* 49: 231–79.

Secord, P. F., and J. E. Muthard. 1955. Personality in faces: IV. A descriptive analysis of the perception of women's faces and identification of some physiognomic determinants. *Journal of Psychology* 39: 269–78.

Spence, J. T., R. Helmreich, and J. Stap. 1974. The Personal Attribute Questionnaire: A measure of sex-role stereotypes and masculinity and femininity. *Journal Supplement Abstract Service Catalog of Selected Documents in Psychology* 4: 43. Ms. No. 617.

Stoessner, S. J., D. L. Hamilton, and D. M. Mackie. 1992. Affect and stereotyping: The effect of induced mood and distinctiveness-based illusory correlations. *Journal of Personality and Social Psychology* 62: 564–76.

U.S. Department of Commerce. 1994. *Statistical abstract of the United States.* Washington, DC: U.S. Government Printing Office.

Zebrowitz, L. A., S. Brownlow, and K. Olson. 1992. Baby talk to the babyfaces. *Journal of Nonverbal Behavior* 16: 143–58.

CHAPTER 20

The Outsider Phenomenon

NANCY A. NAPLES

The purpose of this chapter is to demonstrate the value of a feminist perspective on community studies with particular attention to the debate contrasting insider and outsider ethnographic research.[1] The insider versus outsider debate—whether it is more effective to conduct fieldwork as an insider or an outsider to the communities you study—challenges those of us who use ethnographic methods in our research in the United States to reexamine our taken-for-granted assumptions about what constitutes "indigenous" knowledge and how we use both our commonalities and differences to heighten sensitivity to others' complex and shifting worldviews.

In this feminist revisiting of the insider/outsider debate, I argue that the insider/outsider distinction masks the power differentials and experiential differences between the researcher and the researched. The bipolar construction of insider/outsider also sets up a false separation that neglects the interactive processes through which "insiderness" and "outsiderness" are constructed. Insiderness and outsiderness are not fixed or static positions, rather, they are ever-shifting and permeable social locations that are differentially experienced and expressed by community members. By recognizing the fluidity of insiderness/outsiderness, we also acknowledge three key methodological points: as ethnographers we are never fully outside or inside the community; our relationship to the community is never expressed in general terms but is constantly being negotiated and renegotiated in particular, everyday interactions; and these interactions are themselves located in shifting relationships among community residents. These negotiations simultaneously are embedded in processes that reposition gender, class, and racial-ethnic relations among other socially constructed distinctions. From a feminist perspective, I argue that by shifting the standpoint to those who are marginal to the mythic community insider, certain less visible features of community life are brought into view.

The apparently clear distinction between insiderness and outsiderness falls away as we confront how regional differences, as well as class, gender, age, parenting and marital status, sexuality, race, and ethnicity shape the multiple identities we identify (with) in our research. I start with the assumption that, rather than one insider perspective, we all begin our work from different positions and social experiences that contribute to numerous dimensions on which we can relate to residents in various overlapping communities. Our social location shapes the way we enter the field and how we relate to different members within a particular community. For example, as a woman I have certain experiences that may give me greater insider perspectives on women I meet in the field. However, my research with African American and Puerto Rican women in low income communities in New York City and Philadelphia underscored for me the diverse ways that women's experiences are shaped by race, class, sex, and religious commitment, among other dimensions. On the other hand, as a New York City native and a social worker in Manhattan I was familiar with many more features of social life when conducting this urban-centered research than I was in my research in rural Iowa.

Before I continue, it is necessary to situate myself within my own social cultural background. I was born into a working-class family and lived until August of 1989 in New York City. I spent eight years as a social worker, community resident, and political activist in Manhattan. My dissertation involved research in the South Bronx, Harlem, and the Lower East Side of Manhattan, and with low income communities in Philadelphia. Following the completion of my Ph.D. and much to the amazement of many of my friends, I accepted a faculty position at Iowa State University. The shift from the large urban sprawl of New York City to the small town and largely rural surroundings of Ames, Iowa, inspired a vast array of empirical and theoretical questions that have permanently altered the way I view the world.

When I arrived in Iowa, I was intrigued by the contrast between rural and urban community life. What began as a modest attempt to compare the experiences of low income women in rural Iowa with the urban women I had studied in New York City and Philadelphia has now developed into an extensive and ongoing ethnographic study of the changing gender, class, and racial-ethnic relations in two small towns with populations of under 1,500 residents. With the assistance of a grant from the National Institute of Mental Health, I began an ethnographic study of the social dimensions of rural economic and demographic change. Since so much of my worldview has been shaped within an urban context, I felt very much the outsider when I entered a rural setting. Despite the surface commonality of language, I was completely ignorant of a rural way of life. Ironically, many of those I met in Iowa were baffled by those of us from large urban settings. At the close of a 1991 interview with a farmer, she asked about my background and when I told her she said: "How can you stand having all those people around?" I then described my discomfort with the lack of people in the open spaces of Iowa.

One theme pervading the data gathered in the field is the extent to which residents with a diversity of social, economic, and demographic characteristics experienced feelings of alienation from the perceived community at large. In fact, most people I interviewed in-depth said they were outsiders to the community for a variety of differing reasons. My own feelings of outsiderness became a resource through which I was able to acquire an insider perspective on many residents' perception of alienation from others in their community.

This finding appears to support Georg Simmel's contention that people will share confidences with a stranger that they may not share with friends and acquaintances.[2] Yet the parallel finding that many residents also felt themselves outside the community led me to reexamine the insider/outsider debate and to identify what I have come to call the "outsider phenomenon." Simmel's analysis was based on a rigid conception of social life that assumed an unchanging distinction between the stranger and the insider; an inattention to power in encounters between the stranger and insiders; and a belief in the stranger's greater objectivity. In this feminist revisiting, I highlight the fluidity of outsiderness and insiderness; center attention on power in ethnographic encounters; and challenge reductive and essentialist notions of standpoint. Rather than view insiderness/outsiderness as identifiable and relatively fixed social locations, the concept of outsider phenomenon highlights the processes through which community members are created as others—a process in which all members participate to varying degrees—and by which feelings of otherness are incorporated into self-perceptions and social interactions. The identification of the outsider phenomenon is especially noteworthy given the continued salience of gemeinschaft found in accounts of rural small town life offered by residents and nonresidents alike.

The often used distinction between *gemeinschaft* and *geselleschaft* serves to mask differences in small communities as well as underestimate the close-knit experiences of community in urban areas. The one obvious difference confronted in rural-based research is the obvious paucity of public places/spaces for entry into the field. The lack of public spaces is a disadvantage to an outsider; however, I found access to personal spaces in rural communities easier than in urban settings. As my research progressed, I became more convinced than ever that place profoundly influences the way we see the world around us. Therefore, women of the same class or race background may be unable to bridge the different worldviews shaped by geographic variations in their experiences. On the other hand, as the research progressed, I was surprised to learn that many residents in these two rural towns also felt like outsiders, albeit for different reasons. The mutual outsider feelings became a deeply felt and widely expressed basis for the fieldwork and subsequent analysis. Ironically, my outsider status served as a means by which I became an insider to the outsider feelings of many interviewed for the study. Simultaneously, my insider designation as a faculty member at Iowa State, a popular state university, provided an initial ground for residents' willingness to share their experiences with me.

I interviewed a subset of community members, including clergy, social service workers, and low income women, on two or more occasions. Interviews took place in offices, in homes, at local restaurants, less formally on Main Street, in local businesses during working hours, or while attending community events. The open-ended interview was utilized to generate an oral history of each community resident with special attention to the following areas: background; education and work experiences; attitudes toward his or her community; economic development; gender, race-ethnic, and class relations; participation in community activities; and a description of changes in the town and visions for the future.

One strategy I used to gain a broader understanding of the social construction of community included gathering in-depth information from diverse perspectives—a commonplace fieldwork method. I also utilized group discussions with selected community members to further explore some of the themes identified in the interviews. In these small group discussions, I posed specific questions about the community that were generated from my interviews and other data gathering efforts. Responses from the group helped clarify my findings (or hunches) and, in some instances, redirected my investigations. These discussions often occurred in the course of other activities and sometimes included residents of nearby communities as well as Midtown and Southtown (the pseudonyms for the two towns in this study). These often impromptu discussions were enriched by the presence of nonresidents as they helped further highlight the differences between nonindigenous but contiguous perspectives and indigenous constructions. However, rarely did any one group include a variety of perspectives from within the two towns. Mexicans and Mexican Americans (who had moved to Midtown for employment in an expanding food processing plant located on the outskirts of the town) rarely met informally with non-Spanish-speaking white residents. Low income residents rarely spoke openly about their perceptions and experiences in a group discussion with those they perceived as more economically secure.

As mentioned, a majority of the community residents interviewed reported feelings of alienation from the perceived wider community. Ironically, those who were defined by others as insiders, also said they felt like outsiders who will never be accepted. I often left Midtown and Southtown after a field trip asking: "Who are the insiders here?" I have yet to meet a community resident who feels completely like the mythical community insider. Those named as insiders, such as the owners of the food processing plant and the local bankers, also feel like outsiders as they perceive other community residents' resentment of their economic success and political clout. Erin Landers (a pseudonym), one of the plant owners and a longtime resident of Midtown, reported that she felt a number of community members, particularly older residents who knew her and her husband as children, resented their financial success. She also perceived hostility from community members who were displeased with the number of Mexican and Mexican Americans who had moved to Midtown for employment in the plant.

Embedded in the outsider phenomenon were the patterns of inequality that shaped social life in these two rural towns. While those with more political and economic resources also felt outside for reasons often associated with their power and wealth, those with less resources were more disadvantaged by the social control processes associated with the outsider phenomenon. The mythic construction of a gemeinschaft-like community fed into the outsider pehomenon. The idealized construction of what it meant to be a part of the community and of who were legitimate community members served as both an internalized and externalized means of social control. When someone spoke up to challenge the construction, they were formally silenced or ostracized. Others silenced themselves for fear that they would disrupt the fragile sense of community. Consequently, many members walked around feeling alienated from the mythic community yet were careful not to share their feelings with others who they perceived were more connected to the community. As long as those on the margins felt silenced by the outsider phenomenon they would not challenge the power base and definition of the situation that privileged a small elite who controlled town politics and economic development.

On the other hand, a number of events and shifts in definition we chronicled highlighted the fluidity of the outsider phenomenon. This is most evident when we examine the process of racialization[3] in Midtown. Mexicans and Mexican Americans were most likely to fit into the taken-for-granted definition of newcomer (one important dimension of outsiderness) as they were among the most recent arrivals in Midtown. However, the term *newcomer* was also used to differentiate between

"Americans" and others viewed as temporary and, oftentimes, illegitimate residents. Under this formulation, Mexican Americans were frequently categorized along with undocumented Mexican workers as illegal and posing numerous problems for the so-called legitimate members of the community. However, the process of racialization in Midtown demonstrates that such totalizing conceptualization of the Mexican and Mexican-American residents was unstable and, consequently, quickly fell apart in the face of interactions with different agents of the state, such as the police and agents of the Immigration and Naturalization Service. The totalization was further compromised as young Mexicans and Mexican Americans entered the school system, were adopted by local families, dated white European American teenagers or married local white residents.

The documented shift in construction of outsiderness with regard to the Mexican and Mexican American residents highlights the fluidity of standpoints when viewed over time. Yet the tensions between white European American and Mexican and Mexican American residents remain. As my field investigations focused increasingly on the experiences of the Mexican and Mexican American residents and the process of racialization in Midtown, I was also repositioned by formerly receptive informants, especially those who held positions of power in the town. This repositioning was furthered when I hired bilingual Chicano graduate student Lionel Cantú to assist with the project. Where I found no difficulty moving freely about the town, Mr. Cantú reported being followed by the police, having his mail tampered with, and fearing for his safety.

On the other hand, Mr. Cantú quickly won the trust of many Mexican and Mexican American residents, a trust that would be difficult for me to gain as an Anglo non-Spanish-speaking researcher. In fact, when Anna Ortega (a pseudonym) was concerned with increasing police harassment in the town, she phoned Mr. Cantú in California for assistance. After some deliberation, we decided to mobilize my network of contacts in Iowa who were working as advocates for Latino residents in other parts of the state. My hesitation in connecting her with these advocates related to fear of exposing her position as an informal recruiter of numerous Mexican and Mexican American workers and their families. When Mr. Cantú returned her call and asked if we could give her name to several people who we thought might be able to assist her in dealing with the town officials, she agreed. In her role as recruiter and as a Latina, she felt more responsible for the well-being of those she brought to Midtown than was evidenced by the plant owners who, we suspect, initially sponsored her activities.

Our incorporation into the racialization process in Midtown and our dilemma over how to negotiate a more activist involvement in the community formed but two key tensions we confronted. The racialization process was illustrative of the ways in which the ethnographic field shifted over time and limited our ability to make one unchanging position on any methodological dilemma we faced.

THE PERSONAL POLITICS OF FIELDWORK

I listened with great empathy to the feelings of alienation expressed throughout the ethnographic interviews. One woman asked that I turn the tape recorder off while she composed herself after sharing her sadness over what she saw as the futile attempts of the economic development committee to revitalize the economy of her small town. Yet she had little hope that any other strategies would improve the economic well-being of her neighbors and friends. I also witnessed numerous processes of exclusion that formed the basis of many social exchanges between low income residents, especially single mothers, and more middle class residents. The white European American residents' treatment of the Mexican and Mexican American residents in Midtown was, at times, particularly discriminatory and difficult to witness. Although I harbor no inherent animosity toward the elite of these small towns, I have less empathy with their expressions of outsiderness as I witness their power to define the lives of others. I do admit a certain bias in my empathy toward those on the margins of these small towns that most likely reflects my own feelings of marginalization in many social locations. Yet as a sociologist, I am constantly aware that individual actions are embedded in the wider social cultural and economic processes. For example, I can take the point of view of the owner of a food processing plant who firmly believes that the minimum wage jobs are fair and that all workers are treated equally. However, this plant owner does not find it necessary to take the point of view of the workers in the plant who have different standpoints on the pay and organization of the workplace. From her privileged position, she can deny the power inherent in her ability to ignore the perspectives of those she employs.

How to locate myself in relationship to different community residents continues to haunt me in ongoing as well as sporadic ethnographic encounters. I found a partial solution in Patricia Hill Collins's analysis of the "ethic of caring" in Black feminist thought.[4] She describes the ethic of caring with reference to three interrelated dimensions: an "emphasis on individual uniqueness," "the appropriateness of emotions in dialogues," and "the capacity for empathy." As I gathered data in Midtown and Southtown and identified the outsider phenomenon, I further explored the notion of outsiderness to get underneath residents' public presentations of self. I shared my own feelings to a certain extent and explored the similarities and differences between my experiences and those of the community residents interviewed. I utilized multiple opportunities to dialogue with diverse community members, drawing on my own feelings of outsiderness and enhancing my capacity for empathy in each of these encounters.

Traditional guidelines for ethnographic research include gaining entry, building relationships, preserving objectivity, and maintaining the observer's role. In my own work, I find that gaining entry and building relationships automatically interfere with the third guideline, preserving objectivity (if such a stance were possible at all). As mentioned, one strategy I used to gain a broader understanding of the social construction of community included gathering in-depth information from diverse perspectives. I also took advantage of group discussions with community members to help set the agenda and reflect on the research process. Yet I do not grant all members of the community equal roles in helping me reflect on the research. Certain community members would obviously not be sympathetic to my explicitly feminist, antiracist, and social democratic perspective. I was also careful in sharing my lesbian identity with people in this small town. In fact, the social control processes clearly affected my choice in sharing certain features of my own life with those I interacted with in Midtown and Southtown. As a consequence of my experience of the outsider phenomenon, I relied more heavily on conversations and group discussions with more progressive elements within the community than with others in the two towns.

The second guideline, building relationships, is a direct consequence of the first and raises a basic moral or ethical dilemma for the fieldworker. Most guides to ethnographic research recognize this dilemma but conclude that the benefits of increasing our knowledge about different groups in our social world far outweigh the drawbacks. However, the dilemma continues to surface in our daily encounters in the field. The apparently straightforward question What is data? is often one of the most difficult questions to answer. At times, I clearly understood what was possible and ethical to observe and record. At other times, I had a feeling that to record particular observations or statements would be an invasion of the participants' privacy. There were times I recognized that the researcher role violated the trust gained in the course of the fieldwork. These moments increased as the personal encounters increased. As Susan Stern described in her participatory research project with parents in a public school district outside Washington, D.C., she was often confused about whether a particular encounter with a community resident was data or friendship.[5] The longer she lives in the community, the less data she can accumulate about the community women who are now her friends. On the other hand, Stern argues that friendship is an underexplored basis and rich arena for generating indigenous knowledge. I have continued friendships with two women whom I met through the fieldwork. Each provides me with knowledgeable feedback on the preliminary findings of the research. They constantly challenge my presuppositions and help me clarify terms so that I might remain true to the complex social processes that contribute to the vitality of rural life. I have grown reliant on their wise counsel as I continue to make sense of the social construction of community in rural Iowa.

Building relationships is, of course, a necessary part of gaining trust and access in ethnographic encounters. Less acknowledged in much of the fieldwork literature are the emotional consequences for the researcher when, over the course of fieldwork, more distanced relationships are transformed into friendships. Emotions are always present in personal interactions in ethnographic work. Here the feminist perspective is useful in reminding us that emotions can form an important basis for understanding and analysis. Because a primary goal of feminist research is to uncover how inequality is reproduced and resisted, how we draw on our capacity for empathy and emotion is directly related to a deep commitment to this political project. The use of dialogue as well as emotion and empathy were especially valuable tools for clarifying the tensions between individual narratives and identification of broader processes like racialization and the outsider phenomenon that are hidden from an individual resident's direct sight.

The third guideline, preserving objectivity, is especially troubling for feminist researchers. However, the research process always invites questions of power and control. No matter what kinds of participatory processes we employ in our work, the researcher still retains control over the decisions regarding who benefits from the research, who controls the dissemination of the findings, and who determines the particular processes chosen for the research. The more self-reflective we are about the social structure of research and our own position within that structure, the less we will fall prey to the false belief that we can be objective in our search.

The outsider phenomenon and my methodological reflections on the interaction between my own outsider feelings and those of community members highlights the value of a feminist standpoint methodology for challenging the false divide between insider/outsider research and between so-called objective or scientific and indigenous knowledge. The insights of feminist theories are helpful in examining the differences between ethnographic research in a variety of settings. We start with our position vis-à-vis the community and various community members to determine the personal tensions we confront as we enter different terrains. A consistent theme in feminist approaches includes an emphasis on self-awareness and self-reflection. We need to understand our own cultural biases and assumptions in order to examine the ways they influence the research process and analysis. Our gender, race-ethnicity, class, sexual orientation, age, political perspectives, as well as regional and cultural backgrounds provide a rich canvas on which to evaluate differences and similarities in the field.

Furthermore, this feminist revisiting of the insider/outsider debate demonstrates the limits of Georg Simmel's and other standpoint analyses that neglect the interaction between shifting power relations in a community context. As newcomers to these rural towns, I and my research assistants are implicated in these processes and inevitably become a party to the renegotiations as we interact with different community members whose positions are shifting over time. Identification of the outsider phenomenon and my methodological reflections on the interactions between my own outsider feelings and those of community members highlighted for me how processes of inequality and resistance shaped social life in these small towns. In particular, the process of racialization documented in the course of the fieldwork demonstrated how insider/outsider positions were ever-shifting and permeable social locations. On the other hand, standpoints within the outsider phenomenon are informed by material processes that organize class divisions and gender and racial inequality, among other dimensions. By highlighting processes through which outsiderness was constructed and reconstituted, this feminist analysis reveals how as ethnographers we are never fully outside or inside the community.

I expect to continue this exploration of the outsider phenomenon as I delve deeper into the social construction of community and resistance in rural Iowa. I hope to remain self-conscious of my own assumptions as they influence my relationships with residents in these communities and shape my analysis of the ethnographic data. I can never fully enter into the worldview of those whose lives are shaped by a rural cultural experience nor will I ever fully know the experiences of women from the small towns I study. Yet, keeping aware of the differences I perceive as well as the similarities I discover will help bridge the gap to a certain extent. Acknowledging the tension and shifts between feelings of outsiderness and insiderness for myself as well as for the community residents will help make salient these contrasts. To a certain extent, we all suffer from the outsider phenomenon: yet we can also benefit from it as we recognize how we share this experience with so many others.

NOTES

1. See especially Dorothy E. Smith, *The Everyday World as Problematic: Towards a Feminist Sociology* (Toronto: University of Toronto Press, 1987).

2. Georg Simmel, "The Sociological Significance of the 'Stranger,'" in *Introduction to the Science of Sociology,* ed. R. E. Park and E. W. Burgess (Chicago: University of Chicago Press, 1921).

3. Howard Winant, *Racial Conditions* (Minneapolis: University of Minnesota Press, 1994).

4. Patricia Hill Collins, *Black Feminist Thought.* (Boston: Unwin Hyman, 1990).

5. Susan Stern, *Social Science from Below: Grassroots Knowledge for Science and Emancipation.* Unpublished dissertation, City University of New York, 1994.

CHAPTER 21

The Social Organization of Sexuality and Gender in Alternative Hard Rock

An Analysis of Intersectionality

MIMI SCHIPPERS

Sexuality has held center stage in theoretical and empirical work on the social organization of gender relations, gender inequality, and resistance to male dominance. Theory and research on the gender aspects of sexuality have focused on a myriad of cultural beliefs, patterns of activity, and institutional arrangements that organize sexuality in ways that uphold the gender order of male dominance. (For a review of varying feminist perspectives on sexuality, see Lorber 1999.) By drawing connections between these aspects of sexuality and then placing them within the broader social organization of gender and power, feminists focus on how the gender organization of sexuality reflects, maintains, and in some cases subverts unequal power relations between women and men, among women, and among men. These feminist approaches to sexuality, which include both the social construction of gendered sexuality (e.g., MacKinnon 1989) and compulsory heterosexuality (e.g., Bunch 1978; Rich 1980), are based on an implicit or sometimes explicit contention that sexuality is produced and maintained within gender relations. That is, an analysis of sexuality is necessarily a gender analysis because sexuality is subsumed under gender relations as one mechanism of masculine dominance.

Other theorists have conceptualized the relationship between sexuality and gender differently by focusing on how sexuality, as an analytically distinct feature of social relations, organizes not only gender but social relations more generally. Building on the empirical work of social scientists and historians who demonstrate the importance of sociohistorical context and social processes in the construction of sexual scripts (Gagnon and Simon 1973), sexual identities and communities (Chauncey 1989; D'Emilio 1983; Greenberg 1988; Katz 1976; Lapovsky Kennedy and Davis 1994; Plummer 1975; Weeks 1985) and sexual desire (Ross and Rapp1983; Vance 1984), and on Gayle Rubin's (1984) pathbreaking conceptual separation of sexuality and gender, and on Michel Foucault's (1980) conceptualization of sexual discourse as social control, some theorists (e.g., Ingraham 1996; Sedgewick1990; Seidman 1996; Stein and Plummer 1996; Warner 1993) conceptualize sexuality as not simply one feature of broader gender relations but as a separate organizing principle in its own right and equally central to the workings of power as gender.

These theorists, often referred to as "queer theorists," identify hegemonic sexuality in contemporary Western, industrialized societies as defined in terms of a *hetero-focused binary* that constructs, naturalizes, and stratifies heterosexuality and homosexuality as two halves that make up the whole of human sexuality. Homosexuality and heterosexuality are defined as fixed identities, and heterosexuality is constructed as the norm, while homosexuality is considered marginal or deviant. More important, this construction of sexuality is not simply mapped onto identities but organizes social and institutional relations more generally (Seidman 1996).

Queer theorists conceptualize sexuality and gender as analytically distinct. Sexuality and gender are separate organizing features of social relations but intersect by mutually constituting, reinforcing, and naturalizing each other. Gender relations—which include how masculinity and femininity are mapped onto identities and how gender is displayed, enacted, and understood—naturalize, reinforce, and support sexuality, which includes the display, enactment, and meanings of sexual desire and sexual identities. Likewise, sexuality simultaneously naturalizes, reinforces, and supports gender. Conceptualizing the relationship between sexuality and gender in this way encourages us to think about gender and sexuality as separate, but mutually reinforcing, much like theories of the intersection of race, class, and gender (see, e.g., Combahee River Collective 1983; Hill Collins 1999; hooks 1989; Nakano Glenn 1999; Smith 1990).

Taking seriously the insights of queer theory and theorists of intersectionality, I separated gender and sexuality in an empirical analysis of a rock music subculture. In this article, I will use data derived through participant observation of this subculture to demonstrate the utility and importance of analytically separating sexuality and gender. I will also discuss how conceptualizing sexuality at multiple levels of analysis produced a more robust understanding of how hegemony and resistance operated in this subculture.

METHOD

The main purpose of this study was to identify how women and men negotiate norms for gender performance in face-to-face interaction. For two and one-half years, I conducted an ethnographic study of the face-to-face negotiation of gender in a rock music subculture in Chicago. Observations were made at small rock concerts in local bars and clubs, at the homes of active participants, and at parties attended by active participants. By *active participants,* I mean a loose network of twenty to thirty women and men who regularly attended these rock shows as audience members and/or to play as musicians. While the network was rather large, there was a core group of eight informants with whom I developed a closer relationship. It was mostly with this core group of eight that I spent time outside of the clubs. However, other active participants would attend parties or show up at the homes of these eight people.

I tape-recorded observations when I left the scene and transcribed those recordings the following morning. Field notes were coded and analyzed using the method outlined by Lichterman (1996), which combines the methodological strategies of Burowoy et al. (1991) and Strauss and Corbin (1990). I also conducted twelve in-depth interviews with musicians in and outside Chicago who were associated with this genre of music.[1] These were open-ended interviews that began with questions about specific aspects of their music or performances that I identified as politicized or that specifically challenged sexism. For instance, I asked Donita Sparks of L7 what she meant when she said, "This one goes out to the Supreme Court" before launching into their song "Shitlist." Subsequent questions depended on where the informant went with his or her response. I chose this setting to study the negotiation of gender norms for several reasons. First, rock music has been a public setting where norms for gender, at least in terms of appearance, are more flexible than in other settings. Second, as I will discuss below, this particular subculture, what I call *alternative hard rock,*[2] was one in which participants explicitly incorporated feminist ideology or an explicit opposition to gender inequality into their cultural practices. Third, these concerts took place in public bars and clubs where I had ready access to interaction and where there were few explicit, formalized rules for behavior.

Description of the Subculture: Alternative Hard Rock

The subculture in Chicago is part of a larger genre of music that is most associated with the labels *grunge* or *alternative rock* (see Clawson 1999). The bands that became nationally recognized include Pearl Jam, Hole, L7, Nirvana, Veruca Salt, Soundgarden, and perhaps less known, Babes in Toyland, Poster Children, Silverfish, and 7 Year Bitch. With these bands, the subculture in Chicago shared a musical fusion of the loud, aggressive sound of hard rock (Walser 1993) and the faster tempo and politicized, antiestablishment sentiments of punk (Greil 1990; Hebdige 1979; Laing 1985).

Most important for the purposes of this article, participants in this subculture shared a general rejection of the sexism of mainstream rock (Frith 1983; Groce and Cooper 1990; Weinstein 1991). Thus, there was a concerted effort to do rock music in a way that resisted or challenged hegemonic gender relations. The goal of this article is not to persuade readers that members of this subculture explicitly adopted feminist discourses in their approaches to doing rock music (see Schippers 1997). However, to make my central argument—that separating sexuality and gender and conceptualizing sexuality at multiple levels of analysis is fruitful for students of gender—in the next section I will provide some general background on the gender organization of this subculture, which includes cursory evidence that feminism was important to participants.

THE GENDER ORGANIZATION OF THE ROCK SHOW

In mixed-gender, public discourse and in the interviews with musicians, both women and men expressed a desire to do rock differently to not reproduce the sexism of mainstream rock. For instance, there was an explicit rejection of the groupie scene.

> I think in the last few years there's been a lot of great bands that have killed that stereotype, that male stereotype . . . initially when I got into [rock music] I was like, yeah, guys are dicks, rock bands are pretty stupid, and I want to be in a rock band that doesn't patronize the sexist and racist aspects of rock. Like punk in that

> sense. . . . They're normal people. They're not playing some kind of rock dream of dressing up and getting girls or whatever. (Kim Thayil of Soundgarden [Man])

> I wrote a song called "Out of Step" that said "don't smoke, don't drink, don't fuck. At least I can fuckin' think." And it was sort of about guys around me. That was their big thing, to get fucked up and get laid constantly. That wasn't my priority in life. My priority was to be like a person or whatever. . . . [Punk music] was something that gave me access to a whole 'nother *[sic]* world, and I was challenged on so many levels, like politically, sexually. Everything I thought had to be turned upside down and reexamined. (Ian MacKaye of Fugazi [Man])

> Groupies are mostly a mainstream rock phenomenon. It's a sexist world and groupies are just part of that world. Not any different from any other sexist aspect of society. . . . I don't get into that scene myself, but for some people it works. (Jennifer Finch of L7 [Woman])

> The groupie thing just doesn't happen. It's not part of the sensibility of what we're doing. And the guys that we tour with, you know the Melvins and Wool, it's not like there are groupies back here hanging out with them. It's just not part of what we do. . . . It comes out of punk roots. It's about being more enlightened, having a sense of fairness and not being sexist pigs. You know those guys in like rock bands with all the groupies. That's fine, but they're usually fuckin' pigs trying to prove something. We're just here to rock. (Donita Sparks of L7 [Woman])

These sentiments were also expressed by alternative hard rockers in Chicago. At one show, I was talking about groupies with a few people including a woman in a successful local band.

> I always worried about being called a groupie because I've always dated musicians. But you know that's who I'm around. I admire them and what they do. And I wanted to do what they were doing. I'm a grouper, not a groupie.

Collapsing the dichotomy between musician and groupie worked to situate this woman's behavior outside of the sexualized, gender norms for rock music. The groupie scene of mainstream rock was a relatively common topic of conversation among alternative hard rockers and served as a comparison with which to define their feminist departure.

Alternative hard rockers also developed and enforced norms against men actively pursuing women sexually, or against what participants call "shmoozing," within the confines of the bar. There was a common understanding among participants that the rock show, despite taking place in bars, did not serve as a place to find potential sexual partners. They defined and maintained this normative structure by chastising men who were perceived to be shmoozing or through storytelling.

> BRYAN:[3] Jim can be such an asshole sometimes. It's embarrassing to be with him in public. He totally shmoozes chicks and the way he does it is so fucking obnoxious.
>
> ME: Like what does he do?
>
> BRYAN: Some woman will walk by and he'll like step in front of her and [Here Bryan mimics Jim's behavior by getting really close to me, holds out his hand, smiles broadly, and says, "Hi, You're cute!"].

ME: No way.

BRYAN: All the fucking time. I just walk away and pretend I don't know him.

One night Maddie and I were watching Jim talk to a woman. After a few minutes the woman walked away. Maddie laughed and said, "You shmooze, you lose. He's such an asshole."

Obviously, I did not have access to what men said to each other or how they acted when women were not around. However, I was able to watch men interact in the clubs and, on some occasions, eavesdrop on their conversations. While I have no way of knowing if these norms held when women were not present, it is indicative of the normative gender structure of these rock shows that, for the most part, participants followed these general guidelines.

Although there were norms against sexual interaction between women and men, this does not mean that sexual desire and sexual behavior were absent.

THE SEXUAL ORGANIZATION OF THE ROCK SHOW

At the outset and throughout data collection, feminist conceptualizations of compulsory heterosexuality, social constructions of gendered sexuality, and their relationship to male dominance guided my observations. Thus, my focus, while in the field, was on the ways in which sexual interactions reinforced or challenged hegemonic masculinity and femininity and on whether there was sexual interaction among women or among men. However, as I analyzed the data, I soon realized that conceptualizing sexuality as one facet of gender was not enough. To shed some light on my analysis of the workings of sexual desire, sexual behavior, and sexual norms, I turned to queer theory.

There were two central tenets to queer theory that I brought to my understanding of how gender and sexuality were operating to challenge or maintain gender and sexual hegemony. First, I analyzed how sexualities as stable identities (gay, lesbian, straight) were constructed, understood, and distributed among participants within the subculture. The second was to explore sexuality as having multiple levels of organization, including individual identities, but also as practices; as an organizing feature of face-to-face social interaction; and as an overarching, normative structure for these rock shows. Sexuality at the level of identity was identified by participants' talk about their own and others' sexualities. Sexual practices were coded as expressions of desire and sexual behavior by individuals, such as flirting (winking, licking lips), kissing others, erotic dancing, and genital contact with others. To identify the sexual organization of social interaction, I adopted a symbolic interactionist approach (Blumer 1969; Stryker 1979) and focused on how the heterosexual-homosexual binary took shape in participants' practices and in the ongoing process of negotiated social interaction. This included the social positions constructed during interaction and the meanings attributed to those positions and the activities of people occupying those positions. Finally, I analyzed the overall normative structure for doing sexuality while doing rock music in these clubs and whether a hetero-focused binary was assumed, reproduced, and maintained by those norms.

Sexual Practices

While there were strong norms against heterosexual contact between women and men, there was a great deal of sexual contact among women and overt expressions of sexual desire by women. For instance, women would often engage in playful, sexualized interaction with each other.

> Maddie had a cigarette hanging from her lips and asked Carrie for a light. Carrie leaned in and put her mouth over Maddie's cigarette and pretended to bite it. When she pulled away, Carrie said, "Oh, I thought you said, 'Can I have a bite.' I suppose I could give you a light, but I'd rather give you a bite."

Another time Maddie and Carrie were sitting a few seats away from each other at the bar. Carrie was looking at Maddie winking and licking her lips. After ten or fifteen minutes, Carrie yelled to Maddie, "I'm leaving for a little while, will you miss me?" Maddie responded, "Of course, darling. But we're leaving anyway." Carrie exaggerated a pout and said, "Well then, there's no reason for me to come back."

Women would also express sexual desire for women musicians, as in the following discussion of Kim Gordon of SonicYouth among Maddie, Colleen, and Bryan:

> MADDIE: You met Kim Gordon?!
>
> COLLEEN: Yeah. We went backstage.
>
> MADDIE: I love her. I really, like, have fallen in love with her. . . . She's so cool. They're so good, and she is just so cool.
>
> BRYAN: Oh, I know.
>
> MADDIE: I love Sonic Youth. They're one of those bands that just always puts out good music. . . . I swear, I love her.
>
> COLLEEN: She's totally hot!

At the concerts, it was common to see women rubbing their bodies together and gyrating against each other as they listened to the music. On rare occasions, I observed women kissing.

Interestingly, women's sexual desire was not limited to women and men but was extended to the sound of singers' voices, the sound of guitars, the syncopation of instruments, and other tonal or musical experiences. I heard women talk about wanting to "fuck" the music or about a singer's voice as "totally fuckable." When women particularly enjoyed live or recorded music, a common expression they used to convey this was, "Just fuck me now," or they would sometimes say, "I need a cigarette" or "I'm spent" after a live performance. The sexual references were not addressed to any particular person or people; instead, they were made toward and about the music as an object of desire and as sexually gratifying. As Grossberg (1988) suggests, rock music, especially live rock music, is simultaneously an auditory and bodily experience. At these shows, the music was not only heard but also felt in the body. The rhythm and syncopation between the bass, drums, and guitars gave the bodily experience a sexual valence as expressed by the women. For this reason, it is entirely possible that women's "dirty dancing" together could have been as much about sexualizing the music as it was about their sexual desire for each other (see McRobbie 1984). In other words, sexual desire, as expressed by women in talk and through their actions, was far more diffused and fluid than the hetero-focused binary would have it. This more diffused, fluid sexuality breaks down the relevance of sexual identity labels that are referents to the gender of one's sexual object. For this reason, I want to suggest that women's sexual desire cannot be simplified as bisexual or lesbian but instead can be characterized as queer because it was opened up to include more than other women or even other individuals.

At the same time, it was uncommon to see men moving their bodies to the music, except for "head banging" (vigorously bobbing the head back and forth) or playing "air guitar" (moving the body as if playing an imaginary guitar), so dancing was not something men in this subculture usually did. The men would most often keep their eyes on the stage or each other while conversing between bands, so even overtly "checking women out" was relatively uncommon. At least in the company of women at these shows, men did not usually express sexual desire for, or attraction to, women. On the rare occasion when men did appear to be expressing an overt sexual desire for women, others would invariably make fun of them to keep the counterhegemonic, normative structure intact.

> BRYAN: [A band] had this girl who played guitar. She was so awesome. She played like Angus Young (of AC/DC), you know on stage and stuff. She was so cool. I went up to her once after a show, and she was like "I'm married." I just wanted to talk about music.
>
> [MADDIE, COLLEEN, AND I LAUGH]
>
> COLLEEN: You should have put your dick back in your pants before you went up to talk to her.
>
> BRYAN: I should have taken my coat off my dick and put it back on.
>
> COLLEEN: Hide it behind a newspaper or something.
>
> [LOUD LAUGHTER]

By making Bryan's sexual desire explicit and then mocking it, the women reestablished the norm against men's overt sexual subjectivity. Even Bryan went along with their mocking to demonstrate his acceptance of this norm. In other words, men's sexual subjectivity was constantly monitored and checked as people interacted with each other.

The social control over men's sexual desire is significant because, as described earlier, this is a highly sexualized, public setting where women are overtly expressing and acting on their own sexual desire. The men were, at least within the confines of the bar, taken out of these sexual dynamics. Men did not enact sexual subjectivity in relation to women or to other men, which challenges the hegemonic gender order (Connell 1995). More important, even though men did not overtly watch women, as in most straight bars or at strip clubs, for instance, it is entirely possible that men's sexual desire was limited to the scopophilic view (Mulvey 1990). If this was the case, like pornographic material directed toward heterosexual men that depicts sexual contact among women, this dynamic would reproduce hegemonic gender relations by situating women in the position of sexual objects and men in the position of viewing sexual subjects (Kuhn 1985; MacKinnon 1989). This would also reproduce hegemonic sexual relations by rendering women's sexual contact with each other as heterosexual behavior. However, it is still significant that women experienced and expressed sexual desire for each other publicly and were not subject to men's sexual desire, at least interactively. Also, despite engaging in sexual play with other women, none of the women in the subculture referred to themselves as bisexual or lesbian. As I will discuss below, alternative hard rockers constructed gay men and lesbians as people outside the subculture and therefore as marginalized others, at the same time that the women overtly engaged in intragender sexual behavior. This suggests an important play of gender and sexual hegemony and resistance within the same practices. This mixture of counterhegemonic and hegemonic sexual and gender relations became evident at other levels of social organization as well.

Constructing Sexual Identities through Talk

When alternative hard rockers talked about sexuality, it was most often to confront or challenge homophobia or heterosexism. In their politicized, antiestablishment rock world, it was uncool to be a bigot, and they included heterosexism as bigotry. This stance translated into challenging, chastising, and making ridiculous derogatory talk about gay and lesbian people. More important, these challenges to heterosexism were often used to challenge hegemonic gender relations or to establish alternative norms for femininity or masculinity. For example, one evening, Maddie approached me and angrily said, "Dan is such an asshole sometimes." I asked her what happened:

> I was standing there talking to Dan and Nancy and some other people, and I knew you were waiting, so I was trying to get them to decide what they were going to be doing. I was like, "Come on you guys, could you just make up your minds. Let's go." He was totally ignoring me. So I was like, "Get your thumb out of your ass, and let's do something." He turned to me and said, "Why do you have to be such a dyke all the time?" I said, "Thanks for the compliment. See ya . . ." and left. What a fucking asshole. Can you believe he even said that?

Within the context of this interaction, as reported to me by Maddie, what led to Dan calling Maddie a "dyke" was not that she might have had sex with women but that she was being assertive. Maddie used the opportunity to tell this story to convey her resistive stance toward uses of heterosexism to get women back in line in terms of gender. In response to Dan's explicit attempt to set and enforce gender norms and to implicitly fortify heterosexism, Maddie snapped back, "Thanks for the compliment." By telling of her quick "Thanks," she reconstructed his attempt to insult her into a compliment, suggesting that there was not only nothing wrong with but perhaps something positive about being a "dyke."

While Maddie's story was one of challenging heterosexism, it was also a story about gender resistance. The label *dyke* was redefined as a compliment because, as told by Maddie, it named and made explicit her refusal to enact femininity in a way that reproduced hegemonic gender relations. Maddie used the label *dyke* as a marker of an alternative femininity to shift the meaning of her assertiveness. Her story exposed heterosexism and thus challenged compulsory heterosexuality. At the same time, it challenged the gender order. More important, this illustrates how a positive deployment of the identity *dyke* made gender resistance possible.

However, Maddie's story also reinforced the homosexual-heterosexual binary in her implicit validation of the homosexual label *dyke*. She fully accepted the identity meaning of the label while rejecting its evaluative meaning as negative or inferior. In fact, her story relied on, and fully supported, an underlying assumption that there are "dykes" out there, and that they are admirable because they do femininity in ways that challenge the gender order. The sexual identities and the assumed gender performances attached to those identities were held in place, even though Maddie challenged both compulsory heterosexuality and gender hegemony.

Less often, but not infrequently, alternative hard rockers also challenged compulsory heterosexuality by freely talking about their gay, lesbian, or bisexual friends, roommates, sisters, brothers, mothers, work colleagues, and others. Because of this normalizing talk, there was little question in my analysis that alternative hard rockers challenged compulsory heterosexuality. However, I never heard a participant refer to himself or herself as gay, lesbian, or homosexual, and only on a few isolated occasions did anybody talk about another member of the subculture as gay or lesbian. For the most part, participants constructed gay men and lesbians as people outside the subculture yet also as deserving of all the rights, respect, and happiness of anybody else. More important, words such as *lesbian, gay,* and *dyke* seemed to be the only way in which members of this subculture could talk about their acquaintances, suggesting, as one would expect, that they did not have an elaborate queer language or a language that did not assume stable, sexual identities. That is, while challenging compulsory heterosexuality and challenging hegemonic gender relations, they would fully reinscribe the hegemonic sexual order in their construction of identities through talk and their marginalization of gay and lesbian identities.

The Sexual Organization of Face-to-Face Interaction

In addition to explicit talk about sexual identities, sexuality was also produced through negotiated social interaction. By exaggerating heterosexism or playing different "parts" in sexualized social interaction, alternative hard rockers would sometimes expose sexual bigotry without engaging in any explicit discussions of sexual identity or the politics of sexualities. For example, the first time I met Colleen, Maddie and I were passing by her outside a club before a show. Colleen feigned to whisper to the man she was talking with but said loudly so we could hear, "Did you know she's a lesbian," referring to Maddie. Colleen laughed and then said, "Not only that, but she's a bitch too." Both Maddie and Colleen laughed, hugged, and engaged in a playful banter vying for inclusion in the "lesbian club" and "bitch club." The tone of their exchange indicated that there was something positive about being a lesbian and a bitch. When Maddie and I walked away, Colleen said to me, "Now be careful, she's a lesbian." Maddie quickly responded, "She knows. She's my girlfriend. Jealous?" Colleen laughed and said, "Yeah, but I have my own girlfriend. He (referring to the man she was talking with) is really a she!"

Colleen's initial "whisper" about Maddie being a lesbian mocked the secret of being a lesbian. Colleen immediately invoked the label *bitch,* making fun of that as well. By situating *bitch* in this playful rejection of heterosexism, Colleen implicitly made gender salient. *Bitch,* like *lesbian,* is a derogatory label hurled at women who step out of the bounds of acceptable femininity and is meant to get women back in line. Like Maddie's story about Dan's deployment of *dyke,* both Colleen and Maddie quickly turned the mocked heterosexism and sexism into a verbal competition about who really is a lesbian and who really is a bitch. This shifted the meaning of those labels to positive attributes, which worked as gender resistance because the femininities associated with both challenged hegemonic femininity.

This interaction also challenged compulsory heterosexuality. Maddie and Colleen validated lesbianism through their competitive, interactive volley for the lesbian badge. Also, Colleen's whisper to her man friend could have been a test to see how Maddie would respond to the possibility of sexualizing their relationship. This is more than likely since, not too long after this interaction, Maddie told me she had an especially fine time at a concert the night before because she "made out" with Colleen all night. When I asked her what she meant, she said, "You know. I had my tongue down her throat. She had her tongue down my throat." This story itself was told in the presence of other alternative hard rockers. Whether or not the story was true, when others went along and did not marginalize Maddie, they interactively accepted and validated her position as a woman who "makes out" with other women.

By combining a gender analysis with a sexuality analysis at the level of face-to-face interaction, the data reveal that Colleen's and Maddie's banter involved, first, a queering of sexuality by manipulating gender relations. Colleen's assertion that she has a "lesbian" relationship with a man subverted the homo-hetero binary by destabilizing the meaning of *lesbian* in the context of this interaction. There is no way to see the sexuality organizing this interaction as homosexual, heterosexual, or bisexual, for the identity *woman* was detached from the social position *lesbian.*

Second, this queer sexuality set up subversive gender relations. The man in this interaction became the "girlfriend" of Colleen. That is, Colleen constructed the social roles in the interaction in a way that subverted male dominant power relations—after all, the gender order does not confer masculine power to "girlfriends." In this interaction, queering sexuality and destabilizing gender subverted both hegemonic gender and sexual relations.

However, by also analyzing sexuality as identities constructed through talk, a complicated play of resistance and hegemony is revealed. Although Maddie and Colleen challenged compulsory heterosexuality and complacent femininity at the level of interaction, they simultaneously assumed and bolstered a hetero-focused binary. Their gender resistance was enacted by deploying sexual identity labels. Colleen actually used the word *lesbian* to tease or test Maddie. Again, this was based on a common meaning for *lesbian* as a stable sexual identity with a whole set of corresponding characteristics. Colleen's use of this label also reflected an implicit subcultural norm for heterosexuality.

The Normative Sexual Structure for Alternative Hard Rock

Moving my analysis out to the overarching normative structure of sexuality within the subculture reveals heterosexism in Colleen's pseudowhisper. Even though she might have been testing Maddie's comfort zone with sexualizing their relationship and she made lesbian sexuality a viable possibility by speaking positively of it, Colleen had to have assumed Maddie was heterosexual for the banter about lesbians and bitches to have been not only funny but also effective as gender resistance. If Maddie were indeed a lesbian, this interaction probably would have backfired on Colleen and she would have been chastised as both heterosexist and as supporting sexism. Colleen would never have risked "outing" Maddie if there were any remote possibility that Maddie was a lesbian. Colleen must have safely assumed that people are heterosexual unless proven otherwise. That is, the overarching sexual organization of this music scene was heterosexuality despite participants' rejection of compulsory heterosexuality in their talk and in their subversion of the hetero-focused binary in their practices and interactions.

This play of subversion and hegemony developed in most contexts where alternative hard rockers talked about sexuality. For example, I was at an alternative hard rocker's house with several other people including four men in a local band. The four members of this band were talking about whether it would be a good idea for them to take a gig opening for Tribe 8. Tribe 8 is a band out of San Francisco that consists of five women who are all very much out about their sexual desire for women and who make their sexual desire a central part of their performance.

> Joe (singer and guitarist): Man, I don't know. I don't know if it would be such a good idea. It's going to be a bunch of lesbians who probably would not appreciate a bunch of aggressive guys up there. [Everybody laughs] Shit, I don't want to get my ass kicked! There's no way they'd put up with us if they're waiting to see Tribe 8. I don't think we should.

First, it is important to point out that saying he did not "want to get [his] ass kicked" was not, in the context of this subculture, a derogatory remark about lesbians or about the women in Tribe 8. Men in this subculture often talked about women they admired as able to "kick ass." However, despite this nod of respect, while listening to Joe, I thought that he was probably exaggerating and revealing an underlying heterosexism that fueled his apprehension.

While at the Tribe 8 show, I concluded that Joe's concerns were perhaps heterosexist but at the same time well-founded. The audience consisted of mostly women, there were more overt sexual displays among women than I had seen at other shows, and many of the women were quite aggressive about keeping men out of the space in front of the stage. In other words, the social space was transformed into one where sexual desire among women and women's use of physical aggression framed social interaction and the normative structure more than at other shows.

While Joe might have negative or antagonistic feelings about lesbians, his heterosexism was also apparent in his use of the word *lesbian* to describe the crowd. I noticed that although there were many women there I did not know and who might describe themselves as lesbians or dykes, there were also many women there who consistently attended shows where Joe's band and other local bands played, and who did not refer to themselves as lesbians or dykes. However, the women who were active participants in the alternative hard rock scene in Chicago were indistinguishable in their behavior from most of the women whom I did not recognize. These women did not become lesbians in the identity sense by attending this show but did work with other women to create a counterhegemonic structure for sexual and gender display and interaction. Joe did not have a language to identify the transformation of the normative structure, so he simply said, "It will be a bunch of lesbians"—including Maddie, Colleen, and others. In his talk, Joe only had the label *lesbian,* although it was the practices, interactions, and normative structure that differed at the Tribe 8 show, not the identities of individuals who participated.

This tension between how sexuality was enacted or practiced and the only available identity-based language meant they consistently found it difficult to talk about their practices. For instance, the following field note excerpt demonstrates how, at another concert, Courtney Love of the band Hole vacillated between identity talk and practice talk while revealing to the audience who her sexual partner was at the time.

> Courtney Love says to the audience, "Guess who I'm fucking. If you can guess, I'll tell you. Come on, try to guess." Several people in the audience (including both men and women) raise their hands. Someone from the crowd yells, "Drew!" (The guitarist was dating Drew Barrymore.) Love says, "No. He's fucking Drew (referring to the guitarist), I'm not. I'm not a lesbian. I'm only a part-time muff-muncher." She laughs. "I only munch muff part-time. She (referring to the drummer) is a full-time muff-muncher, and she (the bass player) is a virgin."

When someone in the audience suggested Love was "fucking" Drew Barrymore, she responded by saying, "I'm not a lesbian." What did that mean to Love? It meant that she is only a "part-time muff-muncher," referring to cunnilingus. Although she first used an identity label, and by doing so supported the hetero-focused binary, she quickly shifted the emphasis to what one does in practice to define sexuality. That the bass player was a "virgin" in comparison to herself, a "part-time muff-muncher," and the drummer, a "full-time muff-muncher," meant that not *doing* anything defined one's sexuality. Sexuality was constructed as what you *do* as much as who you *are.* Her immediate shift to who is a "muff-muncher" and who is not transformed an identity into a set of practices. She not only demonstrated the difficulty alternative hard rockers face when talking about sexuality in nonidentity terms but also that sexuality meant something far more complex in practice than identity markers could signify.

While alternative hard rockers fairly consistently reproduced a hetero-focused binary of sexual identities in their talk and in their assumption and reproduction of a heterosexual normative sexual structure, they sometimes queered sexuality in their practices and in their interactions. More important, both the reproduction of sexual identities in their talk and their queering of sexuality in practice worked to undermine male dominance. However, although alternative hard rockers were relatively successful in creating a social setting with norms that challenged gender hegemony, at the same time, they continuously reproduced hegemonic sexuality.

Given the ways in which sexual desire manifested at these shows, I initially concluded that alternative hard rockers were relatively successful in resisting hegemony both in terms of gender and in terms of sexuality. It was only after data were collected and I was analyzing my findings that the importance of a queer theoretical framework became salient. Only by queering my sociological analysis or, to borrow the term from Kimberle Williams Crenshaw (1991) and Patricia Hill Collins (1999), by adopting a perspective of *intersectionality*, did the layers of subversion and hegemony in participants' talk, practices, and interactions become apparent.

IMPLICATIONS AND CONCLUSION

Five main themes emerged from my observations. First, these data suggest that empirical investigations of queer sexuality must be extended to people who identify as heterosexual. Alternative hard rockers' expressions of sexual desire and sexual practices blurred or in some cases rendered meaningless the lines between heterosexual and homosexual despite an overall norm for heterosexual identities. There has been little attention paid to the queer practices of people who identify as heterosexual, and further research in this area is needed. For instance, researchers might compare the queer practices of self-identifying heterosexual people and those of self-identifying gay, lesbian, bisexual, or queer people to better understand the play of gender and sexual hegemony and resistance at different levels of analysis. It would also be fruitful to further explore the workings of hegemony and resistance as men and women negotiate and practice sexual desire as they interact with each other. Mixed-gender, collaborative ethnography might be one way to get at these multiple vectors of gender and sexual relations.

Second, I found a dissonance between how alternative hard rockers talked about sexuality and how they enacted sexual desire. These findings suggest that focusing only on the way people talk about sexuality will leave hidden some of the most important aspects of sexuality, namely, how it is enacted and negotiated in face-to-face interaction. This is significant because it suggests that while alternative hard rockers were facile in, and willing to think about, sexualities in terms of stable homosexual and heterosexual identities, their everyday experience of sexuality, at least to some degree, undermined identity demarcations. My guess is that if asked on a survey or in an interview, alternative hard rockers would be more than willing to "buy into" identity markers and choose one and, more important, in most cases would choose a heterosexual identity. However, survey or interview questions, because they rely on language, would be framing and therefore boxing in alternative hard rockers' sexualities into an identity framework even though in their practices this sometimes is not the case. There were ways in which sexuality was enacted and constructed in face-to-face interaction that stepped out of that framework and would likely disappear empirically if alternative hard rockers were asked to talk about sexuality. This suggests that ethnographic methods or a more innovative formulation of survey and interview questions would greatly enhance our efforts to map and understand sexuality and its relationship to gender and male dominance.

Third, these findings demonstrate that queering sexuality can be an effective form of gender resistance. There is much debate among feminists about whether deconstructing identities is politically expedient (see, e.g., Alcoff 1994; Ault 1996; Butler 1990; DiStefano 1990; Fraser and Nicholson 1990; Fuss 1989). While these findings do not provide any kind of answer to those questions, they do suggest that gender resistance and the subversion of identities are not necessarily incompatible. Further research in other social settings might begin to map the costs and benefits of queering sexuality to undermine male dominance and how social context mediates its effectiveness. It is entirely likely that queering sexuality at a rock concert will have much different outcomes than queering sexuality in a work, school, or family setting. Whether queering sexuality in these settings would be more or less effective is an important empirical question.

Fourth, these data suggest that effective strategies of gender resistance sometimes reinscribe the hegemonic sexual order. Even when participants rejected compulsory heterosexuality, hegemonic norms for sexualized masculinity and femininity, and traditional gender scripts for sexual interaction, they still upheld the hierarchical relationship between heterosexual and homosexual as stable, fixed identities. This supports queer theorists' assertion that sexuality and gender operate separately but articulate each other. This strongly suggests that sociological theorizing and empirical research on gender must take seriously the sexual order as conceptualized by queer theorists and how it intersects with gender. Just as the social organization of race and class crosscut gender relations, the sexual order also does so, and it would do gender sociologists well to incorporate this into their theorizing and research.

Finally, my goal was to demonstrate the importance of conceptualizing and analyzing sexuality at multiple levels of analysis. Without a multilevel analysis, I might have concluded that alternative hard rockers successfully developed a rock music subculture that reproduced neither male dominance nor heterosexual dominance. At the level of practice, identity talk, and interaction, they rejected compulsory heterosexuality and male dominance. However, the same practices and talk that undermined compulsory heterosexuality and worked as effective gender resistance depended on the hegemonic sexual order. This leads to more questions unanswered by this analysis. For instance, what is the relationship between the different levels of sexuality as they intersect with gender? Are certain levels more likely than others to influence beliefs, practices, and broader institutional features of social life? What is the relative importance or weight of each, and how might this vary by social context? How do the different levels of sexuality produce power relations in terms of both sexuality and gender? What levels of sexuality are more important or effective in terms of strategies for social change? Further multilevel theorizing and empirical analyses are needed to begin addressing these and other questions.

If our interests lie in not only understanding but also changing existing relations of domination, seeing these nuances of hegemony and counterhegemony is absolutely necessary. As many have persuasively argued in terms of the relationships between race, ethnicity, class, and gender, adopting a perspective of intersectionality to study the relationship between gender and sexuality at multiple levels of analysis is much needed and long overdue in sociological research.

NOTES

1. I interviewed one or more members of the following bands: L7, Pearl Jam, Soundgarden, 7 Year Bitch, Babes in Toyland, Silverfish, Fugazi, Poster Children.

2. For an in-depth discussion of my use of this term and the subculture, see Schippers (1997).

3. All names used for participants in Chicago are fictitious.

REFERENCES

Alcoff, Linda. 1994. Cultural feminism versus post-structuralism: The identity crisis in feminist theory. In *Culture/power/history: A reader in contemporary social theory,* ed. N. B. Dirks, G. Eley, and S. Ortner, 96–122. Princeton: Princeton University Press.

Ault, Amber. 1996. The dilemma of identity: Bi women's negotiations. In *Queer theory/sociology,* ed. Steven Seidman, 311–30. Cambridge, MA: Blackwell.

Blumer, Herbert. 1969. *Symbolic interactionism: Perspectives and method.* Englewood Cliffs, NJ: Prentice-Hall.

Butler, Judith. 1990. *Gender trouble: Feminism and the subversion of identity.* New York: Routledge.

Bunch, Charlotte. 1978. Lesbians in revolt. In *Feminist frameworks,* ed. A. M. Jaggar and P. R. Struhl, 123–27. New York: McGraw-Hill.

Burowoy, Michael, Alice Burton, Ann Arnett Ferguson, Kathryn J. Fox, Joshua Gamson, Nadine Gartrell, Leslie Hurst, Charles Kurzman, Leslie Salzinger, Josepha Schiffman, and Shiori Ui. 1991. *Ethnography unbound: Power and resistance in modern metropolis.* Berkeley: University of California Press.

Chauncey, George, Jr. 1989. Christian brotherhood or sexual perversion? Homosexual identities and the construction of sexual boundaries in the World War I era. In *Hidden from history: Reclaiming the gay and lesbian past,* ed. Martin Duberman, Martha Vicinus, and George Chauncey Jr., 294–317. New York: Penguin.

Clawson, Mary Ann. 1999. When women play the bass: Instrument specialization and gender interpretation in alternative rock music. *Gender & Society* 13 (2): 193–210.

Combahee River Collective. 1983. The Combahee River collective statement. In *Home girls: A Black feminist anthology,* ed. Barbara Smith, 272–82. New York: Kitchen Table.

Connell, R. W. 1995. *Masculinities.* Berkeley: University of California Press.

D'Emilio, John. 1983. *Sexual politics, sexual communities: The making of a homosexual minority in the United States, 1940–1970.* Chicago: University of Chicago Press.

Di Stefano, C. 1990. Dilemmas of difference: Feminism, modernity, and postmodernism. In *Feminism/postmodernism,* ed. Linda J. Nicholson, 63–82. New York: Routledge.

Foucault, Michele. 1980. *History of sexuality.* Vol. 1. New York: Vintage.

Fraser, Nancy, and Linda J. Nicholson. 1990. Social criticism without philosophy: An encounter between feminism and postmodernism. In *Feminism/postmodernism,* ed. Linda J. Nicholson, 19–38. New York: Routledge.

Frith, Simon. 1983. *Sound effects: Youth, leisure, and the politics of rock.* London: Constable.

Fuss, Diana. 1989. *Essentially speaking: Feminism, nature, and difference.* New York: Routledge.

Gagnon, John, and William Simon. 1973. *Sexual conduct: The social origins of human sexuality.* Chicago: Aldine.

Greenberg, David. 1988. *The construction of homosexuality.* Chicago: University of Chicago Press.

Greil, Marcus. 1990. *Lipstick traces: A secret history of the 20th century.* Cambridge, MA: Harvard University Press.

Groce, S. B., and M. Cooper. 1990. Just me and the boys? Women in local-level rock and roll. *Gender & Society* 4: 220–29.

Grossberg, L. 1988. Putting the pop back in postmodernism. In *Universal abandon? The politics of post-modernism,* ed. A. Ross, 167–90. Minneapolis: University of Minnesota Press.

Hebdige, Dick. 1979. *Subculture: The meaning of style.* New York: Methuen.

Hill Collins, Patricia. 1999. Moving beyond gender: Intersectionality and scientific knowledge. In *Revisioning gender,* ed. Myra Marx Ferree, Judith Lorber, and Beth B. Hess, 261–84. Thousand Oaks, CA: Sage.

hooks, bell. 1989. *Talking back.* Boston: South End.

Ingraham, Chrys. 1996. The heterosexual imaginary: Feminist sociology and theories of gender. In *Queer theory/sociology,* ed. Steven Seidman, 168–93. Cambridge, MA: Blackwell.

Katz, Jonathan. 1976. *Gay American history.* New York: Routledge.

Kuhn, Annette. 1985. *The power of the image: Essays on representation and sexuality.* London: Routledge.

Laing, D. 1985. *One chord wonders: Power and meaning in punk rock.* Milton Keyes, UK: Open University Press.

Lapovsky Kennedy, Elizabeth, and Madeline D. Davis. 1994. *Boot of leather, slippers of gold.* New York: Penguin.

Lichterman, Paul. 1996. *The search for political community: American activists reinventing commitment.* Cambridge: Cambridge University Press.

Lorber, Judith. 1999. Embattled terrain: Gender and sexuality. In *Revisioning gender,* ed. Myra Marx Ferree, Judith Lorber, and Beth B. Hess, 416–48. Thousand Oaks, CA: Sage.

MacKinnon, Catherine. 1989. *Toward a feminist theory of the state.* Cambridge, MA: Harvard University Press.

McRobbie, Angela. 1984. Dance and social fantasy. In *Gender and generation,* ed. Angela McRobbie and M. Nava, 130–61. London: Macmillan.

Mulvey, Laura. 1990.Visual pleasure and narrative cinema. In *Issues in feminist film criticism,* ed. Patricia Erens, 28–40. Bloomington: University of Indiana Press.

Nakano Glenn, Evelyn. 1999. *The social construction and institutionalization of gender and race: An integrative framework.* In *Revisioning gender,* ed. Myra Marx Ferree, Judith Lorber, and Beth B. Hess, 3–43. Thousand Oaks, CA: Sage.

Plummer, Kenneth. 1975. *Sexual stigma: An interactionist account.* London: Routledge.

Rich, Adrienne. 1980. Compulsory heterosexuality and lesbian existence. *Signs: Journal of Women in Culture and Society* 5: 631–60.

Ross, Ellen, and Rayna Rapp. 1983. Sex and society: A research note from social history and anthropology. In *Powers of desire: The politics of sexuality,* ed. Ann Snitow, Christine Stansell, and Sharon Thompson, 51–73. New York: Monthly Review Press.

Rubin, Gayle. 1984. Thinking sex. In *Pleasure and danger: Exploring female sexuality,* ed. Carol Vance, 267–319. Boston: Routledge.

Schippers, Mimi. 1997. Gender maneuvering in alternative hard rock: Women's and men's everyday challenges to the gender order. Ph.D. diss., University of Wisconsin-Madison.

Sedgewick, Eve Kosofsky. 1990. *Epistemology of the closet.* Berkeley: University of California Press.

Seidman, Steven. 1996. Introduction. In *Queer theory/sociology,* ed. Steven Seidman, 1–29. Cambridge, MA: Blackwell.

Smith, Valerie. 1990. Split affinities: The case of interracial rape. In *Conflicts in feminism,* ed. Marianne Hirsch and Evelyn Fox Keller, 271–87. New York: Routledge.

Stein, Arlene, and Ken Plummer. 1996. "I can't even think straight": "Queer" theory and the missing sexual revolution in sociology. In *Queer theory/sociology,* ed. Steven Seidman, 129–44. Cambridge, MA: Blackwell.

Strauss, A., and J. Corbin. 1990. *Basics of qualitative research: Grounded theory procedures and techniques.* Newbury Park, CA: Sage.

Stryker, Sheldon. 1979. *Social interactionism: A social structural approach.* New York: Benjamin-Cummings.

Vance, Carol S. 1984. Pleasure and danger: Toward a politics of sexuality. In *Pleasure and danger: Exploring female sexuality,* ed. Carol S. Vance, 1–27. London: Pandora.

Walser, Robert. 1993. *Running with the devil: Power, gender, and madness in heavy metal music.* Hanover, NH: Wesleyan University Press.

Warner, Michael. 1993. Introduction. In *Fear of a queer planet,* ed. Michael Warner, vii–xxxi. Minneapolis: University of Minnesota Press.

Weeks, Jeffrey. 1985. *Sexuality and its discontents: Meanings, myths, and modern sexualities.* London: Routledge.

Weinstein, Deena. 1991. *Heavy metal: A cultural sociology.* New York: Lexington Books.

Williams Crenshaw, Kimberle. 1991. Mapping the margins: Intersectionality, identity politics, and violence against women of color. *Stanford Law Review* 43: 1241–99.

CHAPTER 22

What's So Feminist about Women's Oral History?

SUSAN GEIGER

There's a long-running revue in Minneapolis called "What's so funny about being female?" While the cast of comedians changes, the show usually features six or seven women whose routines are as diverse as their ages, sizes, delivery styles, and material. On the occasions I've seen this revue, I've found some of the sketches to be very funny while others don't tickle me at all. Among the women I consider very funny, some do what I and they call "feminist humor." But others who don't identify themselves as feminist make me laugh anyway, and not all of the self-identified feminist comics seem funny to me. Nevertheless, all of them think they have something funny to say about being female, and Dudley Riggs, who hires them, thinks so too. But when I'm in the audience, I make up my own mind as to whether the words, the process, and the presentation are funny, feminist, both, or neither. I have certain guidelines and standards for doing this, of course; and I can usually tell by their responses whether others in the audience agree with me.

Just as there is nothing inherently feminist about women comics talking about women, neither is there anything inherently feminist about women's oral histories or women doing women's oral histories. What, then, makes their gathering, production, and publication a feminist act? To answer this, we need to consider a set of prior issues including the objectives of the researcher, the questions addressed in the research, the evidence against which oral data are verified or evaluated, the character of the research relationship, the intended audience for the "product(s)" of the research, and the potential beneficiaries of the transformation of oral into written history. In addition, of course, we need a working definition of the term *feminist,* which I offer under "objectives" below.

OBJECTIVES

It is important to begin with the issue of objectives precisely because oral history is not a new activity or concept; nor is it a new research method. As an activity, it predates writing and transcends research institutions. Women's oral histories are not inherently feminist nor is the telling necessarily a feminist act. Moreover, the gathering of oral histories began long before the current wave of the feminist movement and cannot be considered, automatically, a feminist research method. Nor is the activity of the listener/recorder feminist simply because she is a women researcher.

Oral history only becomes a *method* in the hands of persons whose interests in it go beyond the immediate pleasure of hearing/learning the history being told. As scholars, we *use* information derived from oral history, and, in that way, it becomes a method, and methodological questions arise about it. But it can only become a feminist *methodology* if its use is systematized in particular feminist ways and if the objectives for colleting the oral data are feminist.

Feminist objectives include at least one of the following characteristics: they presuppose gender as a (though not the only) central analytical concept; they generate their problematic from the study of women as embodying and creating historically and situationally specific economic, social, cultural, national, and racial/ethnic realities; they serve as a corrective for androcentric notions and assumptions about what is "normal" by establishing or contributing to a new knowledge base for understanding women's lives and the gendered elements of the broader social world; they accept women's own interpretations of their identities, their experiences, and social worlds as containing and reflecting important truths, and do not categorize and, therefore, dismiss them, for the purposes of generalization, as *simply* subjective.

According to Gelya Frank and Elizabeth Hampsten, feminist objectives emphasize *understanding* rather than *controlling* the material or information generated and conceptualize the interpretive task as one of *opening* rather than *closure.*[1] There are also objectives that may not be feminist but neither are they antifeminist nor inherently "bad." Many of us who call ourselves feminist have certain perfectly reasonable objectives in our scholarly work and research that do not meet or relate to the above criteria. But I believe we deny the term *feminist* all meaning if we insist that it includes everything we happen to do; that it means anything we want it to mean; or that it refers to everything positive and good as opposed to negative and bad.

QUESTIONS

As scholars, we seek and develop methodologies to answer questions that interest us. But what makes our questions feminist? Our objectives will obviously influence the kinds of questions we will address in collecting oral histories. In my view, questions that in their content or formulation presume the accuracy of existing partial, androcentric, or ethnocentric constructions of the lives or situations of women are not feminist. For example, if, as Sally Green suggests, we assume, in our construction of questions to be posed with respect to the lives of Middle Eastern women, that "a 'harem' was a storehouse of lovers . . . and that . . . polygamy and seclusion [are] intrinsically evil"—both elements in the Western image of the Middle East as "Other"—we are unlikely to get beyond "the woman as a black sack of potatoes, shuffling after her husband, as a fleshy, gyrating belly dancer, as a longing face peering though the lattice."[2]

But my own reading of many women's life histories,[3] with a particular focus on the scholarly terms of analysis, has led me to conclude that the problematic for feminists resides most importantly in the fundamental concepts underlying the *fram-*

ing of questions; and that until certain intractable propositions and concepts are shaken up, perfunctory or automatic "answers" to the "wrong" questions are likely to continue to cloud imagination as well as understanding.

Let us consider, for example, two of the most common concepts employed in anthropological and historical analysis of "the person" and available to those of us trained in the Western intellectual tradition: *marginality* and *representativeness.* These concepts have been presented *as if* they are appropriate to objective analysis and somehow identifiable from some stance of "ungendered point of viewlessness."[4] Yet both concepts require that the observer recognize the reality of what Alcoff calls "positionality," a concept she offers to identify not only the relational and "constantly moving" context that constitutes our reality, but as the "place from which values are interpreted and constructed rather than as [the] locus of an already determined set of values."[5]

All too frequently, questions that presume or identify the marginality of an oral historian[6] or the place from which she speaks do not situate the narrator and her world; rather, such questions expose the researcher's preconceived notion of the narrator's world and of her own centrality, or, at least, the *centrality/power* of her own place in the world. For example, if a set of questions put to a woman trader in the Makola #1 market in Accra, Ghana, assumes and adopts the marginalizing economic terminology currently operating in much of the mainstream African literature on trade and commerce (that is, the terms "petty," "informal," "casual," "small-scale"), an understanding of the trader's actual relations in the state to her suppliers and buyers to her fellow traders, and to her own business might well be lost or at best obscured.[7]

Of course, a sense of marginality can, in fact, be expressed in the articulated experience of oral historians. Thus, the Jewish women rabbis interviewed by anthropologist Gelya Frank felt that their own sense of religious experience left them marginalized in the context of mainstream Judaism.[8] On the other hand, neither the lesbian women who created their own bar culture as a space for socializing, nor the African American women writers, studied by Elizabeth Kennedy and Nellie McKay, respectively, considered themselves marginal, thus rendering the concept inappropriate to an interpretation these authors wished to give to their lives.[9]

The point is, then, that marginality cannot be assumed, nor will questions that predict the marginality of the person to whom they are put yield particularly interesting insights into the self-perceptions or life of the oral historian. Marginality is best understood as a relational concept, the "truth" of which depends on the acceptance or affirmation of both parties to that characterization of the relationship, [10] and to the context in which the relationship occurs.

Even when something called marginality can be carefully defined, identified, and contextualized historically and geographically, as Africanist historian Marcia Wright has pointed out, [11] we still do not automatically or necessarily know what it is we have identified or how it operates. Moreover, there are historical circumstances in which even externally imposed economic, social, or political marginalization has been beneficial. In other words, "marginal" is not always a bad way or place to be in the world or in a given society; on the contrary, it can be a protection against certain destructive or negative forces. For example, African women in the Cape, Natal, and Transvaal provinces of South Africa were considered marginal to the wage labor needs of the economy and were therefore exempt, until the 1950s, from the pass requirements and laws through which the white minority regime controlled, intimidated, and oppressed African men.[12]

Questions that derive from the concept of *representativeness* and the assumptions underlying this concept constitute the other side of the same coin. Such questions necessarily presume norms against which the words, position, or experience of the oral historian are measured and in which the validity and, more tellingly, the significance and usefulness of her information is judged. But what determines, in this prior way, what or who is "representative" and, therefore, the norm against which all in a given society are to be judged? Not surprisingly, it is frequently the same scholarly tradition that established marginality as a useful category and concept. This is not to say that these concepts should be completely discarded. My point is simply that questions that presume their relevance ultimately shape and can certainly distort what is learned in the course of oral history work. On the other hand, if an attempt to address the issue of an individual's representativeness within carefully determined parameters follows rather than precedes the formulation of questions, useful contextualization occurs and assists understanding. Thus, Marjorie Shostak, in presenting the life story of Nisa, eventually situates Nisa's life history within a framework that includes the life stories of seven other !Kung women and statistical materials including the age curve of first marriage for !Kung girls, the usual numbers of marriages and children, and so forth. Had Shostak worried about Nisa's "respresentativeness" to begin with, she would have abandoned their interviews on the grounds that Nisa, who was first married at the age of nine, eventually experienced five marriages, had no living children, and was "unusually uninhibited, if not an outright extrovert,"[13] was not sufficiently typical of other !Kung women to bother with.

A particular pitfall for Western feminist scholars is encountered when the concept of "representativeness" gets collapsed into a tendency to "represent" particular "Third World" women, including oral historians, as a kind of universalized "other." As Chandra Mohanty has observed, a homogenization necessarily occurs in this process that creates an "object status" for Third World women. In this scenario, Western feminists remain "true subjects" while Third World women "never rise above their generality . . ."[14] Aihwa Ong further notes that "by portraying women in non-Western societies as identical and interchangeable, and more exploited than women in the dominant capitalist societies, liberal and socialist feminists alike encode a belief in their own cultural superiority."[15]

In some instances, as Julia Swindells has observed, what can be usefully characterized as representative is not, in any case, the individual member of a group but rather the conditions or circumstances within which that person operates. Thus, Hannah Culwick, the Victorian maidservant whose seventeen diaries were written essentially for the pleasure of her master and patron, Arthur Munby, was not herself "representative" of Victorian maidservants; but the general conditions she experienced, far from being unique to herself, were characteristic of her age, time, and class.[16]

An oral history methodology that features as major conceptual organizers the positional markers of marginality and representativeness automatically privileges certain voices and obstructs others through the very framework imposed. As feminists, we should be acutely aware of whose voices are obstructed. In contrast to questions flowing from assumptions of marginality and representativeness, questions that seek larger meaning and relevant concepts from oral historians themselves are likely to yield new and significant insights.

In listening to Italian wage-earning women of Turin talk about their lives between the world wars, historian Luisa Passerini found that models of rebelliousness were frequently exchanged and shared through "habit[s] of reciprocal narration, based, in turn, on family oral traditions."[17] These narratives, juxtaposed against parallel narratives told by the same individuals of their lives as exemplary wives, workers, and mothers, were important symbolically in the context of a tradition of literary representation of women rebels. In discovering both where the models for their lives came from and how these women developed their own counternarratives and models for truth and for a "good life," Passerini moved beyond those questions calling for answers that can be tested for simple factual accuracy. Instead, she concerned herself with the ways of deriving *meaning* from the oral histories and narratives collected. And meaning, as Passerini has so carefully established, lies in the silences and contradictions contained in a life story just as certainly as it lies in what is said.[18] Memory in turn *is* a construction of meaning—significant for feminists only if we are attentive to its shape and importance.

AUTHORITY

I have raised the issue of the validation or dismissal of oral accounts on the basis of a factual standard that privileges certain kinds of historical information, that is, dates, names, and numbers. Qualitative responses, textual evidence, reflections on social consequences of events, the popular memory of "what happened," and so forth are frequently dismissed as insubstantial within the scholarly domain or hedged around with multiple qualifiers designed to demonstrate scholarly skepticism. A related issue concerns the authority against which oral evidence is verified.

The "authority" or "authorities" on whom researchers draw help determine whether or not a methodology is feminist. Most of us have learned to regard information generated by "experts" and found in archives, libraries, classrooms, and universities as "reliable." These are the repositories of knowledge against which we have been taught to measure any "new" information we might collect or discover. If we insist that the validity of women's oral accounts must be—can only be—evaluated against existing knowledge or affirmed through the prism of the "latest" in fashionable social analysis, we are *not* following a feminist methodology in our oral history work with women. The question is this: Why isn't the written word, the received understanding, or the "latest" in analytical virtuosity tested against women's oral testimonies instead of the other way around? This is the method Carolyn Steedman uses in remembering, reconstructing, and presenting the working class childhoods of her mother and herself. Finding that neither the accepted authorities on or iconography of "the working-class" and on working-class motherhood nor those on childhood or femaleness capture the realities or "truths" of her mother's life and how those truths shaped her own, Steedman scrutinizes these authorities for their political and emotional agendas and lacks. She then uses her mother's story "to subvert" idealized accounts of the working class in order that her own, her mother's, and the lives of working-class women should not be found "wanting."[19]

The degree of academic panic or ridicule registered when feminist scholars insist upon the reconsideration and reconceptualization of everything we "know" is often a measure of the general malaise in the fields and disciplines from which these responses emanate. A "crisis of representation" is only a crisis for those who worry that their fundamental beliefs are about to crumble and with them, the power that the centrality of their point of view has brought. This is why many feminists don't consider the "crisis" a crisis at all but, rather, an opportunity. A "feminist" methodology is, in Adrienne Rich's words, prepared to be "disloyal to civilization."[20]

ORAL HISTORIAN/RESEARCHER RELATIONSHIP

The issue of authority—one's own as a scholar, as well as the existing knowledge upon which one depends—is linked to that of the relationship between the researcher and her living "source." It is easier to characterize the possible polarities in this relationship than it is to clearly articulate what might constitute a feminist alternative. At one end of the spectrum of such relationships lies erasure of the *person* of the oral historian through anonymous generalization from her story or through a third-person rendering of her words that objectifies her as just another "text." At the other end lies total identification or attempted merger with the "source" in an attempt to erase not the person herself but the reality of differences and disparities. The latter extreme is often a heartfelt response to the recognition and simultaneous rejection of inequalities separating researcher and oral historian. But it is not a particularly useful response and is, in a sense, as misleading and dishonest as the other extreme. Neither is likely to produce interpretations that have the possibility of transforming our understanding of the world.

In a feminist relationship between oral historian and researcher, existing differences will be recognized and conditions of mutual respect will be sought. Ways of sharing the "authority" expressed in written renditions of the oral account or exchange will be explicitly discussed, as will the nature of the working relationship itself and what is to be produced from it.[21] A feminist research relationship will also be characterized by honesty about its limitations; that is, that the relationship is a particular kind of association, at least with respect to work being done in its context. Whether a different kind of relationship is built into or results from that between scholar and oral historian is another issue. Doing oral history within a feminist methodological framework is about intellectual work and its processes, not about the potential for or realization of a relationship beyond or outside that framework.

This distinction is not always easy to bear in mind because the relationship is obviously being shaped from two directions, and the oral historian's will and intent can be just as strong as the researcher's. Frequently, for example, a young researcher will find herself in the position of being considered a daughter—and certainly a child if the age difference is quite great. Other familial ties may be claimed or asserted, for example, sister, auntie, or mother, if the age difference is closer or reversed. There is something very comforting about having the relationship characterized in familial terms, especially for researchers who have (understandable) doubts about the validity of what they are doing. Moreover, certain kinds of information may only be shared among particular categories of people. Anthropologists have long depended upon, and even capitalized on, this aspect of their chosen form of scholarly work. In almost any circumstance, it is useful to be considered "not-a-stranger." But as feminist researchers, I believe we must think long and hard about these fictive relational assertions and the extent to which we are willing not only to enjoy their benefits but to meet the obligations that necessarily accompany their creation and whatever privileges flow from them.[22]

There is a correlation between what I am trying to suggest with respect to a feminist research relationship and what Bettina Aptheker terms "pivoting the center." As Elsa Barkley Brown notes, this concept calls for the ability to center the experience of another person (or society) without denying the validity of one's own: neither "norm" nor "center"—in the sense of a place from which everything else is "marginal"—are relevant in these conceptualizations.[23]

AUDIENCE

Authority and audience are also linked. Not surprisingly, but all too frequently, they are comprised of the same people. This is the case, for example, if the audience for one's oral history research and production are the gatekeepers and acclaimed superstars of the discipline, the admired mentors/critics whose assessments determine promotion and entrance into an exclusive club of "first rate" scholars. A doubting thesis adviser also constitutes authority and audience in one, as, with increasing frequency, does a self-constituted feminist jury. In any of these cases, it is unlikely that the product(s) resulting from the oral history research can be feminist, and it is, therefore, unlikely that something called a feminist methodology will have been employed.

These audience issues reflect the peopling of our heads with critics whose judgment of our work matters because of the positions they occupy. These critics often have power, both real and imagined, over our scholarly actions and intellectual decisions. It is easier for most of us to identify this audience for ourselves than it is to identify or characterize its opposite: an audience that liberates us from self-censure based on fear and allows us to explore a range of ways of thinking about oral histories that are not easily categorized or contained within preestablished contexts.

In part, it seems to me that a researcher who undertakes oral history work in the context of a feminist methodology needs to image and position as an audience for the "results" several groups of people and perhaps several different "products." Certainly, women of the oral historian's community should be regarded as a significant "audience" for the work and interpretations produced by the researcher. These persons, as individuals and as a collective of sorts, have undoubtedly occupied a prominent place in the researcher's life and mind for the length of the period of collection. To assume that their role and place and function end once their words are recorded on tape or paper is to objectify them as "data."

But identifying this group as part of an audience does not mean that one's interpretation must be *the same as* their interpretation of themselves or their lives; nor does it mean that *everything* a researcher writes must be written in terms or in a context to which oral historians necessarily have direct access.[24] Nevertheless, the oral historians should "be there" in the sense that a feminist methodology cannot be one that wittingly or unwittingly violates the words of the individuals that have become the "subject matter."

Other members of a liberating audience might include fellow feminist scholars working in or with oral histories, feminist students and scholars more generally, and sympathetic "others." I have chosen to emphasize here the audience one constructs in the process and production stages of research. Ultimately, of course, a researcher's audience is not restricted to people visualized or chosen. It includes anyone who happens to have access to what we write and say.

WHO BENEFITS?

The final issue, initially raised as a precursor to, if not determinant of whether oral history might constitute a feminist methodology, concerns the beneficiaries of the relational process and its product(s) or publication(s). The idea that someone besides the researcher should benefit from one's research or its conclusions or findings is hardly unique to feminist scholarship. Much of social science research is presumed to be useful to one group or other: a community, a local government, a society. "Action," participatory or policy-oriented research in anthropology and sociology, history workshop productions, and virtually all of psychology, are designed to be more than intellectual exercises undertaken by scholars for the edification of other scholars. And several of these groups are equally insistent that their studies not harm those who have been studied or those who have participated. "Human Subjects" regulations exist in most universities in order to prevent harm, intended or unintended, to people who constitute the focus of academic research. In any case, to have or claim to have an ethics of caring and concern may well be an aspect of feminist methodology but it is not unique to feminism.[25]

Nevertheless, the conduct of oral history research *does* require an attentiveness to the concerns, interests, and circumstances of oral historians themselves. The specifics of this attentiveness—the way it can be expressed or realized—will vary according to the conditions of collection, the community or social group involved, and the amount of time spent with oral historians, among other factors. The benefits accruing to researcher and to oral historian(s) need not, nor are they likely to be, the same. What constitutes the feminist part of attentiveness to the questions of benefits is a willingness on the part of the researcher to be both flexible and creative—responsive to the fact that oral historians themselves often know how they can and would like to benefit from the work.

In my own research, for example, many of the women whose life histories constitute the base of my understanding of nationalist politics in Tanzania[26] have wanted and received the Swahili transcripts or versions of their life stories. They have wanted these for themselves, their children, and grandchildren, and for other reasons—their reasons. In earlier oral history work,[27] I was asked to find out what had happened to claims regarding a dispute in the 1930s that had been put forward by people I was interviewing in the late 1960s. It is not uncommon to be asked to act as a conduit for the testimonies or explanations of oral historians. And some oral historians may wish further discussion of certain issues because the act of relating has provoked additional thoughts or clarified previously murky ideas. A feminist researcher's methodology must be receptive to these strains in the overall process, even where "strain" has a double meaning as simultaneously "tension" and "strand." This means, of course, that there must be *time* to spare in the research—time that is not seen or experienced by the researcher as "time wasted."[28] And just as feminist objectives validate and concern women centrally and fundamentally, so too it is unimaginable that a feminist methodology should not produce ideas that benefit women through the revelation of historical experience. Finally, as Jacquelyn Dowd Hall points out, men who are open to "multiple voices rather than competing orthodoxies" are likely beneficiaries as well.[29]

TRUTHS AND TRANSFORMATIONS: INTERPRETATIONS AS THE RACIAL ACT IN FEMINIST SCHOLARSHIP

Many of us share the view that in order to be feminist, our methodology must be about transforming the world. Indeed, feminist disillusionment frequently sets in at the point where we presume more power over change than we actually have. This is a major reason, ironically, that women less privileged than ourselves perceive us as *more* rather than *less* like the male imperialists from whom we seek to distance ourselves. If we remember that within our chosen arena of operation, scholarly work, our main contribution will necessarily be an intellectual one, we can relieve ourselves of the immobilizing and counterproductive burdens of frustration and guilt—feelings that too often emerge to inhibit women's ventures into the lives of women different from themselves through a medium such as oral history research.

To be more specific: even as we know that "disloyalty to civilization" must inform a feminist methodology, we need to remain realistic and reasonably modest in our understanding of the part of the transformative project on which we as academics, feminist or otherwise, have some influence. Thus, for example, we cannot usually or in any immediate and substantive way change the lives of women living in tragic or difficult circumstances. What we might be able to do, however, is change the ways their lives are interpreted, appreciated, and understood.

This, in fact, is not such a modest project. It involves engaging in the process and practice of interpretive shifts, large and small, the sum total of which may transform and must certainly complicate thinking on how and why the world is and is *gendered* in the various ways it is and why this matters profoundly in ways with which we are only beginning to come to terms. It is a project that demands placing all accepted texts in question, not with the deconstructionist purpose of upsetting projects of explanation but with the feminist purpose of exposing the interests served by prevailing doctrine. This, in turn, requires understanding the ideological conditions under which norms and binary modes of thought are created and explaining why particular points of view—standpoints—were and are granted the status of (sole) "correct" interpretation and by whom. Most importantly, it involves releasing multiple truths into the scholarly environment.

It is hardly surprising that an acceptance of—indeed, insistence upon—"multiple" or "plural" truths should be expressed in the work and thought of many feminist scholars today. In the recently published volume of essays *Interpreting Women's Lives,* the Personal Narrative Group editing and contributing to the organizational and theoretical framework for the collection settled on "Truths" as the title for the book's concluding essay.[30] Aptheker's insistence on "numerous centers" and the need to "pivot the center";[31] Hall's conclusion that we need to accept the idea of all representations of reality as "partial truths"; Passerini's insight that it is the task of interpreters to discover "in which sense, where, [and] for what purpose" autobiographic memory is true[32]—these assertions all point to our grappling with the meaning of women's experiences over time and in an environment of vital criticism and self-criticism.

There is an interesting parallel, I think, between Jacquelyn Hall's call "for a historical *practice* [my emphasis] that turns on partiality, that is self-conscious about perspective"[33] and the stories and life stories oral historians relate, which are themselves partial, perspectival, and self-conscious. Feminist oral history methodology reflects and values these parallel activities—the practice of the researcher, the practice of the oral historian. Neither practice stands for the other, but if she is careful, the feminist historian's own interpretive product will encompass radical, respectful, newly accessible truths, and realities about women's lives.

NOTES

I want to thank Margaret Strobel, whose critical comments and suggestions on an earlier version of this essay informed my final revision. The gaps and inadequacies remaining are obviously my responsibility.

1. Transcript, "Autobiographies, Biographies, and Life Histories of Women: Interdisciplinary Perspectives" Conference. University of Minnesota, May 23–24, 1986, 9 (Frank); 20, 23–24 (Hampsten).

2. Sally Green, "Reading Middle Eastern Women Writers," *American Book Review* 11 (1989).

3. Susan Geiger, "Women's Life Histories: Method and Content," *Signs* 11 (1986): 334–51.

4. Catherine A. MacKinnon, "Feminism, Marxism, Method, and that State: Toward a Feminist Jurisprudence," *Signs* 8 (1983): 638–39.

5. Linda Alcoff, "Cultural Feminism versus Post-Structuralism: The Identity Crisis in Feminist Theory," *Signs* 13 (1988): 433.

6. I am using the term "oral historian" as Marjorie Mbilinyi uses "life historian" to designate the individual relating history/her history to the researcher. The more commonly employed terms "informant" and even "subject" suggest to me a less important place in the research process and relationship than the term "oral historian," which, despite the fact of who is narrating and who receiving the oral history content, is usually reserved, in academic circles, for the researcher. For Mbilinyi's usage, see Marjorie Mbilinyi, "I'd Have Been a Man," in *Interpreting Women's Lives: Feminist Theory and Personal Narratives,* ed. Personal Narratives Group (Bloomington: Indiana University Press, 1989), 204–27.

7. See Gracia Clark, "Introduction," in *Traders Versus The State: Anthropological Approaches to Unofficial Economics,* ed. Gracia Clark (Boulder: Westview Press, 1988), 1–16.

8. Gelya Frank, Transcript, 5.

9. Elizabeth Kennedy, Transcript, 11–12; Nellie McKay, Transcript, 70–71.

10. This is a view derived from Carolyn Steedman, *Landscape for a Good Woman* (London: Virago, 1986).

11. Marcia Wright, Transcript, 31.

12. See Julia C. Wells, "The War of Degredation: Black Women's Struggle against Orange Free State Pass Laws, 1913," in *Banditry, Rebellion, and Social Protest in Africa,* ed. Donald Crummey (Portsmouth, NH: Heinemann, 1986), 253–70.

13. Marjorie Shostak, "What the Wind Won't Take Away," in *Interpreting Women's Lives,* 231.

14. Chandra Taipade Mohanty, "Under Western Eyes: Feminist Scholarship and Colonial Discourses," *Boundary* 2, 12:3/13, 1 (1984 [published 1986]): 351.

15. Aihwa Ong, "Colonialism and Modernity: Feminist Re-presentations of Women in Non-Western Societies," *Inscriptions* $^3/_4$ (1988): 85.

16. Julia Swindells, Transcript, 238–39.

17. Luisa Passerini, "Women's Personal Narratives: Myths, Experiences, and Emotions," in *Interpreting Women's Lives,* 190.

18. Luisa Passerini, Transcript, 202.

19. Carolyn Steedman, *Landscape,* 7–24, esp. 8–10.

20. Adrinne Rich's phrase "disloyal to civilization" is in turn derived from the insight of Lillian Smith, who notes in "Autobiography as a Dialogue between King and Corpse" (1962), "what [Freud] mistook for her lack of civilization is women's lack of loyalty to civilization." Adrienne Rich, *On Lies, Secrets, and Silence* (New York: Norton, 1979), 277–78.

21. For contrasting but, I believe, equally respectful approaches that take into account the different conditions and contexts of the oral history research, see Margaret Strobel and Sarah Mirza, "Introduction," in *Three Swahili Women: Life Histories from Mombasa, Kenya,* ed. and trans. Sarah Mirza and Margaret Strobel (Bloomington: Indiana University Press, 1989), 4–6; and Marjorie Mbilinyi, "I'd Have Been a Man," in *Interpreting Women's Lives,* 204–27.

22. Carol A. B. Warren, *Gender Issues in Field Research* (Beverly Hills, CA: Sage, 1988) provides a useful overview of the gendered complexities of researcher informant relations. See esp. sections 2 and 3.

23. Elsa Barkley Brown, "African-American Women's Quilting: A Framework for Conceptualizing and Teaching African American Women's History," *Signs* 14 (1989): fn. 1,921–22, citing Bettina Aptheker, *Tapestries of Life: Women's Work, Women's Consciousness, and the Meaning of Daily Life* (Amherst: University of Massachusetts, 1989).

24. Compare this view with Jacquelyn Dowd Hall, "Partial Truths," *Signs* 14 (1989): 911.

25. There are clearly other assertions I make about feminist methodology in this essay that concern ideas and positions that are not the exclusive property of feminists. Here I agree with Deborah Gordon who, in her criticism of *Writing Culture,* points out that to expect "feminist claims to be exclusively feminist (an impossibility by definition as long as the world isn't feminist—at which point the word 'feminism' would cease to exist) . . . creates a double bind. Feminism must produce innovation that is completely distinct from any other; if it doesn't live up to this impossibility then it ceases to be either feminist or innovative." (See Deborah Gordon, "Writing Culture, Writing Feminism: The Poetics and Politics of Experimental Ethnography," *Inscriptions* $^3/_4$ [1988]: 15; also, Frances E. Macia-Lees, Patricia Sharpe, and Colleen Ballerino Cohen, "The Postmodernist Turn in Anthropology: Cautions From A Feminist Perspective," *Signs* 15 [1989]: 7–33.)

26. Susan Geiger, "Women in Nationalist Struggle: TANU Activists in Dar es Salaam," *International Journal of African Historical Studies* 20 (1987): 1–26. But as Margaret Stro-

bel notes, "[I]t is easier to give something back when people themselves are organized and/or have some consciousness [of the significance of documentation]." Of the three women whose life histories she recorded in Mombasa, Kenya, only the youngest, whose political consciousness and sense of history were considerable, wanted a copy of the taped interview and history of the Muslim Women's Institute she had narrated to Strobel. Moreover, Strobel's desire to ensure that Swahili women in Mombasa in general had access to a Swahili version of the three life histories she and Mirza painstakingly transcribed and organized was thwarted by Kenyan publishers who maintained that there was no market for "serious" Swahili literature and were, therefore, not interested in local publication (Margaret Strobel, personal communication, September 29, 1989).

27. Susan [Geiger] Rogers, *The Search for Political Focus on Kilimanjaro: A History of Chagga Politics, 1916–1952, with Special Reference to the Cooperative Movement and Indirect Rule* (Ph.D. dissertation, University of Dar es Salaam, 1973).

28. Compare with Mbilinyi, "I'd have Been a Man," in *Interpreting Women's Lives.*

29. Jacquelyn Dowd Hall, "Partial Truths," 911.

30. See *Interpreting Women's Lives,* 261–64.

31. Elsa Barkley Brown, "African-American Women's Quilting."

32. Luisa Passerini, "Women's Personal Narratives," in *Interpreting Women's Lives.*

33. Jacquelyn Dowd Hall, "Partial Truths," 908.

CHAPTER 23

But Sometimes You're Not Part of the Story

Oral Histories and Ways of Remembering and Telling

ANTOINETTE ERRANTE

> What defines oral history, and sets it apart from other branches of history, is . . . its reliance on memory rather than texts. Yet oral historians seem reluctant to emphasize this, seemingly preferring to treat memory as a set of documents that happen to be in people's heads rather than in the Public Record Office. . . . What is memory? Do we hunt it with a questionnaire, or are we supposed to use a butterfly net?
>
> —FENTRESS AND WICKHAM, *SOCIAL MEMORY*

In recent years, qualitative researchers have demonstrated a growing interest in the personal narrative as a valid articulation of individual and collective experience with the social, political, and cultural worlds of education (e.g., Blake 1997; Davidson 1996; Farrell 1994; Mohanty 1994; Polakow 1993; Weis and Fine 1993). This interest in the "first-person" seems to stem from our ethical and epistemological concerns regarding representation and voice. We increasingly recognize that all narratives, whether oral or written, personal or collective, official or subaltern, are "narratives of identity" (Anderson 1991); that is, they are representations of reality in which narrators also communicate how they see themselves and wish others to see them (Stein 1987; Volkan 1988). Narratives declare narrators' alignments with certain "in" individuals, groups, ideas, and symbols onto which they externalize their most valued, positive, and pride-inducing qualities. Narratives also declare narrators' dissociation from "other" individuals, groups, ideas, and symbols onto which they externalize the least favorable parts of themselves. This articulation of identity—of voice—has thus become understood as a locus of human dignity, much as reason was for the Enlightenment; we can now define a person as one who narrates. Consequently, to deny a person the possibility to narrate his or her own experience is to deny a person's human dignity (Bhabha 1990; Said 1993). And so we celebrate, struggle with, and presume the ability to give, authorize, and enable voice.

As an oral historian, I have been delighted by this celebration of the personal narrative because it has tended to legitimize oral histories as sources of documentation. At the same time, however, the excessive intuitive appeal of "voice" and "narrative" has perhaps bred a certain methodological complacency. Among educational researchers there is more advocacy for the use of narratives as a research strategy than there is detailed discussion of particular methods for engaging in narrative work. Most qualitative methods texts, for example, give little to no attention to personal narratives. But what does it mean to collect and analyze personal narratives? How do persons voice their narratives or narrate their voice? Do conceptions of personhood differ (Schweder and Bourne 1984) and might this influence the nature of voice and what C. Wright Mills called, "the range of the intricate relations" between history and biography, the personal and the collective?

The nature of oral history work coalesces these questions around a particular set of conditions. Like other written and oral narratives, oral histories are a "a context in which identity is practiced" (Friedman 1992, 840). In contrast to written narratives, however, in oral histories, the audience to which the narrator directs his or her story is immediate and interactive. The story's dynamic of personal and collective voice and identity emerges as a result of the interaction between historian (the interviewer) and narrator (the informant). Although the "teller" of the story is the narrator, the story is distorted when we do not take into consideration the historian's participation in the oral history interview (Tonkin 1992). Oral history's identity work, therefore, is also in "the remembering and the telling [which] are themselves events, not only descriptions of events" (Portelli 1981, 175). To some degree, this interviewer-informant dynamic occurs during any kind of interview situation because all interviews are "telling" events. What distinguishes oral histories from other kinds of interviews or oral narratives is that this dynamic is *also* and primarily mediated by the nature and context of remembering. Memory is not simply an exercise of recalling; there are many ways of remembering and different reasons why we may (or may not) want to remember (Fentress and Wickham 1992; Tonkin 1992).

I did not fully appreciate the methodological and epistemological implications of this when I began collecting oral histories of education in Mozambique in 1989. Oral history work is a wondrous experience and I have never lost the sense of privilege I feel that close-to-perfect strangers are willing to share their lives with me. For a brief moment, such apparent openness led me to conclude that there was no individual or collective experience—no voice—that a good oral history could not capture. "Hunting" memory, I thought, was no different from archival work: If I dug long enough, I could eventually find any memory and unleash any voice. I have since realized that there are memories and voices I cannot collect. Historian and narrator may negotiate a story, but some stories lie beyond the oral history event because either the historian or the narrator is not part of the context of remembering in which a particular story is told. In this article, I will take the reader on my journey regarding what I have learned about oral histories, the stories that they tell (and whose), and the ways their narrators tell and remember them.

THE BACKGROUND FOR MY STORY

A thumbnail sketch of the segment of Mozambique's educational history in which I was interested will provide the reader with some context for understanding my oral history work. Mozambique is a former Portuguese colony that was most heavily colonized from the 1930s to 1974 as part of Portugal's authoritarian Salazar-Caetano regime. Portugal established throughout its African colonies a dual educational system: "rudimentary" schools for "natives" operated by the Catholic missions, and official (governmental) schools for whites and assimilated blacks.[1] Similar divisions existed in teacher education: The Catholic missions supervised training schools for "native" teachers while government-run normal schools trained official school teachers. Educational opportunities for blacks remained limited throughout the colonial period, and missionaries did not always support "native" teachers' efforts to improve educational achievement when these exceeded the rigors of the catechism (Cross 1987; Errante 1995). As a result, only about 2 percent of Mozambique's population was literate at the time of independence in 1975 (Isaacman and Isaacman 1983).

Although Mozambique's independence followed a military coup in Lisbon that overthrew Portugal's authoritarian government in 1974, FRELIMO (Frente de Libertação de Mocambique, or Mozambican Liberation Front) had been waging an armed struggle for independence since 1964. Increasingly Marxist in orientation, FRELIMO believed educational opportunity was critical to its mobilization efforts and the development of an independent Mozambique (FRELIMO 1972; 1973). As FRELIMO liberated zones in northern and central Mozambique from Portuguese rule, it established primary schools in these areas and constructed secondary schools on its bases in neighboring Tanzania. The movement recruited heavily among "native" teachers and seminarians for its schools since these constituted some of the country's most educated blacks. The schools of the liberated zones subsequently became the models for postindependence education.

After independence, education remained central to FRELIMO's socialist development agenda. In spite of staggering illiteracy levels, and the loss of 95 percent of its educated human resources with the Portuguese exodus, the country remained buoyed by revolutionary euphoria in the years immediately following independence (Isaacman and Isaacman 1983). Hopeful Mozambicans embarked on wide-scale national reconstruction efforts, including literacy campaigns and the expansion of schooling and health care. But the euphoria was soon disrupted by political instability, economic turmoil, and natural disasters. Mozambique's socialist sympathies made it vulnerable to cold war politics. It was also surrounded by the white minority governments of Rhodesia and South Africa, which felt threatened by Mozambique's black socialist leadership, and its sympathy toward black insurgency movements in both countries. Rhodesia, and then South Africa, launched and supported an insurgency force, RENAMO (Resistencia Nacional de Mocambique), whose initial purpose was to destabilize the Mozambican state. The conflict that followed in the 1980s and early 1990s killed 1.5 million people, including 600,000 children, displaced 5 million people, and decimated the country's infrastructure (Msabaha 1995).

FRELIMO held on to its Marxist development agenda, but as the turmoil mounted, so did the party's tendency to resort to repression; this undermined its popular legitimacy. FRELIMO rejected not only all things colonial but also most cultural practices which party leaders viewed as "traditionally" African, and therefore, obscurantist (Machel 1977). Early postrevolutionary curricula were so loaded with Maoist and Marxist slogans that teachers complained they could not teach the new material because they themselves did not understand it (Mozambique 1979). At the same time, failed collective farming schemes, severe drought, and RENAMO's destabilization efforts left the country near starvation in the mid-1980s. After FRELIMO's first president, Samora Machel, was killed with high-ranking advisors in a suspicious plane crash, FRELIMO blinked. Machel's successor, Joaquim Chissano, moved the country away from socialism in an attempt to end the bloodshed and restore peace (Msabaha 1995). A Peace Accord between FRELIMO and RENAMO was signed in 1992 and multiparty democratic elections were subsequently held in 1994. Educational reforms are currently underway to bring the schools in alignment with the changes in Mozambique's political and economic culture.

MY BIOGRAPHY ABOUT BIOGRAPHIES

My Early Years: Oral Histories as Occasions to Remember

My story opens in 1989, when I began conducting a series of oral histories with Mozambicans as part of a larger study (my dissertation) regarding the socializing role of the primary school in colonial and postcolonial Portugal and Mozambique (Errante 1994). My primary interest was in understanding the role that education—through the values, attitudes, and behaviors it consciously or unconsciously transmitted—might have played in socializing persons to maintain, resist, and transform the colonizer-colonized relationship.

I wanted to examine the segment of the country's educational history I described above as a context for understanding how Mozambicans engaged and interpreted the symbolic and material forms of negotiation and resistance which influenced cultural continuity and change (cf, Comaroff and Comaroff 1992; Ortner 1984, 1997), and social reproduction and change (Fox and Starn 1997; Scott 1990; Tarrow 1991). My perspective was influenced by my reading of studies conflating culture, power, history, and identity (e.g., Dirks, Eley, and Ortner 1994; Sewell 1997). It required grounded work which relied heavily on the phenomenological: to understand how schools socialized to reproduce, resist, and transform the standing order, I also had to understand what the school experiences at different moments of Portuguese and Mozambican history were like and what meaning these experiences had for those who actually lived them.

Oral histories added an invaluable subaltern dimension to this educational history, which was otherwise solely available by reading—and reading against—the official documentation of colonial and postcolonial regimes. They could provide this by adding a measure of history-as-lived-experience. In so doing, and because they represented largely the experiences of groups whose voices were underrepresented in "official" histories, they broadened the range of collective experiences accounted for in the historical record (Tonkin 1992). I triangulated narrators' individual stories with each other and with other published and archival documentation. This not only helped me cross-validate the "facts" narrated, but also gave me a sense of the degree to which personal experiences reflected collective ones. There is a rich tradition of this kind of oral history work with respect to marginalized groups, and this was the basis of my training in African studies.

In this sense, I was guilty, as Fentress and Wickham (1992) charge in their opening quotation above, of treating the oral histories as a set of documents not very different from archival material. Of course, I was aware that oral histories were works of memory (thus the reason to triangulate "facts" with other sources). However, I had a rather limited vision of the nature of memory itself. Anthropologists and historians have begun to give serious attention to the different ways we remember (e.g., Calhoun 1994; Hunt and Benford 1994; Irwin-Zarecka 1996; Stein 1987). Teski and Climo (1995), for instance, argue that there are five different ethnographic categories of memory: remembering, forgetting, reconstructing, metamorphosis of memory, and vicarious memory. My initial approach predisposed me to a particular way of remembering. It is the genre perhaps most of us commonly associate with memory; that is, recall that is dense with detail. This corresponds to the category of memory that Teski and Climo call "remembering":

> When we think about the past and try to bring forth, for example, the name of our first grade teacher . . . we are trying to flesh out our remembered past in a fuller, more satisfying way. We are . . . not consciously trying to change it but to see it as it was. We want to have access to scenes that were real in the past and to somehow preserve these things in our present experience. (3–4)

With this vision of my study and my method, I packed my bags and spent the next two years (1990–1992) in Portugal and Mozambique, going through archival materials, analyzing school textbooks, and collecting oral histories. In Mozambique[2] I collected twenty-seven oral histories with narrators between the ages of twenty-six and ninety-eight whose educational experiences were representative of the different moments of the period in which I was interested (1934–1992): those who attended colonial "native" and official schools, and their respective institutions for teacher training, students and teachers who attended FRELIMO's schools in the liberated zones, and persons who participated in the postindependence socialist reconstruction of Mozambican education, or attended these schools. By oral history standards, this was not a large number of narratives; but my primary interest was in trying to get a sense of the range of colonial and postcolonial educational experiences, and there was sufficient consistency or "theoretical saturation" (Glaser and Strauss 1967) within each group and across the data sets (including written documentation).

I was not only amazed at the details of daily life in school which narrators remembered (e.g., class schedules, names of teachers, names of schoolbooks), but how consistent these details turned out to be with what I could uncover through published documentation. This was not limited to questions of curriculum and routines. For instance, Mr. Cardoso,[3] speaking of the "natives" of his province, recalled: "In my time, [in the mid-50s] there weren't more than four of us who made it to the fourth grade." This might have passed as simple boasting except that consultation of educational statistics of the period for his province revealed that, indeed, only four blacks made it to the fourth grade.

Negotiating Ways of Remembering and Telling or How I Got Narrators to Tell Me What I Wanted to Know

While narrators seemed to have little difficulty remembering, getting them to remember the particular memories I was hunting was another matter. I knew where I hoped the oral histories would take me—to an understanding of the daily life of schools at different historical moments; how these experiences might have shaped narrators' outlooks on life, their culture, and their race; and to any clues regarding how these experiences might have influenced the creation of a critical consciousness toward the standing colonial and postcolonial order. What kinds of questions would elicit this? Some were easier to determine than others. For example, since studies of colonial education tend to view it as a culturally emasculating experience, asking narrators, "When did your education begin?" gave them an opportunity to define for me whether they believed it began with formal schooling or through traditional means, such as with grandparents. Similarly, I asked narrators, "How many languages do you speak?" to see how they characterized African versus European languages. But, through trial and error, I also discovered that there are "watershed questions," which may not appear to solicit the information you are looking for but seem to unlock a stream of memory. By asking, for instance, "What was the relationship between teachers and students?" narrators frequently recalled the smell and layout of schools, disciplinary practices, teacher approaches to instruction, attitudes toward local culture, community perceptions of "native" teachers, and relationships with peers. Having discovered these questions, with some narrators my interview guide was whittled from twenty-five questions to six or seven during a two- to three-hour interview.

I wanted my voice to be minimally heard during the oral history event, and my approach was to ask as few questions as would solicit the information I was looking for. I was interested in how narrators framed their experiences, and so, I allowed[4] them to speak as long as they wished about something they wished to remember, even when this did not seem particularly relevant to my study. Sometimes, narrators would get lost in their memories. They would recall poems they learned as children, songs that their grandmothers sang to them, describe the landscape of their village with poetic vividness. In these moments, narrators made themselves vulnerable by amplifying those memories that were important to them. Their openness often took them by surprise. They would say, "I cannot believe I am telling you this," or, "It's funny, I have not thought about that in years." This does not occur in every interview, but when it does, it is as if both narrator and interviewer enter what Csikszentmihalyi (1990) describes as "flow." These are moments of optimal experience when our sense of self-efficacy is heightened and our social bonds are strong.

Invariably, even memories that seemed extraneous to my immediate objectives enriched my understanding of colonial and postcolonial education's social context. When I asked Mr. Cardoso to describe the family and persons with whom he grew up, I was not expecting him to spend the next twenty minutes describing his earliest memories of his grandmother, who taught him "right from wrong" and the name and medical uses of all the plants in his region. However, these memories gave me cause to think how this education (which was how Mr. Cardoso described this experience) differed from learning the multiplication tables under the stern gaze of a "native" teacher and his paddle.

If narrators chose their moments of vulnerability through what they told and remembered, I was often vulnerable myself. On many occasions I had cause to remember the two pieces of advice I had received during a seminar with two seasoned oral historians, Allen Isaacman and Luise White:

1. "Write down immediately all of your impressions of your informants"; and
2. "Being young and stupid can be a good thing. You will ask the kinds of obvious questions you won't be able to conjure up when you become more familiar with the terrain; narrators will not only not hesitate to set you straight on your stupidity, but in the process reveal their understanding of important events and experiences about which you might not have otherwise asked."

Although I did keep notes, the merits of this only emerged years later. On the latter point, I discovered that indeed, when it comes to "getting the facts straight" narrators rarely hesitated to say, "No, no, no, you do not understand. Now listen and let me explain it to you." I could not hide my youth nor my inexperience, and I sensed this was somewhat endearing to some narrators. Some narrators, particularly former "native" teachers, were almost didactic in relation to me, complimenting me on my choice of questions, and often offering me precious notebooks and schoolbooks, which they had preserved for forty years, so that I might complete my work.

Negotiating the Context of Remembering or How Narrators Got Me To Ask Them What They Wanted Me to Know and How They Wanted Me to Know It

Narrators not only ultimately choose what they wish to remember and tell you; they also participate in negotiating the context of remembering. Narrators also have specific ideas about what constitutes an "interview" and my unstructured style was not always congruent with how they believed stories should be told and remembered. Former "native" teachers, for instance, routinely stopped the interview to suggest questions they felt I should have been asking them, even though they were free to simply volunteer the information the question served to elicit. But for them, the interview context implied a steady stream of questions and answers. I wondered if this "catechetical" way of telling and remembering did not derive from their own educational experiences, which were largely based on biblical as well as political catechisms.

Narrators' views of my role as an academic and what constitutes "scientific information" also come to light in such moments. I have interviewed somewhat reluctant narrators who were not fully convinced they had "useful" information. They begin their narratives with abbreviated responses, as if their elaboration would be an imposition. They tend to need reassurance, interjecting, "I don't know if this is what you want." Although persons may "size you up" before agreeing to participate, it is sometimes difficult for them to understand how their seemingly "ordinary" lives could be of interest to historians. Carefully explaining the purposes of the oral history project does not always clarify this.

This has become a particular challenge since the first multiparty democratic elections were held in Mozambique in 1994. I return to Mozambique annually, and continue to collect oral histories of education whenever I am there, as peace has enabled me to travel more freely through rural areas that were off-limits during the FRELIMO-RENAMO conflict. But some villages, particularly those that were hardest hit by the conflict, have been swamped with largely foreign research teams doing focus group interviews regarding a host of social issues; these interviewers tend to come with structured interview protocols to which they want very specific answers. These researchers also tend to represent international aid organizations that conduct such studies in order to determine their funding priorities. Very often they also pay for villagers' participation. I have found that these experiences have colored villagers' framing of who I am (they assume, erroneously, I represent someone with funds to disburse) and their understanding of the context of sitting down and speaking with a researcher. Regardless of my initial introduction and explanations, there are times when people do not seem altogether convinced that the information they share with me might not reach the ears of someone who could help reconstruct their community.

Narrators' previous interviewing experience not only affects their notion of the context of remembering and telling—in that villagers tend to think I am "after" some very specific responses, and that, perhaps, their responses will determine whether or not the village gets international assistance—but it also seems to influence how they frame their memories. Whether I am speaking casually with villagers about education in the region, or interviewing someone, all memories seem to lead back to discussions of services and forms of assistance the community needs in the present. Can you describe the village where you grew up, I ask a narrator. He responds that it was peaceful and prosperous, unlike today when villagers are struggling because the government and international community have provided them with little assistance to rebuild. Was there a mission in the area during the colonial period, I ask villagers. Yes, they say, and the mission had many schools, unlike today, when the government has yet to send someone to help the community build schools. And the mission, they would add (before I could ask something else), had a fine hospital. It is now in ruins, they tell me, and the authorities in the capital have been promising for three years to build a new one. It would be of no use, someone else adds, because the roads are so bad, no one could get to the hospital in any case, and so what they really need are good roads . . .

The Historian-Narrator Interpersonal Bridge and Ways of Telling and Remembering

How to negotiate moments of flow with narrators whose idea of how their narratives should be told and what they should tell and remember differs from one's own? For the most part, these differences had not hindered my capacity to establish a rapport with narrators and to secure the kind of information I was looking for regarding education's socializing role; and so this question had not concerned me. However, in villages such as the one I described above, I noticed that the drastically different context of remembering began to erode the oral history event: I was less interested in the stories my narrators wanted to tell and they were less open about the stories they were willing to share. Some Mozambicans have become cynical toward the focus group and survey work conducted by internationals. This affected how villagers viewed me. They asked on several occasions why, as a rich foreigner ("rich" and "foreigner" being synonymous in this context), I was making a living by doing research in a country so far away or why they were constantly being asked questions when nothing ever changed for them anyway. It also affected how I began to view narrators. I did not like feeling instrumentalized (as a conduit for funding opportunities) any more than they liked feeling that I was instrumentalizing them. This proved a challenge to constructing an "interpersonal bridge" (Kaufman 1974) between myself and the narrator. This is the "emotional bond that ties people together. . . . Such a bridge involves trust and makes possible experiences of vulnerability and openness. The bridge becomes a vehicle to facilitate mutual understanding, growth and change" (Kaufman 1974, 570).

This interpersonal bridge makes flow possible. Depending on the circumstances of fieldwork, however, there may not be much of an opportunity to build such a relationship before the interview. The oral history event itself must foster this sense of trust, respect, and validation as the remembering and telling and listening and probing unfold. Both narrator and historian must foster this openness. In my earlier interviews, much of the bridge had been constructed in moments of vulnerability. With every intimate, personally important memory that narrators offered, they revealed their humanity. This drew out my own humanity. I stopped listening for what I could extract from the narrative and started listening to the whole person. There is no easy way to translate this into a methodology; it is not an attitude you can feign; but it results in narrators feeling that they have an appreciative and respectful audience. At the same time, my vulnerabilities—my inexperience, my youth, my stupid questions—all revealed my own humanity and this demystified notions narrators might have had about my power and position as a white foreign academic.

I realized this was missing in the interviews I had recently conducted in rural communities so preoccupied with basic survival, after an interview with Mr. Nhamuhuco.[5] I knew from previous conversations with his son and with him personally that he had had a rich life as a "native" teacher. But the oral history event was strained; his responses were short and he kept directing his comments to what he felt the government and aid organizations should be doing to alleviate his community's present economic difficulties. My attempts to have him elaborate about his colonial and postcolonial experiences seemed like I was pulling teeth. Fearing that a long conversation was also a strain to his ailing health, our conversation lasted only about forty minutes. But some time afterward, while I was still visiting with his family, he approached me and said, "That was a very bad interview. I have thought about your questions more and I realize I did not tell you the best parts of my story. You really did want to know about my life didn't you? Won't you please come back and let us try this again?"

I realized that I was at least as much to blame as Mr. Nhamuhuco for our conversation. How could I have not recognized how important it was for me to acknowledge his community's present crisis? Why had I been more willing to listen to "extraneous" memories in other narrators than I was to his stories of a seemingly "irrelevant" present? Ahhh, I thought. I was not listening precisely because I was hunting *memories* and not the present. I had pegged the interview as one of those "instrumental" ones; I had given up on the story also, and so had given Mr. Nhamuhuco few verbal or nonverbal cues that I was interested in *him*. From his perspective, such an attitude must have reinforced his pegging of me as yet another foreign researcher mining for information that will benefit no one but myself. And, I realized, his assessment had been perfectly correct because in hunting down the story I wanted him to tell me, I had shown little respect for the story he needed to tell me.

This lesson in humility reminded me once again of the importance of establishing mutual respect and trust with narrators. I now take more time just engaging in conversation. I explain what oral history work means to me more fully, and the value of narrators' life experiences for the national patrimony. I ask narrators, particularly older ones, to think about what they would like their grandchildren to know about their life and their educational experiences. I ask them if they would like to know something about my life before we start. And I listen first and foremost to the story narrators want to tell me. All of this helps to construct an interpersonal bridge; it gives the narrator and me a chance to get to like each other.

Although this approach has yielded oral history work that has been more satisfying for me, and, I believe, narrators, I did not really consider what I was doing to the context of remembering: By asking narrators to think about what they would like their grandchildren to know about their lives, for instance, I was re-positioning my "place" within the oral history event. I was no longer the sole audience. Until this point I had really not thought about the context in which people remember and tell, and for all of my appreciation regarding the interpersonal bridge, I had not clearly articulated my place in the oral history event. This would have to await another project during which I realized that there were (and had been all along) stories that the oral history context could not capture.

When Mourning Becomes Remembering: Narrating Education as a Site of Social Justice Movements

> Memories carry with them a symbolism that transcends the actual act of telling them. Remembering often evokes pain, and some may choose to "hold on" to their memories as a way of avoiding pain. For these people the step between owning memories privately and allowing them to become a public possession may not be an easy one to take.
>
> —GOBODO-MADZIKIZELA, REMEMBERING AND THE POLITICS OF IDENTITY

Volkan (1988) writes that, "it is through mourning that we accept changes within ourselves and within others, and become able to face reality about our unfulfilled hopes and aspirations" (6). In this sense, grief is the memory of happiness, a particular way of remembering that marks the passing, in the present, of something or someone of value. Although I ultimately interviewed Mozambicans representing a broad range of the racial/ethnic spectrum, about a broad range of experiences, I repeatedly had the sense that the memories of their education in relation to the postrevolutionary transition seemed marked by a sense of loss of something of value.

I hypothesized that the educational experience in Mozambique became a site of grieving because of the symbolic meanings that over the course of this century were attached to it; in particular, that this grief stemmed from the fact that Mozambicans viewed their educational experiences as central to their identification with social movements. Within the political opportunities and constraints afforded them, narrators perceived learning as a form of social protest that aligned them with the important social movements of their day. For these narrators, education was not just one in a series of life events, but a crucial *identifying* experience. And so, "native" teachers viewed their persistent efforts to improve educational attainment in spite of missionaries' objections as a form of resistance in solidarity with FRELIMO's armed struggle for independence (Errante 1995). Those Mozambicans who studied and taught in FRELIMO's schools in the revolutionary and early postindependence period similarly believed that they pursued their education in the name of the social justice ideals of the socialist struggle (Errante 1994). Because the social movement to which narrators aligned their educational experience was important to their overall sense of identity, the *telling* and *remembering* of those educational experiences was an important component of their overall "impression management" (Goffman 1959), that is, how narrators wished others to see them.

If this was pride-inducing, their telling and remembering of the *loss* of their movement's legitimacy seemed to provoke a sense of grief. And so, grief seemed to mark "native" teachers' recollections of the years following Mozambique's independence, when many felt branded as colonial collaborators and rejected by the very movement they had sustained. FRELIMO's cadres of the liberated zones, as well as those who had pressed for revolutionary education during FRELIMO's Marxist heyday, also appeared to become saddened as they recalled how the country's sense of euphoria and commitment to socialism slowly collapsed.

My impression of the narratives was consistent with the research regarding the links between social movements, and the construction of personal and collective identity (Hunt and Benford 1994; Snow and Anderson 1987; Tarrow 1991). They are also consistent with Marris's (1974) discussion of how social change is experienced as a personal loss. Through an analysis of this grief, therefore, I believed we could better understand how personal educational experiences are linked to collective experiences generally.

I returned to Mozambique in the summer of 1997 to conduct further oral histories of education in order to examine this link between identity and grief more systematically. I was confident the oral histories would capture this grief. Not only did my previous oral histories seem to "speak" to me about this, but I had personally experienced some of what I was certain narrators would tell me. My initiation into fieldwork in Mozambique coincided with a turning point in the country's postindependence story. I arrived in July 1989, just as FRELIMO held its Fifth Congress, in which the party formally disestablished socialism in Mozambique. Most Mozambicans I met that summer seemed to be in crisis. My friends had fought to construct a new Mozambican society. They followed the Fifth Congress in visible pain. My journal entry for July 30, 1989, captures some of the mood:

> Yet another evening of collective friendship and misery. I went with some friends to a dinner. The conversation slowly drifted to the war and the [Fifth] Congress, and, as usual, this was not without its moments of humor. In fact, we seemed to alternate laughing and crying about the same things. When it was not some joke related to the shortage of water and electricity, it was about maimed bodies. . . .
>
> The mood turned somber as we watched the Congress on the television news. As Party leaders appeared on camera, people explained (as if to get me up to speed) how each one let the country down. Others argued that it was not their fault; they looked pained when their friends criticized FRELIMO. Instead, they held out that it was the international community and South Africa that had killed "our dream." [Someone] . . . retorted, "Go on and feel sorry for yourselves. Which one of you great Marxist intellectuals smoking your cigarettes and eating a nice curry is watching your kids' limbs being blown to bits?"
>
> I cannot help but feel these webs of emotion are a measure of how deeply they sense this political transformation as a personal one. I was about the only person at the dinner tonight who had not experienced combat (they laughed and cried about those days also); they put their lives on the line for a social project now quickly disintegrating. . . .
>
> What is astonishing is how painful this has been for *me*. . . . I cannot say my feelings have to do with particular political sympathies. Still, socialism seemed like such a struggle to fight the good fight. And now Mozambique—the good guys—lost. But this is not my country. This is not my life. So why does this bother me?

When I returned for a year, 1990–1991, grief and anger seemed all around me. By the time I left, I felt as if I had spent a year grieving: with those who felt they had been betrayed by the revolution, with those who felt they had betrayed the revolution, and with those grieving for the destruction they now attributed to their youthful idealism.[6]

And so, I returned to Mozambique with my tape recorder in the summer of 1997, convinced that I just needed to get on tape what I had heard and experienced. Nothing could be simpler. I was wrong. I found the Mozambican narrators as generous as those I had interviewed earlier. But when the interview turned to the postindependence period, almost unanimously, their entire recollections were reduced to, "And then all that crap happened *[E depois aconteceu aquela porcarião]*." The only variant was, "And then all that confusion happened [*E depois aconteceu aquela confusão*]."

Nonplused, I figured I still had my earlier interviews, which I could reexamine. So I reread the transcripts. To my horror, I could find few traces of grief. Indeed, the transcripts of my earlier interviews were consistent with the narratives I had just collected: even in 1991, most of the informants had confined their comments regarding their postindependence experience to "and then all that confusion happened." As in 1997, with some probing from me, they elaborated, but not with the same effusiveness with which they generally recollected other points in their lives before and since independence.

Had I imagined the grief? I went back and reviewed my interview notes, listened to the tapes, reread my journal, read up on grief. What I discovered was that my journeys through oral histories still left vast expanses of their multidimensional character unexamined.

Narrating in Spite of Themselves: Between Text, Subtext, and Context

First, I had to confront whether these feelings of grief and mourning about Mozambique were simply my own which I had then projected onto others. I could not ignore this. Reading my journal for the first time in eight years (and as was probably evident to readers of my excerpt above) I was struck by how much of my own grief was woven into my overall observations. If I focused so heavily on signs of grief, was it because Mozambique's independence represented something for which I was grieving? Still, I could confirm with colleagues and friends that some of the conversations that had struck me as marked by a sense of loss—and which I was beginning to think I had imagined—really had taken place. Yes, they told me, we were in fact grieving, the death of the socialist dream had been very painful.

This could not tell me whether these sentiments were present in the oral histories, however. I considered whether grief lay in some level of their subtext. Sometimes oral histories yield sentiments "in spite of themselves" (Tonkin 1992). If so, how had this "yielding" occurred? My interest in grief turned out to be significant, because it is a sentiment that we may try to mask. In many cultures, adults hide their grief or may shroud it in other forms of linguistic and paralinguistic expression (Retzinger 1991). This is the case in Mozambique, where many communities consider it inappropriate to express grief outside of intimate circles, or outside of socially sanctioned ritualized contexts (Honwana 1997).

Grief, in other words, is a private memory, and, as Gobodo-Madzikizela (1995) notes in the passage above, we may be reluctant to have such private memories become public possession. In this case, we may not communicate our grief declaratively in our statements to others; instead grief may be "deeply embedded in the moment-by-moment context" of social interaction (Retzinger 1991, 64). As I listened to the tapes and reread my interview notes, I found that I could identify feelings of grief and loss woven over the course of the narrative, in shifts in linguistic, paralinguistic, and behavioral cues; and in the composite dissonance created between narrators' specific phrases and the tone, cadence, and gestures with which they were uttered.

The dissonance between gestures, tone, and phrases was largely produced by what Retzinger (1991) refers to as "verbal hiding" strategies: These are patterns of communication that try to diminish the speakers' actual sense of vulnerability regarding a particular topic of speech. Some of the "verbal hiding behaviors" particularly salient in the oral histories (and illustrated below) include (a) *Mitigation*—a word or phrase that downplays the importance or painfulness of an experience; (b) *Abstraction*—when the narrator begins to speak about an event obliquely, uses passive language to remove agency, or refers to "it" or "they" rather than to anyone directly; (c) *Denial*—of feeling or experience. (This is usually accompanied by prolonged explanations of their feelings.); (d) *Defensiveness*—or irritation, usually resulting from feelings of vulnerability at being "unmasked" by the interviewer. (This may be accompanied by short utterances, in rapid succession.); (e) *Distraction*—the narrator shifts the discussion away from the issue or experience evoking emotion; (f) *Verbal withdrawal*—signaled by changes in patterns of verbal expression, including shorter responses and long pauses (Retzinger argues that pauses over one second may be significant). Painful experiences can also be embedded in largely unconscious paralinguistic cues (Retzinger 1991). The most common in the Mozambican oral histories was a drop in volume.

Verbal hiding patterns are also accompanied by nonverbal cues (Retzinger 1991). It was only at this time that I realized the importance of my professors' advice to jot down all of my impressions of my narrators. I had indeed kept notes, but I had never actually reread them. As I went back to the notes I had kept of the interviews in 1991 and 1992, I found them littered with clues. I had frequently noted that narrators' posture changed at key moments during the oral history event. These changes in narrators' "baseline" carriage occurred while they were recalling their reception and treatment in the postrevolutionary period, or while responding to questions regarding their impression of that period generally.

I illustrate this hiding behavior below in a reconstructed version of an exchange between myself ("A") and a narrator ("N"), alongside a reconstructed excerpt of my fieldnotes regarding the exchange. I have not used actual transcripts or notes because when narrators give their signed consent, they do so on the basis of the memories they make public; I do not believe I have consent to try to reveal their private meaning. Written transcripts, however, can only partially reveal my interpretation. Some of the verbal hiding patterns reflect changes in tone as well as nonverbal gestures. The fieldnotes to some degree reveal changes in body language; however, since gestures, linguistic, and paralinguistic cues all communicate as a single unit, this is no substitute for videotaping the interviews themselves, something which I plan to do, as a result, in future oral history work.

<table>
<tr>
<td>(Without any probing whatsoever, the narrator spends fifteen minutes prior to this describing the important role which "native" teachers played in preparing cadres for independence).
A: What did you do after independence?
N: After independence, well I continued teaching for a while and then I quit.
A: Can you tell me about your' experiences teaching after independence?</td>
<td>Verbal Withdrawal (entire passage below)</td>
</tr>
</table>

N: Humph. . . . What's to tell. I continued to do my job that's all.	Irritation
Then I had enough. I did not want to teach anymore.	Denial
A: You got tired of teaching?	
N: Humph. They got tired of me. We were [lower volume]	Irritation
colonial collaborators. We had been part of the system, so now everything we did was suspect.	Abstraction
Eh. . . . I just got tired of seeing them burning down everything, [lower volume] all those beautiful books.	Mitigation
A: Who was burning books? Why?	
N: Who was burning books, the soldiers that's who. Books, science equipment. If it was Portuguese it had to go.	Irritation
A: What was it like living in Mozambique after Independence?	
N: Well . . . you can see what's become of the place, can't you.	Irritation
Aaaahh, it was all that garbage that happened.	Abstraction
A: What do you mean?	
N: Ohh . . . just . . . things. It's over now. . . .	

My fieldnotes for such an exchange might have said the following:

> Mr. Cruz talked at length of the final years of the struggle for independence. He seemed especially proud of the role which he felt "native" teachers played and discussed this at great length and animatedly. His mood changed considerably once we got to the postindependence period. He volunteered as little as possible and his body language changed. He had been quite formal and polite until this point. Now, he seemed irritated when I asked him about his postindependence teaching experiences. Mr. Cruz is a tall and elegant man, who until this point sat with perfect posture and great command of the space around him. As we discussed his teaching experience after independence, he seemed to deflate in his chair. He responded but would not look at me; instead he started to gaze out into space or look at his hands, which he began rubbing together. I tried for several minutes to get him to elaborate on his experience since Independence, but without much success. His face looked pained and he pressed his lips together when he said that the government viewed "native" teachers as colonial collaborators. He waved his hand as he spoke

of this, as if to indicate this was not of great importance, but he also lowered his head and became very quiet for several seconds. At one point, Mr. Cruz spoke of the missionary schools which FRELIMO troops destroyed after Independence. As he spoke of the books that they had burned, Mr. Cruz stroked his old schoolbook, which was sitting in his lap and which he later offered me.

Attention to such verbal and nonverbal hiding patterns might have gotten me off the hook in terms of reconciling my recollections of grief and their apparent absence in the transcriptions as such. But it really brought me no closer to understanding why and what people *chose* to narrate versus what they did not, and the ways they chose to do so. Why were even narrators who were "in flow" at other points in their narrative so reluctant to share their postrevolutionary memories? Why could I capture other periods of the educational experience and not this one?

Love Me, Love My Memories: Remembering to Forget and Reconstruct the Past

> What happened since independence? That is very recent. I don't remember.
>
> —MR. NHAMUHUCO, PERSONAL INTERVIEW, AUGUST 23, 1997

Our memories not only allow us to remember; they also allow us to forget. At any given time, we may remember, forget, and reinvent certain aspects of our personal and collective pasts because

> individual and . . . collective memories each [try] to validate the view of the past that has become important . . . in the present. Forgetting or changing memories . . . makes the present meaningful and also supports the present with a past that logically leads to a future that the individual or group now finds acceptable. (Teski and Climo 1995, 3)

This is especially true in times of transition, since "all profound changes in consciousness, by their very nature, bring with them characteristic amnesias" (Anderson 1991, 204).

This has epistemological implications in that it blurs the boundary between interpretation of self (our sense of self and whether we exist independent of a collective) and our interpretation of our experiences. Our position in the world not only affects our interpretation of the world (cf, Collins 1990; Harding 1991; Hartsock 1998; hooks 1989); our sense of self mediates our telling and remembering of the world—and our place in it—to others.

I considered whether the period of time during which I collected the oral histories might have influenced what narrators remembered (and forgot) and how they remembered (and forgot) it. For example, I asked Mr. Cordeiro (1991)[7] if he could explain to me who the "New Man" was. The "New Man" *[Homem Novo]* was a term commonly used to refer to decolonized Mozambican consciousness. The objective of the postrevolutionary "New School" was to help create this "New Man" (Vieira 1978). Because it was so central to the socialist educational agenda, it had, by 1990, become a symbol of scorn. Mr. Cordeiro was an important figure in FRELIMO's educational efforts during the struggle for independence and in the early postindependence period. When I spoke with him, he was still active in political life. He spoke freely, but weighed his words carefully in his response to this question, which followed a conspiratorial laugh, and a four–second pause. His grin, as well as his laugh, suggested that he knew that I knew my question was not so innocent (Fieldnotes, July 18, 1991). It was improbable that I could have been in Mozambique for almost a year in those days and not known what the "New Man" meant, and we both knew that the other knew this. The subtext was that I was asking him to comment on the recent criticism of FRELIMO's socialist educational agenda. And so, he did not offer a definition but an explanation, which presupposed I already knew what "the New Man" stood for and that it had become the object of criticism:

> Well . . . [three seconds] others may see it differently but this is my personal interpretation of the meaning of the New Man. I think it was . . . [four seconds] a genuine attempt to call attention to the dignity of the human being, to reconstruct it after so many decades of oppression. That's what it means to me. Others may not agree with me.

Cordeiro's response illustrates how the way we remember becomes a presentation of self and/or the groups with which we identify. But if the telling and remembering of the past to some degree serves needs in the present, it also means that some of those alignments and dissociations that come out during the oral history event may be retroactive. Is this how Cordeiro viewed the ideology of the "New Man" in its heyday? Was this how Cordeiro viewed the "New Man" in the privacy of his own mind as I was recording him? Or was this how he wished posterity to remember the New Man?

This "love-me-love-my-memory" phenomenon made me question the conflation of identity and memory in relation to myself. The more time I spent in Mozambique, the less my narrators' memories and expressions of loss were distinguishable from my own. So for whose memories was I really searching? And whose narrative?

Remembering Vicariously and the Vulnerable Interviewer: When The Personal Becomes Epistemological

I was stunned to find myself asking these questions—again. Was I not well versed in the historical literature exploring the boundaries between the personal and the collective, history and memory (Crane 1996; Knapp 1989; Nora 1989; Teski and Climo 1995)? Had I not followed the debates in post-structuralist and feminist scholarship regarding identity politics (Collins 1990; hooks 1989), practice theories (Bourdieu 1977), and epistemology (Behar and Gordon 1995; Harding 1991; Lather 1991)? Had I not been sufficiently provoked and sensitized by their questions regarding the relationship of the scholar's biography to her intellectual project?

Initially, this scholarship made me feel secure that I had a good grasp of where biography ended and history began, and indeed, whose biography and history I was talking about: I was collecting *their* (narrators') voice, *their* biographies and memories as a way of constructing a history of the Mozambican educational experience. I was well aware that my experiences influenced the manner in which the oral history event unfolded and even my interpretation. But, after all of this reflection, I still I had a nebulous understanding of the way in which *my remembering* influenced my subjectivity.

I was ignoring that the oral history events intersected with another running narrative: my own. This running narrative *also* had memories of the experiences about which I was collecting interviews. These memories not only came from participating in oral history events, but from my experiences of living in Mozambique and listening for countless hours over scotches and beers and curries to very dear friends.

These narrators and friends were people I cared about, and in the process of building those interpersonal bridges, their memories had vicariously become my own. "Vicarious memory . . . happens when the memories of others become a part of reality for those who hear the memories but have not experienced the events to which the memories refer" (Teski and Climo 1995, 9). Teski and Climo argue that vicarious memory is often exploited by states; the commemoration of these inherited memories becomes a virtually shared experience (with those who "lived" them) and a proximally shared experience (with those remembering them vicariously). In a general sense, vicariously sharing in memories can become part of any group's solidarity work by imparting a sense of community. Long-term participant observation and fieldwork can make researchers, and certainly made me, vulnerable to vicarious memory.

I found myself echoing Yow's (1997) doubts: Did I like my narrators too much? Was I so drawn into the power of their narratives that I was losing the capacity to distinguish *their* voice from my own? In the intimacy created while friends and narrators were remembering and telling, I had become a "vulnerable observer" (Behar 1996). This made me sensitive to their sentiments, but it also made it difficult for me, without purposeful examination, to distance my personal experiences from those of the narrators. I realized my identity work through the oral history event is no different from my narrators: Inasmuch as I participated in framing the remembering and the telling, I was also trying to communicate some aspects of myself. And so, if the oral histories did not seem to "capture" the experiences I thought they should, it was partly because I was hoping others would narrate something I was experiencing.

This raises ethical questions regarding representation. When we set out to examine social justice issues, how much of our points of view as researchers is influenced by the personal meaning we externalize onto those ideas or endeavors? What do we feel our participation in such a project says about us? Our academic work may be inextricably linked to our sense of self, but when scholarship is confused with psychotherapy, it takes on an instrumental quality. In oral histories, the narrator becomes almost extraneous to the story, and instead, objectified in a story that is primarily about the interviewer's identity work.

But now that I was beginning to understand my "situation" in the oral history event, one point still troubled me. If I *was* blurring the boundary between my experience and that of my narrators, it suggested, at least, that I was engaged in a "slice" of the Mozambican experience with social change and sense of loss that was "really" happening. So why did the oral histories not capture this mood? Why were they not telling me these stories?

How We Remember Is Also What We Remember: The Intimacy of Context and the Context of Intimacy

My answer to this question came in the middle of a dinner party in Maputo in the summer of 1997. I knew few people there and no one knew my specific interest in oral histories. I walked into the kitchen where people were gathered and found them trading postindependence "war stories." In no time we were all roaring with laughter as people around the dinner table passed the curries and volunteered their favorite memories of the "good old, bad old" days, which were marked by war, drought, famine . . . and camaraderie:

> "Do you remember all the mackerel and cabbage we ate? I must have known about one hundred different ways to cook them;"
>
> "And the lines! We'd get on line at four A.M. without even knowing what it was for because there were lines for everything. Once I waited three hours and all I got was an ugly bra;"
>
> "Do you remember Mrs. X? That woman always had to be first on line. My sister would wake me up extra early just so that we would beat her to the line."

Between the laughter and the storytelling there would be quieter moments, when something would remind everyone that those days were over—and with them, many of the things Mozambicans were longing for in the present. Remembering the past became a way of "forgetting" some of the present they could do without: the hyper-individualism, inequality, child prostitution, corruption, cynicism, and despair. In the historical context of this present, and among friends, it felt good to remember a time when hope sprang eternal, the future was so bright, and there was a sense of purpose and unity. The jokes of hardship mark experiences that people share: everyone ate mackerel and cabbage, everyone waited in lines. It occurred to me that all of the contexts that had generated this kind of remembering and telling—the kind I was searching for—had been in group settings where these discussions furnished occasions for social bonding. In the remembering and the telling, Mozambicans recreated the context of community and camaraderie over which they were grieving. My journal entry cited earlier unwittingly recorded this: "Yet another night of collective friendship and misery."

The oral histories could not really reproduce this rhythm. While they did capture some of the same sense of loss, they could not capture *this* story because this particular way of remembering required a particular context of remembering. The "friendship-in-misery" narrative required a group in which people could throw their narratives into the "memory pool"; having a story signaled your group membership. I could not do this in the oral history interview. It was not only a question of method. This time, it was *I* who was not part of the story. The "voice" narrated in these stories was a "collective" one; it was a "we" experience, and perhaps for this reason, it required a "we" context in order for people to narrate it.

ORAL HISTORIES AS WAYS OF REMEMBERING AND TELLING

What has this odyssey taught me about the manner in which oral histories voice their narrative(s) and narrate their voice(s)? The voice of the oral history narrative not only emerges from the relationship between history and biography, the personal and collective in the narrator, but also within and between narrator and historian. Moreover, the historian-narrator dynamic is mediated in oral history work by the social construction of memory. Although, like other personal narratives, oral histories are supposed to "give voice" to narrators whose experiences often represent those of marginalized groups, both historians and narrators come to the oral history event with stories to remember and tell. Oral historians choose the voices they wish to narrate by choosing some narrators and not others, and they often choose the stories they wish narrators to voice, by hunting for some memories and not others. Rather than being neutral or objective participants in the oral history event, these choices become ways in which oral historians vicariously remember and tell.

This dynamic process of remembering and telling is deeply embedded in the orality of oral histories. Rather than broadening our understanding of oral histories, however, our growing recognition of voice and narrative seems to have restricted our vision of them. Search and retrieval and voice recognition programs have made the transformation of oral histories into written form easier, but in the process, their meaning has been reduced to their transcribable elements. But this reduces the senses (and range of experience) with which we understand how oral histories tell and remember. Much of this lies in the "unspeakable" portions of oral histories—in the gestures and pauses, in what the historian and narrator know is not being said—and in how much the narrator and historian know that the other knows that they know. . . .

At the same time, the stories I could and could not collect have taught me that the ways in which we narrate our voice are inextricably linked to our perceptions of how our stories narrate important aspects of our identity. Our notions of "who we are," and how we express this in the stories we tell and remember, are influenced by local constructions of personhood. But the expression of personhood we attribute to "voice" may not always tell the story—as our Western biases suggest—of a free-floating autonomous agent. Sometimes the personal "I" only exists in relation to the collective "we" (Schweder and Bourne 1984). The ways of remembering I encountered in Mozambique suggest that the point at which the personal meets the collective in "voice" is not fixed from culture to culture, and perhaps even from one experience to another.

If what we remember and tell, and the ways in which we do so, are expressions of local constructions of personhood and voice, then some memories shared by specific communities may require a group-sharing experience to remember and tell. And perhaps some memories are more meaningful when they are shared with some audiences and not others, or best narrated without the presence of an interviewer. What if I had given narrators a tape recorder and asked them to tape themselves as they recounted their educational experiences to their children or grandchildren? What if I had asked Mozambicans to invite whomever they wanted to participate in the oral history event? I don't believe this would distort the accuracy of the "facts" narrators remember. But my odyssey does suggest that stories are optimally recounted in certain contexts and not others.

And so, before we decide whether we should hunt memories with questionnaires or with butterfly nets, we must first understand what specific memories mean to the persons and groups who hold them at any given point in time. Just as we might not use regression analysis to understand the phenomenological, we need to question whether oral history, as it is conventionally conceived, is the best context of narration for capturing those memories. Conversely, we need to be more critical about the meaning behind the particular memories that we do collect during oral history work. I think back to my watershed questions. I thought the most important discovery about them was the questions themselves. Now I think I missed the real point of such a discovery. Why *does* a narrator associate any particular question with a series of seemingly unrelated memories? When we understand how these memories are connected for the narrator, we are much closer to understanding their deeper meaning.

As for my own running narrative, this odyssey has helped me appreciate and yet be more critical of the autobiographical elements of my work. I had forgotten C. Wright Mills's counsel to "trust, yet be skeptical of your own experience. . . . Experience is so important as a source of original intellectual work" (1959, 197). Mills reminds us that the crafting of interesting and meaningful intellectual work lies in our crafting of interesting and meaningful lives. Our attunement to the central questions of human experience depends upon our degree of engagement with the "stuff" of our abstractions, for this is what gives us a stake in the questions we pose and the solutions we look for. It is primarily in this sense that the remembering and telling that take place during oral history events become occasions in which the identities of *both* narrator and historian are practiced (Gluck and Patai 1991; Yow 1997).

NOTES

1. The educational system paralleled a dual legal system that separated "natives" from the Portuguese. Assimilation was a process whereby black Mozambicans could become eligible for Portuguese status. They had to have a fourth-grade education and submit to an examination in which they could prove that they walked, talked, dressed, ate (with silverware), and slept (in beds) like the Portuguese.

2. I conducted parallel work in Portugal, although I will restrict my discussion here to my work in Mozambique.

3. Cardoso, M. (pseud.). Personal interview: May 31, 1991. [Male, born 1934. Born in central Mozambique; Attended missionary primary and normal schools and went on to teach in missionary schools in the early '60s.]

4. If "allowed" seems presumptuous, it should remind the reader of the oral historian's role in voicing narratives. I say "allowed" because I have encountered oral history transcripts where historians interrupt a narrator if he or she begins to stray too far from the historian's topic.

5. Nhamuhuco, Mr. Personal interview: August 24,1997. [Born c.1919. Born in Zavala, Inhambane, Mozambique; Was educated in missionary schools; Attended normal schools for native teachers and taught until retirement in 1972.]

6. These observations permeated my fieldnotes, but were summarized in a journal entry of July 2, 1991, shortly before I left Maputo. Although such perceptions are never generalizable, I caution the reader that this may be especially so in this particular "slice" of Mozambique. Because of the war, movement was restricted to the provincial capitals and road travel was only undertaken at personal peril. Maputo was very much a fishbowl, and as a foreigner, I had access to a sphere of Maputo "society" (artists, politicians, diplomats) one does not usually associate with a graduate student. The closed borders of the city may have contributed to the "stir-crazy" mood and the rapid dispersion of rumors.

7. Cordeiro, M. (pseud.). Personal interview: July 18, 1991. [Male, born 1942.] Although oral histories are an attempt to give a forum to multiple voices, I was required at the time I applied for human subjects review to preserve the confidentiality of the persons I interviewed. Although Mr. Cordeiro was a public official, I did not use his real name since his interview was not done in his public capacity.

REFERENCES

Anderson, B. 1991. *Imagined communities.* London: Verso.

Behar, R. 1996. *The vulnerable observer: Anthropology that breaks your heart.* Boston: Beacon Press.

Behar, R., and D.A. Gordon. 1995. *Women writing culture.* Berkeley: University of California Press.

Bhabha, H. K. 1990. *Nation and narration.* London/New York: Routledge.

Blake, B. E. 1997. *She say, he say: Urban girls write their lives.* Albany: State University of New York Press.

Bourdieu, P. 1977. *Outline of a theory of practice.* Cambridge: Cambridge University Press.

Calhoun, C., ed. 1994. *Social theory and the politics of identity.* Oxford: Blackwell.

Collins, P. H. 1990. *Black feminist thought.* New York: Routledge.

Comaroff, J., and J. Comaroff. 1992. *Ethnography and the historical imagination.* Boulder, CO: Westview Press

Crane, S. A. 1996. (Not) writing history: Rethinking the intersections of personal history and collective memory with Hans von Aufess. *History and Memory* 8(1): 5–29.

Cross, M. 1937. The political economy of colonial education: Mozambique (1930–1975). *Comparative Education Review* 31 (November): 550–69.

Csikszentmihalyi, M. 1990. *Flow.* New York: Harper Perennial.

Davidson, A. L. 1996. *Making and molding identity in schools: Student narratives on race, gender, and academic achievement.* Albany: State University of New York Press.

Dirks, N. B., G. Eley, and S. B. Ortner. 1994. *Culture/power/history: A reader in contemporary social theory.* Princeton: Princeton University Press.

Errante, A. 1994. *The school, the textbook, and national development: Colonial and post-revolutionary primary schooling in Portugal and Mozambique, 1926–1992.* Doctoral dissertation, University of Minnesota.

———. 1995. Growing up assimilating: Oral histories of colonial missionary schooling in Mozambique. *Paedagogica Historica* [Supplemental Series, Vol. 1: Education and the Colonial Experience]: 213–31.

Farrell, E. 1994. *Self and school success: Voices and lore from inner-city students.* Albany: State University of New York Press.

Fentress, J., and C. Wickham. 1992. *Social memory.* Oxford: Blackwell.

Fox, R. G., and O. Starn. 1997. *Between resistance and revolution: Cultural politics and social protest.* New Brunswick, NJ: Rutgers University Press.

FREMILO. 1972. Combater, produzir, estudar [Combat, produce, study]. *A Voz da Revolucao* 9 (April/May): 496–508.

———. 1973. Seminario pedagogico nacional [National pedagogical seminar]. *A Voz da Revolucao* 16 (March): 1.

Friedman, J. 1992. The past in the future: History and the politics of identity. *American Anthropologist* 94: 837–59.

Glaser, B., and A. Strauss. 1967. *The discovery of grounded theory: Strategies for qualitative research.* New York: Aldine de Guyter.

Gluck, S. B., and D. Patai. 1991. *Women's words: The feminist practice of oral history.* New York: Routledge.

Gobodo-Madzikizela, P. 1995. Remembering and the politics of identity. *Psycho-analytic Psychotherapy in South Africa* 3 (Summer): 57–62.

Goffman, E. 1959. *The presentation of self in everyday life.* New York: Anchor Books.

Harding, S. 1991. *Whose science? Whose knowledge? Thinking from women's lives.* Ithaca: Cornell University Press.

Hartsock, N. C. M. 1998. *The feminist standpoint revisited and other essays.* Boulder, CO: Westview Press.

Honwana, A. M. 1997. Healing for peace: Traditional healers and post-war reconstruction in Southern Mozambique. *Peace and Conflict: Journal of Peace Psychology* 3 (3): 293–305.

hooks, b. 1989. *Talking back: Thinking feminist, thinking black.* Boston: South End Press.

Hunt, S. A., and R. D. Benford. 1994. Identity talk in the peace and justice movement. *Journal of Contemporary Ethnography* 22 (4): 488–517.

Irwin-Zarecka, I. 1996. *Frames of remembrance: The dynamics of collective memory.* New Brunswick, NJ: Transaction.

Isaacman, A., and B. Isaacman. 1983. *Mozambique: From colonialism to revolution, 1900–1982.* Boulder, CO: Westview.

Kaufman, G. 1974 The meaning of shame: Toward a self-affirming identity. *Journal of Counseling Psychology* 21: 568–74.

Knapp, S. 1989. Collective memory and the actual past. *Representations* 26 (Spring): 123–49.

Lather, P. 1991. *Getting smart: Feminist research and pedagogy with/in the postmodern.* New York: Routledge.

Machel, S. 1977. *O partido e as classes trabalhadoras Mocambicanas na edificacao da democracia popular* [The party and Mozambique's working classes in the edification of popular democracy]. *Documentos do 3o Congresso da FRELIMO.* Maputo: Departamento de Trabalho Ideologico da FRELIMO.

Marris, P. 1974. *Loss and change.* London: Routledge/Kegan Paul.

Mills, C. W. 1959. On intellectual crahsmanship. In *The sociological imagination,* ed. C. W. Mills, 195–226. New York: Oxford University Press.

Mohanty, C. T. 1994. On race and voice: Challenges for liberal educahon in the 1990s. In *Between borders: Pedagogy and the politics of cultural studies,* ed. H. A. Giroux and P. McLaren, 145–66. New York: Routledge.

Mozambique. 1979. *Primeiro seminario nacional sobre a lingua portuguesa* [First national seminar on Portuguese language]. Maputo: Ministry of Education and Culture.

Msabaha, I. 1995. Negotiating an end to Mozambique's murderous rebellion. In *Elusive peace: Negotiating an end to civil wars,* ed. I. W. Zartmann, 204–30. Washinston DC: Brookings Institute.

Nora, P. 1989. Between memory and history: Les lieux de memoire. *Representations* 26 (Spring): 7–25.

Ortner, S. 1984. Theory in anthropology since the sixties. *Comparative Studies in Society and History* [Great Britain]. 26 (1): 126–66.

Ortner, S. B. 1997. Thick resistance: Death and the cultural construction of agency in Himalayan mountaineering. *Representations* 59 (Summer): 135–62.

Polakow, V. 1993. *Lives on the edge: Single mothers and their children in the other America.* Chicago: University of Chicago Press.

Portelli, A. 1981. "The time of my life": Functions of time in oral history. *International Journal of Oral History* 2 (3): 162–80.

Retzinger, M. S. 1991. *Violent emotions: Shame and rage in marital quarrels.* Newbury Park, CA: Sage.

Said, E. W. 1993. *Culture and imperialism.* New York: Vintage.

Schweder, R. A., and E. J. Bourne. 1984 Does the concept of the person vary cross-culturally? In *Culture theory: Essays on mind, self, and emotion,* ed. R. A. Schweder and R. A. LeVine, 158–99. New York/Cambridge: Cambridge University Press.

Scott, J. C. 1990. *Domination and the arts of resistance.* New Haven: Yale University Press.

Sewell, W. H., Jr., 1997. Geertz, cultural systems, and history: From synchrony to transformation. *Representations* 59 (Summer): 35–55.

Snow, D., and L. Anderson. 1987. Identity work among the homeless: The verbal construction and avowal of personal identities. *American Journal of Sociology* 92: 1336–71.

Stein, H. F. 1987. *Developmental time, cultural space: Studies in psycho-geography.* Norman/London: University of Oklahoma Press.

Tarrow, S. 1991. "Aiming at a moving target": Social science and the recent rebellions in Eastern Europe. *P.S.: Political Science and Politics* 24 (1): 12–20.

Teski, M. C., and J. J. Climo. 1995. *The labyrinth of memory: Ethnographic journeys.* Westport, CT: Bergin and Garvey.

Tonkin, E. 1992. *Narrating our pasts: The social construction of oral history.* Cambridge: Cambridge University Press.

Vieira, S. 1978. O homem novo e um processo [The new man is a process]. *Seara Nova* 1594/1595: 23–32.

Volkan, V. D. 1988. *The need to have enemies and allies: From clinical practice to international relationship.* New York: James Aronson.

Weis, L. and M. Fine, M. 1993. *Beyond silenced voices: Class, race, and gender in United States schools.* Albany: State University of New York Press.

Yow, V. 1997. "Do I like them too much?": Effects of the oral history interview on the interviewer and the vice-versa. *Oral History Review* 24 (1): 55–80.

CPSIA information can be obtained at www.ICGtesting.com
Printed in the USA
BVOW06s0032070716

454533BV00007B/17/P

9 780195 158113